Consumer Behaviour

A European Perspective

Consumer Behaviour

A European Perspective

MICHAEL SOLOMON

GARY BAMOSSY

SØREN ASKEGAARD

FINANCIAL TIMES
Prentice Hall

An imprint of **Pearson Education**

Harlow, England · London · New York · Reading, Massachusetts · San Francisco · Toronto · Don Mills, Ontario · Sydney
Tokyo · Singapore · Hong Kong · Seoul · Taipei · Cape Town · Madrid · Mexico City · Amsterdam · Munich · Paris · Milan

Pearson Education Limited
Edinburgh Gate
Harlow
Essex CM20 2JE
England

and Associated Companies throughout the world

Visit us on the World Wide Web at:
http://www.pearsoneduc.com

Typeset in 10pt Sabon
by Meridian Colour Repro Ltd

Printed and bound by Grafos S.A., Arte sobre papel, Barcelona, Spain

British Library Cataloguing in Publication Data

A catalogue record for this book is available from
the British Library

ISBN 0-13-751983-4

10   9   8   7   6   5   4   3

04   03   02   01   00

Brief contents

Contents

Preface

We wrote this book because we're fascinated by the everyday activities of people. The field of consumer behaviour is, to us, the study of how the world is influenced by the action of marketers. We're fortunate enough to be teachers and researchers whose work allows us to study consumers. Given that we're also consumers, we can find both professional and personal interest in learning more about how this process works. As consumers and future managers, we hope you find this study to be fascinating as well. Whether you're a student, manager, or professor, we're sure you can relate to the trials and tribulations associated with last-minute shopping, preparing for a big night out, agonizing over a purchase decision, fantasizing about a week in the Caribbean, celebrating a holiday, or commemorating a landmark event, such as graduating from university, getting a driver's licence, or (dreaming about) winning the lottery.

Buying, having and being

Our understanding of this field goes beyond looking at the act of *buying* only, but to both *having* and *being* as well. Consumer behaviour is much more than buying things; it also embraces the study about how having (or not having) things affects our lives, and how our possessions influence the way we feel about ourselves and about each other – our state of being. In addition to understanding why people buy things, we also try to appreciate how products, services and consumption activities contribute to the broader social world we experience. Whether shopping, cooking, cleaning, playing football, lying out at the beach, or even looking at ourselves in the mirror, our lives are touched by the marketing system.

The field of consumer behaviour is young, dynamic and in flux. It is constantly being cross-fertilized by perspectives from many different disciplines. We have tried to express the field's staggering diversity in this text. Consumer researchers represent virtually every social science discipline, plus a few represent the physical sciences and the arts for good measure. From this melting pot has come a healthy debate among research perspectives, viewpoints regarding appropriate research methods, and even deeply held beliefs about what are and what are not appropriate issues for consumer researchers to study in the first place.

A European perspective on consumers and marketing strategy

The main objective for this adaptation has been to significantly increase its relevance for European students and scholars, while retaining the accessibility, contemporary approach, and the level of excellence in the discussions of consumer behaviour theory and applications established over the last three editions of Michael Solomon's *Consumer Behavior*. Based on the 4th American edition, we have tried to satisfy the need for a comprehensive consumer behaviour textbook with a significant European content. Hence, we have added illustrative examples and cases which are analyzed and discussed in a European consumer context, as well as numerous European scholarly references. The text also includes a number of advertisements of European origin to visualize various elements in the marketing applications of consumer behaviour theory. These changes, which focus on European consumers and research, have been made throughout the book. However, the most substantial changes have been made in the chapters dealing with demographic groups, subcultures and lifestyles, where the American perspective provided in earlier editions of Solomon's text has been replaced with a European one.

The internationalization of market structures makes it increasingly necessary for business people to acquire a clear perspective and understanding of cultural differences and similarities among consumers from various countries. One of the challenges of writing this book has been to develop materials which illustrate *local* as well as *pan-European* and *global* aspects of consumer behaviour. In this spirit, we have kept a number of American and other non-European examples to illustrate various similarities and differences on the global consumer scene. The book also emphasizes the importance of understanding consumers in formulating marketing strategy. Many (if not most) of the fundamental concepts of marketing are based on the practitioner's ability to know people. To illustrate the potential of consumer research to inform marketing strategy, the text contains numerous examples of specific applications of consumer behaviour concepts by marketing practitioners.

Pedagogical features

Throughout the text there are numerous boxed illustrative examples which highlight particular aspects of the impact and informing role that consumer behaviour has on marketing activities. These colour-coded boxes are labelled: 'Multicultural dimensions', 'Marketing opportunity', and 'Marketing pitfall', and represent examples from several European and global markets. There are several other features within each chapter to assist you in learning and reviewing this text, and to check and critically review your understanding of topics; these include: an opening illustrative Vignette, highlighted Key Terms, a Chapter Summary, and Consumer Behaviour Challenge questions. To familiarize yourself with these features and how they will benefit your study from this text, they are reproduced and described overleaf in the 'Guided Tour' (pages xiii–xiv).

Case study problems

At the end of the text there is a collection of Case Study Problems. The case material covers various companies, industries and countries, and integrates the topics covered in the preceding chapters. The questions at the end of each case study are designed to allow you to apply your understanding to real-life events and consumer behaviour activities, and to develop your analytical skills.

Opening vignette

Each chapter opens with a short, country-specific illustrative scenario, setting the scene for the chapter material and highlighting the inter-relationships between the individual and his or her social realities.

CHAPTER **13**

Age subcultures

It's just a few months before winter weather really sets in, and Joost is lying on his bed 'channel surfing' on the TV and day dreaming about trying out his new ice-hockey skates on the frozen lakes near the flat where he and his father live in the suburbs of Amsterdam. His father tried to convince him to buy the classic 'hoge Noren' – black high-top touring skates with a long blade that have been 'classics' in Holland for decades, but Joost insisted on ice-hockey skates. His response was: 'Your skates are for middle-aged, old-fashioned skaters who are too serious about the whole thing. I want skates I can mess about in. Besides, these skates go well with my new *Fila* winter jacket.'

While Joost is switching from one channel to the next, an advertisement for a skiing holiday comes on the screen and catches his limited attention. Images of 'extreme skiing' are mixed with scenes of young people sitting around a well-stocked breakfast table. Text appears at the bottom of the screen, instructing the viewer to go to the teletext page for more information. The entire advertisement lasts 15 seconds. Joost uses the remote control to switch to the teletext page, and scans the ski package offerings. Great! Ten days in Austria for just 745 guilders. It includes round-trip bus transportation, twin rooms, half-pension and nine days of ski passes. Before moving on to the next channel, he notes down the travel agent's web site address. With the TV still on, he logs on to his computer and checks the web site. He can book the trip on the web. First, he needs to ask a few friends to see if they want to go during the Christmas break. Then he just needs his Dad's permission . . . and his credit card number.

Age and consumer identity

The era in which a consumer is born creates for that person a cultural bond with the millions of others born during the same time period. As we grow older, our needs and preferences change, often in unison with others who are close to our own age. For this reason, a consumer's age exerts a significant influence on his or her identity. All things being equal, we are more likely than not to have things in common with others of our own age. In this chapter, we'll explore some of the important characteristics of some key age groups, and consider how marketing strategies must be modified to appeal to diverse age subcultures.

Age cohorts: 'my generation'

An age cohorts consists of people of similar ages who have undergone similar experiences. They share many common memories about cultural heroes (e.g. Clint Eastwood versus Brad Pitt, or Frank Sinatra versus Kurt Cobain), important historical events (e.g. the 1969 Apollo moon landing versus the 1997 Mars mission), and

Choosing for hockey style ice skates goes well beyond just product and price considerations. Review this chapter's opening consumer vignette for the more complete picture of the complex choice processes of teens.

Key terms

Colour-highlighted within the text where they first appear, and with an icon ━◑ in the margin to assist rapid navigation and revision of the core material.

Colour photographs

Over 80 colour photographs of real company advertisements are integrated throughout the text, bringing consumer behaviour topics to life.

194 CULTURAL INFLUENCES ON CONSUMER BEHAVIOUR

Desacralization

Desacralization occurs when a sacred item or symbol is removed from its special place or is duplicated in mass quantities, becoming profane as a result. For example, souvenir reproductions of sacred monuments such as the leaning Tower of Pisa or the Eiffel Tower, 'pop' artworks of the Mona Lisa or adaptations of important symbols such as the Union Jack by clothing designers, tend to eliminate their special aspects by turning them into unauthentic commodities, produced mechanically and representing relatively little value.[240]

Religion itself has to some extent been desacralized. Religious symbols, such as stylized crosses or New Age crystals, have moved into the mainstream of fashion jewellery.[241] Religious holidays, particularly Christmas, are regarded by many (and criticized by some) as having been transformed into secular, materialistic occasions devoid of their original sacred significance. Benetton, the Italian clothing manufacturer, has been at the forefront in creating vivid (and often controversial) messages exposing us to our cultural categories and prejudices, but also at times have touched upon the issue of desacralization.[242]

Even the clergy are increasingly adopting secular marketing techniques. Especially in the United States, televangelists rely upon the power of television, a secular medium, to convey their messages. The Catholic Church generated a major controversy after it hired a prominent public relations firm to promote its anti-abortion campaign.[243] None the less, many religious groups have taken the secular route, and are now using marketing techniques to increase the number of believers. The question is whether the use of marketing changes the 'product' or 'service' of the churches: true belief and salvation?[244]

Desacralization? This controversial Benetton ad was rejected by some magazines because of what some perceived as offensive religious symbolism.
Photographer: © Toscani for Benetton

SACRED AND PROFANE CONSUMPTION 195

Multicultural dimensions

The American 'market for religious belief' with its televangelists and its heavy promotion of various churches and sects is a very exotic experience for many Europeans. The ad depicted below for a Minneapolis church to help recruit worshippers is typical of the American trend towards secular practices being observed by many organized religions. It even uses a pun (on the curing of a headache?) to pass the message of salvation.

Sacralization

Sacralization occurs when objects, events and even people take on sacred meaning to a culture or to specific groups within a culture. For example, events like the Cannes Film Festival or Wimbledon and people like Elvis Presley or Princess Diana have become sacralized to some consumers.

Objectification occurs when sacred qualities are attributed to mundane items. One way that this process can occur is through *contamination*, where objects associated with sacred events or people become sacred in their own right. This reason explains the desire by many fans for items belonging to, or even touched by, famous people. One standard procedure through which objects become sacralized occurs when they become included in the collection of a museum.

In addition to museum exhibits displaying rare objects, even mundane, inexpensive things may be set apart in private *collections*, where they are transformed from profane items to sacred ones. Name an item, and the odds are that a group of collectors are lusting after it. The contents of collections range from various popular culture memorabilia, rare books and autographs, to Barbie dolls, tea bags, lawn

For fast, fast, fast relief take two tablets.

The ad for The Episcopal Church discussed in the Multicultural dimensions block above.
Courtesy of Church Ad Project. 1021 Diffley Eagan MN 55123

Multicultural dimensions

These illustrative boxes appear within every chapter, highlighting cultural differences in consumer behaviour across countries and continents.

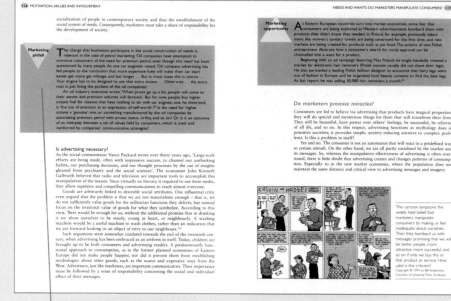

Marketing opportunity

These illustrative boxes appear within every chapter, highlighting how consumer research informs marketing strategy, and the actual or potential application of consumer behaviour concepts by marketing practitioners.

Marketing pitfall

These illustrative boxes appear within every chapter, highlighting the mistakes or ethically suspect marketing activities of companies which have generated controversy.

Chapter summary

The end-of-chapter bullet-points summarize the key concepts and issues, provding a concise check-list of the topics and issues covered.

Key terms list

An alphabetical collation of all the key terms in the chapter including a page reference where each term was first introduced, providing a convenient basis for revision.

Consumer behaviour challenge

Each chapter ends with about 10 short discursive-style questions, encouraging you to review and critically examine topics and issues individually or as part of a group discussion.

Structure of the text

The structure of this textbook is simple: it goes from micro to macro. Think of the book as a sort of photograph album of consumer behaviour: each chapter provides a 'snapshot' of consumers, but the lens used to take each picture gets successively wider. The book begins with issues related to the individual consumer and expands its focus until it eventually considers the behaviours of large groups of people in their social settings. The topics to be covered correspond to the Wheel of Consumer Behaviour presented in the following figure.

Following the Introductory chapter, Part B 'Consumers as individuals', considers the consumer at the most micro level. It examines how the individual receives information from his or her immediate environment and how this material is learned, stored in memory, and used to form and modify individual attitudes – both about products and about oneself. Part C, 'Consumers as decision-makers', explores the ways in which consumers use the information they have acquired to make decisions about consumption activities, both as individuals and as group members. Part D, 'A portrait of European consumers', further expands the focus by considering how the consumer functions as a part of a larger social structure. This structure includes the influence of different social groups with which the consumer belongs and/or identifies, featuring social class and age groups. Finally, Part E, 'Culture and European lifestyles', completes the picture as it examines marketing's impact on mass culture. This discussion focuses on the relationship of marketing to the expression of cultural values and lifestyles, how products and services are related to rituals and cultural myths, and the interface between marketing efforts and the creation of art, music, and other forms of popular culture that are so much a part of our daily lives. It also includes a section on major cultural change processes, analyzed from the perspectives of globalization and postmodernism.

Lecturer supplementary material

A comprehensive **Lecturer Resource Manual** and accompanying **CD-ROM** have been developed to support the preparation and delivery of courses by lecturers adopting this text. The pack includes:

- Chapter-based teaching notes and outlines;
- Answers to the end-of-chapter Consumer Behaviour Challenges;
- Student projects and assignments;
- Debriefs to the Case Study Problems;
- Over 100 PowerPoint presentation slides including key figures and tables from the text.

Website support

The Prentice Hall Europe website (http://www.prenhall.co.uk) includes pages featuring this text, as well as links to the companion PHLIP website for Mike Solomon's *Consumer Behavior* 4th edition.

Acknowledgements

Many of our colleagues from the business world as well as from universities throughout Europe have made significant contributions to this book by helping us identify important issues, and helping us think through them more clearly. We are grateful for their support, enthusiasm, and their willingness to share their knowledge with us. In addition, numerous colleagues developed European case materials and chapter-opening vignettes for this text, or provided valuable comments and feedback in the market research process and reviewing of manuscript drafts. To them, our special thanks:

Christian Alsted, *Alsted Marketing Research, Copenhagen, Denmark*
Anna Trosslöv Aronsson, *Lund University, Sweden*
Suzanne C. Beckmann, *Copenhagen Business School, Denmark*
Peter Bjork, *Swedish School of Economics and Business Administration, Finland*
Josee Bloemer, *Limburgs Universitair Centrum, Belgium*
Janeen Arnold Costa, *University of Utah, USA*
Karin Ekström, *Göteborg University, Sweden*
Basil Englis, *Berry College, Georgia, USA*
A. Fuat Fırat, *Arizona State University West, Phoenix, USA*
James Fitchett, *University of Stirling, Scotland, UK*
Güliz Ger, *Bilkent University, Ankara, Turkey*
David Harvey, *Huddersfield University, UK*
Carina Holmberg, *Stockholm School of Economics, Sweden*
Susan Hayward, *RISC International, Paris, France*
Benoit Heilbrunn, *Ecole de Management de Lyon, France*
Patrick Hetzel, *Université Robert Schuman, Strasbourg, France*
Margaret Hogg, *UMIST, Manchester, UK*
Howard Jackson, *Huddersfield University, UK*
Anne F. Jensen, *Odense University, Denmark*
Madeleen Klaasen, *Consumer Insights Manager, Nike, Hilversum, Netherlands*
Gaynor Lea-Greenwood, *Manchester Metropolitan University, UK*
Eoin Lonergan, *University of North London, UK*
Damien McLoughlin, *University College, Dublin, Ireland*
Raj Minhas, *Sheffield University, UK*
Israel D. Nebenzahl, *Ben-Ilan University, Ramat-Gan, Israel*
Anna Olofsson, *Gazoline Advertising, Umeå, Sweden*
Lara Pearce, *The Henley Centre, London, UK*
Anne Marie Parlevliet, *Amsterdam, Netherlands*
Toygun Ozdem, *Bilkent University, Ankara, Turkey*
Henry S. J. Robben, *Technische Universiteit Delft, Netherlands*
Carolyn Strong, *University of Wales, Cardiff, UK*
Alladi Venkatesh, *University of California, Irvine, USA*
Joop de Vries, *RISC International, Paris, France*

Our thanks also to the contributors of the chapter-opening vignettes:

Anne F. Jensen, *Odense University, Denmark* (chapter 1)
Patrick Hetzel, *Université Robert Schuman, Strasbourg, France* (chapter 2)
Gabriele Morello, *ISIDA, Palermo, Italy* (chapter 3)
Carolyn Strong, *University of Wales, Cardiff* (chapter 7)
Suzanne C. Beckmann, *Copenhagen Business School, Denmark* (chapter 9)
Karin Ekström, *Göteborg University, Sweden* (chapter 10)
Damien McLoughlin, *University College, Dublin, Ireland* (chapter 14)
Güliz Ger, *Bilkent University, Ankara, Turkey* (chapter 16)

Within Prentice Hall Europe, we had everything that authors could hope for in the development of a book. Our editors, Julia Helmsley and Andy Goss were supportive of all our efforts, highly professional in their work standards, and wonderfully personable throughout it all.

We'd also like to express our sincere thanks to our students in Denmark and The Netherlands who gave us suggestions on earlier drafts of this work. In particular, our Student Assistants: Nanine Plaatje (Amsterdam), and Jacob Fiellau-Nikolajsen, Lotte Frederiksen and Mikkel Væde (Odense) were excellent help in collecting material for the book and in reviewing our work-in-progress. Thanks also to our friends and colleagues at Odense Universitet and the Vrije Universiteit, Amsterdam for their support and inspiration throughout this project.

Gary and Søren want to offer a special and personal word of thanks to Mike Solomon. While we were busy getting together the materials for this European edition, Mike was already working hard on the manuscript for the 4th edition of *Consumer Behavior*. He shared materials with us as soon as they were ready, providing us with a pace and structure which kept us focused and on schedule (!). Mike was the perfect senior author – there when we needed something from him, and otherwise a positive source of energy and enthusiasm, coming from a comfortable distance. Ultimately, a great deal of synergy developed in our work together. We ended up sharing new materials, sources of research, and ideas in a mutual process of give and take. Thanks for giving us this opportunity to work with you Mike.

Finally, Gary Bamossy would like to thank Janeen, Joost, Lieke and Jason. There are many time demands in taking on a book project, and as it develops, you recognize that you get an extra amount of support from the people you love. Søren Askegaard would like to thank Caroline and Steen. Caroline, I know I stretched your patience.

Permissions acknowledgements

Grateful acknowledgement is made for permission to reproduce material in this book previously published elsewhere. Every effort has been made to trace the correct copyright holders, but if any have been inadvertently overlooked the publisher will be pleased to make the necessary arrangement at the first opportunity.

PART **A**

Consumers in the marketplace

PART OUTLINE

This introductory part comprises one chapter which previews much of what this book is about, and gives an overview of the field of consumer behaviour. The chapter examines how the field of marketing is influenced by the actions of consumers, and also how we as consumers are influenced by marketers. It also overviews consumer behaviour as a discipline of enquiry, and describes some of the different approaches that researchers use in order better to understand what makes consumers behave as they do.

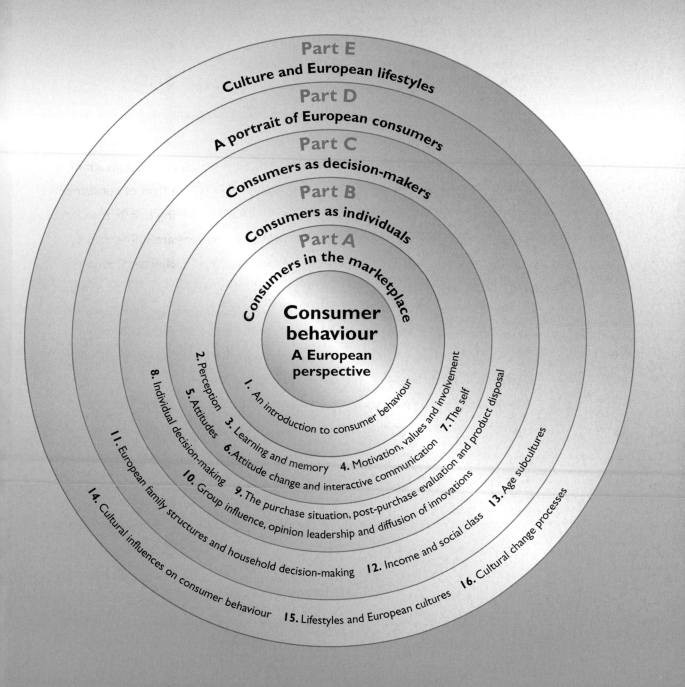

Part E
Culture and European lifestyles

Part D
A portrait of European consumers

Part C
Consumers as decision-makers

Part B
Consumers as individuals

Part A
Consumers in the marketplace

Consumer behaviour
A European perspective

1. An introduction to consumer behaviour

2. Perception   3. Learning and memory   4. Motivation, values and involvement   7. The self

5. Attitudes   6. Attitude change and interactive communication

8. Individual decision-making   9. The purchase situation, post-purchase evaluation and product disposal

10. Group influence, opinion leadership and diffusion of innovations

11. European family structures and household decision-making   12. Income and social class   13. Age subcultures

14. Cultural influences on consumer behaviour   15. Lifestyles and European cultures   16. Cultural change processes

CHAPTER 1

Anne F. Jensen, Odense University, Denmark

Sarah goes to the news-stand to buy a fashion magazine. She has decided to spoil herself by picking any magazine she likes, regardless of the price. Her eyes wander down the endless lines of glossy front covers. She quickly decides on a foreign one – the Danish magazines seem so dull and predictable.

A few years ago, when Sarah worked as a trainee in a provincial hairdressing salon, she would have picked one of the Danish fashion magazines. In fact, she used to buy the same magazine every week. Thursday was the day she would go to the newsagent in the high street after work to buy the magazine and a bag of licorice, and rush home to spend the evening reading about the latest hairstyles and fashions, recipes, or a celebrity.

But Sarah has a different set of friends now who are more cosmopolitan. Now she works in Copenhagen and she feels different. She is a metropolitan woman ready to take on the world, and she wants it to show. The foreign magazines have a sort of metropolitan aura about them, which Sarah likes.

Sarah considers *Vogue*. It has a touch of luxury and elegance which she likes, as opposed to some of the English fashion magazines such as *Attitude*, which often feature styles that Sarah finds downright ugly. Sarah also considers the English version of *Elle*. Helena Christensen, one of her favourite models, features on the front cover, but the main topic today is *shoes and accessories*, and she is really looking for a special edition on party dresses. This is what makes her choose *Cosmopolitan*. Not only do they have a special edition on *Dressing up for Christmas and New Year's Eve*, but they also have a ten-page supplement on the latest hairstyles. What is more, it contains a small sample of that new fragrance from Calvin Klein.

Now she has about half an hour before she is to meet her girlfriend. She finds a capé, sits down and opens the cover . . .

An introduction to consumer behaviour

Consumption in Europe? The European consumer?

This is a book about consumer behaviour written from a European perspective. But what does that mean exactly? Obviously, to write about a 'European' consumer or a 'European's consumer behaviour' is problematic. Some of the general theory about the psychological or sociological influences on consumer behaviour may be common to all Western cultures. Some theory may, on the other hand, be culturally specific. Certain groups of consumers do show similar kinds of behaviour across national borders. On the other hand, the ways in which people live their consumption life are very different from one European country to another, and sometimes even from one region of a country to another. As a student of consumer behaviour, you might want to ask yourself: 'In which consumption situations do I seem to have a great deal in common with fellow students from *other* European countries? And in which ways do I seem to resemble more closely my compatriots? In which ways do subcultures in my country exert a strong influence on my consumption patterns, and how international are these subcultures?'

This book is about consumer behaviour theory in general, and we will illustrate our points with examples from various European markets as well as from the United States (US) and other countries. Each chapter features a box headed 'Multicultural dimensions' which spotlights an international aspect of consumer behaviour, an issue that will be explored in depth in chapters 15 and 16. In chapter 15 in particular we will discuss in greater depth some similarities and differences among European lifestyles and consumer cultures.

Consumer behaviour: people in the marketplace

You can probably relate to at least certain general aspects of Sarah's behaviour. This book is about people like Sarah. It concerns the products and services they buy and use, and the ways these fit into their lives. This introductory chapter briefly describes some important aspects of the field of consumer behaviour, including the topics studied, who studies them and some of the ways these issues are approached by consumer researchers.

But first, let's return to one 'typical' consumer: Sarah. This sketch allows us to highlight some aspects of consumer behaviour that will be covered in the rest of the book.

- As a consumer, Sarah can be described and compared to other individuals in a number of ways. For some purposes, marketers might find it useful to categorize Sarah in terms of her age, sex, income or occupation. These are some examples of descriptive characteristics of a population, or *demographics*. In other cases, marketers would rather know something about Sarah's interests in fashion or music, or the way she spends her leisure-time. This sort of information often comes under the category *psychographics*, which refers to aspects of a person's lifestyle and personality. Knowledge of consumer characteristics plays an extremely important role in many marketing applications, such as defining the market for a product or deciding on the appropriate techniques to employ when targeting a certain group of consumers.

- Sarah's purchase decisions are heavily influenced by the opinions and behaviours of her friends. A lot of product information, as well as recommendations to use or avoid particular brands, is picked up in conversations among real people, rather than by way of television commercials, magazines or advertising hoardings. The bonds among Sarah's group are cemented by the products they all use. There is also pressure on each group member to buy things that will meet with the group's approval, and often a price to pay in the form of group rejection or embarrassment when one does not conform to others' conceptions of what is good or bad, 'in' or 'out'.

- As a member of a large society, people share certain cultural values or strongly held beliefs about the way the world should be structured. Other values are shared by members of *subcultures*, or smaller groups within the culture, such as ethnic groups, teens, people from certain parts of the country, or even 'Hell's Angels'. The people who matter to Sarah – her *reference group* – value the idea that women in their early twenties should be innovative, style-conscious, independent and upfront (at least a little). While many marketers focus on either very young targets or the thirty-somethings, some are recognizing that another segment which ought to be attracting marketers' interest is the rapidly growing segment of older (50+) people.[1]

- When browsing through the magazines, Sarah was exposed to many competing 'brands'. Many magazines did not grab her attention at all; others were noticed but rejected because they did not fit the 'image' with which she identified or to which she aspired. The use of *market segmentation strategies* means targeting a brand only to specific groups of consumers rather than to everybody – even if that means that other consumers will not be interested or may choose to avoid that brand.

- Brands often have clearly defined *images* or 'personalities' created by product advertising, packaging, branding and other marketing strategies that focus on positioning a product a certain way. The purchase of a magazine in particular is very much a lifestyle statement: it says a lot about what a person is interested in, as well as something about the type of person she would like to be. People often choose a product because they like its image, or because they feel its 'personality' somehow corresponds to their own. Moreover, a consumer may believe that by buying and using the product or service, its desirable qualities will somehow magically 'rub off'.

- When a product succeeds in satisfying a consumer's specific needs or desires, as *Cosmopolitan* did for Sarah, it may be rewarded with many years of *brand loyalty*, a bond between product and consumer that is very difficult for competitors to break. Often a change in one's life situation or self-concept is required to weaken this bond and thus create opportunities for competitors.

- Consumers' evaluations of products are affected by their appearance, taste, texture or smell. We may be influenced by the shape and colour of a package, as well as by more subtle factors, such as the symbolism used in a brand name, in an advertisement, or even in the choice of a cover model for a magazine. These judgements are affected by – and often reflect – how a society feels that people should define themselves at that point in time. Sarah's choice of a new hairstyle, for example, says something about the type of image women like her want to project. If asked, Sarah might not be able to say exactly why she considered some magazines and rejected others. Many product meanings are hidden below the surface of the packaging and advertising, and this book will discuss some of the methods used by marketers and social scientists to discover or apply these meanings.

- *Cosmopolitan* has a combined American and international image that appeals to Sarah. A product's image is often influenced by its *country of origin*, which helps to determine its 'brand personality'. In addition, our opinions and desires increasingly are shaped by input from around the world, thanks to rapid advancements in communications and transportation systems. In today's global culture, consumers often prize products and services that 'transport' them to different locations and allow them to experience the diversity of other cultures.

This ad illustrates the local adaptations of a global female magazine, *Cosmopolitan*.

Reprinted with permission from Hearst magazines.

Multicultural dimensions

The 'Cosmo Girl' is an image that is carefully cultivated by the editors of *Cosmopolitan*. In America alone the magazine is read by 2.7 million people each month. The American 'Cosmo Girl', as described by the editor Helen Gurley Brown, expects to get married, but is not in any hurry. She may wait until her late thirties to have children. Sex is 'very important, but not on the first date'. She owns at least one long black skirt with a slit, owns many pairs of shoes and wears big jewellery.

While the American Cosmo Girl is well defined, the magazine also publishes 25 international editions, most of which are separate entities with their own editorial staffs. In some cases local cultures conflict with the Cosmo Girl's liberated image. Latin American editors, for instance, face problems created by a more macho society that often has a double standard for men and women. Advertisers are sometimes reluctant to place ads in a magazine they see as 'perverted', and some parts of the magazine are censored. In places such as Hong Kong, the American image fits better, since women are expected to be more independent and ambitious. In late 1997 the Indonesian version of *Cosmopolitan* was launched, and analysts are divided as to how the Cosmo Girl will be received in the country that is home to the world's largest Muslim population, where most women do not leave home without a headscarf and their bodies fully covered.

What is consumer behaviour?

The field of **consumer behaviour** covers a lot of ground: it is the study of the processes involved when individuals or groups select, purchase, use or dispose of products, services, ideas or experiences to satisfy needs and desires. Consumers take many forms, ranging from a six-year-old child pleading with her mother for Wine Gums to an executive in a large corporation deciding on an extremely expensive computer system. The items that are consumed can include anything from tinned beans, a massage, democracy, rap music, and even other people (e.g. the images of rock stars). Needs and desires to be satisfied range from hunger and thirst to love, status or even spiritual fulfilment. There is a growing interest in consumer behaviour, not only in the field of marketing but from the social sciences in general. This follows a growing awareness of the increasing importance of consumption in our daily lives, in our organization of daily activities, in our identity formation, in politics and economical development, and in the global cultural flows, where consumer culture seems to spread, albeit in new forms, between North America and Europe to other parts of the world.[2] Indeed, consumption can be regarded as playing such an important role in our social, psychological, economical, political and cultural lives that today it has become the 'vanguard of history'.[3]

Consumers are actors on the marketplace stage

The perspective of **role theory**, which this book emphasizes, takes the view that much of consumer behaviour resembles actions in a play,[4] where each consumer has lines, props and costumes that are necessary to a good performance. Since people act out many different roles, they may modify their consumption decisions according to the particular 'play' they are in at the time. The criteria that they use to evaluate products and services in one of their roles may be quite different from those used in another role.

Consumer behaviour is a process

In its early stages of development, the field was often referred to as *buyer behaviour*, reflecting an emphasis on the interaction between consumers and producers at the time of purchase. Marketers now recognize that consumer behaviour is an ongoing process, not merely what happens at the moment a consumer hands over money or a credit card and in turn receives some good or service.

The **exchange**, in which two or more organizations or people give and receive something of value, is an integral part of marketing.[5] While exchange remains an important part of consumer behaviour, the expanded view emphasizes the entire consumption process, which includes the issues that influence the consumer before, during and after a purchase. Figure 1.1 illustrates some of the issues that are addressed during each stage of the consumption process.

Consumer behaviour involves many different actors

A consumer is generally thought of as a person who identifies a need or desire, makes a purchase and then disposes of the product during the three stages in the consumption process. In many cases, however, different people may be involved in the process. The *purchaser* and *user* of a product may not be the same person, as when a parent chooses clothes for a teenager (and makes selections that can result in 'fashion suicide' from the teenager's point of view). In other cases, another person may act as an *influencer*, providing recommendations for (or against) certain products without actually buying or using them. For example, a friend, rather than a parent, accompanying a teenager on a shopping trip may pick out the clothes that he or she decides to purchase.

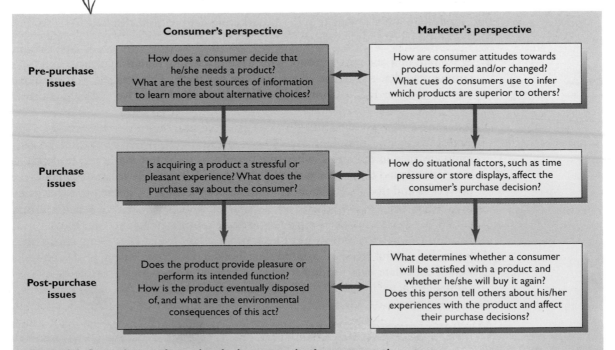

	Consumer's perspective	Marketer's perspective
Pre-purchase issues	How does a consumer decide that he/she needs a product? What are the best sources of information to learn more about alternative choices?	How are consumer attitudes towards products formed and/or changed? What cues do consumers use to infer which products are superior to others?
Purchase issues	Is acquiring a product a stressful or pleasant experience? What does the purchase say about the consumer?	How do situational factors, such as time pressure or store displays, affect the consumer's purchase decision?
Post-purchase issues	Does the product provide pleasure or perform its intended function? How is the product eventually disposed of, and what are the environmental consequences of this act?	What determines whether a consumer will be satisfied with a product and whether he/she will buy it again? Does this person tell others about his/her experiences with the product and affect their purchase decisions?

Figure 1.1 **Some issues that arise during stages in the consumption process**

Finally, consumers may be organizations or groups in which one person may make the decisions involved in purchasing products that will be used by many, as when a purchasing agent orders the company's office supplies. In other organizational situations, purchase decisions may be made by a large group of people – for example, company accountants, designers, engineers, sales personnel and others – all of whom will have a say in the various stages of the consumption process. As we'll see in a later chapter, one important organization is the family, where different family members play pivotal roles in decision-making regarding products and services used by all.

Consumers' impact on marketing strategy

Talking about buying magazines or other products can be a lot of fun – almost as much fun as actually making the purchases! But, on the more serious side, why should managers, advertisers and other marketing professionals bother to learn about this field?

The answer is simple: understanding consumer behaviour is good business. A basic marketing concept states that firms exist to satisfy consumers' needs. These needs can only be satisfied to the extent that marketers understand the people or organizations that will use the products and services they offer, and that they do so *better* than their competitors.

Consumer response is the ultimate test of whether or not a marketing strategy will succeed. Thus, knowledge about consumers is incorporated into virtually every facet of a successful marketing plan. Data about consumers help marketers to define the market and to identify threats and opportunities in their own and other countries that will affect how consumers receive the product. In every chapter, we'll see how developments in consumer behaviour can be used as input to marketing strategies. Boxes headed 'Marketing opportunity' will highlight some of these possibilities. First, here are a few examples of marketing actions that resulted from studies focused on understanding consumers:

- A woman in a consumer group, who were discussing dental hygiene, commented that tartar felt 'like a wall' on her teeth. This imagery was used in ads for Colgate Tartar Control, in which room-sized teeth were shown covered by walls of tartar.[6]
- A Danish firm wanted to introduce a cigarette brand targeted at blue-collar, American males. Unfamiliar with American consumers, it sent researchers to interview men in Arkansas, where the brand was to be test marketed. In-depth interviews found that many potential customers felt sexually frustrated and powerless and that they responded to these deep feelings by getting together with their mates and smoking cigarettes. The company used an ad depicting a brash, confident smoker and challenged these frustrated men to 'Make your move'.[7]
- Researchers for a manufacturer of Swiss chocolate found that many chocolate lovers hide secret 'stashes' around their houses. One respondent confessed to hiding chocolate bars inside her lingerie drawer. The result was an ad campaign theme of 'The True Confessions of Chocaholics'.[8]

Market segmentation: to whom are we marketing?

Whether within or across national boundaries, effective market segmentation delineates segments whose members are similar to one another in one or more characteristics and different from members of other segments. Depending on its goals and resources, a company may choose to focus on just one segment or several, or it may ignore differences among segments by pursuing a mass market strategy.

In many cases, it makes a lot of sense to target a number of market segments. The likelihood is that no one will fit any given segment description exactly and, the issue is whether or not consumers differ from our profile in ways that will affect the chances of their adopting the products we are offering.

Many segmentation variables form the basis for slicing up a larger market, and a great deal of this book is devoted to exploring the ways marketers describe and characterize different segments. The segmentation variables listed in Table 1.1 are grouped into four categories, which also indicate where in the book these categories are considered in more depth.

While consumers can be described in many ways, the segmentation process is valid only when the following criteria are met:

● Consumers within the segment are similar to one another in terms of product needs, and these needs are different from consumers in other segments.
● Important differences among segments can be identified.
● The segment is large enough to be profitable.
● Consumers in the segment can be reached by an appropriate marketing mix.
● The consumers in the segment will respond in the desired way to the marketing mix designed for them.

Demographics are statistics that measure observable aspects of a population, such as birth rate, age distribution or income. The national statistical agencies of European countries and pan-European agencies such as EuroStat are major sources

Table 1.1 Variables for market segmentation

Category	Variables	Location of discussion
Demographics	Age	Chapter 14
	Gender	Chapter 7
	Social class, occupation, income	Chapter 12
	Ethnic group, religion	Chapter 15
	Stage in life	Chapter 11
	Purchaser versus user	Chapter 11
Geographic	Region	Chapter 15
	Country differences	Chapter 15
Psychographic	Self-concept, personality	Chapter 7
	Lifestyle	Chapter 15
Behavioural	Brand loyalty, extent of usage	Chapter 4
	Usage situation	Chapter 9
	Benefits desired	Chapter 4

of demographic data on families, but many private firms gather additional data on specific population groups. The changes and trends revealed in demographic studies are of great interest to marketers, because the data can be used to locate and predict the size of markets for many products, ranging from mortgages to baby food.

In this book, we'll explore many of the important demographic variables that make consumers the same or different from others. We'll also consider other important characteristics that are not so easy to measure, such as psychographics – differences in consumers' personalities and tastes which can't be measured objectively. For now, let's summarize a few of the most important demographic dimensions, each of which will be developed in more detail in later chapters. However, a word of caution is needed here. The last couple of decades have witnessed the growth of new consumer segments that are less dependent on demographics and more likely to borrow behavioural patterns and fashions across formerly more significant borders. It is now not so uncommon to see men and women, or grandmothers and granddaughters, having similar tastes. Hence, as useful as they might be, marketers should beware of using only demographic variables to predict consumer tastes.

Age

Consumers in different age groups have very different needs and wants. While people who belong to the same age group differ in many other ways, they do tend to share a set of values and common cultural experiences that they carry throughout life.[9] Levi Strauss, for example, has been trying to develop the idea that it is a 'brand for life' by introducing products such as Dockers to meet the needs of their consumers as they grow older. As a Levi's marketing executive explained, 'In the 1960s, growth [in the jeans market] was due to adoption of jeans by 15- to 18-year olds . . . . Now these people are 25–49 and Dockers meshes perfectly with what the Levi brand image is about for them.'[10]

Gender

Many products, from fragrances to footwear, are targeted at men or women. Differentiating by sex starts at a very early age – even nappies are sold in pink-trimmed versions for girls and blue for boys. As proof that consumers take these differences seriously, market research has revealed that most parents refuse to put baby boys in pink nappies![11]

One dimension that makes segmenting by gender so interesting is that the behaviours and tastes of men and women are constantly evolving. In the past most marketers assumed that men were the primary decision-makers for car purchases, but this perspective is changing with the times.

Sometimes, the gender segmentation can be an unintended product of an advertising strategy. Wranglers launched a European campaign featuring macho Wild West values such as rodeo riding, after their earlier campaign, featuring a super-model, had made their sales of jeans to women grow 400 per cent but put men off their brand.[12]

Family structure

A person's family and marital status is yet another important demographic variable, since this has such a big effect on consumers' spending priorities. Young bachelors and newlyweds are the most likely to take exercise, go to wine bars and pubs, concerts and the cinema, and to consume alcohol. Families with young children are big purchasers of health foods and fruit juices, while single-parent households and those

Marketers are paying increasing attention to demographic changes in European households.
© The Procter & Gamble Company. Reprinted by permission.

with older children buy more junk food. Home maintenance services are most likely to be used by older couples and bachelors.

Social class and income

People in the same social class are approximately equal in terms of their incomes and social status. They work in roughly similar occupations and tend to have similar tastes in music, clothing, and so on. They also tend to socialize with one another, and share many ideas and values.[13] The distribution of wealth is of great interest to marketers, since it determines which groups have the greatest buying power and market potential.

Race and ethnicity

Immigrants from various countries in Africa and Asia are among the fastest-growing ethnic groups in Europe. As our societies grow increasingly multicultural, new opportunities develop to deliver specialized products to racial and ethnic groups, and to introduce other groups to these offerings.

Sometimes, this adaptation is a matter of putting an existing product or service into a different context. For example, the first motorway service station and cafeteria targeted at the Muslim population recently opened in Great Britain. It has prayer facilities, no pork menus and serves *halal* meat.[14]

Geography

In Europe, most of the evidence points to the fact that cultural differences persist in playing a decisive role in forming our consumption patterns and our unique expressions of consumption. At the same time, global competition tends to have a homogenizing effect in some markets such as music, sports, clothing and entertainment, and multinational companies such as Sony, Pepsi, Nintendo, Nike and Levi Strauss continue to dominate or play important roles in shaping markets.[15] With the creation of the European single market, many companies have begun to consider even more the possibilities of standardized marketing across national boundaries in Europe. The increasing similarity of the brands and products available in Europe does not mean that the consumers are the same, however! Variables such as personal motivation, cultural context, family relation patterns and rhythms of everyday life, all vary substantially from country to country and from region to region. And consumption of various product categories is still very different: in 1995 the per capita consumption of cheese p.a. was 16.9 kg in France and 6.1 kg in Ireland; and consumption of potatoes was 13.8 kg in Italy and 59.9 kg in Finland.[16] In marketing research, the possibility of operating with standard criteria for something as 'simple' as demographics for market segmentation is constantly under discussion. But to date the result is negative.[17]

To sum up, a European segmentation must be able to take into consideration:

- Consumption which is common across cultures (the global or regional, trends, lifestyles and cultural patterns that cross borders); and
- Consumption which is specific between different cultural groups (differences in values, lifestyles, behavioural patterns, etc. among different cultures and subcultures).

Then the problem of specifying the relevant borders arises. Cultural borders do not always follow national borders. Although national borders are still very important for distinguishing between cultures, there may be important regional differences within a country, as well as cultural overlap between two countries.[18] Add to this immigration and the import of foreign (often American) cultural phenomena, and you begin to understand why it is very difficult to talk about European countries as being culturally homogeneous. For example, it is important to distinguish between, say, Dutch *society* with all its multicultural traits and Dutch *culture*, which may be one, albeit dominant, cultural element in Dutch society. Furthermore, Dutch culture (as is the case with all cultures) is not a *static* but a *dynamic* phenomenon, which changes over time and from contact, interaction and integration with other cultures.

Marketing opportunity

New segments

Marketers have come up with so many ways to segment consumers – from the overweight to overachievers – that you might think that they had run out of segments. Hardly. Changes in lifestyle and other characteristics of the population are constantly creating new opportunities. The following are some 'hot' market segments.

The gay community: In more and more societies, the gay minority is becoming increasingly visible. New media featuring homosexual lifestyles and the consumption patterns attached to them flourish and marketers claim that the gay community is as attractive a marketing niche as many other subcultures and that this group form a 'hungry target'.[19] At a trade fair in New York in 1997, a 'gay doll' was launched, a sort of male, gay counterpart to the world-famous 'Barbie'. The product has reportedly been a big success in America, but the producer is waiting 'until the time is right' to launch it in Europe.[20]

The disabled: In the wake of legislation on the rights of the disabled, some marketers are starting to take notice of the estimated 10–15 per cent of the population who have some kind of disability. Initiatives include special phone numbers for hearing-impaired customers and assistance services for disabled people. IBM and Nissan have also used disabled actors in their advertising campaigns.[21] Mattel Inc., who produce Barbie, recently launched a sister-doll, Becky, in a wheelchair – a

<table>
<tr>
<td>

Marketing opportunity continued

</td>
<td>

reflection of the growing awareness of the disabled population in society.

Internet consumers: One huge potential sector is shopping via the internet. For example, it is estimated that 60 per cent of Danish companies will have a web site and that up to 20 per cent of private households in Denmark will have access to the internet in the year 2000. However, there are various problems to be solved. Many shoppers prefer the experience of going to the shops, and there are doubts about the security of credit card payments via the internet. Ad agencies have not yet learned to exploit the interactive medium to the full. Hence the success stories are relatively few in the consumer sector [e.g. amazon (books), Cdnow (music), Virtual Wineyards (wine)], whereas success has been notably greater in the business-to-business market.[22]

</td>
</tr>
</table>

Relationship marketing: building bonds with consumers

Marketers are carefully defining customer segments and listening to people as never before. Many of them have realized that the key to success is building lifetime relationships between brands and customers. Marketers who believe in this philosophy – so-called relationship marketing – are making an effort to keep in touch with their customers on a regular basis, and are giving them reasons to maintain a bond with the company over time. Various types of membership of retail outlets, petrol companies and co-operative movements illustrate this. One co-operative chain offers reductions to its members on such diverse goods as travel, clothing, home appliances, electronics and garden furniture.[23] A new trend is to form consortia of diverse companies from different sectors, supermarkets, banks, petrol retailer, telecommunications and the entertainment and leisure industry. The consortium then issues a loyalty card to help secure a stable clientele.[24]

Some companies establish these ties by offering services that are appreciated by their customers. Many companies donate a small percentage of the purchase price to a charity such as the Red Cross or World Wildlife Fund, or for the care of the poor and marginalized in society. This cements the relationship by giving customers an additional reason to continue buying the company's products year after year.

Another revolution in relationship building is being brought to us by courtesy of **database marketing**. This involves tracking consumers' buying habits by computer and crafting products and information tailored precisely to people's wants and needs.

Keeping close tabs on their customers allows database marketers to monitor their preferences and communicate with those who show an interest in their products or services. Information is passed to the appropriate division for follow-up. Blockbuster Entertainment Corp. is testing a system that makes recommendations based on a consumer's prior video rentals and offers special promotions based on these choices.[25] However, some consumers feel threatened by this kind of surveillance, and resist such marketing efforts. Hence, attempts have been made to ensure that database marketing conforms to the requirements of respondent confidentiality.[26]

Marketing's impact on consumers

For better or worse, we live in a world that is significantly influenced by marketers. We are surrounded by marketing stimuli in the form of advertisements, shops and products competing for our attention and our cash. Much of what we learn about the world is filtered by marketers, whether through conspicuous consumption depicted in glamorous magazine advertising or via the roles played by family members in TV commercials. Ads show us how we ought to act with regard to recycling, alcohol consumption and even the types of house or car we aspire to. In many ways we are 'at the mercy' of marketers, since we rely on them to sell us products that are safe and perform as promised, to tell us the truth about what they are selling, and to price and distribute these products fairly.

Popular culture

Popular culture, the music, films, sports, books and other forms of entertainment consumed by the mass market, is both a product of and inspiration for marketers. Our lives are also affected in more fundamental ways, ranging from how we acknowledge social events such as marriage, death or holidays to how we view societal issues such as air pollution, gambling and addiction. The Football World Cup, Christmas shopping, general elections, newspaper recycling, cigarette smoking and Barbie dolls, all are examples of products and activities that touch many of our lives.

Marketing's role in the creation and communication of popular culture is especially emphasized in this book. This cultural influence is hard to ignore, although many people fail to appreciate the extent to which their view of the world – their film and music icons, the latest fashions in clothing, food and interior design, and even the physical features that they find attractive or not in sexual partners – are influenced by the marketing system.

Consider the product characters that marketers use to create a personality for their products. From the Michelin Man to Ronald McDonald popular culture is peopled with fictional heroes. In fact, it is likely that more consumers will recognize characters such as these than can identify former prime ministers, captains of industry or artists. They may not exist, but many of us feel that we 'know' them, and they certainly are effective *spokes-characters* for the products they promote.

The meaning of consumption

One of the fundamental premises of consumer behaviour is that people often buy products not for what they do, but for what they *mean*. This principle does not imply that a product's primary function is unimportant, but rather that the roles products play in our lives go well beyond the tasks they perform. The deeper meanings of a product may help it to stand out from other, similar goods and services – all things being equal, a person will choose the brand that has an image (or even a personality!) consistent with his or her underlying ideas.

For example, while most people probably can't run faster or jump higher if they are wearing Nikes versus Reeboks, many die-hard loyalists swear by their favourite brand. These arch-rivals are marketed in terms of their image – meanings that have been carefully crafted with the help of legions of rock stars, athletes, slickly produced commercials – and many millions of dollars. So, when you buy a Nike 'swoosh' you may be doing more than choosing footwear – you may also be making a lifestyle statement about the type of person you are, or want to be. For a relatively simple item made of leather and laces, that's quite a feat!

As we have already seen, the hallmark of marketing strategies in the late 1990s is an emphasis on building relationships with customers. The nature of these relationships can vary, and these bonds help us to understand some of the possible

People use brands to express their identities to various degrees. The relationship between consumption and self is the topic of chapter 7.
Photo by Søren Askegaard.

meanings products have for us. Here are some of the types of relationship a person may have with a product.[27]

- *Self-concept attachment* – the product helps to establish the user's identity.
- *Nostalgic attachment* – the product serves as a link with a past self.
- *Interdependence* – the product is a part of the user's daily routine.
- *Love* – the product elicits bonds of warmth, passion or other strong emotion.

One American consumer researcher has developed a classification scheme in an attempt to explore the different ways that products and experiences can provide meaning to people.[28] This consumption typology was derived from a two-year analysis of supporters of a baseball team, but it is easily transferrable to the European context.

This perspective views consumption as a type of action in which people make use of consumption objects in a variety of ways. Focusing on an event such as a football match is a useful reminder that when we refer to consumption, we are talking about intangible experiences, ideas and services (the thrill of a goal or the antics of a team mascot) in addition to tangible objects (like the food and drink consumed at the stadium). This analysis identified four distinct types of consumption activities:

1. *Consuming as experience* – an emotional or aesthetic reaction to consumption objects. This would include activities like the pleasure derived from learning how to interpret the off-side rule, or appreciating the athletic ability of a favourite player.
2. *Consuming as integration* – learning and manipulating consumption objects to express aspects of the self or society. For example, some fans wear hats or scarves in the club's colours to express their solidarity with the team. Attending matches in person rather than watching them on TV allows the fan to integrate his or her experience more completely with that of the team.

3. *Consuming as classification* – the activities that consumers engage in to communicate their association with objects, both to self and to others. For example, spectators might buy souvenirs to demonstrate to others that they are die-hard fans. Unfortunately, the more hard-core express their contempt for opponents' supporters violently. There is a profound 'us' and 'them' dichotomy at stake.

4. *Consuming as play* – consumers use objects to participate in a mutual experience and merge their identities with that of a group. For example, happy fans might scream in unison and engage in an orgy of jumping and hugging when their team scores a goal – this is a different dimension of shared experience compared with watching the game at home.

The global consumer

One highly visible – and controversial – by-product of sophisticated marketing strategies is the movement towards a *global consumer culture*, in which people are united by their common devotion to brand-name consumer goods, film stars and rock stars.[29] Some products in particular have become so associated with an American lifestyle that they are prized possessions around the world. In chapters 15 and 16 we will pay special attention to the good and bad aspects of this cultural homogenization. A 'cousin' of the global consumer is the much debated Euro-consumer. Marketing researchers are heavily involved in a debate about the possibilities of finding market segments that are European rather than national in character. In a study on the consumption of luxury goods, it was concluded that one could draw a demographic portrait of the average European consumer of luxury goods. However, important differences between the countries were also detected. Consumers who expressed more positive attitudes towards cultural change were also more likely to consume luxury goods, independent of their demographics and social class.[30] Given these findings, it is questionable how much is gained from

Levi's jeans have become a world-wide status symbol and an icon for American consumer culture.
Courtesy of Levi Strauss & Co.

Dale color a tu vida con **Levi's** **517** COLLECTION BOOT CUT

working with the concept of the Euro-consumer in terms of segment description. For a product such as cars, which intuitively and in terms of functionality would seem relatively easy to market as a European-wide product, the models still appear in a variety of versions to suit particular national needs and wants. The Euro-consumer will also be discussed in detail in chapter 16.

Marketing ethics

In business, conflicts often arise between the goal to succeed in the marketplace and the desire to conduct business honestly and maximize the well-being of consumers by providing them with safe and effective products and services. Some people argue that by the time people reach university, secondary school or are actually employed by companies, it is a little late to start teaching ethics! Still, many universities and corporations are now focusing very intently on teaching and reinforcing ethical behaviour.

Prescribing ethical standards of conduct

Professional organizations often devise a code of ethics for their members. For example, European or national consumer protection laws or various national marketing associations' codes of ethics provide guidelines for conduct in many areas of marketing practice. These include:

- Disclosure of all substantial risks associated with a product or service.
- Identification of added features that will increase the cost.
- Avoidance of false or misleading advertising.
- Rejection of high-pressure or misleading sales tactics.
- Prohibition of selling or fund-raising under the guise of conducting market research.

Socially responsible behaviour

Whether intentionally or not, some marketers do violate their bond of trust with consumers. In some cases these actions are illegal, as when a manufacturer deliberately mislabels the contents of a package or a retailer adopts a 'bait-and-switch' selling strategy, whereby consumers are lured into the store with promises of inexpensive products with the sole intent of getting them to switch to higher-priced goods.

In other cases, marketing practices have detrimental effects on society even though they are not explicitly illegal. The introduction of so-called alcopops, a mix of alchol and soda or lemonade, targeted more or less explicitly at the teen market, has caused considerable debate in various European countries. Following negative press coverage, sales have gone down in Sweden and the UK, and the two largest retail chains in Denmark have withdrawn these drinks from their product range.[31] Others have run into difficulties by sponsoring commercials depicting groups of people in an unfavourable light to get the attention of a target market. One may recall the heated debate as to whether Benetton's advertising campaigns are attempts to sensitize consumers to the world's real problems, as the company contends, or exploit unfortunate people as in the ads depicting an AIDS victim, a dead Croat soldier or a ship packed with Albanian refugees in order to sell more Benetton clothing.[32]

A crucial barometer of ethical behaviour is what actions a marketer takes once a company is made aware of a problem with its advertising or products. In 1996, a Danish hypermarket chain, which for years had run a campaign guaranteeing the lowest prices compared to competitors, was involved in a scandal when it was discovered that employees were under instruction to change price tags just before a newspaper journalist checked them.[33]

In contrast, Procter & Gamble voluntarily withdrew its 'Rely' tampons following reports of women who had suffered toxic shock syndrome (TSS) after using them. Although scientists did not claim a causal link between Rely and the onset of TSS, the company agreed to undertake extensive advertising notifying women of the symptoms of TSS and asking them to return their boxes of 'Rely' for a refund. The company took a $75 million loss and sacrificed an unusually successful new product which had already captured about 25 per cent of the huge sanitary product market.[34]

Faced with the rising phenomenon of the 'political consumer' – a consumer who expresses his or her political and ethical viewpoints by selecting and avoiding products from companies that are antithetical to these viewpoints – the industry is increasingly coming to realize that ethical behaviour is also good business in the long run, since the trust and satisfaction of consumers translates into years of loyalty from customers. However, many problems remain. Throughout this book, ethical issues related to the practice of marketing are highlighted. Special boxes headed 'Marketing pitfall' feature dubious marketing practices or the possible adverse effects on consumers of certain marketing strategies.

Public policy and consumerism

Concern for the welfare of consumers has been an issue since at least the beginning of the twentieth century. Partly as a result of consumers' efforts, many national and international agencies have been established to oversee consumer-related activities. Consumers themselves continue to have a lively interest in consumer-related issues, ranging from environmental concerns, such as pollution caused by oil spills or toxic waste; the use of additives and genetically manipulated material in food and so on; to excessive violence and sex on television.

Consumer research and consumer welfare

The field of consumer behaviour can play an important role in improving our lives as consumers.[35] Many researchers play a role in formulating or evaluating public policies, such as ensuring that products are labelled accurately, that people can comprehend important information presented in advertising, or that children are not exploited by programme-length toy commercials masquerading as television shows.

Of course, to a large degree consumers are dependent on their governments to regulate and police safety and environmental standards. The extent of supervision may depend on such factors as the national political and cultural climate. Debates within the EU concerning regulation of the use of pesticides and food additives are examples here. In addition, a country's traditions and beliefs may make it more sympathetic to the needs of consumers or producers. In Japan there is a tendency to subvert the needs of consumers to those of manufacturers, and taking legal action against companies is extremely rare. Thus, it is not surprising that no health warnings appear on alcoholic beverages, and that Japanese cigarette packets carry watered-down warning labels, such as 'Because there is a danger of damaging your health, be careful not to smoke too much.'[36]

Table 1.2 The EU priorities for consumer policy

Ten major priorities for the future development of consumer policy have been defined by the Commission:

- Major improvement in the education and information of consumers
- Completion, review and updating of the legislative framework to protect consumer interests in the internal market
- Review of the consumer aspects of financial services
- Review of the protection of consumer interests in the supply of essential public utility services
- Helping consumers to benefit from the information society
- Improving consumer confidence in foodstuffs
- Practical encouragement of sustainable consumption
- Strengthening and increasing consumer representation
- Helping the development of consumer policies in Central and Eastern Europe
- Review of consumer policy in developing countries.

Source: European Commission web page www.cec.org.uk. Used with permission.

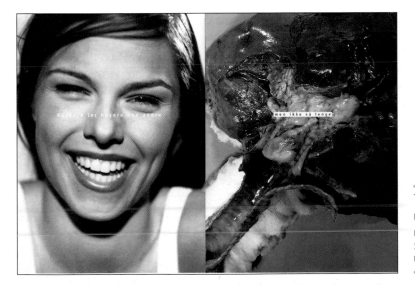

This Norwegian ad represents the many anti-smoking campaigns running in European markets.
Source: Lurzer's vol. 3, 1997.
Used with permission.

Consumer behaviour as a field of study

Although people have been consumers for a very long time, it is only recently that consumption *per se* has been the focus of formal study. In fact, while many business schools now require that marketing students take a consumer behaviour course, most universities and business schools did not even offer such a course until the 1970s. Much of the impetus for the attention now being given to consumer behaviour was the realization by many business people that the consumer really *is* the boss.

Interdisciplinary influences on the study of consumer behaviour

Consumer behaviour is a very new field and, as it grows, it is being influenced by many different perspectives. Indeed, it is hard to think of a field that is more interdisciplinary. People with a background in a very wide range of fields – from psychophysiology to literature – can now be found doing consumer research. Consumer researchers are employed by universities, manufacturers, museums, advertising agencies and governments. Professional groups, such as the Association for Consumer Research, have been formed since the mid-1970s.

Researchers approach consumer issues from different perspectives. You might remember a fable about blind men and an elephant. The gist of the story is that each man touched a different part of the animal, and as a result, the descriptions each gave of the elephant were quite different. This analogy applies to consumer research as well. A similar consumer phenomenon can be studied in different ways and at different levels depending on the training and interests of the researchers studying it.

Figure 1.2 covers some of the disciplines in the field and the level at which each approaches research issues. These disciplines can be loosely characterized in terms of their focus on micro versus macro consumer behaviour topics. The fields closer to the top of the pyramid concentrate on the individual consumer (micro issues), while those towards the base are more interested in the aggregate activities that occur among larger groups of people, such as consumption patterns shared by members of a culture or subculture (macro issues).

To demonstrate that the same marketing issue can be explored at different levels, let's return to the choice faced by Sarah when she was choosing a magazine. Table 1.3 lists research issues that might be of interest to each discipline and provides examples of how these might be applied in the marketing of women's magazines.

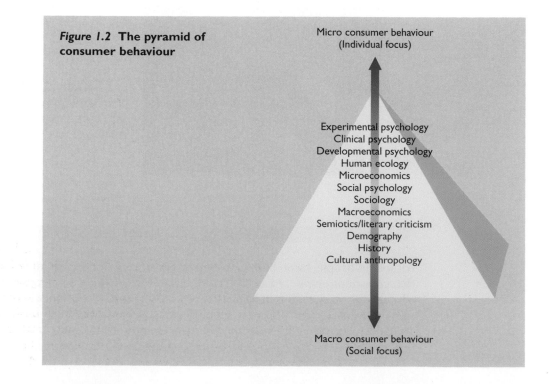

Figure 1.2 **The pyramid of consumer behaviour**

Micro consumer behaviour
(Individual focus)

Experimental psychology
Clinical psychology
Developmental psychology
Human ecology
Microeconomics
Social psychology
Sociology
Macroeconomics
Semiotics/literary criticism
Demography
History
Cultural anthropology

Macro consumer behaviour
(Social focus)

Table 1.3 **Interdisciplinary research issues in consumer behaviour**

Disciplinary focus	Magazine usage sample research issues
Experimental Psychology: product role in perception, learning and memory processes	How specific aspects of magazines, such as their design or layout, are recognized and interpreted; which parts of a magazine are most likely to be read
Clinical Psychology: product role in psychological adjustment	How magazines affect readers' body images (e.g. do thin models make the average woman feel overweight?)
Microeconomics/Human Ecology: product role in allocation of individual or family resources	Factors influencing the amount of money spent on magazines in a household
Social Psychology: product role in the behaviour of individuals as members of social groups	Ways that ads in a magazine affect readers' attitudes towards the products depicted; how peer pressure influences a person's readership decisions
Sociology: product role in social institutions and group relationships	Pattern by which magazine preferences spread through a social group
Macroeconomics: product role in consumers' relations with the marketplace	Effects of the price of fashion magazines and expense of items advertised during periods of high unemployment
Semiotics/Literary Criticism: product role in the verbal and visual communication of meaning	Ways in which underlying messages communicated by models and ads in a magazine are interpreted
Demography: product role in the measurable characteristics of a population	Effects of age, income and marital status of a magazine's readers
History: product role in societal changes over time	Ways in which our culture's depictions of 'femininity' in magazines have changed over time
Cultural Anthropology: product role in a society's beliefs and practices	Ways in which fashions and models in a magazine affect readers' definitions of masculine versus feminine behaviour (e.g. the role of working women, sexual taboos)

The issue of strategic focus

Many people regard the field of consumer behaviour as an applied social science. Accordingly, the value of the knowledge generated has traditionally been evaluated in terms of its ability to improve the effectiveness of marketing practice. Recently, though, some researchers have argued that consumer behaviour should not have a strategic focus at all; the field should not be a 'handmaiden to business'. It should instead focus on understanding consumption for its own sake, rather than because the knowledge can be applied by marketers.[37] This view is probably not held by most consumer researchers, but it has encouraged many to expand the scope of their work beyond the field's traditional focus on the purchase of consumer goods. And it has certainly led to some fierce debates among people working in the field! In fact, it can also be argued that business gets better research from non-strategic research projects because they are unbiased by strategic goals.

This more critical view of consumer research has led to the recognition that not all consumer behaviour and/or marketing activity is necessarily beneficial to individuals or to society. As a result, current consumer research is likely to include attention to the 'dark side' of consumer behaviour, such as addiction, prostitution, homelessness, shoplifting or environmental waste. This activity builds upon the earlier work of researchers who have studied consumer issues related to public policy, ethics and consumerism. There is also a growing movement to develop knowledge about *social marketing*, which attempts to encourage such positive behaviours as increased literacy and to discourage negative activities such as drunk driving.[38]

The issue of two perspectives on consumer research

One general way to classify consumer research is in terms of the fundamental assumptions the researchers make about what they are studying and how to study it. This set of beliefs is known as a **paradigm**. Like other fields of study, consumer behaviour is dominated by a paradigm, but some believe it is in the middle of a *paradigm shift*, which occurs when a competing paradigm challenges the dominant set of assumptions.

The basic set of assumptions underlying the dominant paradigm at this point in time is called **positivism**. This perspective has significantly influenced Western art and science since the late sixteenth century. It emphasizes that human reason is supreme and that there is a single, objective truth that can be discovered by science. Positivism encourages us to stress the function of objects, to celebrate technology and to regard the world as a rational, ordered place with a clearly defined past, present and future.

The emerging paradigm of **interpretivism** questions these assumptions. Proponents of this perspective argue that our society places too much emphasis on science and technology, and that this ordered, rational view of consumers denies the complexity of the social and cultural world in which we live. Others feel that positivism puts too much emphasis on material well-being, and that its logical outlook is dominated by an ideology that stresses the homogeneous views of a predominantly Western and male culture.

Interpretivists on the other hand stress the importance of symbolic, subjective experience, and the idea that meaning is in the mind – that is, we each construct our own meanings based on our unique and shared cultural experiences, so there are no single right or wrong references. To the value we place on products, because they help us to create order in our lives, is added an appreciation of consumption as a set of diverse experiences.

The major differences between these two perspectives are summarized in Table 1.4.

In addition to the cross-cultural differences in consumer behaviour discussed earlier, it is also clear that research styles differ significantly between Europe and North America and also within European countries. For example, studies have shown that European researchers tend to consider the cultural dimension much more than their American counterparts.[39] Further, two special sessions at a recent European consumer research conference revealed that there seem to be important differences between the way consumer behaviour is conceived in Germany and Great Britain, for example.[40]

Table 1.4 **Positivist versus interpretivist approaches to consumer behaviour**

Assumptions	Positivist approach	Interpretivist approach
Nature of reality	Objective, tangible Single	Socially constructed Multiple
Goal	Prediction	Understanding
Knowledge generated	Time free Context independent	Time bound Context dependent
View of causality	Existence of real causes	Multiple, simultaneous shaping events
Research relationship	Separation between researcher and subject	Interactive, co-operative with researcher being part of phenomenon under study

Source: Adapted from Laurel A. Hudson and Julie L. Ozanne, 'Alternative Ways of Seeking Knowledge in Consumer Research', *Journal of Consumer Research* 14 (March 1988): 508–21. Reprinted with the permission of The University of Chicago Press.

An overview of consumer behaviour research methods

There is no single right way or wrong way to conduct consumer behaviour research. Because the field is composed of researchers from so many different disciplines, the researcher's 'toolbox' is filled with a variety of approaches and techniques. The choice depends on the researcher's theoretical orientation and on the nature of the problem. For example, is the researcher's goal to *understand* current behaviour for its own sake, or to *predict* consumers' future behaviour? Is the researcher interested in testing a hypothetical model, or in looking for findings that can be incorporated into a marketing strategy?[41]

The first step in designing the research is defining the general problem to be addressed and specific objectives to be pursued. The problem may be to explore a given consumer phenomenon that is of scientific or public policy interest, for example consumers' use of nutritional information on food packaging. In a case such as this, the objective might be to identify how consumers process packaging information rather than to determine how this affects the sales of a particular brand.

On the other hand, the research problem may be directly related to a marketing manager's goal to improve the performance of a particular brand in the marketplace. In this case, the researcher will address such issues as which version of three different packaging alternatives best communicates the desired image for the product, or how packaging alternatives affect consumers' purchase behaviour in the supermarket.

The researcher's next step is to identify the specific components of the research task. These include the characteristics of the consumer population of interest and the environmental context of the problem (e.g. a brand's performance relative to the prominence of nutritional information on the package, or a brand's performance history when earlier packaging changes were made). The same research components can be approached in radically different ways, according to the researcher's theoretical foundation and assumptions of the problem.

One common way to classify the approaches to consumer behaviour research relies on the distinction between **exploratory** and **problem-solving research**. Although there are exceptions, many researchers equate qualitative methods with exploratory research (which can explore the field, but from which you cannot draw any firm conclusions) and quantitative methods with problem-solving research (which will draw firm conclusions on the basis of the testing of hypotheses). This is due to the different emphasis on the subjective and objective nature of the research process. This distinction is unfortunate, as it gives the false impression that no conclusions can be drawn from interpretive and qualitative research. It is more fruitful to distinguish between positivist and interpretivist paradigms, and between qualitative and quantitative methods, and then conclude that if a researcher subscribes to the positivist paradigm, he or she will be inclined to regard the qualitative studies as being at best exploratory. Interpretivists, on the other hand, may regard qualitative studies as conclusive, again depending on whether the goal is understanding or statistical predictions. So, the distinction between the methods should be complementary rather than mutually exclusive or interdependent (qualitative research as a starter, followed by the main course of quantitative research). Depending on the goal of the research, each method has its strengths and weaknesses. In the following sections, we'll take a brief look at each type.

Qualitative research

The purpose of **qualitative research** is to acquire in-depth knowledge about consumer behaviour issues, to generate ideas for future studies or to test a researcher's initial hunches about a given phenomenon. Because the researchers are not required to provide quantifiable results that are statistically generalizable to large groups of consumers, they have the luxury of being able to undertake in-depth work with small numbers of consumers to understand why these individuals feel or act the way they do. Qualitative research often consists of innovative methods that are used to understand the marketplace from the consumer's point of view. The researcher's experience and personal interpretation of the findings are a crucial facet of the analysis.

The most important qualitative research is the interview, which can be either a **focus group** or **in-depth interview**. Of all qualitative research techniques, focus groups are the most widely used in marketing research.[42] In a focus group interview a series of topics is introduced by a discussion leader or moderator. Each participant is encouraged to express his or her views and to react to the views of others. The group typically consists of 5–9 people who have been screened according to certain criteria, often to represent demographic and/or user characteristics of the target market. In-depth interviews (also called 'long interviews'[43]) are personal semi-structured interviews, during which the interviewer tries to cover as many facets of the informant's life as possible pertaining to the research problem.

Projective techniques

Many qualitative interviews use so-called **projective techniques**. These involve the presentation of an ambiguous, unstructured object, activity or person to which the consumer responds. The person may be asked to explain what the object is, tell a story about it or perhaps draw a picture of it. Projectives are used when it is believed that a consumer will not, or cannot, respond meaningfully to direct questioning.

Projective techniques allow consumers to respond to neutral situations, where, presumably, personal feelings are not at issue and they are freer to respond openly. These techniques assume that a person's responses reflect his or her deep-seated feelings about an issue. Because there are no right or wrong answers, it is hoped that consumers will project their unconscious feelings into their answers.

Consumers enjoy working with pictures, and a number of projective techniques involve the use of pictorial stimuli. Some techniques are simply useful devices to stimulate associations by presenting a consumer with a situation and assessing reactions to it.

Bubble drawings depict a person in an everyday situation (e.g. in a supermarket or driving a car) and require informants to provide a caption. Alternatively, a consumer in the drawing might be shown confronting a new situation, such as a new product or a change in product packaging, and the informant is asked to fill in the consumer's comments in the bubble. In either case the responses are interpreted as the informant's own feelings or doubts about the situation. The bubble drawing in Figure 1.3 allows the informant to voice concerns about trying a new product.

Psychodrawing allows the informant to express his or her perceptions of products or usage situations in a pictorial format. In Figure 1.4, a consumer has projected feelings before, during and after tooth-brushing.

Collage-making is another technique which allows informants to express various aspects of their images, associations and attitudes attached to a product, a service or an attitude towards their own consumption pattern.

Figure 1.3 **A bubble drawing projective instrument. The respondent is asked to supply the shopper's comments**
Source: Wendy Gordon and Roy Langmaid, *Qualitative Market Research* (Hants, England: Gower, 1988), 104. By permission of Gower Publishing Group.

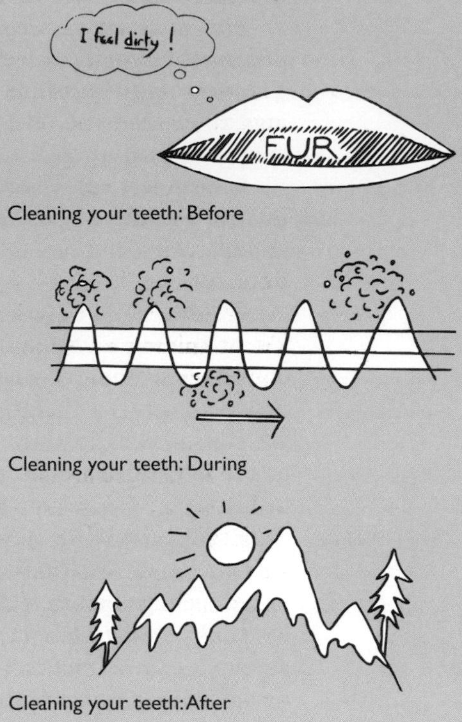

Figure 1.4 **A consumer's psychodrawing of the act of toothbrushing**
Source: Wendy Gordon and Roy Langmaid, *Qualitative Market Research* (Hants, England: Gower, 1988), 104. By permission of Gower Publishing Group.

I feel dirty !

FUR

Cleaning your teeth: Before

Cleaning your teeth: During

Cleaning your teeth: After

Autodriving uses visual and verbal recordings of consumers themselves as projectives. For example, a family might be photographed as it goes about preparing for dinner. These photographs are then shown to family members on a later occasion, and they are asked to talk about them. These interviews can shed light on underlying family dynamics (e.g. how are meal preparation tasks divided up among family members?) or attitudes regarding the use of different food products or appliances.[44]

Verbal projectives. In addition to pictures, researchers also rely on a variety of verbal exercises to allow subjects to project their feelings about products. With a sentence completion technique, for example, the respondent is asked to fill in the missing word(s) in a sentence. In keeping with the intent of projection, the sentences are phrased in the third person. Sentence completion has the advantage of being focused and yielding concise answers. For this reason, it is especially useful in large groups, since it can be given to more than one person at a time and responses across people can be easily compared. Commonly used examples include 'The average person considers television _____' and 'Most people feel that men who use aftershave _____'. Some versions supply a short story and ask people to describe how it ends.

With a **stereotype technique**, informants are given a description of a typical family or person and are asked to supply related information. For example, stereotypical portraits of different types of clients were used in a study investigating associations with and attitudes towards people using different kinds of financial services.[45]

In one of the classic demonstrations of this approach from the 1940s, women were asked to describe two housewives based on their shopping lists.[46] The only difference between the lists was that one included ground coffee, while the other specified instant coffee. The 'instant coffee housewife' was described as lazy and a poor planner. This response revealed the concern of women at that time that buying time-saving products would make their husbands think they were poor housewives.

Naturalistic inquiry

Naturalistic inquiry attempt to generate a 'thick description' of the real-life experiences of people. The emphasis is on getting a lot of in-depth information from relatively few people to gain insights into deeper meanings of experiences or marketing communications. No attempt is made to generalize the experiences to others, although the interpretations of each informant or each group studied can be compared and contrasted to other individuals' and groups' explanations of the same event.

In naturalistic inquiry, the researcher is considered a part of the interpretive process because his or her own beliefs and background influence what is being studied. Due to the interpretivist belief that consumer behaviour cannot be studied in isolation from the context in which it occurs, researchers prefer to travel to the site of consumption activities, rather than bring consumers into a laboratory setting. A consumer's responses in the laboratory cannot be compared to what he or she will reveal to friends or family.

Although relatively new to consumer behaviour research, naturalistic inquiry is gaining popularity. It is being applied to topics ranging from the construction of shopping environments (e.g. the mixing of architectural styles, store types and varieties of ethnic foods in a mall) to the rise of the 'body culture' in our society: consumers alter their body shape through dieting, exercise or surgery to make unique statements about themselves. Some techniques for collecting and analyzing data in such studies have been with us since the early days of consumer behaviour; others are being borrowed from fields such as anthropology and literary criticism, and still others are under development.

Some analytical methods have been adapted from such fields as literature and linguistics to understand better what marketing messages mean. *Semiotics* focuses on the meanings in texts and pictures, and how different elements of a message symbolize deeper meanings. The role played by semiotics in the understanding of how advertising communicates to consumers will be explored further in chapter 2. **Hermeneutics** is a method that stresses that perceivers evaluate messages (such as ads or music videos) by drawing on many preconceived notions, and focuses on how people's notions about themselves, the world and the source of the message, may be changed after being exposed to a message.[47]

One increasingly popular method for studying consumers in their natural 'habitats' is derived from techniques used by anthropologists when studying foreign cultures. This strategy involves *participant observation*, in which the researcher is immersed in the host culture. Although the researcher does not totally 'go native', the aim is to try to understand people on their own terms. This type of in-depth study of a specific group's behaviours, social rules and beliefs is often called **ethnography**. Research is usually done in a natural setting and is reported in the form of a very detailed case study.[48]

The ethnographic approach has come to the forefront of the consumer behaviour research largely as the result of a project called the *Consumer Behaviour Odyssey*, in which a team of marketing professors travelled across the United States in a recreational vehicle to mix with consumers in a wide variety of natural settings, ranging from flea markets and festivals to convents and museums.[49] The project yielded enormous quantities of field notes, still photos and videotapes which documented interviews with a huge diversity of consumers. The Odyssey was one of the first systematic attempts by researchers to study consumers in their natural environments rather than in controlled or laboratory settings. A recent 'sequel' to the Odyssey project took place in Australia, when a team of researchers conducted an ethnography of aboriginal consumer culture.[50]

Quantitative research

Quantitative research is a goal-oriented process in which the researcher wants to make definitive statements about relationships among variables. The emphasis is on descriptive information that is generalizable beyond the sample and quantifiable for comparison across individuals.

In obtaining generalizable data, this research perspective assumes that while there may be some individual variations or effects due to chance, the differences will 'wash out' if enough subjects are studied. In obtaining quantitative data, the aim is to maximize the reliability of the results and make it more likely that the same effect will be observed in future studies. The goal is not to predict the behaviour of any one person, but rather to predict the typical or average response of people who share certain characteristics.

The method for collecting data is considered to require little interpretation on the part of the researcher, who is expected to remain an impartial observer. The responses elicited from the studied consumers can be *physiological* (e.g. eye movements measured in eye-tracking studies to determine what parts of commercials capture the consumers' attention), *verbal* (e.g. responses to questions about commercials the consumers have seen) or *behavioural* (e.g. purchase volume after the consumers have been exposed to a special price promotion).

Quantitative studies include two major types: descriptive and causal. The goal of **descriptive research** is to describe something without necessarily explaining the reason for it. The aim of **causal research** is to obtain evidence of cause-and-effect relationships.

Descriptive research

Descriptive consumer research is usually done to identify the characteristics of a consumer segment or one or more products in the marketplace. For example, a brand manager for a soft drink might want to know the profile of the 'heavy user' of her product as compared with people who drink her competitors' products. Alternatively, the manager might want to track consumption of diet versus regular soft drinks over time. In addition, she might want to know whether changes in promotional expenditures are associated with a change in the brand's sales.

A *longitudinal design* tracks the responses of the same sample of subjects over time. Market researchers often rely on *panel studies*, where a sample of respondents (usually drawn from consumer households), who are statistically representative of a larger market, agree to provide information about purchases on a regular basis. Participants respond to detailed questionnaires about their purchasing habits, media usage, and so on. Most major European research and advertising agencies have their own consumer panel from which they can draw results concerning trends in consumption patterns.

A *cross-sectional design* is most widely used in marketing research. This format involves the collection of information from one or more groups of respondents at only one point in time. Specific types of survey used in cross-sectional designs will be discussed later.

Causal research

Causal research attempts to understand cause-and-effect relationships. Marketers often want to know which **independent variables** cause a phenomenon and which **dependent variables** are affected when the independent variables are changed. To be able to rule out alternative explanations, they must carefully design experiments that test pre-specified relationships among variables.

For example, while a brand manager may find from descriptive research that sales tend to rise when the brand is promoted heavily, he or she cannot be certain that the additional promotional effort really is the cause of the increased sales: another factor may be at work at the same time. For example, people buy more during the Christmas shopping season, so the product may sell more simply because people are out looking for things to buy.

Causal studies may be performed in the laboratory or in carefully controlled field settings, such as shops, restaurants or homes. Whatever the case, the researcher must be able not only to manipulate the independent variables that are under study but to hold constant other factors. If a change in the dependent variable is observed after only the independent variable(s) has been manipulated, the researcher can be more confident in concluding that the independent variable(s) in fact exert(s) a causal (rather than merely correlational) relationship with the dependent variable(s).

For example, a manufacturer might want to assess whether changing the packaging for one of its products (an independent variable) will increase sales (a dependent variable). With the co-operation of a store chain, it might select a number of outlets that are matched in terms of location, customer demographics, and so on. One set of stores might feature the product in its new packaging, while another set would continue to sell the product in its old packaging. Management could then compare sales of the brand between the two sets of stores. If sales rose significantly in stores carrying the new packaging, researchers could conclude with a reasonable degree of confidence that the new packaging did, in fact, exert a causal effect on sales.

Types of data

The actual data collected by consumer researchers can be divided into two general categories: primary data and secondary data. Put simply, **primary data** are any information collected specifically for the purposes of the present study. **Secondary data**, on the other hand, already exist in some form: they were originally collected for another purpose, but may be relevant to the present research.

Primary data

Primary data can take many forms. From a positivist perspective, exploratory research designs often rely on qualitative methods such as those already discussed. Problem-solving research designs involve **experimentation** (in the laboratory or field), **surveys** or observational techniques.

Types of survey questions   Most surveys consist of a questionnaire. The respondent is presented with a set of statements and is asked to respond to them. Questionnaires can take many forms, but the most widely used is a *Likert scale*. The respondent simply ticks or circles a number that indicates how much he or she agrees or disagrees with a statement, for example:

Burger King is a fun place to eat.
Disagree   1   2   3   4   5   Agree

A *semantic-differential scale* is also popular. This consists of a series of bipolar adjectives (e.g. good/bad, pretty/ugly) that anchor either end of a set of numbers; the respondent evaluates a concept along the various dimensions:

The atmosphere at Burger King is
Cold   1   2   3   4   5   Warm

Another measuring device is a *rank-order scale*. Here the respondent is asked to rank products or stores in order of preference according to some criterion:

In terms of places that are fun to eat in, please rank the following from 1 to 4.

_____ Pizzeria
_____ Burger King
_____ traditional restaurant
_____ McDonalds

Modes of survey data collection   Essentially, a researcher who wants to administer a survey to a large number of consumers has three options: use the telephone, use the post or interview people in person.

- *Postal surveys* usually consist of a one-shot questionnaire that is sent to a sample of consumers, often with an incentive to return the survey (the incentive may be a small amount of money attached to the survey or the promise to donate money to the respondent's favourite charity). Alternatively, a consumer may belong to a panel such as those described earlier and receive a packet of materials by post at regular intervals. Postal surveys are relatively easy to administer and offer a high degree of anonymity to respondents. The drawback is that the researcher has little flexibility in the types of question asked, and little control over the circumstances under which the questionnaire is answered (or, for that matter, who actually answers it).
- *Telephone surveys* usually consist of a short phone conversation during which an interviewer reads a series of brief questions. Technological developments have made computer-assisted telephone interviewing much more common; the interviewer reads questions from a computer screen and the respondent's answers are recorded directly into the computer. While telephone interviewing can yield data from large numbers of consumers very quickly, researchers are limited in that the respondent can't be asked to react to any visual stimuli. Furthermore, the proliferation of telemarketing has eroded the willingness of many consumers to participate in phone surveys.
- Personal interviews can be conducted in the respondent's home, although this practice has declined markedly in recent years due to escalating costs and security concerns. More typically, the research conducts a 'mall-intercept' study, when participants are recruited in shopping malls or other public places and asked to respond to a survey. The advantage of being able to tailor the interview based on the responses obtained (e.g. the researcher can probe, or ask further questions, to follow up on what a person has said) may not materialize because respondents are often reluctant to answer questions of a personal nature in a face-to-face context.

Obtaining observational research data   This is a positivistic parallel method to the naturalistic inquiry. Observational research situations are those in which the researcher wishes to record some aspect of consumer behaviour without actually intervening in any way or manipulating the situation. Observational research data can be very useful as a way to corroborate respondents' own reports of what they do.

For example, when mothers were interviewed in focus groups, they claimed they bought a fruit snack made by one company because of its 'wholesomeness'. When researchers observed mothers shopping with their children in supermarkets, however, a different story emerged: children tended to pester their mothers for different food items, and the mothers appeared indifferent as to which brand they bought. In other words, the desire to buy wholesome food was relevant to the category 'fruit snacks', but did not translate into the motivation to buy a specific brand.[51]

- When *personal observation* is employed, the behaviour of people is simply recorded. For example, a researcher might observe customers in a store, noting what questions they ask salespeople and how they handle the product.

- *Mechanical observation* relies on devices to record behaviour. Turnstiles in stores are used to track how many people have visited the establishment over a certain period. The widespread use of the UPC (Universal Product Code) on products has fostered the growth of *scanning technology*, which enables consumers' purchases to be recorded to track buying patterns. In another use of this technology, marketers can tailor their promotions to the specific needs of consumers (e.g. by issuing nappy coupons to consumers who have purchased baby food). Another widespread application of mechanical observation are the various meter methods used by syndicated marketing research agencies to record consumers' television watching. The data obtained from metering devices is used to determine who is watching which programmes. These ratings enable television channels to determine how much they will charge advertisers for commercials (and which programmes are dropped or have a second series).

- **Unobtrusive measures** are methods of data collection that do not require direct human responses. They are also known as trace analysis because they rely on the physical traces, or evidence, of past behaviour. They are often used when the researcher suspects that people will distort their responses, either because they may not be able accurately to recall their behaviour or perhaps they want to portray themselves in a more favourable light. For example, instead of asking a person to report on the products that are currently in his or her home, the researcher might go to the house and perform a 'pantry check', recording the products that are actually on the shelves. One innovative research method, called *garbology*, involves sifting through people's garbage (after it has been collected and anonymously labelled) to determine product usage. This unobtrusive technique is especially useful when the individual is reluctant to report usage truthfully, as may be the case for such sensitive products as alcohol or contraceptives. Another obvious use of this technique is for the study of recycling behaviour.[52]

Secondary data

Secondary data are not directly collected by the researcher. They are usually in the form of published data and are available from a variety of sources, ranging from a company's sales history (internal data generated by the organization itself) to such government sources as the national statistical agencies (external data obtained from a source other than the organization). Secondary data can be helpful in understanding a problem (and interpreting primary data) by placing it in a broader context. Many general business sources of secondary data are available, usually for a fee. These range from business directories and computerized databases to syndicated services that track the purchases, attitudes and lifestyles of different consumer segments.

Chapter summary

- Consumer behaviour is the study of the processes involved when individuals or groups select, purchase, use or dispose of products, services, ideas or experiences to satisfy needs and desires.

- A consumer may purchase, use and/or dispose of a product, but these functions may be performed by different people. In addition, consumers may be thought of as role players who need different products to help them play their various parts.

- Market segmentation is an important aspect of consumer behaviour. Consumers can be segmented along many dimensions, including product usage, demographics (the objective aspects of a population, such as age and sex) and psychographics (psychological and lifestyle characteristics). Emerging developments, such as the new emphasis on relationship marketing and the practice of database marketing, mean that marketers are much more attuned to the wants and needs of different consumer groups.

- Marketing activities exert an enormous impact on individuals. Consumer behaviour is relevant to our understanding of both public policy issues (e.g. ethical marketing practices) and of the dynamics of popular culture.

- The field of consumer behaviour is interdisciplinary; it is composed of researchers from many different fields who share an interest in how people interact with the marketplace. These disciplines can be categorized by the degree to which their focus is micro (the individual consumer) or macro (the consumer as a member of groups or of the larger society).

- There are many perspectives on consumer behaviour, but research orientations can roughly be divided into two approaches. The positivist perspective, which currently dominates the field, emphasizes the objectivity of science and the consumer as a rational decision-maker. The interpretivist perspective, in contrast, stresses the subjective meaning of the consumer's individual experience and the idea that any behaviour is subject to multiple interpretations rather than one single explanation.

- Consumer research can be qualitative or quantitative. Qualitative research is designed to learn more about the nature of a problem or phenomenon, while quantitative research is designed to obtain quantifiable data (how many?, how much? etc.) or to test predictions (hypotheses) based on prior knowledge or models of behaviour. Qualitative methods include the use of focus groups, depth interviews and ethnography. Quantitative methods include the use of controlled experiments, surveys, consumer panels and observational techniques.

- Primary data refer to information that is collected for the purposes of a specific observational or experimental research study, while secondary data refer to existing information that may be adapted to the current study. Secondary data sources include computerized databases, national statistical agencies and many syndicated studies conducted by companies and made available to clients for a fee.

🔑 Key terms

Bubble drawing *(p. 27)*
Causal research *(p. 30)*
Consumer behaviour *(p. 8)*
Database marketing *(p. 15)*
Demographics *(p. 11)*
Dependent variables *(p. 31)*
Descriptive research *(p. 30)*
Ethnography *(p. 29)*
Exchange *(p. 9)*
Experimentation *(p. 31)*
Exploratory research *(p. 26)*
Focus groups *(p. 26)*
Hermeneutics *(p. 29)*
Independent variables *(p. 31)*
In-depth interview *(p. 26)*
Interpretivism *(p. 24)*

Naturalistic inquiry *(p. 29)*
Paradigm *(p. 24)*
Popular culture *(p. 16)*
Positivism *(p. 24)*
Primary data *(p. 31)*
Problem-solving research *(p. 26)*
Projective techniques *(p. 26)*
Pschodrawing *(p. 27)*
Psychographics *(p. 12)*
Qualitative research *(p. 26)*
Quantitative research *(p. 30)*
Role theory *(p. 8)*
Secondary data *(p. 31)*
Stereotype technique *(p. 28)*
Surveys *(p. 31)*
Unobtrusive measures *(p. 33)*

Consumer behaviour challenge

1. This chapter states that people play different roles and that their consumption behaviours may differ depending on the particular role they are playing. State whether you agree or disagree with this perspective, giving examples from your own life.

2. Some researchers believe that the field of consumer behaviour should be a pure, rather than an applied, science. That is, research issues should be framed in terms of their scientific interest rather than their applicability to immediate marketing problems. Do you agree?

3. Name some products or services that are widely used by your social group. State whether you agree or disagree with the notion that these products help to form the group bonds, and support your argument with examples from your list of products used by the group.

4. Although demographic information on large numbers of consumers is used in many marketing contexts, some people believe that the sale of data on customers' incomes, buying habits, and so on constitutes an invasion of privacy and should be banned. Comment on this issue from both a consumer's and a marketer's point of view.

5. List the three stages in the consumption process. Describe the issues that you considered in each of these stages when you made a recent important purchase.

6. State the differences between the positivist and interpretivist approaches to consumer research. For each type of inquiry, give examples of product dimensions that would be more usefully explored using that type of research over the other.

7. What aspects of consumer behaviour are likely to be of interest to a financial planner? To a university administrator? To a graphic arts designer? To a social worker in a government agency? To a nursing instructor?

8. Select a product and brand that you use frequently and list what you consider to be the brand's determinant attributes. Without revealing your list, ask a friend who is approximately the same age but of the opposite sex to make a similar list for the same product (the brand may be different). Compare and contrast the identified attributes and report your findings.

9. Collect ads for five different brands of the same product. Report on the segmentation variables, target markets and emphasized product attributes in each ad.

PART B

Consumers as individuals

PART OUTLINE

In this part, we focus on the internal dynamics of consumers. While 'no man is an island', each of us is to some degree a self-contained receptor for information from the outside world. We are constantly confronted with advertising messages, products, other people persuading us to buy, and reflections of ourselves. Each chapter in this part will consider a different aspect of the consumer – sensations, memories and attitudes – that is invisible to others.

Chapter 2 describes the process of perception, in which information from the outside world about products and other people is absorbed by the individual and interpreted. Chapter 3 focuses on the ways this information is mentally stored and how it adds to our existing knowledge about the world as it is learned. Chapter 4 discusses our reasons or motivations for absorbing this information and how particular needs and wants influence the way we think about products.

Chapters 5 and 6 discuss how attitudes – our evaluations of all these products, ad messages, and so on – are formed and (sometimes) changed by marketers. When all of these 'internal' parts are put together, the unique role of each individual consumer as a self-contained agent in the marketplace will be clear. The last chapter in this part, Chapter 7, further explores how our views about ourselves affect what we do, want and buy.

Part E
Culture and European lifestyles

Part D
A portrait of European consumers

Part C
Consumers as decision-makers

Part B
Consumers as individuals

Part A
Consumers in the marketplace

Consumer behaviour
A European perspective

1. An introduction to consumer behaviour
2. Perception
3. Learning and memory
4. Motivation, values and involvement
5. Attitudes
6. Attitude change and interactive communication
7. The self
8. Individual decision-making
9. The purchase situation, post-purchase evaluation and product disposal
10. Group influence, opinion leadership and diffusion of innovations
11. European family structures and household decision-making
12. Income and social class
13. Age subcultures
14. Cultural influences on consumer behaviour
15. Lifestyles and European cultures
16. Cultural change processes

CHAPTER 2

Patrick Hetzel, Université Robert Schuman, Strasbourg, France

Fabienne is a 35-year-old mother of two and works at the French National Railway Company's headquarters in Lyon Part Dieu. Twice a week she uses her two-hour lunch break to go to the nearby shopping centre, the biggest in Lyon. Today she had just two things in mind: a quick bite to eat and a present for her son, Georges-Hubert. As she enters the shopping centre she is immediately drawn to the appetizing aroma of pizza coming from a nearby fast-food restaurant. She decides to stop and buy a slice and a small bottle of mineral water. Next she decides to go to a shop called 'Nature et Découvertes', the French version of the Californian 'Nature Company'. She has never been there before, but Catherine, her 14-year-old daughter, says that all her friends are talking about it. It seems to be the perfect place to buy a small microscope for Georges-Hubert's birthday.

On entering the shop she is very surprised. As in all shops her eyes are immediately and highly stimulated, but what makes this shop different is that there is more to it than that: all five of her senses are appealed to. The background music lets Fabienne discover birdsong, the sound of the forest, nature itself. As she is able to handle the products, Fabienne can familiarize herself with new shapes, new materials. An appeal is also made to her sense of taste when she is offered a cup of herbal tea. Finally, the natural aromas from the woods and plants combined with synthetic aromatics recreate the delicious atmosphere of the undergrowth to appeal to her sense of smell.

Fabienne likes the shop very much and for half an hour loses all sense of time. She wanders round as if in a trance. When she finally goes to the cash desk she realizes that not only does she have the little microscope in her hands, but a candle as well, and a book on trees.

Perception

Introduction

We live in a world overflowing with sensations. Wherever we turn, we are bombarded by a symphony of colours, sounds and odours. Some of the 'notes' in this symphony occur naturally, such as the barking of a dog, the shadows of the evening sky or the heady smell of a rosebush. Others come from people; the person sitting next to you might have dyed blonde hair, bright pink jeans, and be wearing enough perfume to make your eyes water.

Marketers certainly contribute to this commotion. Consumers are never far from advertisements, product packages, radio and television commercials, and advertising hoardings that clamour for their attention. Each of us copes with this bombardment by paying attention to some stimuli and screening out others. When we do make a decision to purchase, we are responding not only to these influences but to our interpretations of them. The aim of 'Nature et Découvertes' is to open the doors to the emotions, to a sense of wonder, to get in touch with one's capacity for pleasure. Unlike many other sales outlets there is an overdetermined motivation to create sensory effects to the utmost, to play on all five senses simultaneously. In a situation like this, the appeal is not so much to Fabienne's mind as to her perceptions, her emotions.

This chapter focuses on the process of perception, in which sensations are absorbed by the consumer and used to interpret the surrounding world. After discussing the stages of this process, the chapter examines how the five senses (sight, smell, sound, touch and taste) affect consumers. It also highlights some of the ways in which marketers develop products and communications that appeal to the senses.

The chapter emphasizes that the way in which a marketing stimulus is presented plays a role in determining whether the consumer will make sense of it or even notice it at all. The techniques and marketing practices that make messages more likely to be noticed are discussed. Finally, the chapter discusses the process of interpretation, in which the stimuli that are noticed by the consumer are organized and assigned meaning.

The perceptual process

As you sit in a lecture hall, you may find your attention shifting. One minute you are concentrating on the lecture, and in the next, you catch yourself daydreaming about the weekend ahead before you realize that you are missing some important points and tune back into the lecture.

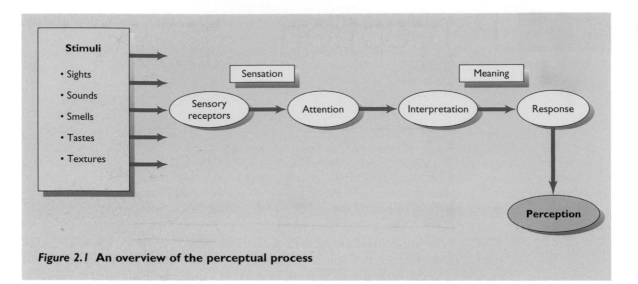

Figure 2.1 **An overview of the perceptual process**

People undergo stages of information processing in which stimuli are input and stored. However, we do not passively process whatever information happens to be present. Only a very small number of the stimuli in our environment are ever noticed. Of these, an even smaller number are attended to. And the stimuli that do enter our consciousness are not processed objectively. The meaning of a stimulus is interpreted by the individual, who is influenced by his or her unique biases, needs and experiences. These three stages of *exposure (or sensation)*, *attention* and *interpretation* make up the process of perception. The stages involved in selecting and interpreting stimuli are illustrated in Figure 2.1, which provides an overview of the perceptual process.

From sensation to perception

Sensation refers to the immediate response of our sensory receptors (e.g. eyes, ears, nose, mouth, fingers) to such basic stimuli as light, colour and sound. **Perception** is the process by which these stimuli are selected, organized and interpreted. We process raw data (sensation); however, the study of perception focuses on what we add to or take away from these sensations as we assign meaning to them.

The subjective nature of perception is demonstrated by a controversial advertisement developed for Benetton. Because a black man and a white man were handcuffed together, the ad was the target of many complaints about racism after it appeared in magazines and on hoardings, even though the company has a reputation for promoting racial tolerance. People interpreted it to mean that the black man had been arrested by a white man.[1] Even though both men are dressed identically, people's prior assumptions shaped the ad's meaning. Of course, the company's goal was exactly that: to expose us to our own perceptual prejudice through the ambiguity of the photo.

Such interpretations or assumptions stem from the **schemas**, or organized collections of beliefs and feelings. That is, we tend to group the objects we see as having similar characteristics, and the schema to which an object is assigned is a crucial determinant of how we choose to evaluate this object at a later time.

UNITED COLORS
OF BENETTON.

One in a series of
controversial ads from
Benetton, trying to
expose our prejudice to
ourselves.
Courtesy of Benetton.

The perceptual process can be illustrated by the purchase of a new aftershave.
We have learned to equate aftershave with romantic appeal, so we search for cues
that (we believe) will increase our attractiveness. We make our selection by considering such factors as the image associated with each alternative and the design of the
bottle, as well as the actual scent. We thus access a small portion of the raw data
available and process it to be consistent with our wants. These expectations are
largely affected by our cultural background. For example, a male consumer self-
conscious about his masculinity may react negatively to an overtly feminine brand
name, even though other men may respond differently.

A perceptual process can be broken down into the following stages:[2]

1. *Primitive categorization*, in which the basic characteristics of a stimulus are
   isolated: our male consumer feels he needs to bolster his image, so he chooses
   aftershave.
2. *Cue check*, in which the characteristics are analyzed in preparation for the
   selection of a schema: everyone has his own unique, more or less developed
   schemas or categories for different types of aftershave, such as 'down-to-earth
   macho', 'mysterious' or 'fancy French'. We use certain cues, such as the colour
   of the bottle, to decide in which schema a particular cologne fits.
3. *Confirmation check*, in which the schema is selected: the consumer may decide
   that a brand falls into his 'mysterious' schema.
4. *Confirmation completion*, in which a decision is made as to what the stimulus
   is: the consumer decides he has made the right choice, and then reinforces this
   decision by considering the colour of the bottle and the interesting name of the
   aftershave.

Such experiences illustrate the importance of the perceptual process for product
positioning. In many cases, consumers use a few basic dimensions to categorize
competing products or services, and then evaluate each alternative in terms of its relative standing on these dimensions.

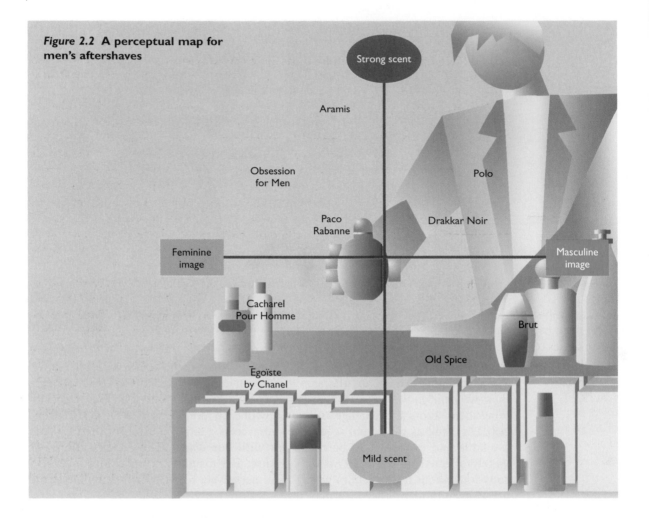

Figure 2.2 **A perceptual map for men's aftershaves**

This tendency has led to the use of a very useful positioning tool – a **perceptual map**. By identifying the important dimensions and then asking consumers to place competitors within this space, marketers can answer some crucial strategic questions, such as which product alternatives are seen by consumers as similar or dissimilar, and what opportunities exist for new products that possess attributes not represented by current brands? Figure 2.2 is a simple perceptual map illustrating a fictive but possible perception of competing aftershaves. What strategic insights might a marketer obtain from such a map?

Marketing pitfall

A recent controversy illustrates what can happen when the perceptual categorization process backfires. The retailer Toys 'R' Us announced that it would stop selling 'realistic' toy guns following the shooting of two children whose toy guns were mistaken for the real thing by police officers in New York. The decision comes as many parents are expressing their unhappiness with the sales of these toys.[3]

Sensory systems

External stimuli, or sensory inputs, can be received on a number of channels. We may see an advertising hoarding, hear a jingle, feel the softness of a cashmere sweater, taste a new flavour of ice cream or smell a leather jacket.

The inputs picked up by our five senses constitute the raw data that generate many types of responses. For example, sensory data emanating from the external environment (e.g. hearing a song on the radio) can generate internal sensory experiences when the song on the radio triggers a young man's memory of his first dance and brings to mind the smell of his date's perfume or the feel of her hair on his cheek. Sensory inputs evoke historical imagery, in which events that actually occurred are recalled. Fantasy imagery results when an entirely new, imaginary experience is the response to sensory data. These responses are an important part of **hedonic consumption**, or the multi-sensory, fantasy and emotional aspects of consumers' interactions with products.[4] The data that we receive from our sensory systems determine how we respond to products.

Although we usually trust our sensory receptors to give us an accurate account of the external environment, new technology is making the linkage between our senses and reality more questionable. Computer-simulated environments, or *virtual reality*, allow surgeons to 'cut into' a person without drawing blood or an architect to see a building design from different perspectives. This technology, which creates a three-dimensional perceptual environment which the viewer experiences as being virtually real, is already being adapted to everyday pursuits, such as virtual reality games.

Enterprising business people will no doubt continue to find new ways to adapt this technology for consumers' entertainment – perhaps by developing 'virtual catalogues' which allow a person to browse through a shop without leaving his or her armchair. Until that time, though, we are mostly affected by marketers' ability to manipulate real sensory inputs along five distinct channels. In this section, we'll take a brief look at some of the processes involved in the business applications of sensory stimuli.

This ad for a luxury car emphasizes the contribution of all our senses to the evaluation of a driving experience. Lexus use a lot of sensory imagery in their campaigns. In a recent British campaign, Lexus used the slogan 'The loudest sound you will hear inside the Lexus is yourself thinking', thereby alluding to a classic campaign for Rolls Royce, which in the 1950s stated: 'At sixty miles an hour, the loudest sound you'll hear is the electric clock'.[5]
©1993 by Lexus, a division of Toyota Motor Sales, USA, Inc. Used by permission.

Vision

Marketers rely heavily on visual elements in advertising, store design and packaging. Meanings are communicated on the visual channel through a product's size, styling, brightness and distinctiveness compared with competitors.

Colour in the marketplace

Colours are rich in symbolic value and cultural meanings. For example, the display of red, white and blue evokes feelings of patriotism for both British and French people. Such powerful cultural meanings make colour a central aspect of many marketing strategies. Colour choices are made with regard to packaging, advertising and even shop fittings. Indeed, there is evidence to suggest that some colours (particularly red) are arousing while others (such as blue) are relaxing. The power of colours to evoke positive and negative feelings makes this an important consideration in advertising design. The popularity of different colours varies greatly across cultures. For example, in the mid-1980s while the British seemed to prefer avocado bathrooms, the French tended to opt for blue.[6]

A special use of colour was introduced in a TV commercial by the brand 'Circle Coffee'. This showed an orange circle with a coffee bean inside and the voice-over told the viewer to stare at the bean for 30 seconds; then, when the screen went black, a blue circle 'magically' appeared on the screen. This illusion is created by the perceptual law of complementary colours – a fitting illusion, given that another of the company's coffee brands is 'Blue Circle'.[7]

The ability of colours to 'colour' our expectations is frequently exploited by marketers. Recently, marketers of products from beer and soft drinks to deodorant and petrol have launched new 'clear' products, which are intended to convey such qualities as purity and simplicity as a counter to over-elaborate product claims.[8] Green too has been gaining in popularity as consumers' ecological consciousness has grown.

The text in the ad reads: 'Where would the bright orange be without Dreft?' Orange is the national colour of the Netherlands, so the ad simultaneously underlines the colour-protecting qualities of the product and, through the national colour code, refers to the strength of the Dutch nation.
Source: Lurzer's 1997.
Used with permission.

Multicultural dimensions

Cultural differences in colour preferences create the need for marketing strategies tailored to different countries. While many northern European women now believe that heavy makeup is unprofessional and not very flattering, traditional femininity is still valued by Latin Americans. Mexican women, for example, are passionate in their love for vibrant lipsticks and nail varnish. Mexican girls are taught to be attentive to their appearance from early childhood. Baby girls have pierced ears, and housewives typically get dressed up in brightly coloured high heels to go to the supermarket. For these women, the 'natural look' is out. As one legal secretary in Mexico City explained, 'When you don't wear makeup, men look at you like you are sick or something.'[9]

Today colour is a key issue in package design. But the choice used to be made casually. The familiar Campbell's soup can was produced in red and white because a company executive liked the football kit at a particular university! Now colour is a serious business, and companies frequently employ consultants to assist in these decisions. In Switzerland an instant coffee container was redesigned with diagonal strips of mauve. The package won a design award, but sales dropped off significantly. Consumers did not associate the colour mauve with coffee.[10]

Some colour combinations come to be so strongly associated with a particular corporation that they become known as the company's livery, and the company may even be granted exclusive use of the colours. Eastman Kodak is one such company and has successfully protected its yellow, black and red in court. As a rule, however, this protection is granted only if there is the possibility that consumers might be confused about what they are buying if a competitor uses the same colour combination.[11]

Since the number of competing brands has proliferated for many types of products, colour can be a critical spur to sales. When introducing a white cheese as a 'sister product' to an existing blue 'Castello' cheese, a Danish company launched it in a red package and under the name of Castello Bianco. The red package was chosen for maximum visibility and signal effect. Although taste tests were very positive, sales were disappointing. A semiotic analysis of consumer interpretations showed that the red packaging and the name gave the consumers the wrong association about the product type and its degree of sweetness (due to associations with the vermouth 'Martini Bianco'). It was relaunched in a white packaging and with the name 'white Castello', and almost immediately sales figures more than doubled.[12]

In a given year, certain colours appear to be 'hot' and show up over and over again in clothing, home furnishings, cars, and so on. But favourite colours disappear as fast as they come, to be replaced by another set of 'hot' colours the next year or season.

Consumers' colour choices may be affected by these trends. One simple reason is that consumers' choices are largely limited by the colours available in the stores. Few people, however, realize the extent to which these 'hot' colours result from choices made by industry insiders, in a process known as colour forecasting. Colour experts in various consulting groups meet periodically to predict what colours will best reflect a season in one year's, five years' and sometimes even ten years' time. Members make colour predictions based on cultural and social trends, and these recommendations are then used by manufacturers in production forecasting.

As the old saying goes, 'A picture is worth a thousand words'. The visual elements of a marketing message often speak volumes about a product's attributes. In this case, the message about roominess conveyed by this Singaporean ad for Mitsubishi is clear.
Courtesy of Euro RSCG Ball Partnership, Singapore.

Smell

Odours can stir the emotions or have a calming effect. They can invoke memories or relieve stress. Some of our responses to scents result from early associations with other experiences. As one marketer noted, an example 'is a baby-powder scent that is frequently used in fragrances because the smell connotes comfort, warmth, and gratification'.[13]

Consumers' love of fragrances has contributed to a very large industry. Because this market is extremely competitive (30–40 new scents are introduced each year) and expensive (it costs an average of £30 million to introduce a new fragrance), manufacturers are scrambling to find new ways to expand the use of scents and odours in our daily lives. While traditional floral scents, such as rose and jasmine, are still widely used, newer fragrances feature such scents as melon peach (Elizabeth Arden's Sunflowers) and a blend of peach, mandarin orange, waterlily and white cloud rose (Sun Moon Stars by Karl Lagerfeld).[14] A later trend, supported by the marketing efforts of, among others, Calvin Klein, are perfumes positioned as unisex. In addition to the perfume market, home fragrance products, consisting primarily of potpourri, room sprays and atomizers, drawer liners, sachets and scented candles, represent important markets. But the use of smell goes further than that. An association of employers in the wood industry used a scratch'n'sniff card to convince potential apprentices of the advantages of smell in the wood industry compared with other professions.[15]

Sound

Music and sound are also important to marketers. Consumers spend vast amounts of money each year on compact discs and cassettes, advertising jingles maintain brand awareness and background music creates desired moods.[16] In a recent development, greeting card manufacturers are prospering by selling consumers the ability to send their own sounds to others: Hallmark Cards Inc. sells 'Recordable Greeting Cards' that allow the sender to record a personal 10-second message on a microchip. The message plays automatically when the card is opened.[17]

Many aspects of sound affect people's feelings and behaviours. One British company stresses the importance of the sound a packaging gives when opened, after having watched consumers open, close and reopen it several times during a test, clearly also listening to the right sound of the opening procedure.[18] Two areas of research that have widespread applications in consumer contexts are the effects of background music on mood and the influence of speaking rate on attitude change and message comprehension.

Muzak is heard by millions of people every day. This so-called 'functional music' is played in stores, shopping malls and offices either to relax or stimulate consumers. There is general agreement that muzak contributes to the well-being and buying activities of customers, but no scientific proof exists. *Time compression* is a technique used by broadcasters to manipulate perceptions of sound. It is a way to pack more information into a limited time by speeding up an announcer's voice in commercials. The speaking rate is typically accelerated to about 120–30 per cent of normal. Most people fail to notice this effect.

The evidence for the effectiveness of time compression is mixed. It has been shown to increase persuasion in some situations but to reduce it in others. One explanation for a positive effect is that the listener uses a person's speaking rate to infer whether the speaker is confident; people seem to think that fast talkers must know what they are talking about.

Another explanation is that the listener is given less time to elaborate on the assertions made in the commercial. The acceleration disrupts normal responses to the ad and changes the cues used to form judgements about its content. This change can either hinder or facilitate attitude change, depending on other conditions.[19]

Touch

Although relatively little research has been done on the effects of tactile stimulation on consumer behaviour, common observation tells us that this sensory channel is important. Moods are stimulated or relaxed on the basis of sensations of the skin, whether from a luxurious massage or the bite of a winter wind.

This ad metaphorically illustrates the natural quality and taste sensation of a lemon as a substitute for salt.
Used with permission.

Table 2.1 Tactile oppositions to fabrics

Perception	Male		Female	
High-class	Wool		Silk	Fine
Low-class	Denim		Cotton	↕
	Heavy	⟵⟶	Light	Coarse

Touch has even been shown to be a factor in sales interactions. There are considerable cultural differences in the world as well as within Europe concerning the appropriate amount and kind of touching in interpersonal interactions. In general, northern Europeans touch less than their southern European counterparts. Many British think the French shake hands excessively.[20]

Tactile cues have symbolic meaning. People associate the textures of fabrics and other products with underlying product qualities. The perceived richness or quality of the material in clothing, bedding or upholstery is linked to its 'feel', whether it is rough or smooth, soft or stiff. A smooth fabric such as silk is equated with luxury, while denim is considered practical and durable. Some of these tactile/quality associations are summarized in Table 2.1. Fabrics that are composed of rare materials or that require a high degree of processing to achieve their smoothness or fineness tend to be more expensive and thus are seen as being classier. Similarly, lighter, more delicate textures are assumed to be feminine. Roughness is often positively valued for men, while smoothness is sought by women.

Just as fabrics are prized for their textures, some types of alcohol are rated according to their 'feel'. The British Lexus ad mentioned on page 43 quotes a car magazine saying that the engine is 'as velvety as the finest malt whisky'. This ad for a Scotch malt whisky emphasizes the product's smoothness metaphorically by equating its taste with the experience of gliding over ice.
Courtesy of William Grant & Sons, Inc.

Taste

Our taste receptors contribute to our experience of many products. Sensory analysis is used to account for the human perception of sensory product qualities. One study used sensory analysis to assess butter biscuits: the crispness, buttery-taste, rate of melt, density, 'molar packing' (the amount of cookie that sticks to the teeth) and the 'notes' of the biscuit, such as sweetness, saltiness or bitterness.[21]

Food companies go to great lengths to ensure that their products taste as they should. Companies may use a group of 'sensory panelists' as tasters. These consumers are recruited because they have superior sensory abilities, and are then given six months' training. Or they rely on lay people, i.e. ordinary consumers. In a blind taste test, panelists rate the products of a company and its competitors on a number of dimensions. The results of such studies are important to discover both different consumer preferences and, thus, different consumer segments, and the positioning of a company or a brand in terms of the most important sensory qualities of the product.[22]

Are blind taste tests worth their salt? While taste tests often provide valuable information, their results can be misleading when it is forgotten that objective taste is only one component of product evaluation. The most famous example of this mistake concerns New Coke, Coca-Cola's answer to the Pepsi Challenge.[23] The new formulation was preferred to Pepsi in blind taste tests (in which the products were not identified) by an average of 55 per cent to 45 per cent in seventeen markets, yet New Coke ran into problems when it replaced the older version. People do not buy a cola for taste alone; they are buying intangibles like brand image as well.

Sometimes taste test failures can be overcome by repositioning the product. For example, Vernor's ginger ale did poorly in a taste test against leading ginger ales. When the research team introduced it as a new type of soft drink with a tangier taste, it won easily. As an executive noted, 'People hated it because it didn't meet the preconceived expectations of what a ginger ale should be.'[24]

Sensory thresholds

If you have ever blown a dog whistle and watched pets respond to a sound you cannot hear, you know that there are some stimuli that people simply are not capable of perceiving. And, of course, some people are better able to pick up sensory information than are others.

The science that focuses on how the physical environment is integrated into our personal, subjective world is known as **psychophysics.** By understanding some of the physical laws that govern what we are capable of responding to, this knowledge can be translated into marketing strategies.

The absolute threshold

When we define the lowest intensity of a stimulus that can be registered on a sensory channel, we speak of a threshold for that receptor. The **absolute threshold** refers to the minimum amount of stimulation that can be detected on a sensory channel. The sound emitted by a dog whistle is too high to be detected by human ears, so this stimulus is beyond our auditory absolute threshold. The absolute threshold is an important consideration in designing marketing stimuli. A hoarding might have the most entertaining story ever written, but this genius is wasted if the print is too small for passing motorists to read it.

The differential threshold

The **differential threshold** refers to the ability of a sensory system to detect changes or differences between two stimuli. A commercial that is intentionally produced in black-and-white might be noticed on a colour television because the intensity of colour differs from the programme that preceded it. The same commercial being watched on a black and white television would not be seen as different and might be ignored altogether.

The issue of when and if a change will be noticed is relevant to many marketing situations. Sometimes a marketer may want to ensure that a change is noticed, such as when merchandise is offered at a discount. In other situations, the fact that a change has been made is downplayed, as in the case of price increases or when the size of the product is decreased (e.g. a chocolate bar).

A consumer's ability to detect a difference between two stimuli is relative. A whispered conversation that might be unintelligible on a noisy street can suddenly become public and embarrassing knowledge in a quiet library. It is the relative difference between the decibel level of the conversation and its surroundings, rather than the loudness of the conversation itself, that determines whether the stimulus will register.

The minimum change in a stimulus that can be detected is also known as the **JND**, which stands for just noticeable difference. In the nineteenth century, Ernst Weber, a psychophysicist, found that the amount of change that is necessary to be noticed is related to the original intensity of the stimulus. The stronger the initial stimulus, the greater the change must be for it to be noticed. This relationship is known as **Weber's Law.** Many companies choose to update their packages periodically, making small changes that will not necessarily be noticed at the time. When a product icon is updated, the manufacturer does not want people to lose their identification with a familiar symbol.

Figure 2.3 **The slight changes in the design of Campbell's canned soups illustrate the company's efforts to keep the central, traditional features of the brand packaging while making sure that the product does not begin to look dated.**
Courtesy of Campbell's Inc.

Perceptual selection

Although we live in an 'information society', we can have too much of a good thing. Consumers are often in a state of sensory overload, exposed to far more information than they are capable or willing to process. People in a noisy, crowded bar or party for several hours may feel the need to step outside periodically to take a break. A consumer can experience a similar feeling of being overwhelmed after being forced to sift through the claims made by hundreds of competing brands. Further, the competition for our attention is increasing steadily with the increasing number of exposures to television commercials and other types of advertising.

Because the brain's capacity to process information is limited, consumers are very selective about what they pay attention to. **Perceptual selectivity** means that people attend to only a small portion of stimuli to which they are exposed. Consumers practise a form of psychic economy, picking and choosing among stimuli, to avoid being overwhelmed by *advertising clutter*. This overabundance of advertising stimuli highlights two important aspects of perceptual selectivity as they relate to consumer behaviour: exposure and attention.

Marketing pitfall

Consumers and marketers are increasingly annoyed by advertising clutter. Advertising professionals feel that the proliferation of ads in both traditional media as well as non-traditional locations, such as in cinemas and on TV monitors in doctors' waiting rooms, is threatening the quality of their work. They fear that consumers will be so bombarded by competing stimuli that they won't be in a receptive frame of mind when their messages are transmitted. Consumers are also fed up. More and more surveys reveal that it takes a very good ad to avoid consumer boredom and hold the attention: either a good joke, nice aesthetics or some real information – whatever these are.

Exposure

Exposure is the degree to which people notice a stimulus that is within range of their sensory receptors. Consumers concentrate on certain stimuli, are unaware of others, and even go out of their way to ignore some messages. An experiment by a bank illustrates consumers' tendencies to miss or ignore information in which they are not interested. After a law was passed in America requiring banks to explain details about money transfer in electronic banking, the Northwestern National Bank distributed a pamphlet to 120,000 of its customers at considerable cost to provide the required information – hardly exciting bedtime reading. In 100 of the leaflets, a phrase in the middle of the pamphlet offered the reader $10.00 just for finding that paragraph. Not a single person claimed it.[25]

Selective exposure

Experience, which is the result of acquiring stimulation, is one factor that determines how much exposure to a particular stimulus a person accepts. Perceptual filters based on consumers' past experiences influence what we decide to process.

Perceptual vigilance is a factor in selective exposure. Consumers are more likely to be aware of stimuli that relate to their current needs. These needs may be conscious or unconscious. A consumer who rarely notices car ads will become very much conscious of them when he or she is in the market for a new car. A newspaper ad for a fast food restaurant that would otherwise go unnoticed becomes significant when one glances at the paper during a 5 o'clock class.

The advent of the video recorder has allowed consumers armed with remote control fast-forward buttons to be much more selective about which TV messages they are exposed to. By 'zipping', viewers fast-forward through commercials when watching their favourite programmes. A video recorder marketed by Mitsubishi can remove the need for zipping. It distinguishes between the different types of TV signals used to broadcast programmes and commercials and automatically pauses during ads.[26]

Zipping has enhanced the need for advertising creativity. Interesting commercials do not get zipped as frequently. Evidence indicates that viewers are willing to stop fast-forwarding to watch an appealing or novel commercial. In addition, longer commercials and those that keep a static figure on the screen (such as a brand name or a logo) appear to counteract the effects of zipping; they are unaffected by a speed increase, since the figure remains in place.[27]

Adaptation

Another factor affecting exposure is **adaptation**, or the degree to which consumers continue to notice a stimulus over time. The process of adaptation occurs when consumers no longer pay attention to a stimulus because it is so familiar. Almost like drug addiction, a consumer can become 'habituated' and require increasingly stronger 'doses' of a stimulus for it to continue to be noticed. For example, a consumer on the way to work might read a new advertising hoarding, but after a few days it becomes part of the passing scenery.

Several factors can lead to adaptation:

- *Intensity:* Less intense stimuli (e.g. soft sounds or dim colours) habituate because they have less of a sensory impact.
- *Duration:* Stimuli that require relatively lengthy exposure in order to be processed tend to habituate because they require a long attention span.
- *Discrimination:* Simple stimuli tend to habituate because they do not require attention to detail.
- *Exposure:* Frequently encountered stimuli tend to habituate as the rate of exposure increases.
- *Relevance:* Stimuli that are irrelevant or unimportant will habituate because they fail to attract attention.

Attention

Attention is the degree to which consumers focus on stimuli within their range of exposure. Because consumers are exposed to so many advertising stimuli, marketers are becoming increasingly creative in their attempts to gain attention for their products.

A dynamic package is one way to gain this attention. Some consulting firms have established elaborate procedures to measure package effectiveness, using such instruments as an angle meter, which measures package visibility as a shopper moves down the aisle and views the package from different angles. Also, data from eye-tracking tests, in which consumers' eye movements as they look at packages and ads are followed and measured, can result in subtle but powerful changes that influence their impact. Eye tracking tests are also used to evaluate in-store displays.[28]

Countering advertising clutter

Many marketers are attempting to counter the sensory overload caused by advertising clutter in order to call attention to their products. One expensive strategy involves buying large blocks of advertising space in order to dominate consumers' attention. IBM has experimented with buying two or three consecutive full-page newspaper ads. And Coca-Cola once bought a full 5-minute block of TV commercial time on Danish television shortly before Christmas.

Other companies are using 'bookend ads', where a commercial for one product is split into parts that are separated by commercials for other products. The first part creates conflict, and the second resolves it. This technique motivates the viewer to keep watching in order to get the rest of the story. For example, a TV commercial for Tuborg's special Christmas brew beer showed a cartoon Santa Claus in his sleigh going from one side of the screen to the other. After a couple of other commercials, he reappears, this time meeting a Tuborg delivery van going in the opposite direction. He quickly turns his sleigh round and follows the van as Tuborg wishes everybody a merry Christmas and a happy new year.

Some advertisers have taken to printing part of their ads upside down to get the reader's attention. Perhaps reflecting differences in level of cultural involvement in advertising, the editor of the Starch-Tested Copy newsletter noted, 'I find people don't like to work at reading their ads! Americans don't like it. There's a disorienting aspect they find uncomfortable. The English, on the other hand, like it.'[29]

Another solution has been to put ads in unconventional places, where there will be less competition for attention. These include the backs of supermarket shopping trolleys, underground pedestrian passes, floors of sports stadiums and even films, as the growing interest in product placement has shown.[30] More obscure places where advertisements can be found are public toilets,[31] petrol pump handles and on the steps in the London Underground.[32] And, of course, runner Linford Christie's specially designed contact lenses with the Puma logo created a lot of publicity.[33] An executive at Campbell's Soup, commenting on the company's decision to place ads in church bulletins, noted, 'We have to shake consumers up these days in order to make them take notice . . . . Television alone won't do that. Now we have to hit them with our ads where they shop and play and on their way to work.'[34] Of course, such a policy may backfire if people are getting more and more weary of the difficulty of finding advertising-free moments in their life. One of the more grotesque examples of 'new media' were the rumours that Nike would buy Brazilian footballer Ronaldo for $64 million. Having him play for just one club was considered a too narrow utilization of his name and sales effects. Instead he was supposed to play in a new club each year, according to where he could be most useful for Nike's marketing efforts.[35] The deal was not completed.

Creating contrast

When many stimuli are competing to be noticed, one will receive attention to the extent that it differs from those around it. Stimuli that fall into unpredictable patterns often command a lot of attention. Size and colour differences are also powerful ways to achieve contrast. A black-and-white object in a colour ad is quite noticeable, as is a block of printed type surrounded by large amounts of white space. The size of the stimulus itself in contrast to the competition is also important.

The music industry is trying new formats to reach potential buyers. MCA Records paid a major cinema chain to screen a music video by Tom Petty and the Heartbreakers prior to showing its scheduled films, while Mercury Records launched a bus placard campaign in eighteen cities to promote a new John Mellencamp album. As the senior vice-president of marketing for MCA noted, 'There is a real strong corollary between people who see films and buy music. And one thing you know for sure is that when they are in a movie house, you've got them. They are all looking at the screen.'[36]

A more and more frequently used way of creating contrast is by using advertising clichés and then giving them a twist. The Energizer Bunny™ cropping up in what looks like a completely different commercial is one example of this (cf. the discussion of semiotics below). A mortgage company used the cliché of a homecoming soldier and the young waiting wife to advertise new restoration loans. After seeing the woman gazing out of the window and the soldier in the troop transport, he finally arrives – only to hit his head hard on a low-hanging tie beam.[37] In general, self-referential advertisements where sympathy and credibility are created by mocking advertising or other cultural stereotypes are becoming more and more common.[38]

Interpretation: deciding what things mean

Interpretation refers to the meaning that people assign to sensory stimuli. Just as people differ in terms of the stimuli that they perceive, the eventual assignment of meanings to these stimuli varies as well. Two people can see or hear the same event, but their interpretation of it may be completely different.

Consumers assign meaning to stimuli based on the *schema*, or set of beliefs, to which the stimulus is assigned. During a process known as **priming**, certain properties of a stimulus are more likely to evoke a schema than others. As evidenced by the case of Castello cheese quoted earlier, a brand name can communicate expectations about product attributes and colour consumers' perceptions of product performance by activating a schema.

Stimulus ambiguity occurs when a stimulus is not clearly perceived or when it conveys a number of meanings. In such cases, consumers tend to project their own wishes and desires to assign meaning. Although ambiguity in product advertisements is normally seen as undesirable to marketers, it is used creatively more and more frequently to generate contrast, paradox, controversy or interest. For example, a popular ad for Benson & Hedges cigarettes featured a group of people sitting around a dinner table, while a man wearing only pyjama bottoms stands in the background. This ambiguous character yielded valuable publicity for the company as people competed to explain the meaning of the mysterious 'pyjama man'.

Stimulus organization

People do not perceive a single stimulus in isolation. Our brains tend to relate incoming sensations to imagery of other events or sensations already in memory based on some fundamental organizational principles. A number of perceptual principles describe how stimuli are perceived and organized.

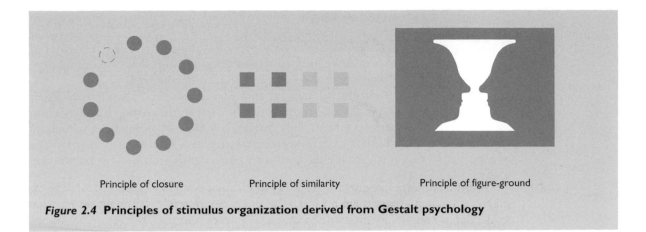

Principle of closure   Principle of similarity   Principle of figure-ground

Figure 2.4 **Principles of stimulus organization derived from Gestalt psychology**

The gestalt

These principles are based on work in **gestalt psychology**, a school of thought maintaining that people derive meaning from the totality of a set of stimuli, rather than from any individual stimulus. The German word *Gestalt* roughly means whole, pattern or configuration, and this perspective is best summarized by the saying 'the whole is greater than the sum of its parts'. A piecemeal perspective that analyzes each component of the stimulus separately will be unable to capture the total effect. The gestalt perspective provides several principles relating to the way stimuli are organized. Three of these principles, or perceptual tendencies, are illustrated in Figure 2.4.

The gestalt **principle of closure** implies that consumers tend to perceive an incomplete picture as complete. That is, we tend to fill in the blanks based on our prior experience. This principle explains why most of us have no trouble reading a

This J&B ad illustrates the use of the principle of closure, in which people participate in the ad by mentally filling in the gaps.
Reprinted with permission from the Paddington Corporation ©.

neon sign, even if one or two of its letters are burned out, or filling in the blanks in an incomplete message, as illustrated by the J&B ad shown here. The principle of closure is also at work when we hear only part of a jingle or theme. Utilization of the principle of closure in marketing strategies encourages audience participation, which increases the chance that people will attend to the message.

The **principle of similarity** tells us that consumers tend to group together objects that share similar physical characteristics. That is, they group like items into sets to form an integrated whole. This principle is used by companies who have extended product lines, but wish to keep certain features similar, such as the shape of a bottle, so that it is easy for the consumer to recognize that he is in fact buying a shampoo of brand X.

Another important gestalt concept is the **figure-ground principle**, in which one part of a stimulus (the figure) will dominate while other parts recede into the background. This concept is easy to understand if one thinks of a photograph with a clear and sharply focused object (the figure) in the centre. The figure is dominant, and the eye goes straight to it. The parts of the configuration that will be perceived as figure or ground can vary depending on the individual consumer as well as other factors. Similarly, in marketing messages that use the figure-ground principle, a stimulus can be made the focal point of the message or merely the context that surrounds the focus.

'What makes life a little greener . . . ?' This ad (one of a long-running and very successful campaign) for one of the Tuborg beer brands ('Tuborg Green Label') uses a colour coding referring to both green as part of the brand name and the positive associations with the colour green: Spring, Freshness, Nature . . . At the same time, it uses the figure-ground principle to invite people to recognize the well-known shapes of a beer bottle and the unique 8-like shape of the Green Tuborg label in the ad.
Courtesy of Tuborg Breweries.

The role of symbolism in interpretation

When we try to make sense of a marketing stimulus, whether a distinctive package, an elaborately staged television commercial or perhaps a model on the cover of a magazine, we do so by interpreting its meaning in the light of associations we have with these images. For this reason much of the meaning we take away is influenced by what we make of the symbolism we perceive. After all, on the surface many marketing images have virtually no literal connection to actual products. What does a cowboy have to do with a bit of tobacco rolled into a paper tube? How can a celebrity such as the football star Gary Lineker enhance the image of a potato crisp?

For assistance, in understanding how consumers interpret the meanings of symbols, some marketers are turning to a field of study known as **semiotics**, which examines the correspondence between signs and symbols and their role in the assignment of meaning.[39] Semiotics is important to the understanding of consumer behaviour, since consumers use products to express their social identities. Products have learned meanings, and we rely on advertising to work out what those meanings are. As one set of researchers put it, 'advertising serves as a kind of culture/ consumption dictionary; its entries are products, and their definitions are cultural meanings.'[40]

According to the semiotician Charles Sanders Peirce, every message has three basic components: an object, a sign and an interpretant. A marketing message such as a Marlboro ad, can be read on different levels. On the lowest level of reading, the **object** would be the product that is the focus of the message (e.g. Marlboro cigarettes). The **sign** is the sensory imagery that represents the intended meanings of the object (the contents of the ad, in this case, the cowboy). The **interpretant** is the meaning derived (e.g. this man smokes these cigarettes). But this man is not any man. He is a cowboy – and not just any cowboy. The interpretant 'man (cowboy) smoking these cigarettes' in itself becomes a sign, especially since we have already seen many examples of these ads from this company. So, on the second, connotative level, this sign refers to the fictive personality of 'the Marlboro Man', and its interpretant consists of all the connotations attached to the Marlboro Man, for example him being a 'rugged, individualistic American'. On the third level, called the ideological level, the interpretant of the 'rugged, individualistic American' becomes a sign for what is stereotypically American. So its object is 'America', and the interpretant all the ideas and characteristics that we might consider as typically and quintessentially American. This semiotic relationship is shown in Figure 2.5. By means of such a chain of meanings, the Marlboro ad both borrows from and contributes to reinforce a fundamental 'myth of America'. We will return to the discussion of myths and consumption in chapter 14.

From the semiotic perspective of Peirce, signs are related to objects in one of three ways. They can resemble objects, be connected to them with some kind of causal or other relation, or be conventionally tied to them.[41] An **icon** is a sign that resembles the product in some way (e.g. Apple Computers uses the image of an apple to represent itself). An index is a sign that is connected to a product because they share some property (e.g. the pine tree on certain cleaning products conveys the shared property of fresh, natural scent). A symbol is a sign that is related to a product through purely conventional associations (e.g. the Mercedes star which in addition to the Mercedes-Benz company provides associations with German industrial quality and ingenuity).

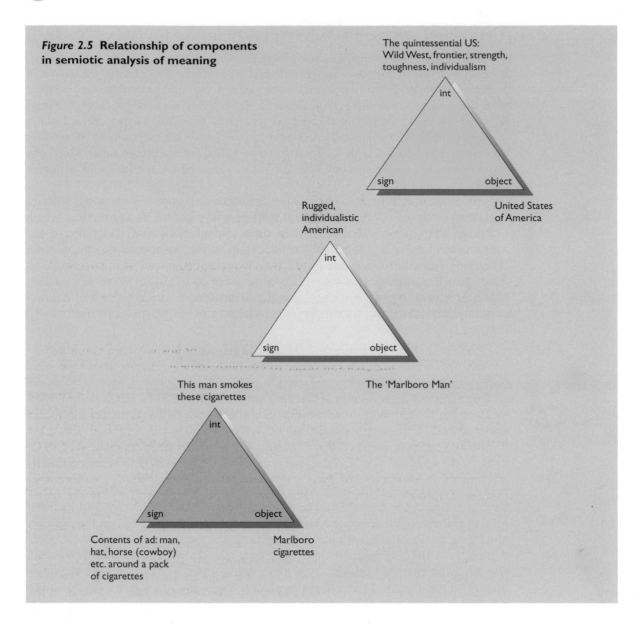

Figure 2.5 **Relationship of components in semiotic analysis of meaning**

The quintessential US: Wild West, frontier, strength, toughness, individualism

int

sign   object

United States of America

Rugged, individualistic American

int

sign   object

The 'Marlboro Man'

This man smokes these cigarettes

int

sign   object

Contents of ad: man, hat, horse (cowboy) etc. around a pack of cigarettes

Marlboro cigarettes

The Cognac Hennessy ad illustrates some of the subtle semiotic processes that convey meaning in advertising. The product, cognac, is a luxury alcoholic beverage associated with a soft, smooth taste, luxurious surroundings, and a large price tag. The label is an icon – it literally represents the product. Silk is used as an index that shares properties with the cognac – it is smooth and also associated with luxury. The woman wrapped in a silk gown is a symbol – she stands for sex appeal, smoothness and luxury. The creators of the ad hope that these properties will transfer to people's perceptions of the product.

The use of symbols provides a powerful means for marketers to convey product attributes to consumers. For example, expensive cars, designer fashions and diamond jewellery – all widely recognized symbols of success – frequently appear in ads to associate products with affluence or sophistication. The rhetoric of advertising is an additional field of analysis which has been useful for the discussion of how adver-

An illustration of how to read an advertisement semiotically. Note again the reference to smoothness, also found in some of the other alcohol ads in this chapter.
Reprinted with permission by Schieffelin & Somerset Co.

tising communicates its messages.[42] Semiotic analysis of ads has been connected to product and brand life cycles in order to establish some guidelines about when to use the most complex advertising forms.[43]

One aspect of the semiotics of consumption, which used to be relatively neglected compared to the semiotics of advertising, is the semiotics of goods as such. In recent years, instead of studying messages about commodities there has been an increased number of studies of commodities as messages.[44] Semiotics of consumer goods, then, focus on the ability of goods to communicate either by themselves or in connection to other goods. A related field of study is symbolic consumption,[45] which focuses not so much on the good as sign *per se*, but rather on the meanings attached to the act of consuming the good. Here, in many cases, the good becomes an indexical sign for some attributes that characterize the consumer, such as trendiness, wealth, femininity or other attributes placing the consumer in some subcultural context.

Other uses of semiotics include industrial design[46] and design of distribution outlets. For example, in a semiotic study of the meanings and expectations consumers' would attach to a new hypermarket, the researchers generated four different value profiles among potential customers. These profiles were linked to preferences for different designs of the hypermarket and its interior, thus helping the planners to conceive a type of hypermarket that was pleasing to most consumers.[47]

Semiotics plays a central role in much of the recent challenging consumer behaviour theory. Due to the fact that consumers have become increasingly aware of how they communicate through their consumption as well as what they communicate has led to the designation of the present world as a 'semiotic world'.[48] Furthermore, it has been argued that we feel more confident in creating our own messages rather than just following what is proposed by marketing or fashion statements. This tendency to eclecticism means that we are more and more likely to match things, such as articles of clothing, furniture or even lifestyles that traditionally have not been perceived as fitting together.

As we have already argued, one of the hallmarks of modern advertising is that it creates a condition where advertising is becoming self-referential. An increasing number of ads and commercials are referring, often ironically or tongue-in-cheek,

The popular pink Energizer Bunny™, gaily marching though fake commercials, creates
a condition of hyperreality in which product symbols take on a life of their own.
Courtesy of the Eveready Battery Company Inc.

to other advertisements, and thus create a universe of their own, which in many
ways is independent from the goods actually advertised. Advertising thus becomes
an art in itself and is appreciated as such rather than as deceptive information about
products.[49] **Hyperreality** refers to the becoming real of what is initially simulation
or 'hype'.[50] Advertisers create new relationships between objects and interpretants
by inventing new connections between products and benefits, such as equating
Marlboro cigarettes with the American frontier spirit.[51] To a large extent, over time
the relationship between the symbol and reality is increasingly difficult to discern,
and the 'artificial' associations between advertisement symbols, product symbols
and the real world may take on a life of their own.

For example, Tasters' Choice coffee perfected the concept of an ongoing series
of 'soap opera' commercials where a romantic relationship is slowly cultivated
between two actors, a commercial form later adopted by other coffee brands such
as Nestlé's Gold Blend. The pink Energizer Bunny™, who began life in regular
Eveready Battery commercials, now goes gaily marching through fake commercials
for such totally unrelated products as 'Alarm' bath and shower soap – where the
Bunny is appropriately dressed in rain gear. As illustrated by the film stills shown
here, the Bunny's antics take the actors in these simulated commercials by surprise
and usually the viewers as well.

Hyperreality will be discussed again in the final chapter of the book, because it
has been linked to the concept of postmodernism, the idea that we are living in a
period of radical cultural change where certain hitherto dominant features and
assumptions of modern societies are challenged.

Chapter summary

- Perception is the process by which physical sensations such as sights, sounds
  and smells are selected, organized and interpreted. The eventual interpretation
  of a stimulus allows it to be assigned meaning. A perceptual map is a widely
  used marketing tool which evaluates the relative standing of competing brands
  along relevant dimensions.
- Marketing stimuli have important sensory qualities. We rely on colours,
  odours, sounds, tastes and even the 'feel' of products when forming
  evaluations of them.

- Not all sensations successfully make their way through the perceptual process. Many stimuli compete for our attention, and the majority are not noticed or comprehended.
- People have different thresholds of perception. A stimulus must be presented at a certain level of intensity before it can be detected by sensory receptors. In addition, a consumer's ability to detect whether two stimuli are different (the differential threshold) is an important issue in many marketing contexts, such as changing a package design, altering the size of a product or reducing its price.
- Some of the factors that determine which stimuli (above the threshold level) do get perceived are the amount of exposure to the stimulus, how much attention it generates and how it is interpreted. In an increasingly crowded stimulus environment, advertising clutter occurs when too many marketing-related messages compete for attention.
- A stimulus that is attended to is not perceived in isolation. It is classified and organized according to principles of perceptual organization. These principles are guided by a gestalt, or overall, pattern. Specific grouping principles include closure, similarity and figure-ground relationships.
- The final step in the process of perception is interpretation. We make sense of the world through the interpretation of signs: icons, indexes and symbols. This interpretation is often shared by others, thus forming common languages and cultures. The degree to which the symbolism is consistent with our previous experience affects the meaning we assign to related objects. Every marketing message contains a relationship between the product, the sign or symbol, and the interpretation of meaning. A semiotic analysis involves the correspondence between message elements and the meaning of signs.
- Signs function on several levels. The intended meaning may be literal (e.g. an icon like a street sign with a picture of children playing). The meaning may be indexical; it relies on shared characteristics (e.g. the horizontal stripe in a stop sign means do not pass beyond this). Finally, meaning can be conveyed by a symbol, where an image is given meaning by convention or by agreement by members of a society (e.g. stop signs are octagonal, while yield signs are triangular).

🔑 Key terms

Absolute threshold *(p. 49)*	**Object** *(p. 57)*
Adaptation *(p. 52)*	**Perception** *(p. 40)*
Attention *(p. 52)*	**Perceptual map** *(p. 42)*
Differential threshold *(p. 50)*	**Perceptual selectivity** *(p. 51)*
Exposure *(p. 51)*	**Principle of closure** *(p. 55)*
Figure-ground principle *(p. 56)*	**Principle of similarity** *(p. 56)*
Gestalt psychology *(p. 55)*	**Psychophysics** *(p. 49)*
Hedonic consumption *(p. 43)*	**Schema** *(p. 40)*
Hyperreality *(p. 60)*	**Semiotics** *(p. 57)*
Icon *(p. 57)*	**Sensation** *(p. 40)*
Interpretant *(p. 57)*	**Sign** *(p. 57)*
Interpretation *(p. 54)*	**Stimulus ambiguity** *(p. 54)*
JND *(p. 50)*	**Weber's Law** *(p. 50)*

Consumer behaviour challenge

1. Many studies have shown that our sensory detection abilities decline as we grow older. Discuss the implications of the absolute threshold for marketers attempting to appeal to the elderly.

2. Interview 3–5 male and 3–5 female friends regarding their perceptions of both men's and women's fragrances. Construct a perceptual map for each set of products. Based on your map of perfumes, do you see any areas that are not adequately served by current offerings? What (if any) gender differences did you obtain regarding both the relevant dimensions used by raters and the placement of specific brands along these dimensions?

3. Assume that you are a consultant for a marketer who wants to design a package for a new premium chocolate bar targeted to an affluent market. What recommendations would you provide in terms of such package elements as colour, symbolism and graphic design? Give the reasons for your suggestions.

4. Do you believe that marketers have the right to use any or all public spaces to deliver product messages? Where would you draw the line in terms of places and products that should be restricted?

5. Find one ad that is rich in symbolism and perform a semiotic analysis of it. Identify each type of sign used in the ad and the product qualities being communicated by each. Comment on the effectiveness of the signs that are used to communicate the intended message.

6. Using magazines archived in the library, track the packaging of a specific brand over time. Find an example of gradual changes in package design that may have been below the JND.

7. Collect a set of current ads for one type of product (e.g. personal computers, perfumes, laundry detergents or athletic shoes) from magazines, and analyze the colours employed. Describe the images conveyed by different colours, and try to identify any consistency across brands in terms of the colours used in product packaging or other aspects of the ads.

8. Look through a current magazine and select one ad that captures your attention over the others. Give the reasons why.

9. Find ads that utilize the techniques of contrast and novelty. Give your opinion of the effectiveness of each ad and whether the technique is likely to be appropriate for the consumers targeted by the ad.

Gabriele Morello, ISIDA, Palermo, Italy

Mario Rossi is a 60-year-old Italian insurance man, and still very active in his field. He is a pleasant, sociable and easy-going fellow, and has made a very good career for himself. Together with his wife and four children, he lives in a comfortable flat in the suburbs of Rome. Although Rome is full of historical sites to visit, Mario is a staunch nature-lover, and he prefers to 'get back to nature' in his free time.

Coming home late after work, the dog Raphael recognizes the sound of his old Fiat drawing up outside. Mario's 'first love' was a Fiat 126, and in spite of his good income, he keeps the old car running. Relaxing and sipping a glass of Chianti is just what he needs after a hard day's work. The furniture in his sitting room, and even his television set, are not the latest models, but he likes it that way – the old objects give him a sense of security. Slowly winding down, he looks forward to spending the weekend with his family and friends at his house in the countryside. He grew up there, and is very attached to the old villa and everything in it.

He often imagines what it will be like when he retires when he will be able to live there permanently, surrounded by his family. It will be like the good old days, when he was a boy and life was uncomplicated, less chaotic. He pictures them all sitting around the table enjoying a leisurely meal (with pasta, of course!) made from home-grown produce, and afterwards sitting together.

This peaceful fantasy is in stark contrast to the reality of last weekend! His two eldest sons had gone off to a football match. The youngest ones restlessly complained about the fact that there still was no internet connection in the house, and then went into another room to settle down in front of the television for what they called an afternoon's entertainment!

Learning and memory

Learning refers to a relatively permanent change in behaviour which comes with experience. This experience does not have to affect the learner directly; we can learn vicariously by observing events that affect others.[1] We also learn even when we are not trying to do so. Consumers, for example, recognize many brand names and can hum many product jingles, even for those product categories they themselves do not use. This casual, unintentional acquisition of knowledge is known as **incidental learning**. Like the concept of perception discussed in the last chapter, learning is a process. Our knowledge about the world is constantly being revised as we are exposed to new stimuli and receive feedback that allows us to modify behaviour in other, similar situations. The concept of learning covers a lot of ground, ranging from a consumer's simple association between a stimulus such as a product logo (e.g. Coca-Cola) and a response (e.g. 'refreshing soft drink') to a complex series of cognitive activities (e.g. writing an essay on learning for a consumer behaviour exam). Psychologists who study learning have advanced several theories to explain the learning process. These range from those focusing on simple stimulus–response associations to perspectives that regard consumers as complex problem-solvers who learn abstract rules and concepts by observing others.

Behavioural learning theories

Behavioural learning theories assume that learning takes place as the result of responses to external events. Psychologists who subscribe to this viewpoint do not focus on internal thought processes. Instead, they approach the mind as a 'black box' and emphasize the observable aspects of behaviour, as depicted in Figure 3.1. The observable aspects consist of things that go into the box (the stimuli, or events perceived from the outside world) and things that come out of the box (the responses, or reactions to these stimuli).

This view is represented by two major approaches to learning: classical conditioning and instrumental conditioning. People's experiences are shaped by the feedback they receive as they go through life. Similarly, consumers respond to brand names, scents, jingles and other marketing stimuli based on the learned connections they have formed over time. People also learn that actions they take result in rewards and punishments, and this feedback influences the way they respond in similar situations in the future. Consumers who are complimented on a product choice will be more likely to buy that brand again, while those who get food poisoning at a new restaurant will not be likely to patronize it in the future.

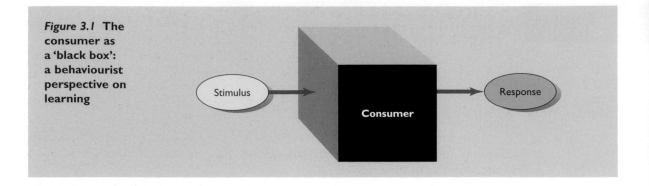

Figure 3.1 **The consumer as a 'black box': a behaviourist perspective on learning**

Classical conditioning

Classical conditioning occurs when a stimulus that elicits a response is paired with another stimulus that initially does not elicit a response on its own. Over time, this second stimulus causes a similar response because it is associated with the first stimulus. This phenomenon was first demonstrated in dogs by Ivan Pavlov, a Russian physiologist doing research on digestion in animals.

Pavlov induced classically conditioned learning by pairing a neutral stimulus (a bell) with a stimulus known to cause a salivation response in dogs (he squirted dried meat powder into their mouths). The powder was an unconditioned stimulus (UCS) because it was naturally capable of causing the response. Over time, the bell became a conditioned stimulus (CS); it did not initially cause salivation, but the dogs learned to associate the bell with the meat powder and began to salivate at the sound of the bell only. The drooling of these canine consumers over a sound, now linked to feeding time, was a conditioned response (CR).

This basic form of classical conditioning primarily applies to responses controlled by the autonomic (e.g. salivation) and nervous (e.g. eye blink) systems. That is, it focuses on visual and olfactory cues that induce hunger, thirst or sexual arousal. When these cues are consistently paired with conditioned stimuli, such as brand names, consumers may learn to feel hungry, thirsty or aroused when later exposed to the brand cues.

Classical conditioning can have similar effects for more complex reactions, too. Even a credit card becomes a conditioned cue that triggers greater spending, especially since it is a stimulus that is present only in situations where consumers are spending money. People learn they can make larger purchases when using credit cards, and they also have been found to leave larger tips than they do when using cash.[2] Small wonder that American Express® reminds us, 'Don't leave home without it.' Conditioning effects are more likely to occur after the conditioned and unconditioned stimuli have been paired a number of times.[3] Repeated exposures increase the strength of stimulus–response associations and prevent the decay of these associations in memory.

Conditioning will not occur or will take longer if the CS is only occasionally presented with the UCS. One result of this lack of association may be **extinction**, which occurs when the effects of prior conditioning are reduced and finally disappear. This can occur, for example, when a product is overexposed in the marketplace so that its original allure is lost. The Lacoste polo shirt, with its distinctive crocodile logo, is a good example of this effect. When the once-exclusive crocodile started to appear on baby clothes and many other items, it lost its cachet and was soon replaced by other contenders, such as the Lauren polo player.[4]

Stimulus generalization refers to the tendency of stimuli similar to a CS to evoke similar, conditioned responses.[5] Pavlov noticed in subsequent studies that his dogs would sometimes salivate when they heard noises that only resembled a bell (e.g. keys jangling). People react to other, similar stimuli in much the same way they responded to an original stimulus. A chemist shop's bottle of own-brand mouthwash deliberately packaged to resemble Listerine mouthwash may evoke a similar response among consumers who assume that this 'me-too' product shares other characteristics of the original.

Stimulus discrimination occurs when a stimulus similar to a CS is not followed by a UCS. In these situations, reactions are weakened and will soon disappear. Part of the learning process involves making a response to some stimuli but not to other, similar stimuli. Manufacturers of well-established brands commonly urge consumers not to buy 'cheap imitations' because the results will not be what they expect.

Operant conditioning

Operant conditioning, also known as instrumental conditioning, occurs as the individual learns to perform behaviours that produce positive outcomes and to avoid those that yield negative outcomes. This learning process is most closely associated with the psychologist B. F. Skinner, who demonstrated the effects of instrumental conditioning by teaching animals to dance, pigeons to play ping-pong, and so on, by systematically rewarding them for desired behaviours.[6]

While responses in classical conditioning are involuntary and fairly simple, those in instrumental conditioning are made deliberately to obtain a goal and may be more complex. The desired behaviour may be learned over a period of time, as intermediate actions are rewarded in a process called shaping. For example, the owner of a new shop may award prizes to shoppers just for coming in, hoping that over time they will continue to drop in and eventually buy something.

Also, classical conditioning involves the close pairing of two stimuli. Instrumental learning occurs as a result of a reward received following the desired behaviour and takes place over a period in which a variety of other behaviours are attempted and abandoned because they are not reinforced. A good way to remember the difference is to keep in mind that in instrumental learning the response is performed because it is instrumental to gaining a reward or avoiding a punishment. Consumers over time come to associate with people that reward them and to choose products that make them feel good or satisfy some need.

Operant conditioning (instrumental learning) occurs in one of three ways. When the environment provides **positive reinforcement** in the form of a reward, the response is strengthened, and appropriate behaviour is learned. For example, a woman who is complimented after wearing Obsession perfume will learn that using this product has the desired effect, and she will be more likely to keep buying the product. **Negative reinforcement** also strengthens responses so that appropriate behaviour is learned. A perfume company, for example, might run an ad showing a woman sitting alone on a Saturday night because she did not use its fragrance. The message to be conveyed is that she could have avoided this negative outcome if only she had used the perfume. In contrast to situations wherein we learn to do certain things in order to avoid unpleasantness, punishment occurs when a response is followed by unpleasant events (such as being ridiculed by friends for wearing an offensive-smelling perfume). We learn not to repeat these behaviours.

When trying to understand the differences among these mechanisms, keep in mind that reactions from a person's environment to behaviour can be either positive or negative and that these outcomes or anticipated outcomes can be applied or removed. That is, under conditions of both positive reinforcement and punishment, the person receives a reaction after doing something. In contrast, negative reinforcement occurs when a negative outcome is avoided; the removal of something negative is pleasurable and hence is rewarding. Finally, when a positive outcome is no longer received, extinction is likely to occur, and the learned stimulus–response connection will not be maintained (as when a woman no longer receives compliments on her perfume). Thus, positive and negative reinforcement strengthen the future linkage between a response and an outcome because of the pleasant experience. This tie is weakened under conditions of both punishment and extinction because of the unpleasant experience. The relationships among these four conditions are easier to understand by referring to Figure 3.2.

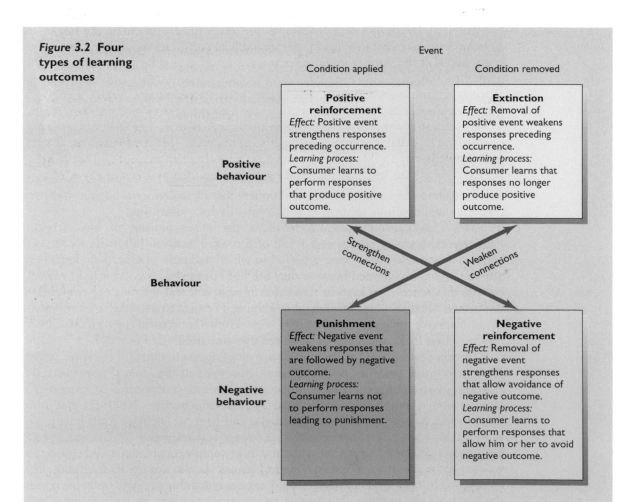

Figure 3.2 **Four types of learning outcomes**

Event

Condition applied

Condition removed

Positive reinforcement
Effect: Positive event strengthens responses preceding occurrence.
Learning process: Consumer learns to perform responses that produce positive outcome.

Extinction
Effect: Removal of positive event weakens responses preceding occurrence.
Learning process: Consumer learns that responses no longer produce positive outcome.

Positive behaviour

Strengthen connections

Weaken connections

Behaviour

Punishment
Effect: Negative event weakens responses that are followed by negative outcome.
Learning process: Consumer learns not to perform responses leading to punishment.

Negative reinforcement
Effect: Removal of negative event strengthens responses that allow avoidance of negative outcome.
Learning process: Consumer learns to perform responses that allow him or her to avoid negative outcome.

Negative behaviour

An important factor in operant conditioning is the set of rules by which appropriate reinforcements are given for a behaviour. The issue of what is the most effective reinforcement schedule to use is important to marketers, because it relates to the amount of effort and resources they must devote to rewarding consumers in order to condition desired behaviours.

- *Fixed-interval reinforcement.* After a specified period has passed, the first response that is made brings the reward. Under such conditions, people tend to respond slowly immediately after being reinforced, but their responses speed up as the time for the next reinforcement approaches. For example, consumers may crowd into a store for the last day of its seasonal sale and not reappear again until the next one.
- *Variable-interval reinforcement.* The time that must pass before reinforcement is delivered varies around some average. Since the person does not know exactly when to expect the reinforcement, responses must be performed at a consistent rate. This logic is behind retailers' use of so-called secret shoppers – people who periodically test for service quality by posing as customers at unannounced times. Since store employees never know exactly when to expect a visit, high quality must be constantly maintained.
- *Fixed-ratio reinforcement.* Reinforcement occurs only after a fixed number of responses. This schedule motivates people to continue performing the same behaviour over and over again. For example, a consumer might keep buying groceries at the same store in order to earn a gift after collecting 50 books of trading stamps.
- *Variable-ratio reinforcement.* The person is reinforced after a certain number of responses, but he or she does not know how many responses are required. People in such situations tend to respond at very high and steady rates, and this type of behaviour is very difficult to extinguish. This reinforcement schedule is responsible for consumers' attraction to slot machines. They learn that if they keep feeding money into the machine, they will eventually win something (if they don't go broke first).

Cognitive learning theory

Cognitive learning occurs as a result of mental processes. In contrast to behavioural theories of learning, cognitive learning theory stresses the importance of internal mental processes. This perspective views people as problem-solvers who actively use information from the world around them to master their environment. Supporters of this viewpoint also stress the role of creativity and insight during the learning process.

The issue of consciousness

A lot of controversy surrounds the issue of whether or when people are aware of their learning processes. While behavioural learning theorists emphasize the routine, automatic nature of conditioning, proponents of cognitive learning argue that even these simple effects are based on cognitive factors; that is, expectations are created that a stimulus will be followed by a response (the formation of expectations requires mental activity). According to this school of thought, conditioning occurs because subjects develop conscious hypotheses and then act on them.

On the one hand, there is some evidence for the existence of nonconscious procedural knowledge. People apparently do process at least some information in an automatic, passive way, which is a condition that has been termed mindlessness.[7] When we meet someone new or encounter a new product, for example, we have a tendency to respond to the stimulus in terms of existing categories, rather than taking the trouble to formulate different ones. Our reactions are activated by a trigger feature, some stimulus that cues us towards a particular pattern. For example, men in one study rated a car in an ad as superior on a variety of characteristics if a seductive woman (the trigger feature) was present, despite the fact that the men did not believe the woman's presence actually had an influence.[8]

None the less, many modern theorists are beginning to regard some instances of conditioning as cognitive processes, especially where expectations are formed about the linkages between stimuli and responses. Indeed, studies using masking effects, wherein it is difficult for subjects to learn CS/UCS associations, show substantial reductions in conditioning.[9] For example, an adolescent girl may observe that women on television and in real life seem to be rewarded with compliments and attention when they smell nice and wear alluring clothing. She works out that the probability of these rewards occurring is greater when she wears perfume and deliberately wears a popular scent to obtain the payoff of social acceptance.

Observational learning

Observational learning occurs when people watch the actions of others and note the reinforcements they receive for their behaviours. This type of learning is a complex process; people store these observations in memory as they accumulate knowledge, perhaps using this information at a later point to guide their own behaviours. This process of imitating the behaviour of others is called modelling. For example, a woman shopping for a new kind of perfume may remember the reactions a friend received when wearing a certain brand several months earlier; and she will base her behaviour on her friend's actions. In order for observational learning in the form of modelling to occur, four conditions must be met.[10] These factors are summarized in Figure 3.3.

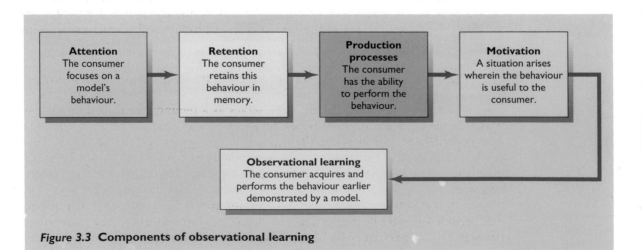

Figure 3.3 **Components of observational learning**

1. The consumer's attention must be directed to the appropriate model who, for reasons of attractiveness, competence, status or similarity, is desirable to emulate.
2. The consumer must remember what is said or done by the model.
3. The consumer must convert this information into actions.
4. The consumer must be motivated to perform these actions.

Marketing applications of learning principles

Understanding how consumers learn is very important to marketers. After all, many strategic decisions are based on the assumption that consumers are continually accumulating information about products and that people can be 'taught' to prefer some alternatives over others.

Behavioural learning applications

Many marketing strategies focus on the establishment of associations between stimuli and responses. Behavioural learning principles apply to many consumer phenomena, ranging from the creation of a distinctive brand image to the perceived linkage between a product and an underlying need.

How marketers take advantage of classical conditioning principles

The transfer of meaning from an unconditioned stimulus to a conditioned stimulus explains why 'made-up' brand names like Marlboro, Coca-Cola or IBM can exert such powerful effects on consumers. The association between the Marlboro Man and the cigarette is so strong that in some cases the company no longer even includes the brand name in its ad. When nonsense syllables (meaningless sets of letters) are paired with such evaluative words as beauty or success, the meaning is transferred to the nonsense syllables. This change in the symbolic significance of initially meaningless words shows that complex meanings can be conditioned.[11]

These conditioned associations are crucial to many marketing strategies that rely on the creation and perpetuation of positive brand equity, in which a brand has strong positive associations in a consumer's memory and commands a lot of loyalty as a result.[12] As we will see in the next chapter, a product with brand equity holds a tremendous advantage in the marketplace.

Repetition One advertising researcher argues that more than three exposures are wasted. The first creates awareness of the product, the second demonstrates its relevance to the consumer, and the third serves as a reminder of the product's benefits.[13] However, even this bare-bones approach implies that repetition is needed to ensure that the consumer is actually exposed to (and processes) the ad at least three times. Marketers attempting to condition an association must ensure that the consumers they have targeted will be exposed to the stimulus a sufficient number of times.

On the other hand, it is possible to have too much of a good thing. Consumers can become so used to hearing or seeing a marketing stimulus that they cease to pay attention to it (see chapter 2). This problem, known as advertising wearout, can be reduced by varying the way in which the basic message is presented.

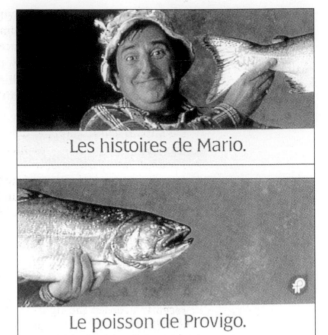

Les histoires de Mario.

Le poisson de Provigo.

One innovative way to employ repetition without causing wearout is illustrated by these related advertising hoarding images.
Courtesy of Cossette Communications Marketing for Provigo Supermarkets, 1986.

Conditioning product associations Advertisements often pair a product with a positive stimulus to create a desirable association. Various aspects of a marketing message, such as music, humour or imagery, can affect conditioning. In one study, subjects who viewed a slide of pens paired with either pleasant or unpleasant music were more likely later to select the pen that appeared with pleasant music.[14]

The order in which the conditioned stimulus and the unconditioned stimulus is presented can affect the likelihood that learning will occur. Generally speaking, the unconditioned stimulus should be presented prior to the conditioned stimulus. The technique of backward conditioning, such as showing a soft drink (the CS) and then playing a jingle (the UCS) is generally not effective.[15] Because sequential presentation is desirable for conditioning to occur, classical conditioning is not very effective in static situations, such as in magazine ads, where (in contrast to TV or radio) the marketer cannot control the order in which the CS and the UCS are perceived.

Just as product associations can be formed, they can be extinguished. Because of the danger of extinction, a classical conditioning strategy may not be as effective for products that are frequently encountered, since there is no guarantee they will be accompanied by the CS. A bottle of Pepsi paired with the refreshing sound of a carbonated beverage being poured over ice may seem like a good example of conditioning. Unfortunately, the product would also be seen in many other contexts where this sound was absent, reducing the effectiveness of the conditioning.

By the same reasoning, a novel tune should be chosen over a popular one to pair with a product, since the popular song might also be heard in many situations in which the product is not present.[16] Music videos in particular may serve as effective UCSs because they often have an emotional impact on viewers and this effect may transfer to ads accompanying the video.[17]

Applications of stimulus generalization The process of stimulus generalization is often central to branding and packaging decisions that attempt to capitalize on consumers' positive associations with an existing brand or company name, as exemplified by a hairdressing establishment called United Hairlines.[18] In one 20-month period, Procter & Gamble introduced almost 90 new products. Not a single product carried a new brand name. In fact, roughly 80 per cent of all new products are actually extensions of existing brands or product lines.[19] Strategies based on stimulus generalization include the following:

- *Family branding*, in which a variety of products capitalize on the reputation of a company name. Companies such as Campbell's, Heinz, Philips and Sony rely on their positive corporate images to sell different product lines.
- *Product line extensions*, in which related products are added to an established brand. Dole, which is associated with fruit, was able to introduce refrigerated juices and juice bars, while Sun Maid went from raisins to raisin bread. Other recent extensions include Woolite rug cleaner, and the various models of Nike Air shoes.[20]
- *Licensing*, in which well-known names are 'rented' by others. This strategy is increasing in popularity as marketers try to link their products and services with well-established figures. Companies as diverse as McDonald's and Harley-Davidson have authorized the use of their names on products. Japan Airlines recently licensed the rights to use Disney characters, and, in addition to painting Mickey Mouse and Donald Duck on several of its planes, the carrier is requiring its flight attendants to wear mouse ears on some domestic flights![21]
- Marketers increasingly are capitalizing on the public's enthusiasm for films and popular TV programmes by developing numerous product tie-ins.
- *Look-alike packaging*, in which distinctive packaging designs create strong associations with a particular brand. This linkage often is exploited by makers of generic or private-label brands who wish to communicate a quality image by putting their products in very similar packages. As one chemist chainstore executive commented, 'You want to tell the consumer that it's close to the national brand. You've got to make it look like, within the law, close to the national brand. They're at least attracted to the package.'[22]

Many marketing strategies focus on the establishment of associations between stimuli and responses. Associating products with the imagery of the popular TV programme *The X Files* is one example of this stimulus–reponse application.
Used with permisson.

Applications of stimulus discrimination An emphasis on communicating a product's distinctive attributes *vis-à-vis* its competitors is an important aspect of positioning, in which consumers learn to differentiate a brand from its competitors (see chapter 2). This is not always an easy task, especially in product categories where the brand names of many of the alternatives look and sound alike. For example, a recent survey showed that many consumers have a great deal of trouble distinguishing among products sold by the top computer manufacturers. With a blur of names like OmniPlex, OptiPlex, Premmia, Premium, ProLinea, ProLiant, etc., this confusion is not surprising.[23]

Companies with a well-established brand image try to encourage stimulus discrimination by promoting the unique attributes of their brands. Thus, the constant reminders for American Express® traveller's cheques: 'Ask for them by name . . . .' On the other hand, a brand name that is used so widely that it is no longer distinctive becomes part of the public domain and can be used by competitors, as has been the case for such products as aspirin, cellophane, yo-yo and escalator.

How marketers take advantage of instrumental conditioning principles

Principles of instrumental conditioning are at work when a consumer is rewarded or punished for a purchase decision. Businesspeople shape behaviour by gradually reinforcing consumers for taking appropriate actions. For example, a car dealer might encourage a reluctant buyer to try sitting in a showroom model, then suggest a test drive, and so on.

Marketers have many ways to reinforce consumers, ranging from a simple thank you after a purchase to substantial rebates and follow-up phone calls. For example, a life insurance company obtained a much higher rate of policy renewal among a group of new customers who received a thank you letter after each payment compared to a control group that did not receive any reinforcement.[24]

A popular technique known as **frequency marketing** reinforces regular purchasers by giving them prizes with values that increase along with the amount purchased. This operant learning strategy was pioneered by the airline industry, which introduced 'frequent-flyer' programmes in the early 1980s to reward loyal customers. Well over 20 per cent of food stores now offer trading stamps or some other frequent-buyer promotion. Manufacturers in the fast moving consumer goods (FMCG) category also make use of this technique in food stores. For example, Douwe Egberts, the coffee manufacturer owned by Sara Lee offers stamps which can be saved and redeemed for a whole range of coffee related products such as expresso makers, service sets and coffee grinders, including their classic (and nostalgic) hand coffee grinder.

In some industries, these reinforcers take the form of clubs, including a Hilton Hotel Club. Club members usually earn bonus points to set against future purchases, and some get such privileges as magazines and free telephone numbers and sometimes even invitations to exclusive outings.

How marketers take advantage of cognitive learning principles

Consumers' ability to learn vicariously by observing how the behaviour of others is reinforced makes the lives of marketers much easier. Because people do not have to be directly reinforced for their actions, marketers do not necessarily have to reward or punish them for purchase behaviours. Instead, they can show what happens to

This cosmetics ad illustrates the principle of vicarious reinforcement. The model uses the product and is shown reaping the reward – the approval of her boyfriend.
Courtesy of Maybelline, Inc.

desirable models who use or do not use their products and know that consumers will often be motivated to imitate these actions at a later time. For example, a perfume commercial may depict a woman surrounded by a throng of admirers who are providing her with positive reinforcement for using the product. Needless to say, this learning process is more practical than providing the same personal attention to each woman who actually buys the perfume!

Consumers' evaluations of models go beyond simple stimulus–response connections. For example, a celebrity's image is often more than a simple reflexive response of good or bad.[25] It is a complex combination of many attributes. In general, the degree to which a model will be emulated depends upon his or her social attractiveness. Attractiveness can be based upon several components, including physical appearance, expertise or similarity to the evaluator.

These factors will be further addressed in chapter 6, which discusses personal characteristics that make a communication's source more or less effective in changing consumers' attitudes. In addition, many applications of consumer problem-solving are related to ways information is represented in memory and recalled at a later date. This aspect of cognitive learning is the focus of the next section.

The role of learning in memory

Memory involves a process of acquiring information and storing it over time so that it will be available when needed. Contemporary approaches to the study of memory employ an information-processing approach. They assume that the mind is in some ways like a computer; data are input, processed and output for later use in revised form. In the **encoding** stage, information is entered in a way the system will recognize. In the **storage** stage, this knowledge is integrated with what is already

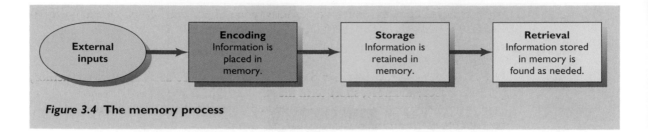

Figure 3.4 The memory process

in memory and 'warehoused' until needed. During **retrieval**, the person accesses the desired information.[26] The memory process is summarized in Figure 3.4.

As suggested by Mario's memories and musings at the beginning of the chapter, many of our experiences are locked inside our heads, and we maintain those memories and recall those experiences if prompted by the right cues. Marketers rely on consumers to retain information they have learned about products and services, trusting that it will later be applied in situations where purchase decisions must be made. During the consumer decision-making process, this internal memory is combined with external memory – which includes all the product details on packages in shopping lists, and through other marketing stimuli – to permit brand alternatives to be identified and evaluated.[27]

Encoding of information for later retrieval

The way information is encoded or mentally programmed helps to determine how it will be represented in memory. In general, incoming data that are associated with other information already in memory stand a better chance of being retained. For example, brand names that are linked to physical characteristics of a product category (e.g. Coffee Mate creamer or Sani-Flush toilet bowl cleaner) or that are easy to visualize (e.g. Tide detergent) tend to be more easily retained in memory than more abstract brand names.[28]

Types of memory

A consumer may process a stimulus simply in terms of its sensory meaning, such as its colour or shape. When this occurs, the meaning may be activated when the person sees a picture of the stimulus. We may experience a sense of familiarity on seeing an ad for a new snack food we recently tasted, for example.

In many cases, though, meanings are encoded at a more abstract level. Semantic meaning refers to symbolic associations, such as the idea that rich people drink champagne or that fashionable men wear an earring.

Episodic memories are those that relate to events that are personally relevant, such as Mario's.[29] As a result, a person's motivation to retain these memories will be strong. Couples often have 'their song' that reminds them of their first date or wedding. The memories that might be triggered upon hearing this song would be quite different and unique for them.

Commercials sometimes attempt to activate episodic memories by focusing on experiences shared by many people. Recall of the past may have an effect on future behaviour. A university fund-raising campaign can get higher donations by evoking pleasant memories. Some especially vivid associations are called _flashbulb_ memories. These are usually related to some highly significant event. As one example, many people claim to remember exactly what they were doing when President Kennedy was assassinated in 1963.

Memory systems

According to the information-processing perspective, there are three distinct memory systems: sensory memory, short-term memory (STM) and long-term memory (LTM). Each plays a role in processing brand-related information. The interrelationships of these memory systems are summarized in Figure 3.5.

Sensory memory permits storage of the information we receive from our senses. This storage is very temporary; it lasts a couple of seconds at most. For example, a person might be walking past a bakery and get a brief, but enticing whiff of bread baking inside. While this sensation would only last for a few seconds, it would be sufficient to allow the person to determine if he or she should investigate further. If the information is retained for further processing, it passes through an attentional gate and is transferred to short-term memory.

Short-term memory also stores information for a limited period of time, and its capacity is limited. Similar to a computer, this system can be regarded as working memory; it holds the information we are currently processing. Verbal input may be stored acoustically (in terms of how it sounds) or semantically (in terms of its meaning).[30]

The information is stored by combining small pieces into larger ones in a process known as 'chunking'. A chunk is a configuration that is familiar to the person and can be manipulated as a unit. For example, a brand name can be a chunk that summarizes a great deal of detailed information about the brand.

Initially, it was believed that STM was capable of processing 5–9 chunks of information at a time, and for this reason phone numbers were designed to have seven digits.[31] It now appears that 3–4 chunks is the optimum size for efficient retrieval (seven-digit phone numbers can be remembered because the individual digits are chunked, so we may remember a three-digit exchange as one piece of information).[32]

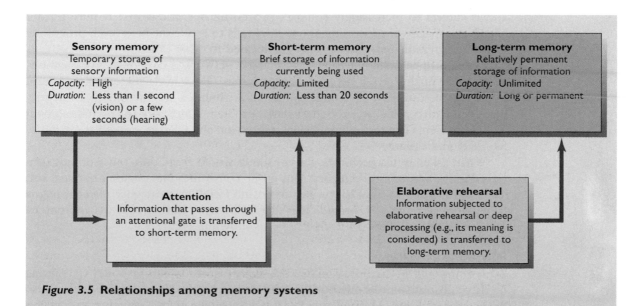

Figure 3.5 **Relationships among memory systems**

Long-term memory is the system that allows us to retain information for a long period of time. In order for information to enter into long-term memory from short-term memory, elaborative rehearsal is required. This process involves thinking about the meaning of a stimulus and relating it to other information already in memory. Marketers sometimes assist in the process by devising catchy slogans or jingles that consumers repeat on their own.

Storing of information in memory

Relationships among the types of memory are a source of some controversy. The traditional perspective, known as multiple-store, assumes that STM and LTM are separate systems. More recent research has moved away from the distinction between the two types of memory, instead emphasizing the interdependence of the systems. This work argues that, depending upon the nature of the processing task, different levels of processing occur that activate some aspects of memory rather than others. These approaches are called **activation models of memory**.[33] The more effort it takes to process information (so-called deep processing), the more likely it is that information will be placed in long-term memory.

Activation models propose that an incoming piece of information is stored in an associative network containing many bits of related information organized according to some set of relationships. The consumer has organized systems of concepts relating to brands, stores, and so on.

Knowledge structures

These storage units, known as **knowledge structures**, can be thought of as complex spiders' webs filled with pieces of data. This information is placed into nodes, which are connected by associative links within these structures. Pieces of information that are seen as similar in some way are chunked together under some more abstract category. New, incoming information is interpreted to be consistent with the structure already in place.[34] According to the hierarchical processing model, a message is processed in a bottom-up fashion: processing begins at a very basic level and is subject to increasingly complex processing operations that require greater cognitive capacity. If processing at one level fails to evoke the next level, processing of the ad is terminated, and capacity is allocated to other tasks.[35]

Links form between nodes as an associative network is developed. For example, a consumer might have a network for 'perfumes'. Each node represents a concept related to the category. This node can be an attribute, a specific brand, a celebrity identified with a perfume, or even a related product. A network for perfumes might include concepts like the names Chanel, Obsession and Charlie, as well as attributes like sexy and elegant.

When asked to list perfumes, the consumer would recall only those brands contained in the appropriate category. This group constitutes that person's **evoked set**. The task of a new entrant that wants to position itself as a category member (e.g. a new luxury perfume) is to provide cues that facilitate its placement in the appropriate category. A sample network for perfumes is shown in Figure 3.6.

Spreading activation

A meaning can be activated indirectly; energy spreads across nodes of varying levels of abstraction. As one node is activated, other nodes associated with it also begin to be triggered. Meaning thus spreads across the network, bringing up concepts

Hierachical processing model.

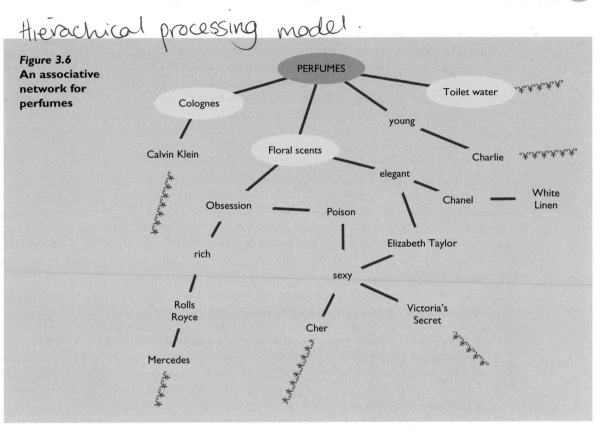

Figure 3.6
**An associative
network for
perfumes**

including competing brands and relevant attributes that are used to form attitudes towards the brand.

This process of spreading activation allows consumers to shift back and forth between levels of meaning. The way a piece of information is stored in memory depends upon the type of meaning assigned to it. This meaning type will, in turn, determine how and when the meaning is activated. For example, the memory trace for an ad could be stored in one or more of the following ways:

- Brand-specific – in terms of claims made for the brand.
- Ad-specific – in terms of the medium or content of the ad itself.
- Brand identification – in terms of the brand name.
- Product category – in terms of how the product works, where it should be used, or experiences with the product.
- Evaluative reactions – in terms of whether 'that looks like fun'.[36]

Levels of knowledge

Knowledge is coded at different levels of abstraction and complexity. Meaning concepts are individual nodes (e.g. elegant). These may be combined into a larger unit, called a proposition (also known as a belief). A proposition links two nodes together to form a more complex meaning, which can serve as a single chunk of information. For example, a proposition might be that 'Chanel is a perfume for elegant women.'

Propositions are, in turn, integrated to produce a complex unit known as a schema. As was noted at the beginning of the chapter, a schema is a cognitive framework that is developed through experience. Information that is consistent with an existing schema is encoded more readily.[37] The ability to move up and down among levels of abstraction greatly increases processing flexibility and efficiency. For this reason, young children, who do not yet have well-developed schemas, are not able to make efficient use of purchase information compared to older children.[38]

One type of schema that is relevant to consumer behaviour is a script, a sequence of procedures that is expected by an individual. For example, consumers learn service scripts that guide expectations and purchasing behaviour in business settings. Consumers learn to expect a certain sequence of events, and they may become uncomfortable if the service departs from the script. A service script for your visit to the dentist might include such events as (1) driving to the dentist, (2) reading old magazines in the waiting room, (3) hearing your name called and sitting in the dentist's chair, (4) having the dentist probe your teeth, (5) having the dentist scale and polish your teeth, and so on. This desire to follow a script helps to explain why such service innovations as automatic bank machines and self-service petrol stations have met with resistance by some consumers, who have trouble adapting to a new sequence of events.[39]

Retrieving of information for purchase decisions

Retrieval is the process whereby information is accessed from long-term memory. As evidenced by the popularity of the game Trivial Pursuit, people have a vast quantity of information stored in their heads that is not necessarily available on demand. Although most of the information entered in long-term memory does not go away, it may be difficult or impossible to retrieve unless the appropriate cues are present.

Factors influencing retrieval

Some differences in retrieval ability are physiological. Older adults consistently display inferior recall ability for current items, such as prescription information, though events that happened to them when they were younger may be recalled with great clarity.[40]

Other factors are situational, relating to the environment in which the message is delivered. Not surprisingly, recall is enhanced when the consumer pays more attention to the message in the first place. Some evidence indicates that information about a pioneering brand (the first brand to enter a market) is more easily retrieved from memory than follower brands because the product's introduction is likely to be distinctive and, in the short term, no competitors divert the consumer's attention.[41] In addition, descriptive brand names are more likely to be recalled than are those that do not provide adequate cues as to what the product is.[42]

The viewing environment of a marketing message also can affect recall. For example, commercials shown during baseball games yield the lowest recall scores among sports programmes because the activity is stop-and-go rather than continuous. Unlike football or basketball, the pacing of baseball gives many opportunities for attention to wander even during play. Similarly, General Electric found that its commercials do better in television programmes with continuous activity, such as stories or dramas, compared to variety or talk shows, which are punctuated by a series of acts.[43]

State-dependent retrieval In a process termed state-dependent retrieval, people are better able to access information if their internal state is the same at the time of recall as it was when the information was learned.

Trivial Pursuit, a popular board game, tests consumers' memories of cultural happenings.
TRIVIAL PURSUIT® is a registered trademark of Horn Abbot Ltd., under exclusive licence to Parker Brothers and used with permission.

This phenomenon, called the mood congruence effect, underscores the desirability of matching a consumer's mood at the time of purchase when planning exposure to marketing communications. A consumer is more likely to recall an ad, for example, if his or her mood or level of arousal at the time of exposure is similar to that in the purchase environment. By recreating the cues that were present when the information was first presented, recall can be enhanced.

Familiarity and recall   As a general rule, prior familiarity with an item enhances its recall. Indeed, this is one of the basic goals of marketers who are trying to create and maintain awareness of their products. The more experience a consumer has with a product, the better use that person is able to make of product information.[44]

However, there is a possible fly in the ointment: as noted earlier in the chapter, some evidence indicates that over-familiarity can result in inferior learning and/or recall. When consumers are highly familiar with a brand or an advertisement, they may attend to fewer attributes because they do not believe that any additional effort will yield a gain in knowledge.[45] For example, when consumers are exposed to the technique of radio replay, where the audio track from a television ad is replayed on the radio, they do very little critical, evaluative processing and instead mentally replay the video portion of the ad.[46]

Salience and recall   The salience of a brand refers to its prominence or level of activation in memory. As noted in chapter 2, stimuli that stand out in contrast to their environment are more likely to command attention, which, in turn, increases the likelihood they will be recalled. Almost any technique that increases the novelty of a stimulus also improves recall (a result known as the von Restorff effect).[47] This effect explains why unusual advertising or distinctive packaging tends to facilitate brand recall.[48]

As we saw in chapter 2, introducing a surprise element in an ad (e.g. the Energizer Bunny™ who unexpectedly marches through a commercial) can be particularly effective. This strategy aids recall even if the stimulus is not relevant to the factual information being presented.[49] In addition, so-called mystery ads, where the brand is not identified until the end, are more effective at building associations in memory between the product category and that brand – especially in the case of novel brands.[50]

Pictorial versus verbal cues   There is some evidence for the superiority of visual memory over verbal memory, but this advantage is unclear because it is more difficult to measure recall of pictures.[51] However, the available data indicate that information presented in pictorial form is more likely to be recognized later.[52] Certainly, visual aspects of an ad are more likely to grab a consumer's attention. In fact, eye-movement studies indicate that about 90 per cent of viewers look at the dominant picture in an ad before they bother to view the copy.[53]

While pictorial ads may enhance recall, however, they do not necessarily improve comprehension. One study found that television news items presented with illustrations (still pictures) as a backdrop result in improved recall for details of the news story, even though understanding of the story's content does not improve.[54] Visual imagery can be especially effective when it includes verbal cues that relate to the consumer's existing knowledge.

Factors influencing forgetting

Marketers obviously hope that consumers will not forget their products. However, in a poll of more than 13,000 adults, over half were unable to remember any specific ad they had seen, heard or read in the previous 30 days.[55] Forgetting is obviously a problem for marketers.

Early memory theorists assumed that memories fade due to the simple passage of time. In a process of decay, the structural changes in the brain produced by learning simply go away. Forgetting also occurs due to **interference**; as additional information is learned, it displaces the earlier information.

Stimulus–response associations will be forgotten if the consumers subsequently learn new responses to the same or similar stimuli in a process known as retroactive interference. Or prior learning can interfere with new learning, a process termed proactive interference. Since pieces of information are stored as nodes in memory that are connected to one another by links, a meaning concept that is connected by a larger number of links is more likely to be retrieved. But, as new responses are learned, a stimulus loses its effectiveness in retrieving the old response.[56]

These interference effects help to explain problems in remembering brand information. Consumers tend to organize attribute information by brand.[57] Additional attribute information regarding a brand or similar brands may limit the person's ability to recall old brand information. Recall may also be inhibited if the brand name is composed of frequently used words. These words cue competing associations and result in less retention of brand information.[58]

In one study, brand evaluations deteriorated more rapidly when ads for the brand appeared with messages for twelve other brands in the same category than when the ad was shown with ads for twelve dissimilar products.[59] By increasing the salience of a brand, the recall of other brands can be impaired.[60] On the other hand, calling a competitor by name can result in poorer recall for one's own brand.[61]

Finally, a phenomenon known as the part-list cueing effect allows marketers strategically to utilize the interference process. When only a portion of the items in a category are presented to consumers, the omitted items are not as easily recalled.

For example, comparative advertising that mentions only a subset of competitors (preferably those that the marketer is not very worried about) may inhibit recall of the unmentioned brands with which the product does not favourably compare.[62]

Products as memory markers

Products and ads can themselves serve as powerful retrieval cues. Indeed, the three types of possessions most valued by consumers are furniture, visual art and photos. The most common explanation for this attachment is the ability of these things to summon memories of the past.[63] Products are particularly important as markers when our sense of past is threatened, as when a consumer's current identity is challenged due to some change in role caused by divorce, moving, graduation, and so on.[64] Products have mnemonic qualities that serve as a form of external memory by prompting consumers to retrieve episodic memories. For example, family photography allows consumers to create their own retrieval cues, with the 11 billion amateur photos taken annually forming a kind of external memory bank for our culture.

Researchers are just beginning to probe the effects of autobiographical memories on buying behaviour. These memories appear to be one way that advertisements create emotional responses; ads that succeed in getting us to think about our own past also appear to get us to like these ads more – especially if the linkage between the nostalgia experience and the brand is strong.[65]

The power of nostalgia

Nostalgia has been described as a bitter-sweet emotion, where the past is viewed with both sadness and longing. References to 'the good old days' are increasingly common, as advertisers call up memories of distant youth – feelings they hope will translate to what they're selling today. A stimulus is at times able to evoke a weakened response much later, an effect known as spontaneous recovery, and this re-established connection may explain consumers' powerful nostalgic reactions to songs or pictures they have not been exposed to in many years.

Many other European companies are making use of nostalgic appeals, some of which are not based on the too distant past! Berlin's Humboldt University and City Museum have staged a fashion show of the sixties, displaying clothes, appliances and posters from the communist era. The show, entitled 'Ostalgie' which is a play on words for 'East Nostalgia' in the German language, gave a nostalgic view of a time when goods might have been shoddy, but when there was no unemployment or homelessness. There's growing interest in the Trabant (the joke used to be that you could double the value of a Trabant by filling it with sand) which has resulted in the Son of Trabant, built in the same factory where they used to build the original. Likewise, Western European multinationals are relaunching local brands of East European origin in response to a backlash against the incursion of foreign products. From cigarettes to yogurt, multinationals are trying to lure consumers by combining yesteryear's product names with today's quality. Local brands like Nestlé's Chokito or Unilever's Flora margarine brands are now among the companies' best selling products in Eastern European markets. Considerable care goes into the production values of campaigns which are intended to evoke nostalgia. Mulino Bianco, the Italian producer of cakes, biscuits and cereals, carefully developed a campaign depicting the quiet aspects of rural life to increase sales of cakes, which are typically served only on special occasions. The campaign showed a white farmhouse on a green hill, next to a water mill. Parents, children and friends are shown

The rebirth of the Beetle

Hoping to win back former buyers – and to lure new ones – Volkswagen will soon unveil an updated version of the small round-shouldered car that became a generational icon in the US in the 1960s and 1970s. Back in those days, the 'Bug' was cramped and noisy, but was a hit because it was relatively cheap, fuel-efficient, and had symbolic value as a protest against Detroit's 'big boats'. In contrast to the Bug of old, the new one will cater to consumers craving for space, with more headroom and legroom in front. If all goes as planned, VW believes the US comeback of both its Volkswagen and Audi brands will be assured. Jens Neumann, the VW executive in charge of North America feels 'The Beetle is the core of the VW soul. If we put it back in people's minds, they will think of our other products more.' The revised Beetle's resemblance to the old one is literally skin deep. Unlike the original, which had an air-cooled engine in the rear, the new Beetle will be packed with the latest German technology, including an optional fuel-efficient turbo-diesel direct-injection motor. Otherwise the car is essentially a Golf with a number of Beetle-type characteristics to evoke nostalgia: curvy body panels; round dashboard dials and controls; circular sideview mirrors; side running boards; and indented door handles you grip to open. Apart from its nostalgic value, the car's fate will surely depend on price. VW officials say the base Beetle will cost 5–10 per cent more than a comparable Golf, which sells for $13,470 in the US. The first Bugs sold in the US in 1949 cost $800, and the last sedans sold in the US in 1977 cost $3600, while the convertible went for $6,495. This time, VW is deliberately pricing the Bug above cars that appeal to most first-time buyers because it intends to attract far more than the college-age market. 'It is a classless car, and the Beetle will target a broad swathe of people who simply *love* the car, and aren't just looking for a utilitarian commuting box.' Following the reintroduction of the Beetle in the US, Volkswagen will also sell the nolstalgic Bug in Europe.[66]

in a slow, relaxed, informal atmosphere, far from the hectic urban commitments of work. The object was to evoke a relationship between 'the good old days' and cakes, and to present cakes as genuine food to be eaten every day during normal meals. In Italy, where the tension to escape from the hectic urban life is high, the campaign was quite successful. In France, where eating habits are different, and the appeal to rural life is weaker, the same campaign was not successful.[67]

Memory and aesthetic preferences

In addition to liking ads and products that remind us of our past, our prior experiences also help to determine what we like now. Some recent research indicates that people's tastes in such products as films and clothing are influenced by what was popular during certain critical periods of their youth. For example, liking for specific songs appears to be related to how old a person was when those songs were popular; on average, songs that were popular when an individual was 23–24 years old are the most likely to be favoured.[68] In the United States, the Nickelodeon cable network programmes its Nick at Nite segment, which features repeats, by selecting the shows that were highly rated when its major audience was 12 years old.[69] Similar programming strategies are followed by several satellite stations throughout Europe. In addition, it seems that men form preferences for women's clothing styles that were in vogue when these men were in their early twenties.[70]

With an eye on the future, and nostalgia for the past: the Mercedes and the Trabant represent different aspects of learning, memory and aesthetics for consumers in the eastern part of Germany.
Photo by Julia Helmsley.

More generally, many marketers understand that life-long brand loyalties are formed at a fairly early age; they view the battle for the hearts (and wallets) of students and young adults as a long-term investment. These age-related preferences will be further addressed in chapter 13.

Measuring memory for advertising

Because advertisers pay so much money to place their messages in front of consumers, they are naturally concerned that people will actually remember these messages at a later point. It seems that they have good reason to be concerned. In one study, less than 40 per cent of television viewers made positive links between commercial messages and the corresponding products; only 65 per cent noticed the brand name in a commercial; and only 38 per cent recognized a connection to an important point.[71]

More worryingly, only 7 per cent of television viewers can recall the product or company featured in the most recent television commercial they watched. This figure represents less than half the recall rate recorded in 1965 and may be attributed to such factors as the increase of 30- and 15-second commercials and the practice of airing television commercials in clusters rather than in connection with single-sponsor programmes.[72]

Recognition versus recall

One indicator of good advertising is, of course, the impression it makes on consumers. But how can this impact be defined and measured? Two basic measures of impact are recognition and recall. In the typical recognition test, subjects are shown ads one at a time and asked if they have seen them before. In contrast, free recall tests ask consumers to produce independently previously acquired information and then perform a recognition test on it.

Under some conditions, these two memory measures tend to yield the same results, especially when the researchers try to keep the viewers' interest in the ads constant.[73] Generally, though, recognition scores tend to be more reliable and do not decay over time in the way recall scores do.[74] Recognition scores are almost always better than recall scores because recognition is a simpler process and more retrieval cues are available to the consumer.

Both types of retrieval play important roles in purchase decisions. Recall tends to be more important in situations where consumers do not have product data at their disposal, and so they must rely upon memory to generate this information.[75] On the other hand, recognition is more likely to be an important factor in a store, where consumers are confronted with thousands of product options and information (i.e. where external memory is abundantly available) and where the task may simply be to recognize a familiar package. Unfortunately, package recognition and familiarity can have a negative consequence in that warning labels may be ignored, since their existence is taken for granted and not really noticed.[76]

The Starch Test

A widely used commercial measure of advertising recall for magazines is called the Starch Test, a syndicated service founded in 1932. This service provides scores on a number of aspects of consumers' familiarity with an ad, including such categories as 'noted', 'associated' and 'read most'. It also scores the impact of the component parts of an overall ad, giving such information as 'seen' for major illustrations and 'read some' for a major block of copy.[77] Such factors as the size of the ad, whether it appears towards the front or the back of the magazine, if it is on the right or left page, and the size of illustrations play an important role in affecting the amount of attention given to an ad as determined by Starch scores.

Problems with memory measures

While the measurement of an ad's memorability is important, the ability of existing measures to assess these dimensions accurately has been criticized for several reasons.

Response biases Results obtained from a measuring instrument are not necessarily due to what is being measured, but rather to something else about the instrument or the respondent. This form of contamination is called a **response bias**. For example, people tend to give 'yes' responses to questions, regardless of what is

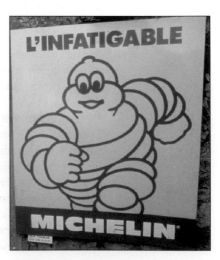

A picture is worth a thousand words. Product icons – like the Michelin Man who has appeared in ads and on packaging for more than 30 years – are a significant factor in product recognition.
Used with permission.

asked. In addition, consumers often are eager to be 'good subjects' by pleasing the experimenter. They will try to give the responses they think he or she is looking for. In some studies, the claimed recognition of bogus ads (ads that have not been seen before) is almost as high as the recognition rate of real ads.[78]

Memory lapses People are also prone to forgetting information unintentionally. Typical problems include omitting (the leaving out of facts), averaging (the tendency to 'normalize' things and not report extreme cases), and telescoping (the inaccurate recall of time).[79] These distortions call into question the accuracy of various product usage databases that rely upon consumers to recall their purchase and consumption of food and household items. In one study, for example, people were asked to describe what portion of various foods – small, medium or large – they ate in a normal meal; however, different definitions of 'medium' were used (e.g. 185ml versus 375ml). Regardless of the measurement specified, about the same number of people claimed they normally ate medium portions.[80]

Memory for facts versus feelings Although techniques are being developed to increase the accuracy of memory scores, these improvements do not address the more fundamental issue of whether recall is necessary for advertising to have an effect. In particular, some critics argue that these measures do not adequately tap the impact of 'feeling' ads where the objective is to arouse strong emotions rather than to convey concrete product benefits. Many ad campaigns, including those for Hallmark cards, Chevrolet and Pepsi use this approach.[81] An effective strategy relies on a long-term build-up of feeling rather than on a one-shot attempt to convince consumers to buy the product.

Also, it is not clear that recall translates into preference. We may recall the benefits touted in an ad but not believe them. Or the ad may be memorable because it is so obnoxious, and the product becomes one we 'love to hate'. The bottom line is that while recall is important, especially for creating brand awareness, it is not necessarily sufficient to alter consumer preferences. To accomplish this, marketers need more sophisticated attitude-change strategies. These issues will be discussed in chapters 5 and 6.

Chapter summary

- Learning is a change in behaviour that is caused by experience. Learning can occur through simple associations between a stimulus and a response or via a complex series of cognitive activities.
- Behavioural learning theories assume that learning occurs as a result of responses to external events. Classical conditioning occurs when a stimulus that naturally elicits a response (an unconditioned stimulus) is paired with another stimulus that does not initially elicit this response. Over time, the second stimulus (the conditioned stimulus) comes to elicit the response, as well.
- This response can also extend to other, similar stimuli in a process known as stimulus generalization. This process is the basis for such marketing strategies as licensing and family branding, in which a consumer's positive associations with a product are transferred to other contexts.
- Operant or instrumental conditioning occurs as the person learns to perform behaviours that produce positive outcomes and avoid those that result in

negative outcomes. While classical conditioning involves the pairing of two stimuli, instrumental learning occurs when reinforcement is delivered following a response to a stimulus. Reinforcement is positive if a reward is delivered following a response. It is negative if a negative outcome is avoided by not performing a response. Punishment occurs when a response is followed by unpleasant events. Extinction of the behaviour will occur if reinforcement is no longer received.

● Cognitive learning occurs as the result of mental processes. For example, observational learning takes place when the consumer performs a behaviour as a result of seeing someone else performing it and being rewarded for it.

● Memory refers to the storage of learned information. The way information is encoded when it is perceived determines how it will be stored in memory. The memory systems known as sensory memory, short-term memory and long-term memory each play a role in retaining and processing information from the outside world.

● Information is not stored in isolation; it is incorporated into knowledge structures, where it is associated with other related data. The location of product information in associative networks and the level of abstraction at which it is coded help to determine when and how this information will be activated at a later time. Some factors that influence the likelihood of retrieval include the level of familiarity with an item, its salience (or prominence) in memory and whether the information was presented in pictorial or written form.

● Products also play a role as memory markers; they are used by consumers to retrieve memories about past experiences (autobiographical memories) and are often valued for their ability to do this. This function also contributes to the use of nostalgia in marketing strategies.

● Memory for product information can be measured either through recognition or recall techniques. Consumers are more likely to recognize an advertisement if it is presented to them than to recall one without being given any cues.

🔑 Key terms

Activation models of memory (p. 78)
Behavioural learning theories (p. 65)
Brand equity (p. 71)
Classical conditioning (p. 66)
Cognitive learning (p. 69)
Encoding (p. 75)
Evoked set (p. 78)
Extinction (p. 66)
Frequency marketing (p. 74)
Interference (p. 82)
Knowledge structures (p. 78)
Learning (p. 65)
Long-term memory (p. 78)

Memory (p. 75)
Negative reinforcement (p. 67)
Nostalgia (p. 83)
Observational learning (p. 70)
Operant conditioning (p. 67)
Positive reinforcement (p. 67)
Punishment (p. 68)
Response bias (p. 86)
Retrieval (p. 76)
Schema (p. 79)
Sensory memory (p. 77)
Short-term memory (p. 77)
Stimulus discrimination (p. 67)
Stimulus generalization (p. 67)
Storage (p. 75)

Consumer behaviour challenge

1. Identify three patterns of reinforcement and provide an example of how each is used in a marketing context.
2. Describe the functions of short-term and long-term memory. What is the apparent relationship between the two?
3. Devise a 'product jingle memory test'. Compile a list of brands that are or have been associated with memorable jingles, such as Opal Fruits or Heinz Baked Beans. Read this list to friends, and see how many jingles are remembered. You may be surprised at the level of recall.
4. Identify some important characteristics for a product with a well-known brand name. Based on these attributes, generate a list of possible brand extension or licensing opportunities, as well as some others that would most likely not be accepted by consumers.
5. Collect some pictures of 'classic' products that have high nostalgia value. Show these pictures to consumers and allow them to free associate. Analyze the types of memories that are evoked, and think about how these associations might be employed in a product's promotional strategy.

It's been two years since Peter gave up smoking, drinking and junk food. He now devotes the same enthusiasm to working out that he used to bring to partying. Peter has become a dedicated triathlete. Participating in this sport, which involves running, swimming and cycling, has become so important to Peter that he now structures his entire life around his training regime. He even passed on an important class he would have liked to take because it was on at the same time he did his daily run.

Peter has become so engrossed in the sport that his friends hardly see him – he spends most of his free time (when not in training) reading magazines dedicated to the sport, shopping for special equipment such as running shoes and Lycra tights for winter training, or travelling to triathalon events all over Europe. His girlfriend complains that lately he likes looking at himself in the mirror more than he likes looking at her.

Peter remains committed – he's nothing if not dedicated to the cause . . .

Motivation, values and involvement

Introduction

Introduction

Some people are so involved in an activity that they can be termed *fanatic consumers*. Whether they are training for a triathalon, watching television or playing music, these people tend to become totally engrossed in an activity to the point where such involvement has been called a 'positive addiction'. One survey of triathletes (like Peter) found that intense commitment to the sport resulted in a highly modified daily schedule, unwillingness to stop training even if injured, major dietary changes and – most relevant to marketers – a substantial financial commitment to travel to races, specialized clothing and health club membership.[1]

The forces that drive people to buy and use products can sometimes seem quite straightforward, as when a person purchases a box of cornflakes after consuming the previous one. But some questions remain unanswered, such as why do we eat cornflakes rather other things? And why do we buy one brand rather than another? As hard-core triathletes like Peter demonstrate, the consumption of an everyday product such as running shoes may be related to deep-seated experiences. In some cases, these emotional responses create a deep commitment to the product. Sometimes, people are not even fully aware of the forces that drive them towards some products and away from others. Often these choices are influenced by the person's *values* – his or her priorities and beliefs about the world.

To understand motivation is to understand *why* consumers do what they do. Why do people choose to bungy jump from a bridge or go white-water rafting, while others spend their leisure time playing chess or gardening? Everything that we do is rooted in a number of reasons, whether to quench a thirst, kill boredom or attain a deep spiritual experience. Marketing students are taught from day one that the goal of marketing is to satisfy consumers' needs. However, this insight is useless unless we can discover *what* those needs are and *why* they exist.

The motivation process

Motivation refers to the processes that cause people to behave as they do. From a *psychological perspective*, it occurs when a need is aroused that the consumer wishes to satisfy. Once a need has been activated, a state of tension exists that drives the consumer to attempt to reduce or eliminate the need. This need may be predominantly utilitarian (i.e. a desire to achieve some functional or practical benefit, as when a person requires a pair of durable sneakers) or it may be predominantly hedonic (i.e. an experiential need, involving emotional responses or fantasies, as when Peter buys special running shoes for a triathalon event). The distinction between the two is, however, a matter of degree. The desired end-state is the consumer's **goal.** Marketers try to create products and services that will provide the desired benefits and permit the consumer to reduce this tension.

Whether the need is utilitarian or hedonic, a discrepancy exists between the consumer's present state and some ideal state. This gulf creates a state of tension. The magnitude of this tension determines the urgency the consumer feels to reduce the tension, and this degree of arousal is called a drive. A basic need can be satisfied any number of ways, and the specific path a person chooses is influenced by his or her unique set of experiences, cultural background, and so on.

These personal and cultural factors combine to create a **want**, which is one manifestation of a need. For example, hunger is a basic need that must be satisfied by all; the lack of food creates a tension state that can be reduced by the intake of such products as pizzas, chocolate biscuits, raw fish or bean sprouts. Throughout the world, the consumer's specific route to hunger reduction is culturally determined.

Once the goal is attained, tension is reduced and the motivation recedes (temporarily). Motivation can be described in terms of its strength, or the pull it exerts on the consumer, and its direction, or the particular way the consumer attempts to reduce motivational tension.

Motivational strength

The degree to which a person is willing to expend energy to reach one goal as opposed to another reflects his or her underlying motivation to attain that goal. Many theories have been advanced to explain why people behave the way they do. Most share the basic idea that people have some finite amount of energy that must be directed toward certain goals.

Biological versus learned needs

Early work on motivation ascribed behaviour to instinct, the innate patterns of behaviour that are universal in a species. This view is now largely discredited. For one thing, the existence of an instinct is difficult to prove or disprove. The instinct is inferred from the behaviour it is supposed to explain (this type of circular explanation is called a *tautology*).[2] It is like saying that a consumer buys products that are status symbols because he or she is motivated to attain status, which is hardly a satisfying explanation.

Drive theory

Drive theory focuses on biological needs that produce unpleasant states of arousal (e.g. your stomach rumbles during a morning class). We are motivated to reduce the tension caused by this arousal. Tension reduction has been proposed as a basic mechanism governing human behaviour.

In marketing, tension refers to the unpleasant state that exists if a person's consumption needs are not fulfilled. A person may be irritable if he hasn't eaten, or he may be dejected or angry if he cannot afford the new car he wants. This state activates goal-oriented behaviour, which attempts to reduce or eliminate this unpleasant state and return to a balanced one, known as **homeostasis**

Those behaviours that are successful in reducing the drive by eliminating the underlying need are strengthened and tend to be repeated. (This aspect of the learning process was discussed in chapter 3.) Your motivation to leave class early in order to grab a snack would be greater if you hadn't eaten in 24 hours than if you had eaten only two hours earlier. If you did sneak out and got indigestion after, say, wolfing down a packet of crisps, this behaviour would be less likely to be repeated the next time you wanted a snack. One's degree of motivation, then, depends upon the distance between one's present state and the goal.

Drive theory, however, runs into difficulties when it tries to explain some facets of human behaviour that run counter to its predictions. People often do things that *increase* a drive state rather than decrease it. For example, people may delay gratification. If you know you are going out for a five-course dinner, you might decide to forgo a snack earlier in the day even though you are hungry at that time. In other cases, people deliberately watch porn movies, even though these stimuli often increase sexual arousal rather than diminish it.

Expectancy theory

Most current explanations of motivation focus on cognitive factors rather than biological ones to understand what drives behaviour. **Expectancy theory** suggests that behaviour is largely pulled by expectations of achieving desirable outcomes – *positive incentives* – rather than pushed from within. We choose one product over another because we expect this choice to have more positive consequences for us. Thus the term *drive* is used here more loosely to refer to both physical and cognitive, i.e. learned processes.

Motivational direction

Motives have direction as well as strength. They are goal-oriented in that specific objectives are desired to satisfy a need. Most goals can be reached by a number of routes, and the objective of marketers is to convince consumers that the alternative they offer provides the best chance to attain the goal. For example, a consumer who decides that he needs a pair of jeans to help him reach his goal of being accepted by others or projecting an appropriate image can choose among Levi's, Wranglers, Calvin Klein, and many other alternatives, each of which promises to deliver certain benefits.

Needs versus wants

The specific way a need is satisfied depends on the individual's unique history, learning experiences and his or her cultural environment. The particular form of consumption used to satisfy a need is termed a want. For example, two classmates may feel their stomachs rumbling during a lunchtime lecture. If neither has eaten since the night before, the strength of their respective needs (hunger) would be about the same. However, the way each person goes about satisfying this need might be quite different. The first person may be a health fanatic who fantasizes about a big bowl of salad, while the second person may be equally aroused by the prospect of a greasy slice of pizza.

A start to the discussion of needs and wants can best be illustrated by considering two basic types of need. People are born with a need for certain elements necessary to maintain life, such as food, water, air and shelter. These needs can be viewed as *biogenic needs*. People have many other needs, however, that are not innate. *Psychogenic needs* are acquired in the process of becoming a member of a culture. These include the need for status, power, affiliation, and so on. Psychogenic needs reflect the priorities of a culture, and their effect on behaviour will vary in different environments. For example, a French consumer may be driven to devote a good chunk of his income to products that permit him to display his wealth and status, while his Scandinavian counterpart may work equally hard to ensure that he does not stand out from his group. These cultural differences in the expression of consumer values will be discussed more fully in chapter 15.

This distinction is revealing because it shows how difficult it is to distinguish needs from wants. How can we tell what part of the motivation is a psychogenic need and what part is a want? Both are profoundly formed by culture, so the distinction is problematic at best. As for the biogenic needs, we know from anthropology that satisfaction of these needs are some of the most symbolically rich and culturally based activities of humankind. The ways we want to eat, dress, drink and provide shelter are far more interesting to marketers than our need to do so. And, in fact, human beings need very little in the strict sense of the word. Charles Darwin was astonished to see the native Americans of Tierra del Fuego sleep naked in the snow. Hence, the idea of satisfaction of biogenic needs is more or less a given thing for marketing and consumer research because it is on the most basic level nothing more than a simple prerequisite for us to be here. Beyond that level, and of much greater interest (and challenge!) to marketers, is a concept embedded in culture such as wants.[3]

As we have seen, another traditional distinction is between the motivation to satisfy either utilitarian or hedonic needs. The satisfaction of utilitarian needs implies that consumers will emphasize the objective, tangible attributes of products, such as fuel economy in a car; the amount of fat, calories and protein in a cheeseburger; and the durability of a pair of blue jeans. Hedonic needs are subjective and experiential. Here, consumers may rely on a product to meet their needs for excitement, self-confidence, fantasy, and so on. Of course, consumers may be motivated to purchase a product because it provides *both* types of benefit. For example, a mink coat may be bought because it feels soft and luxurious against the skin and because it keeps one warm on a snowy day. But again the distinction tends to hide more than it reveals, because functionality can bring great pleasure to people and is an important value in the modern world.[4]

Most recently, researchers have begun to discuss the importance of the concept of **desire** for understanding consumer behaviour, since it better captures the seductive spirit of the positioning of many contemporary brands and the deep feelings involved in consumer goods' contribution to the formation of consumers' self-images. The concept of desire also emphasizes that, even though desires, needs and wants are felt psychologically, the concept of society (often called 'the Other' in the literature on desire) is very central to the understanding of desire. Thus, desire would refer to the *sociogenic* nature of needs.[5]

One study of consumer desires in Denmark, Turkey and the United States concluded that desires were much more profound than wants, that desire is cyclical and basically insatiable, that what is desired is more often various kinds of social relationship mediated by consumption experiences rather than consumption in itself,

An example of a collage used to explore consumer desire, as described in text.

and finally that desire is potentially harmful because it contains an important element of excess and lack of control over oneself.[6] The study used collages among other techniques to explore consumer desire, and the collage shown here illustrates some of the featured findings: that desire is positive but potentially harmful if out of control (the balance, the fight with one's own shadow) and can lead to impossible dreams (the ugly man and the model) or to excess and violation of norms (Hugh Grant and the prostitute).

Motivational conflicts

A goal has *valence*, which means that it can be positive or negative. A positively valued goal is one towards which consumers direct their behaviour; they are motivated to *approach* the goal and will seek out products that will be instrumental in attaining it. Peter used his athletic equipment to help him improve his triathalon performance, his goal. However, not all behaviour is motivated by the desire to approach a goal. Sometimes, consumers are motivated to *avoid* a negative outcome. They will structure their purchases or consumption activities to reduce the chances of attaining this end-result. For example, many consumers work hard to avoid rejection, a negative goal. They will stay away from products that they associate with social disapproval. Products such as deodorants and mouthwashes frequently rely

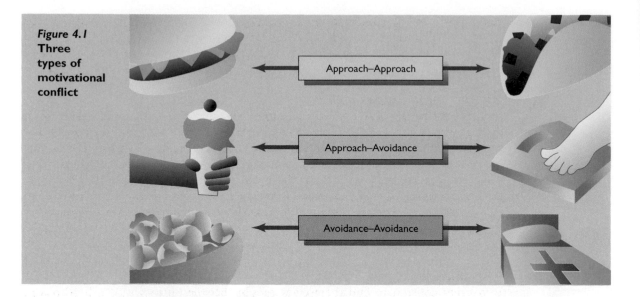

Figure 4.1
Three types of motivational conflict

Approach–Approach

Approach–Avoidance

Avoidance–Avoidance

upon consumers' negative motivation by depicting the onerous social consequences of underarm odour or bad breath. Peter would most likely be especially vigilant about avoiding junk food as he prepared for a forthcoming meet.

Because a purchase decision may involve more than one source of motivation, consumers often find themselves in situations where different motives, both positive and negative, conflict with one another. Since marketers are attempting to satisfy consumers' needs, they can also be helpful by providing possible solutions to these dilemmas. As shown in Figure 4.1, three general types of conflicts can occur: approach–approach, approach–avoidance and avoidance–avoidance.

Approach–approach conflict

In an approach–approach conflict, a person must choose between two desirable alternatives. A student might be torn between going home for the holidays or going on a skiing trip with friends. Or he or she might have to choose between two compact discs.

The **theory of cognitive dissonance** is based on the premise that people have a need for order and consistency in their lives and that a state of tension is created when beliefs or behaviours conflict with one another. The conflict that arises when choosing between two alternatives may be resolved through a process of cognitive dissonance reduction, in which people are motivated to reduce this inconsistency (or dissonance) and thus eliminate unpleasant tension.[7]

A state of dissonance occurs when there is a psychological inconsistency between two or more beliefs or behaviours. It often occurs when a consumer must make a choice between two products, where both alternatives usually possess both good and bad qualities. By choosing one product and not the other, the person gets the bad qualities of the chosen product and loses out on the good qualities of the one not chosen.

This loss creates an unpleasant, dissonant state that the person is motivated to reduce. People tend to convince themselves after the fact that the choice they made was the right one by finding additional reasons to support the alternative they chose, or perhaps by 'discovering' flaws with the option they did not choose. A marketer can try to resolve an approach–approach conflict by bundling several benefits together. For example, many low calorie products claim that they have 'all the taste' *and* 'half the calories' allowing the consumer to avoid the choice of better taste or fewer calories.

Approach–avoidance conflict

Many of the products and services we desire have negative consequences attached to them as well. We may feel guilty or ostentatious when buying a high-status product or feel like a glutton when contemplating a box of chocolates. When we desire a goal but wish to avoid it at the same time, an approach–avoidance conflict exists. Some solutions to these conflicts include the proliferation of fake furs, which eliminate guilt about killing animals to make a fashion statement, and the above-mentioned low calorie foods that promise good food without the calories. Many marketers try to overcome guilt by convincing consumers that they deserve luxuries (e.g. when the model for L'Oreal cosmetics claims 'Because I'm worth it!').

Avoidance–avoidance conflict

Sometimes consumers find themselves caught 'between a rock and a hard place'. They may face a choice with two undesirable alternatives. A person may be faced with the option of either throwing more money into an old car or buying a new one. Marketers frequently address this conflict by messages that stress the unforeseen benefits of choosing one option (e.g. by emphasizing special credit plans to ease the pain of new car payments).

Classifying consumer needs

Much research has been done on classifying human needs. On the one hand, some psychologists have tried to define a universal inventory of needs that could be traced systematically to explain virtually all behaviour. Others have focused on specific needs (which often are included in general models) and their ramifications for behaviour. For example, one study of working women found that those who were high in achievement motivation were more likely to choose clothing they considered businesslike, and less likely to be interested in apparel that accentuated their femininity.[8]

Maslow's hierarchy of needs

One influential approach to motivation was proposed by the psychologist Abraham Maslow. Maslow's approach is a general one originally developed to understand personal growth and the attainment of 'peak experiences'.[9] Maslow formulated a hierarchy of needs, in which levels of motives are specified. A hierarchical approach implies that the order of development is fixed – that is, a certain level must be attained before the next, higher one is activated. This universal approach to motivation has been adapted by marketers because it (indirectly) specifies certain types of product benefits people might be looking for, depending upon the different stages in their development and/or their environmental conditions.

These levels are summarized in Figure 4.2. At each level, different priorities exist in terms of the product benefits a consumer is looking for. Ideally, an individual progresses up the hierarchy until his or her dominant motivation is a focus on 'ultimate' goals, such as justice and beauty. Unfortunately, this state is difficult to achieve (at least on a regular basis); most of us have to be satisfied with occasional glimpses or peak experiences.

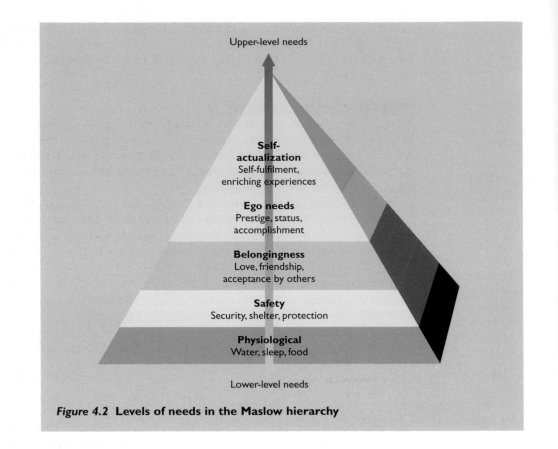

Upper-level needs

Self-actualization
Self-fulfilment,
enriching experiences

Ego needs
Prestige, status,
accomplishment

Belongingness
Love, friendship,
acceptance by others

Safety
Security, shelter, protection

Physiological
Water, sleep, food

Lower-level needs

Figure 4.2 **Levels of needs in the Maslow hierarchy**

The implication of Maslow's hierarchy is that one must first satisfy basic needs before progressing up the ladder (i.e. a starving man is not interested in status symbols, friendship or self-fulfilment). This hierarchy is not set in stone. Its use in marketing has been somewhat simplistic, especially since the same product or activity can satisfy a number of different needs.

Sex, for example, is characterized as a basic biological drive. While this observation is true throughout most of the animal kingdom, it is obviously a more complicated phenomenon for humans. Indeed, this activity could conceivably fit into every level of Maslow's hierarchy. A sociobiologist, who approaches human behaviour in terms of its biological origins, might argue that reproductive behaviour provides security because it ensures continuation of a person's gene pool and the provision of children to care for the person in old age. Sex can also express love and affiliation at the belongingness level. In addition, sex is often used as a vehicle to attain status, domination over another and to satisfy ego needs; it can be a significant determinant of self-respect. Finally, a sexual experience can be self-actualizing in that it may provide an ecstatic, transcendental experience. The same thing could be said for almost any kind of consumer experience. While eating certainly is necessary for our survival, it also is very much a social act (belongingness), a status act as in the consumption of champagne or other expensive wines, and an act through which the gourmet or the caring, cooking mother or father can obtain self-actualization. The house gives us shelter, but is also a security device, a home for the family, a status object and a field for actualizing our personal aspirations.

Another problem with taking Maslow's hierarchy too literally is that it is culture-bound. The assumptions of the hierarchy may be restricted to a highly rational, materialistic and individualistic Western culture, and people in other cultures may question the order of the levels as specified. A religious person who has taken a vow of celibacy would not necessarily agree that physiological needs must be satisfied for self-fulfilment to occur. Neither do all people in Western cultures seem to live according to Maslow's hierarchy. In fact, research based on visual rather than verbal data has indicated that spiritual survival is a stronger motivator than physical survival, as can be seen from patriots giving their life for the idea of nation, religious fanatics for their God, or suicidal people, drawing the consequence of a 'spiritual death' by ending their physical lives.[10]

Similarly, many Asian cultures operate on the premise that the welfare of the group (belongingness needs) are more highly valued than needs of the individual (esteem needs). The point is that this hierarchy, while widely applied in marketing, should be valued because it reminds us that consumers may have different need priorities at different times (i.e. you have to walk before you can run) rather than because it *exactly* specifies a consumer's progression up the ladder of needs.

Consumer involvement

As we have seen, a consumer's motivation to attain a goal influences his or her desire to expend the effort necessary to attain the products or services believed to be instrumental in satisfying that objective. However, not everyone is motivated to the same extent – one person might be convinced he or she can't live without the latest style or modern convenience, while another is not interested in this item at all. **Involvement** refers to 'the level of perceived personal importance and/or interest evoked by a stimulus (or stimuli) within a specific situation'.[11] This definition implies that aspects of the person, the product and the situation combine to determine the consumer's motivation to process product-related information at a given point in time. When consumers are intent on doing what they can to satisfy a need, they will be motivated to pay attention and process any information felt to be relevant to achieving their goals.

On the other hand, a person may not bother to pay any attention to the same information if it is not seen as relevant to satisfying some need. One person who prides himself on his knowledge of exercise equipment may read anything he can find about the subject, spend his spare time in sports stores, and so on, while another person may skip over this information without giving it a second thought. Involvement can be viewed as the motivation to process information.[12] To the degree that there is a perceived linkage between a consumer's needs, goals or values, and product knowledge, the consumer will be motivated to pay attention to product information. When relevant knowledge is activated in memory, a motivational state is created that drives behaviour (e.g. shopping). This subjective feeling of personal relevance is termed felt involvement. As felt involvement with a product increases, people devote more attention to ads related to the product, exert more cognitive effort to understand these ads, and focus their attention on the product-related information in them.[13] However, this kind of 'rational' involvement may be the exception rather than the rule, even for such products as stereos, TVs and VCRs, as a company executive from Philips once argued.[14]

Levels of involvement: from inertia to passion

The type of information processing that will occur thus depends upon the consumer's level of involvement. It can range from *simple processing*, where only the basic features of a message are considered, all the way to *elaboration*, where the incoming information is linked to one's pre-existing knowledge systems.[15]

A person's degree of involvement can be conceived as a continuum, ranging from absolute lack of interest in a marketing stimulus at one end, to obsession at the other. Consumption at the low end of involvement is characterized by **inertia**, where decisions are made out of habit because the consumer lacks the motivation to consider alternatives. At the high end of involvement, we can expect to find the type of passionate intensity reserved for people and objects that carry great meaning to the individual. For the most part, however, a consumer's involvement level with products falls somewhere in the middle, and the marketing strategist must determine the relative level of importance to understand how much elaboration of product information will occur.

Marketing opportunity

The passion of some consumers for famous people demonstrates the high end of the involvement continuum. Celebrity worship is evident in activities ranging from autograph collections to the sky-high prices paid for possessions that used to belong to stars such as John Lennon, Elton John or Jimi Hendrix can fetch at auctions. Consumers can be described in terms of the intensity of their admiration for a celebrity. At the bottom of this intensity ladder are people who are uninvolved, oblivious or even hostile to a celebrity.

As identification with a star increases, so does the consumer's degree of passion and desire to accumulate artefacts belonging to that star, or even to make actual contact with him or her. Groupies, for example, are people who follow celebrities, and often attempt to become a part of stars' lives by seducing them or even harassing them.

Fan clubs are composed of people who share a common devotion to an individual, whether a musician, racing driver or soap opera star. While some clubs are spontaneously created by devoted fans, others are deliberately engineered by the stars themselves to perpetuate their adulation.

The many faces of involvement

As previously defined, involvement can take many forms. Peter could certainly be said to be involved with his running shoes, since they help to define and bolster his self-concept. This involvement seems to increase at certain times, as when he must prove himself in a triathalon. Alternatively, the act of buying the shoes may be very involving for people who are passionately devoted to shopping. To complicate matters further, advertisements, such as those produced for Nike or Adidas, may themselves be involving for some reason (e.g. because they make us laugh, cry or inspire us to work harder).

It seems that involvement is a fuzzy concept, because it overlaps with other things and means different things to different people. Indeed, the consensus is that there are actually several broad types of involvement.[16]

Product involvement is related to a consumer's level of interest in making a particular purchase. Many sales promotions are designed to increase this type of involvement.

Message-response involvement refers to the consumer's interest in processing marketing communications.[17] Television is considered a low-involvement medium, because it requires a passive viewer who exerts relatively little control (remote control 'zipping' notwithstanding) over content. In contrast, print is a high-involvement medium. The reader is actively involved in processing the information and is able to pause and reflect on what he or she has read before moving on.[18] The role of message characteristics in changing attitudes is further discussed in chapter 6.

Marketing opportunity

Quick Burger, France's second largest fast-food chain, discovered a route to increasing customers' involvement. The company became a partner in a marketing programme called Multipoints, which is an interactive service that lets consumers collect points that can then be redeemed for discounts and prizes. More than 70,000 French consumers signed up for the service. Using a device that resembles a calculator, participants entered codes they find in print ads and advertising hoardings or hear on radio programmes. They can even hold the device against their TV screens during programming that is specially encoded to dispense credits. People can win points for playing along with certain game shows and answering questions correctly. They can then redeem their points for merchandise at Quick Burger restaurants and other locations (including selected travel agencies and news-stands) by plugging their device into a computer terminal. The hamburger chain gives consumers 500 free points per week just for visiting, which gives them additional motivation to patronize Quick Burger instead of arch-rival McDonald's.[19]

Ego involvement (sometimes termed *enduring involvement*) refers to the importance of a product to a consumer's self-concept. This concept implies a high level of social risk; the prospect of the product not performing its desired function may result in embarrassment or damage to the consumer's self-concept (chapter 7 is devoted to the importance of the self-concept for consumer behaviour issues). For example, Peter's running shoes are clearly an important part of his self-identity (they are said to have high sign value). This type of involvement is independent of particular purchase situations. It is an ongoing concern related to the self and hedonic experiences (e.g. the emotions felt as a result of using the product).[20]

Measuring involvement

The measurement of involvement is important for many marketing applications. For example, research evidence indicates that a viewer who is more involved with a television show will also respond more positively to commercials contained in that show, and that these slots will have a greater chance of influencing his or her purchase intentions.[21] The many conceptualizations of involvement have led to some confusion about the best way to measure the concept. The scale shown in Table 4.1 is one widely used method.[22]

Table 4.1 A scale to measure product involvement

		To me (object to be judged) is	
1.	important	_:_:_:_:_:_:_	unimportant*
2.	boring	_:_:_:_:_:_	interesting
3.	relevant	_:_:_:_:_:_	irrelevant*
4.	exciting	_:_:_:_:_:_	unexciting*
5.	means nothing	_:_:_:_:_:_	means a lot to me
6.	appealing	_:_:_:_:_:_	unappealing*
7.	fascinating	_:_:_:_:_:_	mundane*
8.	worthless	_:_:_:_:_:_	valuable
9.	involving	_:_:_:_:_:_	uninvolving*
10.	not needed	_:_:_:_:_:_	needed

Source: Judith Lynne Zaichkowsky, 'The Personal Involvement Inventory: Reduction, Revision, and Application to Advertising', *Journal of Advertising* 23(4) (December 1994): 59–70.
Note: Totalling the ten items gives a score from a low of 10 to a high of 70.
*Indicates item is reverse scored. For example, a score of 7 for item no. 1 (important/unimportant) would actually be scored as 1.

A pair of French researchers have argued that no single component of involvement is predominant. Recognizing that consumers can be involved with a product because it is a risky purchase and/or its use reflects upon or affects the self, they advocate the development of an *involvement profile* containing five components:[23]

- The personal interest a consumer has in a product category.
- The perceived importance of the potential negative consequences of a bad purchase.
- The probability of making a bad purchase.
- The pleasure value of the product category.
- The sign value of the product category.

These researchers asked a sample of housewives to rate a set of fourteen product categories on each of the above facets of involvement. The results are shown in Table 4.2. These data indicate that no single component captures consumer involvement, since this quality can occur for different reasons. For example, the purchase of a durable product such as a vacuum cleaner is seen as risky, because one is stuck with a bad choice for many years. However, the vacuum cleaner does not provide pleasure (hedonic value), nor is it high in sign value (i.e. its use is not related to the person's self-concept). In contrast, chocolate is high in pleasure value but is not seen as risky or closely related to the self. Dresses and bras, on the other hand, appear to be involving for a combination of reasons.

Table 4.2 **Involvement profiles for a set of French consumer products**

	Importance of negative consequences	Subjective probability of mispurchase	Pleasure value	Sign value
Dresses	121	112	147	181
Bras	117	115	106	130
Washing machines	118	109	106	111
TV sets	112	100	122	95
Vacuum cleaners	110	112	70	78
Irons	103	95	72	76
Champagne	109	120	125	125
Oil	89	97	65	92
Yoghurt	86	83	106	78
Chocolate	80	89	123	75
Shampoo	96	103	90	81
Toothpaste	95	95	94	105
Toilet soap	82	90	114	118
Detergents	79	82	56	63

Average product score = 100.
Source: Gilles Laurent and Jean-Nöel Kapferer, 'Measuring Consumer Involvement Profiles', *Journal of Marketing Research* 22 (February 1985): 45, Table 3. By permission of American Marketing Association.

Multicultural dimensions

A recent study compared involvement levels of consumers from different countries for a number of products and services. When the researchers compared regular users of these items across countries, some differences in involvement emerged (as measured by the scale in Table 4.1).[24]

- The Chinese are more involved with beer than are South Americans. Otherwise, the study found little differences for this category across countries.
- Involvement with soft drinks was relatively low in Canada and Sweden, but relatively high in (what was then) Yugoslavia and China.
- Blue jeans got the highest involvement score from Austrian consumers and the lowest from Swedes.
- Americans scored relatively high on involvement with air travel; Swedes, relatively low.
- French and Chinese subjects were most likely to be involved with going to the cinema, while Mexicans were the least.

Segmenting by involvement levels

A measurement approach of this nature allows consumer researchers to capture the diversity of the involvement construct, and it also provides the potential to use involvement as a basis for market segmentation. For example, a yoghurt manufacturer might find that even though its product is low in sign value for one group of consumers, it might be highly related to the self-concept of another market segment, such as health food enthusiasts or avid dieters. The company could adapt its strategy to account for the motivation of different segments to process information about the product. These variations are discussed in chapter 6. Note also that involvement with a product class may vary across cultures. While this sample of French consumers rated champagne high in both sign value and personal value, the ability of champagne to provide pleasure or be central to self-definition might not transfer to other countries. For example, whereas a typical French family would find champagne an absolutely essential part of the celebration of a marriage, a Danish family, especially from a rural area, might find consumption of champagne an excessive luxury and perhaps also to some extent a sign of decadence.[25]

Strategies to increase involvement

Although consumers differ in their level of involvement with respect to a product message, marketers do not have to sit back and hope for the best. By being aware of some basic factors that increase or decrease attention, they can take steps to increase the likelihood that product information will get through. A consumer's motivation to process relevant information can be enhanced fairly easily by the marketer who uses one or more of the following techniques:[26]

- Appeal to the consumers' hedonic needs. For example, ads using sensory appeals generate higher levels of attention.[27]
- Use novel stimuli, such as unusual cinematography, sudden silences or unexpected movements in commercials.
- Use prominent stimuli, such as loud music and fast action to capture attention in commercials. In print formats, larger ads increase attention. Also, viewers look longer at coloured pictures as opposed to black-and-white.
- Include celebrity endorsers to generate higher interest in commercials. This strategy will be discussed in chapter 6.
- Build a bond with consumers by maintaining an ongoing relationship with them. The routes to cultivating brand loyalty will be further discussed in chapter 8.

Values

Generally speaking, a **value** can be defined as a belief about some desirable end-state that transcends specific situations and guides selection of behaviour.[28] Thus, values are general and different from attitudes in that they do not apply to specific situations only. A person's set of values plays a very important role in his or her consumption activities, since many products and services are purchased because (it is believed) they will help us to attain a value-related goal.

As we'll see in chapters 15 and 16, the specific values that motivate people vary across cultures, yet within each culture there is usually a set of underlying goals that most members of that culture agree are important. One comparison of management practices concerning industrial buying behaviour in Europe and North America concluded that in Europe, development of relationships is seen as more important, whereas in North America, rigour and competitiveness were the key issues.[29] Such differences may be interpreted as pointing at fundamental differences in values in the business worlds of the two continents. But also within Europe, large differences can be detected, for example between the Anglo-Saxon approach, which is closer to the American model described above, and the Germanic-Alpine (including Scandinavia) model which is more oriented towards the relationship approach.[30]

Core values

Every culture has a set of values that it imparts to its members.[31] For example, people in one culture might feel that being a unique individual is preferable to subordinating one's identity to the group, while another group may emphasize the virtues of group membership. In many cases, values are universal. Who does not desire health, wisdom or world peace?

One perspective on the study of values stresses that what sets cultures apart is the *relative importance*, or ranking, of these universal values. This set of rankings constitutes a culture's **value system.**[32] To illustrate a difference in value systems, consider the results of a comparison between the adherence to a set of values in Norway, Germany and the US (see Table 4.3).[33] The value of sense of belonging is very important in Germany and Norway, but much less so in the US, which is coherent with many other studies underlining the individualistic character of the American culture. Likewise, the value of security is very important in Germany and US but much less so in Norway. The results seem to indicate that the value of security in the US is understood in terms of social security, whereas in Germany it is understood more in terms

Table 4.3 **Distribution of values in different countries (%)**

	Germany	United States	Norway
Sense of belonging	28.6	7.9	33.4
Fun and enjoyment in life	6.4	4.5	3.6
Warm relationships with others	7.9	16.2	13.4
Self-fulfilment	4.8	9.6	7.7
Being well respected	6.1	8.8	8.4
Excitement	3.7	_a	_a
Self-respect	12.9	21.1	16.6
Security	24.1	20.6	10.0
Sense of accomplishment	5.4	11.4	6.8

Note: a. The value excitement was collapsed into fun and enjoyment because just a negligible percentage of US and Norwegian respondents selected this as most important value.
Source: Reprinted from *Journal of Business Research* 20, S.C. Grunert and G. Scherhorn: 'Consumer Values in West Germany: Underlying Dimensions and Cross-cultural Comparison with North America', pp. 97–107. Copyright 1990, by permission of Elsevier Science.

of social relationships. In Norway it is interpreted much as in the US, but it does not represent the same importance due to the elaborate social security of the Norwegian welfare state.

Every culture is characterized by its members' endorsement of a value system. These end-states may not be equally endorsed by everyone, and in some cases, values may even seem to contradict one another (e.g. Westerners in general appear to value both conformity and individuality and seek to find some accommodation between the two). None the less, it is usually possible to identify a general set of *core values* which uniquely define a culture. These beliefs are taught to us by *socialization agents*, including parents, friends and teachers. The process of learning the beliefs and behaviours endorsed by one's own culture is termed enculturation. In contrast, the process of learning the value system and behaviours of another culture (often a priority for those who wish to understand consumers and markets in foreign countries) is called acculturation.

As we saw in the example above, such core values must be understood in the local context, that is the meaning of the values change when the cultural context shifts. 'Security' is *not* the same for English, Scandinavian, German and Italian consumers. This is a serious challenge to the idea that it is possible to compare value systems by studying the rankings of universal sets of values across countries.

Applications of values to consumer behaviour

Despite their importance, values have not been widely applied to direct examinations of consumer behaviour. One reason is that such broad-based concepts as freedom, security or inner harmony are more likely to affect general purchasing patterns than to differentiate between brands within a product category. For this reason, some researchers have found it convenient to make distinctions among such broad-based *cultural values* as security or happiness, *consumption-specific values* such as convenient shopping or prompt service, and such *product-specific values* such as ease of use or durability.[34] However, such a distinction may border on abusing the value concept, since it is normally taken to represent the most general and profound level in the social psychological hierarchy.

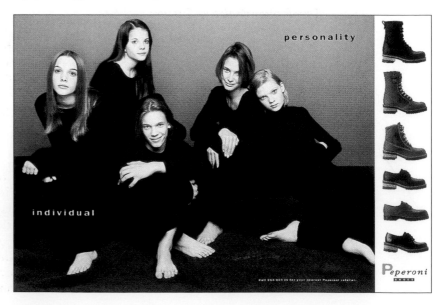

This Swedish shoe ad appeals to the value of individuality.
Courtesy of LT Skor, Sweden.

Whether it's a swift horse, a smart hound or an agile car, the English have long known the importance of good breeding.

JAGUAR

This ad clearly states the connection between consumption and traditional values.

Since values drive much of consumer behaviour (at least in a very general sense), it could be said that virtually all types of consumer research ultimately are related to the identification and measurement of values. This process can take many forms, ranging from qualitative research techniques such as ethnography to quantitative techniques such as laboratory experiments and large-scale surveys. An overview of these approaches was provided in chapter 1. This section describes some attempts by researchers to measure cultural values and apply this knowledge to marketing strategy. A number of companies track changes in values through large-scale surveys. The results of these studies are then sold to marketers, who pay a fee to receive regular updates on changes and trends. Some of these services are discussed in chapter 15.

The Rokeach Value Survey

The psychologist Milton Rokeach identified a set of **terminal values**, or desired end-states, that apply (to various degrees) to many different cultures. *The Rokeach Value Survey*, a scale used to measure these values, also includes a set of **instrumental values**, which are composed of actions needed to achieve these terminal values.[35] These two sets of values appear in Table 4.4. This set of values has been used in many studies, for example to investigate the changes in the value system of post-Soviet Russia.[36]

The List of Values (LOV)

Although some evidence indicates that differences on these global values do translate into product-specific preferences and differences in media usage, the Rokeach Value Survey has not been widely applied to consumer behaviour issues.[37] As an alternative, the List of Values scale (**LOV**) was developed to isolate values with more direct marketing applications.[38]

This instrument identifies nine consumer values which can be related to differences in consumption behaviours. The instrument includes the following values: sense of belonging, fun and enjoyment in life, warm relationships with others,

Table 4.4 **Two types of values in the Rokeach Value Survey**

Instrumental values	Terminal values
Ambitious	A comfortable life
Broadminded	An exciting life
Capable	A sense of accomplishment
Cheerful	A world at peace
Clean	A world of beauty
Courageous	Equality
Forgiving	Family security
Helpful	Freedom
Honest	Happiness
Imaginative	Inner harmony
Independent	Mature love
Intellectual	National security
Logical	Pleasure
Loving	Salvation
Obedient	Self-respect
Polite	Social recognition
Responsible	True friendship
Self-controlled	Wisdom

Source: Richard W. Pollay, 'Measuring the Cultural Values Manifest in Advertising', *Current Issues and Research in Advertising* (1983): 71–92. Reprinted by permission of University of Michigan Division of Research.

self-fulfilment, being well-respected, excitement, sense of accomplishment, security and self-respect. This was the instrument used in the studies in Germany, Norway and USA quoted above. Likewise, in a comparative study of French and German consumers, the values of sense of belonging and self-respect were much more popular in Germany, whereas the values of fun and enjoyment in life, self-fulfilment and self-accomplishment were significantly more often chosen as most important value in France.[39]

However, it should be noticed that the cross-cultural validity of such value instruments is, at best, difficult to obtain since the meaning of values as already said may differ significantly in different cultural contexts.[40] For example, the LOV did not do very well in a test of its cross-cultural validity.[41]

Schwartz value survey

This very elaborate set of values containing 56 different values organized in 11 so-called motivational domains has been demonstrated to be among the more cross-culturally valid instruments.[42] This instrument was used to profile Danish consumers with environmentally friendly attitudes and behaviour, where it turned out that such values as 'protecting the environment' and 'unity with nature' but also 'mature love', 'broadminded' and 'social justice' characterized the 'green' segment, whereas values such as 'authority', 'social power', 'national security' and 'politeness' were the most characteristic of the non-green segment.[43] (See also chapter 9.)

Multicultural dimensions

Japanese culture is well known for its emphasis on cleanliness. The Shinto religion requires a ritual washing of hands and mouth before entering shrines, and people always take off their shoes at home to avoid dirtying the floors. People give money as wedding gifts and may actually iron it before putting it in the envelope. Some laundromats even allow customers to rinse out the inside of a machine before using it.

This value has reached new proportions since a food poisoning epidemic in the summer of 1996. Demand for products such as antiseptic bicycle grips, karaoke microphones and gauze masks is skyrocketing, and a rash of sterilized products ranging from stationery and floppy disks to telephones and dishwashers is invading the market. Pentel makes a germ-free pen decorated with a medical blue cross; the popular brand is advertised with the slogan: 'The pen is mightier than the bacterium'. Japan's Sanwa Bank literally 'launders money' for its customers in specially designed ATM machines, while Tokyo's Mitsubishi Bank opened a 'Total Anti-Germ Branch' featuring ATMs with surfaces made of plastics saturated with chemicals that resist bacteria and fungus. A bank spokesman noted the branch is especially popular with young female customers who say they 'don't want to touch things handled by middle-aged men'. But how successful are the efforts to live in a sanitized world? A Japanese sociologist comments, 'Young people today think they can banish germs from their lives with a few gimmicks. But after you use your antiseptic ATM, you still walk out the door into a world of germs'.[44] None the less, they keep trying ...

The means–end chain model

Another research approach that incorporates values is termed a **means–end chain** model. This approach assumes that very specific product attributes are linked at levels of increasing abstraction to terminal values. The person has valued end states, and he or she chooses among alternative means to attain these goals. Products are thus valued as the means to an end. Through a technique called **laddering**, consumers' associations between specific attributes and general consequences are uncovered. Consumers are helped to climb up the 'ladder' of abstraction that connects functional product attributes with desired end-states.[45]

To understand how laddering works, consider somebody who expresses a liking for a light beer. Probing might reveal that this attribute is linked to the consequence of not getting drunk. A consequence of not getting drunk is that s/he will be able to lead more interesting conversations, which in turn means that s/he will be more sociable. Finally, a better sociability results in better friendship, a terminal value for this person.[46]

Laddering is not without problems however, since the laddering technique might generate invalid answers if the respondent is pushed up the ladder by a too strong emphasis on the sequence in the means–end chain. Consumers should be allowed to jump back and forth, to make loops and forks and blind alleys, which requires more skill of the interviewer but is also a more accurate representation of the respondent's thought processes.[47] Furthermore, it has been argued that in researching the demand for status goods, using laddering techniques can be problematic since motivations for conspicuous consumption are difficult for consumers to express or reveal.[48]

MECCAs

The notion that products are consumed because they are instrumental to attaining more abstract values is central to one application of this technique, called the Means–End Conceptualization of the Components of Advertising Strategy (**MECCAs**). In this approach, researchers first generate a map depicting relationships between functional product or service attributes and terminal values. This information is then used to develop advertising strategy by identifying such elements as:[49]

- *Message elements*: the specific attributes or product features to be depicted.
- *Consumer benefit*: the positive consequences of using the product or service.
- *Executional framework*: the overall style and tone of the advertisement.
- *Leverage point*: the way the message will activate the terminal value by linking it with specific product features.
- *Driving force*: the end-value upon which the advertising will focus.

This technique was used to develop an advertising strategy for the Danish fish trade organization. In spite of the country's huge fishing industry and the supply of fresh fish, the Danish per capita consumption of fish was considerably lower than in several other European countries. A study was carried out using a means–end approach to investigate Danish consumers' attitudes to eating fish. It was concluded that some of the main problems were found in the lack of ideas in preparation and variation of fish-based meals among Danish housewives. This was in sharp contrast to the traditional driving force used by the organization, stressing that fish is healthy.[50]

Based on these results, an advertising campaign was created. Its message elements emphasized fish as a convenient and delicious food. The consumer benefit was the quick and easy preparation, which made dinner or lunch an easy task to accomplish. The executional framework was a humorous one. Two middle-aged, traditional-looking people are portrayed in various situations, where the male is sceptical about the idea of eating fish for lunch or dinner. In one of the TV spots, the wife is talking to somebody else over the telephone. Her remarks lead the TV viewers (and the husband listening in the background) to think that they are talking about the other family's sex life ('You do it TWICE a week!', 'It takes FIFTEEN minutes!!!', 'so HE likes that'). In fact, a friend is telling her about how she prepares fish for dinner. The leverage point is that these recipes allow the wife to prepare delicious meals very quickly, which in turn provides a happy family life, the driving force (terminal value). Almost immediately after the campaign, the trade organization registered an increase in the interest and the consumption of fresh fish.[51]

Figure 4.3 shows two different hierarchical value maps, or sets of ladders, from the fish study. The two ladders are very similar with the exception of the elaboration and central position of negative, demotivating elements. The one with only a few demotivating elements are the aggregate ladders for consumers who are highly

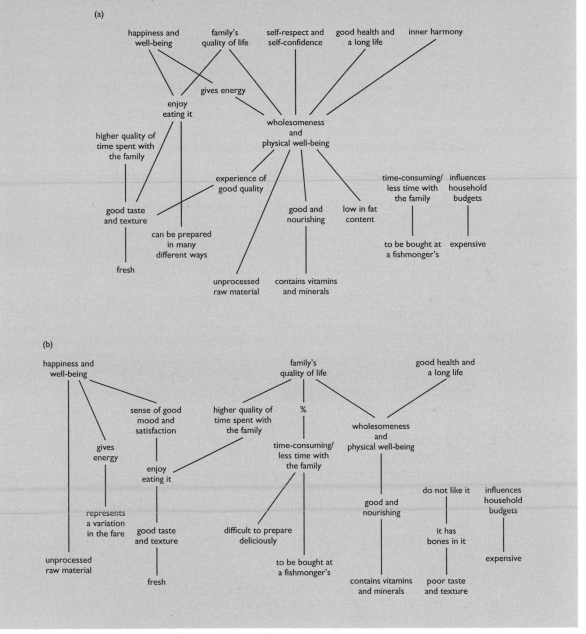

Figure 4.3 **Hierarchical value map for fish for (a) more experienced and (b) less experienced respondents**
Source: E. Sørensen, K.G. Grunert and N.A. Nielsen, 'The Impact of Product Experience, Product Involvement, and Verbal Processing Style on Consumers' Cognitive Structures with Regard to Fresh Fish', MAPP Working Paper No. 42 (The Aarhus School of Business, October 1996).

experienced fish consumers, whereas the other one shows the ladders for the less experienced segment of consumers. These ladders, in addition to the nature of the means–end technique, illustrate the central importance of the concept of product experience for consumers' motivation structures.

Hidden motives: probing beneath the surface

A motive is an underlying reason for behaviour and not something researchers can see or easily measure. Furthermore, the same behaviour can be caused by a configuration of different motives. To compound the problem of identifying motives, the consumer may be unaware of the actual need/want he or she is attempting to satisfy, or alternatively he or she may not be willing to admit that this need exists. Because of these difficulties, motives must often be *inferred* by the analyst. Although some consumer needs undoubtedly are utilitarian and fairly straightforward, some researchers feel that a great many purchase decisions are not the result of deliberate, logical decisions. On the contrary, people may do things to satisfy motives of which they are not even aware.

Consumer behaviour on the couch: Freudian theory

Sigmund Freud had a profound, if controversial, impact on many basic assumptions of human behaviour. His work changed the way we view such topics as adult sexuality, dreams and psychological adjustment. Freud developed the idea that much of human behaviour stems from a fundamental conflict between a person's desire to gratify his or her physical needs and the necessity to function as a responsible member of society. This struggle is carried out in the mind among three systems. (Note that these systems do not refer to physical parts of the brain.)

The **id** is entirely oriented towards immediate gratification – it is the 'party animal' of the mind. It operates according to the pleasure principle; behaviour is guided by the primary desire to maximize pleasure and avoid pain. The id is selfish and illogical. It directs a person's psychic energy towards pleasurable acts without regard for the consequences.

The **superego** is the counterweight to the id. This system is essentially the person's conscience. It internalizes society's rules (especially as communicated by parents) and works to prevent the id from seeking selfish gratification.

Finally, the **ego** is the system that mediates between the id and the superego. It is in a way a referee in the fight between temptation and virtue. The ego tries to balance these two opposing forces according to the reality principle. It finds ways to gratify the id that will be acceptable to the outside world. These conflicts occur on an unconscious level, so the person is not necessarily aware of the underlying reasons for behaviour.

According to Freudian theory, a person's development hinges on the way these systems interact in childhood. Aspects of Freudian theory are controversial, and his observations are not always accepted literally. For example, the bulk of Freud's insights were based on his own patients, a limited sample composed primarily of affluent Viennese women. Many feminists object to Freud's assumptions about the inferiority of women, ideas that were widely accepted in his time. None the less, Freud had a profound impact on the fields of psychiatry and clinical psychology.

Some of Freud's ideas have also been adapted by consumer researchers. In particular, his work highlights the potential importance of unconscious motives underlying purchases. The implication is that consumers cannot necessarily tell us their true motivation for choosing a product, even if we can devise a sensitive way to ask them directly.

The Freudian perspective also hints at the possibility that the ego relies on the symbolism in products to compromise between the demands of the id and the prohibitions of the superego. The consumer channels his or her unacceptable desire into acceptable outlets by using products that signify these underlying desires. This is the connection between product symbolism and motivation: the product stands for, or represents, a consumer's true goal, which is socially unacceptable or unattainable. By acquiring the product, the person is able vicariously to experience the forbidden fruit.

Most Freudian applications in marketing are related to the sexuality of products. For example, some analysts have speculated that a sports car is a substitute for sexual gratification for many men. Indeed, some men do seem inordinately attached to their cars and may spend many hours lovingly washing and polishing them. Others focus on male-oriented symbolism – so-called phallic symbols – that appeals to women. Although Freud himself joked that 'sometimes a cigar is just a cigar', many pop applications of Freud's ideas revolve around the use of objects that resemble sex organs (e.g. cigars, trees or swords for men; tunnels for women). This focus stems from Freud's analysis of dreams, which were often interpreted as communicating repressed desires through symbols.

Motivational research

The first attempts to apply Freudian ideas to understand the deeper meanings of products and advertisements were made in the 1950s as a perspective known as **motivational research** was developed. This approach was largely based on psychoanalytic (Freudian) interpretations, with a heavy emphasis on unconscious motives. A basic assumption is that socially unacceptable needs are channelled into acceptable outlets. Product use or avoidance is motivated by unconscious forces which often are determined in childhood.

This form of research relies on *depth interviews* probing deeply into each person's purchase motivations. These can be derived only after questioning and interpretation on the part of a carefully trained interviewer. This work was pioneered by Ernest Dichter, a psychoanalyst who was trained in Vienna in the early part of the twentieth century. Dichter conducted in-depth interview studies on over 230 different products, and many of his findings have been incorporated in marketing campaigns.[52] For example, Esso (or Exxon) for many years reminded consumers to 'Put a Tiger in Your Tank' after Dichter found that people responded well to this powerful animal symbolism containing vaguely suggestive overtones.

Criticisms of motivational research

Motivational research has been attacked for two quite opposite reasons. Some feel it does not work, while others feel it works *too* well. On the one hand, social critics attacked this school of thought for giving advertisers the power to manipulate consumers.[53] On the other hand, many consumer researchers felt the research lacked sufficient rigour and validity, since interpretations were subjective and indirect.[54] Because conclusions are based on the analyst's own judgement and are derived from discussions with a small number of people, some researchers are doubtful as to the degree to which these results can be generalized to a large market. In addition, because the original motivational researchers were heavily influenced by orthodox Freudian theory, their interpretations usually carried strong sexual overtones. This emphasis tends to overlook other plausible causes for behaviour. It is worth noting that it has been argued that such over-interpretations and disregard of the more mundane and obvious were more common in the American market than in the British for example, leading to a greater discredit in the USA than in Europe of qualitative research in general and motivational research in particular.[55]

The positive side of motivational research

Motivational research had great appeal at least to some marketers for several reasons, some of which are detailed here. Motivational research tends to be less expensive than large-scale, quantitative survey data because interviewing and data processing costs are relatively small.

The knowledge derived from motivational research may help in the development of marketing communications that appeal to deep-seated needs and thus provide a more powerful hook to relate a product to consumers. Even if they are not necessarily valid for all consumers in a target market, these insights can be valuable when used in an exploratory way. For example, the rich imagery that may be associated with a product can be used creatively when developing advertising copy.

Some of the findings seem intuitively plausible after the fact. For example, motivational studies concluded that coffee is associated with companionship, that people avoid prunes because they remind them of old age, and that men fondly equate the first car they owned as a young man with the onset of their sexual freedom.

Other interpretations were hard for some people to accept, such as the observation that to a woman baking a cake symbolizes giving birth, or that men are reluctant to give blood because they feel that their vital fluids are being drained. On the other hand, some people do refer to a pregnant woman as 'having a bun in the oven'.[56] Motivational research for the Red Cross did find that men (but not women) tend to overestimate drastically the amount of blood that is taken during a donation. This group counteracted the fear of loss of virility by symbolically equating the act of giving blood with fertilization: 'Give the gift of life'. Despite its drawbacks, motivational research continues to be employed as a useful diagnostic tool. Its validity is enhanced, however, when used in conjunction with the other research techniques available to the consumer researcher.

Needs and wants: do marketers manipulate consumers?

One of the most common and stinging criticisms of marketing is that marketing techniques (especially advertising) are responsible for convincing consumers that they 'need' many material goods and that they will be unhappy and somehow inferior if they do not have these 'necessities'. The issue is complex, and one that is certainly worth considering: do marketers give people what they want, or do they tell people what they ought to want?

Philosophers have approached this issue when considering the concept of free will. It has been argued that in order to claim that consumers are acting autonomously in response to ads, the capacity for free will and free action must be present. That is, the consumer must be capable of deciding *independently* what to do, and not be prevented from carrying out that decision. This, it has been argued, is probably true for purely informative advertising, where only the product or store information required to make a rational decision is provided, whereas the case for advertising, where imagery or underlying motivations are tapped, is not as clear.[57] Such a view presupposes that informative advertising is somehow more objective than imagery-based advertising. But functionality and utility are also important images of a specific cultural context that uses references to our reason to seduce us.[58] Three issues related to the complex relationship between marketing practices and consumers' needs are considered here.

Do marketers create artificial needs?

The marketing system has come under fire from both ends of the political spectrum. On the one hand, some conservative traditionalists believe that advertising contributes to the moral breakdown of society by presenting images of hedonistic pleasure. On the other hand, some leftists argue that the same misleading promises of material pleasure function to buy off people who would otherwise be revolutionaries working to change the system.[59] Through advertising, then, the system creates demand that only its products can satisfy.

One possible response to such criticism is that a need is a basic biological motive, while a want represents one way that society has taught us that the need can be satisfied. For example, while thirst is biologically based, we are taught to want Coca-Cola to satisfy that thirst rather than, say, goat's milk. Thus, the need is already there; marketers simply recommend ways to satisfy it. A basic objective of advertising is to create awareness that these needs exist, rather than to create them.

However, marketers are important engineers of our environment. And beyond the level of banality, needs are always formed by the social environment. Thus, in a sense, needs are always 'artificial' because we are interested in needs only in their social form. Alternatively, needs are never artificial because they are always 'real' to the people who feel them. 'Needs' are something we are socialized to have. In the case of the Coca-Cola vs. goat's milk example, it should be remembered that we do not eat and drink solely to satisfy a biological need. We eat and drink for a number of reasons, all of them embedded in our cultural context. What is the need of a sofa? A TV? A car? A textbook on consumer behaviour? Thus a better response would be that marketers do not create artificial needs, but they do contribute heavily to the

This ad was created by the American Association of Advertising Agencies to counter charges that ads create artificial needs. Compare this message with the marketing opportunity on page 117. What is your conclusion?
Courtesy of American Association of Advertising Agencies.

socialization of people in contemporary society and thus the establishment of the *social* system of needs. Consequently, marketers must take a share of responsibility for the development of society.

Marketing pitfall

The charge that businesses participate in the social construction of needs is relevant in the case of petrol marketing. Oil companies have attempted to convince consumers of the need for premium petrol, even though this need has been questioned by many people. As one car engineer noted, 'Oil company advertising has led people to the conclusion that more expensive fuels will make their car start easier, get more gas mileage, and last longer ... But in most cases this is untrue ... Your engine has to be designed to use that extra octane ... Otherwise ... the extra cost is just lining the pockets of the oil companies.'

An oil industry executive wrote, 'When prices go up a bit, people will come to their senses and premium volumes will diminish'. But for now, people buy higher octane fuel for reasons that have nothing to do with car engines; one, he theorized, is 'the use of premium as an expression of self-worth'.[60] Is the need for higher octane a 'genuine' one, or something manufactured by the oil companies by associating premium petrol with power, status, virility, and so on? Or is it an outcome of an interplay between a set of values held by consumers, which is used and reinforced by companies' communicative strategies?

Is advertising necessary?

As the social commentator Vance Packard wrote over thirty years ago, 'Large-scale efforts are being made, often with impressive success, to channel our unthinking habits, our purchasing decisions, and our thought processes by the use of insights gleaned from psychiatry and the social sciences'. The economist John Kenneth Galbraith believed that radio and television are important tools to accomplish this manipulation of the masses. Since virtually no literacy is required to use these media, they allow repetitive and compelling communications to reach almost everyone.

Goods are arbitrarily linked to desirable social attributes. One influential critic even argued that the problem is that we are not materialistic enough – that is, we do not sufficiently value goods for the utilitarian functions they deliver, but instead focus on the irrational value of goods for what they symbolize. According to this view, 'Beer would be enough for us, without the additional promise that in drinking it we show ourselves to be manly, young at heart, or neighbourly. A washing machine would be a useful machine to wash clothes, rather than an indication that we are forward-looking or an object of envy to our neighbours.'[61]

Such arguments seem somewhat outdated towards the end of the twentieth century, when advertising has been embraced as an artform in itself. Today, children are brought up to be both consumers and advertising readers. A predominantly functional approach to consumption, as in the former planned economies of Eastern Europe did not make people happier, nor did it prevent them from establishing mythologies about other goods, such as the scarce and expensive ones from the West. Advertisers, just like marketers, are important communicators. Their importance must be followed by a sense of responsibility concerning the social and individual effect of their messages.

Marketing opportunity

As Eastern European countries turn into market economies, some fear that consumers are being exploited as Western advertisements bombard them with products they didn't know they needed. In Poland, for example, previously taboo items like women's sanitary towels are being advertised for the first time, and new markets are being created for products such as pet food. The actions of one Polish entrepreneur illustrate how a consumer's search for social approval can be channelled into a want for a product.

Beginning with an ad campaign featuring Miss Poland, he single-handedly created a market for electronic hair removers (Polish women usually did not shave their legs). He also persuaded a leading Polish fashion designer to announce that hairy legs were out of fashion in Europe, and he organized local beauty contests to find the best legs. At last report, he was selling 30,000 hair removers a month.[62]

Do marketers promise miracles?

Consumers are led to believe via advertising that products have magical properties; they will do special and mysterious things for them that will transform their lives. They will be beautiful, have power over others' feelings, be successful, be relieved of all ills, and so on. In this respect, advertising functions as mythology does in primitive societies; it provides simple, anxiety-reducing answers to complex problems. Is this a problem in itself?

Yes and no. The consumer is not an automaton that will react in a predefined way to certain stimuli. On the other hand, we are all partly socialized by the market and its messages. So, whereas the manipulative effectiveness of advertising is often overstated, there is little doubt that advertising creates and changes patterns of consumption. Especially so in the new market economies, where the population does not maintain the same distance and critical view to advertising messages and imagery.

This cartoon lampoons the widely held belief that marketers manipulate consumers by making us feel inadequate about ourselves. Then they bombard us with messages promising that we will be better people, more attractive, more successful, and so on if only we buy this or that product or service. How valid is this criticism?
Copyright © 1994 by Bill Watterston. Courtesy of Universal Press Syndicate.

But the effect is in general more subtle than simple manipulative persuasion. In most cases, advertisers simply do not know enough about people to manipulate them directly. Consider that the failure rate for new products ranges from 40 to 80 per cent. The main effect of advertising may often be found on the more general level in the promotion of the idea that your self and your personal relationships, your success and your image are all dependent on your consumer choices.

Chapter summary

- Marketers have claimed that they try to satisfy consumer needs, but the reason why any product is purchased can vary widely. The identification of consumer motives is an important step in ensuring that the appropriate needs and wants will be met by a product.

- Traditional approaches to consumer behaviour have focused on the abilities of products to satisfy rational needs (utilitarian motives), but hedonic motives (e.g. the need for exploration or for fun) also play a role in many purchase decisions.

- The same product can satisfy different needs, depending upon the consumer's state at the time. In addition, the consumer's degree of involvement with the product must be considered.

- Since consumers are not necessarily able or willing to communicate their underlying needs to marketers, various techniques such as projective tests can be employed to indirectly assess needs.

- Consumer motivations often are driven by underlying values. In this context, products take on meaning because they are seen as being instrumental in helping the person to achieve some goal that is linked to a value, such as individuality or freedom.

- Values are basic, general principles used to judge the desirability of end-states. All cultures form a value system, which sets it apart from other cultures. Some researchers have developed lists to account for such value systems and used them in cross cultural comparisons.

- One approach to the study of values is the means–end chain, which tries to link product attributes to consumer values via the consequences that usage of the product will have for the consumer.

- It is often heard that marketers create artificial needs. Although this criticism is oversimplified, it is true that marketers must accept their share of the responsibility for how society develops and what is considered necessary to have and what is acceptable, nice and fun to do within society.

⚷ Key terms

Acculturation *(p. 106)*	**Laddering** *(p. 109)*
Desire *(p. 94)*	**LOV** *(p. 107)*
Drive theory *(p. 92)*	**Means–end chain** *(p. 109)*
Ego *(p. 112)*	**MECCAs** *(p. 110)*
Ego involvement *(p. 101)*	**Motivation** *(p. 91)*
Enculturation *(p. 106)*	**Motivational research** *(p. 113)*
Expectancy theory *(p. 93)*	**Superego** *(p. 112)*
Goal *(p. 92)*	**Terminal values** *(p. 107)*
Homeostasis *(p. 92)*	**Theory of cognitive dissonance** *(p. 96)*
Id *(p. 112)*	
Inertia *(p. 100)*	**Value** *(p. 104)*
Instrumental values *(p. 107)*	**Value system** *(p. 105)*
Involvement *(p. 99)*	**Want** *(p. 92)*

Consumer behaviour challenge

1. Describe three types of motivational conflicts, citing an example of each from current marketing campaigns.
2. Should consumer researchers have the right to probe into the consumer's unconscious? Is this a violation of privacy, or just another way to gather deep knowledge of purchase motivations?
3. Devise separate promotional strategies for an article of clothing, each of which stresses one of the levels of Maslow's hierarchy of needs.
4. What is the difference between a want and a need? Do marketers have the power to create needs?
5. Describe how a man's level of involvement with his car would affect how he is influenced by different marketing stimuli. How might you design a strategy for a line of car batteries for a segment of low-involvement consumers, and how would this strategy differ from your attempts to reach a segment of men who are very involved in working on their cars?
6. Interview members of a celebrity fan club. Describe their level of involvement with the 'product', and devise some marketing opportunities to reach this group.
7. 'High involvement is just a fancy term for expensive'. Do you agree?
8. Collect a sample of ads that appear to appeal to consumers' values. What value is being communicated in each, and how is this done? Is this an effective approach to designing a marketing communication?
9. Construct a hypothetical means–end chain model for the purchase of a bouquet of roses. How might a florist use this approach to construct a promotional strategy?

It's Saturday night, and Nancy, Lynn and Terri are out on the town. When the barman at The Wagon & Horses pub comes to take their drink orders, Nancy immediately orders her usual: a dry Stolichnaya martini, straight up, with a twist. Nancy takes her vodka seriously. She's tried them all, and nothing else will do. Lynn, on the other hand, is indecisive. She doesn't drink often, and she can't really tell one concoction from another. Finally she says, 'Oh, I don't care. I guess your house white wine will be fine.'

Terri shrugs and says, 'Looks like it's going to be Pepsi for me. I'm the designated driver tonight.' Dave the barman is impressed. 'Now that's a nice change. It looks like all the publicity about drunk driving has finally got through to you.' Terri replies, 'Look, things are different these days! People know they can't party without facing the consequences.' When the drinks are served, Nancy and Lynn settle back and enjoy their beverages. Terri eyes their glasses as she drinks her Pepsi. 'These two owe me one', she thinks, anticipating next Saturday night . . .

Attitudes

The power of attitudes

An **attitude** is a lasting, general evaluation of people (including oneself), objects or issues.[1] Anything towards which one has an attitude, whether it is tangible, such as a brand of vodka, or intangible, such as drunk driving, is called an **attitude object** (**A$_o$**). This chapter will consider the contents of an attitude, how attitudes are formed and how they can be measured, and will review some of the surprisingly complex relationships between attitudes and behaviour. In the next chapter, we'll take a closer look at how attitudes can be changed – an issue of prime importance to marketers. First, though, let's take a brief look at how marketers are attempting to influence the behaviour of people like Terri to benefit society as a whole.

As Terri's willingness to serve as a designated driver (on a Saturday night!) shows, marketers can have a big impact on consumers' attitudes regarding many facets of their everyday lives. **Social marketing** involves the promotion of causes and ideas, such as responsible drinking, energy conservation and population control.[2] For example, public health care organizations in many European countries regularly run public service mass media campaigns to inform target markets about the health risks of smoking, drinking and healthy eating.[3]

Attitudes towards products are formed and perpetuated in many ways, ranging from persuasive messages delivered by celebrities who endorse these items on television and in magazines, to observations of brands that are bought and used by friends or parents. Consumers' attitudes can also be influenced by the behaviours of media role models, who act as communications sources even when not explicitly endorsing a product. Unfortunately, the behaviour of television characters too often encourages irresponsible behaviour by glamourizing greed, promiscuity, excessive alcohol and drug use, and so on. For example, the depiction of sexual activity on television is increasing, but the consequences of these acts in terms of unwanted pregnancies and sexually transmitted diseases are rarely mentioned.[4]

Some social marketers are turning their attention to the possibility that attitudes can be changed more effectively by influencing the consumption activities depicted in popular media. As one television executive observed, 'If you put a cigarette in a character's hand, you are announcing that he smells bad and doesn't take care of himself. And if you are going to give them a drink, it had better be wine with a fancy, multiple name'.[5]

The power of television to mould behaviour was used successfully in America by a public service campaign called the Harvard Alcohol Project. This was the first attempt to change consumer behaviour by coordinating the subtle messages conveyed by a number of popular television programmes. To promote the use of

designated drivers by people who are out drinking, the scripts of peak-viewing programmes were deliberately written to mention designated drivers. Within one year,
the project reported a 10 per cent increase in the proportion of consumers who
claimed to have used a designated driver.[6]

The content of attitudes

The term attitude is widely used in popular culture. You might be asked, 'What is
your attitude towards abortion?' A parent might scold, 'Young man, I don't like
your attitude'. Some bars even euphemistically refer to happy hour as 'an attitude
adjustment period'.

An attitude is *lasting* because it tends to endure over time. It is *general* because
it applies to more than a momentary event, like hearing a loud noise (though over
time you might develop a negative attitude towards all loud noises). Consumers
have attitudes towards very product-specific behaviours (e.g. using Mentodent
rather than Colgate toothpaste), as well as towards more general consumption-
related behaviours (e.g. how often you should brush your teeth). Attitudes help to
determine who a person goes out with, what music he or she listens to, whether he or
she will recycle or discard cans, or whether he or she chooses to become a consumer
researcher for a living.

The functions of attitudes

The **functional theory of attitudes** was initially developed by the psychologist
Daniel Katz to explain how attitudes facilitate social behaviour.[7] According to this
pragmatic approach, attitudes exist because they serve a function for the person.
That is, they are determined by a person's motives. Consumers who expect that they
will need to deal with similar information at a future time will be more likely to start
forming attitudes in anticipation of this event.[8]

Two people can each have the same attitude towards an object for very different
reasons. As a result, it can be helpful for a marketer to know why an attitude is held
before attempting to change it. The following are attitude functions as identified by
Katz:

- *Utilitarian function.* The utilitarian function is related to the basic principles of
  reward and punishment. We develop some of our attitudes towards products
  simply on the basis of whether these products provide pleasure or pain. If a
  person likes the taste of a cheeseburger, that person will develop a positive
  attitude towards cheeseburgers. Ads that stress straightforward product
  benefits (e.g. you should drink Diet Coke 'just for the taste of it') appeal to the
  utilitarian function.
- *Value-expressive function.* Attitudes that perform a value-expressive function
  express the consumer's central values or self-concept. A person forms a
  product attitude not because of its objective benefits, but because of what the
  product says about him or her as a person (e.g., 'What sort of woman reads
  Elle?'). Value-expressive attitudes are highly relevant to lifestyle analyses,
  where consumers cultivate a cluster of activities, interests and opinions to
  express a particular social identity.

- *Ego-defensive function.* Attitudes that are formed to protect the person, either from external threats or internal feelings, perform an ego-defensive function. An early marketing study indicated that housewives in the 1950s resisted the use of instant coffee because it threatened their conception of themselves as capable homemakers.[9] Products that promise to help a man project a 'macho' image (e.g. Marlboro cigarettes) may be appealing to his insecurities about his masculinity. Another example of this function is deodorant campaigns that stress the dire, embarrassing consequences of underarm odour.
- *Knowledge function.* Some attitudes are formed as the result of a need for order, structure or meaning. This need is often present when a person is in an ambiguous situation or is confronted with a new product (e.g. 'Bayer wants you to know about pain relievers').

An attitude can serve more than one function, but in many cases a particular one will be dominant. By identifying the dominant function a product serves for consumers (i.e. what benefits it provides), marketers can emphasize these benefits in their communications and packaging. Ads relevant to the function prompt more favourable thoughts about what is being marketed and can result in a heightened preference for both the ad and the product.

One American study determined that for most people coffee serves more of a utilitarian function than a value-expressive function. As a consequence, subjects responded more positively to copy for a fictitious brand of coffee that read, 'The delicious, hearty flavour and aroma of Sterling Blend coffee comes from a blend of the freshest coffee beans' (i.e utilitarian appeal) than they did to copy that read, 'The coffee you drink says something about the type of person you are. It can reveal your rare, discriminating taste' (i.e. value-expressive function). In European countries with a strong 'coffee culture', such as Germany, the Benelux and Scandinavian countries, ads are more likely to stress the value-expressive function, wherein the more social and ritualistic aspects of coffee consumption are expressed.[10]

The ABC model of attitudes and hierarchies of effects

Most researchers agree that an attitude has three components: affect, behaviour and cognition. **Affect** refers to the way a consumer feels about an attitude object. **Behaviour** involves the person's intentions to do something with regard to an attitude object (but, as will be discussed later, an intention does not always result in an actual behaviour). **Cognition** refers to the beliefs a consumer has about an attitude object. These three components of an attitude can be remembered as the ABC model of attitudes.

This model emphasizes the interrelationships between knowing, feeling and doing. Consumers' attitudes toward a product cannot be determined simply by identifying their beliefs about it. For example, a researcher may find that shoppers 'know' a particular camcorder has an 8:1 power zoom lens, auto-focus and a flying erase head, but such findings do not indicate whether they feel these attributes are good, bad or irrelevant, or whether they would actually buy the camcorder.

While all three components of an attitude are important, their relative importance will vary depending upon a consumer's level of motivation with regard to the attitude object. The differences in drink choices among the three friends at the bar illustrate how these elements can be combined in different ways to create attitudes. Attitude researchers have developed the concept of a *hierarchy of effects* to

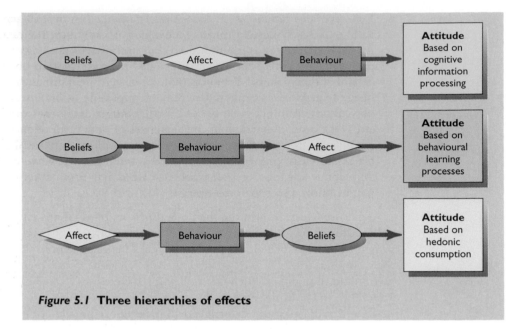

Figure 5.1 **Three hierarchies of effects**

explain the relative impact of the three components. Each hierarchy specifies that a fixed sequence of steps occurs en route to an attitude. Three different hierarchies are summarized in Figure 5.1.

The standard learning hierarchy

Nancy's choice of a favourite drink closely resembles the process by which most attitudes have been assumed to be constructed. A consumer approaches a product decision as a problem-solving process. First, he or she forms beliefs about a product by accumulating knowledge (beliefs) regarding relevant attributes. Next, the consumer evaluates these beliefs and forms a feeling about the product (affect). Over time, Nancy integrated information about alternative vodka brands and formed a preference for one kind.

Finally, based on this evaluation, the consumer engages in a relevant behaviour, such as buying the product. This careful choice process often results in the type of brand loyalty displayed by Nancy; the consumer 'bonds' with the product over time and is not easily persuaded to experiment with other brands. The standard learning hierarchy assumes that a consumer is highly involved in making a purchase decision.[11] The person is motivated to seek a lot of information, carefully weigh alternatives and come to a thoughtful decision. As we saw in chapter 4, this process is likely to occur if the decision is important to the consumer or in some way central to the consumer's self-concept.

The low-involvement hierarchy

In sharp contrast to Nancy, Lynn's interest in the attitude object (a particular brand of alcoholic beverage) is at best lukewarm. She has collected only a minimal amount of information before acting and has an emotional response only after consuming the beverage. Lynn is typical of a consumer who forms an attitude via the low-involvement hierarchy of effects. In this sequence, the consumer initially does not have a strong preference for one brand over another, but instead acts on the basis of limited knowledge and then forms an evaluation only after the fact.[12] The attitude is likely to come about through behavioural learning, where the consumer's choice is reinforced by good or bad experiences with the product after purchase.

The possibility that consumers simply don't care enough about many decisions to assemble a set of product beliefs carefully and then evaluate them is important because it implies that all the concern about influencing beliefs and carefully communicating information about product attributes may be largely wasted. Consumers aren't necessarily going to pay attention anyway; they are more likely to respond to simple stimulus–response connections when making purchase decisions. For example, a male shopper in a supermarket faced with the task of choosing among paper towels might choose the brand which is on special offer rather than bothering to compare all of the brands on the shelf systematically.

The notion of low involvement on the part of consumers is a bitter pill for some marketers to swallow. Who wants to admit that what they market is not very important or involving? A brand manager for, say, a brand of chewing gum or cat food may find it hard to believe that consumers don't put that much thought into purchasing her product since she spends many of her waking (and perhaps sleeping) hours thinking about it.

For marketers, the ironic silver lining to this low-involvement cloud is that under these conditions, consumers are not motivated to process a lot of complex brand-related information. Instead, they will be swayed by principles of behavioural learning, such as the simple responses caused by conditioned brand names, point-of-purchase displays, and so on. This results in what we might call the involvement paradox: that is, the less important the product is to consumers, the more important are many of the marketing stimuli (e.g. packages, jingles) that must be devised to sell it.

The experiential hierarchy

Researchers in recent years have begun to stress the significance of emotional response as a central aspect of an attitude. According to the experiential hierarchy of effects, consumers act on the basis of their emotional reactions (just as Terri felt strongly about drunk drivers). Although the factors of beliefs and behaviour are recognized as playing a part, a consumer's overall evaluation of an attitude object is considered by many to be the core of an attitude.

This perspective highlights the idea that attitudes can be strongly influenced by intangible product attributes such as package design, and by consumers' reactions towards accompanying stimuli such as advertising and even the brand name. As discussed in chapter 4, resulting attitudes will be affected by consumers' hedonic motivations, such as how the product makes them feel or the fun its use will provide.

One important debate about the experiential hierarchy concerns the independence of cognition and affect. On the one hand, the *cognitive-affective model* argues that an affective judgement is the last step in a series of cognitive processes. Earlier steps include the sensory registration of stimuli and the retrieval of meaningful information from memory to categorize these stimuli.[13]

On the other hand, the *independence hypothesis* takes the position that affect and cognition involve two separate, partially independent systems; affective responses do not always require prior cognitions.[14] The number one song on the 'Top Ten Hit Parade' may possess the same attributes as many other songs (dominant bass guitar, raspy vocals, persistent downbeat), but beliefs about these attributes cannot explain why one song becomes a classic while another sharing the same characteristics ends up in the bargain bin at the local record store. The independence hypothesis does not eliminate the role of cognition in experience. It simply balances this traditional, rational emphasis on calculated decision-making by paying more attention to the impact of aesthetic, subjective experience. This type of holistic processing is more likely to occur when the product is perceived as primarily expressive or delivers sensory pleasure rather than utilitarian benefits.[15]

There's more to marketing than product attitudes

Marketers who are concerned with understanding consumers' attitudes have to contend with an even more complex issue: in decision-making situations, people form attitudes towards objects other than the product itself that can influence their ultimate selections. One additional factor to consider is attitudes towards the act of buying in general. As we'll see later in the chapter, sometimes people are reluctant, embarrassed or just too lazy to expend the effort to obtain a desired product or service.

In addition, consumers' reactions to a product, over and above their feelings about the product itself, are influenced by their evaluations of its advertising. Our evaluation of a product can be determined solely by our appraisal of how it is depicted in marketing communications – that is, we don't hesitate to form attitudes about products we've never even seen in person, much less used.

The **attitude towards the advertisement (A_{ad})** is defined as a predisposition to respond in a favourable or unfavourable manner to a particular advertising stimulus during a particular exposure occasion. Determinants of A_{ad} include the viewer's attitude towards the advertiser, evaluations of the ad execution itself, the mood evoked by the ad and the degree to which the ad affects viewers' arousal levels.[16] A viewer's feelings about the context in which an ad appears can also influence brand attitudes. For example, attitudes about an ad and the brand depicted will be influenced if the consumer sees the ad while watching a favourite TV programme.[17] The effects demonstrated by A_{ad} emphasize the importance of an ad's entertainment value in the purchase process.[18]

The feelings generated by advertising can have a direct impact on brand attitudes. Commercials can evoke a wide range of emotional responses, from disgust to happiness. Further, there is evidence that emotional responses will vary from one group of consumers to another. In an empirical study of students and housewives in Belgium and Holland, the results showed that the Belgians were more positive towards the hedonic and socio-cultural aspects of advertising than their Dutch counterparts. In the UK, Ford's ad campaign research on the Ford *Ka*, which is targeting an image-oriented market, showed it annoyed 41 per cent of 55–64 year olds, compared with only 18 per cent of 25–34 year olds. These feelings can be influenced both by the way the ad is done (i.e. the specific advertising execution) and by the consumer's reactions to the advertiser's motives. For example, many advertisers who are trying to craft messages for adolescents and young adults are encountering problems because this age group, having grown up in a 'marketing society', tends to be sceptical about attempts to persuade them to buy things.[19] These reactions can, in turn, influence memory for advertising content.[20] At least three emotional dimensions have been identified in commercials: pleasure, arousal and intimidation.[21] Specific types of feelings that can be generated by an ad include the following:[22]

- Upbeat feelings – amused, delighted, playful
- Warm feelings – affectionate, contemplative, hopeful
- Negative feelings – critical, defiant, offended.

Forming attitudes

We all have lots of attitudes, and we don't usually question how we got them. No one is born with the conviction that, say, Pepsi is better than Coke or that heavy metal music liberates the soul. Where do these attitudes come from?

An attitude can form in several different ways, depending on the particular hierarchy of effects in operation. It can occur because of classical conditioning, wherein an attitude object, such as the name Pepsi, is repeatedly paired with a catchy jingle ('You're in the Pepsi Generation . . .'). Or, it can be formed through instrumental conditioning, in which consumption of the attitude object is reinforced (e.g. Pepsi quenches the thirst). Alternatively, the learning of an attitude can be the outcome of a very complex cognitive process. For example, a teenager may come to model the behaviour of friends and media figures who drink Pepsi because she believes that this act will enable her to fit in with the desirable images of the Pepsi Generation.

It is thus important to distinguish among types of attitudes, since not all are formed the same way.[23] A highly brand-loyal consumer like Nancy, the Stolichnaya drinker, has an enduring, deeply held positive attitude towards an attitude object, and this involvement will be difficult to weaken. On the other hand, another consumer like Lynn, the occasional wine drinker, may be more fickle: she may have a mildly positive attitude towards a product, but be quite willing to abandon it when something better comes along. This section will consider the differences between strongly and weakly held attitudes and briefly review some of the major theoretical perspectives that have been developed to explain how attitudes form and relate to one another in the minds of consumers.

Levels of commitment to an attitude

Consumers vary in their commitment to an attitude; the degree of commitment is related to their level of involvement with the attitude object, as follows:[24]

- *Compliance*: At the lowest level of involvement, compliance, an attitude is formed because it helps in gaining rewards or avoiding punishments from others. This attitude is very superficial; it is likely to change when the person's behaviour is no longer monitored by others or when another option becomes available. A person may drink Pepsi because that is the brand the café sells and it is too much trouble to go elsewhere for a Coca-Cola.
- *Identification*: A process of identification occurs when attitudes are formed in order for the consumer to be similar to another person or group. Advertising that depicts the social consequences of choosing some products over others is relying on the tendency of consumers to imitate the behaviour of desirable models.
- *Internalization*: At a high level of involvement, deep-seated attitudes are internalized and become part of the person's value system. These attitudes are very difficult to change because they are so important to the individual. For example, many consumers had strong attitudes towards Coca-Cola and reacted quite negatively when the company attempted to switch to the New Coke

formula. This allegiance to Coke was obviously more than a minor preference for these people; the brand had become intertwined with their social identities, taking on patriotic and nostalgic properties.

The consistency principle

Have you ever heard someone say, 'Pepsi is my favourite soft drink. It tastes terrible', or 'I love my husband. He's the biggest idiot I've ever met?' Perhaps not very often, because these beliefs or evaluations are not consistent with one another. According to the **principle of cognitive consistency**, consumers value harmony among their thoughts, feelings and behaviours, and they are motivated to maintain uniformity among these elements. This desire means that, if necessary, consumers will change their thoughts, feelings or behaviours to make them consistent with their other experiences. The consistency principle is an important reminder that attitudes are not formed in a vacuum. A significant determinant of the way an attitude object will be evaluated is how it fits with other, related attitudes already held by the consumer.

Cognitive dissonance theory revisited

In the last chapter, we discussed the role played by cognitive dissonance when consumers are trying to choose between two desired products. Cognitive dissonance theory has other important ramifications for attitudes, since people are often confronted with situations in which there is some conflict between their attitudes and behaviours.[25]

The theory proposes that, much like hunger or thirst, people are motivated to reduce this negative state by making things fit with one another. The theory focuses on situations where two cognitive elements are inconsistent with one another.

A cognitive element can be something a person believes about himself, a behaviour he performs or an observation about his surroundings. For example, the two cognitive elements 'I know smoking cigarettes causes cancer' and 'I smoke cigarettes' are dissonant. This psychological inconsistency creates a feeling of discomfort that

This public service advertisement hopes to form young people's attitudes towards drinking. Of course, individuals will vary in their level of commitment towards drinking. Does this ad strike you primarily at a cognitive, or an emotional level? What is your attitude towards the ad?
Used with permission.

the smoker is motivated to reduce. The magnitude of dissonance depends upon both the importance and number of dissonant elements.[26] In other words, the pressure to reduce dissonance is more likely to be observed in high-involvement situations in which the elements are more important to the individual.

Dissonance reduction can occur either by eliminating, adding or changing elements. For example, the person could stop smoking (eliminating) or remember Great-Aunt Sophia, who smoked until the day she died at age 90 (adding). Alternatively, he might question the research that links cancer and smoking (changing), perhaps by believing industry-sponsored studies that try to refute this connection.

Dissonance theory can help to explain why evaluations of a product tend to increase after it has been purchased, i.e. post-purchase dissonance. The cognitive element 'I made a stupid decision' is dissonant with the element 'I am not a stupid person', so people tend to find even more reasons to like something after buying it.

A field study performed at a horse race demonstrates post-purchase dissonance. Gamblers evaluated their chosen horses more highly and were more confident of their success after they had placed a bet than before. Since the gambler is financially committed to the choice, he or she reduces dissonance by increasing the attractiveness of the chosen alternative relative to the unchosen ones.[27] One implication of this phenomenon is that consumers actively seek support for their purchase decisions, so marketers should supply them with additional reinforcement to build positive brand attitudes.

While the consistency principle works well in explaining our desire for harmony among thoughts, feelings and behaviours, and subsequently in helping marketers understand their target markets, it isn't a perfect predictor of the way in which we hold seemingly *related* attitudes. Consider the results of a large European study of young adults, wherein attitudes towards the environment were being analyzed. Figure 5.2 shows the percentage of 16–24 year olds who agree with the statement: 'We must take radical action to cut down on how we use our cars'. A few preliminary conclusions can be made from this graph. First, European youth's attitude towards addressing cutting down on the use of cars seems generally positive. Not only is it positive, but the attitude seems to be gaining in support over time (from 1993 to 1996), with the exception of the sample from The Netherlands. Now compare the results of attitudes towards car usage with the results of paying more for environmentally friendly products, shown in Figure 5.3 (both results are from the same samples). Here, the attitude of *not* having to pay more for environmentally friendly products is strong, stable over time, and across countries, with the Dutch sample reporting a somewhat greater willingness to pay more for environmental products. So, while congruity theory would predict that seemingly related attitudes are positively correlated, consumers can and do hold attitudes which are not always consistent, at least on the surface!

Self-perception theory

Do attitudes necessarily change following behaviour because people are motivated to feel good about their decisions? **Self-perception theory** provides an alternative explanation of dissonance effects.[28] It assumes that people use observations of their own behaviour to determine what their attitudes are, just as we assume that we know the attitudes of others by watching what they do. The theory states that we maintain consistency by inferring that we must have a positive attitude towards an object if we have bought or consumed it (assuming that we freely made this choice). Thus, Nancy might say to herself, 'I must like this brand of vodka. I seem to order it a lot'.

Self-perception theory is relevant to the low-involvement hierarchy, since it involves situations in which behaviours are initially performed in the absence of a

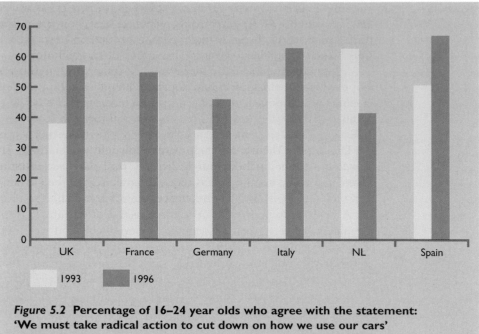

Figure 5.2 **Percentage of 16–24 year olds who agree with the statement: 'We must take radical action to cut down on how we use our cars'**
Source: The Henley Centre

strong internal attitude. After the fact, the cognitive and affective components of attitude fall into line. Thus, buying a product out of habit may result in a positive attitude towards it after the fact – namely, why would I buy it if I didn't like it?

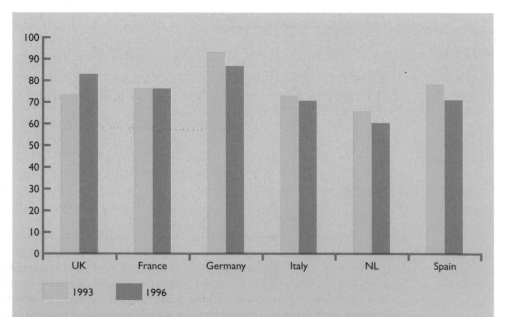

Figure 5.3 **Percentage of 16–24 year olds who agree with the statement: 'I should *not* have to pay more for environmentally friendly products'**
Source: The Henley Centre

Self-perception theory helps to explain the effectiveness of a sales strategy called the **foot-in-the-door technique**, which is based on the observation that a consumer is more likely to comply with a request if he or she has first agreed to comply with a smaller request.[29] The name of this technique comes from the practice of door-to-door selling, when the salesperson was taught to plant his or her foot in a door so the prospect could not slam it shut. A good salesperson knows that he or she is more likely to get an order if the customer can be persuaded to open the door and talk. By agreeing to do so, the customer has established that she or he is willing to listen. Placing an order is consistent with this self-perception. This technique is especially useful for inducing consumers to answer surveys or to donate money to charity. Such factors as the time-lag between the first and second request, the similarity between the two requests, and whether the same person makes both requests have been found to influence their effectiveness.[30]

Social judgement theory

Social judgement theory assumes that people assimilate new information about attitude objects in the light of what they already know or feel.[31] The initial attitude acts as a frame of reference, and new information is categorized in terms of this existing standard. Just as our decision that a box is heavy depends in part on other boxes we have lifted, we develop a subjective standard when making judgements about attitude objects.

One important aspect of the theory is the notion that people differ in terms of the information they will find acceptable or unacceptable. They form **latitudes of acceptance and rejection** around an attitude standard. Ideas that fall within a latitude will be favourably received, while those falling outside of this zone will not. Since Terri had a favourable attitude towards the use of designated drivers, she is likely to be receptive to communications urging her to play this role before leaving for an evening out. If she were opposed to this practice, these messages would probably not be considered.

Messages that fall within the latitude of acceptance tend to be seen as more consistent with one's position than they actually are. This process is called an assimilation effect. On the other hand, messages falling in the latitude of rejection tend to be seen as even further from one's position than they actually are, resulting in a contrast effect.[32]

As a person becomes more involved with an attitude object, his or her latitude of acceptance shrinks. In other words, the consumer accepts fewer ideas that are removed from his or her own position and tends to oppose even mildly divergent positions. This tendency is evident in ads that appeal to discriminating buyers, which claim that knowledgeable people will reject anything but the very best (e.g. 'Choosy mothers choose Jif'). On the other hand, relatively uninvolved consumers will consider a wider range of alternatives. They are less likely to be brand-loyal and will be more likely to be brand-switchers.[33]

Balance theory

Balance theory considers relations among elements a person might perceive as belonging together.[34] This perspective involves relations (always from the perceiver's subjective point of view) among three elements, so the resulting attitude structures are called *triads*. Each triad contains (1) a person and his or her perceptions of (2) an attitude object and (3) some other person or object.

These perceptions can be positive or negative. More importantly, people *alter* these perceptions in order to make relations among them consistent. The theory specifies that people desire relations among elements in a triad to be harmonious, or balanced. If they are not, a state of tension will result until perceptions are changed and balance is restored.

Elements can be perceived as going together in one of two ways. They can have a *unit relation*, where one element is seen as belonging to or being a part of the other (something like a belief) or a sentiment relation, where the two elements are linked because one has expressed a preference (or dislike) for the other. A couple might be seen as having a positive sentiment relation. If they marry, they will have a positive unit relation. The process of divorce is an attempt to sever a unit relation.

To see how balance theory might work, consider the following scenario:

- Monica would like to go out with Anthony, who is in her consumer behaviour class. In balance theory terms, Monica has a positive sentiment relation with Anthony.
- One day, Anthony attends class wearing clothing that allows his fellow students to see his tattoo. Anthony has a positive unit relation with the tattoo. It belongs to him and is literally a part of him.
- Monica does not like tattooed men. She has a negative sentiment relation with tattoos.

According to balance theory, Monica faces an unbalanced triad, and she will experience pressure to restore balance by altering some aspect of the triad, as shown in Figure 5.4. She could, for example, decide that she does not like Anthony after

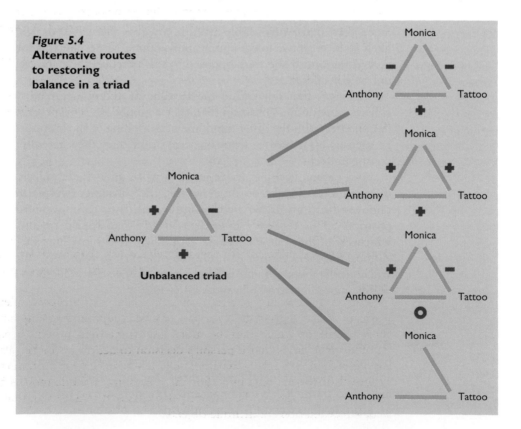

**Figure 5.4
Alternative routes
to restoring
balance in a triad**

Unbalanced triad

all. Or her liking for Anthony could prompt a change in her attitude towards tattoos. Finally, she could choose to 'leave the field' by thinking no more about Anthony and his controversial tattoo. Note that while the theory does not specify which of these routes will be taken, it does predict that one or more of Monica's perceptions will have to change in order to achieve balance. While this distortion is an oversimplified representation of most attitude processes, it helps to explain a number of consumer behaviour phenomena.

Balance theory reminds us that when perceptions are balanced, attitudes are likely to be stable. On the other hand, when inconsistencies are observed, we are more likely to observe changes in attitudes. Balance theory also helps to explain why consumers like to be associated with positively valued objects. Forming a unit relation with a popular product (e.g. buying and wearing fashionable clothing or driving a high-performance car) may improve one's chances of being included as a positive sentiment relation in other people's triads.

Finally, balance theory is useful in accounting for the widespread use of celebrities to endorse products. In cases where a triad is not fully formed (e.g. one involving perceptions about a new product or one about which the consumer does not yet have a well-defined attitude), the marketer can create a positive sentiment relation between the consumer and the product by depicting a positive unit relation between the product and a well-known personality. In other cases, behaviours are discouraged when admired people argue against them, as is the goal when athletes feature in government-sponsored anti-drug campaigns.

This 'balancing act' is at the heart of celebrity endorsements, in which it is hoped that the star's popularity will transfer to the product. This strategy will be considered at length in the next chapter. But, it pays to remember that this creation of a unit relation between product and star can backfire if the public's opinion of the celebrity endorser shifts from positive to negative, as happened when Madonna was associated with a controversial music video involving religion and sex. Pepsi withdrew an ad featuring her. The strategy can also cause trouble if the star–product unit relation is questioned, as happened when the singer Michael Jackson, who also did promotions for Pepsi, subsequently confessed that he does not drink the brand.

Attitude models

A consumer's overall evaluation of a product sometimes accounts for the bulk of his or her *attitude* towards it. When market researchers want to assess attitudes, it can often be sufficient for them simply to ask the consumer, 'How do you feel about Heineken?', or 'How do you feel about the proposed introduction of the Euro?'

However, as we saw earlier, attitudes can be a lot more complex than that. One problem is that a product or service may be composed of many attributes, or qualities – some of which may be more important than others to particular people. Another problem is that a person's decision to act on his or her attitude is affected by other factors, such as whether it is felt that buying a product will meet with approval of friends or family. For these reasons, attitude models have been developed that try to specify the different elements that might work together to influence people's evaluations of attitude objects.

Multiattribute attitude models

A simple response does not always tell us everything we need to know about why the consumer has certain feelings towards a product or about what marketers can do to change the consumer's attitude. For this reason, **multiattribute attitude models** have been extremely popular among marketing researchers. This type of model assumes that a consumer's attitude (evaluation) of an attitude object (A_o) will depend on the beliefs he or she has about several or many attributes of the object. The use of a multiattribute model implies that an attitude towards a product or brand can be predicted by identifying these specific beliefs and combining them to derive a measure of the consumer's overall attitude. We'll describe how these work, using the example of a consumer evaluating a complex attitude object that should be very familiar: a university.

Basic multiattribute models specify three elements:[35]

- *Attributes* are characteristics of the A_o. Most models assume that the relevant characteristics can be identified. That is, the researcher can include those attributes that consumers take into consideration when evaluating the A_o. For example, scholarly reputation is an attribute of a university.
- *Beliefs* are cognitions about the specific A_o (usually relative to others like it). A belief measure assesses the extent to which the consumer perceives that a brand possesses a particular attribute. For example, a student might have a belief that Oxford Colleges have a strong academic standing.
- *Importance weights* reflect the relative priority of an attribute to the consumer. Although an A_o can be considered on a number of attributes, some will be more important than others (i.e. they will be given greater weight), and these weights are likely to differ across consumers. In the case of universities, for example, one student might stress the school's library resources, while another might assign greater weight to the social environment in which the university is located.

Measuring attitude elements

Suppose a supermarket chain wanted to measure shoppers' attitudes towards its retail outlets. The firm might administer one of the following types of attitude scales to consumers by mail, phone or in person (see chapter 1).[36]

Single-item scales   One simple way to assess consumers' attitudes towards a store or product is to ask them for their general feelings about it. Such a global assessment does not provide much information about specific attributes, but it does give managers some sense of consumers' overall attitudes. This single-item approach often uses a Likert scale, which measures respondents' overall level of agreement or feelings about an attitude statement.

How satisfied are you with your grocery store?
Very satisfied   Somewhat satisfied   Satisfied   Not at all satisfied

Multiple-item batteries   Attitude models go beyond such a simple measure, since they acknowledge that an overall attitude may often be composed of consumers' perceptions about multiple elements. For this reason, many attitude measures assess a set of beliefs about an issue and combine these reactions into an overall score. For example, the supermarket might ask customers to respond to a set of Likert scales and combine their responses into an overall measure of store satisfaction.

1. My supermarket has a good selection of produce.
2. My supermarket maintains sanitary conditions.
3. I never have trouble finding exotic foods at my supermarket.

| Agree
strongly | Agree
somewhat | Neither agree
nor disagree | Disagree
somewhat | Disagree
strongly |

The *semantic-differential scale* is useful for describing a person's set of beliefs about a company or brand, and it is also used to compare the images of competing brands. Respondents rate each attribute on a series of rating scales, where each end is anchored by adjectives or phrases, such as this one:

My supermarket is
Dirty 1 — 2 — 3 — 4 — 5 — 6 — 7 Clean

Semantic-differential scales can be used to construct a profile analysis of the competition, where the images of several stores or products can be compared visually by plotting the mean ratings for each object on several attributes of interest. This simple technique can help to pinpoint areas where the product or store diverges sharply from the competitors (in either a positive or a negative way). The fictitious profiles of three different types of cinemas are shown in Figure 5.5. Based on these findings, the management of a multi-screen cinema might want to emphasize its wide selection of films and/or try to improve its image as a modern cinema, or improve its cleanliness.

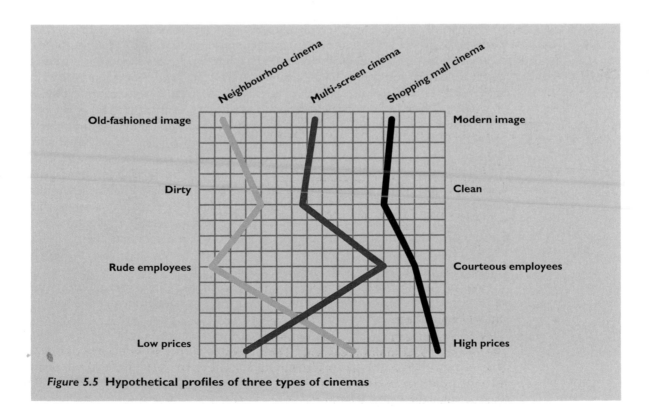

Figure 5.5 **Hypothetical profiles of three types of cinemas**

The Fishbein model

The most influential multiattribute model is the Fishbein model, named after its primary developer.[37] The model measures three components of attitude.

1. *Salient beliefs* people have about an A₀ (i.e. those beliefs about the object that are considered during evaluation).
2. *Object-attribute linkages*, or the probability that a particular object has an important attribute.
3. *Evaluation* of each of the important attributes.

Note, however, that the model makes some assumptions that may not always be warranted. It assumes that we have been able to specify adequately all the relevant attributes that, for example, a student will use in evaluating his or her choice about which college to attend. The model also assumes that he or she will go through the process (formally or informally) of identifying a set of relevant attributes, weighing them and summing them. Although this particular decision is likely to be highly involving, it is still possible that his or her attitude will be formed by an overall affective response (a process known as affect-referral).

By combining these three elements, a consumer's overall attitude towards an object can be computed. (We'll see later how this basic equation has been modified to increase its accuracy.) The basic formula is

$$A_{ijk} = \Sigma B_{ijk} I_{ik}$$

where i = attribute; j = brand; k = consumer; I = the importance weight given attribute i by consumer k; B = consumer k's belief regarding the extent to which brand j possesses attribute i; and A = a particular consumer k's attitude score for brand j.

The overall attitude score (A) is obtained by multiplying a consumer's rating of each attribute for all the brands considered by the importance rating for that attribute.

To see how this basic multiattribute model might work, let's suppose we want to predict which college a middle-school graduate is likely to attend. After months of waiting, Sandra has been accepted at four colleges. Since she must now decide among these, we would first like to know which attributes Sandra will consider in forming an attitude towards each college. We can then ask Sandra to assign a rating regarding how well each college performs on each attribute and also determine the relative importance of the attributes to her. An overall attitude score for each college can then be computed by summing scores on each attribute (after weighing each by its relative importance). These hypothetical ratings are shown in Table 5.1. Based on this analysis, it seems that Sandra has the most favourable attitude towards Smith. She is clearly someone who would like to attend an all-woman's college with a solid academic reputation rather than a college that offers a strong athletics programme or a party atmosphere.

Strategic applications of the multiattribute model

Imagine you are the director of marketing for Northland University, another institution Sandra is considering. How might you use the data from this analysis to improve your image?

Capitalize on relative advantage If one's brand is viewed as being superior on a particular attribute, consumers like Sandra need to be convinced that this particular attribute is an important one. For example, while Sandra rates Northland's social atmosphere highly, she does not believe this attribute is a valued aspect for a college. As Northland's marketing director, you might emphasize the importance of an active

Table 5.1 The basic multiattribute model: Sandra's college decision

Attribute (i)	Importance (I)	Smith	Beliefs (b) Princeton	Rutgers	Northland
Academic reputation	6	8	9	6	3
All women	7	9	3	3	3
Cost	4	2	2	6	9
Proximity to home	3	2	2	6	9
Athletics	1	1	2	5	1
Party atmosphere	2	1	3	7	9
Library facilities	5	7	9	7	2
Attitude score		163	142	153	131

Note: These hypothetical ratings are scored from 1 to 10, and higher numbers indicate 'better' standing on an attribute. For a negative attribute (e.g. cost), higher scores indicate that the school is believed to have 'less' of that attribute (i.e. to be cheaper).

social life, varied experiences or even the development of future business contacts forged through strong school friendships.

Strengthen perceived product/attribute linkages A marketer may discover that consumers do not equate his or her brand with a certain attribute. This problem is commonly addressed by campaigns that stress the product's qualities to consumers (e.g. 'new and improved'). Sandra apparently does not think much of Northland's academic quality, sports facilities or library. You might develop an informational campaign to improve these perceptions (e.g. 'Little known facts about Northland').

Add a new attribute Product marketers frequently try to create a distinctive position from their competitors by adding a product feature. Northland might try to emphasize some unique aspect, such as a supervised work-experience programme for business graduates, which takes advantage of links with the local community.

Influence competitors' ratings Finally, you might try to decrease the positive rating of competitors. This type of action is the rationale for a strategy of comparative advertising. One tactic might be to publish an ad that lists the tuition fees of a number of local colleges, as well as their attributes with which Northland can be favourably compared, as the basis for emphasizing the value for money obtained at Northland.

Using attitudes to predict behaviour

Although multiattribute models have been used by consumer researchers for many years, they have been plagued by a major problem: in many cases, knowledge of a person's attitude is not a very good predictor of behaviour. In a classic demonstration of 'do as I say, not as I do', many studies have obtained a very low correlation between a person's reported attitude towards something and his or her actual behaviour towards it. Some researchers have been so discouraged that they have questioned whether attitudes are of any use at all in understanding behaviour.[38] This questionable linkage can be a big headache for advertisers when consumers love a commercial yet fail to buy the product. A Norwegian charity recently won an award for a popular advertising campaign on which it spent 3 million Nkr (£300,000) only to find that it resulted in just 1.7 million Nkr in donations.[39]

The extended Fishbein model

The original Fishbein model, which focused on measuring a consumer's attitude towards a product, has been extended in a number of ways to improve its predictive ability. The revised version is called the **theory of reasoned action**.[40] The model is still not perfect, but its ability to predict relevant behaviour has been improved.[41] Some of the modifications to this model are considered here.

Intentions versus behaviour

Many factors might interfere with actual behaviour, even if the consumer's intentions are sincere. He or she might save up with the intention of buying a stereo system. In the interim, though, any number of things – being made redundant or finding that the desired model is out of stock – could happen. It is not surprising, then, that in some instances past purchase behaviour has been found to be a better predictor of future behaviour than is a consumer's behavioural intention.[42] The theory of reasoned action aims to measure behavioural intentions, recognizing that certain uncontrollable factors inhibit prediction of actual behaviour.

Social pressure

The theory acknowledges the power of other people in influencing behaviour. Many of our behaviours are not determined in isolation. Much as we may hate to admit it, what we think others would like us to do may be more relevant than our own individual preferences.

In the case of Sandra's college choice, note that she is very positive about going to an all-female institution. However, if she feels that this choice would be unpopular (perhaps her friends will think she is mad), she might ignore or downgrade this preference when making her final decision. A new element, the subjective norm (SN), was thus added to include the effects of what we believe other people think we should do. The value of SN is arrived at by including two other factors: (1) the intensity of a normative belief (NB) that others believe an action should be taken or not taken, and (2) the motivation to comply (MC) with that belief (i.e. the degree to which the consumer takes others' anticipated reactions into account when evaluating a course of action or a purchase).

Attitude towards buying

The model now measures **attitude towards the act of buying (A_{act})**, rather than only the attitude towards the product itself. In other words, it focuses on the perceived consequences of a purchase. Knowing how someone feels about buying or using an object proves to be more valid than merely knowing the consumer's evaluation of the object itself.[43]

To understand this distinction, consider a problem that might arise when measuring attitudes towards condoms. Although a group of college students might have a positive attitude towards condom use, does this necessarily predict that they will buy and use them? A better prediction would be obtained by asking the students how likely they are to buy condoms. While a person might have a positive A_o towards condoms, A_{act} might be negative due to the embarrassment or the trouble involved.

Obstacles to predicting behaviour

Despite improvements to the Fishbein model, problems arise when it is misapplied. In many cases, the model is used in ways for which it was not intended or where certain assumptions about human behaviour may not be warranted.[44] Other obstacles to predicting behaviour are as follows:

- The model was developed to deal with actual behaviour (e.g. taking a slimming pill), not with the outcomes of behaviour (e.g. losing weight) which are assessed in some studies.
- Some outcomes are beyond the consumer's control, such as when the purchase requires the cooperation of other people. For instance, a woman might seek a mortgage, but this intention will be worthless if she cannot find a banker to give her one.
- The basic assumption that behaviour is intentional may be invalid in a variety of cases, including those involving impulsive acts, sudden changes in one's situation, novelty-seeking or even simple repeat-buying. One study found that such unexpected events as having guests, changes in the weather or reading articles about the health qualities of certain foods exerted a significant effect on actual behaviours.[45]
- Measures of attitude often do not really correspond to the behaviour they are supposed to predict, either in terms of the A_o or when the act will occur. One common problem is a difference in the level of abstraction employed. For example, knowing a person's attitude towards sports cars may not predict whether he or she will purchase a Porsche 9-11. It is very important to match the level of specificity between the attitude and the behavioural intention.
- A similar problem relates to the time-frame of the attitude measure. In general, the longer the time between the attitude measurement and the behaviour it is supposed to assess, the weaker the relationship will be. For example, predictability would improve markedly by asking consumers the likelihood that they would buy a house in the next week as opposed to within the next five years.
- Attitudes formed by direct, personal experience with an A_o are stronger and more predictive of behaviour than those formed indirectly, such as through advertising.[46] According to the attitude accessibility perspective, behaviour is a function of the person's immediate perceptions of the A_o in the context of the situation in which it is encountered. An attitude will guide the evaluation of the object, but only if it is activated from memory when the object is observed. These findings underscore the importance of strategies that induce trial (e.g. by widespread product sampling to encourage the consumer to try the product at home, by taste tests, test-drives, etc.) as well as those that maximize exposure to marketing communications.

Multicultural dimensions

The theory of reasoned action has primarily been applied in the West. Certain assumptions inherent in the model may not necessarily apply to consumers from other cultures. Several of the following diminish the universality of the theory of reasoned action.

- The model was developed to predict the performance of any voluntary act. Across cultures, however, many consumer activities, ranging from taking exams and entering military service to receiving an inoculation or even choosing a marriage partner, are not necessarily voluntary.
- The relative impact of subjective norms may vary across cultures. For example, Asian cultures tend to value conformity and face-saving, so it is possible that subjective norms involving the anticipated reactions of others to the choice will have an even greater impact on behaviour for many Asian consumers.
- The model measures behavioural intentions and thus presupposes that consumers are actively anticipating and planning future behaviours. The intention concept assumes that consumers have a linear time sense, i.e. they think in terms of past, present and future. As will be discussed in a later chapter, this time perspective is not held by all cultures.
- A consumer who forms an intention is (implicitly) claiming that he or she is in control of his or her actions. Some cultures tend to be fatalistic and do not necessarily believe in the concept of free will. Indeed, one study comparing students from the United States, Jordan and Thailand found evidence for cultural differences in assumptions about fatalism and control over the future.[47]

Tracking attitudes over time

An attitude survey is like a snapshot taken at a single point in time. It may tell us a lot about the position of a person, issue or object at that moment, but it does not permit many inferences about progress made over time or any predictions about possible future changes in consumer attitudes. To accomplish these tasks, it is necessary to develop an attitude-tracking programme. This activity helps to increase the predictability of behaviour by allowing researchers to analyze attitude trends over an extended period of time. It is more like a film than a snapshot. For example, a longitudinal survey, conducted by The Henley Centre, of Europeans' attitudes regarding the process of moving towards European Union shows how attitudes can shift over time, and how the shift can be different for different age cohorts. Figure 5.6 shows the results of a large-scale study carried out in six countries. The percentage of respondents reporting that they 'feel as much European as they do a citizen of their own country' is not particularly strong (especially in the UK), and the percentage of the population supporting the sentiment seems to be declining over time (1991–96).

These results would suggest that as Europe moves towards a more integrated union with a common currency at the turn of the century, consumers from individual countries are holding more closely to their own national identity. Now compare these findings from the general population with the results of the same question put to European young adults (16–24 years) (Figure 5.7). The margin of sampling error would account for the generally small differences across time and countries, with the exception of the UK, where there has been a significant increase over the five-year period in the percentage of young adults who support the statement (albeit at a much lower level than the other countries in the survey).

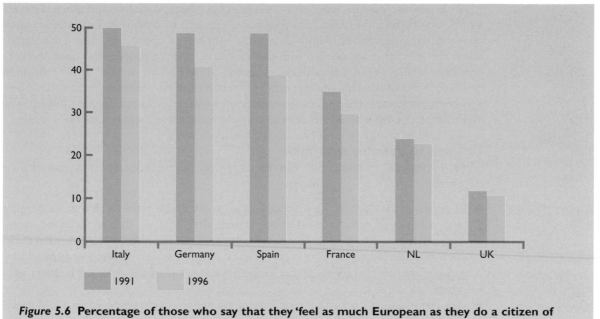

Figure 5.6 **Percentage of those who say that they 'feel as much European as they do a citizen of own country'**
Source: The Henley Centre

Tracking studies

Attitude tracking involves the administration of an attitude survey at regular intervals. Preferably, the same methodology will be used each time so that results can be reliably compared. Several services, such as Gallup, The Henley Centre or the Yankelovich Monitor, track consumer attitudes over time.

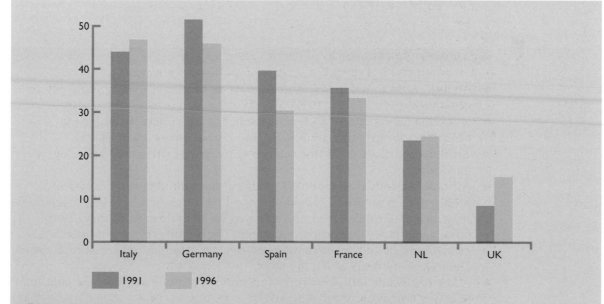

Figure 5.7 **Percentage of 16–24 year olds who say that they 'feel as much European as they do a citizen of own country'**
Source: The Henley Centre

This activity can be extremely valuable for strategic decision-making. For example, one financial services firm monitored changes in consumer attitudes towards one-stop banking centres. Although a large number of consumers were enthusiastic about the idea when it was first introduced, the number of people who liked the concept did not increase over time despite the millions of dollars invested in advertising to promote the centres. This finding indicated some problems with the way the concept was being presented, and the company decided to 'go back to the drawing board', and eventually came up with a new way to communicate the advantages of this service.

Changes to look for over time

Some of the dimensions that can be included in attitude tracking include the following:

- *A focus on changes in different age groups.* Attitudes tend to change as people age (a life-cycle effect). In addition, cohort effects occur, that is, members of a particular generation (e.g. teens, generation X, or the elderly) tend to share certain outlooks. Also, historical effects can be observed as large groups of people are affected by profound cultural changes (e.g. the democratization of Eastern Europe).
- *Scenarios about the future.* Consumers are frequently tracked in terms of their future plans, confidence in the economy, and so on. These measures can provide valuable data about future behaviour and yield insights for public policy. For example, Americans tend to overestimate how much they will earn after retirement, which is potentially a dangerous miscalculation.
- *Identification of change agents.* Social phenomena can change people's attitudes towards basic consumption activities over time, as when consumers' willingness to buy fur products shifts. Or people's likelihood to seek divorce may be affected by such facilitators as changes in the legal system that make this easier, or by inhibitors, such as the prevalence of AIDS and the value of two salaries in today's economy.[48]

Chapter summary

- An attitude is a predisposition to evaluate an object or product positively or negatively.
- Social marketing refers to attempts to change consumers' attitudes and behaviours in ways that are beneficial to the society as a whole.
- Attitudes are made up of three components: beliefs, affect and behavioural intentions.
- Attitude researchers traditionally assumed that attitudes were learned in a predetermined sequence, consisting first of the formation of beliefs (cognitions) regarding an attitude object and followed by an evaluation of that object (affect) and then some action (behaviour). Depending on the consumer's level of involvement and the circumstances, though, attitudes can result from other hierarchies of effects.
- A key to attitude formation is the function the attitude plays for the consumer (e.g. is it utilitarian or ego defensive?).
- One organizing principle of attitude formation is the importance of consistency among attitudinal components – that is, some parts of an attitude may be

altered to conform with others. Such theoretical approaches to attitudes as cognitive dissonance theory, balance theory and congruity theory stress the vital role of consistency.

- The complexity of attitudes is underscored by multiattribute attitude models, in which sets of beliefs and evaluations are identified and combined to predict an overall attitude. Factors such as subjective norms and the specificity of attitude scales have been integrated into attitude measures to improve predictability.

Key terms

Affect *(p. 123)*
Attitude *(p. 121)*
Attitude object (A₀) *(p. 121)*
Attitude towards the act of buying (A_{act}) *(p. 138)*
Attitude towards the advertisement (A_{ad}) *(p. 126)*
Balance theory *(p. 131)*
Behaviour *(p. 123)*
Cognition *(p. 123)*
Foot-in-the-door technique *(p. 131)*
Functional theory of attitudes *(p. 122)*

Hierarchy of effects *(p. 123)*
Latitudes of acceptance and rejection *(p. 131)*
Multiattribute attitude models *(p. 134)*
Principle of cognitive consistency *(p. 128)*
Self-perception theory *(p. 129)*
Social judgement theory *(p. 131)*
Social marketing *(p. 121)*
Theory of reasoned action *(p. 138)*

Consumer behaviour challenge

1. Contrast the hierarchies of effects outlined in the chapter. How will strategic decisions related to the marketing mix be influenced by which hierarchy is operative among target consumers?

2. List three functions played by attitudes, giving an example of how each function is employed in a marketing situation. To examine European countries' attitudes towards a wide variety of issues, go to the website: *http://europa.eu.int/en/comm/dg10/infcom/epo/eo.html*
   Which sorts of attitudes expressed in different countries seem utilitarian, value-expressive or ego-defensive? Why?

3. Think of a behaviour exhibited by an individual that is inconsistent with his

or her attitudes (e.g. attitudes towards cholesterol, drug use or even buying things to attain status or be noticed). Ask the person to elaborate on why he or she does the behaviour, and try to identify the way the person has resolved dissonant elements.

4. Using a series of semantic-differential scales, devise an attitude survey for a set of competing automobiles. Identify areas of competitive advantage or disadvantage for each model you incorporate.

5. Construct a multiattribute model for a set of local restaurants. Based on your findings, suggest how restaurant managers can improve their establishments' image using the strategies described in the chapter.

For Margaret, the unthinkable was about to happen. Here she was, with a big cigar in her mouth. A few short months ago, Margaret believed that cigars were smoked by large, foul-smelling, older men. Lately, though, her attitudes had started to change. First, her friend Mary Ann, returning from business trips to Stockholm and New York, reported that cigar-smoking among women was definitely more commonplace there than in Manchester. Then, she seemed to be reading more and more news stories about famous women lighting up. The clincher was coming across her heroine, supermodel Linda Evangelista, on the cover of *Cigar Aficionado*. Somehow, knowing that an elegant woman like Linda was a cigar fan put to rest any anxieties Margaret had about sacrificing her femininity if she took a puff now and then. Now, the signs were everywhere – women were shedding their disdain for smoke-filled rooms and flocking to cigar bars. The Consolidated Cigar Corporation picked up early on this sea-change and introduced its Cleopatra Collection, featuring versions of its cigars tapered at both ends to make it easier for women to light and hold in their mouths.[1]

Apparently, many women have taken up cigar smoking as a way to navigate the 'old boy network', and as a form of rebellion. That didn't worry Margaret, but she did find that she actually liked to relax after a good meal and savour the taste. Seemingly overnight, her beliefs about the unsavoury characteristics of cigar smokers had changed – and several of her friends admired her pluck for lighting up in public. She even went so far as to surf the net for more information about cigar products. She particularly liked the cigar.com web site, where she could access several cigar retailers, read about people's experiences with different brands and even access short stories about cigars.

Attitude change and interactive communications

Changing attitudes through communication

Prominent women from Marlene Dietrich to Madonna have sported cigars for their shock value and as a way to communicate the notion of rebellion and political incorrectness. More recently, though, the cigar industry itself has climbed on the bandwagon as some canny marketers realized the potential to nurture a new market by persuading 'everyday' women like Margaret to light up. Of course, inspiring such a radical change in behaviour first required an equally drastic change in the way women felt about the product and their beliefs about who used it and what this usage said about the type of people they were.

As consumers we are constantly bombarded by messages inducing us to change our attitudes. These attempts can range from logical arguments to graphic pictures, and from intimidation by peers to exhortations by celebrities. To make things even more complicated, communications flow both ways – the consumer may choose to access information in order to learn more about these options, as Margaret did by surfing the net.

This chapter will review some of the factors that help to determine the effectiveness of such communication devices. Our focus will be on some basic aspects of

Supermodel Linda Evangelista posing as
Cigar Aficionado's cover girl.
Used with permission.

"They're beautiful have them Strangled"

It takes the painful death of up to 40 animals to make one fur coat.
Animals caught in barbaric steel traps take days to die. "Farmed" wild animals are kept in wire cages before they're chased by car exhaust, have their necks broken or are electrocuted anally. If you think you look good wearing a fur coat, think again.

RSPCA AGAINST FUR

This anti-fur ad ran in Hong Kong. It relies on a graphic description of fur industry practices to discourage consumers from considering the purchase of a fur coat.
Courtesy of Bates Hong Kong Ltd.

communication that specifically help to determine how and if attitudes will be created or modified. This objective relates to **persuasion**, which refers to an active attempt to change attitudes. Persuasion is, of course, the central goal of many marketing communications.

Decisions, decisions

Suppose that a cigar company wants to create an advertising campaign for a new product targeted at female smokers. As it plans this campaign, it must develop a message that will create desire for the cigar by potential customers – many of whom

One way that the fur industry is trying to counteract the graphic messages of anti-fur groups is to position the debate as one involving the curtailment of the personal right to buy what one chooses. This ad that was placed by a Scandinavian fur marketer is typical; it wraps the fur wearer in images of a wholesome family scene and positions the decision to buy a fur as representing freedom of choice.
Courtesy of Saga Furs of Scandinavia.

Some people are opposed to a very basic luxury:
Your freedom of choice.

SAGA MINK OF SCANDINAVIA

(like Margaret) have been raised to believe that cigars are about the last thing any woman would want. To craft persuasive messages that might change this attitude, a number of questions must be answered:

- *Who will be featured smoking a cigar in an ad?* Should it be linked to a glamorous celebrity? A career woman? A rock star? The source of a message helps to determine consumers' acceptance of it as well as their desire to try the product.
- *How should the message be constructed?* Should it emphasize the negative consequences of being left out while others are enjoying themselves in the cigar bar? Should it directly compare the cigar with others already on the market, or perhaps present a fantasy where a tough-minded female executive meets a dashing stranger while ducking out of a board meeting for a smoke? Product benefits can be expressed in many ways.
- *What media should be used to transmit the message?* Should it be depicted in a print ad? On television? Sold door-to-door? If a print ad is produced, should it be run in the pages of *Vogue*? *Good Housekeeping*? *Cigar Aficionado*? Sometimes *where* something is said can be as important as *what* is said. Ideally, the attributes of the product should be matched to those of the medium. For example, magazines with high prestige are more effective at communicating messages about overall product image and quality, while specialized, expert magazines do a better job at conveying factual information.[2]
- *What characteristics of the target market might influence the ad's acceptance?* If targeted users are frustrated in their daily lives, these women might be more receptive to a fantasy appeal. If they don't smoke cigars or know anyone who does, they may not pay any attention to a traditional cigar ad at all.

The elements of communication

Marketers and advertisers have traditionally tried to understand how marketing messages can change consumers' attitudes by thinking in terms of the **communications model**, which specifies that a number of elements are necessary for communication to be achieved. In this model, a *source* must choose and encode a message (i.e. initiate the transfer of meaning by choosing appropriate symbolic images which represent that meaning). For example, the publishers of *Cigar Aficionado* magazine attempted to send the message that it's 'cool' for women to light up by highlighting famous females who are cigar fans. This meaning must be put in the form of a *message*. There are many ways to say something, and the structure of the message has a major effect on how it is perceived. In the example shown at the beginning of this chapter a visual image of a well-known supermodel holding a cigar spoke volumes about the sexiness and trendiness of cigars. The message must be transmitted via a *medium*, which could be television, radio, magazines, advertising hoardings, personal contact, and so on. In this case, the message appeared in a specialized magazine targeted to current – and prospective – cigar smokers. The message is then decoded by one or more *receivers*, like Margaret, who interpret the symbols in the light of their own experiences. Finally, *feedback* must be received by the source, who uses the reactions of receivers to modify aspects of the message. Favourable reactions by readers led *Cigar Aficionado* to continue to feature prominent women in its pages. The traditional communications process is depicted in Figure 6.1.

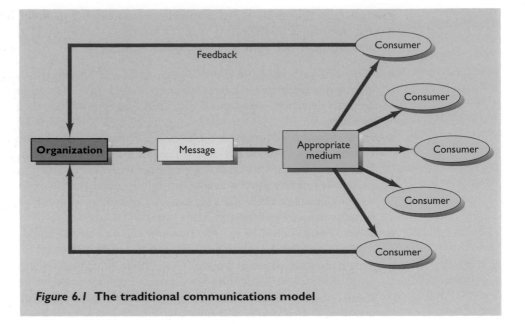

Figure 6.1 **The traditional communications model**

An updated view: interactive communications

While the traditional communications model is not entirely wrong, it doesn't tell the whole story – especially in today's dynamic world of interactivity.[3] The traditional model was developed to understand mass communications, where information is transferred from a producer (source) to many consumers (receivers) at one time – typically via newspaper, television or radio. This perspective essentially views advertising as the process of transferring information to the buyer before a sale. A message is perishable – it is repeated (perhaps frequently) for a fairly short period of time and then 'vanishes' as a new 'campaign' is substituted.

This traditional communications model was strongly influenced by a group of theorists known as the Frankfurt School, which dominated mass communications research for most of the twentieth century. In this view, the media exert direct and powerful effects on individuals, and often are used by those in power to brainwash and exploit them. The receiver is basically passive and is simply the receptacle for many messages, and may often be duped or persuaded to act based on what he or she hears or sees.

Uses and gratifications

Is this an accurate picture of the way we relate to marketing communications? Proponents of **uses and gratifications theory** argue that consumers are an active, goal-directed audience who draw on mass media as a resource to satisfy needs. Instead of asking what media do for or to people, they ask what people do *with* their media.[4]

The uses and gratifications approach emphasizes that media compete with other sources to satisfy needs, and that these needs include diversion and entertainment as well as information. This means that the line between marketing information and entertainment is continuing to blur – especially as companies are being forced to design more attractive retail outlets, catalogues and web sites in order to induce consumers to stop at them. Toyota's site (www.toyota.com) provides a lot more than the latest specifications about available car options; it includes interests like gardening, travel and sports.

Indeed, research with young people in Great Britain finds that they rely on advertising for many gratifications including entertainment (some report that the 'adverts' are better than the programmes), escapism, play (some report singing along with jingles, others make posters out of magazine ads) and self-affirmation (ads can reinforce their own values or provide role models). It's important to note that this perspective is not arguing that media play a uniformly positive role in our lives, only that recipients are making use of the information in a number of ways. For example, marketing messages have the potential to undermine self-esteem. A comment by one study participant illustrates this negative impact. She observes that when she's watching TV with her boyfriend '. . . really, it makes you think "Oh no, what must I be like?" I mean you're sitting with your boyfriend and he's saying "Oh, look at her. What a body!"'[5]

An interactionist perspective on communication

The **interactionist** perspective on communication does not describe human communication as 'mechanistically' as does the classic communications model. Briefly, interactionism relies on three basic premises about communication, which focus on the meaning of objects, ideas and actions:[6]

1. Human beings act towards objects on the basis of the meanings that objects have for them.

2. The meaning of objects is derived from the social interaction that one has.

3. These meanings are processed and modified through an interpretive process which a person uses in dealing with the object encountered.

The interactionist perspective tones down the importance of the external stimuli, and views consumers as 'interpreters', wherein meaning does not arise from the objects themselves, nor from the psyche, but from interaction patterns. This view argues that meanings are not given 'once and for all' and are readily retrievable from memory. Rather, they are re-created and interpreted anew in each communicative action. Hence, the central role of the 'communicating self' must be taken into consideration. The self is seen as an active participant in the creation of meaning from the various signs in the marketplace rather than as a passive decoder of meanings, which may be inherent in the message. Thus, from an interactionist perspective, there is no sender and receiver as such, only *communicators* who are always engaged in mutual sending and receiving of messages. Here, the self is both an object (a 'me') and a subject ('I') of action. The 'me' contains the consciousness of the acting self seen in relation to past experiences of the self and of others. There is thus a constant interpretation of both the self and the other as objects, as well as the object of the communication (the 'message' in the traditional communication model) going on. Figure 6.2 provides an overview of this interactionist communication model.

The model is comprised of several components.[7] The first component is that of 'role and role taking'. Here, the communicator performs a role, following some scripts of past experiences, interpreting the situation and act accordingly. These are efforts of seeing the 'other' from the perspective of 'self'. But the role playing also involves taking the role of the 'other' to see oneself or seeing the self from the perspective of the other (imagining the image that the other may have).

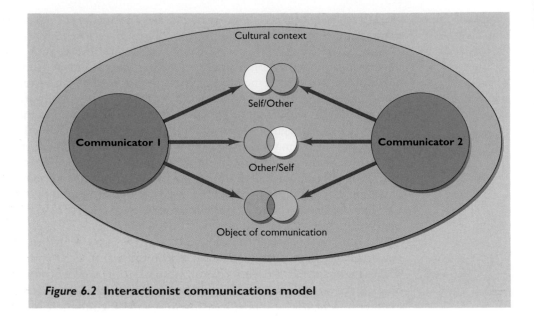

Figure 6.2 **Interactionist communications model**

The second component is orientation, which suggests that these roles we carry out are oriented towards an object. This object might be one of the communicators but also any other idea, thing, or person. To the extent that the interpretive orientations of the communicators are similar, we can say that there is agreement, or congruence between them, and that the communicators share the meanings pertaining to themselves and the object. Congruence is typically a matter of degree, and neither total congruence nor total incongruence are possible. Finally, there is the component of cultural embeddedness which suggests that the symbols and other communicative devices used in the communicative process occur in a cultural context.

As an example, consider a company and its advertising agency. As part of the creative process, the ways in which the ad agency see themselves, the selected target market, the product and campaign in question, and the cultural context of the country will play a role for how they interpret the message they are about to create and send out. Likewise, the consumer's past experiences with this company's products, the meanings that the consumer attaches, based on cultural background and present context (e.g., present aspirations), coupled with the campaign seen in relation to former campaigns, all are important to the interpretation of the campaign's elements and the subsequent interpretation of the whole message.

Who's in charge of the remote?

Technological and social developments are making it increasingly obvious to everybody that people are playing an interactive role in communications. In other words, consumers are to a greater extent becoming active partners, not only in interpreting but also in forming messages in the communications process; their input is helping to shape the messages they and others like them receive, and furthermore they may seek out these messages rather than sit at home and wait to see them on television and in the newspaper.

One of the early signs of this communications revolution was the humble hand-held remote control device. As VCRs became commonplace in the home, consumers had more say in what they wanted to watch – and when. No longer were they at the mercy

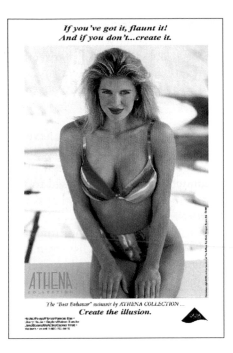

If you've got it, flaunt it!
And if you don't...create it.

ATHENA
COLLECTION

The "Bust Enhancer" swimsuit by ATHENA COLLECTION ...
Create the illusion.

The traditional communication model takes the view that information is transfered from a source (manufacturer) to a receiver (consumer), in a relatively one-way, passive fashion. A more dynamic view of how consumers relate to marketing communication comes from Uses and Gratification theory, which sees consumers as an active, goal directed audience. This perspective would suggest that some consumers would simply ignore the advert on the left. Others may reject it, develop counter-arguments about the message, or elaborate on the message in terms of what it means to them. Whether ignored, rejected, accepted, or elaborated on, messages serve as a dynamic link between senders and receivers.
Used with permission.

of the TV networks to decide when to see their favourite programme; nor did they necessarily have to forsake one programme because it conflicted with another's time slot.

Caller ID devices and answering machines allow us to decide if we will accept a phone call during dinner, and to know the source of the message before picking up the phone. A bit of surfing allows us to identify kindred spirits around the globe, to request information about products, and even to provide suggestions to product designers and market researchers.

As a final example, consider a technology called the *radio data system* (RDS), which has been adopted by the BBC in the UK. This allows a radio station to transmit data on the unused portion of its frequency, known as a subcarrier. RDS is the concept behind Coupon Radio, a car radio system now being tested that allows listeners to 'capture' information and give stations and advertisers feedback about their choices. A driver who hears a new song he or she likes could request more information about the musicians, or get the names and addresses of retailers that sell an advertised product.[8]

Levels of interactive response

The key to understanding the dynamics of interactive marketing communications is to consider exactly what is meant by a response.[10] The early perspective on communications primarily regarded feedback in terms of behaviour – did the recipient go out and buy the soap powder after being exposed to an ad for it?

However, a variety of other responses are possible as well, including building awareness of the brand, informing us about product features, reminding us to buy a new package when we've run out and – perhaps most importantly – building a long-term relationship. Therefore a transaction is *one* type of response, but forward-thinking marketers realize that customers can interact with them in other valuable ways as well. For this reason it is helpful to distinguish between two basic types of feedback.

First-order response   Direct marketing vehicles such as catalogues and television infomercials are interactive – if successful, they result in an order which is most definitely a response! So, let's think of a product offer that directly yields a transaction as a *first-order response*. In addition to providing revenue, sales data are a valuable source of feedback which allow marketers to gauge the effectiveness of their communications efforts.

Second-order response   However, a marketing communication does not have to result in an immediate purchase to be an important component of interactive marketing. Messages can prompt useful responses from customers, even though these recipients do not necessarily place an order immediately after being exposed to the communication. Customer feedback in response to a marketing message that is not in the form of a transaction is a *second-order response*.

A second-order response may take the form of a request for more information about a good, service or organization, or perhaps receipt of a 'wish list' from the customer that specifies the types of product information he or she would like to get in the future. This response may even be in the form of recommendations for other potential customers. The two telephone giants MCI and British Telecom offer a 20 per cent discount to customers who give them the phone numbers of people they call regularly. The phone company then targets these people with promotion messages to get *them* to switch companies as well.

A second-order response programme, the *Pepperidge Farm No Fuss Pastry Club*, illustrates how a firm communicates directly with users without trying to make an immediate sale. The club boasts more than 30,000 members who have been generated through a combination of promotion efforts, including a magazine mail-in offer, an offer on packages of Pepperidge Farm products, publicity created by news reports about the club and a sign-up form available in grocery stores. Pepperidge Farm uses surveys to determine members' attitudes towards issues related to its business, and the company also collects valuable information on how these people use frozen puff pastry products.[11] Though the company's immediate goal is not to generate the first-order response of selling frozen pastry, it knows that the second-order responses received from club members will result in loyal customers over time – and many more first-order responses as a result.

The source

Regardless of whether a message is received by 'snail mail' or e-mail, common sense tells us that the same words uttered or written by different people can have very different effects. Research on *source effects* has been carried out for over thirty years. By attributing the same message to different sources and measuring the degree of attitude change that occurs after listeners hear it, it is possible to determine what aspects of a communicator will induce attitude change.[12]

Under most conditions, the source of a message can have a big impact on the likelihood the message will be accepted. The choice of a source to maximize attitude change can tap into several dimensions. The source can be chosen because he or she is an expert, attractive, famous or even a 'typical' consumer who is both likable and trustworthy. Two important source characteristics are *credibility* and *attractiveness*.[13]

How do marketing specialists decide which dimension to stress? There should be a match between the needs of the recipient and the potential rewards offered by the source. When this match occurs, the recipient is more motivated to process the message. People who tend to be sensitive about social acceptance and the opinions of others, for example, are more persuaded by an attractive source, while those who are more internally oriented are swayed by a credible, expert source.[14]

The choice may also depend on the type of product. While a positive source can help to reduce risk and increase message acceptance, particular types of sources are more effective at reducing different kinds of risk. Experts are effective at changing attitudes towards utilitarian products that have high *performance risk*, such as vacuum cleaners (i.e. they may be complex and not work as expected). Celebrities are more effective when they focus on products such as jewellery and furniture that have high *social risk*; the user of such products is aware of their effect on the impression others have or him or her. Finally, 'typical' consumers, who are appealing sources because of their similarity to the recipient, tend to be most effective when endorsing everyday products that are low risk, such as biscuits.[15]

Source credibility

Source credibility refers to a source's perceived expertise, objectivity or trustworthiness. This characteristic relates to consumers' beliefs that a communicator is competent and willing to provide the necessary information to evaluate competing products adequately. A credible source can be particularly persuasive when the consumer has not yet learned much about a product or formed an opinion of it.[16]

Building credibility
Credibility can be enhanced if the source's qualifications are perceived as relevant to the product being endorsed For example, the footballer Gary Lineker is popularly known in the UK as 'Mr Nice' – a personality type which was a natural for the crisp manufacturer Walker to tie into their advertising campaign that Walker's crisps are 'so nice that the nicest people would nick [steal] them'. Before the campaign unprompted awareness of Walker's ads was around 40 per cent. Following Lineker's antics of stealing packets of crisps from little boys, awareness never fell below 60 per cent, and sales have soared.[17] Similarly, Ronald Biggs, whose claim to fame was his role in the British 'Great Train Robbery' in 1963, successfully served as a spokesman in Brazil, where he lives in exile, for a company that makes door locks – a topic about which he is presumably knowledgeable![18]

Source biases
A consumer's beliefs about a product's attributes can be weakened if the source is perceived to be the victim of bias in presenting information.[19] *Knowledge bias* implies that a source's knowledge about a topic is not accurate. *Reporting bias* occurs when a source has the required knowledge, but his or her willingness to convey it accurately is compromised – for example, when an expert endorses a product. While his or her credentials might be appropriate, the fact that the expert is perceived as a 'hired gun' compromises credibility.

Source attractiveness

Source attractiveness refers to the source's perceived social value. This quality can emanate from the person's physical appearance, personality, social status or his or her similarity to the receiver (we like to listen to people who are like us).

Star power: celebrities as communications sources

The sight of a supermodel holding a cigar had a big impact on Margaret's attitudes towards cigar smoking. The use of celebrity endorsers is an expensive but commonly used strategy. While a celebrity endorsement strategy is expensive, it can pay off handsomely.[20] Oasis soft drinks is a case in point. Oasis had a very successful soft drink launch in 1995 and is market leader in the adult soft drinks sector of the UK. The drink capitalized on the vibrant nature of the TV personality and transvestite, Lily Savage, who provided the voice-over for the ads. Ms Savage was seen as ideal for launching the Oasis brand because of her 'larger than life persona, memorable personality and appeal to young people. She is seen as very down-to-earth, very British and with a witty sense of humour – exactly the kind of attitude the brand wanted to own'.[21]

When used properly, famous or expert spokespeople can be of great value in improving the fortunes of a product. Celebrities increase awareness of a firm's advertising and enhance both company image and brand attitudes.[22] One reason for this effectiveness is that consumers are better able to identify products that are associated with a spokesperson.[23]

More generally, star power works because celebrities represent *cultural meanings* – they symbolize important categories such as status and social class (e.g. a 'working-class heroine' like Roseanne), gender (e.g. a 'manly man' like Sylvester Stallone or Paul Hogan), age (e.g. the boyish Michael J. Fox) and even personality types (e.g. the eccentric Kramer from *Seinfeld*). Ideally, the advertiser decides what meanings the product should convey (that is, how it should be positioned in the marketplace), and then chooses a celebrity who has come to evoke that meaning. The product's meaning thus moves from the manufacturer to the consumer, using the star as a vehicle.[24]

Famous people can be effective because they are credible, attractive or both, depending on the reasons for their fame. The computer guru Bill Gates is unlikely to be a 'sex symbol', but he may be quite effective at influencing people's attitudes towards unrestricted access to the internet. On the other hand, Elizabeth Hurley may not be perceived as an expert in cosmetics, but Estee Lauder is expecting her to be a persuasive source for a message about perfumes and cosmetics.

The effectiveness of celebrities as communications sources often depends upon their perceived credibility. Consumers may not trust a celebrity's motives for endorsing a product, or they may question the star's competence to evaluate the product's claims. This 'credibility gap' appears to be widening. In a recent one-year period, for example, the number of consumers who find celebrity advertising 'less than credible' jumped to 52 per cent. The greatest erosion of confidence comes from younger consumers, 64 per cent of whom thought that celebrities appeared in ads just for the money.[25] The lack of credibility is aggravated by incidences where celebrities

Multicultural dimensions

Some celebrities choose to maintain their credibility by endorsing products only in other countries. Many celebrities who do not do many American advertisements appear frequently in Japan. Mel Gibson endorses Asahi beer, Sly Stallone appears for Kirin beer, Sean Connery plugs Ito hams and the singer Sheena was featured in ads for Shochu liquor – dressed in a kimono and wig. Even the normally reclusive comedian and film director Woody Allen featured in a campaign for a large Tokyo department store.[26]

Marketing pitfall

For celebrity campaigns to be effective, the endorser must have a clear and popular image. In addition, the celebrity's image and that of the product he or she endorses should be similar – this effect is known as the match-up hypothesis.[27] Many promotional strategies employing stars fail because the endorser has not been selected very carefully – some marketers just assume that because a person is 'famous' he or she will serve as a successful spokesperson.

The images of celebrities can, however, be pre-tested to increase the probability of consumer acceptance. One widely used technique is the so called 'Q' rating (Q stands for quality) developed by a market research company. This rating considers two factors in surveys: consumers' level of familiarity with a name and the number of respondents who indicate that a person, programme, or character is a favourite. While not the most sophisticated research technique, the Q rating acknowledges that familiarity with a celebrity's name in itself is not sufficient to gauge popularity since some widely known people are also widely disliked. Celebrities with a low Q rating include Michael Jackson, Madonna and Cyndi Lauper. Those with high ratings include Stevie Wonder, Billy Joel, Phil Collins, Whitney Houston, Cher and Dolly Parton.[28] However, even a high Q rating does not guarantee success if the celebrity's specific image doesn't match up with the featured product.

Another potential problem is what to do about celebrity endorsers who 'misbehave'. Pepsi had to abandon its sponsorship of Michael Jackson after the singer was accused of child abuse. Madonna met a similar fate following the release of her controversial *Like a Prayer* music video. Then, of course, there's always O.J. Simpson ... To avoid some of these problems, most endorsement contracts now contain a morality clause which allows the company to release the celebrity if so warranted.[29] Other advertisers are looking a lot more favourably at characters like Bugs Bunny, who tend to stay out of trouble!

endorse products that they do not really believe in, or in some cases do not use. After Pepsi paid over $5 million to singer Michael Jackson in an endorsement deal, the company was not pleased by his later confession that he doesn't drink cola – and cola fans weren't too impressed either.[30]

In spite of this 'credibility gap', there are some celebrities who endorse so many products that they can be seen as 'serial advertisers'. John Cleese, for example, endorses nine different organizations, promoting everything from soft drinks to telecommunications to anti-smoking campaigns (Schweppes, Sainsbury's, Talking Pages, American Express, Sony, Compaq, Cellnet, Norwich Union Direct and anti-smoking!). Here, the concept of interactive communications discussed earlier in the chapter comes into play: 'There is a complicity between the audience and someone like Cleese. He knows that we know that he knows he is selling something, but if he entertains, engages, or surprises us, then we'll forgive him'.[31]

'What is beautiful is good'

Almost everywhere we turn, beautiful people are trying to persuade us to buy or do something. Our society places a very high premium on physical attractiveness, and we tend to assume that people who are good-looking are cleverer, more fashionable, and so on. Such an assumption is called a *halo effect*, which occurs when persons who rank high on one dimension are assumed to excel on others as well. The effect can be explained in terms of the consistency principle discussed in chapter 5, which

Beverages: Non-Alcoholic

Nunca mais vá à praia de **camis**eta.

DIET PEPSI

Escolha pelo sabor.

You'll never have to go to the beach in a T-shirt again.

The logic behind the celebrity match-up hypothesis can be applied to the selection of models who are physically attractive, even if they are not (yet) famous. Certain beauty 'types' are distinguishable, and are believed to match up with specific brand images. This Brazilian ad for Diet Pepsi portrays a 'wholesome' beauty type whose figure becomes associated with the Diet softdrink, Pepsi.[32]

Used with permission.

Marketing opportunity

'*The best a man can get*' each morning is a clean, close shave with a razor, shaving cream and same-brand toiletries, according to the global ad campaign of Gillette Co., the Boston-based shaving industry giant. But is a wet shave with a razor the best a European woman can get, too? That's the question facing Gillette and other companies as they pitch their new generation of designed-for-women shaving systems in Europe, hoping to entice women to wet shave. Currently, the world's biggest markets are the US, India and Russia. In Eastern Europe, razor blades were in short supply during the communist era. Today, sales of premium-shaving systems are exploding in countries such as Russia and Poland.

The market potential in Western Europe is huge. Only 30 per cent of European women wet shave, compared to 75 per cent in the United States. What's more, there is still a large number of European women who don't remove hair from their underarms and legs at all. If the percentage of women wet shaving in Europe were to reach American levels, the total sales of blades would increase by 500 million annually.

Unlike in the US, where women have been removing body hair for decades, attitudes differ in Europe, and are often deeply rooted in cultural traditions, economic conditions and varying perceptions of beauty. Many of these behaviours are learned from the family or from female role models, and changing culturally linked behaviour is difficult. In France and the UK, for example, most women share behaviours of their American counterparts and wet shave. Spanish women also remove body hair – a habit which can be traced back to the Moorish influence – but Spaniards usually go to waxing salons, or they wax at home. In Germany, shaving has more of a generational influence, with wet shaving being more common among younger women who have been influenced by the media, cinema, foreign travel and super-models with sleek legs and underarms.

Marketing opportunity continued   Due to the complex market structure, shaving companies confront two challenges: one is to convince women who wet shave (but usually grab a simple disposable razor for use in the shower) to switch to new shaving systems which include ergonomically designed razors, pastel colours, built-in lubricants and special blade design elements to avoid nicks and cuts. The other major goal is to introduce women to hair removal – and wet shaving as the preferred method.[33]

states that people are more comfortable when all of their judgements about a person go together. This notion has been termed the 'what is beautiful is good' stereotype.[34]

A physically attractive source tends to facilitate attitude change. His or her degree of attractiveness exerts at least modest effects on consumers' purchase intentions or product evaluation.[35] How does this happen?

One explanation is that physical attractiveness functions as a cue that facilitates or modifies information-processing by directing consumers' attention to relevant marketing stimuli. Some evidence indicates that consumers pay more attention to ads that feature attractive models, though not necessarily to the ad copy.[36] In other words, an ad with a beautiful person may stand a better chance of getting noticed, but is not necessarily read. While we may enjoy looking at a beautiful or handsome person, these positive feelings do not necessarily affect product attitudes or purchase intentions.[37]

Beauty can also function as a source of information. The effectiveness of highly attractive spokespeople in ads appears to be largely limited to those situations where the advertised product is overtly related to attractiveness or sexuality.[38] The *social adaptation perspective* assumes that information seen to be instrumental in forming an attitude will be more heavily weighted by the perceiver. We filter out irrelevant information to minimize cognitive effort.

Under the right circumstances, an endorser's level of attractiveness constitutes a source of information instrumental to the attitude-change process and thus functions as a central, task relevant cue.[39] An attractive spokesperson, for this reason, is more likely to be an effective source when the product is relevant to attractiveness. For example, attractiveness affects attitudes towards ads for perfume or aftershave (where attractiveness is relevant) but not for coffee ads, where attractiveness is not. Finally, in the global marketplace, the notions of what comprises 'beauty' and 'attractiveness' are certainly culturally based (see the 'Marketing opportunity' for Gillette on page 156).

The sleeper effect

While in general more positive sources tend to increase attitude change, exceptions can occur. Sometimes a source can be obnoxious or disliked and still manage to be effective at getting the product's message across. In some instances the differences in attitude change between positive sources and less positive sources seem to get erased over time. After a while people appear to 'forget' about the negative source and change their attitudes anyway. This process is known as the **sleeper effect**.[40]

The explanation for the sleeper effect is the subject of debate, as is the more basic question regarding whether and when it really exists. Initially, the *dissociative cue hypothesis* proposed that over time the message and the source become disassociated in the consumer's mind. The message remains on its own in memory, causing the delayed attitude change termed the sleeper effect.[41] A more recent explanation is the *availability-valence hypothesis*, which emphasizes the selectivity of memory owing to limited capacity.[42] If the associations linked to the negative source are less available than those linked to the message information, the residual impact of the message enhances persuasion. Consistent with this view, the sleeper effect has been obtained only when the message was encoded deeply; it had stronger associations in memory than did the source.[43]

Countries as product endorsers?

Do you take care to distinguish between Australian and Chilean wines, take pride in original Greek feta cheese, or go to some lengths to convince guests that they will like authentic Italian grappa? If so, then you're like most consumers, who *sometimes* pay real attention to the influence that country-of-origin information has on the process of evaluating and choosing products. The crucial word here is *sometimes*, since the effects of country-of-origin information can range from strong to weak to non-existent. At the cognitive level, there are many products for which the additional information of country origin plays little or no role in our decision process. For example, most consumers would have no doubts about buying a pocket calculator made in China or the Philippines, because we believe that this 'simple' technology has diffused across borders, and that these less industrialized countries can make calculators as well as any other country.

Fashion and clothing manufacturing technology has also diffused around the world, but would you prefer to buy an Armani suit made in Italy or in the Philippines? Research has shown that a strong brand name can compensate for a product manufactured in a country with an unknown or weak image. Sony consumer electronics may be assembled in less industrialized countries, but as consumers we have beliefs about the quality which underlies Sony's name. A shirt with the sound-alike name Ralph Loren or LaCost may be sewn in the Maldives or Sri Lanka, but consumers believe that the fashion designing and quality controls will be consistent with their image of the brand name. Honda has even shipped cars produced in the US back to Japan, as a statement of their belief in the quality of the 'American-made' Hondas!

Like brand names, country-of-origin information provides consumers with cognitive-based information, as well as prompting affective-based reactions. Although the research results on country-of-origin effects are mixed, it is clear that the 'made in' label can be important to us, depending on the consumption situation (Russian caviar might make a good impression on your boss, but how about picking her up in a Russian car?) and the level of involvement we feel towards the product or service. With the rise in patriotism, regionalism and ethnic identity around the world, multinational and regional countries, as well as country-sponsored export agencies will continue to promote their country, and its positive associations.[44]

The message

A major study of over 1,000 commercials identified factors that appear to determine whether or not a commercial message will be persuasive. The single most important feature was whether the communications contained a brand-differentiating message.

In other words, did the communication stress a unique attribute or benefit of the product? Other good and bad elements are depicted in Table 6.1.[45]

Characteristics of the message itself help to determine its impact on attitudes. These variables include how the message is said as well as what is said. Some of the issues facing marketers include the following:

- Should the message be conveyed in words or pictures?
- How often should the message be repeated?
- Should a conclusion be drawn, or should this be left up to the listener?
- Should both sides of an argument be presented?
- Is it effective to make an explicit comparison with competitors' products?
- Should blatant sexual appeal be used?
- Should negative emotions, such as fear, ever be aroused?
- How concrete or vivid should the arguments and imagery be?
- Should the ad be funny?

Sending the message

The saying 'one picture is worth a thousand words' captures the idea that visual stimuli can deliver a big impact economically, especially when the communicator wants to influence receivers' emotional responses. For this reason, advertisers often place great emphasis on vivid and creative illustrations or photography.[46]

But a picture may not be as effective at communicating factual information. Ads that contain the same information, presented in either visual or verbal form, have been found to elicit different reactions. The verbal version affects ratings on the utilitarian aspects of a product, while the visual version affects aesthetic evaluations.[47] Verbal elements are more effective when reinforced by an accompanying picture, especially if the illustration is *framed* (the message in the picture is strongly related to the copy).[48]

Table 6.1 Positive and negative effects of elements in television commercials

Positive effects	Negative effects
Showing convenience of use	Extensive information on components, ingredients or nutrition
Showing new product or improved features	
Casting background (i.e. people are incidental to message)	Outdoor setting (message gets lost)
	Large number of on-screen characters
Indirect comparison to other products	Graphic displays
Demonstration of the product in use	
Demonstration of tangible results (e.g. bouncy hair)	
An actor playing the role of an ordinary person	
No principal character (i.e. more time is devoted to the product)	

Source: Adapted from David W. Stewart and David H. Furse, 'The Effects of Television Advertising Execution on Recall, Comprehension, and Persuasion', *Psychology & Marketing* 2 (Fall 1985): 135–60. Copyright © 1985 by John Wiley & Sons, Inc. Reprinted by permission.

Which one makes a
beer taste great?

☐ Blondes in bikinis
☐ Sports stars
☐ Catchy jingles
☐ Snow-capped mountains

Just being the best is enough.

This ad pokes fun at the typical elements one would expect to see in a persuasive communication targeted at beer drinkers.
Courtesy of Heineken USA, Inc., White Plains, NY.

Because it requires more effort to process, a verbal message is most appropriate for high-involvement situations, such as in print contexts where the reader is motivated to pay close attention to the advertising. Because verbal material decays more rapidly in memory, more frequent exposures are needed to obtain the desired effect. Visual images, in contrast, allow the receiver to 'chunk' information at the time of encoding (see chapter 3). Chunking results in a stronger memory trace which aids retrieval over time.[49]

Visual elements may affect brand attitudes in one of two ways. First, the consumer may form inferences about the brand and change his or her beliefs because of an illustration's imagery. For example, people who saw an ad for a box of tissues accompanied by a photo of a sunset were more likely to believe that the brand came in attractive colours. Second, brand attitudes may be affected more directly; for example, a strong positive or negative reaction elicited by the visual elements will influence the consumer's attitude towards the ad (A_{ad}), which will then affect brand attitudes (A_b). This *dual component model* of brand attitudes is illustrated in Figure 6.3.[50]

Vividness

Pictures and words may both differ in *vividness*. Powerful descriptions or graphics command attention and are more strongly embedded in memory. The reason may be because they tend to activate mental imagery, while abstract stimuli inhibit this process.[51] Of course, this effect can cut both ways: negative information presented in a vivid manner may result in more negative evaluations at a later time.[52]

The concrete discussion of a product attribute in ad copy also influences the importance of that attribute, because more attention is drawn to it. For example, the copy for a watch that read 'According to industry sources, three out of every four watch breakdowns are due to water getting into the case' was more effective

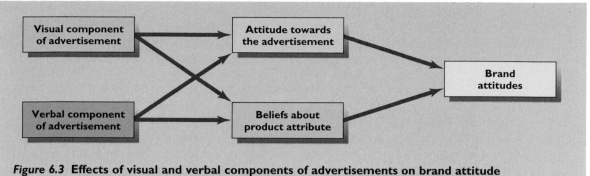

Figure 6.3 Effects of visual and verbal components of advertisements on brand attitude
Source: Andrew A. Mitchell, 'The Effect of Verbal and Visual Components of Advertisements on Brand Attitudes and Attitude Toward the Advertisement', *Journal of Consumer Research* 13 (June 1986): 21. Reprinted by permission of The University of Chicago Press.

than this version: 'According to industry sources, many watch breakdowns are due to water getting into the case.'[53]

Repetition

Repetition can be a two-edged sword for marketers. As noted in chapter 3, multiple exposures to a stimulus are usually required for learning (especially conditioning) to occur. Contrary to the saying 'familiarity breeds contempt', people tend to like things that are familiar to them, even if they were not keen on them initially.[54] This is known as the *mere exposure* phenomenon. On the other hand, as we saw in chapter 2, too much repetition creates *habituation*, so that the consumer no longer pays attention to the stimulus out of fatigue or boredom. Excessive exposure can cause *advertising wear-out*, which can result in negative reactions to an ad after seeing it too much.[55]

The fine line between familiarity and boredom has been explained by the **two-factor theory**, which proposes that two separate psychological processes are operating when a person is repeatedly exposed to an ad. The positive side of repetition is that it increases familiarity and thus reduces uncertainty about the product. The negative side is that, over time, boredom increases with each exposure. At some point the amount of boredom incurred begins to exceed the amount of uncertainty reduced, resulting in wear-out. This pattern is depicted in Figure 6.4. Its effect is especially pronounced in cases where each exposure is of a fairly long duration (such as a 60-second commercial).[56]

The theory implies that advertisers can overcome this problem by limiting the amount of exposure per repetition (such as using 15-second spots). They can also maintain familiarity but alleviate boredom by slightly varying the content of ads over time through campaigns that revolve around a common theme, although each spot may be different.

Constructing the argument

Many marketing messages are similar to debates or trials, where someone presents arguments and tries to convince the receiver to shift his or her opinion accordingly. The way the argument is presented can thus be very important.

One versus two-sided arguments

Most messages merely present one or more positive attributes about the product or reasons to buy it. These are known as *supportive arguments*. An alternative is to use a *two-*

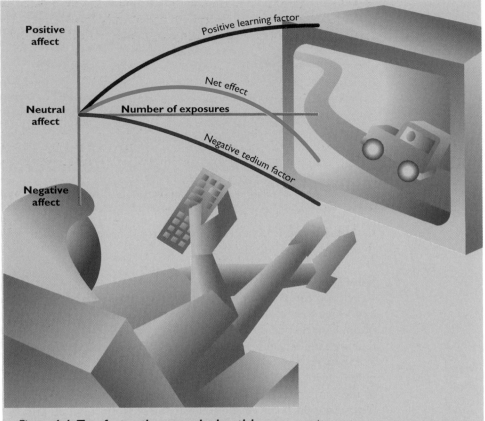

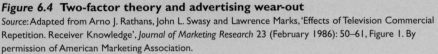

Figure 6.4 **Two-factor theory and advertising wear-out**
Source: Adapted from Arno J. Rathans, John L. Swasy and Lawrence Marks, 'Effects of Television Commercial Repetition. Receiver Knowledge', *Journal of Marketing Research* 23 (February 1986): 50–61, Figure 1. By permission of American Marketing Association.

sided message, where both positive and negative information is presented. Research has indicated that two-sided ads can be quite effective, yet they are not widely used.[57]

Why would a marketer want to devote advertising space to publicizing a product's negative attributes? Under the right circumstances, the use of *refutational arguments*, where a negative issue is raised and then dismissed, can be quite effective. This approach can increase source credibility by reducing reporting bias. Also, people who are sceptical about the product may be more receptive to a balanced argument instead of a 'whitewash'.[58] In one novel application, a Château Potelle winery ad included both positive and negative reviews of a wine by two experts. The ad suggested that consumers develop their own taste rather than relying on reviews in wine magazines.[59]

This is not to say that the marketer should go overboard in presenting major problems with the product. In the typical refutational strategy, relatively minor attributes which may present a problem or fall short when compared with competitors, are discussed. These drawbacks are then refuted by emphasizing positive, important attributes. For example, the car-hire firm Avis got a lot of mileage out of claiming to be only 'No. 2', while an ad for Volkswagen woefully described one of its cars as a 'lemon' because there was a scratch on the glove compartment chrome strip.[60] A two-sided strategy appears to be the most effective when the audience is well educated (and is presumably more impressed by a balanced argument).[61] It is also best to use when receivers are not already loyal to the product: 'preaching to the converted' about possible drawbacks may raise doubts unnecessarily.

Drawing conclusions

A related factor is whether the argument should draw conclusions, or whether the points should merely be presented, permitting the consumer to arrive at his or her own. Should the message say 'Our brand is superior', or should it add 'You should buy our brand'? On the one hand, consumers who make their own inferences instead of having them spoon-fed will form stronger, more accessible attitudes. On the other, leaving the conclusion ambiguous increases the chance that the desired attitude will not be formed.

The response to this issue depends on the consumers' motivation to process the ad and the complexity of the arguments. If the message is personally relevant, people will pay attention to it and spontaneously form inferences. However, if the arguments are hard to follow or consumers' motivation to follow them is absent, it is safer for the ad to draw conclusions.[62]

Types of message appeals

Emotional versus rational appeals

A few years ago, both Toyota and Nissan introduced a large luxury car that sold for over £30,000. The two companies chose very different ways to communicate their product's attributes, as seen in the ads shown here. Toyota's advertising for its Lexus model used a rational appeal, with ads concentrating on the large number of technical advancements incorporated in the car's design. Print ads were dominated by copy describing these engineering features.

In sharp contrast, Nissan's controversial campaign for its Infiniti used an emotional appeal. The new model was introduced with a series of print and television

These ads demonstrate rational versus emotional message appeals. At the time of the initial ad campaign for the new Infiniti models, the ads for rival Lexus (top) emphasized design and engineering, while the ads for Infiniti (bottom) did not even show the car.
Courtesy of Lexus. Courtesy of INFINITI®. A division of Nissan Motor Corporation, USA.

ads that did not discuss the car at all. Instead the ads focused on the Zen-like experience of driving and featured long shots of serene landscapes. As one executive involved with the campaign explained, 'We're not selling the skin of the car; we're selling the spirit'.[63] While these ads were innovative, most American consumers had trouble grasping the Japanese conception of luxury. Later ads for the Infiniti emphasized functional features of the car to compensate for this initial confusion.

The goal of an emotional appeal is to establish a connection between the product and the consumer, a strategy known as *bonding*.[64] Emotional appeals have the potential to increase the chance that the message will be perceived, they may be more likely to be retained in memory and they can also increase the consumer's involvement with the product. Although Nissan's gamble on emphasizing the aesthetic aspects of its product did not pay off in this case, other emotional appeals are quite effective. Many companies turned to this strategy after realizing that consumers do not find many differences among brands, especially those in well-established, mature categories. Ads for products ranging from cars (Lincoln Mercury) to cards (Hallmark) focus instead on emotional aspects. Mercury's capitalization on emotional attachments to old rock songs succeeded in lowering the median age of their consumers for some models by ten years.[65]

The precise effects of rational versus emotional appeals are hard to gauge. Though recall of ad contents tends to be better for 'thinking' ads than for 'feeling' ads, conventional measures of advertising effectiveness (e.g. day-after recall) may not be adequate to assess cumulative effects of emotional ads. These open-ended measures are oriented towards cognitive responses, and feeling ads may be penalized because the reactions are not as easy to articulate.[66]

While they can make a strong impression, emotional appeals also run the risk of not getting across an adequate amount of product-related information. This potential problem is reminding some advertisers that the arousal of emotions is functional only to the extent that it sells the product. Procter & Gamble's original ads for Bounce fabric softener showed a happy young couple dancing to the song 'Jump', with the message that Bounce is for clothes 'you can't wait to jump into'. In more recent spots, a woman discusses why the product makes her clothes feel and smell

Marketing pitfall

As the foot soldiers of Nike Inc. first set out to conquer foreign lands and win World War Shoe, they marched forth under this doctrine: *Speak loudly and carry a big shtick*. 'Europe, Asia, and Latin America: Barricade your stadiums. Hide your trophies. Invest in some deodorant', blared a Nike ad in *Soccer America* magazine. At least on Europe's hallowed football (or 'soccer') fields, the early results are not nearly as victorious as Nike would have liked. Their television ads throughout Europe have inspired controversy, frenzy and outrage – just the way that Nike typically likes it. But Nike is discovering that its iconoclastic culture is not as universal as it thought. With annual sales approaching $9 billion, Nike is pinning its future on the international sneaker and sportswear markets. The company believes its domestic sales in America, which average an astounding $20 per person, may be peaking. By contrast, per capita Nike sales in Japan are $4, in Germany $3, and in China just over 2 cents. The trick will be for Nike to keep their cool edge which has appealed to America's sneaker-buying culture, while recognizing that sometimes subtlety is better than shock tactics, and homage better than outrage, when dealing with tradition-bound European and Asian cultures.[67]

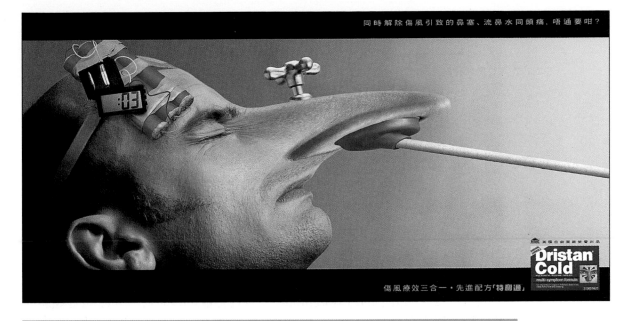

同時解除傷風引致的鼻塞、流鼻水同頭痛，唔通要咁？

傷風療效三合一・先進配方「特和通」

Dristan Cold multi-symptom formula

This humorous ad for Dristan cold medicine, which ran in Hong Kong, reads: 'Is this the only way to get rid of a stuffed-up runny nose and the headaches a cold can bring?' Visual humour is often an effective way to get attention and cut through advertising clutter.
Courtesy of Bates Hong Kong, Ltd.

better. It is still somewhat emotional and experiential, but the main selling point of 'softness without static cling' is driven home.[68]

Sex appeals

Under the assumption that 'sex sells', many campaigns – for everything from perfumes to cars – feature erotic suggestions that range from subtle hints to blatant displays of flesh. Perhaps not surprisingly, female nudity in print ads generates negative feelings and tension among female consumers, while men's reactions are more positive.[69]

Does sex work? Although the use of sex does appear to draw attention to an ad, its use may actually be counterproductive to the marketer. Ironically, a provocative picture can be too effective; it attracts so much attention that it hinders processing and recall of the ad's contents. Sexual appeals appear to be ineffective when used merely as an attention-grabber. They do, however, appear to work when the product is *itself* sexually related.

Humorous appeals

The use of humour can be problematic, particularly since what is funny to one person may be offensive or incomprehensible to another. Different cultures may have different senses of humour and use funny material in diverse ways. For example, commercials in the UK are more likely to use puns and satire than those in the US.[70]

Does humour work? Overall, humorous advertisements do get attention. One study found that recognition scores for humorous alcohol ads were better than average. However, the verdict is mixed as to whether humour affects recall or product attitudes in a significant way.[71] One function it may play is to provide a source of

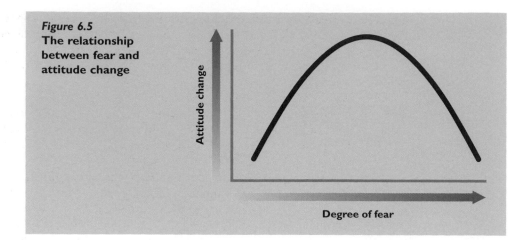

Figure 6.5
The relationship between fear and attitude change

distraction. A funny ad inhibits the consumer from counterarguing, thereby increasing the likelihood of message acceptance.[72]

Humour is more likely to be effective when the brand is clearly identified and the funny material does not 'swamp' the message. This danger is similar to that of beautiful models diverting attention from copy points. Subtle humour is usually better, as is humour that does not make fun of the potential consumer. Finally, humour should be appropriate to the product's image. An undertaker or a bank might want to avoid humour, while other products adapt to it quite well. Sales of Sunsweet pitted prunes improved dramatically based on the claim, 'Today the pits, tomorrow the wrinkles'.[73]

Fear appeals

Fear appeals highlight the negative consequences that can occur unless the consumer changes a behaviour or an attitude. This strategy is widespread; fear appeals

Fear appeals have a greater chance of being effective if they also provide consumers with a possible solution to the problem. Here, celebrity Cher gives concrete advice about breast self-examinations.
Courtesy of Coors Brewing Company and AMC Cancer Research Center.

are used in over 15 per cent of all television ads.[74] The arousal of fear is a common tactic for social policy issues, such as convincing consumers to stop smoking or to drive safely (i.e. to reduce physical risk). It can also be applied to social risk issues by threatening one's success with the opposite sex, career, and so on. This tactic has been half-jokingly called 'slice of death'.

Does fear work? Fear appeals are usually most effective when only a moderate amount of fear is induced.[75] As shown in Figure 6.5, increasing levels of fear do not result in increased change; the relationship instead resembles an inverted U-shaped curve. If the threat is too great, the audience tends to deny that it exists as a way to rationalize the danger.

A study that manipulated subjects' degree of anxiety about AIDS, for example, found that condom ads were evaluated positively when a moderate amount of fear was induced. In this context, copy that promoted the use of the condom because 'sex is a risky business' (moderate fear) resulted in more attitude change than either a low fear appeal that emphasized the product's sensitivity or a high fear appeal that discussed the certainty of death from AIDS.[76] Similarly, scare tactics have not been as effective as hoped in getting teenagers to cut down on their consumption of alcohol or drugs. Teenagers simply tune out the message or deny its relevance to them.[77]

Fear appeals appear to be most effective when the consumer is already afraid of the problem discussed in the ad. The threats should not be excessive and a solution to the problem should be presented (otherwise, consumers will tune out the ad since they can do nothing to solve the problem).[78] Appeals also work better when source credibility is high.[79]

Multicultural dimensions

American gun manufacturers are capitalizing on women's fears regarding self- and home defence. According to the National Rifle Association, 15–20 million American women own guns. At least three manufacturers have introduced guns for women. One company makes a .32 magnum model called a 'Bonnie', to go with a .38 'Clyde' for his-and-hers shooting. Smith & Wesson introduced the LadySmith, a revolver with a slimmed-down grip.[80] The company's ads have been criticized for preying on the fears of women. They include such copy as 'The world is different today than when you grew up' and 'Personal security is a very real issue'. A magazine called *Women & Guns* now has a readership of over 25,000.[81] In addition to gun safety, it features articles on firearm fashions. The cover of a recent issue featured an attractive woman wearing a pistol holder strapped above her knee with the caption 'Self-Defense Goes Thigh High'.

The message as artform: metaphors be with you

Marketers may be thought of as storytellers who supply visions of reality similar to those provided by authors, poets and artists. These communications take the form of stories because the product benefits they describe are intangible and must be given tangible meaning by expressing them in a form that is concrete and visible. Advertising creatives rely (consciously or not) on various literary devices to communicate these meanings. For example, a product or service might be personified by a character such as the Jolly Green Giant or the California Raisins. Many ads take the form of an allegory, where a story is told about an abstract trait or concept that has been personified as a person, animal, vegetable, and so on.

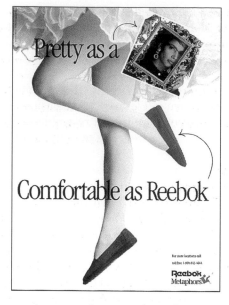

Reebok uses the metaphor 'pretty as a picture' to promote its line of Metaphors shoes.
Reprinted by permission of Reebok International Ltd.

A **metaphor** involves the use of an explicit comparison, such as A is B (e.g. 'United Airlines is your friend in faraway places'). The device was used literally by Reebok to equate its Metaphors line of shoes with comfort, as seen in the ad shown here. Metaphors allow the marketer to activate meaningful images and apply them to everyday events. In the stock market, 'white knights' battle 'hostile raiders' using 'poison pills', while Tony the Tiger allows us to equate Frosties cereal with strength, and Merrill Lynch's bull sends the message that the company is 'a breed apart'.[82]

Resonance is another type of literary device that is frequently used in advertising. It is a form of presentation that combines a play on words with a relevant picture. Table 6.2 gives some examples of actual ads that rely on the principle of resonance.

Table 6.2 Some examples of advertising resonance

Product/headline	Visual
Embassy Suites: 'This Year, We're Unwrapping Suites by the Dozen'	Chocolate kisses with hotel names underneath each
Toyota auto parts: 'Our Lifetime Guarantee May Come as a Shock'	Man holding a shock absorber
Bucks filter cigarettes: 'Herd of These?'	Cigarette pack with a picture of a stag
Bounce fabric softener: 'Is There Something Creeping Up Behind You?'	Woman's dress bunched up on the back of her due to static
Pepsi: 'This Year, Hit the Beach Topless'	Pepsi bottle cap lying on the sand
ASICS athletic shoes: 'We Believe Women Should Be Running the Country'	Woman jogging in a rural setting

Source: Adapted from Edward F. McQuarrie and David Glen Mick, 'On Resonance: A Critical Pluralistic Inquiry into Advertising Rhetoric', *Journal of Consumer Research* 19 (September 1992): 182, Table 1. Reprinted with permission of The University of Chicago Press.

While metaphor substitutes one meaning for another, resonance uses an element that has a double meaning, such as a pun where there is a similarity in the sound of a word but a difference in meaning.

For example, an ad for a diet strawberry shortcake dessert might bear the copy 'berried treasure' so that qualities associated with buried treasure – being rich, hidden and associated with adventurous pirates – are conveyed for the brand. Because the text departs from expectations, it creates a state of tension or uncertainty on the part of the viewer until he or she works out the wordplay. Once the consumer 'gets it', he or she may prefer the ad to a more straightforward message.[83]

Forms of story presentation

Just as a story can be told in words or pictures, the way the audience is addressed can also make a difference. Commercials are structured like other artforms, borrowing conventions from literature and art as they communicate their messages.[84]

One important distinction is between a *drama* and a *lecture*.[85] A lecture is like a speech where the source speaks directly to the audience in an attempt to inform them about a product or persuade them to buy it. Because a lecture clearly implies an attempt at persuasion, the audience will regard it as such. Assuming listeners are motivated to do so, the merits of the message will be weighed, along with the credibility of the source. Cognitive responses, such as counter-arguments, will occur. The appeal will be accepted to the extent that it overcomes objections and is congruent with a person's beliefs.

In contrast, a drama is similar to a play or film. While an argument holds the viewer at arm's length, a drama draws the viewer into the action. The characters only indirectly address the audience; they interact with each other about a product or service in an imaginary setting. Dramas attempt to be experiential – to involve the audience emotionally. In *transformational advertising*, the consumer associates the experience of product usage with some subjective sensation. Thus, ads for the Infiniti attempted to transform the 'driving experience' into a mystical, spiritual event.

The source versus the message: sell the steak or the sizzle?

Two major components of the communications model, the source and the message, have been reviewed. Which aspect has more impact on persuading consumers to change their attitudes? Should marketers worry about *what* is said, or *how* it's said and *who* says it?

The answer is, it depends. Variations in a consumer's level of involvement, as discussed in chapter 4, result in the activation of very different cognitive processes when a message is received. Research indicates that this level of involvement will determine which aspects of a communication are processed. The situation appears to resemble a traveller who comes to a fork in the road: one or the other path is chosen, and this path has a big impact on the factors that will make a difference in persuasion attempts.

The elaboration likelihood model

The **elaboration likelihood model (ELM)** assumes that once a consumer receives a message he or she begins to process it.[86] Depending on the personal relevance of this information, one of two routes to persuasion will be followed. Under conditions of high involvement, the consumer takes the *central route to persuasion*. Under conditions of low involvement, a *peripheral route* is taken instead. This model is shown in Figure 6.6.

The central route to persuasion

When the consumer finds the information in a persuasive message to be relevant or somehow interesting, he or she will carefully attend to the message content. The person is likely to think actively about the arguments presented and generate *cognitive responses*. On hearing a radio message warning about drinking alcohol while pregnant, an expectant mother might say to herself, 'She's right. I really should stop drinking alcohol now that I'm pregnant.' Or, she might offer *counter-arguments*, such as, 'That's a load of nonsense. My mother had a cocktail every night when she was pregnant with me, and I turned out OK.' If a person generates counter-arguments in response to a message, it is less likely that he or she will yield to the message, while the generation of further supporting arguments increases the probability of compliance.[87]

The central route to persuasion is likely to involve the traditional hierarchy of effects, as discussed in chapter 5. Beliefs are carefully formed and evaluated, and the resulting strong attitudes will be likely to guide behaviour. The implication is that message factors, such as the quality of arguments presented, will be important in determining attitude change. Prior knowledge about a topic results in more thoughts about the message and also increases the number of counter-arguments.[88]

The peripheral route to persuasion

In contrast, the peripheral route is taken when the person is not motivated to think deeply about the arguments presented. Instead, the consumer is likely to use other cues in deciding on the suitability of the message. These cues may include the product's package, the attractiveness of the source or the context in which the message is presented. Sources of information extraneous to the actual message content are called *peripheral cues* because they surround the actual message.

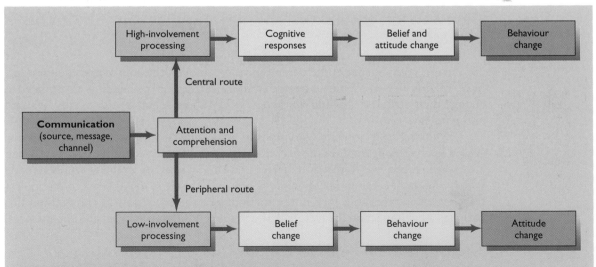

***Figure 6.6* The elaboration likelihood model of persuasion**

Reprinted with the permission of Macmillan Publishing Company from *Consumer Behavior*, 2nd edn, by John C. Mowen. Copyright © 1990 by Macmillan Publishing Company.

The peripheral route to persuasion highlights the paradox of low involvement discussed in chapter 4: when consumers do not care about a product, the stimuli associated with it increase in importance. The implication here is that low-involvement products may be purchased chiefly because the marketer has done a good job in designing a 'sexy' package, choosing a popular spokesperson or perhaps just creating a pleasant shopping environment.

Support for the ELM model

The ELM model has received a lot of research support.[89] In one study, undergraduates were exposed to one of several mock advertisements for Break, a new brand of low-alcohol beer. Using the technique of *thought-listing*, they were asked to provide their thoughts about the ads, which were later analyzed. Two versions of the ads are shown here.[90] Three independent variables crucial to the ELM model were manipulated.

1. *Message processing involvement*: Some subjects were motivated to be highly involved with the ads. They were promised a gift of low-alcohol beer for participating in the study and were told that the brand would soon be available in their area. Low-involvement subjects were not promised a gift and were told that the brand would be introduced in a distant area.
2. *Argument strength*: One version of the ad used strong, compelling arguments to drink Break (e.g. 'Break contains one-half of the amount of alcohol of regular beers and, therefore, has less calories than regular beer…'), while the other listed only weak arguments (e.g. 'Break is just as good as any other regular beer').
3. *Source characteristics*: While both ads contained a photo of a couple drinking the beer, their relative social attractiveness was varied by their dress, their posture and nonverbal expressions, and the background information given about their educational achievements and occupations.

Consistent with the ELM model, high-involvement subjects had more thoughts related to the ad messages than did low-involvement subjects, who devoted more

Source: J. Craig Andrews and Terence A. Shimp, 'Effects of Involvement, Argument, Strength, and Source Characteristics on Central and Peripheral Processing in Advertising', *Psychology & Marketing* 7 (Fall 1990): 195–214.

cognitive activity to the sources used in the ad. The attitudes of high-involvement subjects were more likely to be swayed by powerful arguments, while the attitudes of low-involvement subjects were more likely to be influenced by the ad version using attractive sources. The results of this study, paired with others, indicate that the relative effectiveness of a strong message and a favourable source depends on consumers' level of involvement with the product being advertised.

These results underscore the basic idea that highly involved consumers look for the 'steak' (e.g. strong, rational arguments). Those who are less involved are more affected by the 'sizzle' (e.g. the colours and images used in packaging or endorsements by famous people). It is important to remember, however, that the *same* communications variable can be both a central and a peripheral cue, depending on its relation to the attitude object. The physical attractiveness of a model might serve as a peripheral cue in a car commercial, but her beauty might be a central cue for a product such as shampoo, where the product's benefits are directly tied to enhancing attractiveness.[91]

Chapter summary

- *Persuasion* refers to an attempt to change consumers' attitudes.
- The *communications model* specifies the elements needed to transmit meaning. These include a source, message, medium, receiver and feedback.
- Two important characteristics that determine the effectiveness of a source are its *attractiveness* and *credibility*. While celebrities often serve this purpose, their credibility is not always as strong as marketers hope.
- Some elements of a message that help to determine its effectiveness are whether it is conveyed in words or pictures, whether an emotional or a rational appeal is employed, the frequency with which it is repeated, whether a conclusion is drawn, whether both sides of the argument are presented, and whether the message includes fear, humour or sexual references.
- Advertising messages often incorporate such elements from art or literature as dramas, lectures, metaphors, allegories and resonance.
- The relative influence of the source versus the message depends upon the receiver's level of involvement with the communication. The *elaboration likelihood model* specifies that a less-involved consumer is more likely to be swayed by source effects, while a more involved consumer is more likely to attend to and process components of the actual message.

🔑 Key terms

Communications model *(p. 147)*	**Persuasion** *(p. 146)*
Elaboration likelihood model **(ELM)** *(p. 169)*	**Resonance** *(p. 168)*
	Sleeper effect *(p. 157)*
Fear appeals *(p. 166)*	**Source attractiveness** *(p. 153)*
Interactionist *(p. 149)*	**Source credibility** *(p. 153)*
Match-up hypothesis *(p. 155)*	**Two-factor theory** *(p. 161)*
Metaphor *(p. 168)*	**Uses and gratifications theory** *(p. 148)*

Consumer behaviour challenge

1. The chapter's opening vignette discusses the theoretical and managerial issues in changing attitudes through communications. Identify and discuss the ethical issues of using marketing techniques which promote the use of tobacco. Are these issues similar to the ethical issues in promoting 'wet shaving' among European women? Why or why not?

2. Create a list of celebrities who match up with products in your country. What are the elements of the celebrities and products which make for a 'good match'? Why? Which celebrities have a global or European-wide appeal, and why?

3. A government agency wants to encourage the use of designated drivers by people who have been drinking. What advice would you give the organization about constructing persuasive communications? Discuss factors that might be important, including the structure of the communications, where they should appear and who should deliver them. Should fear appeals be used, and if so, how?

4. Are infomercials ethical? Should marketers be allowed to use any format they want to present product-related information?

5. Why would a marketer consider saying negative things about his or her product? When is this strategy feasible? Can you find examples of it?

6. A marketer must decide whether to incorporate rational or emotional appeals in a communications strategy. Describe conditions that are more favourable to using one or the other.

7. Collect ads that rely on sex appeal to sell products. How often are benefits of the actual product communicated to the reader?

8. To observe the process of counter-argumentation, ask a friend to talk through a commercial. Ask him or her to respond to each point in the ad or to write down reactions to the claims made. How much scepticism regarding the claims can you detect?

9. Make a log of all the commercials shown on one television channel over a 6-hour period. Categorize each according to product category, and whether they are presented as drama or argument. Describe the types of messages used (e.g. two-sided arguments), and keep track of the types of spokespeople (e.g. television actors, famous people, animated characters). What can you conclude about the dominant forms of persuasive tactics currently employed by marketers?

10. Collect examples of ads that rely on the use of metaphors or resonance. Do you feel these ads are effective? If you were working with the products, would you feel more comfortable with ads that use a more straightforward, 'hard-sell' approach? Why or why not?

CHAPTER 7

Carolyn Strong, University of Wales, Cardiff

Gareth, a Marketing Director in his thirties, is a happily married man, and his two children aged four and three provide immense joy in his life. However, at 36 he feels younger than his years, and somewhat anxious about his totally family-oriented life – he has a nice house, a magnificent garden and takes regular family holidays in rural France. But he has begun to feel the loss of his previous, extravagant, care-free life, one in which he perceived himself to be a well-dressed, admired individual of good taste and discernment who always turned heads when he entered the room. He is apprehensive that his 'Gareth the family man' role has totally taken over his life's spirit. It's a life he loves and one which has his complete commitment, but one which he also views as 'prudent and sensible'.

Some months into the development of these feelings, Gareth is contacted by his company's Personnel Department about replacing his company car. Three years earlier he had selected a sensible Audi 80 with the family needs in mind. In the meantime, his wife has bought a Volvo Estate which is always used for family travel. He has an exorbitant budget allocated to car purchase, due to his long-term commitment and excellent contribution to company performance over the last 18 months. As a result he can select almost any car he desires. After a prolonged search and extensive thought he decides on a Porsche Boxer.

The Porsche Boxer, a well-designed and admired car, for the driver of good taste and discernment, has the image of a sporty, confident, powerful individual. The current press campaign displays a successful thirty-something man being admired at the traffic lights, in the office car parks *and* at the local school collecting his children. Whilst driving home Gareth plays his CD collection at full volume, exceeds the legal speed limit when he believes it is 'safe' to do so, and generally feels more like the much revered Gareth who graduated fifteen years ago.

The self

Perspectives on the self

Gareth is not alone in feeling that his self-image and possessions affect his 'value' as a person. Consumers' insecurities about their appearance are rampant: it has been estimated that 72 per cent of men and 85 per cent of women are unhappy with at least one aspect of their appearance.[1] Many products, from cars to after-shave, are bought because the person is trying to highlight or hide some aspect of the self. In this chapter, we'll focus on how consumers' feelings about themselves shape their consumption habits, particularly as they strive to fulfil their society's expectations about how a male or female should look and act.

Does the self exist?

The 1980s were called the 'Me Decade' because for many this time was marked by an absorption with the self. While it seems natural to think about each consumer having a self, this concept is actually a relatively new way of regarding people and their relationship to society. The idea that each human life is unique, rather than a part of a group, developed in late medieval times (in Europe). The notion that the self is an object to be pampered is even more recent. In addition, the emphasis on the unique nature of the self is much greater in Western societies.[2] Many Eastern cultures by contrast stress the importance of a collective self, where the person's identity is derived in large measure from his or her social group.

Both Eastern and Western cultures see the self as divided into an inner, private self and an outer, public self. But where they differ is in terms of which part is seen as the 'real you'. The West tends to subscribe to an independent construal of the self, which emphasizes the inherent separateness of each individual. Non-Western cultures, in contrast, tend to focus on an interdependent self, where one's identity is largely defined by the relationships one has with others.[3]

For example, a Confucian perspective stresses the importance of 'face' – others' perceptions of the self and maintaining one's desired status in their eyes. One dimension of face is *mien-tzu* – reputation achieved through success and ostentation. Some Asian cultures developed explicit rules about the specific garments and even colours that certain social classes and occupations were allowed to display, and these live on today in Japanese style manuals which provide very detailed instructions for dressing and addressing a particular individual.[4] That orientation is at odds with such Western practices as 'Casual Fridays', which encourage employees to express their unique selves. The self can be understood from many different theoretical vantage-points. As discussed in a previous chapter, a psychoanalytical or Freudian perspective regards the self as a system of competing forces riddled with conflict. In chapter 3 we also noted that behaviourists tend to regard the self as a collection of conditioned responses. From a cognitive orientation, the self is an information processing system, an organizing force that serves as a nucleus around which new information is processed.[5]

Self-concept

The **self-concept** refers to the beliefs a person holds about his or her attributes, and how he or she evaluates these qualities. While one's overall self-concept may be positive, there certainly are parts of the self that are evaluated more positively than others. For example, Gareth felt better about his professional identity than he did about his pending 'middle age' identity.

Components of the self-concept

The self-concept is a very complex structure. It is composed of many attributes, some of which are given greater emphasis when the overall self is being evaluated. Attributes of self-concept can be described along such dimensions as their content (e.g. facial attractiveness versus mental aptitude), positivity or negativity (i.e. self-esteem), intensity, stability over time and accuracy (i.e. the degree to which one's self-assessment corresponds to reality).[6] As we'll see later in the chapter, consumers' self-assessments can be quite distorted, especially with regard to their physical appearance.

Self-esteem

Self-esteem refers to the positivity of a person's self-concept. People with low self-esteem do not expect that they will perform very well, and they will try to avoid embarrassment, failure or rejection. In developing a new line of snack cakes, for example, Sara Lee found that consumers low in self-esteem preferred portion-controlled snack items because they felt they lacked self-control.[7] In contrast, people with high self-esteem expect to be successful, will take more risks and are more willing to be the centre of attention.[8] Self-esteem often is related to acceptance by others. As you probably remember, teenagers who are members of high-status groups have higher self-esteem than their excluded classmates.[9]

Marketing communications can influence a consumer's level of self-esteem. Exposure to ads can trigger a process of *social comparison*, where the person tries to evaluate his or her self by comparing it to the people depicted in these artificial images. This form of comparison appears to be a basic human motive, and many marketers have tapped into this need by supplying idealized images of happy, attractive people who just happen to be using their products.

A recent study illustrates the social comparison process. It showed that female college students do tend to compare their physical appearance with advertising models. Furthermore, study participants who were exposed to beautiful women in advertisements afterwards expressed lowered satisfaction with their own appearance, as compared to controls.[10] Another study demonstrated that young women's perceptions of their own body shapes and sizes can be altered after being exposed to as little as 30 minutes of television programming.[11]

Self-esteem advertising attempts to change product attitudes by stimulating positive feelings about the self.[12] One strategy is to challenge the consumer's self-esteem and then show a linkage to a product that will provide a remedy. For example, the

US Marine Corps uses this strategy with its theme targeted at young men, 'If you have what it takes . . .'. Another strategy is outright flattery, as when Virginia Slims cigarettes proclaims to women, 'You've come a long way, baby'.

Sometimes such compliments are derived by comparing the person to others. For instance, many consumers are socialized to consider body odour as repulsive and are motivated to protect their self-image by denying the existence of these odours in themselves. This attitude explains the success of the theme of *Dial* soap's advertising: 'Aren't you glad you use *Dial*, don't you wish everyone did?'[13]

Real and ideal selves

Self-esteem is influenced by a process where the consumer compares his or her actual standing on some attribute to some ideal. A consumer might ask 'Am I as attractive as I would like to be?', 'Do I make as much money as I should?', and so on. The **ideal self** is a person's conception of how he or she would like to be, while the **actual self** refers to our more realistic appraisal of the qualities we have or lack.

The ideal self is partly moulded by elements of the consumer's culture, such as heroes or people depicted in advertising, who serve as models of achievement or appearance.[14] Products may be purchased because they are believed to be instrumental in helping us achieve these goals. Some products are chosen because they are perceived to be consistent with the consumer's actual self, while others are used to help in reaching the standard set by the ideal self.

Fantasy: bridging the gap between the selves

While most people experience a discrepancy between their real and ideal selves, for some consumers this gap is larger than for others. These people are especially good targets for marketing communications that employ *fantasy* appeals.[15] A **fantasy** or daydream is a self-induced shift in consciousness, which is sometimes a way of compensating for a lack of external stimulation or of escaping from problems in the real world.[16] Many products and services are successful because they appeal to consumers' tendency to fantasize. These marketing strategies allow us to extend our vision of ourselves by placing us in unfamiliar, exciting situations or by permitting us to try interesting or provocative roles.

Multiple selves

In a way, each of us really is a number of different people – your mother probably would not recognize the 'you' that emerges while you're on vacation with a group of friends! We have as many selves as we do different social roles. Depending on the situation, we act differently, use different products and services, and we even vary in terms of how much we like ourselves. A person may require a different set of products to play a desired role: she may choose a sedate, understated perfume when she is being her professional self, but splash on something more provocative on Saturday night as she becomes her *femme fatale* self. The dramaturgical perspective on consumer behaviour views people much like actors who play different roles. We each play many roles, and each has its own script, props and costumes.[17]

The self can be thought of as having different components, or *role identities*, and only some of these are active at any given time. Some identities (e.g. husband, boss, student) are more central to the self than others, but other identities (e.g. stamp collector, dancer or advocate for greater equality in the workplace) may be dominant in specific situations. For example, executives in a survey undertaken in the US, UK

If I had a Nissan 240SX … it would be a red coupe.

Wait! A silver fastback. And I'd go for a spin up Route 7, the twisty part.

Just me and Astro …

no, Amy.

Heck, Christie Brinkley!

Wow! Yeah, me and Christie …

in my silver – no, red 240SX … driving into the sunset.

This storyboard for a Nissan 240SX ad illustrates the use of the fantasy theme, which allows consumers to try out new roles and extend their vision of the ideal self.

This photo
shows the
working
woman in one
of her many
(relatively
new) roles.
Used with
permission.

and some Pacific Rim countries said that different aspects of their personalities come into play depending on whether they are making purchase decisions at home or at work. Not surprisingly, they report being less time-conscious, more emotional and less disciplined in their home roles.[18]

Symbolic interactionism

If each person potentially has many social selves, how does each develop and how do we decide which self to 'activate' at any point in time? The sociological tradition of **symbolic interactionism** stresses that relationships with other people play a large part in forming the self.[19] This perspective maintains that people exist in a symbolic environment, and the meaning attached to any situation or object is determined by the interpretation of these symbols. As members of society, we learn to agree on shared meanings. Thus, we 'know' that a red light means stop, or that McDonald's 'golden arches' means fast food.

Like other social objects, the meanings of consumers themselves are defined by social consensus. The consumer interprets his or her own identity, and this assessment is continually evolving as he or she encounters new situations and people. In symbolic interactionist terms, we *negotiate* these meanings over time. Essentially the consumer poses the question: 'Who am I in this situation?' The answer to this question is greatly influenced by those around us: 'Who do *other people* think I am?' We tend to pattern our behaviour on the perceived expectations of others in a form of *self-fulfilling prophecy*. By acting the way we assume others expect us to act, we may confirm these perceptions. This pattern of self-fulfilling behaviour is often expressed in our 'gendered roles', as will be seen later in this chapter.

The looking-glass self

This process of imagining the reactions of others towards us is known as 'taking the role of the other', or the **looking-glass self**.[20] According to this view, our desire to define ourselves operates as a sort of psychological sonar: we take readings of our own identity by 'bouncing' signals off others and trying to project what impression they have of us. The looking-glass image we receive will differ depending upon whose views we are considering.

Like the distorted mirrors in a funfair, our appraisal of who we are can vary, depending on whose perspective we are taking and how accurately we are able to predict their evaluations of us. A successful man like Gareth may have self-doubts about his role as a middle-aged 'family man' as it conflicts with his earlier self-image as dapper and care-free (whether these perceptions are true or not). A self-fulfilling prophecy may be at work here, since these 'signals' can influence Gareth's actual behaviour. If he doesn't believe he's dapper, he may choose clothing and behaviours that actually make him less dapper. On the other hand, his self-confidence in a professional setting may cause him to assume that others hold his 'executive self' in even higher regard than they actually do (we've all known people like that!).

Self-consciousness

There are times when people seem to be painfully aware of themselves. If you have ever walked into a class in the middle of a lecture and noticed that all eyes were on you, you can understand this feeling of *self-consciousness*. In contrast, consumers sometimes behave with shockingly little self-consciousness. For example, people may do things in a stadium, a riot or a student party that they would never do if they were highly conscious of their behaviour.[21]

Some people seem in general to be more sensitive to the image they communicate to others (on the other hand, we all know people who act as if they're oblivious to the impression they are making!). A heightened concern about the nature of one's public 'image' also results in more concern about the social appropriateness of products and consumption activities.

Several measures have been devised to measure this tendency. Consumers who score high on a scale of *public self-consciousness*, for example, are also more interested in clothing and are heavier users of cosmetics.[22] A similar measure is *self-monitoring*. High self-monitors are more attuned to how they present themselves in their social environments, and their product choices are influenced by their estimates of how these items will be perceived by others.[23] Self-monitoring is assessed by consumers' extent of agreement with such items as 'I suppose I put on a show to impress or entertain others', or 'I would probably make a good actor'.[24] High self-monitors are more likely to evaluate products consumed in public in terms of the impressions they make on others than are low self-monitors.[25] Similarly, some recent research has looked at aspects of *vanity*, such as a fixation on physical appearance or on the achievement of personal goals. Perhaps not surprisingly, groups like body builders and fashion models tend to score higher on this dimension.[26]

Consumption and self-concept

By extending the dramaturgical perspective a bit further, it is easy to see how the consumption of products and services contributes to the definition of the self. For an actor to play a role convincingly, he or she needs the correct props, stage setting, and so on. Consumers learn that different roles are accompanied by *constellations* of products and activities which help to define these roles.[27] Some 'props' are so important to the roles we play that they can be viewed as a part of the *extended self*, a concept to be discussed shortly.

Products that shape the self: you are what you consume

Recall that the reflected self helps to shape self-concept, which implies that people see themselves as they imagine others see them. Since what others see includes a person's clothing, jewellery, furniture, car, and so on, it stands to reason that these products also help to determine the perceived self. A consumer's products place him or her in a social role, which helps to answer the question 'Who am I *now*?'

People use an individual's consumption behaviours to help them make judgements about that person's social identity. In addition to considering a person's clothes, grooming habits, and so on, we make inferences about personality based on a person's choice of leisure activities (e.g. squash versus soccer), food preferences (e.g. vegetarians versus 'steak and chips' people), cars, home decorating choices, and so on. People who are shown pictures of someone's sitting room, for example, are able to make surprisingly accurate guesses about his or her personality.[28] In the same way that a consumer's use of products influences others' perceptions, the same products can help to determine his or her *own* self-concept and social identity.[29]

A consumer exhibits *attachment* to an object to the extent that it is used by that person to maintain his or her self-concept.[30] Objects can act as a sort of security blanket by reinforcing our identities, especially in unfamiliar situations. For example, students who decorate their room or house with personal items are less likely to drop out. This coping process may protect the self from being diluted in an unfamiliar environment.[31]

The use of consumption information to define the self is especially important when an identity is yet to be adequately formed, something that occurs when a consumer plays a new or unfamiliar role. **Symbolic self-completion theory** predicts that people who have an incomplete self-definition tend to complete this identity by acquiring and displaying symbols associated with it.[32] Adolescent boys, may use 'macho' products like cars and cigarettes to bolster their developing masculinity; these items act as a 'social crutch' to be leaned on during a period of uncertainty about identity.

Loss of self

The contribution of possessions to self-identity is perhaps most apparent when these treasured objects are lost or stolen. One of the first acts performed by institutions that want to repress individuality and encourage group identity, such as prisons or convents, is to confiscate personal possessions.[33] Victims of burglaries and natural disasters commonly report feelings of alienation, depression or of being 'violated'. One consumer's comment after being robbed is typical: 'It's the next worse thing to being bereaved; it's like being raped'.[34] Burglary victims exhibit a diminished sense of community, reduced sense of privacy and take less pride in their house's appearance than do their neighbours.[35]

The dramatic impact of product loss is highlighted by studying post-disaster conditions, when consumers may literally lose almost everything but the clothes on their backs following a fire, hurricane, flood or earthquake. Some people are reluctant to undergo the process of recreating their identity by acquiring all new possessions. Interviews with disaster victims reveal that some are reluctant to invest the self in new possessions and so become more detached about what they buy. This comment from a woman in her fifties is representative of this attitude: 'I had so much love tied up in my things. I can't go through that kind of loss again. What I'm buying now won't be as important to me.'[36]

Self/product congruence

Because many consumption activities are related to self-definition, it is not surprising to learn that consumers demonstrate consistency between their values (see chapter 4) and the things they buy.[37] **Self-image congruence models** predict that products will be chosen when their attributes match some aspect of the self.[38] These models assume a process of cognitive matching between these attributes and the consumer's self-image.[39]

While results are somewhat mixed, the ideal self appears to be more relevant as a comparison standard for highly expressive social products such as perfume. In contrast, the actual self is more relevant for everyday, functional products. These standards are also likely to vary by usage situation. For example, a consumer might want a functional, reliable car to commute to work everyday, but a flashier model with more 'zing' when going out on a date in the evening. Sadly, there are examples of using products wherein the goal of enhancing the ideal self ends up conflicting and damaging the actual self. The body-building craze which has swept through the US and the north-east of England has resulted in an increasing number of young men who use anabolic steroids for body-building. This steroid use may 'bulk up' the physique (and provide a faster attainment of the ideal self), but it also damages the actual self, since the steroids cause male infertility.[40]

Research tends to support the idea of congruence between product usage and self-image. One of the earliest studies to examine this process found that car owners' ratings of themselves tended to match their perceptions of their cars – drivers of the sporty Pontiac model saw themselves as more active and flashier than did Volkswagen drivers.[41] Congruity also has been found between consumers and their most preferred brands of beer, soap, toothpaste and cigarettes relative to their least preferred brands, as well as between consumers' self-images and their favourite shops.[42] Some specific attributes that have been found to be useful in describing some of the matches between consumers and products include rugged/delicate, excitable/calm, rational/emotional and formal/informal.[43]

While these findings make some intuitive sense, we cannot blithely assume that consumers will always buy products whose characteristics match their own. It is not clear that consumers really see aspects of themselves in down to earth, functional products that don't have very complex or human-like images. It is one thing to consider a brand personality for an expressive, image-oriented product like perfume and quite another to impute human characteristics to a toaster.

Another problem is the old 'chicken-and-egg' question: do people buy products because the products are seen as similar to the self, or do they *assume* that these products must be similar because they have bought them? The similarity between a person's self-image and the images of products purchased does tend to increase with ownership, so this explanation cannot be ruled out.

The extended self

As noted earlier, many of the props and settings consumers use to define their social roles in a sense become a part of their selves. Those external objects that we consider a part of us comprise the **extended self**. In some cultures, people literally incorporate objects into the self – they lick new possessions, take the names of conquered enemies (or in some cases eat them) or bury the dead with their possessions.[44] We don't usually go that far, but many people do cherish possessions

Blending self-concepts with product attributes, Maybelline evokes images of the real and ideal self. Used with permission.

as if they were a part of them. Many material objects, ranging from personal possessions and pets to national monuments or landmarks, help to form a consumer's identity. Just about everyone can name a valued possession that has a lot of the self 'wrapped up' in it, whether it is a treasured photograph, a trophy, an old shirt, a car or a cat. Indeed, it is often possible to construct a pretty accurate 'biography' of someone just by cataloguing the items on display in his or her bedroom or office.

In one study on the extended self, people were given a list of items that ranged from electronic equipment, facial tissues and television programmes to parents, body parts and favourite clothes. They were asked to rate each in terms of its closeness to the self. Objects were more likely to be considered a part of extended self if 'psychic energy' was invested in them by expending effort to obtain them or because they were personalized and kept for a long time.[45]

Four levels of the extended self were described. These range from very personal objects to places and things that allow people to feel like they are rooted in their larger social environments.[46]

- *Individual level*: Consumers include many of their personal possessions in self-definition. These products can include jewellery, cars, clothing, and so on. The saying 'You are what you wear' reflects the belief that one's things are a part of what one is.
- *Family level*: This part of the extended self includes a consumer's residence and its furnishings. The house can be thought of as a symbolic body for the family and often is a central aspect of identity.
- *Community level*: It is common for consumers to describe themselves in terms of the neighbourhood or town from which they come. For farming families or residents with close ties to a community, this sense of belonging is particularly important.
- *Group level*: Our attachments to certain social groups can be considered a part of self. A consumer may feel that landmarks, monuments or sports teams are a part of the extended self.

Gender roles

Sexual identity is a very important component of a consumer's self-concept. People often conform to their culture's expectations about how those of their gender should act, dress, speak, and so on. Of course, these guidelines change over time, and they can differ radically across societies. Some societies are highly dichotomized, with little tolerance for deviation from gender norms. In other societies this is not the case, and greater freedom in behaviour, including behaviour stemming from sexual orientation, is allowed. In certain societies, lip-service is paid to gender equality, but inequalities are just under the surface; in others, there is greater sharing of power, of resources and of decision-making. To the extent that our culture is everything that we learn, then virtually all aspects of the consumption process must be affected by culture. It is not always clear to what extent sex differences are innate versus culturally shaped – but they're certainly evident in many consumption decisions![47]

Consider the gender differences market researchers have observed when comparing the food preferences of men and women. Women eat more fruit; men are more likely to eat meat. As one food writer put it, 'Boy food doesn't grow. It is hunted or killed'. Men are more likely to eat Frosted Flakes or Corn Flakes, while women prefer multigrain cereals. Men are more likely than women to consume soft drinks, while women account for the bulk of sales of bottled water. The sexes also differ sharply in the quantities of food they eat: when researchers at Hershey's discovered that women eat smaller amounts of sweets, the company created a white chocolate confection called Hugs, one of the most successful food launches of all time.

Gender differences in socialization

A society's assumptions about the proper roles of men and women is communicated in terms of the ideal behaviours that are stressed for each sex (in advertising, among other places). It is likely, for instance, that many women eat smaller quantities because they have been 'trained' to be more delicate and dainty.

Gender goals and expectations

In many societies, males are controlled by **agentic goals**, which stress self-assertion and mastery. Females, on the other hand, are taught to value **communal goals**, such as affiliation and the fostering of harmonious relations.[48]

Every society creates a set of expectations regarding the behaviours appropriate for men and women, and finds ways to communicate these priorities. This training begins very young; even children's birthday stories reinforce sex roles. A recent analysis showed that while stereotypical depictions have decreased over time, female characters in children's books still are far more likely to take on nurturant roles such as baking and gift-giving. The adult who prepares the birthday celebration is almost always the mother – often no adult male is present at all. On the other hand, the male figure in these stories is often cast in the role of a miraculous provider of gifts.[49]

Macho marketers?

Marketing has historically been largely defined by men, so it still tends to be dominated by male values. Competition rather than cooperation is stressed, and the language of warfare and domination is often used. Strategists often use distinctly masculine concepts: 'market penetration' or 'competitive thrusts', for example. Marketing articles in academic journals also emphasize agentic rather than communal goals. The most pervasive theme is power and control over others. Other themes include instrumentality (manipulating people for the good of an organization) and competition.[50] This bias may diminish in years to come, as more marketing researchers begin to stress such factors as emotions and aesthetics in purchase decisions, and as increasing numbers of women graduate in marketing!

Gender versus sexual identity

Sex role identity is a state of mind as well as body. A person's biological gender (i.e. male or female) does not totally determine whether he or she will exhibit **sex-typed traits**, or characteristics that are stereotypically associated with one sex or the other. A consumer's subjective feelings about his or her sexuality are crucial as well.[51]

Unlike maleness and femaleness, masculinity and femininity are *not* biological characteristics. A behaviour considered masculine in one culture may not be viewed as such in another. For example, the norm in Northern Europe, and Scandinavia in particular, is that men are stoic, while cultures in Southern Europe and in Latin America allow men to show their emotions. Each society determines what 'real' men and women should and should not do.

Sex-typed products

Many products also are *sex-typed*; they take on masculine or feminine attributes, and consumers often associate them with one sex or another.[52] The sex-typing of products is often created or perpetuated by marketers (e.g. Princess telephones, boys' and girls' toys, and babies' colour-coded nappies). Even brand names appear to be sex-typed: those containing alphanumerics (e.g., Formula 409, 10W40, Clorox 2) are assumed to be technical and hence masculine.[53] Our gender also seems to influence the instrumentality of the products we buy. Studies have shown that men tend to buy instrumental and leisure items impulsively projecting independence and activity, while women tend to buy symbolic and self-expressive goods concerned with appearance and emotional aspects of self. Other research has shown for example that men take a more self-oriented approach to buying clothes, stressing its use as expressive symbols of personality and functional benefits, whilst women have 'other-oriented' concerns, choosing to use clothes as symbols of their social and personal interrelatedness with others.[54] Some sex-typed products are listed in Table 7.1.

Table 7.1 Sex-typed products

Masculine	Feminine
Pocket knife	Scarf
Tool kit	Baby oil
Shaving cream	Bedroom slippers
Briefcase	Hand lotion
Camera (35 mm)	Clothes dryer
Stereo system	Food processor
Scotch	Wine
Wall paint	Facial tissue

Source: Adapted from Kathleen Debevec and Easwar Iyer, 'Sex Roles and Consumer Perceptions of Promotions, Products, and Self: What Do We Know and Where Should We Be Headed', in *Advances in Consumer Research*, ed. Richard J. Lutz (Provo, UT: Association for Consumer Research 13, 1986): 210–14.

Androgyny

Masculinity and femininity are not opposite ends of the same dimension. **Androgyny** refers to the possession of both masculine and feminine traits.[55] Researchers make a distinction between *sex-typed people*, who are stereotypically masculine or feminine, and *androgynous people*, whose mixture of characteristics allows them to function well in a variety of social situations.

Differences in sex-role orientation can influence responses to marketing stimuli, at least under some circumstances.[56] For example, research evidence indicates that females are more likely to undergo elaborate processing of message content, so they tend to be more sensitive to specific pieces of information when forming a judgement, while males are more influenced by overall themes.[57] In addition, women with a relatively strong masculine component in their sex-role identity prefer ad portrayals that include non-traditional women.[58] Some research indicates that sex-typed people are more sensitive to the sex-role depictions of characters in advertising, although women appear to be more sensitive to gender role relationships than are men.

In one study, subjects read two versions of a beer advertisement, couched in either masculine or feminine terms. The masculine version contained phrases like 'X Beer has the strong aggressive flavour that really asserts itself with good food and good company . . .', while the feminine version made claims like 'Brewed with tender care, X Beer is a full-bodied beer that goes down smoothly and gently . . .' People who rated themselves as highly masculine or highly feminine preferred the version that was described in (respectively) very masculine or feminine terms.[59] Sex-typed people in general are more concerned with ensuring that their behaviour is consistent with their culture's definition of gender appropriateness.

Female gender roles

Gender roles for women are changing rapidly. Social changes, such as the dramatic increase in the proportion of women in waged work, have led to an upheaval in the way women are regarded by men, the way they regard themselves and in the products they choose to buy. Modern women now play a greater role in decisions regarding

In spite of many changes in 'gendered behaviour' over the past years, some sex-role stereotypes continue to endure.
Used with permission.

One of the most marked changes in gender roles is occurring in Japan. Traditional Japanese wives stay at home and care for their children while their husbands work late and entertain clients. The good Japanese wife is expected to walk two paces behind her husband. However, these patterns are changing as women are less willing to live vicariously through their husbands. More than half of Japanese women aged between 25 and 29 are either working or looking for a job.[60] Japanese marketers and advertisers are beginning to depict women in professional situations (though still usually in subservient roles), and even to develop female market segments for such traditionally male products as automobiles.

traditionally male purchases. For example, more than 60 per cent of new car buyers under the age of 50 are female, and women even buy almost half of all condoms sold.[61]

Segmenting women

In the 1949 movie *Adam's Rib*, Katharine Hepburn played a stylish and competent lawyer. This film was one of the first to show that a woman can have a successful career and still be happily married. Historically, married women have worked outside the home, especially during wartime. However, the presence of women in a position of authority is a fairly recent phenomenon. The evolution of a new managerial class of women has forced marketers to change their traditional assumptions about women as they target this growing market.

Ironically, it seems that in some cases marketers have overcompensated for their former emphasis on women as housewives. Many attempts to target the vast market of females employed outside the home tend to depict all these women in glamorous, executive positions. This portrayal ignores the facts that the majority of women do not hold such jobs, and that many work because they have to, rather than for self-fulfilment. This diversity means that not all women should be expected to respond to marketing campaigns that stress professional achievement or the glamour of the working life.

The character of Rosie the Riveter was created during the Second World War to symbolize the efforts of American women to take the place of men on factory production lines.
Used with permission.

Whether or not they work outside the home, many women have come to value greater independence and respond positively to marketing campaigns that stress the freedom to make their own lifestyle decisions. American Express has been targeting women for a long time, but the company found that its 'Do you know me?' campaign did not appeal to women as much as to men. A campaign aimed specifically at women featured confident women using their American Express cards. By depicting women in active situations, the company greatly increased its share of the woman's credit card market.[62]

Cheesecake: the depiction of women in advertising

As implied by the ads for Virginia Slims cigarettes – 'You've come a long way, baby!' – attitudes about female sex roles have changed remarkably in the twentieth century. Still, women continue to be depicted by advertisers and the media in stereotypical ways. Analyses of ads in such magazines as *Time*, *Newsweek*, *Playboy* and even *Ms*. have shown that the large majority of women included were presented as sex objects (so-called 'cheesecake' ads) or in traditional roles.[63] Similar findings have been obtained in the United Kingdom.[64] One of the biggest culprits may be rock videos, which tend to reinforce traditional women's roles.

Ads may also reinforce negative stereotypes. Women often are portrayed as stupid, submissive, temperamental or as sexual objects who exist solely for the pleasure of men. An ad for Newport cigarettes illustrates how the theme of female submission may be perpetuated. The copy 'Alive with pleasure!' is accompanied by a photo of a woman in the woods, playfully hanging from a pole being carried by two men. The underlying message may be interpreted as two men bringing home their captured prey.[65]

Although women continue to be depicted in traditional roles, this situation is changing as advertisers scramble to catch up with reality. For example, Avon Products is trying to shed its old-fashioned image by focusing on the concerns of contemporary women. As one recent ad proclaims, 'After all, you have more on your mind than what's on your lips. And Avon thinks that's beautiful.'[66] Women are now as likely as men to be central characters in television commercials. Still, while males increasingly are depicted as spouses and parents, women are still more likely than men to be seen in domestic settings. Also, about 90 per cent of all narrators in commercials are male. The deeper male voice apparently is perceived as more authoritative and credible.[67]

Some ads now feature *role reversal*, where women occupy traditional men's roles. In other cases, women are portrayed in romantic situations, but they tend to be more sexually dominant. Ironically, current advertising is more free to emphasize traditional female traits now that sexual equality is becoming more of an accepted

| Marketing pitfall | Marketers continue to grapple with ways to entice female customers for traditionally male-oriented products, such as cars and computers, without offending them. One early effort by Tandy Corp. illustrates the potential for these efforts to backfire. When the company decided to market personal computers to women in 1990, it did so by packaging them with software for doing such 'feminine' tasks as making Christmas lists, taking inventory of silverware and china, and generating recipes. Women were not amused by the homemaker stereotype, and the campaign failed.[68] |

While you don't necessarily dress for men, it doesn't hurt, on occasion, to see one drool like the pathetic dog that he is.

This ad illustrates the 'men-bashing' approach taken by some advertisers who are trying to appeal to women. *Advertising Age* (1994).
Photo courtesy of Goldsmith/Jeffrey and Bodyslimmers.

fact. This freedom is demonstrated in a German poster for a women's magazine. The caption reads 'Today's women can sometimes show weakness, because they are strong'.

Male sex roles

While the traditional conception of the ideal male as a tough, aggressive, muscular man who enjoys 'manly' sports and activities is not dead, society's definition of the male role is evolving. Men in the late 1990s are allowed to be more compassionate and to have close friendships with other men. In contrast to the depiction of macho men who do not show feelings, some marketers are promoting men's 'sensitive' side. An emphasis on male bonding has been the centrepiece of many ad campaigns, especially for beers.[69]

The prototype of the 'new man' was expressed in the positioning statement for Paco Rabanne Pour Homme, an aftershave that attempted to focus on this new lifestyle: 'Paco Rabanne Pour Homme is a prestige men's fragrance for the male who is not a clichéd stereotype, the man who understands and accepts the fluidity of male/female relationships.' The ideal personality of the target consumer for the aftershave was described by the company with adjectives like confident, independent, romantic, tender and playful.[70]

Marketing opportunity

As sex roles for males evolve, formerly 'feminine products' like fragrances and hair colouring have been successfully marketed to men in recent years. Cosmetics companies such as Aramis, Clinique and Urban Decay are attempting to expand the male market even further. Even nail varnish is slowly making its way onto men's shelves – the Hard Candy line offers its Candy Man collection which includes a metallic gold called Cowboy and a forest green shade named Oedipus.[71]

Marketing opportunity continued The companies ironically have been boosted by the recent trend towards corporate 'downsizing', which seems to have spurred interest among men for shortcuts to looking younger and perhaps less likely to be made redundant because of their age. American men are spending $9.5 billion a year on face-lifts, toupees, cosmetics, girdles and other items in pursuit of the Fountain of Youth.[72] They are flocking to products like Rogaine to thicken their hair, Bodyslimmers underwear that nips in the waist, and Super Shaper Briefs that round out the buttocks (for an extra $5 the buyer can get an 'endowment pad' that slips in the front). A corporate recruiter has nicknamed the customer for these products 'The Bionic Executive'. [73]

The joys of fatherhood

Males' lifestyles are changing to allow greater freedom of expression in clothing choices, hobbies such as cooking, and so on. Men are getting more involved in bringing up children, and advertising campaigns for such companies as Kodak, Omega watches and Pioneer electronics stress the theme of fatherhood.[74] Still, this change is coming slowly. A commercial for 7–11 stores (a corner shop chain in America and Western Europe) showed two men out for a walk, each with a pushchair. As they near a 7–11, they begin to push faster until they are racing each other. The campaign's creative director explained, 'We showed them engaged in a competition to make it easier for men to accept the concept of taking care of children'.[75]

Beefcake: the depiction of men in advertising

Men as well as women are often depicted in a negative fashion in advertising. They frequently come across as helpless or bumbling. As one advertising executive put it, 'The woman's movement raised consciousness in the ad business as to how women can be depicted. The thought now is, if we can't have women in these old-fashioned traditional roles, at least we can have men being dummies.'[76]

Just as advertisers are criticized for depicting women as sex objects, the same accusations can be made about how males are portrayed – a practice correspondingly known as 'beefcake'.[77] An ad campaign for Sansabelt trousers featured the theme 'What women look for in men's pants'. Ads feature a woman who confides, 'I always lower my eyes when a man passes [pause] to see if he's worth following'. One female executive commented, 'turnabout is fair play . . . If we can't put a stop to sexism in advertising . . . at least we can have some fun with it and do a little leering of our own.'[78]

Gay and lesbian consumers

Gay and lesbian consumers are still largely ignored by marketers. This situation is starting to change, however, as some marketers are acknowledging the upmarket demographic profile of these consumers.[79] IKEA, the Swedish furniture retailer with outlets throughout Europe and in several major US cities, broke new ground by running a TV spot featuring a gay male couple who purchase a dining room table at the store.[80] Other major companies making an effort to market to homosexuals include AT&T, Anheuser-Busch, Apple Computer, Benetton, Philip Morris, Seagram and Sony.[81] Gay consumers can even get their own credit card – a Rainbow Visa card issued by Travelers Bank USA. Using tennis star Martina Navratilova as its spokeswoman, users of the card benefit such groups as the National Center for

Lesbian Rights. The card allows people who don't qualify based on income to apply with a same-sex partner.[82]

The percentage of the population that is gay and lesbian is difficult to determine, and efforts to measure this group have been controversial.[83] However, the respected research company Yankelovich Partners Inc., which has tracked consumer values and attitudes since 1971 in its annual Monitor™ survey, now includes a question about sexual identity in its survey. This study was virtually the first to use a sample that reflects the population as a whole instead of polling only smaller or biased groups (such as readers of gay publications) whose responses may not be as representative of all consumers. About 6 per cent of respondents identify themselves as gay/homosexual/lesbian.

As civil rights gains are made by gay activists, the social climate is becoming more favourable for firms targeting this market segment.[84] In one of the first academic studies in this field, the conclusion was that gays and lesbians did not qualify as a market segment because they did not satisfy the traditional criteria of being identifiable, accessible and of sufficient size.[85] Subsequent studies have argued that the segmentation criteria rely on outdated assumptions regarding the nature of consumers, marketing activities and the ways in which media are used in the contemporary marketplace. Here, the argument is that identifiability is an unreliable construct for socially subordinated groups, and really isn't the issue anyway. How marketers segment (i.e. by race, ethnicity, gender, or in this case, sexuality) isn't as important as whether the group itself expresses consumption patterns in identifiable ways. Similarly, the accessible criterion continues with the assumption of active marketers who contact passive consumers. This criterion also needs to take into account the dramatic changes in media over the past two decades, in particular the use of speciality media by marketers to access special interest segments. Finally, sufficient size assumes separate campaigns are necessary to reach each segment, an assumption that ignores consumers' ability and willingness to explore multiple media.[86]

At least in some parts of the US and Europe, homosexuality appears to be becoming more mainstream and accepted. Mattel even sells an Earring Magic Ken doll, complete with *faux*-leather vest, lavender mesh shirt and two-tone hair (though the product has become a favourite of gay men, the company denied it was targeted to that group).

This German ad for New West cigarettes features a gay wedding. The headline focuses on the brand's strong taste, depicting it as the choice of fearless individuals. *Advertising Age* (Global Gallery), 8 March 1993, p. 40. Photo courtesy of Scholz & Friends, Hamburg.

Subaru ad targeted to lesbian consumers.
Used with permission.

Body image

A person's physical appearance is a large part of his or her self-concept. **Body image** refers to a consumer's subjective evaluation of his or her physical self. As was the case with the overall self-concept, this image is not necessarily accurate. A man may think of himself as being more muscular than he really is, or a woman may think she is fatter than is the case. In fact, it is not uncommon to find marketing strategies that exploit consumers' tendencies to distort their body images by preying upon insecurities about appearance, thereby creating a gap between the real and ideal physical self and, consequently, the desire to purchase products and services to narrow that gap.

Body cathexis

A person's feelings about his or her body can be described in terms of **body cathexis**. Cathexis refers to the emotional significance of some object or idea to a person, and some parts of the body are more central to self-concept than are others. One study of young adults' feelings about their bodies found that these respondents were the most satisfied with their hair and eyes and had the least positive feelings about their waists. These feelings were related to consumption of grooming products. Consumers who were more satisfied with their bodies were more frequent users of such 'preening' products as hair conditioner, hairdryers, aftershave, artificial tanning products, toothpaste and pumice soap.[88] In a large-scale study of older women in six European countries, the results showed that women would like to 'grow old beautifully', and that they were prepared to follow diets, exercise and use cosmetics to reach this goal. Wrinkles were the biggest concern, and Greek and Italian women were by far the most concerned about how to combat ageing, with northern European women expressing more agreement with the statement that ageing was natural and inevitable.[89]

Ideals of beauty

A person's satisfaction with the physical image he or she presents to others is affected by how closely that image corresponds to the image valued by his or her culture. In fact, infants as young as two months show a preference for attractive faces.[90] An **ideal of beauty** is a particular model, or exemplar, of appearance. Ideals of beauty for both men and women may include physical features (e.g. big breasts or small, bulging muscles or not) as well as clothing styles, cosmetics, hairstyles, skin tone (pale versus tan) and body type (petite, athletic, voluptuous, etc.).

Is beauty universal?

Recent research indicates that preferences for some physical features over others are 'wired in' genetically, and that these reactions tend to be the same among people around the world. Specifically, people appear to favour features associated with good health and youth, attributes linked to reproductive ability and strength. Men also are more likely to use a woman's body shape as a sexual cue, and it has been theorized that this is because feminine curves provide evidence of reproductive potential. During puberty a typical female gains almost 15kg of 'reproductive fat'

As suggested by this Benetton ad, a global perspective on ideals of beauty is resulting in more ways to be considered attractive.
Photo by Oliviero Toscani for Benetton.

around hips and thighs which supply the approximately 80,000 extra calories needed for pregnancy. Most fertile women have waist : hip ratios of 0.6 : 0.8, an hourglass shape that happens to be the one men rank highest. Even though preferences for total weight change, waist : hip ratios tend to stay in this range – even the superthin model Twiggy (who pioneered the 'waif' look decades before Kate Moss!) had a ratio of 0.73.[91] Other positively valued female characteristics include a higher forehead than average, fuller lips, a shorter jaw and a smaller chin and nose. Women, on the other hand, favour men with a heavy lower face, those who are slightly above average height and males with a prominent brow.

Of course, the way these faces are 'packaged' still varies enormously, and that's where marketers come in. Advertising and other forms of mass media play a significant role in determining which forms of beauty are considered desirable at any point in time. An ideal of beauty functions as a sort of cultural yardstick. Consumers compare themselves to some standard (often advocated by the fashion media) and are dissatisfied with their appearance to the extent that they don't match up to it. These mass media portrayals have been criticized not only on social grounds, but on issues of health as well. In a study of New Zealand print advertisements over the period 1958–88, the findings confirmed that advertising models became thinner and less curvaceous over the 30-year period, resulting in contemporary models being approximately 8.5 kg lighter than they would be if they had the same body shape as models of the late 1950s. To achieve the currently fashionable body shape, a young woman of average height would weigh approximately 42 kg, which is far below the recommended level for good health.[92]

Ideals of beauty over time

While beauty may be only skin deep, throughout history and across cultures women in particular have worked very hard to attain it. They have starved themselves, painfully bound their feet, inserted plates into their lips, spent countless hours under hairdryers, in front of mirrors and beneath ultraviolet lights, and have undergone breast reduction or enlargement operations to alter their appearance and meet their society's expectations of what a beautiful woman should look like.

Periods of history tend to be characterized by a specific 'look', or ideal of beauty. American history can be described in terms of a succession of dominant ideals. For example, in sharp contrast to today's emphasis on health and vigour, in the early 1800s it was fashionable to appear delicate to the point of looking ill. The poet John Keats described the ideal woman of that time as 'a milk white lamb that bleats for man's protection'. Other looks have included the voluptuous, lusty woman as epitomized by Lillian Russell, the athletic Gibson Girl of the 1890s, and the small, boyish flapper of the 1920s as exemplified by Clara Bow.[93]

Throughout much of the nineteenth century, the desirable waistline for American women was 18 inches, a circumference that required the use of corsets pulled so tight that they routinely caused headaches, fainting fits, and possibly even the uterine and spinal disorders common among women of the time. While modern women are not quite as 'straitlaced', many still endure such indignities as high heels, body waxing, eye-lifts and liposuction. In addition to the millions spent on cosmetics, clothing, health clubs and fashion magazines, these practices remind us that – rightly or wrongly – the desire to conform to current standards of beauty is alive and well.

The ideal body type of Western women has changed radically over time, and these changes have resulted in a realignment of *sexual dimorphic markers* – those aspects of the body that distinguish between the sexes. For example, analyses of the

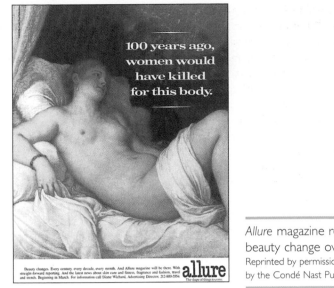

Allure magazine reminds us that ideals of beauty change over time.
Reprinted by permission of *Allure* magazine. Copyright © 1990 by the Condé Nast Publications, Inc.

measurements of *Playboy* centrefolds over a twenty-year period, 1958 to 1978, show that these ideals got thinner and more muscular. The average hip measurement went from 36 inches in 1958 to just over 34 inches in 1978. Average bust size shrunk from almost 37 inches in 1958 to about 35 inches in 1978.[94]

The first part of the 1990s saw the emergence of the controversial 'waif' look, where successful models (notably Kate Moss) were likely to have bodies resembling those of young boys. More recently, the pendulum seems to be shifting back a bit, as the more buxom, 'hourglass figure' popular in the 1950s (exemplified by the Marilyn Monroe ideal) has reappeared.[95] One factor leading to this change has been the opposition to the use of super-thin models by feminist groups, who charge that these role models encourage starvation diets and eating disorders among women who want to emulate the look.[96] These groups have advocated boycotts against companies like Coca-Cola and Calvin Klein who have used wafer-thin models in their advertising. Some protesters have even taken to pasting stickers over these ads that read 'Feed this woman', or 'Give me a cheeseburger'.

We can also distinguish among ideals of beauty for men in terms of facial features, musculature and facial hair – who could confuse Tom Cruise with Mr Bean? In fact, one recent national survey which asked both men and women to comment on male aspects of appearance, found that the dominant standard of beauty for men is a strongly masculine, muscled body – though women tend to prefer men with less muscle mass than men themselves strive to attain.[97] Advertisers appear to have the males' ideal in mind – a recent study of men appearing in advertisements found that most sport the strong and muscular physique of the male stereotype.[98]

Working on the body

Because many consumers are motivated to match up to an ideal appearance, they often go to great lengths to change aspects of their physical selves. From cosmetics to plastic surgery, tanning salons to diet drinks, a multitude of products and services are directed towards altering or maintaining aspects of the physical self in order

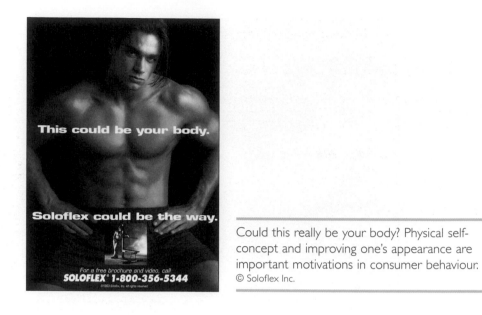

Could this really be your body? Physical self-concept and improving one's appearance are important motivations in consumer behaviour.
© Soloflex Inc.

to present a desirable appearance. It is difficult to overstate the importance of the physical self-concept (and the desire by consumers to improve their appearance) to many marketing activities.

Sizeism

As reflected in the expression 'you can never be too thin or too rich', many Western societies have an obsession with weight. Even primary school children perceive obesity as worse than being disabled.[99] The pressure to be slim is continually reinforced both by advertising and by peers. Americans in particular are preoccupied by what they weigh. They are continually bombarded by images of thin, happy people.

How realistic are these appearance standards? There is a small consumer movement urging people to stop judging people by the pound – a coalition of pro-fat groups holds an International No-Diet Day, and a group in Seattle held a scale-smashing event.[100] Still, many consumers focus on attaining an unrealistic ideal weight, sometimes by relying on height and weight charts which show what one should weigh. These expectations are communicated in subtle ways. Even fashion dolls, such as the ubiquitous Barbie, reinforce the ideal of thinness. The dimensions of these dolls, when extrapolated to average female body sizes, are unnaturally long and thin.[101] In spite of Americans' obsession about weight, as a country, they continue to have a greater percentage of obesity in the general population relative to all European countries, as shown in Figure 7.1.

Body image distortions

While many people perceive a strong link between self-esteem and appearance, some consumers unfortunately exaggerate this connection even more, and sacrifice greatly to attain what they consider to be a desirable body image. Women tend to be taught to a greater degree than men that the quality of their bodies reflects their self-worth, so it is not surprising that most major distortions of body image occur among females.

Men do not tend to differ in ratings of their current figure, their ideal figure and the figure they think is most attractive to women. In contrast, women rate both the figure they think is most attractive to men and their ideal figure as much thinner

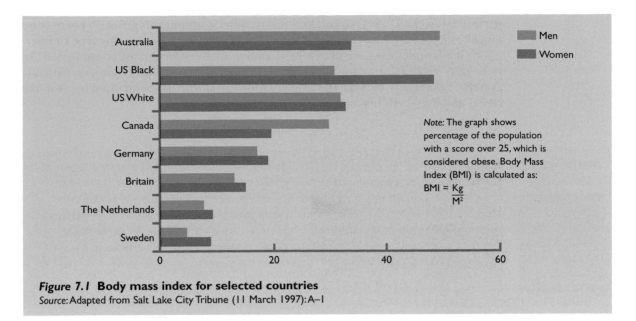

Figure 7.1 Body mass index for selected countries
Source: Adapted from Salt Lake City Tribune (11 March 1997): A–1

than their actual figure.[102] In one survey, two-thirds of college women admitted resorting to unhealthy behaviour to control weight. Advertising messages that convey an image of slimness help to reinforce these activities by arousing insecurities about weight.[103]

A distorted body image has been linked to the rise of eating disorders, which are particularly prevalent among young women. People with anorexia regard themselves as fat, and starve themselves in the quest for thinness. This condition may be accompanied by bulimia, which involves two stages: first, binge eating occurs (usually in private), where more than 5,000 calories may be consumed at one time. The binge is then followed by induced vomiting, abuse of laxatives, fasting and/or overly strenuous exercise – a 'purging' process that reasserts the woman's sense of control.

Most eating disorders are found in white, teenaged girls and students. Victims often have brothers or fathers who are hypercritical of their weight. In addition, binge eating may be encouraged by one's peers. Groups such as athletic teams, and social clubs at school may develop positive norms regarding binge eating. In one study of a female social club, members' popularity within the group increased the more they binged.[104]

Eating disorders do affect some men as well. They are common among male athletes who must also conform to various weight requirements, such as jockeys, boxers and male models.[105] In general, though, most men who have distorted body images consider themselves to be too light rather than too heavy: society has taught them that they must be muscular to be masculine. Men are more likely than women to express their insecurities about their bodies by becoming addicted to exercise. In fact, striking similarities have been found between male compulsive runners and female anorexics. These include a commitment to diet and exercise as a central part of one's identity and susceptibility to body image distortions.[106]

Cosmetic surgery

American consumers are increasingly electing to have cosmetic surgery to change a poor body image.[107] More than half a million cosmetic surgical procedures are performed in the US every year, and this number continues to grow.[108] There is no longer much (if any) psychological stigma associated with having this type of operation; it is commonplace and accepted among many segments of consumers.[109] In fact, men now account for as much as 20 per cent of plastic surgery patients. Popular operations include the implantation of silicon pectoral muscles (for the chest) and even calf implants to fill out 'chicken legs'. [110]

Multicultural dimensions

Belly button reconstruction is now a popular form of cosmetic surgery in Japan, as women strive for the perfect navel they can show off as they wear the midriff fashions now popular there. The navel is an important part of Japanese culture, and mothers often save a baby's umbilical cord. In Japanese, a 'bent navel' is a grouch, and the phrase which would roughly mean 'give me a break' translates as 'yeah, and I brew tea in my belly button'. A popular insult among children: 'Your mother has an outie [protruding belly button].'[111]

Many women turn to surgery either to reduce weight or to increase sexual desirability. The use of liposuction, where fat is removed from the thighs with a vacuum-like device, has almost doubled since it was introduced in the United States in 1982.[112] Some women believe that larger breasts will increase their allure and undergo breast augmentation procedures. Although some of these procedures have generated controversy due to possible negative side effects, it is unclear whether potential medical problems will deter large numbers of women from choosing surgical options to enhance their (perceived) femininity. The importance of breast size to self-concept resulted in an interesting and successful marketing strategy undertaken by an underwear company. While conducting focus groups on bras, an analyst noted that small-chested women typically reacted with hostility when discussing the subject. They would unconsciously cover their chests with their arms as they spoke and felt that their needs were ignored by the fashion industry. To meet this overlooked need, the company introduced a line of A-cup bras called 'A-OK' and depicted wearers in a positive light. A new market segment was born. Other companies are going in the opposite direction by promoting bras that create the illusion of a larger cleavage. In Europe and the US, both Gossard and Playtex are aggressively marketing specially designed bras offering 'cleavage enhancement' which use a combination of wires and internal pads to create the desired effect.

Body decoration and mutilation

The body is adorned or altered in some way in every culture. Decorating the self serves a number of purposes.[113]

● *To separate group members from non-members*: Chinook Indians of North America used to press the head of a newborn baby between two boards for a year, permanently altering its shape. In our society, teenagers go out of their way to adopt distinctive hair and clothing styles that will distinguish them from adults.

Multicultural dimensions

Cosmetic surgeons often try to mould their patients into a standard ideal of beauty, using the features of such Caucasian classic beauties as Grace Kelly or Katharine Hepburn as a guide. The aesthetic standard used by surgeons is called the *classic canon*, which spells out the ideal relationships among facial features. For example, it states that the width of the base of the nose should be the same as the distance between the eyes.

However, this standard applies to the Caucasian ideal, and is being revised as people from other ethnic groups are demanding less rigidity in culture's definition of what is beautiful. Some consumers are rebelling against the need to conform to the Western ideal. For example, a rounded face is valued as a sign of beauty by many Asians, and thus giving cheek implants to an Asian patient would remove much of what makes her face attractive.

Some surgeons who work on African-Americans are trying to change the guidelines they use when sculpting features. For example, they argue that an ideal African-American nose is shorter and has a more rounded tip than does a Caucasian nose. Doctors are beginning to diversify their 'product lines', offering consumers a broader assortment of features that better reflect the diversity of cultural ideals of beauty in a heterogeneous society.[114]

Racial differences in beauty ideals also surfaced in a recent study of teenagers. White girls who were asked to describe the 'ideal' girl agreed she should be 5'7", weigh between 45–50 kg, and have blue eyes and long flowing hair – in other words, she should look a lot like a Barbie doll. Almost 90 per cent of the girls in this study said they were dissatisfied with their weight.

In contrast, 70 per cent of the black girls in the same study responded that they were *satisfied* with their weight. They were much less likely to use physical characteristics to describe the ideal girl, instead emphasizing someone who has a personal sense of style and who gets along with others. It was only when prodded that they named such features as fuller hips, large thighs and a small waist, which, the authors of the study say, are attributes valued by black men.[115]

- *To place the individual in the social organization*: Many cultures engage in rites of passage at puberty when a boy symbolically becomes a man. Young men in Ghana paint their bodies with white stripes to resemble skeletons to symbolize the death of their child status. In Western culture, this rite may involve some form of mild self-mutilation or engaging in dangerous activities.

- *To place the person in a gender category*: The Tchikrin Indians of South America insert a string of beads in a boy's lip to enlarge it. Western women wear lipstick to enhance femininity. At the turn of the century, small lips were fashionable because they represented women's submissive role at that time.[116] Today, big, red lips are provocative and indicate an aggressive sexuality. Some women, including a number of famous actresses and models, have collagen injections or lip inserts to create large, pouting lips (known in the modelling industry as 'liver lips').[117]

- *To enhance sex-role identification*: Wearing high heels, which podiatrists agree are a prime cause of knee and hip problems, backaches and fatigue, can be compared with the traditional Oriental practice of foot-binding to enhance femininity. As one doctor observed, 'When they [women] get home, they can't get their high-heeled shoes off fast enough. But every doctor in the world could yell from now until Doomsday, and women would still wear them.'[118]

- *To indicate desired social conduct*: The Suya of South America wear ear ornaments to emphasize the importance placed in their culture on listening and obedience. In Western society gay men may wear an earring to signal how they expect to be treated.

- *To indicate high status or rank*: The Hidates Indians of North America wear feather ornaments that indicate how many people they have killed. In our society, some people wear glasses with clear lenses, even though they do not have eye problems, to increase their perceived status.

- *To provide a sense of security*: Consumers often wear lucky charms, amulets, rabbits' feet, and so on to protect them from the 'evil eye'. Some modern women wear a 'mugger whistle' around their necks for a similar reason.

Tattoos

Tattoos – both temporary and permanent – are a popular form of body adornment. This body art can be used to communicate aspects of the self to onlookers and may serve some of the same functions that other kinds of body painting do in primitive cultures. Tattoos (from the Tahitian *ta-tu*) have deep roots in folk art. Until recently, the images were crude and were primarily either death symbols (e.g. a skull), animals (especially panthers, eagles and snakes), pin-up women or military designs. More current influences include science fiction themes, Japanese symbolism and tribal designs.

A tattoo may be viewed as a fairly risk-free (?) way of expressing an adventurous side of the self. Tattoos have a long history of association with people who are social outcasts. For example, the faces and arms of criminals in sixth-century Japan were tattooed as a way of identifying them, as were Massachusetts prison inmates

Body decoration can be permanent, or (hopefully!) temporary in order to distinguish oneself, shock others, signify group membership, or express a particular mood or message.
Used with permission.

in the nineteenth century. These emblems are often used by marginal groups, such as bikers or Japanese *yakuze* (gang members), to express group identity and solidarity.

Body piercing

Decorating the body with various kinds of metallic inserts has evolved from a practice associated with some fringe groups to become a popular fashion statement. Piercings can range from a hoop protruding from a navel to scalp implants, where metal posts are inserted in the skull (do not try this at home!). Publications such as *Piercing Fans International Quarterly* are seeing their circulations soar and web sites featuring piercings and piercing products are attracting numerous followers. This popularity is not pleasing to hard-core piercing fans, who view the practice as a sensual consciousness-raising ritual and are concerned that now people just do it because it's trendy. As one customer waiting for a piercing remarked, 'If your piercing doesn't mean anything, then it's just like buying a pair of platform shoes'.[119]

Chapter summary

- Consumers' *self-concepts* are reflections of their attitudes towards themselves. Whether these attitudes are positive or negative, they will help to guide many purchase decisions; products can be used to bolster self-esteem or to 'reward' the self.
- Many product choices are dictated by the consumer's perceived similarity between his or her personality and attributes of the product. The *symbolic interactionist perspective* on the self implies that each of us actually has many selves, and a different set of products is required as props to play each. Many things other than the body can also be viewed as part of the self. Valued objects, car, homes and even attachments to sports teams or national monuments are used to define the self, when these are incorporated into the extended self.
- A person's *sex-role identity* is a major component of self-definition. Conceptions about masculinity and femininity, largely shaped by society, guide the acquisition of 'sex-typed' products and services.
- Advertising and other media play an important role in socializing consumers to be male and female. While traditional women's roles have often been perpetuated in advertising depictions, this situation is changing somewhat. The media do not always portray men accurately either.
- Sometimes these activities are carried to an extreme, as people try too hard to live up to cultural ideals. One example is found in eating disorders, where women in particular become obsessed with thinness.
- A person's conception of his or her body also provides feedback to self-image. A culture communicates certain ideals of beauty, and consumers go to great lengths to attain these. Many consumer activities involve manipulating the body, whether through dieting, cosmetic surgery, tattooing, or so forth.

Key terms

Actual self *(p. 177)*
Agentic goals *(p. 184)*
Androgyny *(p. 186)*
Body cathexis *(p. 192)*
Body image *(p. 192)*
Communal goals *(p. 184)*
Extended self *(p. 182)*
Fantasy *(p. 177)*
Ideal of beauty *(p. 193)*

Ideal self *(p. 177)*
Looking-glass self *(p. 179)*
Self-concept *(p. 176)*
Self-image congruence models
  (p. 182)
Sex-typed traits *(p. 185)*
Symbolic interactionism *(p. 179)*
Symbolic self-completion theory
  (p. 181)

Consumer behaviour challenge

1. How might the creation of a self-conscious state be related to consumers who are trying on clothing in dressing rooms? Does the act of preening in front of a mirror change the dynamics by which people evaluate their product choices? Why?
2. Is it ethical for marketers to encourage infatuation with the self?
3. List three dimensions by which the self-concept can be described.
4. Compare and contrast the real versus the ideal self. List three products for which each type of self is likely to be used as a reference point when a purchase is considered.
5. Watch a series of ads featuring men and women on television. Try to imagine the characters with reversed roles (i.e. the male parts played by women, and vice versa). Can you see any differences in assumptions about sex-typed behaviour?
6. To date, the bulk of advertising targeted at gay consumers has been placed in exclusively gay media. If it was your decision, would you consider using mainstream media to reach gays, who constitute a significant proportion of the general population? Or, bearing in mind

that members of some targeted segments have serious objection to this practice, especially when the product (e.g. alcohol, cigarettes) may be viewed as harmful in some way, do you think gays should be singled out at all by marketers?
7. Do you agree that marketing strategies tend to have a male-oriented bias? If so, what are some possible consequences for specific marketing activities?
8. Construct a 'consumption biography' of a friend or family member. Make a list and/or photograph his or her favourite possessions, and see if you or others can describe this person's personality just from the information provided by this catalogue.
9. Some consumer advocates have protested at the use of super-thin models in advertising, claiming that these women encourage others to starve themselves in order to attain the 'waif' look. Other critics respond that the media's power to shape behaviour has been overestimated, and that it is insulting to people to assume that they are unable to separate fantasy from reality. What do you think?

Consumers as decision-makers

PART OUTLINE

This part explores how we make consumption decisions and discusses the many influences exerted by others in this process. Chapter 8 focuses on the basic sequence of steps we undergo when making a decision. Chapter 9 considers how the particular situation we find ourselves in affects these decisions and how we go about evaluating what we've bought afterwards. Chapter 10 provides an overview of group processes and discusses the reasons we are motivated to conform to the expectations of our fellow group members. It also considers how some individuals in particular (called 'opinion leaders') are likely to influence the consumption behaviour of others in a group.

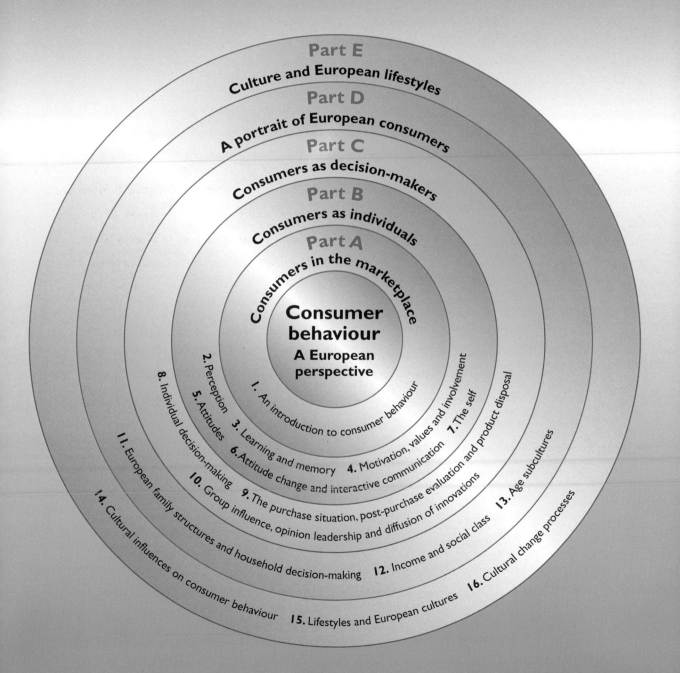

Part E
Culture and European lifestyles

Part D
A portrait of European consumers

Part C
Consumers as decision-makers

Part B
Consumers as individuals

Part A
Consumers in the marketplace

Consumer behaviour
A European perspective

1. An introduction to consumer behaviour
2. Perception
3. Learning and memory
4. Motivation, values and involvement
5. Attitudes
6. Attitude change and interactive communication
7. The self
8. Individual decision-making
9. The purchase situation, post-purchase evaluation and product disposal
10. Group influence, opinion leadership and diffusion of innovations
11. European family structures and household decision-making
12. Income and social class
13. Age subcultures
14. Cultural influences on consumer behaviour
15. Lifestyles and European cultures
16. Cultural change processes

Andy has had enough. He can no longer bear to go on watching TV on his tiny, antiquated, black-and-white set. It was bad enough trying to listen to the scratchy music on videos and squinting through *The Simpsons* and *Beavis & Butthead*. The final straw was when he couldn't tell Manchester United from Ajax during last Wednesday night's football match! When he went next door to watch the second half on Mark's big set, he really realized what he had been missing. Budget or not, it was time to act. A man has to have his priorities.

Andy thinks he'll probably get a good selection (at an affordable price) in one of those new warehouse stores. Arriving at The London Appliance Emporium, Andy heads straight for the Video Zone – barely noticing the rows of toasters, microwave ovens and stereos en route. Within minutes, he's intercepted by a smiling salesman wearing a cheap suit. Even though he could use some help, Andy tells the salesman he's just browsing – these guys don't know what they're talking about, and they're only interested in closing a sale, no matter what.

Andy starts to examine some of the features on the 52 cm colour sets. He knows his friend Carol has a set by Prime Wave which she really likes, and his sister Diane has warned him to stay away from the Kamashita. Although Andy finds a Prime Wave model with lots of features such as a sleep timer, on-screen programming menu, cable compatible tuner and remote control, he chooses the less expensive Precision 2000X because it has one feature that really catches his fancy: stereo broadcast reception. Later that day, Andy is a happy man as he sits in his easy chair, watching *No Doubt* on video. If he's going to be a couch potato, he's doing it in style . . .

Individual decision-making

A consumer purchase is a response to a problem, which in Andy's case is the perceived need for a new TV. His situation is similar to that encountered by consumers virtually every day of their lives. He realizes that he wants to make a purchase, and he goes through a series of steps in order to make it. These steps can be described as (1) problem recognition, (2) information search, (3) evaluation of alternatives, and (4) product choice. Of course, after the decision is made, the quality of that decision affects the final step in the process, when learning occurs based on how well the choice worked out. This learning process influences the likelihood that the same choice will be made the next time the need for a similar decision occurs.

An overview of this decision-making process is shown in Figure 8.1. The chapter begins by considering various approaches consumers use when faced with a purchase decision. It then focuses on three of the steps in the decision process: how consumers recognize the problem, or need for a product; their search for information about product choices; and the ways in which they evaluate alternatives to arrive at a decision. Chapter 9 considers influences in the actual purchase situation, as well as the person's satisfaction with the decision.

Since some purchase decisions are more important than others, the amount of effort we put into each differs. Sometimes the decision-making process is done almost automatically; we seem to make snap judgements based on very little information. At other times, reaching a purchase decision begins to resemble a full-time job. A person may spend literally days or weeks thinking about an important purchase such as a new home, even to the point of obsession.

Perspectives on decision-making

Traditionally, consumer researchers have approached decision-makers from a rational perspective. In this view, people calmly and carefully integrate as much information as possible with what they already know about a product, painstakingly weigh the pluses and minuses of each alternative, and arrive at a satisfactory decision. This process implies that steps in decision-making should be carefully studied by marketing managers in order to understand how information is obtained, how beliefs are formed, and what product choice criteria are specified by consumers. Products can then be developed that emphasize appropriate attributes, and promotional strategies can be tailored to deliver the types of information that are most likely to be desired in the most effective formats.[1]

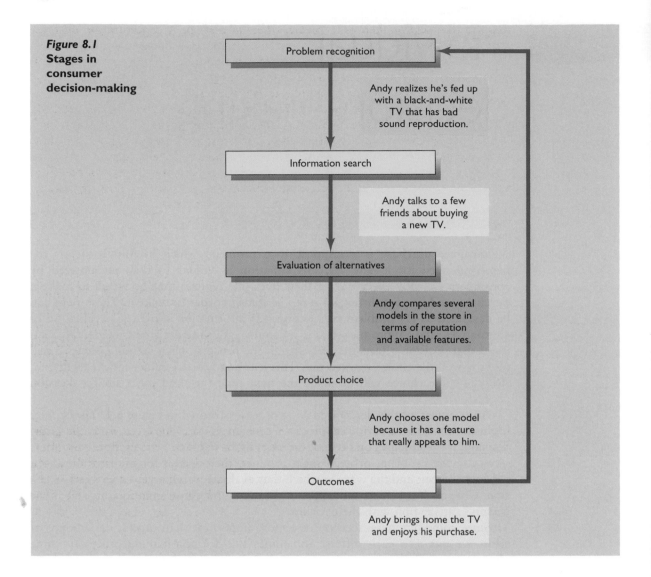

Figure 8.1 Stages in consumer decision-making

While the steps in decision-making are followed by consumers for some purchases, such a process is not an accurate portrayal of many purchase decisions.[2] Consumers simply do not go through this elaborate sequence for every decision. If they did, their entire lives would be spent making such decisions, leaving them very little time to enjoy the things they eventually decide to buy.

Researchers are now beginning to realize that decision-makers actually possess a repertoire of strategies. A consumer evaluates the effort required to make a particular choice, and then he or she chooses a strategy best suited to the level of effort required. This sequence of events is known as *constructive processing.* Rather than using a big club to swat a fly, consumers tailor their degree of cognitive 'effort' to the task at hand.[3]

Some decisions are made under conditions of low involvement, as discussed in chapter 4. In many of these situations, the consumer's decision is a learned response to environmental cues (see chapter 3), as when he or she decides to buy something on impulse that is promoted as a 'special offer' in a shop. A concentration on these types of decision can be described as the **behavioural influence perspective**. Under these circumstances, managers must concentrate on assessing the characteristics of the environment, such as the design of a retail outlet or whether a package is enticing, that influence members of a target market.[4]

In other cases, consumers are highly involved in a decision, but still the selections made cannot wholly be explained rationally. For example, the traditional approach is hard-pressed to explain a person's choice of art, music or even a spouse. In these cases, no single quality may be the determining factor. Instead, the **experiential perspective** stresses the gestalt, or totality, of the product or service. Marketers in these areas focus on measuring consumers' affective responses to products or services, and develop offerings that elicit appropriate subjective reactions.

Types of consumer decisions

One helpful way to characterize the decision-making process is to consider the amount of effort that goes into the decision each time it must be made. Consumer researchers have found it convenient to think in terms of a continuum, which is anchored on one end by **habitual decision-making** and at the other extreme by **extended problem-solving**. Many decisions fall somewhere in the middle and are characterized by **limited problem-solving**. This continuum is presented in Figure 8.2.

Extended problem-solving

Decisions involving extended problem-solving correspond most closely to the traditional decision-making perspective. As indicated in Table 8.1, the extended problem-solving process is usually initiated by a motive that is fairly central to the self-concept (see chapter 7), and the eventual decision is perceived to carry a fair degree of risk. The consumer tries to collect as much information as possible, both from memory (internal search) and from outside sources (external search). Based on

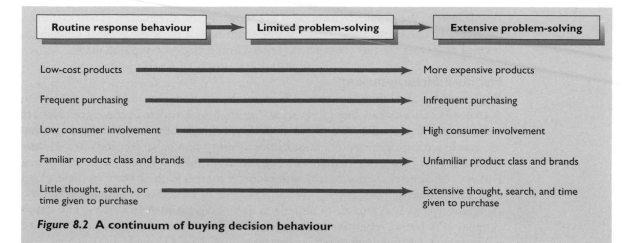

Figure 8.2 **A continuum of buying decision behaviour**

Table 8.1 **Characteristics of limited versus extended problem-solving**

	Limited problem-solving	*Extended problem-solving*
Motivation	Low risk and involvement	High risk and involvement
Information search	Little search	Extensive search
	Information processed passively	Information processed actively
	In-store decision likely	Multiple sources consulted prior to store visits
Alternative evaluation	Weakly held beliefs	Strongly held beliefs
	Only most prominent criteria used	Many criteria used
	Alternatives perceived as basically similar	Significant differences perceived among alternatives
	Non-compensatory strategy used	Compensatory strategy used
Purchase	Limited shopping time; may prefer self-service	Many outlets shopped if needed
	Choice often influenced by store displays	Communication with store personnel often desirable

the importance of the decision, each product alternative is carefully evaluated. The evaluation is often done by considering the attributes of one brand at a time and seeing how each brand's attributes shape up to some set of desired characteristics.

Limited problem-solving

Limited problem-solving is usually more straightforward and simple. Buyers are not as motivated to search for information or to evaluate each alternative rigorously. People instead use simple *decision rules* to choose among alternatives. These cognitive shortcuts (more about these later) enable them to fall back on general guidelines, instead of having to start from scratch every time a decision is to be made.

Habitual decision-making

Both extended and limited problem-solving modes involve some degree of information search and deliberation, though they vary in the degree to which these activities are undertaken. At the other end of the choice continuum, however, are decisions that are made with little or no conscious effort. Many purchase decisions are so routinized that we may not realize we've made them until we look in our shopping trolleys. Choices characterized by *automaticity* are performed with minimal effort and without conscious control.[5] While this kind of thoughtless activity may seem dangerous or at best stupid, it actually is quite efficient in many cases. The development of habitual, repetitive behaviour allows consumers to minimize the time and energy spent on mundane purchase decisions.

Problem recognition

Problem recognition occurs whenever the consumer sees a significant difference between his or her current state of affairs and some desired or ideal state. The consumer perceives there is a problem to be solved, which may be small or large, simple or complex. A person who unexpectedly runs out of petrol on the motorway has a problem, as does the person who becomes dissatisfied with the image of his or her car, even though there is nothing mechanically wrong with it. Although the quality of Andy's TV had not changed, for example, his *standard of comparison* had changed, and he was confronted with a need he did not have prior to watching his friend's TV.

Problem creation

Figure 8.3 shows that a problem can arise in one of two ways. As in the case of the person running out of petrol, the quality of the consumer's *actual state* can move downward (*need recognition*). On the other hand, as in the case of the person who craves a high-performance car, the consumer's *ideal state* can move upward (*opportunity recognition*). Either way, a gulf occurs between the actual state and the ideal state.[6] In Andy's case, a problem was perceived as a result of opportunity recognition; his ideal state in terms of television reception quality was altered.

Need recognition can occur in several ways. The quality of the person's actual state can be diminished simply by running out of a product, by buying a product that turns out not to satisfy needs adequately, or by creating new needs (e.g. buying a house can set off an avalanche of other choices, since many new things will be needed to furnish the house). Opportunity recognition often occurs when a consumer is exposed to different or better quality products. This shift often occurs because the person's circumstances have somehow changed, as when an individual goes to college or gets a new job. As the person's frame of reference shifts, purchases are made to adapt to the new environment.

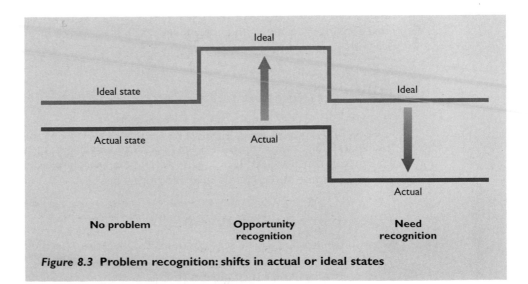

Figure 8.3 **Problem recognition: shifts in actual or ideal states**

Marketing pitfall

A common structure for advertisements has been to present a person who has a physical or social problem, and then 'miraculously' show how the product will resolve it. Some marketers have gone so far as to *invent* a problem and then offer a remedy for it. In the 1940s, for example, the Talon zipper was touted as a cure for 'gaposis', the horrifying condition that develops when puckers appear around the buttons on a woman's skirt. Listerine, a mouthwash, which was originally sold to fight dandruff, carried warnings about 'bottle bacillus', which caused 'infectious dandruff'. Geritol gave us a remedy for 'tired blood', and Wisk detergent drew our attention to the shame of 'ring around the collar'.[7]

Even when real problems are depicted in ads, the offered solutions are sometimes too simplistic, implying that the problem will disappear if the product is used. One analysis of over 1,000 television ads found that about 80 per cent suggest that the problem will be resolved within seconds or minutes after using the product. In addition, 75 per cent of the ads make definite claims that the product will solve the problem, and over 75 per cent imply that this solution is a one-step process – all the consumer needs to do is buy the product, and the problem will go away.[8] Consumers, however, are becoming more cynical and less susceptible to such claims. As many marketers are discovering, consumers of the 1990s are more receptive to realistic ads that provide solid information about the product. In addition, both the government and consumer groups are now taking a more active interest in product claims, and marketers are more cautious about the content of their ads.

Marketers' role in problem creation

While problem recognition can and does occur naturally, this process is often spurred by marketing efforts. In some cases, marketers attempt to create *primary demand*, where consumers are encouraged to use a product or service regardless of the brand they choose. Such needs are often encouraged in the early stages of a product's life cycle, as, for example, when microwave ovens were first introduced. *Secondary demand*, where consumers are prompted to prefer a specific brand to others, can occur only if primary demand already exists. At this point, marketers must convince consumers that a problem can best be solved by choosing their brand over others in a category.

Information search

Once a problem has been recognized, consumers need adequate information to resolve it. **Information search** is the process in which the consumer surveys his or her environment for appropriate data to make a reasonable decision. This section will review some of the factors involved in this search.

Types of information search

A consumer may explicitly search the marketplace for specific information after a need has been recognized (a process called *pre-purchase search*). On the other hand, many consumers, especially veteran shoppers, enjoy browsing just for the fun of it, or because they like to stay up-to-date on what's happening in the marketplace. They are engaging in *ongoing search.*[9] Some differences between these two search modes are described in Table 8.2.

Table 8.2 A framework for consumer information search

Pre-purchase search	Ongoing search
Determinants	
Involvement in the purchase	Involvement with the product
Market environment	Market environment
Situational factors	Situational factors
Motives	
Making of better purchase decisions	Building of a bank of information for future use
	Experiencing of fun and pleasure
Outcomes	
Increased product and market knowledge	Increased product and market knowledge leading to
Better purchase decisions	• future buying efficiencies
Increased satisfaction with the purchase outcome	• personal influence
	Increased impulse buying
	Increased satisfaction from search and other outcomes

Source: Peter H. Bloch, Daniel L. Sherrell and Nancy M. Ridgway, 'Consumer Search: An Extended Framework', *Journal of Consumer Research* 13 (June 1986): 120. Reprinted with permission by The University of Chicago Press.

This ad for Arm & Hammer demonstrates the strategy of identifying new problems an existing product can solve.
By permission of Church & Dwight Co., Inc.

Internal versus external search

Information sources can roughly be broken down into two kinds: internal and external. As a result of prior experience and simply living in a consumer culture, each of us often has some degree of knowledge about many products already in memory. When confronted with a purchase decision, we may engage in *internal search* by scanning our own memory banks to assemble information about different product alternatives (see chapter 3). Usually, though, even the most market-aware of us needs to supplement this knowledge with external search, where information is obtained from advertisements, friends, or just plain people-watching.

Deliberate versus 'accidental' search

Our existing knowledge of a product may be the result of *directed learning*, where on a previous occasion we had already searched for relevant information or experienced some of the alternatives. A parent who bought a birthday cake for one child last month, for example, probably has a good idea of the best kind to buy for another child this month.

Alternatively, we may have acquired information in a more passive manner. Even though a product may not be of interest, exposure to advertising, packaging and sales promotion activities may result in *incidental learning*. Mere exposure over time to conditioned stimuli and observations of others results in the learning of much material which may not be needed for some time after the fact, if ever. For marketers, this result is a benefit of steady, 'low-dose' advertising, since product associations are established and maintained until the time they are needed.[10]

In some cases, we may be so expert about a product category (or at least believe we are) that no additional search is undertaken. Frequently, however, our existing state of knowledge is not satisfactory to make an adequate decision, and we must look elsewhere for more information. The sources we consult for advice vary: they may be impersonal and marketer-dominated sources, such as retailers and catalogues; they may be friends and family members; or they may be unbiased third parties such as *Which?* magazine or other consumer reports which are published in a number of European countries.[11]

Marketing opportunity	Advances in technology are helping to feed consumers' growing appetite for information about products and services. One in three American households and one in five European has a computer, and the number of households accessing the internet grows by millions each year. A survey by the research firm Find/SVP shows that consumers in developed market economies spend almost $500 per year on 'pure' information – papers, magazines, reference books, non-entertainment videos and online services.[12]

Ironically, the problem for many is too much information rather than too little. The World Wide Web is a victim of its own success – the volume of available information is staggering, and noise and congestion makes it hard to attract visitors and keep them coming back.

Now, the ability to *narrowcast* is promising to turn the net into a personalized broadcast system, where the user can obtain only the information he or she requests and not have to sift through all the rest. Programs called 'tuners' organize information into 'channels' and 'push delivery' gets it out to 'viewers' who have completed a profile specifying what they want – and providers are gambling that

Marketing opportunity *continued*

viewers will be willing to pay for this customized service. Retailers such as Lands' End and Tesco PLC are experimenting with direct marketing on-line and, via the internet, notifying subscribers of promotions and sending them order forms. By the year 2000 Webcasting is projected to generate a third of the $14 billion in net advertising, subscriptions and retail revenues. Major players developing push technology include America Online, Marimba (which can send programs and applets along with content), Microsoft, Netscape Constellation and Pointcast.[13]

The Adfinity software package illustrates one way push technology can simplify decision-making. When a surfer first visits a web site, he or she is asked for some basic facts in exchange for access to the site's content. Adfinity will connect with files on that user from participating company databases and send ads fine-tuned to his or her interests. For example, someone who has purchased golfing holiday packages in the past might be offered a discount at a golf course as an incentive to fly with a participating airline. Of course, a strategy that requires several corporations to pool their knowledge about customers can backfire, if consumers get scared away by the spectre of Big Brother and issues of privacy are not respected.[14] Push technology can be a two-edged sword which can cut the wrong way in the wrong hands.

The economics of information

The traditional decision-making perspective incorporates the *economics-of-information* approach to the search process; it assumes that consumers will gather as much data as is needed to make an informed decision. Consumers form expectations of the value of additional information and continue to search to the extent that the rewards of doing so (what economists call the *utility*) exceed the costs. This utilitarian assumption implies that the most valuable units of information will be collected first. Additional pieces will be absorbed only to the extent that they are seen as adding to what is already known.[15] In other words, people will put themselves out to collect as much information as possible, as long as the process of gathering it is not too onerous or time consuming.[16]

Do consumers always search rationally?

This assumption of rational search is not always supported. The amount of external search for most products is surprisingly small, even when additional information would most likely benefit the consumer. For example, lower-income shoppers, who have more to lose by making a bad purchase, actually search *less* prior to buying than do more affluent people.[17] Like our friend Andy, some consumers typically visit only one or two stores and rarely seek out unbiased information sources prior to making a purchase decision, especially when little time is available to do so.[18] This pattern is especially prevalent for decisions regarding durables like appliances or cars, even when these products represent significant investments. One study of Australian car buyers found that more than a third had made only one or two trips to inspect cars prior to buying one. Finally, there is some evidence that even having information available on the package does not necessarily mean that consumers make use of it. Environmentally friendly products in Finland are beginning to carry the Nordic Environmental Label to assist consumers in their choice for environmentally safe products. In a study which asked Finnish consumers to evaluate detergent and batteries choices, little use and little trust were given to the 'green label' on the packages, in spite of the positive attitudes that Finnish citizens have towards the environment. The results suggest that marketers have a long way to go in order to provide clear, easily comprehensible and unbiased information regarding 'green' products.[19]

This tendency to avoid external search is less prevalent when consumers consider the purchase of symbolic items, such as clothing. In those cases, not surprisingly, people tend to do a fair amount of external search, although most of it involves seeking the opinions of peers.[20] While the stakes may be lower financially, these self-expressive decisions may be seen as having dire social consequences if the wrong choice is made. The level of perceived risk, a concept to be discussed shortly, is high.

In addition, consumers often are observed to engage in *brand-switching*, even if their current brand satisfies their needs. For example, researchers for the British brewer Bass Export who were studying the American beer market discovered a consumer trend towards having a repertoire of 2–6 favourite brands, rather than sticking to just one. This preference for brand-switching led the firm to begin exporting their Tennent's 1885 lager to the US, positioning the brew as an alternative to young drinkers' usual favourite brands.[21]

Sometimes, it seems that people just like to try new things – they are interested in *variety seeking*, where the priority is to vary one's product experiences, perhaps as a form of stimulation or to reduce boredom. Variety seeking is especially likely to occur when people are in a good mood, or when there is relatively little stimulation elsewhere in their environment.[22] On the other hand, when the decision situation is ambiguous or when there is little information about competing brands, consumers tend to opt for the safe choice by selecting familiar brands and maintaining the status quo.

Brand familiarity influences confidence about a brand, which in turn affects purchase intention.[23] Still, the tendency of consumers to shift brand choices over time means that marketers can never relax in the belief that once they have won a customer, he or she is necessarily theirs forever.[24]

Biases in the decision-making process

Consider the following scenario: you've been given a free ticket to the finals of a world-class tennis tournament. At the last minute, a snowstorm makes getting to the stadium dangerous. Would you go? Now, assume the same final and snowstorm, but this time you have paid handsomely for the ticket. Would you go?

Analyses of people's responses to this situation and to others illustrate principles of *mental accounting*, where decisions are influenced by the way a problem is posed (called *framing*), and by whether it is put in terms of gains or losses.[25] For example, people are more likely to risk their personal safety in the storm if they paid for the tennis ticket. Only the most diehard fan would fail to recognize that this is an irrational choice, since the risk to the person is the same regardless of whether he or she got a great deal on the ticket. This decision-making bias is called the *sunk-cost fallacy* – having paid for something makes us reluctant to waste it.

Another bias is known as *loss aversion*. People place much more emphasis on loss as they do on gain. For example, for most people losing money is more unpleasant than gaining money is pleasant. *Prospect theory*, a descriptive model of choice, finds that utility is a function of gains and losses, and risk differs when the consumer faces options involving gains versus those involving losses.[26]

To illustrate this bias, consider the following. For each, would you take the safe bet or choose to gamble?

Option 1. You're given £30 and then offered a chance to flip a coin: Heads you win £9, tails you lose £9.
Option 2. You're given a choice of getting £30 outright or accepting a coin flip that will win you either £39 or £21.

In one study, 70 per cent of those given option 1 chose to gamble, compared to just 43 per cent of those offered option 2. Yet, the odds are the same for both options! The difference is that people prefer 'playing with the house money'; they are more willing to take risks when they perceive they're using someone else's resources. So, contrary to a rational decision-making perspective, we value money differently depending on its source. This explains why someone might choose to spend a big bonus on a frivolous purchase, while they would never consider taking that amount from their savings account for the same purpose.

Finally, research in mental accounting demonstrates that extraneous characteristics of the choice situation can influence our selections, even though they shouldn't if we were rational decision-makers. As one example, participants in a survey were provided with one of two versions of this scenario:

> You are lying on the beach on a hot day. All you have to drink is iced water. For the last hour you have been thinking about how much you would enjoy a nice cold bottle of your favourite brand of beer. A companion gets up to go and make a phone call and offers to bring back a beer from the only nearby place where beer is sold (either a smart hotel or a small, run-down grocery store, depending on the version you're given). He says that the beer might be expensive and so asks how much you are willing to pay for it. What price do you tell him?

In this survey, the median price given by participants who were in the 'smart hotel' version was the equivalent of $2.65, while those given the cheaper 'grocery store version' were only willing to pay $1.50! In both versions the consumption act is the same, the beer is the same and no 'atmosphere' is consumed since the beer is being brought back to the beach.[27] So much for rational decision-making!

How much search occurs?

As a general rule, search activity is greater when the purchase is important, when there is a need to learn more about the purchase and/or when the relevant information is easily obtained and utilized.[28]

Consumers differ in the amount of search they tend to undertake, regardless of the product category in question. All things being equal, younger, better-educated people who enjoy the shopping/fact-finding process tend to conduct more information search. Women are more inclined to search than men, as are those who place greater value on style and the image they present.[29]

The consumer's prior expertise
Should prior product knowledge make it more or less likely that consumers will engage in search? Product experts and novices use very different procedures during decision-making. Novices who know little about a product should be the most motivated to find out more about it. However, experts are more familiar with the product category, so they should be able to understand better the meaning of any new product information they might acquire.

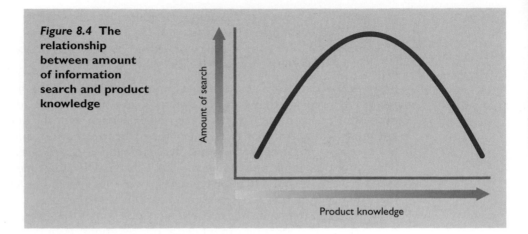

Figure 8.4 **The relationship between amount of information search and product knowledge**

So, who searches more? The answer is neither: search tends to be greatest among those consumers who are *moderately* knowledgeable about the product. There is an inverted-U relationship between knowledge and external search effort, as shown in Figure 8.4. People with very limited expertise may not feel they are capable of searching extensively. In fact, they may not even know where to start. Andy, who did not spend a lot of time researching his purchase, is representative of this situation. He visited one store, and he only looked at brands with which he was already familiar. In addition, he focused on only a small number of product features.[30]

The *type* of search undertaken by people with varying levels of expertise differs as well. Because experts have a better sense of what information is relevant to the decision, they tend to engage in *selective search*, which means their efforts are more focused and efficient. In contrast, novices are more likely to rely on the opinions of others and to rely on 'non-functional' attributes, such as brand name and price, to distinguish among alternatives. They may also process information in a 'top-down' rather than a 'bottom-up' manner, focusing less on details than on the big picture. For instance, they may be more impressed by the sheer amount of technical information presented in an ad than by the actual significance of the claims made.[31]

Perceived risk

As a rule, purchase decisions that involve extensive search also entail some kind of perceived risk, or the belief that the product has potentially negative consequences. Perceived risk may be present if the product is expensive or is complex and difficult to understand. Alternatively, perceived risk can be a factor when a product choice is visible to others, and we run the risk of embarrassment if the wrong choice is made.

Figure 8.5 lists five basic kinds of risk – including both objective (e.g. physical danger) and subjective factors (e.g. social embarrassment) – as well as the products that tend to be affected by each type. As this figure notes, consumers with greater 'risk capital' are less affected by perceived risks associated with the products. For example, a highly self-confident person would be less worried about the social risk inherent in a product, while a more vulnerable, insecure consumer might be reluctant to take a chance on a product that might not be accepted by peers.

Minolta features a No-Risk Guarantee as a way of reducing the perceived risk in buying an office copier.
Courtesy of Minolta Corporation.

Figure 8.5
Five types of perceived risk

	Buyers most sensitive to risk	Purchases most subject to risk
Monetary risk	Risk capital consists of money and property. Those with relatively little income and wealth are most vulnerable.	High-price items that require substantial expenditures are most subject to this form of risk.
Functional risk	Risk capital consists of alternate means of performing the function or meeting the need. Practical consumers are most sensitive.	Products or services whose purchase and use requires the buyer's exclusive commitment and precludes redundancy are most sensitive.
Physical risk	Risk capital consists of physical vigour, health and vitality. Those who are elderly, frail, or in ill health are most vulnerable.	Mechanical or electrical goods (such as vehicles or flammables), drugs and medical treatment, and food and beverages are most sensitive.
Social risk	Risk capital consists of self-esteem and self-confidence. Those who are insecure and uncertain are most sensitive.	Socially visible or symbolic goods, such as clothes, jewellery, cars, homes, or sports equipment are most subject to it.
Psychological risk	Risk capital consists of affiliations and status. Those lacking self-respect or attractiveness to peers are most sensitive.	Expensive personal luxuries that may engender guilt; durables; and services whose use demands self-discipline or sacrifice are most sensitive.

Marketing opportunity

The spread of the HIV virus has created a boom in home-testing kits which encourage people to find out if they have been infected in a less threatening environment than a clinic or a doctor's surgery. The typical kit allows the consumer to send a blood sample to a testing lab, and results are returned in 3–7 days. While high-risk groups such as adolescents and gay men are most likely to need the kits, some speculate that sales will come primarily from the 'worried well', those who are less likely to be infected in the first place. Companies are taking different approaches, ranging from humorous to provocative to serious, as they try to find the best way to reach people who are unlikely to go to a clinic to be tested. In one ad for *Home Access*, the copy (targeted at young straight males) reads: 'Nothing arouses a woman like knowing you're responsible'.[32]

Evaluation of alternatives

Much of the effort that goes into a purchase decision occurs at the stage where a choice must be made from the available alternatives. After all, modern consumer society abounds with choice. In some cases, there may be dozens of different brands (as in cigarettes) or different variations of the same brand (as in shades of lipstick), each clamouring for our attention.

Just for fun, ask a friend to name all the brands of perfume she can think of. The odds are she will reel off three to five names quickly, then pause before coming up with a few more. It is likely that the first set of brands are those with which she is highly familiar, and she probably wears one or more of these. The list may also contain one or two brands that she does not like and would perhaps like to forget. Note also that there are many, many more brands on the market she did not name at all.

If your friend were to go to a shop to buy perfume, she would probably consider buying some or most of the brands she listed initially. She might also consider a few more if these were forcefully brought to her attention while in the shop – for example,

Focusing on reduction of monetary, functional and social risk, Volkswagen introduces the Passat as a car for the 1990s. Used with permission.

if she is approached by an employee who is spraying scent samples on shoppers, which is a common occurrence in some department stores.

Identifying alternatives

How do we decide which criteria are important, and how do we narrow down product alternatives to an acceptable number and eventually choose one in preference to the others? The answer varies depending upon the decision-making process used. A consumer engaged in extended problem-solving may carefully evaluate several brands, while someone making a habitual decision may not consider any alternatives to their normal brand. Some evidence indicates that more extended processing occurs in situations where negative emotions are aroused due to conflicts among the choices available.[33]

The alternatives actively considered during a consumer's choice process are his or her **evoked set**. The evoked set is composed of those products already in memory (the retrieval set), plus those prominent in the retail environment. For example, recall that Andy did not know much about the technical aspects of television sets and had only a few major brands in memory. Of these, two were acceptable possibilities and one was not. The alternatives that the consumer is aware of but would not consider buying are his or her _inept set,_ while those not under consideration at all comprise the _inert set._ You can easily guess in which set a marketer wants its brand to appear! These categories are depicted in Figure 8.6.

Consumers often include a surprisingly small number of alternatives in their evoked set. One study combined results from several large-scale investigations of consumers' evoked sets and found that the number of products included in these sets is limited, although there are some marked variations by product category and across countries. For example, the average evoked set size for American beer consumers was one or two, while Canadian consumers typically considered seven brands. In contrast, while car buyers in Norway studied two alternatives, American consumers on average looked at more than eight models before making a decision.[34]

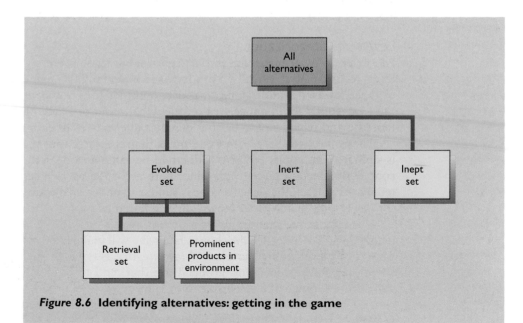

Figure 8.6 **Identifying alternatives: getting in the game**

For obvious reasons, a marketer who finds that her or his brand is not in the evoked set of a target market has cause to worry. A product is not likely to be placed in the evoked set after it has previously been considered and rejected. Indeed, a new brand is more likely to be added to the evoked set than is an existing brand that was previously considered but passed over, even after additional positive information has been provided for that brand.[35] For marketers, this unwillingness to give a rejected product a second chance underscores the importance of ensuring that it performs well from the time it is introduced.

Product categorization

Remember that when consumers process product information, they do not do so in a vacuum. Instead, a product stimulus is evaluated in terms of what people already know about a product or those things to which it is similar. A person evaluating a particular 35 mm camera will most likely compare it to other 35 mm cameras rather than to a Polaroid camera, and the consumer would certainly not compare it to a slide projector or VCR. Since the category in which a product is placed determines the other products it will be compared to, *categorization* is a crucial determinant of how a product is evaluated.

The products in a consumer's evoked set are likely to be those that share similar features. It is important to understand how this knowledge is represented in a consumer's **cognitive structure**, which refers to a set of factual knowledge about products (i.e. beliefs) and the way these beliefs are organized in people's minds.[36] These knowledge structures were discussed in chapter 4. One reason is that marketers want to ensure that their products are correctly grouped. For example, General Foods brought out a new line of Jell-O flavours such as Cranberry Orange which it called 'Jell-O Gelatin Flavors for Salads'. Unfortunately, the company discovered that people would use it only for salad since the name encouraged them to put the product in their 'salad' structure rather than in their 'dessert' structure. The line had to be dropped.[37]

Levels of categorization

People not only group things into categories, but these groupings occur at different levels of specificity. Typically, a product is represented in a cognitive structure at one of three levels. To understand this idea, consider how someone might respond to these questions about an ice cream cone: what other products share similar characteristics, and which would be considered as alternatives to eating a cone?

These questions may be more complex than they first appear. At one level, a cone is similar to an apple, because both could be eaten as a dessert. At another level, a cone is similar to a piece of pie, since both are eaten as a dessert and both are fattening. At still another level, a cone is similar to an ice cream sundae. Both are eaten for dessert, are made of ice cream and are fattening.

It is easy to see that the items a person associates with – say, the category 'fattening dessert' – influence the choices he or she will make for what to eat after dinner. The middle level, known as a *basic level category*, is typically the most useful in classifying products, since items grouped together tend to have a lot in common, but still permit a range of alternatives to be considered. The broader *superordinate category* is more abstract, while the more specific *subordinate category* often includes individual brands.[38] These three levels are depicted in Figure 8.7.

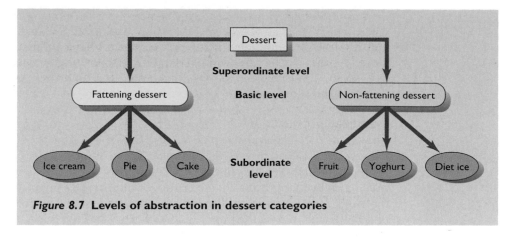

Figure 8.7 **Levels of abstraction in dessert categories**

Of course, not all items fit equally well into a category. Apple pie is a better example of the subordinate category 'pie' than is rhubarb pie, even though both are types of pie. Apple pie is thus more *prototypical*, and would tend to be considered first, especially by category novices. In contrast, pie experts will tend to have knowledge about both typical and atypical category examples.[39]

Strategic implications of product categorization

Product categorization has many strategic implications. The way a product is grouped with others has very important ramifications for determining both its competitors for adoption and what criteria will be used to make this choice.

Product positioning

The success of a *positioning strategy* often hinges on the marketer's ability to convince the consumer that his or her product should be considered within a given category. For example, the orange juice industry tried to reposition orange juice as a drink that could be enjoyed all day long ('It's not just for breakfast anymore'). On the other hand, soft drink companies are now attempting the opposite by portraying carbonated drinks as suitable for breakfast consumption. They are trying to make their way into consumers' 'breakfast drink' category, along with orange juice, grapefruit juice and coffee. Of course, this strategy can backfire, as Pepsi-Cola discovered when it introduced Pepsi A.M. and positioned it as a coffee substitute. The company did such a good job of categorizing the drink as a morning beverage that consumers wouldn't drink it at any other time and the product failed.[40]

Identifying competitors

At the abstract, superordinate level, many different product forms compete for membership. Both bowling and the ballet may be considered as subcategories of 'entertainment' by some people, but many would not necessarily consider the substitution of one of these activities for the other. Products and services that on the surface are quite different, however, actually compete with each other at a broad level for consumers' discretionary money. While football or ballet may not be a likely tradeoff for many people, it is feasible, for example, that a symphony might try to lure season ticketholders to the ballet by positioning itself as an equivalent member of the category 'cultural event'.[41]

Consumers often are faced with choices between non-comparable categories, where a number of attributes exist that cannot be directly related to one another (the old problem of comparing apples and oranges). The comparison process is easier when consumers can derive an overlapping category that encompasses both items (e.g. entertainment, value, usefulness) and then rate each alternative in terms of that superordinate category.[42]

Exemplar products

As we saw with the case of apple versus rhubarb pie, if a product is a really good example of a category it is more familiar to consumers, and is more easily recognized and recalled.[43] Judgements about category attributes tend to be disproportionately influenced by the characteristics of category exemplars.[44] In a sense, brands that are strongly associated with a category 'call the shots' by defining the evaluative criteria that should be used to evaluate all category members.

Being a bit less than prototypical is not necessarily a bad thing, however. Products that are moderately unusual within their product category may stimulate more information-processing and positive evaluations, since they are neither so familiar that they will be taken for granted nor so discrepant that they will be dismissed.[45] A brand that is strongly discrepant may occupy a unique niche position, while those that are moderately discrepant remain in a distinct position within the general category.[46]

Locating products

Product categorization may affect consumers' expectations regarding the places they can locate a desired product. If products do not clearly fit into categories (e.g. is a *carpet* furniture?), consumers' ability to find them or make sense of them may be diminished. For instance, a frozen dog food that had to be thawed and cooked failed in the market, partly because people could not adapt to the idea of buying dog food in the 'frozen foods for people' section of their supermarket.

Product choice: selecting among alternatives

Once the relevant options from a category have been assembled and evaluated, a choice must be made among them.[47] Recall that the decision rules guiding choice can range from very simple and quick strategies to complicated processes requiring a lot of attention and cognitive processing. The choice can be influenced by integrating information from such sources as prior experience with the product, information present at the time of purchase and beliefs about the brands that have been created by advertising.[48]

Evaluative criteria

When Andy was looking at different television sets, he focused on one or two product features while completely ignoring several others. He narrowed down his choice by considering only two specific brand names, and from the Prime Wave and Precision models he chose one that had a stereo capability.

Evaluative criteria are the dimensions used to judge the merits of competing options. In comparing alternative products, Andy could have chosen from among any number of criteria, ranging from very functional attributes ('does this TV come with remote control?') to experiential ones ('does this TV's sound reproduction make me imagine I'm in a concert hall?').

Claiming the product is 'full of strength', this ad for Pucko, a Swedish chocolate drink, emphasizes an evaluation criterion based on nutritional value, whereas American consumers might evaluate a similar product based on taste or calorie content.
Photographer Kurt Wass. Courtesy of Forsman and BodenFors.

Another important point is that criteria on which products *differ* from one another carry more weight in the decision process than do those where the alternatives are *similar*. If all brands being considered rate equally well on one attribute (e.g. if all TVs come with remote control), consumers will have to find other reasons to choose one over another. The attributes actually used to differentiate among choices are *determinant attributes*.

Marketers can play a role in educating consumers about which criteria should be used as determinant attributes. For example, consumer research indicated that many consumers view the use of natural ingredients as a determinant attribute. The result was promotion of a toothpaste made from baking soda, which the company already manufactured for its Arm & Hammer brand.[49]

The decision about which attributes to use is the result of *procedural learning*, where a person undergoes a series of cognitive steps before making a choice. These steps include identifying important attributes, remembering whether competing brands differ on those attributes, and so on. In order for a marketer to recommend a new decision criterion effectively, his or her communication should convey three pieces of information:[50]

1. It should point out that there are significant differences among brands on the attribute.
2. It should supply the consumer with a decision making rule, such as *if* (deciding among competing brands), *then* . . . (use the attribute as a criterion).
3. It should convey a rule that can be easily integrated with how the person has made this decision in the past. Otherwise, the recommendation is likely to be ignored, since it requires too much mental work.

Heuristics: mental shortcuts

Do we actually perform complex mental calculations every time we make a purchase decision? Of course not! To simplify decisions, consumers often employ decision rules that allow them to use some dimensions as substitutes for others. For example, Andy relied on certain assumptions as substitutes for prolonged information search.

In particular, he assumed the selection at The London Appliance Emporium would be more than sufficient, so he did not bother to investigate any of Emporium's competitors. This assumption served as a shortcut to more extended information processing.[51]

Especially where limited problem-solving occurs prior to making a choice, consumers often fall back on **heuristics**, or mental rules-of-thumb, that lead to a speedy decision. These rules range from the very general (e.g. 'Higher priced products are higher quality products' or 'Buy the same brand I bought last time') to the very specific (e.g. 'Buy Silver Spoon, the brand of sugar my mother always bought').[52]

Sometimes these shortcuts may not be in consumers' best interests. A consumer who personally knows one or two people who have had problems with a particular make of car might assume he or she would have similar trouble with it and thus overlook the model's overall excellent repair record.[53] The influence of such assumptions may be enhanced if the product has an unusual name, which makes it *and* the experiences with it more distinctive.[54]

Relying on a product signal

One frequently used shortcut is the tendency to infer hidden dimensions of products from observable attributes. The aspect of the product that is visible acts as a *signal* of some underlying quality. Such inferences explain why someone trying to sell a used car takes great pains to be sure the car's exterior is clean and shiny: potential buyers often judge the vehicle's mechanical condition by its appearance, even though this means they may drive away in a shiny, clean death trap.[55]

When product information is incomplete, judgements often are derived from beliefs about *covariation*, or perceived associations among events which may or may not actually influence one another.[56] For example, a consumer may form an association between product quality and the length of time a manufacturer has been in business. Other signals or attributes believed to coexist with good or bad products include well-known brand names, country of origin, price and the retail outlets that carry the product.

Unfortunately, consumers tend to be poor estimators of covariation. Their beliefs persist despite evidence to the contrary. Similar to the consistency principle discussed in chapter 5, people tend to see what they are looking for. They will look for product information that confirms their guesses. In one experiment, consumers sampled four sets of products to determine if price and quality were related. Those who believed in this relationship prior to the study elected to sample higher-priced products, thus creating a sort of self-fulfilling prophecy.[57]

Market beliefs: is it better if I have to pay more for it?

Consumers often form assumptions about companies, products and shops. These **market beliefs** then become the shortcuts that guide their decisions – whether or not they are accurate.[58] Recall, for instance, that Andy chose to shop at a large 'electronics supermarket' because he *assumed* the selection would be better than if he went to a specialized shop. A large number of market beliefs have been identified. Some of these are listed in Table 8.3. How many do you share?

Do higher prices mean higher quality? The assumption of a *price–quality relationship* is one of the most pervasive market beliefs.[59] Novice consumers may in fact consider price as the *only* relevant product attribute. Experts also consider this information, although in these cases price tends to be used for its informational value, especially for products (e.g. pure new wool) that are known to have wide quality variations in the marketplace. When this quality level is more standard or strictly

Table 8.3 Common market beliefs

Brand	All brands are basically the same.
	Generic products are just name brands sold under a different label at a lower price.
	The best brands are the ones that are purchased the most.
	When in doubt, a national brand is always a safe bet.
Store	Specialized shops are good places to familiarize yourself with the best brands; but once you know what you want, it's cheaper to buy it at a discount outlet.
	A store's character is reflected in its window displays.
	Sales people in specialized shops are more knowledgeable than other sales personnel.
	Larger stores offer better prices than small stores.
	Locally owned stores give the best service.
	A store that offers a good value on one of its products probably offers good values on all of its items.
	Credit and return policies are most lenient at large department stores.
	Stores that have just opened usually charge attractive prices.
Prices/Discounts/Sales	Sales are typically run to get rid of slow-moving merchandise.
	Stores that are constantly having sales don't really save you money.
	Within a given store, higher prices generally indicate higher quality.
Advertising and sales promotion	'Hard-sell' advertising is associated with low-quality products.
	Items tied to 'giveaways' are not a good value (even with the freebie).
	Coupons represent real savings for customers because they are not offered by the store.
	When you buy heavily advertised products, you are paying for the label, not for higher quality.
Product/Packaging	Largest-sized containers are almost always cheaper per unit than smaller sizes.
	New products are more expensive when they're first introduced; prices tend to settle down as time goes by.
	When you are not sure what you need in a product, it's a good idea to invest in the extra features, because you'll probably wish you had them later.
	In general, synthetic goods are lower in quality than goods made of natural materials.
	It's advisable to stay away from products when they are new to the market; it usually takes the manufacturer a little time to work the bugs out.

Source: Adapted from Calvin P. Duncan, 'Consumer Market Beliefs: A Review of the Literature and an Agenda for Future Research', in Marvin E. Goldberg, Gerald Gorn and Richard W. Pollay (eds.), *Advances in Consumer Research* 17 (Provo, UT: Association for Consumer Research, 1990): 729–35.

regulated (e.g. Harris Tweed sportsjackets), experts do not weigh price in their decisions. For the most part, this belief is justified; you do tend to get what you pay for. However, let the buyer beware: The price–quality relationship is not always justified.[60]

Country of origin as a product signal

Modern consumers choose among products made in many countries. European consumers may buy Italian or Brazilian shoes, Japanese cars, clothing imported from Taiwan or microwave ovens built in South Korea. Consumers' reactions to these imports are mixed. In some cases, people have come to assume that a product made overseas is of better quality (e.g. cameras, cars), while in other cases the knowledge that a product has been imported tends to lower perceptions of product quality (e.g. apparel).[61] In general, people tend to rate their own country's products more favourably than do foreigners, and products from industrialized countries are better rated than are those from developing countries.

As briefly discussed in chapter 6 on persuasive communication, a product's *country of origin* in some cases is an important piece of information in the decision-making process.[62] Of course, the extent to which this is a factor depends on the product category. In a recent Gallup Poll of American consumers, only 3 per cent of respondents felt that this information is important when they buy shoes and only 7 per cent relied on it for toy purchases, but 51 per cent said country of origin is a key factor when they buy clothing, and 54 per cent agreed that a car's country of origin is important.[63]

A product's origin, then, often is used as a signal of quality. Certain items are strongly associated with specific countries, and products from those countries often attempt to benefit from these linkages. Country of origin can function as a *stereotype* – a knowledge structure based on inferences across products. These stereotypes may be biased or inaccurate, but they do play a constructive role in simplifying complex choice situations.[64] For example, a Brazilian soft drink company is now trying to market a beverage it is calling Samba in the US. Samba is made from the guaraná berry; this sweet, flowery-tasting soft drink is extremely popular in Brazil. The company is capitalizing on the care-free, partying image that many Americans have of Brazilians to get them to try it. In its commercials, a scantily-clad woman says, 'In Brazil we do things a little differently. We laugh a little more, wear a little less and dance the samba. Dance the dance. Drink the drink.'[65]

Recent evidence indicates that learning of a product's country of origin is not necessarily good or bad. Instead, it has the effect of stimulating the consumer's interest in the product to a greater degree. The purchaser thinks more extensively about the product and evaluates it more carefully.[66] The origin of the product thus can act as a product attribute which combines with other attributes to influence evaluations.[67] In addition, the consumer's own expertise with the product category moderates the effects of this attribute. When other information is available, experts tend to ignore country of origin information while novices continue to rely upon it. However, when other information is unavailable or ambiguous, both experts and novices will rely on this attribute to make a decision.[68]

Multicultural dimensions

Japanese consumers have a strong interest in European and American products, and other countries work hard to cultivate a favourable image in the discriminating Japanese market. Dentsu, the largest Japanese advertising agency, has conducted several studies for the Commission of the European Communities to determine how Japanese consumers perceive European countries, the US and some Asian countries, and how they evaluate products from those countries.

The study, involved personal interviews with 1,600 consumers ranging in age from 15 to 59. Respondents rated countries on such overall dimensions as 'rich in history/tradition', 'abundant natural scenery', and 'would like to visit', as well as on

Multicultural dimensions *continued*

product-related characteristics, such as 'high-quality, performance products' and 'well-designed, stylish products'. The results showed that the Japanese public associates Europe with history, tradition and well-designed products, while American advanced technology and agriculture are highly rated (products from South Korea and Taiwan tended to be rated lower than those from the US or Europe).

Overall, respondents told the researchers that foreign products (i.e. non-Japanese) are well regarded in terms of style, but are assumed to be lower in technological sophistication than most Japanese products. There was also widespread sentiment that many non-Japanese products are not well suited to Japanese needs. These consumers felt that many foreign goods are too expensive and need more thorough after-sales service.

A perceptual map (these were described in chapter 2) summarizing Japanese consumers' images of European countries and the US is shown in Figure 8.8. The five countries in Group 1 have the most 'image wealth'; they are strong in both overall appeal and in ratings of product quality. Germany is the sole country in Group 2, indicating that its products are better regarded than is the country as a whole. The countries in Group 3 have positive images, but have yet to transfer these good feelings to their products. Finally, the countries in Group 4 appear to have their work cut out if they hope to win over the hearts and wallets of Japanese consumers.[69]

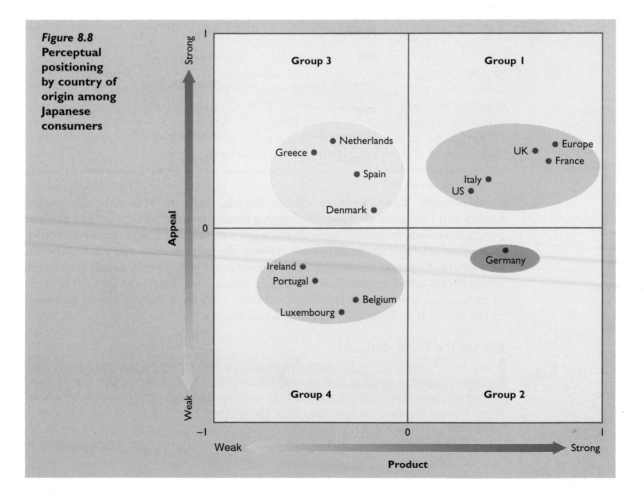

Figure 8.8 Perceptual positioning by country of origin among Japanese consumers

Choosing familiar brand names: loyalty or habit?

Branding is a marketing strategy which often functions as a heuristic. People form preferences for a favourite brand, and then they literally may never change their minds in the course of a lifetime. In a study of the market leaders in 30 product categories by the Boston Consulting Group, it was found that 27 of the brands that were number one in 1930 remain at the top today. These include such perennial American favourites as Ivory Soap, Campbell's Soup and Gold Medal Flour.[70]

A brand that exhibits that kind of staying power is treasured by marketers, and for good reason. Brands that dominate their markets are as much as 50 per cent more profitable than their nearest competitors.[71] A survey on brand power in Asia, Australia, South Africa, Europe and the US calculated brand scores to produce the following list of the most positively regarded brand names around the world.[72]

	1990	1996
1.	Coca-Cola	McDonald's
2.	Kellogg's	Coca-Cola
3.	McDonald's	Disney
4.	Kodak	Kodak
5.	Marlboro	Sony
6.	IBM	Gillette
7.	American Express	Mercedes-Benz
8.	Sony	Levi's
9.	Mercedes-Benz	Microsoft
10.	Nescafé	Marlboro

Consumers' attachments to certain brands, such as Marlboro, Coca-Cola, Gerber and Levi's, are so powerful that this loyalty is often considered as a positive product attribute in and of itself. Brand equity actually can be quantified in terms of *goodwill*, defined as the difference between the market value and the book value of a brand. Recently, the British company Grand Metropolitan decided to record brand names it had acquired on its balance sheets, including these intangible assets in its financial reports to shareholders.[73] Marlboro is the most valuable brand name in the world. It was recently valued at $31.2 billion.[74]

Inertia: the fickle customer

Many people tend to buy the same brand almost every time they go to a shop. This consistent pattern often is due to inertia, where a brand is bought out of habit merely because less effort is required. If another product is introduced which for some reason is easier to buy (e.g. it is cheaper, or the original product is out of stock), the consumer will not hesitate to do so. A competitor who is trying to change a buying pattern based on inertia can do so quite easily, because little resistance to brand-switching will be encountered if the right incentive is offered. Since there is little or no underlying commitment to the product, such promotional tools as point-of-purchase displays, extensive couponing or noticeable price reductions may be sufficient to 'unfreeze' a consumer's habitual pattern.

Brand loyalty: a 'friend', tried-and-true

This kind of fickleness will not occur if true brand loyalty exists. In contrast to inertia, brand loyalty is a form of repeat purchasing behaviour reflecting a *conscious* decision to continue buying the same brand.[75] For brand loyalty to exist, a pattern of repeat purchase must be accompanied by an underlying positive attitude towards the brand. Brand loyalty may be initiated by customer preference based on objective reasons, but after the brand has existed for a long time and is heavily advertised it can also create an emotional attachment, either by being incorporated into the consumer's self-image or because it is associated with prior experiences.[76] Purchase decisions based on brand loyalty also become habitual over time, though in these cases the underlying commitment to the product is much firmer.

Compared to inertia where the consumer passively accepts a brand, a brand-loyal consumer is actively (sometimes passionately) involved with his or her favourite. Because of the emotional bonds that can be created between brand-loyal consumers and products, 'true-blue' users react more vehemently when these products are altered, redesigned or withdrawn.[77] Recall, for example, the national call-in campaigns, boycotts and other protests when Coca-Cola replaced its tried-and-true formula with New Coke.

In recent years, marketers have struggled with the problem of *brand parity*, which refers to consumers' beliefs that there are no significant differences among brands. For example, one survey found that more than 70 per cent of consumers worldwide believe that all paper towels, soaps and crisps are alike.[78] Some analysts even proclaimed that brand names are dead, killed off by own-label or generic products which offer the same value for less money.

However, the reports of this death appear to be premature – major brands are making a comeback. This renaissance is attributed to information overload – with too many alternatives (many of them unfamiliar names) to choose from, people are looking for a few clear signals of quality. Following a period in the late 1980s and early 1990s when people had strong doubts about the ability of large companies to produce quality products, more recent surveys indicate consumers slowly are beginning to trust major manufacturers again.[79] Brand names are very much alive.

Decision rules

Consumers consider sets of product attributes by using different rules, depending upon the complexity of the decision and the importance of the decision to them. As we have seen, in some cases these rules are quite simple: people simply rely on a 'shortcut' to make a choice. In other cases, though, more effort and thought is put into carefully weighing alternatives before coming to a decision.

One way to differentiate among decision rules is to divide them into those that are *compensatory* versus those that are *non-compensatory*. To aid the discussion of some of these rules, the attributes of TV sets considered by Andy are summarized in Table 8.4. Now, let's see how some of these rules result in different brand choices.

Table 8.4 **Hypothetical alternatives for a television set**

Attribute	Importance ranking	Prime wave	Brand ratings Precision	Kamashita
Size of screen	1	Excellent	Excellent	Excellent
Stereo broadcast capability	2	Poor	Excellent	Good
Brand reputation	3	Excellent	Excellent	Poor
On-screen programming	4	Excellent	Poor	Poor
Cable-ready capability	5	Good	Good	Good
Sleep timer	6	Excellent	Poor	Good

 ## Non-compensatory decision rules

Simple decision rules are non-compensatory, meaning that a product with a low standing on one attribute cannot make up for this position by being better on another. In other words, people simply eliminate all options that do not meet some basic standards. A consumer like Andy who uses the decision rule 'Only buy well-known brand names' would not consider a new brand, even if it was equal or superior to existing ones. When people are less familiar with a product category or are not very motivated to process complex information, they tend to use simple, non-compensatory rules, which are summarized below:[80]

When the *lexicographic rule* is used, the brand that is the best on the most important attribute is selected. If two or more brands are seen as being equally good on that attribute, the consumer then compares them on the second most important attribute. This selection process goes on until the tie is broken. In Andy's case, since both the Prime Wave and Precision models were tied on his most important attribute (a 52 cm screen), the Precision was chosen because of its rating on this second most important attribute – its stereo capability.

Using the *elimination-by-aspects rule*, brands also are evaluated on the most important attribute. In this case, though, specific cutoffs are imposed. For example, if Andy had been more interested in having a sleep timer on his TV (i.e. if it had a higher importance ranking), he might have stipulated that his choice 'must have a sleep timer'. Since the Prime Wave model had one and the Precision did not, the Prime Wave would have been chosen.

While the two former rules involve processing by attribute, the *conjunctive rule* entails processing by brand. As with the elimination-by-aspects procedure, cutoffs are established for each attribute. A brand is chosen if it meets all the cutoffs, while failure to meet any one cutoff means it will be rejected. If none of the brands meets all the cutoffs, the choice may be delayed, the decision rule may be changed or the cutoffs may be modified.

If Andy had stipulated that all attributes had to be rated 'good' or better, he would not have been able to choose any of the options. He might then have modified his decision rule, conceding that it was not possible to attain these high standards in the price range he was considering. In this case, Andy might have decided that he could live without on-screen programming, so the Precision model could again be considered.

Compensatory decision rules

Unlike non-compensatory decision rules, **compensatory decision rules** give a product a chance to make up for its shortcomings. Consumers who employ these rules tend to be more involved in the purchase, and thus are willing to exert the effort to consider the entire picture in a more exacting way. The willingness to off-set good product qualities against bad ones can result in quite different choices. For example, if Andy were not concerned about having stereo reception, he might have chosen the Prime Wave model. But because this brand did not feature this highly ranked attribute, it doesn't stand a chance when he uses a non-compensatory rule.

Two basic types of compensatory rules have been identified. When using the *simple additive rule*, the consumer merely chooses the alternative having the largest number of positive attributes. This choice is most likely to occur when his or her ability or motivation to process information is limited. One drawback to this approach for the consumer is that some of these attributes may not be very meaningful or important. An ad containing a long list of product benefits may be persuasive, despite the fact that many of the benefits included actually are standard within the product class and aren't determinant attributes at all.

The more complex version is known as the *weighted additive rule*.[81] When using this rule, the consumer also takes into account the relative importance of positively rated attributes, essentially multiplying brand ratings by importance weights. If this process sounds familiar, it should. The calculation process strongly resembles the multiattribute attitude model described in chapter 5.

Chapter summary

- Consumers are faced with the need to make decisions about products all the time. Some of these decisions are very important and entail great effort, while others are made more or less automatically.
- Perspectives on decision-making range from a focus on habits that people develop over time to novel situations involving a great deal of risk, where consumers must carefully collect and analyze information prior to making a choice.
- A typical decision process involves several steps. The first is *problem recognition*, where the consumer first realizes that some action must be taken. This realization may be prompted in a variety of ways, ranging from the actual malfunction of a current purchase to a desire for new things based on exposure to different circumstances or advertising that provides a glimpse into what is needed to 'live the good life'.
- Once a problem has been recognized and is seen as sufficiently important to warrant some action, *information search* begins. This search may range from simply scanning memory to determine what has been done to resolve the problem in the past, to extensive fieldwork where the consumer consults a variety of sources to amass as much information as possible. In many cases, people engage in surprisingly little search. Instead, they rely on various mental shortcuts, such as brand names or price, or they may simply imitate others.

- In the *evaluation of alternatives* stage, the product alternatives that are considered comprise the individual's evoked set. Members of the *evoked set* usually share some characteristics; they are categorized similarly. The way products are mentally grouped influences which alternatives will be considered, and some brands are more strongly associated with these categories than are others (i.e. they are more prototypical).

- When the consumer eventually must make a *product choice* from among alternatives, a number of decision rules may be used. *Non-compensatory rules* eliminate alternatives that are deficient on any of the criteria the consumer has chosen to use. *Compensatory rules*, which are more likely to be applied in high-involvement situations, allow the decision-maker to consider each alternative's good and bad points more carefully to arrive at the overall best choice.

- Very often *heuristics*, or mental rules of thumb, are used to simplify decision-making. In particular, people develop many market beliefs over time. One of the most common beliefs is that price is positively related to quality. Other heuristics rely on well-known brand names or a product's country of origin as signals of product quality. When a brand is consistently purchased over time, this pattern may be due to true *brand loyalty*, or simply to *inertia* because it's the easiest thing to do.

🔑 Key terms

Behavioural influence perspective (p. 209)
Brand loyalty (p. 231)
Cognitive structure (p. 222)
Compensatory decision rules (p. 233)
Evaluative criteria (p. 224)
Evoked set (p. 221)
Experiential perspective (p. 209)
Extended problem-solving (p. 209)
Habitual decision-making (p. 209)

Heuristics (p. 226)
Inertia (p. 230)
Information search (p. 212)
Limited problem-solving (p. 209)
Market beliefs (p. 226)
Non-compensatory decision rule (p. 232)
Perceived risk (p. 218)
Problem recognition (p. 211)
Rational perspective (p. 207)

Consumer behaviour challenge

1. If people are not always rational decision-makers, is it worth the effort to study how they reach decisions? What techniques might be employed to understand experiential consumption and to translate this knowledge into marketing strategy?

2. List three product attributes that can be used as quality signals and provide an example of each.

3. Explain the 'evoked set'. Why is it difficult to place a product in a consumer's evoked set after it has already been rejected? What strategies might a marketer use in an attempt to accomplish this goal?

4. Define the three levels of product categorization described in the chapter. Draw a diagram of these levels for a health club.

5. Discuss two different non-compensatory decision rules and highlight the difference(s) between them. How might the use of one rule versus another result in a different product choice?

6. Choose a friend or parent who purchases groceries on a regular basis and keep a log of their purchases of common consumer products over the term. Can you detect any evidence of brand loyalty in any categories based on consistency of purchases? If so, talk to the person about these purchases. Try to determine if his or her choices are based on true brand loyalty or on inertia. What techniques might you use to differentiate between the two?

7. Find a person who is about to make a major purchase. Ask that person to make a chronological list of all the information sources consulted prior to making a decision. How would you characterize the types of sources used (i.e. internal versus external, media versus personal, etc.)? Which sources appeared to have the most impact on the person's decision?

8. Perform a survey of country-of-origin stereotypes. Compile a list of five countries and ask people what products they associate with each. What are their evaluations of the products and likely attributes of these different products? The power of a country stereotype can also be demonstrated in another way. Prepare a brief description of a product, including a list of features, and ask people to rate it in terms of quality, likelihood of purchase, and so on. Make several versions of the description, varying only the country from which it comes. Do ratings change as a function of the country-of-origin?

9. Ask a friend to 'talk through' the process he or she used to choose one brand over others during a recent purchase. Based on this description, can you identify the decision rule that was most likely employed?

CHAPTER 9

Suzanne C. Beckmann, Copenhagen Business School, Denmark

Helmut's old VW barely resembled a car any more. His friends at the last Green Party meeting commented on the fading Greenpeace sticker and the growing oil spots on the road under his old car. They had also discussed with great enthusiasm the new ecologically sound hybrid cars soon to be introduced on the German market and suggested that Helmut ought to think about getting one. His colleagues at the bank where he worked joked about his car making theirs look bad in the staff car park. With the coming of spring Helmut's heart turned to love – and sports cars. After much encouragement from his work colleagues, he replaced his faithful old beetle with a new BMW. Both he and his friends were elated. The staff car park was much improved and his problems were over – or so he thought. The old VW was still in his garage and he could not decide whether to sell it for a few hundred Deutschmarks which he could use now, or have the car recycled at a significant cost. The next Green Party meeting was at hand and, recalling their advice, he wondered whether he should have opted for a less stylish hybrid car. His anxiety was so high about being 'exposed' as a closet yuppie that he even considered driving the old VW to the meeting, if it would start. He could not help wondering whether he had done the right thing in buying the BMW, but it seemed like such a good idea at the time.

The purchase situation, post-purchase evaluation and product disposal

Introduction

Helmut's dilemma highlights the importance of the purchase situation (it is spring, one wants to feel more 'seductive') and the post-purchase evaluation (was it the right choice?). On top of this, the experience of service linked to the act of purchasing and evaluating the purchase play central roles. In a recent British poll, 80 per cent of consumers said that they would change suppliers if they are unhappy with the service; and 86 per cent said that they expect better service today than five years ago.[1] Further, the issue of environmental friendliness is becoming more and more important for many purchase decisions, just as it was for Helmut, even though environmentalism in this case was overruled by other desires.

Helmut's experience illustrates some of the concepts to be discussed in this chapter. Making a purchase is often not a simple, routine matter of going to a store and picking out something. As illustrated in Figure 9.1, a consumer's choices are affected by many personal factors, such as mood, time pressure and the particular situation or context for which the product is needed. In some situations, like the purchase of a car or a home, the salesperson or the reference group (which we will discuss in chapter 10) play a pivotal role in the final choice.

The store environment also exerts a major influence: shopping is like a stage performance, with the customer involved either as a member of the audience or as an active participant. The quality of the performance is affected by the other *cast*

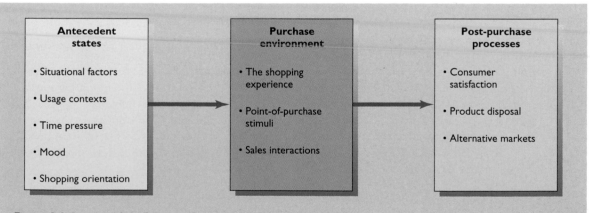

Figure 9.1 Issues related to purchase and post-purchase activities

members (salespeople or other shoppers), as well as by the *setting* of the play (the image of a particular store and the 'feeling' it imparts) and *props* (store fittings and promotional material which try to influence the shopper's decisions).

In addition, a lot of important consumer activity occurs *after* a product has been purchased and brought home. After using a product, the consumer must decide whether he or she is satisfied with it. The satisfaction process is especially important to marketers who realize that the key to success is not selling a product once, but rather forging a relationship with the consumer so that he or she will continue to buy in the future. Finally, just as Helmut thought about the resale of his car, we must also consider how consumers go about disposing of products and how secondary markets (e.g. secondhand car dealers) often play a pivotal role in product acquisition. This chapter considers many issues related to purchase and post-purchase phenomena.

Situational effects on consumer behaviour

A *consumption situation* is defined by factors over and above characteristics of the person and of the product. Situational effects can be behavioural (e.g. entertaining friends) or perceptual (e.g. being depressed, or feeling pressed for time).[2] Common sense tells us that people tailor their purchases to specific occasions or that the way we feel at a specific point in time affects what we feel like buying or doing.

One reason for this variability is that the role a person plays at any time is partly determined by his or her *situational self-image*: 'Who am I right now?' (cf. chapter 7).[3] Someone trying to impress his girlfriend by playing the role of 'man-about-town' may spend more lavishly, ordering champagne rather than beer and buying flowers – purchases he would never consider when he is with his male friends in a pub and playing the role of 'one of the boys'. As this example demonstrates, knowledge of what consumers are doing at the time a product is consumed may improve predictions of product and brand choice.[4] As one renowned European consumer researcher has pointed out, the question '*where* is consumer behaviour' has been surprisingly little investigated. This researcher more specifically proposed a neo-behaviourist model operating with four general types of consumer situations: accomplishment, pleasure, accumulation and maintenance.[5]

Marketing pitfall

Sometimes a marketing strategy can work *too* well. This is the case with Nabisco's Grey Poupon mustard brand, which the company has successfully positioned as a premium product. The problem is that consumers tend to save the brand for special occasions rather than spreading the mustard on just any old sandwich.

Grey Poupon's 'special' cachet is due to its long-running ad campaign, in which toffee-nosed aristocrats pass the mustard through the windows of their limousines. The campaign is so well known that the familiar tag line, 'Pardon me, would you have any Grey Poupon?' was even repeated in the movie *Wayne's World*.

To dig themselves out of this situational hole, the brand's advertising agency developed a new advertising campaign, with magazine ads that feature simpler occasions, such as a picnic. In the ad shown here, readers are reminded to 'Poupon the potato salad' or 'class up the cold cuts'.[6]

Courtesy of Nabisco, Inc.

Situational segmentation

By systematically identifying important usage situations, market segmentation strategies can be developed to position products that will meet the specific needs arising from these situations.[7] Many product categories are amenable to this form of segmentation. For example, consumers' furniture choices are often tailored to specific settings. We prefer different styles for a town-flat, country cottage or an executive suite. The South African ad for Volkswagen shown here emphasizes the versatility of the Volkswagen bus for different situations.

This South African ad for Volkswagen emphasizes that brand criteria can differ depending upon the situation in which the product will be used. Courtesy of Volkswagen of South Africa.

Table 9.1 A person-situation-segmentation matrix for suntan lotion

Situation	Young children		Teenagers		Adult women		Adult men		Benefits/features
	Fair skin	Dark skin	Fair skin	Dark skin	Fair skin	Dark skin	Fair skin	Dark skin	
Beach/boat sunbathing	Combined insect repellent				Summer perfume				a. Product serves as windburn protection b. Formula and container can stand heat c. Container floats and is distinctive (not easily lost)
Home-poolside sunbathing					Combined moisturizer				a. Product has large pump dispenser b. Product won't stain wood, concrete, furnishings
Sunlamp bathing					Combined moisturizer and massage oil				a. Product is designed specifically for type of lamp b. Product has an artificial tanning ingredient
Snow skiing					Winter perfume				a. Product provides special protection from special light rays and weather b. Product has antifreeze formula
Person benefit/features	Special protection a. Protection is critical b. Formula is non-poisonous		Special protection a. Product fits in jeans pocket b. Product used by opinion leaders		Special protection Female perfume		Special protection Male perfume		

Source: Adapted from Peter R. Dickson, 'Person-Situation: Segmentation's Missing Link', *Journal of Marketing* 46 (Fall 1982): 62. By permission of American Marketing Association.

Constructing a situational segmentation matrix

Table 9.1 gives one example of how situations can be used to fine-tune a segmentation strategy. By listing the major contexts where a product is used (e.g. skiing and sunbathing, for a suntan lotion) and the different users of the product, a matrix can be constructed that identifies specific product features which should be emphasized for each situation. For example, a suntan lotion manufacturer might promote the fact that the bottle floats and is hard to lose during the summer, but tout its anti-freeze formula during the winter season.

Social and physical surroundings

A consumer's physical and social environment can make a big difference in motives for product usage and also affect how the product is evaluated. Important cues include the person's physical surroundings, as well as the amount and type of other consumers also present in that situation.

As we shall see in the next chapter, many of a consumer's purchase decisions are significantly affected by the groups or social settings in which these occur. In some cases, the presence or absence of other patrons ('*co-consumers*') in a setting can be a determinant attribute (see chapter 8), such as when an exclusive resort or boutique promises to provide privacy to privileged customers. At other times, the presence of others can have positive value. A sparsely attended football match or an empty bar can be depressing sights.

The presence of large numbers of people in a consumer environment increases arousal levels, so a consumer's subjective experience of a setting tends to be more intense. This polarization, however, can be both positive and negative. While the presence of other people creates a state of arousal, the consumer's actual experience depends on his or her *interpretation* of this arousal. It is important to distinguish between *density* and *crowding* for this reason. The former term refers to the actual number of people occupying a space, while the psychological state of crowding exists only if a negative affective state occurs as a result of this density.[8] For example, 100 students packed into a classroom designed for 75 may be unpleasant for all concerned, but the same number of people jammed together at a party occupying a room of the same size might just make for a great party.

In addition, the type of consumers who patronize a store or service can serve as a store attribute. We may infer something about a store by examining its customers. For this reason, some restaurants require men to wear a jacket for dinner, and bouncers of some 'hot' nightspots hand-pick patrons based on whether they have the right 'look' for the club. To paraphrase the comedian Groucho Marx, 'I would never join a club that would have me for a member'.

Multicultural dimensions

As we shall discuss later in this chapter, American retailers are probably the most innovative when it comes to 'putting on a show' for the customers. Developments in the coin-operated laundry business illustrate how a traditionally depressing experience can be repositioned as a fun, social event. Many laundries have taken to installing bars, tanning salons and exercise machines to encourage customers to look forward to doing their laundry. The Videotown Laundrette in Manhattan features a 6,000 title videocassette library, and Suds & Duds in Greensboro, North Carolina, has a snack bar, pool hall and big-screen television.[9]

Temporal factors

Time is one of consumers' most limiting resources. We talk about 'making time' or 'spending time', and we are frequently reminded that 'time is money'. Our perspectives on time can affect many stages of decision-making and consumption, such as needs that are stimulated, the amount of information search we undertake, and so on. Common sense tells us that more careful information search and deliberation occurs when we have the luxury of taking our time. A meticulous shopper who would normally check the price of an item in three different shops before buying it might be found running through the mall at Christmas just before closing time, frantically scooping up anything left on the shelves that might serve as a last-minute gift.

Economic time

Time is an economic variable; it is a resource that must be divided among activities.[10] Consumers try to maximize satisfaction by allocating time to the appropriate combination of tasks. Of course, people's allocation decisions differ; we all know people who seem to play all of the time, and others who are workaholics. An individual's priorities determine his or her **time style**.[11] Time style, it has been suggested, incorporates such dimensions as economic time, past orientation, future orientation, time submissiveness and time anxiety.[12]

Many consumers believe they are more pressed for time than ever before. This feeling may, however, be due more to perception than to fact. People may simply have more options for spending their time and feel pressured by the weight of it all. The average working day at the turn of the century was 10 hours (6 days per week), and women did 27 hours of housework per week, compared to under 5 hours now. Of course, one reason for this difference is that men are sharing these burdens more.[13]

This sense of *time poverty* has made consumers very responsive to marketing innovations that allow them to save time. As an executive at Campbell's Soup observed, 'Time will be the currency of the 1990s'.[14] This priority has created new opportunities for services as diverse as photograph processing, optometrists and car repair, where speed of delivery has become an important attribute.[15] To cater to this need, a Chicago funeral director even offers a drive-through service, where viewers can see a loved one on a screen without taking the time to leave their cars. The owner notes, 'The working person doesn't have time to come in. They want to see the body but they don't want to wait.'[16]

With the increase in time poverty, researchers also are noting a rise in *polychronic activity*, where consumers do more than one thing at a time.[17] One area where this type of activity is especially prevalent is eating. Many consumers often do not allocate a specific time to dining, but do something else while eating. As one food industry executive commented, 'We've moved beyond grazing and into gulping'.[18] On the other hand, counter-trends of slow food are also found among other segments. In the UK, three other food cultures have been reported in addition to the globalized fast food culture: expatriate food (interest in 'authentic' foreign cuisines), food nostalgia (classic British cuisine) and creolization (a mixing of tastes and cuisines) (cf. chapter 16).[19]

Psychological time

The psychological dimension of time, or how it is experienced, is an important actor in *queuing theory*, the mathematical study of waiting in queues. A consumer's experience of waiting can radically influence his or her perceptions of service quality. Although we assume that something must be good if we have to wait for it, the negative feelings aroused by long waits can quickly deter customers.[20] There are large cross-cultural differences in the acceptance of waiting time. Twenty per cent of Sicilians consider a waiting time of 30 minutes for a dental appointment reasonable, and the average waiting time at a bank counter is 24 minutes.[21] What do you think?

Marketers have adopted a variety of 'tricks' to minimize psychological waiting time. These techniques range from altering customers' perceptions of a queue's length to providing distractions that divert attention away from waiting.[22] However, one study concluded that differences in queuing systems had only a minor effect on perceived waiting time compared to differences in waiting environment attractiveness and actual waiting time.[23]

- One hotel chain, after receiving numerous complaints about the wait for lifts, installed mirrors near the lift entrances. People's natural tendency to check their appearance reduced complaints, even though the actual waiting time was unchanged.
- Airline passengers often complain of the time they have to wait to claim their baggage. In one airport, it would take them one minute to walk from the plane to the baggage carousel where they would wait seven minutes for their luggage. By changing the layout so that the walk to the carousel took six minutes and bags arrived two minutes after that, complaints were almost entirely eliminated.

Multicultural dimensions

Even though the Western time concept may become more and more dominant, at least in the international business world, this conception of time is far from universal. Large cultural differences exist in terms of people's time perspectives.[24] Some cultures run on procedural time and ignore the clock completely. People decide to do something 'when the time is right'. Much of the world appears to live on 'event time'; for example, in Burundi people might arrange to meet when the cows return from the watering hole, while in Madagascar the response if someone asks how long it takes to get to the market might be 'the time it takes to cook rice'.[25]

Alternatively, in circular or cyclic time, people are governed by natural cycles, such as the regular occurrence of the seasons (a perspective found in many Latino cultures). To these consumers, the notion of the future does not make sense, because that time will be much like the present. Since the concept of future value does not exist, these consumers often prefer to buy an inferior product that is available now to waiting for a better one that will become available later. Also, it is hard to convince people who function on circular time to buy insurance or save for the future.

A social scientist recently compared the pace of life in 31 cities around the world as part of a study of time styles. He and his assistants timed how long it takes pedestrians to walk 60 feet and postal clerks to sell a stamp. Based on these responses, the fastest countries were claimed to be:

1. Switzerland, 2. Ireland, 3. Germany, 4. Japan, 5. Italy.

and the slowest countries:

31. Mexico, 30. Indonesia, 29. Brazil, 28. El Salvador, 27. Syria.

Obviously, such national results depend on the actual place of measurement: consider, for example, the difference of Sicilian time compared with Milan time.[26]

● McDonald's uses a multiple queue system, where each server deals with a separate queue of people. Other fast food outlets use a multi-stage system, where the first server takes orders, the second prepares burgers, the third pours drinks, and so on. While such queues are longer, customers move continuously through stages, so signs of progress can be seen and psychological time is reduced. Similarly, Disneyland often disguises the length of its queues by leading them around corners so that customers cannot judge the length of the queue or the anticipated waiting time.

Social time

Social time has been proposed as an important but overlooked time dimension in consumer behaviour.[27] Social refers to the time in relation to social processes and rhythms and schedules in society. It takes into account how determined our lives are by interrelated temporal phenomena, such as working hours, opening hours, eating hours and other institutionalized schedules. For example, the liberalized shop opening hours in Denmark, introduced in 1995, which allow grocery shops and supermarkets to stay open after 5.30 p.m. have meant a shift away from the kiosks and petrol stations (which did not have similar opening restrictions) and may, in the long run, make a significant difference to Danish families' daily social and temporal shopping and consumption patterns.[28]

To most Western consumers, time is something that is neatly compartmentalized: we wake up in the morning, go to school or work, come home, eat, go out, go to bed, then do it all over again. This perspective is called linear separable time (or Christian time); events proceed in an orderly sequence and different times are well defined: 'There's a time and a place for everything'. In this world-wide 'modernized' conception of time, there is a clear sense of past, present and future, and the present is preferred to the past, whereas the future is generally rated better than the present.[29] Many activities are performed as the means to an end that will occur at a future point, as when people 'save for a rainy day'.

But even in North European and American cultures, the very linear and compartmentalized chronological time is not hegemonic, as indicated by the above-mentioned psychological time patterns, which call for a more relativistic and complex approach to time structures in societies most influenced by economic time concepts.[30]

When groups of university students were asked to draw a picture of time, the resulting sketches (Figure 9.2) illustrated some of these different temporal perspectives.[31] The drawing at the top represents procedural time; there is lack of direction

Marketing pitfall

An emphasis on speed resulted in some serious public relations problems for the American pizza delivery company Domino's Pizza, which guarantees delivery within 30 minutes. Critics claimed that this policy encouraged reckless driving and backed up this charge with some damaging statistics. In 1989, more than a dozen lawsuits, stemming from death or serious injuries caused by delivery people rushing to make the half-hour deadline, were filed against the company. The employee death rate was 50 per 100,000, equal to that suffered in the mining industry.[32] Domino's no longer offers the guarantee.

Figure 9.2 Drawings of time
Source: Esther S. Page-Wood, Carol J. Kaufman and Paul M. Lane, 'The Art of Time', *Proceedings of the Academy of Marketing Science* (1990).

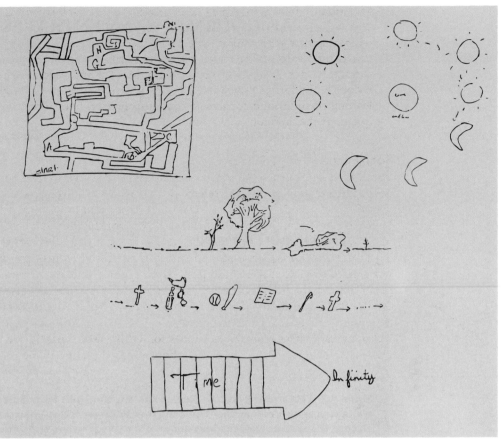

from left to right and little sense of past, present and future. The two drawings in the middle denote cyclical time, with regular cycles designated by markers. The bottom drawing represents linear time, with a segmented time line moving from left to right in a well-defined sequence.

Some products and services are believed to be appropriate for certain times and not for others. One scholar illustrated this by producing a mock restaurant menu, which was very appropriate in terms of delicacy and nutrition but totally inappropriate in terms of timing and constellation of food items (Figure 9.3). Also, we may be more receptive to advertising messages at certain times (who wants to hear a beer commercial at 7 a.m.?). Some products crossing cultural borders are also crossing over from one time of day consumption to another. In its home country of Italy, the capuccino is known as a breakfast coffee. Now it has become popular all over Europe, and in these new markets it is drunk at all times of the day whenever a cup of regular coffee would traditionally have been appropriate. So the capuccino has moved from a 'breakfast time' category to a more general 'coffee time' category.[33]

AU GOURMET SANS ENTRAVES

Restaurant
* * *

MENU

Breakfast	*Dinner*
(10.30 – 13.30)	*(15.00 – 19.30)*
Salad of Exotic	*Season's Salad*
Fruits	*Wild Salmon Escalope with*
Spaghetti alla Carbonara	*Beef Marrow*
Onion Soup with	*Soup Du Barry*
Toast	*Sorbets*
Ice Tea	*Capuccino*
	Butter Croissants
	Liqueur or Kir
	Royal

Figure 9.3 **This menu from the restaurant 'Au Gourmet Sans Entraves' (which translates as something like 'The Gourmet Without Rules') illustrates how culture shapes our expectations about what to eat when, and with what. How many broken rules can you find? This is probably culture-dependent. Remember that it was constructed by a Frenchman, who obviously had a certain set of inappropriate constellations and timings in mind.**
Source: Claude Fischler, *L'homnivore* (Paris: Editions Odile Jacob, 1990). Used with permission.

Antecedent states

A person's mood or physiological condition active at the time of purchase can have a major impact on what is bought and can also affect how products are evaluated.[34] One reason is that behaviour is directed towards certain goal states, as was discussed in chapter 3. In addition, the person's particular social identity, or role that is being played at a given time, will be influential.[35]

Mood

A consumer's mood will impact on purchase decisions. For example, stress can reduce a consumer's information-processing and problem-solving abilities.[36] Two dimensions determine whether a shopper will react positively or negatively to a store environment: *pleasure* and *arousal*. A person can enjoy or not enjoy a situation, and he or she can feel stimulated or not. As Figure 9.4 indicates, different combinations of pleasure and arousal levels result in a variety of emotional states. For example, an arousing situation can be either distressing or exciting, depending on whether the

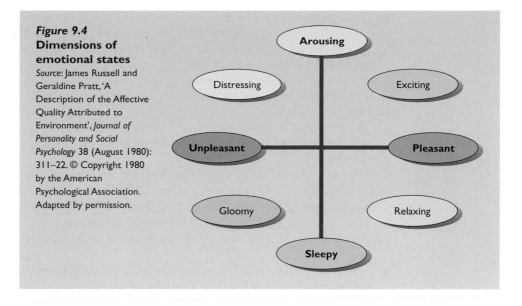

Figure 9.4
Dimensions of emotional states
Source: James Russell and Geraldine Pratt, 'A Description of the Affective Quality Attributed to Environment', *Journal of Personality and Social Psychology* 38 (August 1980): 311–22. © Copyright 1980 by the American Psychological Association. Adapted by permission.

context is positive or negative (e.g. a street riot versus a street festival). Maintaining an upbeat mood in a pleasant context is one factor behind the success of theme parks such as Disneyland, which try to provide consistent doses of carefully calculated stimulation to patrons.[37]

A specific mood is some combination of these two factors. For example, the state of happiness is high in pleasantness and moderate in arousal, while elation would be high on both dimensions.[38] In general, a mood state (either positive or negative) biases judgements of products and service in that direction.[39] Put simply, consumers like things better when they are in a good mood (this may explain the popularity of the business lunch!).

Moods can be affected by store design, the weather or other factors specific to the consumer. In addition, music and television programming can affect mood; this has important consequences for commercials.[40] When consumers hear happy music or watch happy programmes, they have more positive reactions to commercials and products, especially when the marketing appeals are aimed at arousing emotional reactions.[41]

Shopping motives

People often shop even though they do not necessarily intend to buy anything at all, while others have to be dragged to a mall. Shopping is a way to acquire needed products and services, but social motives for shopping also are important. Thus, shopping is an activity that can be performed for utilitarian (functional or tangible) or hedonic (pleasurable or intangible) reasons.[42]

These different motives are illustrated by scale items used by researchers to assess people's underlying reasons for shopping. One item that measures hedonic value is 'During the trip, I felt the excitement of the hunt'. When that type of sentiment is compared to a functionally related statement such as 'I accomplished just what I wanted to on this shopping trip', the contrast between these two dimensions is clear.[43] Hedonic shopping motives can include the following:[44]

● *Social experiences*: The shopping centre or department store has replaced the traditional town square or county fair as a community meeting place. Many people (especially in suburban or rural areas) may have nowhere else to go to spend their leisure-time.

● *Sharing of common interests*: Shops frequently offer specialized goods which allow people with shared interests to communicate.

● *Interpersonal attraction*: Shopping centres are a natural place to congregate. The shopping arcade has become a central meeting place for teenagers. It also represents a controlled, secure environment for other groups, such as the elderly.

● *Instant status*: As every salesperson knows, some people love the experience of being waited on, even though they may not necessarily buy anything. One men's clothing salesman offered this advice: 'remember their size, remember what you sold them last time. Make them feel important! If you can make people feel important, they are going to come back. Everybody likes to feel important!'[45]

● *'The thrill of the chase'*: Some people pride themselves on their knowledge of the marketplace. They may relish the process of haggling and bargaining, viewing it almost as a sport.

Do people hate to shop or love it? It varies. Consumers can be segmented in terms of their **shopping orientation**, or general attitudes about shopping. These orientations may vary depending on the particular product categories and store types considered. Many people feel insecure about shopping for a car, but they may love to browse in record stores. Several shopping types have been identified, although the following list does not cover the whole range of possible shopping types:[46]

● *The economic consumer*: a rational, goal-oriented shopper who is primarily interested in maximizing the value of his or her money.

● *The personalized consumer*: a shopper who tends to form strong attachments to store personnel ('I shop where they know my name').

● *The ethical consumer*: a shopper who likes to help out the underdog and will support local shops rather than chainstores.

● *The apathetic consumer*: one who does not like to shop and sees it as a necessary but unpleasant chore.

● *The recreational shopper*: a person who views shopping as a fun, social activity – a preferred way to spend leisure time.

The purchase environment

We see bumper stickers and T-shirts everywhere: 'Shop 'til you drop', 'When the going gets tough, the tough go shopping', 'Born to shop'. Like it or not, shopping is a major activity for many consumers. The competition for shoppers is getting tougher amongst retailers. Retailers must now offer something extra to lure shoppers, whether that something is excitement or just plain bargains.[47] One prominent trend is the tendency to blur the boundaries between types of outlet. For example, supermarket and hypermarket chains are now posing a serious threat to the petrol companies by taking larger and larger shares of their market (in France, the supermarkets' share is about 50 per cent).[48] In Denmark and other countries, the petrol stations are striking back, increasing their share of the market for daily groceries. Two of the major companies, Shell and Statoil, had a turnover in groceries in 1996 of more than 2 billion Danish kroner and turnover growth of over 30 per cent.[49] On the contrary, in Great Britain, there has been a tendency to place yet more supermarkets in tandem with petrol stations, thus countering this type of competition.[50]

Another European trend is the increase of trade from kiosks, smaller stores with extended opening hours carrying a small selection of daily goods as well as snack products, sweets, newspapers, etc., sometimes more or less like the 7–11 concept imported from the United States. In many countries, such kiosks are well established and are often run by Middle Eastern or North African immigrants. But in countries such as Finland, where the introduction of kiosks is more recent, it has created a whole new situation for a certain part of the retail system.[51]

In order to be able to compete in the European single market, many retail chains have undergone an internationalization process. For example, of the top 25 European retail chains of daily goods, only one (no. 25) is not internationalized or at least participating in an international network of cooperating chains. The ten biggest companies control 30 per cent of the turnover in daily goods in Europe and the concentration is growing.[52]

Non-store shopping

The competition for customers is becoming even more intense as non-store alternatives that bring retail services to the home continue to multiply. Popular non-store alternatives include mail order catalogues, television shopping networks, salespersons who make house calls and home shopping parties (e.g. Tupperware). Electronic home shopping has often been mentioned as one of the potentially most significant changes in the retail structure for many years. Whereas growth is still relatively slow, many are waiting for the breakthrough because of the opportunities of saving in costs of the distribution chain and transport.[53] The growth of electronic home shopping systems have been especially rapid in France, where the Minitel System offers thousands of information services and is connected to millions of home terminals. One American source identified the segment most open to internet shopping as being the 'fast laners', 14 per cent of the population and predominantly in their teens and twenties.[54]

The shopping experience

Store-loyal consumers are valued by retailers. They will routinely visit a small set of stores without considering others or doing much in the way of comparative pre-purchase search. However, consumers now have an abundance of choices regarding where to shop, including the non-store alternatives. For this reason, people do not tend to be as store-loyal as they once were.[55] In Great Britain, the retail chain Tesco was the biggest spender on marketing among British retailers in 1990–94. Together with the introduction of a customer loyalty card, their marketing strategy helped them to take over from their rival Sainsbury as the biggest British retailer. Sainsbury finally gave up its initial resistance to the introduction of loyalty cards in 1996. Their new card became an instant success: between June and August of that year they issued more than 5 million loyalty cards and gained 1 per cent market share increase.[56]

Retailing as theatre

Shopping can no longer be regarded as a simple act of purchasing.[57] A retail culture has arisen,[58] where acts of shopping have taken on new entertainment and/or experiential dimensions as retailers compete for customers' attention, not to speak of their loyalty. The act of shopping ties into a number of central existential aspects of human life such as sexuality.[59] Furthermore, the customer may not be regarded as a passive recipient of the offerings of the purchase environment but rather as an active co-creator of this very environment and the meanings attached to it,[60] in a situation analogous to the focus among 'marketing mavens' on flexibility in the product supply and tailor-made marketing mixes for the individual consumer.[61] One of the most obvious trends in the retailing sector in Europe is the construction of shopping malls, most often modelled on American prototypes. In the US today, the mall is often a focal point in a community: 94 per cent of adults visit a mall at least once a month and more than half of all retail purchases (excluding cars and petrol) are made in a mall.[62] Malls are also flourishing in Europe, where, once introduced into an area, they often bring with them a whole new combination of leisure activities, shopping and social encounters in safe environments.[63]

Malls are becoming giant entertainment centres, almost to the point where their traditional retail occupants sometimes seem like an afterthought.[64] It is now common to find such features as carousels, miniature golf or batting cages in a suburban mall. As one retailing executive put it, 'Malls are becoming the new mini-amusement parks'.[65] The importance of creating a positive, vibrant and interesting image has led innovative marketers to blur the line between shopping and the theatre. Shopping malls and individual stores have to create environments that stimulate people and allow them to shop and be entertained at the same time.[66] Thematized shopping centres and stores bear witness to the multitude of styles that flourish in the attempt to attract consumers who seek more than just a distribution outlet.[67] The Hard Rock Café, established in London over 25 years ago, now has over 45 restaurants around the world, and has become a sort of pilgrimage place in itself. Some consumers make a point of collecting as many Hard Rock Café merchandise items (T-shirts etc.) from as many HRCs in the world as possible.

The classic European counterpart to the American malls is the department store.[68] The first department stores can be seen as marking the introduction of a modern consumer culture, nourished by dreams of abundance.[69] Department stores often hold elaborate store-wide promotions based, for example, on the culture of a selected country. During these events the entire store is transformed, with each department featuring unusual merchandise from the country. These promotions are accompanied by lavish parties, food and entertainment associated with that country.

The following are two examples of elaborate American 'performers' in the retailing theatre:[70]

- Babyland (the home of Cabbage Patch dolls) does not have a sales staff. Instead, the company offers 'doctors', 'nurses' and 'adoption officers'. Dolls are never 'sold', they are adopted. Every 15 minutes, Bunny Bees hover over the cabbage patch and inseminate the cabbages. These cabbages quiver and the leaves open, displaying a newborn Cabbage Patch baby.
- Ralph Lauren's Madison Avenue store is in a refurbished mansion, and the decor is consistent with the company's image of aristocratic gentility and the good life. The store is furnished with expensive antiques and tapestries, and cocktails and canapés are served in the evening. Even cleaning supplies are carried by maintenance staff in Lauren shopping bags.

Nike Towns, stores specialized in Nike Products, are often highly thematized and use a lot of references to the Nike celebrity endorsers used over time. This Nike Town store in Portland, Oregon provides an innovative, futuristic atmosphere designed to enhance the shopping.
© Christopher Kean.

Multicultural dimensions

American retailers, including Blockbuster Video, Original Levi's stores, Foot Locker, Toys'R'Us and The Gap, are exporting their version of the dynamic retail environment to Europe – with some adaptations. These 'invasions' often begin in Britain, since cultural differences seems smaller, bureaucratic hurdles lower and personnel costs reduced. The Gap found that it needed to stock smaller sizes than in the US, and that many of its European customers prefer darker colours. Also, some retailers have done away with 'greeters' who stand at the entrance in many American stores – Europeans tend to find them intimidating.[71]

Store image

With so many stores competing for customers, how do consumers select one rather than another? Like products, stores may be thought of as having 'personalities'. Some stores have very clearly defined images (either good or bad); others tend to blend into the crowd. They may not have anything distinctive about them and may be over-looked for this reason. This personality, or **store image**, is composed of many dif-ferent factors. The design and general image of the store is central to the perception of the goods displayed there, whether we are talking about fashion,[72] food products[73] or any other type of good. Store features, coupled with such consumer characteristics as shopping orientation, help to predict which shopping outlets people will prefer.[74] Some of the important dimensions of a store's profile are location, merchandise suit-ability and the knowledge and congeniality of the sales staff.[75]

When shoppers think about stores, they may not say, 'Well, that place is fairly good in terms of convenience, the salespeople are acceptable and service is good'. They are more likely to say, 'That place gives me the creeps', or 'I always enjoy shopping there'. Consumers evaluate stores in terms of both their specific attributes *and* a global evaluation, or the **store gestalt** (see chapter 2).[76] This overall feeling may have more to do with such intangibles as interior design and the types of people one finds in the store than with such aspects as return policies or credit availability. As a result, some stores are likely to be consistently in consumers' minds, while others will never be considered.

Because a store's gestalt is now recognized as a very important aspect of the retailing mix, attention is increasingly paid to **atmospherics**, or the 'conscious designing of space and its various dimensions to evoke certain effects in buyers'.[77] These dimensions include colours, scents and sounds. For example, stores done out in red tend to make people tense, while a blue decor imparts a calmer feeling.[78]

Many elements of store design can be cleverly controlled to attract customers and produce desired effects on consumers. Light colours impart a feeling of spaciousness and serenity, and signs in bright colours create excitement. In one subtle but effective application, fashion designer Norma Kamali replaced fluorescent lights with pink ones in department store dressing rooms. The light had the effect of flattering the face and banishing wrinkles, making female customers more willing to try on (and buy) the company's bathing suits.[79]

In addition to visual stimuli, all sorts of cues can influence behaviours.[80] For example, music can affect eating habits. A study found that diners who listened to loud, fast music ate more food. In contrast, those who listened to Mozart or Brahms ate less and more slowly. The researchers concluded that diners who choose soothing music at mealtimes can increase weight loss by at least five pounds a month![81]

In-store decision making

Despite all their efforts to 'pre-sell' to consumers through advertising, marketers increasingly are recognizing the significant degree to which many purchases are influenced by the store environment. A Danish survey indicated that nine out of ten customers did not plan the purchase of at least one third of the goods they acquired.[82] The proportion of unplanned purchases is even higher for some product categories. For the US market it is estimated that the purchase of 85 per cent of sweets and chewing gum, almost 70 per cent of cosmetics and 75 per cent of oral hygiene purchases is unplanned.[83]

Spontaneous shopping

When a shopper is prompted to buy something while in a shop, one of two different processes may be at work: *unplanned buying* may occur when a person is unfamiliar with a store's layout or perhaps when under some time pressure; or a person may be reminded to buy something by seeing it on a shelf.[84]

Impulse buying

In contrast, **impulse buying** occurs when the person experiences a sudden urge that he or she cannot resist.[85] For this reason, so-called impulse items such as sweets and chewing gum are conveniently placed near the checkout. Similarly, many supermarkets have installed wider aisles to encourage browsing, and the widest tend to contain products with the highest margin. Low mark-up items that are purchased regularly tend to be stacked high in narrower aisles, to allow shopping trolleys to speed through.[86] A more recent high-tech tool has been added to encourage impulse buying: a device called 'The Portable Shopper' is a personal scanning gun which allows customers to ring up their own purchases as they shop. The gun was initially developed for Albert Heijn, The Netherlands' largest grocery chain, to move customers through the store more quickly. It is now in use in over 150 groceries world-wide.[87]

Shoppers can be categorized in terms of how much advance planning they do. *Planners* tend to know what products and specific brands they will buy beforehand, *partial planners* know they need certain products, but do not decide on specific brands until they are in the store, and *impulse purchasers* do no advance planning whatsoever.[88] Figure 9.5 was drawn by a consumer, participating in a study on consumers' shopping experiences, who was asked to sketch a typical impulse purchaser.

Point-of-purchase stimuli

Because so much decision-making apparently occurs while the shopper is in the purchasing environment, retailers are beginning to pay more attention to the amount of information in their stores, as well as to the way it is presented. It has been estimated that impulse purchases increase by 10 per cent when appropriate displays are used. Each year, American companies spend more than $13 billion on **point-of-purchase stimuli (POP)**. A point-of-purchase stimulus can be an elaborate product display or demonstration, a coupon-dispensing machine, or someone giving out free samples of a new biscuit in the grocery aisle.

In-store advertising is becoming very sophisticated, as marketers come to appreciate the influence of the shopping environment in steering consumers toward promoted items. The problem has been that the effect of in-store advertising and other POP is difficult to assess. High-tech solutions such as hand-held computers which will process filmed as well as alphanumerical data are used by Reebok to show whether their in-store efforts are used correctly and which type works best, in comparison to competitors.[89]

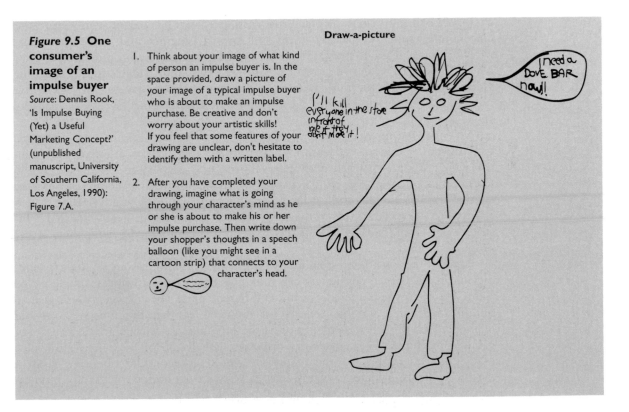

Figure 9.5 One consumer's image of an impulse buyer
Source: Dennis Rook, 'Is Impulse Buying (Yet) a Useful Marketing Concept?' (unpublished manuscript, University of Southern California, Los Angeles, 1990): Figure 7.A.

Draw-a-picture

1. Think about your image of what kind of person an impulse buyer is. In the space provided, draw a picture of your image of a typical impulse buyer who is about to make an impulse purchase. Be creative and don't worry about your artistic skills! If you feel that some features of your drawing are unclear, don't hesitate to identify them with a written label.

2. After you have completed your drawing, imagine what is going through your character's mind as he or she is about to make his or her impulse purchase. Then write down your shopper's thoughts in a speech balloon (like you might see in a cartoon strip) that connects to your character's head.

In-store *displays* are another commonly used device to attract attention in the store environment. While most displays consist of simple racks that dispense the product and/or related coupons, some highlight the value of regarding retailing as theatre by supplying the 'audience' with elaborate performances and scenery. For example, POP displays are one of the most important tools in the annual toy acquisition peak before Christmas, and the winners are the large and established brands like Barbie, Lego, etc. as well as newcomers who know how to make an impressive visual impact. In the UK market for construction toys, Lego has long dominated, with Meccano as a distant second. However, by using an aggressive POP strategy, K'Nex came close to a 20 per cent market share in 1996 from a standing start that same year.[90] Others among the more dramatic POP displays have included:[91]

- *Timex*: A still-ticking watch sits in the bottom of a filled aquarium.
- *Kellogg's Corn Flakes*: A button with a picture of Cornelius the Rooster is placed within the reach of children near Corn Flakes. When a child presses the button, he hears the rooster cock-a-doodle-doo.
- *Elizabeth Arden*: The company introduced 'Elizabeth', a computer and video makeover system which allows customers to try out their images with different shades of makeup, without having to apply the products first.

Place-based media

Advertisers are also being more aggressive about hitting consumers with their messages, wherever they may be. *Place-based media* is a specialized medium that is growing in popularity: it targets consumers based on locations in which the message is delivered. These places may be anything from airports, doctors' offices, university campuses or health clubs. Turner Broadcasting System has begun such ventures as Checkout Channel for grocery stores and Airport Channel, and it has even tested McDTV for McDonald's restaurants.[92] Even MTV is getting in on the act: its new Music Report, to be shown in record stores, is a two-hour 'video capsule' featuring video spots and ads for music retailers and corporate sponsors. An MTV executive observed, 'They're already out there at the retail environment. They're ready to spend money'.[93]

Much of the growth in point-of-purchase activity has been in new electronic technologies.[94] Some stores feature talking posters that contain a human body sensor which speaks up when a shopper approaches. The Point-of-Purchase Radio Corporation offers in-store radio networks which are now used by about sixty grocery chains.[95] Some shopping trolleys have a small screen that displays advertising, which is keyed to the specific areas of the store through which the trolley is wheeled.[96] In-store video displays allow advertisers to reinforce major media campaigns at the point of purchase.[97]

Some of the most interesting innovations can be found in state-of-the-art vending machines. French consumers can purchase Levi's jeans from a machine called 'Libre Service', which offers jeans in ten different sizes. The customer uses a belt to find his or her size, and the jeans sell for about £6 less than the same versions sold in shops. Due to their frenetic lifestyles, the Japanese are particularly avid users of vending machines. These machines dispense virtually all of life's necessities, plus many luxuries people in other countries would not consider obtaining from a machine. The list includes jewellery, fresh flowers, frozen beef, pornography, business cards, underwear and even the names of possible dates.[98]

Exchange relationships

One of the most important in-store factors is the salesperson, who attempts to influence the buying behaviour of the customer.[99] This influence can be understood in terms of **exchange theory**, which stresses that every interaction involves an exchange of value. Each participant gives something to the other and hopes to receive something in return.[100]

Resource exchange

What 'value' does the customer look for in a sales interaction? There are a variety of resources a salesperson might offer. He or she, for example, might offer expertise about the product to make the shopper's choice easier. Alternatively, the customer may be reassured because the salesperson is an admired or likeable person whose tastes are similar and is seen as someone who can be trusted.[101] In fact, research data attest to the impact of a salesperson's appearance on sales effectiveness. In sales, as in much of life, attractive people appear to hold the upper hand.[102]

The sales interaction

A buyer/seller situation is like many other dyadic encounters (two-person groups); it is a relationship where some agreement must be reached about the roles of each participant: a process of *identity negotiation* occurs.[103] For example, if the salesperson immediately establishes him- or herself as an all-knowing expert (and the customer accepts this position), the salesperson is likely to have more influence over the customer through the course of the relationship. Some of the factors that help to determine a salesperson's role (and relative effectiveness) are his or her age, appearance, educational level and motivation to sell.[104]

In addition, more effective salespersons usually know their customers' traits and preferences better than do ineffective salespersons, since this knowledge allows them to adapt their approach to meet the needs of the specific customer.[105] The ability to be adaptable is especially vital when customers and salespeople differ in terms of their *interaction styles*.[106] Consumers, for example, vary in the degree of assertiveness they bring to interactions. At one extreme, non-assertive people believe that complaining is not socially acceptable and may be intimidated in sales situations. Assertive people are more likely to stand up for themselves in a firm but non-threatening way, while aggressives may resort to rudeness and threats if they do not get their way.[107]

Relationship marketing

The strategic perspective that stresses the long-term, human side of buyer/seller interactions is called **relationship marketing**. It focuses on the importance of developing long-lasting relational exchanges, for example, by building commitment and trust with the customer.[108] Relationship marketing has been hailed as one of the most promising concepts within recent marketing theory development, most notably because it potentially brings marketing theory back to the experienced reality of managers.[109] Like a romantic involvement, long-term sales relationships have been seen as going through five phases.[110]

1. *Awareness*: The buyer enters the market, perhaps becoming aware of local brands.
2. *Exploration*: The buyer undergoes search and trial. A minimal investment is made in the relationship. Norms and expectations begin to develop.

3. *Expansion*: The buyer and seller start to become more interdependent as the relationship becomes solidified.
4. *Commitment*: A pledge is made (it may be done implicitly) to continue the relationship (e.g. a customer may come to refer to someone as 'my hairdresser').
5. *Dissolution*: The relationship will dissolve, unless steps are taken to keep it together. One way for the seller to prevent dissolution is to construct *exit barriers*, making it difficult for the buyer to separate. Examples of exit barriers include delayed rebates (customers must accumulate proof-of-purchase seals over time), frequent-flier programmes (which make it less tempting to switch airlines) or rental deposits.

Post-purchase satisfaction

Consumer satisfaction/dissatisfaction (CS/D) is determined by the overall feelings, or attitude, a person has about a product after it has been purchased. Consumers are engaged in a constant process of evaluating the things they buy as these products are integrated into their daily consumption activities.[111] Customer satisfaction has a real impact on profitability: a recent study conducted among a large sample of Swedish consumers found that product quality affects customer satisfaction, which in turn results in increased profitability among firms who provide quality products.[112] Quality is more than a marketing 'buzzword'.

Perceptions of product quality

Just what do consumers look for in products? The answer's easy: they want quality and value. Especially because of foreign competition, claims of product quality have become strategically crucial to maintaining a competitive advantage.[113] Consumers use a number of cues to infer quality, including brand name, price and even their own estimates of how much money has been put into a new product's advertising campaign.[114] These cues, as well as others such as product warranties and follow-up letters from the company, are often used by consumers to relieve perceived risk and assure themselves that they have made smart purchase decisions.[115]

What is quality?

In *Zen and the Art of Motorcycle Maintenance*, a cult book from the mid-1970s, the hero literally goes mad trying to work out the meaning of quality.[116] Marketers appear to use the word quality as a catch-all term for 'good'. Because of its wide and imprecise usage, the attribute 'quality' threatens to become a meaningless claim. If everyone has it, what good is it?

One way to define quality is to establish uniform standards to which products from around the world must conform. This is the intent of the International Standards Organization, a Geneva-based organization that does just that. A set of quality criteria were initially developed in 1987 to regulate product quality. The broad set of guidelines are known as **ISO standards**. These standards exist in different versions and cover issues related to the manufacture and installation of products, post-sale servicing but also sustainability and environmentally friendly production processes.

The importance of expectations

Global standards for quality help to ensure that products work as promised, but consumers' evaluations of those products are a bit more complex. Satisfaction or dissatisfaction is more than a reaction to the actual performance quality of a product or service. It is influenced by prior expectations regarding the level of quality. According to the **expectancy disconfirmation model**, consumers form beliefs about product performance based upon prior experience with the product and/or communications about the product that imply a certain level of quality.[117] When something performs the way we thought it would, we may not think much about it. If, on the other hand, it fails to live up to expectations, negative affect may result. And if performance exceeds our expectations, we are satisfied and pleased.

To understand this perspective, think about different types of restaurant. People expect to be provided with sparkling clear glassware in high-class restaurants, and they might become upset if they are offered a grimy glass. On the other hand, we may not be surprised to find fingerprints on our mug at a local 'greasy spoon'; we may even shrug it off because it contributes to the place's 'charm'. An important lesson emerges for marketers from this perspective: don't overpromise.[118]

One approach to customer satisfaction, known as the *Kano-model*, operates with three kinds of expectation: basis, performance and enthusiasm expectations. The first includes the implicit and taken-for-granted qualities expected from a product. If these are not satisfied, the product will never be able to live up to the customer's requirements, but even if fulfilled, they do not profile the product because these qualities are taken for granted as a minimum. For the performance expectations satisfaction is proportional to how well the product lives up to the expectations. Such quality requirements are often specified and articulated by the customer. In fact, it is wrong to call the enthusiasm-related product features expectations, since their essential character is that they are *not* expected by the customer. Therefore, such positive surprises can lead to a very great feeling of satisfaction, since the product quality was even better than expected.[119] Furthermore, research evidence indicates that product experience is important for customer satisfaction. When people have no experiences they are relatively easy to satisfy, but with growing experience, they become harder to satisfy. Then, when they reach a certain level of experience, satisfaction again becomes easier to obtain, since consumers are now 'experts' and this facilitates choice and generates more realistic expectations.[120] A general conclusion which one should draw from such a discussion is that consumer goals may be multiple and the product or service offer so complex to evaluate that any measurement of satisfaction must be used with caution.[121]

Quality and product failures

The power of quality claims is most evident when they are not fulfilled, as when a company's product fails. Here, consumers' expectations are dashed, and dissatisfaction results. In these situations, marketers immediately take steps to reassure customers. When the company confronts the problem candidly, consumers often are willing to forgive and forget, as was the case with Perrier when traces of benzene were found in the water. When a company appears to be dragging its heels or attempting a cover-up, on the other hand, consumer resentment will grow, as occurred during Union Carbide's disaster in Bhopal, India and with Exxon following the massive oil spill in Alaska caused by its tanker, the *Exxon Valdez*.

Acting on dissatisfaction

If a person is not happy with a product or service, what can be done? Essentially, a consumer has one or more different courses of action to take:[122]

1. *Voice response*: The consumer can appeal directly to the retailer for redress (e.g. a refund).
2. *Private response*: Express dissatisfaction about the store or product to friends and/or boycott the store. As will be discussed in chapter 10, negative word of mouth (WOM) can be very damaging to a store's reputation.
3. *Third-party response*: The consumer can take legal action against the merchant, register a complaint with the Ombudsman, or perhaps write a letter to the newspaper.

A number of factors influence which route is taken. The consumer may in general be assertive or meek. Action is more likely to be taken for expensive products such as household durables, cars and clothing than for inexpensive products.[123] Also, if the consumer does not believe that the store will respond positively to a complaint, the person will be more likely to switch brands than fight.[124] Ironically, marketers should *encourage* consumers to complain to them: people are more likely to spread the word about unresolved negative experiences to their friends than they are to boast about positive occurrences.[125]

Product disposal and environmentalism

Because people often do form strong attachments to products, the decision to dispose of something may be a painful one. One function performed by possessions is to serve as anchors for our identities: our past lives on in our things.[126] This attachment is exemplified by the Japanese, who ritually 'retire' worn-out sewing needles, chopsticks and even computer chips by burning them as thanks for good service.[127]

Although some people have more trouble than others in discarding things, even a 'magpie' does not keep everything. Consumers must often dispose of things, either because they have fulfilled their designated functions, or possibly because they no longer fit with consumers' view of themselves. Concern about the environment coupled with a need for convenience has made ease of product disposal a key attribute in categories from razors to nappies.

Disposal options

When a consumer decides that a product is no longer of use, several choices are available. The person can either (1) keep the item, (2) temporarily dispose of it, or (3) permanently dispose of it. In many cases, a new product is acquired even though the old one still functions. Some reasons for this replacement include a desire for new features, a change in the person's environment (e.g. a refrigerator is the wrong colour for a freshly painted kitchen) or a change in the person's role or self-image.[128] Figure 9.6 provides an overview of consumers' disposal options.

Recycling

The issue of product disposition and **recycling** is doubly vital because of its enormous public policy implications. We live in a throw-away society, which creates problems for the environment and also results in a great deal of unfortunate waste. Training consumers to recycle has become a priority in many countries. Japan recycles about 40 per cent of its waste, and this relatively high rate of compliance is partly due to the social

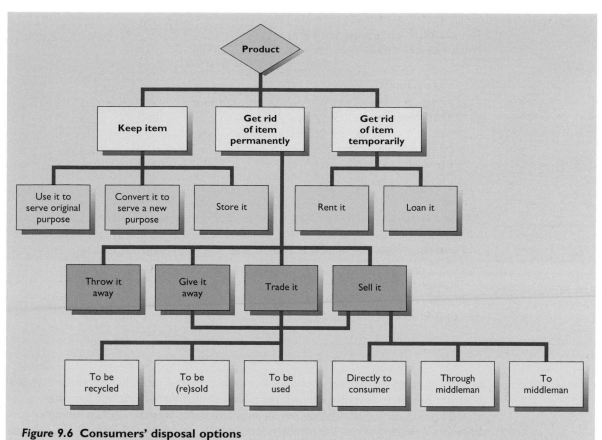

Figure 9.6 Consumers' disposal options
Source: Adapted from Jacob Jacoby, Carol K. Berning and Thomas F. Dietvorst, 'What About Disposition?', Journal of Marketing 41 (April 1977): 23. By permission of American Marketing Association.

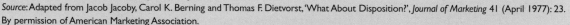

value the Japanese place on recycling: citizens are encouraged by waste disposal lorries which periodically rumble through the streets playing classical music or children's songs.[129] Companies continue to search for ways to use resources more efficiently, often at the prompting of activist consumer groups. For example, McDonald's restaurants bowed to pressure by eliminating the use of styrofoam packages, and its outlets in Europe are experimenting with edible breakfast platters made of maize.[130]

Several studies have examined the relevant goals consumers have to recycle. It used a means–end chain analysis of the type described in chapter 4 to identify how specific instrumental goals are linked to more abstract terminal values. The most important lower-order goals identified were 'avoid filling up landfills', 'reduce waste', 're-use materials' and 'save the environment'. These were linked to the terminal values of 'promote health/avoid sickness', 'achieve life-sustaining ends' and 'provide for future generations'. Another study reported that the perceived effort involved in recycling was the best predictor of whether people would go through the trouble – this pragmatic dimension outweighed general attitudes towards recycling and the environment in predicting intention to recycle.[131] Yet, another (European) study concluded, among other things, that one major motivating factor for recycling was a high perceived effectiveness of the action, that is, whether the consumer thinks it makes a difference if he/she recycles[132] By applying such techniques to study recycling and other product disposal behaviours, it will be easier for social marketers to design

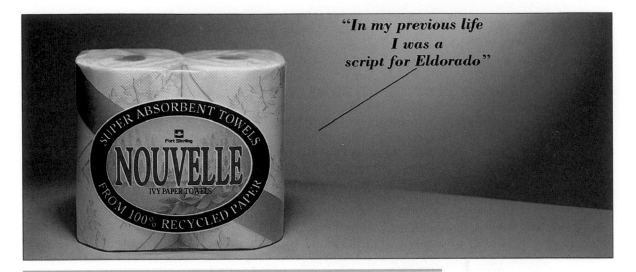

This British ad for paper towels takes a humorous route to emphasize that the paper towels are made from recycled paper.
Lurzer's Archiv, 1994, 91. Photo courtesy of BDH, Manchester, UK. Creative Team; Wayne Hanson, Graham Daldry.

advertising copy and other messages that tap into the underlying values that will motivate people to increase environmentally responsible behaviour.[133]

Even considering the difficulties in measurement, statistics reveal that the production of waste differs enormously among the countries of Europe. In the late 1980s, the yearly municipal solid waste per capita in Western European countries ranged from 231 kg in Portugal to 608 kg in Finland. As a comparison, the corresponding figure in the US was 864 kg. The different levels of waste generation are due to differences in general income level and to differences in consumption styles.[134]

Waste management also differs among countries. Different types of recycling programmes in Denmark encourage people to cut down on household waste and recycle as much as possible, as the municipal waste management systems charge consumers according to weight or volume of the household waste.[135] The Danish model of waste management, which stresses local responsibility for source separation programmes, is now marketed globally through on-site visits and video cassettes.[136] In Germany, producers are required by law to be responsible for the redistribution and recycling of used products.[137] In addition to recycling, other disposal programmes have caught the authorities' interest. In several European countries, including Spain, Italy, France and Denmark, economic incentives have been offered

Marketing opportunity Some enterprising entrepreneurs have found profitable ways to encourage recycling by creating fashion items out of recycled materials. Two young jewellery designers in New York created a fad by making necklaces out of old bottle caps. They even pay homeless people to collect the caps. A company called Little Earth Productions Inc. makes all its products from recycled materials. They sell backpacks decorated with old license plates, a shoulder bag made from rubber and hubcaps, and even purses crafted from discarded tuna cans.[138]

En als u erop uitgekeken bent,
ruimen we hem weer netjes op.

This Dutch Volkswagen ad focuses on recycling. The copy says, 'And when you've had enough of it, we'll clear it away nicely'.
Lurzer's Archiv, 1994. Photo courtesy of Volkswagen and DDB Needham Worldwide BV Amsterdam.

by the state to encourage car owners to replace their old car with a newer one, in order to reduce air pollution and increase road safety.[139]

Lateral cycling: junk versus 'junque'

Interesting consumer processes occur during **lateral cycling**, where already purchased objects are sold to others or exchanged for yet other things. Many purchases are made secondhand, rather than new. The re-use of other people's things is especially important in our throw-away society because, as one researcher put it, 'there is no longer an "away" to throw things to'.[140]

Flea markets, garage sales, classified advertisements, bartering for services, hand-me-downs and the black market all represent important alternative marketing systems which operate in addition to the formal marketplace. In the US the number of used-merchandise retail establishments has grown at about ten times the rate of other stores.[141] While traditional marketers have paid little attention to the secondhand market, factors such as concern about the environment, demands for quality and cost and fashion consciousness are conspiring to make these 'secondary' markets more important.[142] Interest in antiques, period accessories and specialized magazines catering for this niche is increasing. Other growth areas include markets for used computers and ski swaps, where used ski equipment is exchanged. A new generation of secondhand shopkeepers is developing markets for everything from used office equipment to cast-off kitchen sinks. Many are non-profit ventures started with government funding. These efforts remind us that recycling is actually the last step in the familiar mantra of the environmental movement: reduce, re-use, recycle. Only if no use is found for an item should it be shredded and made into something else.

From recycling to environmentalism and the political consumer

Recycling has proved to be only the beginning of a more profound process, taking into consideration not only recyclability but also environmental issues connected to the production process. Concern for the environment, or the **green movement**, is no longer confined to recycling but to all aspects of the production and consumption processes and is affecting marketing strategies for products ranging from nappies to fast food. For example, Ecover, a highly environmentally conscious Belgian producer of detergents and cleaning products, appealed to consumers' environmental concerns in a tongue-in-cheek way by recycling its competitors' old TV commercials. The company used five black-and-white commercials from the 1950s and superimposed a colour picture of its brand over the competing brand while a voice-over explained that the old commercial had been recycled.[143] It has been argued that environmental concern is gradually becoming a new universal value, not in its militant form but as a more tacit precondition for the degree of acceptability of products.[144] One commentator expressed it in a paradox: 'Environmentalism means that we will no longer have ecological milk. We will have milk and industrial milk.' This might also lead to more sensitivity towards various kinds of natural products and products from smaller independent producers. Different consumer groups are thus increasing pressure on producers to demonstrate that they are producing in such a way as to preserve nature and resources rather than exploit them.

Certain retail chains in Europe have been pioneering the environmentally friendly policies. Migros, the largest Swiss retail chain, has cut down on packaging material, increased its use of train transportation, and introduced various forms of non-toxic, well-insulated stores to cut energy consumption, etc. Tengelmann of Germany (chlorine-free products, milk dispensing machines for recyclable milk containers), Otto, the world's largest mail-order company (environmental friendliness as corporate culture, collaborations with the World Wildlife Fund), Sainsbury (recycled plastic bags, a 'Penny Back Scheme' donating refunded pennies to charity) and Tesco (comprehensive labelling, healthy eating programme and organically grown produce) of the UK are among the pioneering retailers for environmental issues.[145]

There are obvious differences among various European countries concerning the role of environmentalism. It is a politically more important issue in such countries as Germany, Denmark and Sweden. A study of the relative importance of environmental concern in car purchases ranked Germany first, followed by the UK, France and Spain.[146]

Environmentalist attitudes and behaviours have proved hard to predict. Some have argued that the trend is waning since an organization such as Greenpeace has experienced a decline in membership. Others have concluded that while attitudes are 'green', actual behaviour is less likely to change. This was the conclusion of one 1991 study of Danish consumers.[147] Since then, the demand for ecological produce in the dairy, egg and vegetable sectors has exploded, in Denmark as in many other countries. One major indication that environmentalism is becoming a (more or less) global value and is not just a passing fad is the role that concern for the environment plays in youth-oriented media such as MTV and, not least, in school curricula.[148]

Many consumer studies have tried to establish a distinct value profile for environmentally oriented consumers,[149] discussing, for example, whether they are more individually or socially oriented.[150] Values such as 'close relationships to others' and 'social justice' have been identified as being associated with a higher degree of environmentally conscious attitudes and behaviour.[151]

An environmentally related issue such as the use of growth hormones in milk and beef is a major problem in trade negotiations between Europe and the US. Some argue by references to scientific data stating that there is no risk,[152] but others

LOOKING FOR PACKAGING THAT IS ECOLOGICALLY SOUND?

Plastic. Glass. Metal. All everyday packaging materials. But not all degradable.
If we want to avoid leaving a mountain of waste behind us, in a world whose natural resources we've plundered and squandered, we need to find packaging materials that are in harmony with nature.
Nature makes only disposable packaging. This has satisfied its needs for millions of years and, naturally, is ecologically sound. It is part of the natural cycle in which materials are broken down and then used again.
We can learn from this.

FRÖVI ALONE.
FRÖVI is the only manufacturer of unbleached, coated board in Europe.
Because the board is based entirely on wood fibre sourced from Swedish forests, it is recyclable, degradable and renewable. Fully integrated into the natural cycles. Born of the earth, it is returned to the earth.
The board's combination of inherent properties – strength, purity and elegance – gives our customers the freedom to choose packaging that is ideal in every respect. Even ecologically.

CREATIVE PACKAGING.
We are suppliers of raw materials to the European packaging industry, committed to influencing the direction of future developments.
Working closely with the leading plant manufacturers, the conversion industry, the retail industry and the end users, we are constantly fine-tuning our products and advancing our knowledge.
Given the increasing environmental awareness in Europe, you need ecologically sound packaging. We can supply the right basic material.

 FRÖVI

FRÖVI CARTONBOARD SALES LTD.
- A MEMBER OF THE ASSI GROUP.
FRÖVI HOUSE, 284 B CHASE ROAD, SOUTHGATE
LONDON N14 6HF. PHONE 081-882 63 73.

This Swedish ad for a manufacturer of ecologically friendly packaging materials reflects the desire of many marketers to participate in the green movement.
Courtesy of Ehrenstrahle & Co., BBDO, Stockholm, SWEDEN.

maintain the argument that it is a matter of production and consumption ethics more than of actual risks to consumers. Whatever the case, many consumers are highly sceptical about such things as genetically manipulated produce (15 per cent acceptance in France; 31 per cent in the UK).[153] Thus, what is at stake on the consumer level, disregarding the international economic interests involved, seems to be the confrontation of an economic versus a moral logic.

The political consumer

The green consumer has recently been followed by, or maybe turned into, the concept of the **political consumer**. The political consumer uses her or his buying pattern as a weapon against and support for the companies that reflect values similar to the consumer's own. This consumer type selects products according to the company's ethical behaviour, which includes respect for human rights, animal protection, environmental friendliness and support for various benevolent causes. Companies such as The Body Shop are founded on the idea of natural and non-animal tested products and a maximum of environmental concern. But their con-

The Body Shop's Ruby, a Barbie look-alike doll but with considerably rounder forms, introduced in order to fight the tyranny of thinness and impossible body ideal of the supermodels and also reinforced by Barbie's shape.
©The Body Shop International PLC 1997. This material is reproduced with the permission of The Body Shop International Arts PLC.

cerns are becoming directed towards a broader array of social values. They recently took up the debate of beauty ideals by introducing 'Ruby', a Barbie look-alike doll but with considerably rounder forms in order to fight the tyranny of thinness and the impossible body ideal of the supermodels also endorsed by Barbie's shape. The reaction was predictable: Mattel Inc., the producers of Barbie, took out an injunction against The Body Shop because Ruby's face was too like Barbie's.

Many other companies are now working proactively to avoid the sort of trouble Shell ran into in Denmark, the Netherlands and Germany with the Brent Spar case, or the difficulties French exporters experienced in the wake of nuclear testing in 1996. Just to mention a few cases, the mineral water company Ramlösa is campaigning for clean water acts in the third world together with the Red Cross in Scandinavia under the slogan 'Water for Life',[154] and British Telecom has run a campaign underlining their work for elderly and disabled people.[155] The two brewery giants Heineken and Carlsberg both withdrew plans for large-scale investments in Myanmar (Burma) after consumers' protests against what was seen as direct support for the repressive military government there.

There is a risk that the political consumer may become an even more moralizing politically correct consumer, as has occurred in the US's political and cultural climate. In fact, some British consumer groups have taken action against the

Botanical and natural extracts
No animal testing
Nothing but earth-friendly inks
Recycled packaging
And every time you buy it, money goes
to preserving the Rainforest

It's the way you
care
teach
think
dream
believe

Love's
Clean
& Natural
It's the way you live.

Introducing Clean & Natural Cologne Splash, All-Over
Body Spray, Shower Gel, Moisturizer, Body Powder & Deodorant.

©1991 MEM Company Inc. Northvale, N.J. 07647

This American ad for a range of body powders and oils is positioned to appeal to people who are ecologically minded. It hits many of the political consumer issues: no animal testing, packaging is recycled and a part of the profits goes to help the rain forests.
Love's Clean & Natural, MEM Company, Inc.

companies which screened commercials during the TV broadcast of the controversial film *The Last Temptation of Christ*.[156] The question is: where is the dividing line between morality and moralizing?

Chapter summary

- The *act of purchase* can be affected by many factors. These include the consumer's antecedent state (e.g. his/her mood, time pressure or attitude to shopping). Time is an important resource which often determines how much effort and search will go into a decision. Mood can be affected by the degree of pleasure and arousal present in a store environment.
- The *usage context* of a product can be a basis for segmentation; consumers look for different product attributes depending on the use to which they intend to put their purchase. The presence or absence of other people – and the types of people they are – can also affect a consumer's decisions.
- The *shopping experience* is a pivotal part of the purchase decision. In many cases, retailing is like theatre – the consumer's evaluation of stores and products may depend on the type of 'performance' he or she witnesses. This evaluation can be influenced by the actors (e.g. salespeople), the setting (the store environment) and props (e.g. store displays). A *store image*, like a brand personality, is determined by a number of factors, such as perceived convenience, sophistication, knowledgeability of salespeople, and so on. With increasing competition from non-store alternatives, the creation of a positive shopping experience has never been more important.

- Since many purchase decisions are not made until the time the consumer is actually in the store, *point-of-purchase* (POP) stimuli are very important sales tools. These include product samples, elaborate package displays, place-based media and in-store promotional materials such as 'shelf talkers'. POP stimuli are particularly useful in stimulating impulse buying, where a consumer yields to a sudden urge for a product.
- The consumer's encounter with a salesperson is a complex and important process. The outcome can be affected by such factors as the salesperson's similarity to the customer and his or her perceived credibility.
- The perspective called *relationship marketing* stresses the desirability of building a long-term relationship with the consumer. Like a romantic relationship, it develops in stages of increasing familiarity and identification.
- *Consumer satisfaction* is determined by the person's overall feeling towards the product after purchase. Many factors influence perceptions of product quality, including price, brand name and product performance. Satisfaction is often determined by the degree to which a product's performance is consistent with the consumer's prior expectations of how well it will function.
- *Product disposal* is an increasingly important problem. Recycling is one option which will continue to be stressed as consumers' environmental awareness grows. Products may also be introduced by consumers into secondary markets during a process of *lateral cycling*, which occurs when objects are bought and sold secondhand, 'fenced' or bartered.
- The *green movement* is a common denominator in the trend towards increased attention to the environmental impact of human activities. In terms of consumption, this has broadened the scope of enviromental judgement from recycling of scarce resources to attention to the whole production and distribution process.
- The green movement may be an indication of an even broader trend towards more conscious reflection on the ethical aspects of consumption. The *political consumer* 'votes with his/her shopping basket' in an attempt to influence companies to care for the natural as well as the human environment, adding issues such as human rights to the set of dimensions that influence purchases.

Key terms

Atmospherics *(p. 252)*
Consumer
   satisfaction/dissatisfaction
   (CS/D) *(p. 256)*
Exchange theory *(p. 255)*
Expectancy disconfirmation
   model *(p. 257)*
Green movement *(p. 261)*
Impulse buying *(p. 252)*
ISO standards *(p. 256)*

Lateral cycling *(p. 261)*
Point-of-purchase stimuli (POP)
   (p. 253)
Political consumer *(p. 263)*
Recycling *(p. 258)*
Relationship marketing *(p. 255)*
Shopping orientation *(p. 248)*
Store gestalt *(p. 251)*
Store image *(p. 251)*
Time style *(p. 242)*

Consumer behaviour challenge

1. Discuss some of the motivations for shopping as described in the chapter. How might a retailer adjust his or her strategy to accommodate these motivations?

2. What are the positive and negative aspects of requiring employees who interact with customers to wear some kind of uniform or to impose a dress code in the office?

3. The store environment is heating up as more and more companies put their promotional means into point-of-purchase efforts. Shoppers are now confronted by videos at the checkout, computer monitors attached to their shopping trolleys, and so on. Place-based media expose us to ads in non-shopping environments. Do you feel that these innovations are unacceptably intrusive? At what point might shoppers rebel and demand some peace while shopping? Do you see any market potential in the future for stores that 'counter-market' by promising a 'hands-off' shopping environment?

4. List the five stages of a long-term service relationship. How can a practitioner of relationship marketing incorporate each stage into his or her strategy?

5. Discuss the concept of 'timestyle'. Based on your own experiences, how might consumers be segmented in terms of their timestyles?

6. Compare and contrast different cultures' conceptions of time. What are the implications for marketing strategy within each of these frameworks?

7. The movement away from a 'disposable consumer society' towards one that emphasizes creative recycling creates many opportunities for marketers. Can you identify some?

8. Conduct naturalistic observation at a local mall, shopping centre or supermarket. Sit in a central location and observe the activities of mall staff and customers. Keep a log of the non-retailing activity you observe (e.g. special performances, exhibits, socializing, etc.). Does this activity enhance or detract from business conducted at the mall?

9. Select three competing clothing shops in your area and conduct a store image study for each one. Ask a group of consumers to rate each store on a set of attributes and plot these ratings on the same graph. Based on your findings, are there any areas of competitive advantage or disadvantage you could bring to the attention of store management? (This technique was described in chapter 5.)

10. Using Table 9.1 as a model, construct a person/situation segmentation matrix for a brand of perfume.

11. In your opinion, in which areas have the environmental issues had the biggest impact on consumer behaviour? Why do you think that is the case?

12. Is the 'political consumer' a fad or a new and growing challenge for marketers and producers? Discuss.

13. Go to your local supermarket to check the selection of ecological products. How are they presented in the store? What does that say about the way these products are regarded?

14. Try to provide an estimate about how often environmental issues are mentioned in advertising. Are these messages credible? Why or why not?

15. What do you think about boycotts as consumers' response to what is perceived as companies' unethical behaviour?

CHAPTER 10

Karin Ekstrom, Göteburg University, Sweden

It was December and Björn had been thinking of snowboards all day after seeing a brilliant ad for a store called Summit in the morning newspaper with the headline 'Sweaty feet free of charge'. Maybe he could ask his dad if he could have a snowboard for Christmas? How could he convince him? Well, most of his friends had one, and it would make winter holidays in the Swedish mountains with the family much more fun. He couldn't bear the thought of coming back and telling his friends he had been downhill skiing! And it wouldn't be as expensive because the ad said that if you bought the snowboard now, you would get the boots free.

Björn thought about what clothes to wear. Snowboarders used to wear baggy, knitted clothes which absorbed the snow. But not anymore. Goretex is definitely the best material. Maybe his grandmother would pitch in on a jacket? She liked to see him happy and definitely knew that quality matters. If he bought a good, high-tech jacket, it could also be used for mountain climbing. According to his friends, the best brand was Vampire. The Swedish national snowboard team uses Goldwin, and Ingemar Stenmark, the famous downhill skier, is involved in that design. Björn had read about cross-over trends in a sports magazine, that is, that clothing styles for skiers and snowboarders were becoming more similar.

Björn wondered if the snowboard brands in the ad were any good. He would ask his friends and also the salespeople at Summit. The famous Swedish snowboarder Ingmar Backman apparently uses Four Square and United Rewind. Of course, the snowboard and brand depended on whether he was going to practise alpine, halfpipe or boarder-cross. Bright colours were out; he definitely wanted a black snowboard. He could just see himself snowboarding at Riksgränsen, on the border of northern Sweden.

Group influence, opinion leadership and diffusion of innovations

Introduction

Skiing and snowboarding are an important part of Björn's identity, and his friends influence many of his buying decisions. Fellow snowboarders are united in their consumption choices so that total strangers feel an immediate bond with each other when they meet.

Humans are social animals. We all belong to groups, try to please others and pick up cues about how to behave by observing the actions of those around us. In fact, our desire to 'fit in' or to identify with desirable individuals or groups is the primary motivation for many of our purchases and activities. We often go to great lengths to please the members of a group whose acceptance we covet.

This chapter focuses on how other people, whether fellow skiers, co-workers, friends and family, or just casual acquaintances influence our purchase decisions. It considers how our preferences are shaped by our group memberships, by our desire to please or be accepted by others, even by the actions of famous people whom we've never even met. Finally, it explores why some people are more influential than others in affecting consumers' product preferences, and how marketers go about finding those people and enlisting their support in the persuasion process.

Reference groups

Björn doesn't model himself on *any* snowboarder – only the people with whom he really identifies can exert that kind of influence. For example, Björn primarily identifies with other Swedish snowboarders. Essentially, only the Swedes comprise Björn's *reference group*.

A **reference group** is 'an actual or imaginary individual or group conceived of having significant relevance upon an individual's evaluations, aspirations, or behaviour'.[1] There are three reference group influences: *informational*, *utilitarian* and *value-expressive*. These are described in Table 10.1 and discussed in this chapter.

Types of reference groups

Although two or more people are normally required to form a group, the term reference group is used more loosely to describe *any* external influence that provides social cues.[2] The referent may be a cultural figure and have an impact on many

Table 10.1 **Three forms of reference group influence**

Informational influence	The individual seeks information about various brands from an association of professionals or independent group of experts.
	The individual seeks information from those who work with the product as a profession.
	The individual seeks brand-related knowledge and experience (such as how Brand A's performance compares to Brand B's) from those friends, neighbours, relatives, or work associates who have reliable information about the brands.
	The brand the individual selects is influenced by observing a seal of approval of an independent testing agency.
	The individual's observation of what experts do (such as observing the type of car that police drive or the brand of television that repairmen buy) influences his or her choice of a brand.
Utilitarian influence	So that he or she satisfies the expectation of fellow work associates, the individual's decision to purchase a particular brand is influenced by their preferences.
	The individual's decision to purchase a particular brand is influenced by the preferences of people with whom he or she has social interaction.
	The individual's decision to purchase a particular brand is influenced by the preferences of family members.
	The desire to satisfy the expectations that others have of him or her has an impact on the individual's brand choice.
Value-expressive influence	The individual feels that the purchase or use of a particular brand will enhance the image others have of him or her.
	The individual feels that those who purchase or use a particular brand possess the characteristics that he or she would like to have.
	The individual sometimes feels that it would be nice to be like the type of person that advertisements show using a particular brand.
	The individual feels that the people who purchase a particular brand are admired or respected by others.
	The individual feels that the purchase of a particular brand would help show others what he or she is or would like to be (such as an athlete, successful business person, good parent, etc.)

Source: Adapted from C. Whan Park and V. Parker Lessig, 'Students and Housewives: Differences in Susceptibility to Reference Group Influence', *Journal of Consumer Research* 4 (September 1977): 102. Reprinted with permission by The University of Chicago Press.

people (e.g. the late Mother Theresa or members of royal families) or a person or group whose influence is confined to the consumer's immediate environment (e.g. Björn's skiing friends). Reference groups that affect consumption can include parents, fellow skiing, motorcycle or other leisure activity enthusiasts, a political party or even sports clubs such as Manchester United and bands such as U2.

Some groups and individuals exert a greater influence than others and for a broader range of consumption decisions. For example, our parents may play a pivotal role in forming our values towards many important issues, such as attitudes about marriage or where to go to college. This **normative influence** helps to set and enforce fundamental standards of conduct. In contrast, a Harley-Davidson club might exert **comparative influence**, where decisions about specific brands or activities are affected.[3]

| **Multicultural dimensions**  | '**C**ommon man' or 'slice-of-life' depictions, which highlight 'real' people, are more realistic and thus more credible than celebrities or superstars. While we admire perfect people, it can be frustrating to compare ourselves with them and their actually using the product may seem improbable. By including people who are successful but not perfect, consumers' identification with them is often enhanced. This strategy has been successfully employed in the classic 'Dewar's Profiles', a series of ads describing the lifestyles of non-celebrity high achievers who happen to drink Dewar's Scotch Whisky. Since the strategy uses real people from many different walks of life, the company has expanded its ad campaigns to focus on accomplished people in different countries. For example, a Thai ad highlights a successful architect who lives in Bangkok, while a Spanish campaign features a 29-year-old flight instructor, as seen in the ad shown here.[4] |

Dewar's has successfully used non-celebrities as endorsers in its 'Profiles' campaign, which is now being adapted to other countries, as this Spanish ad illustrates.
Courtesy of Schenley Industries, Inc.

Formal versus informal groups

A reference group can take the form of a large, formal organization that has a recognized structure, regular meeting times and officers. Or it can be small and informal, such as a group of friends or students living in a dormitory. Marketers tend to have more control over their influencing of formal groups because they are more easily identifiable and accessible.

In general, small, informal groups exert a more powerful influence on individual consumers. These groups tend to be more involved in our day-to-day lives and to be more important to us, because they are high in normative influence. Larger, formal groups tend to be more product- or activity-specific and thus are high in comparative influence.

Membership versus aspirational reference groups

While some reference groups consist of people the consumer actually knows, others are composed of people the consumer can *identify with* or admire. Not surprisingly, many marketing efforts that specifically adopt a reference group appeal concentrate on highly visible, widely admired figures, such as well-known athletes.

Identificational reference groups

Since people tend to compare themselves with others who are similar, they are often swayed by knowing how people like themselves conduct their lives. For this reason, many promotional strategies include 'ordinary' people whose consumption activities provide informational social influence. For example, in the campaign for fish consumption, discussed in chapter 4, the endorsing actors performed as very ordinary people to underline the message that special fish dishes are not difficult to prepare or are for high-class gourmets only.[5]

The likelihood that people will become part of a consumer's identificational reference group is affected by several factors, including:

- *Propinquity*: As physical distance between people decreases and opportunities for interaction increase, relationships are more likely to form. Physical nearness is called *propinquity*. An early study of friendship patterns in a housing estate showed this factor's strong effects: residents were much more likely to be friends with the people next door than with those who lived only two doors away. People who lived next to a stairway had more friends than those at the end of a corridor (presumably, they were more likely to bump into people using the stairs).[6] Physical structure has a lot to do with whom we get to know and how popular we are.
- *Mere exposure*: We grow to like persons or things simply as a result of seeing them more often: the *mere exposure phenomenon*.[7] Greater frequency of contact, even if unintentional, may help to determine one's set of local referents. The same effect holds when evaluating works of art, or even political candidates.[8] One study predicted 83 per cent of the winners in a political election solely by the amount of media exposure given to candidates.[9]
- *Group cohesiveness*: The degree to which members of a group are attracted to each other and value their group membership is called cohesiveness. As the value of the group to the individual increases, so too does the likelihood that the group will guide consumption decisions. Smaller groups tend to be more cohesive, because it is more difficult to relate to larger groups of people. By the same token, groups often try to restrict membership to a select few, which

increases the value of membership to those who are admitted. Exclusivity of membership is a benefit often touted by credit card companies, book clubs, and so on, even though the actual membership base might be fairly large.

It is an old, established truth in marketing that while the consumer may have no direct contact with reference groups, they can have powerful influences on his or her tastes and preferences, because they provide guidance as to the types of products used by admired people.[10] *Aspirational reference groups* are composed of idealized figures such as successful business people, athletes or performers. Many ads featuring such groups rely on the aspirational reference group perspective to appeal to people who aspire to be successful just as the role models depicted in the ad.

For example, one study that included business students who aspired to the 'executive' role found a strong relationship between products they associated with their *ideal selves* (see chapter 7) and those they assumed would be owned or used by executives.[11]

Positive versus negative reference groups

Reference groups may exert either a positive or a negative influence on consumption behaviours. In most cases, consumers model their behaviour to be consistent with what they think the group expects of them. In some cases, though, a consumer may try to distance him- or herself from other people or groups who function as *avoidance groups*. He or she may carefully study the dress or mannerisms of a disliked group and scrupulously avoid buying anything that might identify him or her with that group.[12] For example, rebellious adolescents often resent parental influence and may deliberately do the opposite of what their parents would like as a way of making a statement about their independence. As Romeo and Juliet discovered, nothing makes a partner more attractive than a little parental opposition.

When reference groups are important

Reference group influences are not equally powerful for all types of products and consumption activities. For example, products that are not very complex, that are low in perceived risk and that can be tried prior to purchase are less susceptible to personal influence.[13] In addition, the specific impact of reference groups may vary. At times they may determine the use of certain products rather than others (e.g. owning or not owning a computer, eating junk food versus health food), while at other times they may have specific effects on brand decisions within a product category (e.g., wearing Levi's versus Calvin Klein jeans, or smoking Marlboro cigarettes instead of a national brand).

Two dimensions that influence the degree to which reference groups are important are whether the purchase is to be consumed publicly or privately and whether it is a luxury or a necessity. As a rule, reference group effects are more robust for purchases that are (1) luxuries rather than necessities (e.g. yachts), since products that are purchased with discretionary income are subject to individual tastes and preferences, while necessities do not offer this range of choices; and (2) socially conspicuous or visible to others (e.g. living room furniture or clothing) since consumers do not tend to be swayed as much by the opinions of others if their purchases will never be observed by anyone but themselves.[14] The relative effects of reference group influences on some specific product classes are shown in Figure 10.1. This obviously does not mean that a reference group cannot exert influence on the consumption of private necessities.

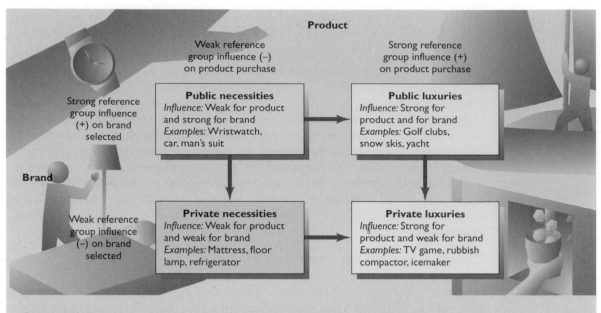

Figure 10.1 Relative reference group influence on purchase decisions
Adapted from William O. Bearden and Michael J. Etzel, 'Reference Group Influence on Product and Brand Purchase Decisions', *Journal of Consumer Research* (September 1982): 185. Reprinted with permission by The University of Chicago Press.

Marketing opportunity

Group membership has entered cyberspace, as 'netizens' around the world rapidly form virtual communities. Members are linked to one another via their computer modems, and all of their interactions are digital.[15] This electronic anonymity opens exciting new vistas for many, especially those who have difficulty interacting in face-to-face settings (e.g. the net has made a dramatic difference in the lives of many disabled people who can now interact with others around the globe without having to leave home). New technologies allow people to chat about their mutual interests, to help one another with enquiries and suggestions, and to get suggestions for new products and services.

The power of reference groups

Social power refers to 'the capacity to alter the actions of others'.[16] To the degree that you are able to make someone else do something, whether they do it willingly or not, you have power over that person. The following classification of *power bases* can help us to distinguish among the reasons a person can exert power over another, the degree to which the influence is allowed voluntarily, and whether this influence will continue to have an effect in the absence of the power source.[17]

Referent power

If a person admires the qualities of a person or a group, he or she will try to imitate those qualities by copying the referent's behaviours (e.g. choice of clothing, cars, leisure activities) as a guide to forming consumption preferences, just as Björn's preferences were affected by his fellow snowboarders. Prominent people in all walks of life can affect people's consumption behaviours by virtue of product endorsements (e.g. Eric Cantona for Nike), distinctive fashion statements (e.g. Madonna's use of lingerie as outerwear), or championing causes (e.g. Brigitte Bardot's work against fur). Referent power is important to many marketing strategies because consumers voluntarily change behaviours to please or identify with a referent.

Information power

A person can have **information power** simply because he or she knows something others would like to know. Editors of trade publications in the fashion industry often possess power due to their ability to compile and disseminate information that can make or break individual designers or companies. People with information power are able to influence consumer opinion by virtue of their (assumed) access to the 'truth'.

Legitimate power

Sometimes people are granted power by virtue of social agreements, such as the power given to the police and professors. The legitimate power conferred by a

Marketing opportunity

One of the most recent and widespread applications of reference group influences to consumer behaviour is affinity marketing. This strategy allows consumers to underscore their identification with some organization by attaching the group's identification to aspects of their personal life.

In the most common form of affinity marketing, the endorsement of a group leader or the coupling of a company with insignia of a special reference group is used to sell to members of that group. This technique has been mostly used in the credit card market where depictions of rock stars, sports stars or other publicly identifiable reference persons have been depicted on the bank's credit cards,[18] but is now spreading to other types of markets as well.[19]

This anti-tobacco advertisement recognizes the role of reference groups. Many teens start smoking due to peer influence. This message uses the same reference group approach to discourage smoking.
Brogan and Partners. Used with permission.

uniform is recognized in many consumer contexts, including teaching hospitals, where medical students don white coats to enhance their aura of authority with patients, and organizations where uniforms communicate trustworthiness.[20] This form of power may be 'borrowed' by marketers to influence consumers. For example, an ad featuring a model wearing a nurse's uniform can add an aura of legitimacy or authority to the presentation of the product, as seen in TV advertising campaigns in the baby's nappy market.

Expert power

Expert power is derived from possessing a specific knowledge or skill. Consumers are often influenced by experts who are assumed to be able to evaluate products in an objective, informed way. This power base also underlies the appeal of television shows, where panels of authorities – often a mix of journalists and professional experts – discuss issues of interest to consumers.

Reward power

When a person or group has the means to provide positive reinforcement (see chapter 4), that entity will have power over a consumer to the extent that this reinforcement is valued or desired. The reward may be tangible, as occurs when an employee is given a pay rise. Or, the reward may be intangible: social approval or acceptance is often what is exchanged in return for moulding one's behaviour to a group or buying the products expected of group members. However, this kind of power is perhaps wearing thin in advertising, since an over-exploitation of reward arguments has left such campaigns with little credibility. The Sprite soft drink campaign under the slogan 'Image is nothing, thirst is everything, obey your thirst' makes fun of other commercials' use of reward power by suggesting something seen as more basic, thirst. However, the slogan in itself paradoxically promises a reward in the form of an image – of somebody who does not fall for cheap tricks.[21]

Coercive power

While coercive power often is effective in the short term, it does not tend to produce permanent attitudinal or behavioural change. Surveillance of some sort is usually required to make people do something they do not wish to do. Fortunately, coercive power is rarely employed in marketing situations. However, elements of this power base are evident in fear appeals, intimidation in personal selling and campaigns that emphasize the negative consequences that can occur if people do not use a product.

Conformity

Conformity refers to a change in beliefs or actions as a reaction to real or imagined group pressure. In order for a society to function, its members develop **norms,** or informal rules that govern behaviour. If such a system of agreements did not evolve, chaos would result. Imagine the confusion if a simple norm such as stopping for a red traffic light did not exist. While norms change slowly over time, there is general agreement within a society about which ones should be obeyed, and we adjust our way of thinking to conform to these norms.

Unspoken rules govern many aspects of consumption. In addition to norms regarding appropriate use of clothing and other personal items, we conform to rules that include gift-giving (we expect birthday presents from loved ones and get upset if they do not materialize), sex roles (men often are expected to pick up the bill on a first date) and personal hygiene (we are expected to shower or bathe regularly to avoid offending others).

Types of social influence

Just as the bases for social power can vary, the process of social influence operates in several ways.[22] Sometimes a person is motivated to model the behaviour of others because this mimicry is believed to yield rewards such as social approval or money. At other times, the social influence process occurs simply because the person honestly does not *know* the correct way to respond and is using the behaviour of the other person or group as a cue to ensure that he or she is responding correctly.[23] **Normative social influence** occurs when a person conforms to meet the expectations of a person or group.

In contrast, **informational social influence** refers to conformity that occurs because the group's behaviour is taken as evidence of reality: if other people respond in a certain way in an ambiguous situation, we may mimic their behaviour because this appears to be the correct thing to do.[24]

Reasons for conformity

Conformity is not an automatic process, and many factors contribute to the likelihood that consumers will pattern their behaviour on others.[25] Among the factors that affect the likelihood of conformity are the following:

- *Cultural pressures.* Different cultures encourage conformity to a greater or lesser degree. The American slogan 'Do your own thing' in the 1960s reflected a movement away from conformity and towards individualism. In contrast, Japanese society is characterized by the dominance of collective well-being and group loyalty over individuals' needs. Most European societies are situated somewhere between these two in this respect 'extreme' cultures. In an analysis of the reading of a soft drink TV commercial, Danish consumers stressed the group solidarity that they saw in the ad, an aspect not mentioned at all by the American sample.[26]
- *Fear of deviance.* The individual may have reason to believe that the group will apply *sanctions* to punish behaviour that differs from the group's. It is not unusual to observe adolescents shunning a peer who is 'different' or a corporation passing over a person for promotion because he or she is not a 'team player'.
- *Commitment.* The more a person is dedicated to a group and values membership in it, the more motivated he or she will be to follow the dictates of the group. Rock groupies and followers of religious sects may do anything that is asked of them, and terrorists (or martyrs, depending on the perspective) may be willing to die for the good of their cause. According to the *principle of least interest*, the person or group that is least committed to staying in a relationship has the most power, because that party won't be susceptible to threatened rejection.[27]
- *Group unanimity, size and expertise.* As groups gain in power, compliance increases. It is often harder to resist the demands of a large number of people than just a few, and this difficulty is compounded when the group members are perceived to know what they are talking about.

- *Susceptibility to interpersonal influence:* This trait refers to an individual's need to identify or enhance his or her image in the opinion of significant others. This enhancement process often is accompanied by the acquisition of products the person believes will impress his or her audience, and by the tendency to learn about products by observing how others use them.[28] Consumers who are low on this trait have been called *role relaxed*; they tend to be older, affluent and have high self-confidence. Based on research identifying role-relaxed consumers, Subaru created a communications strategy to reach these people. In one commercial, a man is heard saying, 'I want a car . . . Don't tell me about wood panelling, about winning the respect of my neighbours. They're my neighbours. They're not my heroes . . .'

Social comparison: 'How am I doing?'

Informational social influence implies that sometimes we look to the behaviour of others to provide a yardstick about reality. **Social comparison theory** asserts that this process occurs as a way of increasing the stability of one's self-evaluation, especially when physical evidence is unavailable.[29] Social comparison even applies to choices for which there is no objectively correct answer. Such stylistic decisions as tastes in music and art are assumed to be a matter of individual choice, yet people often assume that some types are 'better' or more 'correct' than others.[30] If you have ever been responsible for choosing the music to play at a party, you can probably appreciate the social pressure involved in choosing the right 'mix'.

Choosing comparison groups

Although people often like to compare their judgements and actions with those of others, they tend to be selective about precisely whom they will use as benchmarks. Similarity between the consumer and others used for social comparison boosts confidence that the information is accurate and relevant (though we may find it more threatening to be outperformed by someone similar to ourselves).[31] We tend to value the views of obviously dissimilar others only when we are reasonably certain of our own.[32]

In general people tend to choose a *co-oriented peer*, or a person of equivalent standing, when undergoing social comparison. For example, a study of adult cosmetics users found that women were more likely to seek information about product choices from similar friends to reduce uncertainty and to trust the judgements of similar others.[33] The same effects have been found for evaluations of products as diverse as men's suits and coffee.[34]

Compliance and obedience

The discussion of persuasive communications in chapter 6 indicated that source and message characteristics have a large impact on the likelihood of influence. Influencers have been found to be more successful at gaining compliance if they are perceived to be confident or expert.[35]

Tactical requests

The way a request for compliance is phrased or structured can make a difference. One well-known sales tactic is known as the *foot-in-the-door technique*, where the consumer is first asked a small request and then is 'hit' for something bigger.[36] This term is adapted from door-to-door selling. Experienced salespeople know that they are much more likely to make a sale if they first convince a customer to let them into the house to deliver their sales pitch. Once the person has agreed to this small request, it is more difficult to refuse a larger one, since the consumer has legitimized the salesperson's presence by entering into a dialogue. He or she is no longer a threatening stranger at the door.

Other variations on this strategy include the *low-ball technique*, where a person is asked a small favour and is informed after agreeing to it that it will be very costly, or the *door-in-the-face technique*, where a person is first asked to do something extreme (a request that is usually refused) and then is asked to do something smaller. In each of these cases, people tend to go along with the smaller request, possibly because they feel guilty about denying the larger one.[37]

Group effects on individual behaviour

With more people in a group, it becomes less likely that any one member will be singled out for attention. People in larger groups or those in situations where they are likely to be unidentified tend to focus less attention on themselves, so normal restraints on behaviour are reduced. You may have observed that people sometimes behave more wildly at costume parties or on Hallowe'en night than they do normally. This phenomenon is known as **deindividuation**, where individual identities get submerged within a group.

There is some evidence that decisions made by groups differ from those made by an individual. In many cases, group members show a greater willingness to consider riskier alternatives following group discussion than they would if each member made his or her own decision with no discussion. This change is known as the **risky shift**.[38]

Several explanations have been advanced to explain this increased riskiness. One possibility is that something similar to social loafing occurs. As more people are involved in a decision, each individual is less accountable for the outcome, so *diffusion of responsibility* occurs.[39] Another explanation is termed the *value hypothesis*. In this case, riskiness is a culturally valued characteristic, and social pressures operate on individuals to conform to attributes valued by society.[40]

Evidence for the risky shift is mixed. A more general effect appears to be that group discussion tends to increase decision polarization. Whichever direction the group members were leaning before discussion began, towards a risky choice or towards a conservative choice, becomes even more extreme in that direction after discussion. Group discussions regarding product purchases tend to create a risky shift for low-risk items, but they yield even more conservative group decisions for high-risk products.[41]

Shopping patterns

Shopping behaviour changes when people do it in groups. For example, people who shop with at least one other person tend to make more unplanned purchases, buy more and cover more areas of a store than those who go alone.[42] These effects are due to both normative and informational social influence. Group members may be convinced to buy something to gain the approval of the others, or they may simply be exposed to more products and stores by pooling information with the group. For these reasons, retailers would be well advised to encourage group shopping activities.

Marketing opportunity

The institution of home shopping parties, as epitomized by Tupperware, capitalize on group pressures to boost sales.[43] A company representative makes a sales presentation to a group of people who have gathered in the home of a friend or acquaintance. This format is effective because of informational social influence: participants model the behaviour of others who can provide them with information about how to use certain products, especially since the home party is likely to be attended by a relatively homogeneous group (e.g. neighbourhood housewives) that serves as a valuable benchmark. Normative social influence also operates because actions are publicly observed. Pressures to conform may be particularly intense and may escalate as more and more group members begin to 'cave in' (this process is sometimes termed the *bandwagon effect*). In addition, deindividuation and/or the risky shift may be activated: as consumers get caught up in the group, they may find themselves willing to try new products they would not normally consider.

Resistance to influence

Many people pride themselves on their independence, unique style or ability to resist the best efforts of salespeople and advertisers to buy products.[44] Indeed, individuality should be encouraged by the marketing system: innovation creates change and demand for new products and styles.

Anti-conformity versus independence

It is important to distinguish between *independence* and *anti-conformity*, where defiance of the group is the actual object of behaviour.[45] Some people will go out of their way *not* to buy whatever happens to be in fashion. Indeed, they may spend a lot of time and effort to ensure that they will not be caught in style. This behaviour is a bit of a paradox, since in order to be vigilant about not doing what is expected, one must always be aware of what is expected. In contrast, truly independent people are oblivious to what is expected, they 'march to their own drummers'.

Reactance and the need for uniqueness

People have a deep-seated need to preserve freedom of choice. When they are threatened with a loss of freedom, they try to overcome this loss. This negative emotional state is termed **reactance**.[46] For example, efforts to censor books, television or rock music because some people find the content objectionable may result in an *increased* desire for these products by the public.[47] Similarly, extremely overbearing promotions that tell consumers they must or should use a product may lose customers in the long run, even those who were already loyal to the advertised brand! Reactance is more likely to occur when the perceived threat to one's freedom increases and as the threatened behaviour's importance to the consumer also increases.

If you have ever arrived at a party wearing the same outfit as someone else, you know how upsetting it can be. Some psychologists believe this reaction is a result of a need for uniqueness.[48] Consumers who have been led to believe they are not unique are more likely to try to compensate by increasing their creativity, or even to engage in unusual experiences. In fact, this need could be one explanation for the purchase of relatively obscure brands. People may try to establish a unique identity by deliberately *not* buying market leaders.

This desire to carve out a unique identity was the rationale behind Saab's shift from stressing engineering and safety in its marketing messages to appealing to people to 'find your own road'. According to a Saab executive, 'Research companies tell us we're moving into a period where people feel good about their choices because it fits their own self-concept rather than social conventions'.[49]

Word-of-mouth communication

Despite the abundance of formal means of communication (such as newspapers, magazines and television), much information about the world is conveyed by individuals on an informal basis. If you think carefully about the content of your own conversations in the course of a normal day, you will probably agree that much of what you discuss with friends, family members or fellow employees is product-related: whether you compliment someone on her dress and ask her where she bought it, recommend a new restaurant to a friend or complain to your neighbour about the shoddy treatment you got at the bank, you are engaging in **word-of-mouth communication (WOM)**. Recall, for example, that many of Björn's equipment purchases were directly initiated by comments and suggestions from his friends. This kind of communication can be an efficient marketing tool. When the British Triumph motor cycle was relaunched in the American market in 1991, they relied almost totally on the nostalgia of the brand and the efficiency of word-of-mouth communications among motor bike fans.[50]

Information obtained from those we know or talk to directly tends to be more reliable and trustworthy than that received through more formal channels, and unlike advertising, it is often backed up by social pressure to conform with these recommendations.[51] Another important factor for the importance of WOM is the decline in people's faith in institutions. As traditional endorsers are becoming increasingly problematical to use, celebrities because they can be unreliable and classical authority figures because of the withering of their authority, and, indeed, as people are becoming more cynical about all sorts of commercial communications, they turn to sources which they feel are above commercial exploitation: friends and family.[52] The importance of personal, informal product communication to marketers is further underscored by one advertising executive, who stated, 'Today, 80 per cent of all buying decisions are influenced by someone's direct recommendations.'[53]

The dominance of WOM

In the 1950s communications theorists began to challenge the assumption that advertising is the primary determinant of purchases: it is now generally accepted that advertising is more effective at reinforcing existing product preferences than at creating new ones.[54] Studies in both industrial and consumer purchase settings underscore the idea that while information from impersonal sources is important for creating brand awareness, word-of-mouth is relied upon in the later stages of evaluation and adoption.[55] The more positive information a consumer gets about a product from peers, the more likely it is that he or she will adopt the product.[56] The influence of others' opinions is at times even more powerful than one's own perceptions. In one study of furniture choices, consumers' estimates of how much their friends would like the furniture was a better predictor of purchase than their *own* evaluations.[57]

Factors encouraging WOM

Most WOM campaigns happen spontaneously, as a product begins to develop a regional or a subcultural following but occasionally, a 'buzz' is intentionally created. For example, when launching a new brand of beer, called 'Black Sheep', bottles were distributed and maximum exposure to opinion leaders in the trade ensured in order to pave the way for a massive word-of-mouth effect, intended as the vehicle carrying the new brand towards success.[58]

Product-related conversations can be motivated by a number of factors.[59]

- A person might be highly involved with a type of product or activity and enjoy talking about it. Computer hackers, avid bird-watchers and 'fashion plates' seem to share the ability to steer a conversation towards their particular interest.
- A person might be knowledgeable about a product and use conversations as a way to let others know it. Thus, word-of-mouth communication sometimes enhances the ego of the individual who wants to impress others with his or her expertise.
- A person might initiate such a discussion out of a genuine concern for someone else. We often are motivated to ensure that people we care about buy what is good for them, do not waste their money, and so on.
- One way to reduce uncertainty about the wisdom of a purchase is to talk about it. Talking gives the consumer an opportunity to generate more supporting arguments for the purchase and to garner support for this decision from others.

Efficiency of WOM

Interpersonal transmissions can be quite rapid. The producers of *Batman* showed a trailer to 300 Batman fans months before its release to counteract widespread anger about the casting of Michael Keaton as the hero. The filmmakers attribute the film's eventual huge success to the positive word-of-mouth that quickly spread following the screening.[60]

WOM is especially powerful in cases where the consumer is relatively unfamiliar with the product category. Such a situation would be expected in cases where the product is new (e.g. medication to prevent hair loss) or is technologically complex (e.g. CD players). As one example, the strongest predictor of a person's intention to buy a residential solar water heating system was found to be the number of solar heating users the person knows.[61]

Negative WOM

Word-of-mouth is a two-edged sword that can cut both ways for marketers. Informal discussions among consumers can make or break a product or store. And negative word-of-mouth is weighted *more* heavily by consumers than are positive comments. According to one study, 90 per cent of unhappy customers will not do business with a company again. Each of these people is likely to share their grievance with at least nine other people, and 13 per cent of these disgruntled customers will go on to tell *more than thirty* people of their negative experience.[62] Especially when making a decision about trying a product innovation, the consumer is more likely to pay attention to negative information than positive information and to relate news of this experience to others.[63] Negative WOM has been shown to reduce the credibility of a firm's advertising, and to influence consumers' attitudes towards a product as well as their intention to buy it.[64]

Rumours

In the 1930s, 'professional rumourmongers' were hired to organize word-of-mouth campaigns to promote clients' products and criticize those of competitors.[65] A **rumour**, even if it has no basis in fact, can be a very dangerous thing. As information is transmitted among consumers, it tends to change. The resulting message ceases to resemble the original.

Social scientists who study rumours have examined the process by which information gets distorted. The British psychologist Frederic Bartlett used the method of *serial reproduction* to examine this phenomenon. A subject is asked to reproduce a stimulus, such as a drawing or a story. Another subject is given this reproduction and asked to copy that, and so on. This technique is shown in Figure 10.2. Bartlett found that distortions almost inevitably follow a pattern: they tend to change from ambiguous forms to more conventional ones as subjects try to make them consistent with pre-existing schemas. This process, known as *assimilation*, is characterized by *levelling*, where details are omitted to simplify the structure, or *sharpening*, where prominent details are accentuated.

In general, people have been shown to prefer transmitting good news rather than bad, perhaps because they like to avoid unpleasantness or dislike arousing hostility. However, this reluctance does not appear to occur when companies are the topic of

Figure 10.2 **The transmission of misinformation These drawings provide a classic example of the distortions that can occur as information is transmitted from person to person. As each person reproduces the figure, it gradually changes from an owl to a cat.**
Source: Kenneth J. Gergen and Mary Gergen, *Social Psychology* (New York: Harcourt Brace Jovanovich, 1981): 365. Figure 10.2 adapted from F.C. Bartlett, *Remembering* (Cambridge: Cambridge University Press, 1932).

Original drawing

Marketing pitfall

After a very successful launching of the combined shampoo and conditioner 'Wash&Go' on the Danish market in January 1990, where the company reached a market share (value) of more than 20 per cent in September that same year, a negative rumour caused a severe blow to the company. First, hairdressers complained about problems with doing colourings and perms on clients using the new product. Procter & Gamble denied the complaint, but did not dispel the rumour and soon had to deal with a second rumour: that the use of the product caused significant loss of hair. Their market share fell from 20 to 5 per cent.[66]

Most rumours have some 'kernel of truth', and it is very important for the company facing the rumour to detect it. The silicon in Wash&Go actually did cause problems for certain perm or colouring products, but this was not immediately acknowledged. Instead, the denial of the first rumour without producing substantial factual documentation led to the spreading of the second rumour, perhaps as an attempt to 'get even with' the 'aggressive' marketer. Large foreign companies are often targets of such negative word-of-mouth.[67] Procter & Gamble first tried to ignore the rumour by denial, then to refute it with reference to their own research, a source of information which had little credibility and probably strengthened the rumour rather than weakened it. Only when they asked the state environmental agency to conduct independent tests could Procter & Gamble disprove the rumours and slowly begin to regain the lost market shares.[68]

conversation. Corporations such as Procter & Gamble and McDonald's have been the subjects of rumours about their products, sometimes with marked effects on sales.

Rumours are thought to reveal the underlying fears of a society. One of the most (in)famous rumours in modern European history concerned the white slave trade and reflected a tacit anti-Semitism in society. The rumour said that young women were kidnapped from fitting-rooms in Jewish shopkeepers' fashion boutiques in the French city of Orléans to be sent to the Middle East. The rumour in turn generated rumours about an anti-Semitic conspiracy against Jewish businesspeople.[69] Another rumour regarding snakes coming out of teddy bears imported from the Orient was interpreted to signify Western consumers' apprehensions about Asian influences. While rumours sometimes die out by themselves, in other instances a company may take direct action to counteract them. A French margarine was rumoured to contain contaminants, and the company addressed this in its advertising by referring to the story as 'The rumour that costs you dearly'.[70]

Multicultural dimensions

Multinational firms are especially prone to damage from rumours, since they may have less control over product quality, content or word-of-mouth. Several marketers in Indonesia, including Nestlé, have been damaged by rumours that their foods contain pork, which is prohibited to the 160 million Muslim consumers in that country. Islamic preachers, or mullahs, responded to these rumours by warning consumers not to buy products that might be tainted with pork fat. Nestlé spent more than $250,000 on an ad campaign to counteract the rumours.[71] A beer brewery was hit by a product-tampering scare in China. Rumours about poisoned bottles spread quickly, apparently following an incident where home-brewed beer was poured into empty bottles from this brewery and resold.[72]

Consumer boycotts

We live in a period when many consumers are becoming increasingly aware that their consumption pattern is part of a global political and economic system, to the extent that they become political consumers, as discussed in the previous chapter. Sometimes a negative experience can trigger an organized and devastating response, as when a consumer group organizes a *boycott* of a company's products. These efforts can include protests against everything from investing in a politically undesirable country (as when Carlsberg withdrew their investments from Myanmar as mentioned in chapter 9, or Shell was accused of tolerating pollution and political repression of the people of the Ogoni region of Nigeria) to efforts to discourage consumption of products from certain companies or countries (as during the boycott of French wines and other products during the nuclear testing in the Pacific in 1996, an action which was especially strongly felt in The Netherlands and in the Scandinavian countries). In the United States, the inclusion of obscene or inflammatory lyrics led to boycott threats as when law enforcement organizations threatened to boycott Time Warner after it distributed a rap song by Ice-T entitled 'Cop Killer'.

One well-known case was the boycott of Shell following its plans to dump an old drilling platform, Brent Spar, in the North Sea. In Germany, the company's revenue fell by almost 30 per cent; the boycott was felt in Denmark and The Netherlands too. Ironically, Shell's quick reversal of the decision to dump the platform only seemed to confirm to consumers that they were indeed guilty, in spite of evidence that deep-water disposal was the most environmentally friendly solution to the problem.[73]

Boycotts are not always effective – studies show that normally only a limited percentage of a country's consumers participate in them. However, those who do are disproportionately vocal and well educated, so they are a group companies especially don't want to alienate. The negative PR that arises from media coverage of the boycott may be problematic for the company in the long run, since competitors may gain relative advantages. After the boycott of French wines in Denmark had calmed down, the French wines had lost 20 per cent market share. However, that was not seen as the biggest problem, since the general impression was that consumers could be persuaded to switch back to French wines. But many supermarket shelves had been reorganized in order to give more space to Italian and Spanish wines, and this was considered a more serious problem.[74]

One increasingly popular solution used by marketers is setting up a joint task force with the boycotting organization to try to iron out the problem. In the US, McDonald's used this approach with the Environmental Defence Fund, which was concerned about its use of polystyrene containers and bleached paper. The company agreed to test a composting programme and to switch to plain brown bags.[75]

Opinion leadership

Although consumers get information from personal sources, they do not tend to ask *anyone* for advice about purchases. If you decide to buy a new stereo, you are most likely to seek advice from a friend who knows a lot about sound systems. This friend may own a sophisticated system, or he or she may subscribe to specialist magazines and spend time browsing in electronics stores. On the other hand, you may have another friend who has a reputation for being stylish and who spends *his* free time reading fashion and lifestyle magazines and shopping in trendy boutiques. While you might not bring your stereo problem to him, you may take him with you to shop for a new wardrobe.

This so-called opinion leadership is an important influence on a brand's popularity in many categories. The market for sports accessories is among these, where both celebrity endorsements (chapter 6) and sponsorship in order to form opinions are major marketing tools. The American Gatorade sports drink company made its entrance on the British market on an exclusive opinion leadership basis, sponsoring sports events and professionals like the captain of the national cricket team, but without any major promotion of the product itself. This suspense strategy created curiosity, interest and inquiries, and probably pre-shaped a lot of opinion leaders' opinions about the product before its major launch in distribution outlets.[76]

However, there is some discussion as to whether endorsement of individual athletes is a better communication vehicle than official sponsorship of events. Nike outscored many official sponsors at the Euro '96 Football Championship in England thanks to its campaign based on individual players, even though some of them didn't make it to their respective national teams. In many ways, this 'blunder' may have created even more mention and awareness of Nike than if the players had actually played.[77]

The nature of opinion leadership

Everyone knows people who are knowledgeable about products and whose advice is taken seriously by others. These individuals are **opinion leaders**. An opinion leader is a person who is frequently able to influence others' attitudes or behaviours.[78] Opinion leaders are extremely valuable information sources for a number of reasons.

1. They are technically competent and thus are convincing because they possess expert power.[79]
2. They have pre-screened, evaluated and synthesized product information in an unbiased way, so they possess knowledge power.[80] Unlike commercial endorsers, opinion leaders do not represent the interests of one company. They are more credible because they have no 'axe to grind'.
3. They tend to be socially active and highly interconnected in their community.[81] They are likely to hold office in community groups and clubs and to be active outside the home. As a result, opinion leaders often have legitimate power by virtue of their social standing.
4. They tend to be similar to the consumer in terms of their values and beliefs, so they possess referent power. Note that while opinion leaders are set apart by their interest or expertise in a product category, they are more convincing to the extent that they tend to be just slightly higher in terms of status and educational attainment than those they influence, but not so high as to be in a different social class.
5. Opinion leaders often are among the first to buy new products, so they absorb much of the risk. This experience reduces uncertainty for others who are not as courageous. And, while company-sponsored communications tend to focus exclusively on the positive aspects of a product, this hands-on experience makes opinion leaders more likely to impart *both* positive and negative information about product performance.

BUY THIS 24-YEAR-OLD
AND GET ALL HIS FRIENDS
ABSOLUTELY FREE.

This ad for MTV focuses on the importance of young opinion leaders in shaping their friends' preferences.
Courtesy of Viacom, International.

Whereas individual behavioural and psychological traits are the most important in identifying opinion leaders, there are some indications that opinion leadership does not function the same way in different cultures. For example, there are cultural differences in how much people rely on impersonal versus personal information. In a study of opinion leadership in fourteen European countries plus USA and Canada, the countries most characterized by the use of impersonal information seeking (e.g. from consumer magazines, etc.) were Denmark, Norway, Sweden and Finland, whereas the countries least characterized by impersonal information seeking were Italy, Portugal and Spain.[82]

The extent of an opinion leader's influence

When marketers and social scientists initially developed the concept of the opinion leader, it was assumed that certain influential people in a community would exert an overall impact on group members' attitudes. Later work, however, began to question the assumption that there is such a thing as a *generalized opinion leader*, somebody whose recommendations are sought for all types of purchases. Very few people are capable of being expert in a number of fields. Sociologists distinguish between those who are *monomorphic*, or experts in a limited field, and those who are *polymorphic*, or experts in several fields.[83] Even the opinion leaders who are polymorphic tend to concentrate on one broad domain, such as electronics or fashion.

Research on opinion leadership generally indicates that while opinion leaders do exist for multiple product categories, expertise tends to overlap across similar categories. It is rare to find a generalized opinion leader. An opinion leader for home appliances is likely to serve a similar function for home cleaners, but not for cosmetics. In contrast, a *fashion opinion leader* whose primary influence is on clothing choices may also be consulted for recommendations on cosmetics purchases, but not necessarily on microwave ovens.[84]

Opinion leaders versus other consumer types

Early conceptions of the opinion leader role also assumed a static process: the opinion leader absorbs information from the mass media and in turn transmits these data to opinion receivers. This view has turned out to be over-simplified; it confuses the functions of several different types of consumers. Furthermore, research has shown some evidence that the flow of influence is not one-way but two-way, so that opinion leaders are influenced by responses of their followers.[85] This would reflect a more complex communication situation as described by the interactive communication model discussed in chapter 6.

Opinion leaders may or may not be purchasers of the products they recommend. Early purchasers are known as *innovators*. Opinion leaders who are also early purchasers have been termed **innovative communicators**. One study identified a number of characteristics of male university students who were innovative communicators for fashion products. These men were among the first to buy new fashions, and their fashion opinions were incorporated by other students in their own clothing decisions. Other characteristics included:[86]

- They were socially active.
- They were appearance-conscious and narcissistic (i.e. they were quite fond of themselves and self-centred).
- They were involved in rock culture.
- They were heavy magazine readers.
- They were likely to own more clothing, and a broader range of styles, than other students.
- Their intellectual interests were relatively limited.

Opinion leaders also are likely to be **opinion seekers**. They are generally more involved in a product category and actively search for information. As a result, they are more likely to talk about products with others and to solicit others' opinions as well. Contrary to the static view of opinion leadership, most product-related conversation does not take place in a 'lecture' format, where one person does all of the talking. A lot of product-related conversation is prompted by the situation and occurs in the context of a casual interaction rather than as formal instruction.[87] One study, which found that opinion seeking is especially high for food products, revealed that two-thirds of opinion seekers also view themselves as opinion leaders.[88]

Consumers who are expert in a product category may not actively communicate with others, while other consumers may have a more general interest in being involved in product discussions. A consumer category called the **market maven** has been proposed to describe people who are actively involved in transmitting marketplace information of all types. Market mavens are not necessarily interested in certain products and may not necessarily be early purchasers of products. They come closer to the function of a generalized opinion leader because they tend to have a solid overall knowledge of how and where to procure products.[89] A scale that has been used to identify market mavens is shown in Figure 10.3.

In addition to everyday consumers who are influential in influencing others' purchase decisions, a class of marketing intermediary called the surrogate consumer is an active player in many categories. A **surrogate consumer** is a person who is hired to provide input into purchase decisions. Unlike the opinion leader or market maven, the surrogate is usually compensated for this involvement.

Interior decorators, stockbrokers or professional shoppers can all be thought of as surrogate consumers. Whether or not they actually make the purchase on behalf of the consumer, surrogates' recommendations can be enormously influential. The consumer in essence relinquishes control over several or all decision-making functions, such as information search, evaluation of alternatives or the actual purchase. For

1. I like introducing new brands and products to my friends.

2. I like helping people by providing them with information about many kinds of products.

3. People ask me for information about products, places to shop, or sales.

4. If someone asked me where to get the best buy on several types of products, I could tell him or her where to shop.

5. My friends think of me as a good source of information when it comes to new products or sales.

6. Think about a person who has information about a variety of products and likes to share this information with others. This person knows about new products, sales, stores, and so on, but does not necessarily feel he or she is an expert on one particular product. How well would you say this description fits you?

Figure 10.3 Scale items used to identify market mavens

Source: Adapted from Lawrence Feick and Linda Price, 'The Market Maven: A Diffuser of Marketplace Information', *Journal of Marketing* 51 (January 1987): 83–7. Used by permission of American Marketing Association.

example, a client may commission an interior decorator, while a broker may be entrusted to make crucial buy/sell decisions on behalf of investors. The involvement of surrogates in a wide range of purchase decisions tends to be overlooked by many marketers, who may be mistargeting their communications to end-consumers instead of to the surrogates who are actually sifting through product information.[90]

Identifying opinion leaders

Because opinion leaders are so central to consumer decision-making, marketers are quite interested in identifying influential people for a product category. In fact, many ads are intended to reach these influentials rather than the average consumer, especially if the ads contain a lot of technical information. The average television purchaser probably would not be excited by an ad for a Pioneer projection television that claims to have a lens with a 'maximum bore of 160 mm' and a 'new high-voltage stabilizing circuit'. On the other hand, an electronics buff might be quite impressed by this information and in turn take it into consideration when recommending a projection television to a more naive friend.

Professional opinion leaders

Perhaps the easiest way to find opinion leaders is to target people who are paid to give expert opinions. *Professional opinion leaders* are people such as doctors or scientists who obtain specialized information from technical journals and other practitioners.

Marketers who are trying to gain consumer acceptance for their products sometimes find it easier to try to win over professional opinion leaders, who (they hope) will, in turn, recommend their products to customers. A case in point is the recent effort by Roc S.A., maker of Europe's leading brand of hypoallergenic lotions to break into the lucrative American market for skin-care products. Instead of competing head-to-head with the lavish consumer advertising of Revlon or Estée Lauder, the French company decided first to gain medical acceptance by winning over pharmacists and dermatologists. In 1994 the company began advertising in medical journals, and the product was distributed to dermatologists and to pharmacies patronized by patients of dermatologists. A free telephone number was established to provide interested consumers with the names of pharmacies carrying the range.[91]

Of course, this approach may backfire if it is carried to an extreme and compromises the credibility of professional opinion leaders. In several countries, the medical industry has a dubious reputation of 'bribing' doctors with invitations to product presentations disguised as conferences, often held in glamorous places.

Consumer opinion leaders

Since most opinion leaders are everyday consumers and are not formally included in marketing efforts, they are harder to find. A celebrity or an influential industry executive is by definition easy to locate. He or she has national or at least regional visibility or may be listed in published directories. In contrast, opinion leaders tend to operate at the local level and may influence 5–10 consumers rather than an entire market segment. In some cases, companies have been known to identify influentials and involve them directly in their marketing efforts, hoping to create a 'ripple effect' as these consumers sing the company's praises to their friends. Many department stores, for example, have fashion 'panels', usually composed of adolescent girls, who provide input into fashion trends, participate in fashion shows, and so on.

Because of the difficulties involved in identifying specific opinion leaders in a large market, most attempts to do so focus on exploratory studies where the characteristics of representative opinion leaders can be identified and then generalized to the larger market. This knowledge helps marketers to target their product-related information to appropriate settings and media. For example, one attempt to identify financial opinion leaders found that these consumers were more likely to be involved in managing their own finances and tended to use a computer to do so. They also were more likely to follow their investments on a daily basis and to read books and watch television programmes devoted to financial issues.[92]

The self-designating method

The most commonly used technique to identify opinion leaders is simply to ask individual consumers whether they consider themselves to be opinion leaders.

However, there are obvious problems with self-designation. While respondents who report a greater degree of interest in a product category are more likely to be opinion leaders, the results of surveys intended to identify self-designated opinion leaders must be viewed with some scepticism. Some people have a tendency to inflate their own importance and influence, while others who really are influential might not admit to this quality.[93] Just because we transmit advice about products does not mean other people *take* that advice. For someone to be considered a *bona fide* opinion leader, his or her advice must actually be heard and heeded by opinion seekers. An alternative is to select certain group members (*key informants*) who in turn are asked to identify opinion leaders. The success of this approach hinges on locating those who have accurate knowledge of the group and on minimizing their response biases (e.g. the tendency to inflate one's own influence on the choices of others).

While the self-designating method is not as reliable as a more systematic analysis (where individual claims of influence can be verified by asking others whether the person is really influential), it does have the advantage of being easy to administer to a large group of potential opinion leaders. In some cases not all members of a community are surveyed. One of the original measurement scales developed for self-designation of opinion leaders is shown in Figure 10.4.

Please rate yourself on the following scales relating to your interactions with friends and neighbours regarding _____.

1. In general, do you talk to your friends and neighbours about _____:

very often				never
5	4	3	2	1

2. When you talk to your friends and neighbours about _____ do you:

give a great deal of information			give very little information	
5	4	3	2	1

3. During the past six months, how many people have you told about a new _____?

told a number of people			told no one	
5	4	3	2	1

4. Compared with your circle of friends, how likely are you to be asked about new _____?

very likely to be asked			not at all likely to be asked	
5	4	3	2	1

5. In discussion of new _____, which of the following happens most?

you tell your friends about _____			your friends tell you about _____	
5	4	3	2	1

6. Overall in all of your discussions with friends and neighbours are you:

often used as a source of advice			not used as a source of advice	
5	4	3	2	1

Figure 10.4 A revised and updated version of the opinion leadership scale

Source: Adapted from Terry L. Childers, 'Assessment of the Psychometric Properties of an Opinion Leadership Scale', *Journal of Marketing Research* 23 (May 1986): 184–8; and Leisa Reinecke Flynn, Ronald E. Goldsmith and Jacqueline K. Eastman, 'The King and Summers Opinion Leadership Scale: Revision and Refinement', *Journal of Business Research* 31 (1994): 55–64.

Sociometry

A web-based service has been created that is based on the popular play *Six Degrees of Separation*. The basic premise of the plot is that everyone on the planet is separated by only six other people. The web site (www.sixdegrees.com) allows a person to register and provide names and e-mail addresses of other people, so that when the user needs to network a connection is made with others in the database.[94]

This site is a digital version of more conventional **sociometric methods**, which trace communication patterns among group members, allow researchers systematically to map out the interactions that take place among group members. By interviewing participants and asking them whom they go to for product information, those who tend to be sources of product-related information can be identified. While this method is the most precise, it is expensive to implement, since it involves very close study of interaction patterns in small groups. For this reason, sociometric techniques are best applied in a closed, self-contained social setting, such as in hospitals, prisons and army bases, where members are largely isolated from other social networks.

Many professionals and services marketers depend primarily on word-of-mouth to generate business. In many cases consumers recommend a service provider to a friend or fellow worker, and in other cases other businesspeople will make recommendations to their customers.

Sociometric analyses can be used to understand better *referral behaviour* and to locate strengths and weaknesses in terms of how one's reputation is communicated through a community. *Network analysis* focuses on communication in social systems, considers the relations among people in a *referral network* and measures the *tie strength* among them. Tie strength refers to the nature of the bond between people. It can range from strong primary (e.g. one's spouse) to weak secondary (e.g. an acquaintance that one rarely sees). A strong tie relationship may be thought of as a primary reference group; interactions are frequent and important to the individual.

While strong ties are important, weak ties can perform a *bridging function*. This type of connection allows a consumer access between subgroups. For example, you might have a regular group of friends who serve as a primary reference group (strong ties). If you have an interest in tennis, say, one of these friends might introduce you to a group of people who play on the tennis team. As a result, you gain access to their valuable expertise through this bridging function. This referral process demonstrates the strength of weak ties.

One study analyzed the referral networks of a services marketer (in this case, a piano tuner) to demonstrate how referral patterns can be better understood. The researchers contacted all the piano tuner's customers and asked them how they found out about him (referral paths). The paths were identified, and the researchers were able to describe where business was being generated (whether through friends, business contacts, etc.) and also to pinpoint opinion leaders in the system (i.e. people who were a referral source for more than one customer).[95] This technique could conceivably be applied by many service providers to identify those customers who are responsible for generating a lot of business.

The diffusion of innovations

New products and styles termed innovations constantly enter the market. These new products or services occur in both consumer and industrial settings. Innovations may take the form of a clothing style (e.g. Jean-Paul Gaultier's skirts for men), a new manufacturing technique, or a novel way to deliver a service. If an innovation is successful (most are not), it spreads through the population. First it is bought and/or used by only a few people, and then more and more consumers decide to adopt it, until, in some cases, it seems that almost everyone has bought or tried the innovation. Diffusion of innovations refer to the process whereby a new product, service or idea spreads through a population.

Adopting innovations

A consumer's adoption of an innovation may resemble the decision-making sequence discussed in chapter 8. The person moves through the stages of awareness, information search, evaluation, trial and adoption, although the relative importance of each stage may differ depending on how much is already known about a product,[96] as well as on cultural factors that may affect people's willingness to try new things.[97]

However, even within the same culture, not all people adopt an innovation at the same rate. Some do so quite rapidly, and others never do at all. Consumers can be placed into approximate categories based upon the likelihood of adopting an innovation. The categories of adopters, shown in Figure 10.5, can be related to phases of the product-life cycle concept used widely by marketing strategists.

As can be seen in Figure 10.5, roughly one-sixth of the population (innovators and early adopters) are very quick to adopt new products, and one-sixth of the people (laggards) are very slow. The other two-thirds are somewhere in the middle, and these majority adopters represent the mainstream public. In some cases people

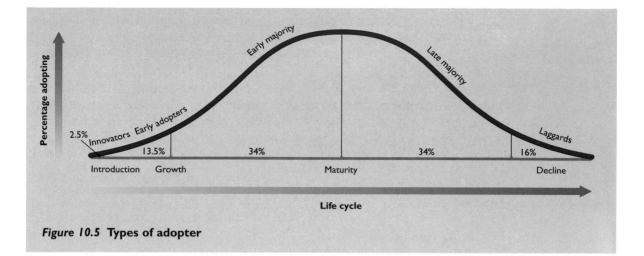

Figure 10.5 Types of adopter

deliberately wait before adopting an innovation because they assume that its technological qualities will be improved or that its price will fall after it has been on the
market.[98] Keep in mind that the proportion of consumers falling into each category
is an estimate; the actual size of each depends upon such factors as the complexity
of the product, its cost and other product-related factors, but possibly also varies
from country to country.

Even though innovators represent only 2.5 per cent of the population, marketers
are always interested in identifying them. According to standard theory, these are
the brave souls who are always on the lookout for novel developments and will be
the first to try a new offering. Just as generalized opinion leaders do not appear to
exist, innovators tend to be category-specific. A person who is an innovator in one
area may even be a laggard in another. For example, someone who prides himself on
being at the cutting edge of fashion may have no conception of new developments
in recording technology and stereo equipment.

Despite this qualification, some generalizations can be offered regarding the profile of innovators.[99] Not surprisingly they tend to have more favourable attitudes
towards taking risks. They are also, at least in an American context, likely to have
higher educational and income levels and to be socially active. However, in a
European study of the fashion and clothing market, the same correlation between
socio-demographic variables and innovative or early adopting behaviour could not
be found.[100]

Early adopters share many of the same characteristics as innovators, but an
important difference is their degree of concern for social acceptance, especially with
regard to expressive products such as clothing, cosmetics, and so on. Generally
speaking, an early adopter is receptive to new styles because he or she is involved in
the product category and also places high value on being in fashion. The universality of the dichotomy of innovators and adopters has been challenged by research
pertaining to health foods, suggesting that (1) three groups can be distinguished,
namely innovators, more-involved adaptors and less involved adaptors, and (2)
there is not a big difference between the purchase rate of new products between
innovators and adaptors; rather the difference lies in the kind of innovations tried
and the approach to trying new products.[101] Table 10.2 gives a brief description of
the different types of consumers and their approach to new product trials.

Table 10.2 **Decision styles of market segments based on adoption, innovation and personal involvement**

Adoption decision process stage	Less-involved adaptors	Innovators	More-involved adaptors
Problem recognition	Passive, reactive	Active	Proactive
Search	Minimal, confined to resolution of minor anomalies caused by current consumption patterns	Superficial but extensively based within and across product class boundaries	Extensive within relevant product category; assiduous exploration of all possible solutions within that framework
Evaluation	Meticulous, rational slow and cautious; objective appraisal using tried and tested criteria	Quick, impulsive, based on currently accepted criteria; personal and subjective	Careful, confined to considerations raised by the relevant product category: but executed confidently and (for the Adaptor) briskly within that frame of reference
Decision	Conservative selection within known range of products, continuous innovations preferred	Radical: easily attracted to discontinuously new product class and able to choose quickly within it. Frequent trial, followed by abandonment	Careful selection within a product field that has become familiar through deliberation, vicarious trial, and sound and prudent pre-purchase comparative evaluation
Post-purchase evaluation	Meticulous, tendency to brand loyalty if item performs well	Less loyal; constantly seeking novel experiences through purchase and consumption	Loyal if satisfied but willing to try innovations within the prescribed frame of reference; perhaps tends towards dynamically-continuous innovations

Source: Gordon R. Foxall and Seema Bhate, 'Cognitive Style and Personal Involvement as Explicators of Innovative Purchasing of Health Food Brands', *European Journal of Marketing* 27(2)(1993): 5–16. Used with permission.

Types of innovations

Innovations can contain a technological level and involve some functional change (e.g. car air bags) or be of a more intangible kind, communicating a new social meaning (i.e. a new hair style). However, contrary to what much literature states,[102] both are symbolic in the sense that one refers to symbols of technical performance, safety and the other to less tangible symbols, such as courage and individuality. Both types refer to symbols of progress.[103] New products, services and ideas have characteristics that determine the degree to which they will probably diffuse. Innovations that are more novel may be less likely to diffuse, since they require bigger changes in people's lifestyles and thus more effort. On the other hand, most innovations are close to being of the 'me too' kind, and thus do not necessarily possess qualities that would persuade the consumer to shift from existing product types.

In any case, it should be noted that in spite of all the good intentions of the marketing concept to ensure that there is a market before the product is developed, the failure rate of new products is as high as ever, if not higher.[104]

Behavioural demands of innovations

Innovations can be categorized in terms of the degree to which they demand changes in behaviour from adopters. Three major types of innovation have been identified, though these three categories are not absolutes. They refer, in a relative sense, to the amount of disruption or change they bring to people's lives.

A **continuous innovation** refers to a modification of an existing product, as when a breakfast cereal is introduced in a sugar-coated version, or Levi's promoted 'shrink-to-fit' jeans. This type of change may be used to set one brand apart from its competitors. Most product innovations are evolutionary rather than revolutionary. Small changes are made to position the product, add line extensions or merely to alleviate consumer boredom.

Consumers may be lured to the new product, but adoption represents only minor changes in consumption habits, since innovation perhaps adds to the product's convenience or to the range of choices available. A typewriter company, for example, many years ago modified the shape of its product to make it more user friendly. One simple change was the curving of the tops of the keys, a convention that was carried over on today's computer keyboards. One of the reasons for the change was that secretaries had complained about the difficulty of typing with long fingernails on the flat surfaces.

A **dynamically continuous innovation** is a more pronounced change in an existing product, as represented by self-focusing cameras or touch-tone telephones. These innovations have a modest impact on the way people do things, creating some behavioural changes, although the touch-tone telephone is an expression of a larger innovation involving many discontinuous renewals of daily life: the digitalization of communication. When introduced, the IBM electric typewriter, which used a 'golf ball' rather than individual keys, enabled typists to change the typeface of manuscripts simply by replacing one ball with another.

A **discontinuous innovation** creates major changes in the way we live. Major inventions, such as the aeroplane, the car, the computer and television have radically changed modern lifestyles, although, as can be seen from these examples, major changes normally take some time from the point of introduction. The personal computer has, in many cases, supplanted the typewriter, and it has created the phenomenon of 'telecommuters' by allowing many people to work from their homes. Of course, the cycle continues, as new innovations (e.g. new versions of software) are constantly being made; dynamically continuous innovations such as the keyboard 'mouse', compete for adoption; and discontinuous innovations like wristwatch personal computers loom on the horizon.

Prerequisites for successful adoption

Regardless of how much behavioural change is demanded by an innovation, several factors are desirable for a new product to succeed.[105]

● **Compatibility**. The innovation should be compatible with consumers' lifestyles. As an illustration, a manufacturer of personal care products tried unsuccessfully several years ago to introduce a hair remover cream for men as a substitute for razors and shaving cream. This formulation was similar to that

The personal computer is an innovation that has significantly changed the way we live. And in a few years' time, the integrated interactive communications system including computer, TV, telephone/fax, etc. will change our lives again.

Photographs reproduced courtesy of International Business Machines Corporation.

used widely by women to remove hair from their legs. Although the product was simple and convenient to use, it failed because men were not interested in a product they perceived to be too feminine and thus threatening to their masculine self-concepts.

- **Trialability**. Since an unknown is accompanied by high perceived risk, people are more likely to adopt an innovation if they can experiment with it prior to making a commitment. To reduce this risk, companies often choose the expensive strategies of distributing free 'trial-size' samples of new products. For example, the Swedish coffee brand Gevalia has distributed free samples targeted especially at young people, because there is some evidence that fewer young people are drinking coffee, and those that do, begin later in life.

- **Complexity**. The product should be low in complexity. A product that is easier to understand and use will often be preferred to a competitor. This strategy requires less effort from the consumer, and it also lowers perceived risk. Manufacturers of videocassette recorders, for example, have put a lot of effort into simplifying VCR usage (such as on-screen programming) to encourage adoption.

- **Observability**. Innovations that are easily observable are more likely to spread, since this quality makes it more likely that other potential adopters will become aware of its existence. The rapid proliferation of 'bum bags' (pouches worn around the waist in lieu of wallets or purses) was due to their high visibility. It was easy for others to see the convenience offered.
- **Relative advantage**. Most importantly, the product should offer relative advantage over alternatives. The consumer must believe that its use will provide a benefit other products cannot offer. For example, the success of many environmentally friendly product alternatives may be due to the fact that, once consumers have been convinced about the environmental advantages of the product, it is a clear and easily understandable advantage compared to competing products.

The social context of innovations

One critical but relatively little researched aspect is the importance of the social context of product adoption behaviour.[106] This is linked to the importance of visibility of the product innovation as well as the influence of the reference group which is seen as related to the new product. For example, Western products are admired in many contexts in Asia and Africa, or the marketizing economies of Eastern Europe, for the sole reason of being linked to the status of the Western world, which is seen as 'better', more 'developed' and generally of a higher status.[107] Likewise, in Europe the association of new products with the American way of life will have a significant impact on the adopting behaviour of various groups in society but will differ in different European countries.

Another aspect of the social dimension of innovation is the pitfall of being caught up in too many continuous innovations due to an ever finer market segmentation and customization approach. This may take resources away from more strategic considerations of changing 'the way things are done'.[108] For example, a British bank had created such a complex structure of financial services and accounts, as well as charges attached to these services, that customers began to complain about waiting time and lack of understanding of their own financial affairs. The bank simplified the structure to one account type and a much simpler charge system and successfully made this a unique selling proposition in a market dominated by more complex offerings.[109]

Chapter summary

- Consumers belong to or admire many different groups and are often influenced in their purchase decisions by a desire to be accepted by others.
- Individuals have influence in a group to the extent that they possess *social power*; types of power include information power, referent power, legitimate power, expert power, reward power and coercive power.
- We conform to the desires of others for one of two basic reasons. People who model their behaviour on others because they take others' behaviour as evidence of the correct way to act are conforming because of *informational social influence*. Those who conform to satisfy the expectations of others and/or to be accepted by the group are affected by *normative social influence*.
- Group members often do things they would not do as individuals because their identities become merged with the group; they become *deindividuated*.

- Individuals or groups whose opinions or behaviour are particularly important to consumers are *reference groups*. Both formal and informal groups influence the individual's purchase decisions, although the impact of reference group influence is affected by such factors as the conspicuousness of the product and the relevance of the reference group for a particular purchase.

- *Opinion leaders* who are knowledgeable about a product and whose opinions are highly regarded tend to influence others' choices. Specific opinion leaders are somewhat hard to identify, but marketers who know their general characteristics can try to target them in their media and promotional strategies.

- Other influencers include *market mavens*, who have a general interest in marketplace activities, and *surrogate consumers*, who are compensated for their advice about purchases.

- Much of what we know about products comes about through *word-of-mouth communication* (WOM) rather than formal advertising. Product-related information tends to be exchanged in casual conversations.

- While word-of-mouth often is helpful for making consumers aware of products, it can also hurt companies when damaging product *rumours* or negative word-of-mouth occurs.

- *Sociometric methods* are used to trace referral patterns. This information can be used to identify opinion leaders and other influential consumers.

- The *diffusion of innovations* refers to the process whereby a new product, service or idea spreads through a population. A consumer's decision to adopt a new item depends on his or her personal characteristics (i.e. if he or she is inclined to try new things) and on the characteristics of the item. Products sometimes stand a better chance of being adopted if they demand relatively little change in behaviour from consumers and are compatible with current practices. They are also more likely to diffuse if they can be tested prior to purchase, if they are not complex, if their use is visible to others, and, most importantly, if they provide a relative advantage *vis-à-vis* existing products.

🔑 Key terms

Comparative influence *(p. 271)*
Compatibility *(p. 295)*
Complexity *(p. 296)*
Conformity *(p. 276)*
Continuous innovation *(p. 295)*
Deindividuation *(p. 279)*
Discontinuous innovation *(p. 295)*
Dynamically continuous innovation *(p. 295)*
Early adopters *(p. 293)*
Information power *(p. 275)*
Informational social influence *(p. 277)*
Innovative communicators *(p. 288)*
Market maven *(p. 288)*
Normative influence *(p. 271)*
Normative social influence *(p. 277)*

Norms *(p. 276)*
Observability *(p. 297)*
Opinion leaders *(p. 286)*
Opinion seekers *(p. 288)*
Reactance *(p. 280)*
Reference group *(p. 269)*
Referent power *(p. 274)*
Relative advantage *(p. 297)*
Risky shift *(p. 279)*
Rumour *(p. 283)*
Social comparison theory *(p. 278)*
Sociometric methods *(p. 291)*
Surrogate consumer *(p. 288)*
Trialability *(p. 296)*
Word-of-mouth communication (WOM) *(p. 281)*

Consumer behaviour challenge

1. Compare and contrast the five bases of power described in the text. Which are most likely to be relevant for marketing efforts?

2. Why is referent power an especially potent force for marketing appeals? What are factors that help to predict whether reference groups will or will not be a powerful influence on a person's purchase decisions?

3. Evaluate the strategic soundness of the concept of affinity marketing. For what type of linkages is this strategy most likely to be a success?

4. Discuss some factors that determine the amount of conformity likely to be observed among consumers.

5. Under what conditions are we more likely to engage in social comparison with dissimilar others versus similar others? How might this dimension be used in the design of marketing appeals?

6. Discuss some factors that influence whether or not membership groups will have a significant influence on a person's behaviour.

7. Why is word-of-mouth communication often more persuasive than advertising?

8. Is there such a thing as a generalized opinion leader? What is likely to determine if an opinion leader will be influential with regard to a specific product category?

9. The adoption of a certain brand of shoe or apparel by athletes can be a powerful influence on students and other fans. Should high school and college coaches be paid to determine what brand of athletic equipment their players will wear?

10. The power of unspoken social norms often becomes obvious only when these norms are violated. To witness this result first hand, try one of the following: stand facing the back wall in a lift; serve dessert before the main course; offer to pay cash for dinner at a friend's home; wear pyjamas to class; or tell someone not to have a nice day.

11. Identify a set of avoidance groups for your peers. Can you identify any consumption decisions that are made with these groups in mind?

12. Identify fashion opinion leaders on your university or business school. Do they fit the profile discussed in the chapter.

13. Conduct a sociometric analysis within your dormitory or neighbourhood. For a product category such as music or cars, ask each individual to identify other individuals with whom they share information. Systematically trace all of these avenues of communication, and identify opinion leaders by locating individuals who are repeatedly named as providing helpful information.

A portrait of European consumers

PART OUTLINE

The chapters in this part consider some of the social influences that help to determine who we are, with an emphasis on the various subcultures to which we belong. Chapter 11 provides a discussion of family structures in Europe, and identifies the many instances in which our purchase decisions are made in conjunction with the family. Chapter 12 focuses on factors that define our social classes, and how membership in a social class exerts a strong influence on what we buy with the money we make. Chapter 13 discusses the strong influence that age has on our behaviour as consumers, with an emphasis on the bonds we share with others who were born at roughly the same time.

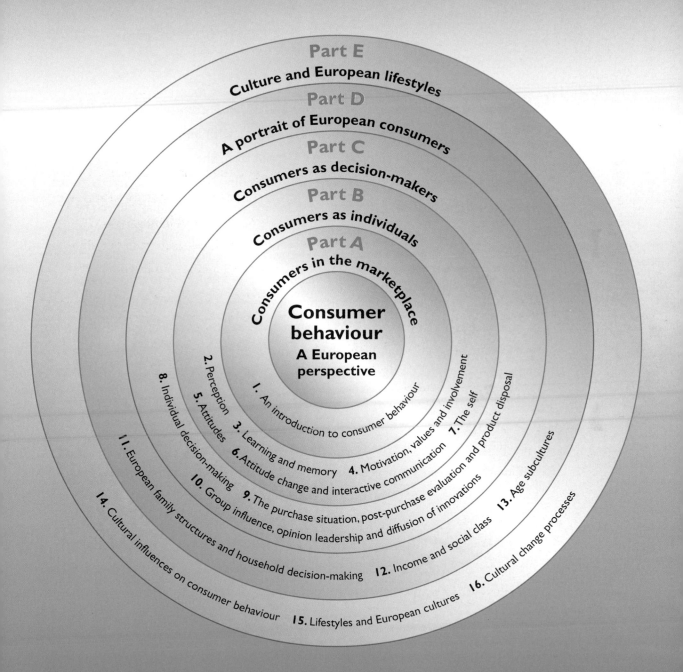

Part E
Culture and European lifestyles

Part D
A portrait of European consumers

Part C
Consumers as decision-makers

Part B
Consumers as individuals

Part A
Consumers in the marketplace

Consumer
behaviour
A European
perspective

1. An introduction to consumer behaviour

2. Perception   3. Learning and memory   4. Motivation, values and involvement   7. The self

5. Attitudes   6. Attitude change and interactive communication

8. Individual decision-making   9. The purchase situation, post-purchase evaluation and product disposal

10. Group influence, opinion leadership and diffusion of innovations

11. European family structures and household decision-making   12. Income and social class   13. Age subcultures

14. Cultural influences on consumer behaviour   15. Lifestyles and European cultures   16. Cultural change processes

Saturday is the main shopping day, and Steen is accompanying his mother to the supermarket. He doesn't usually go with her, and he suspects that Caroline, his mum, would rather go without him. She spends less and gets home faster without him, she says. But he's going today anyway, partly to be sure that she picks out the right stuff for his eleventh birthday party. The Power Rangers tablecloth and biscuits were OK last year, but he's almost a teenager now and he plans to push heavily for the right food and decorations. He wants a party with the 'right atmosphere' – maybe some music by L.L. Cool J or The Kelly Family. Even though these two groups are really different he's seen a lot of them on TV, and his friends at school talk about both groups all the time. If he could just get his mum to buy *both* CDs, he would have a better idea of which to play for 'setting the mood' at his party.

First, though, they have to get the family's regular shopping out of the way. Caroline gets a little exasperated as Steen and his little sister Anna argue over the best type of dog food to get for Baggins, their new puppy. Finally, at Caroline's urging, they move on to the next aisle, where she quickly throws two cans of tuna fish into the trolley. She starts to move on, but from behind her she hears Steen say: 'You're not really going to buy that brand, are you? Don't you know that they still use nets to catch their tuna and those nets kill hundreds of innocent dolphins every year!' This was news to Caroline. After getting over her initial irritation at being told how to shop by a child who can't even tidy his room, she realizes that Steen is making a lot of sense.

As she puts the offending cans back on the shelf, she remarks, 'Well, Steen, I think I should send you to do the shopping from now on. Maybe I can get you to go shopping with your father too – sometimes I think he could use a little more common sense on those rare occasions when he steps into the supermarket.'

European family structures and household decision-making

Children are becoming a major force in persuading their parents to clean up their act when it comes to the environment. One study showed that one-third of parents have changed their shopping habits to be more environmentally conscious because of information they received from their children. Teenagers have been instrumental in projects ranging from home and school recycling to persuading tuna companies to stop buying tuna caught in nets that also trap dolphins. Many companies are becoming aware of young people's influence in everyday family buying decisions, and some are trying hard to convince 'green teens' that their products are environmentally friendly.[1]

Steen's influence on Caroline's choice of an environmentally safe product illustrates that many consumer decisions are made jointly. The individual decision-making process described in detail in chapter 8 is, in many cases, too simplistic since more than one person may be involved in any stage of the problem-solving sequence, from initial problem recognition and information search to evaluation of alternatives and product choice. For example, the decision to get a pet is often made jointly by family members. The children may be instrumental in persuading their reluctant parents to get a dog or a cat, while the parents may be responsible for the information search to determine what breed to get or where to get it. Then, the entire family may be involved in selecting the puppy or kitten that will soon become another family member.

Whether they are choosing a can of tuna or buying a new PC for the home, consumers commonly work together. This chapter examines issues related to *collective decision-making*, where more than one person is involved in the purchasing process for products or services that may be used by multiple consumers. We focus specifically on one of the most important organizations to which we all claim membership – the family unit. We'll consider how members of a family negotiate among themselves, and how important changes in modern family structure are affecting this process. The chapter concludes by discussing how 'new employees' – children – learn to become consumers.

The family

Constructing and deconstructing the family in Europe

While it might still be too early to draw definite conclusions, it's reasonable to speculate that historians will regard the 1990s as one of the most politically, socially and economically turbulent decades in modern history. Radical political and market changes throughout Western and Eastern Europe are reflections and outcomes of intense social change in European societies that have been underway since the 1950s. While the extent and pace of changes, and the national perceptions of social change have differed from one country to another, it is clear that many of our social institutions have been altered over the past four decades, not least of which is the notion of 'family'.

Before moving on to a discussion of the forces that have changed our notions of family, and what these changes mean in terms of consumer behaviour, we need to spend a moment tackling the thorny question 'What is the family, and how do we gather data about it?' There is a great deal of family diversity throughout Europe, and the conceptualization of *family* is based on ideology, popular mythology and conventions that are firmly rooted in each country's historical, political, economic and cultural traditions. Certainly, European governments have had a strong history of requiring regular and up-to-date socio-demographic information on the behaviour of families (birth rates, fertility rates, divorce rates), and about family forms (size, structure and organization). This sort of information is an essential component in governments' policy-making processes.

Yet, despite a long history of international collaboration and the growing need for reliable information about demographic trends in Europe, by the mid-1990s data on households and families in the European Union were still far from comparable.[2] Attempts to standardize data collection methods across countries have had to deal with issues such as national political priorities and ideologies, the centralization and autonomy of the organizations responsible for data collection, and the reluctance of some governments to accept decisions taken at the supranational level. As an example of the problems of comparing families across Europe, consider the problem of dealing with the *age of children living at home*. In most EU member states, no age limit was applied during the 1991 census. However, in Denmark, Finland and Sweden, children were considered as part of the family up to the age of 18, and in Luxumbourg to 25. France applied a limit of 25 years until 1982, but this was abolished for the 1991 census, which increased the proportion of lone-parent families by 35 per cent! Eurostat's 1991 census reported that the 'traditional family' (man, woman and children under one roof) made up just 54 per cent of the European population, while their 1996 report (using a new sampling frame and method) concluded that the traditional one-family household is still predominant throughout Europe, comprising 72 per cent of the population.[3] As Europe moves into the new millennium, more standardized and comparable forms of data about the family will be collected.

Marketing opportunity

Under the same roof:
living arrangements in the European Union

The first data from the *European Community Household Panel* (ECHP) is now available, which focuses on living conditions, income and many aspects of social well-being. Some highlights from this first report include the following descriptions: The traditional one-family household is still predominant throughout Europe, comprising 72 per cent of the population. There is also the persistence of multi-generational households: around 20 per cent in Greece, Spain and Portugal. In Spain, Italy, Portugal and Ireland the percentage of individuals living in households where at

Marketing opportunity *continued* least one child over the age of 16 is still living with his or her parents amounts to around a third of all individuals. However, the 'traditional family norm' is being eroded by other living arrangements. Living alone has become important in the EU (10 per cent of the population), and there is a growth of cohabitation, particularly among young people (70 per cent in Denmark).

Results also suggest that there is a different pattern of living emerging between northern countries, and southern countries plus Ireland. In the Mediterranean countries and Ireland, children tend to live in the parental home until they are ready to form new, usually legalized, family units. Also, more than one generation share the same household. In northern countries, the transition from the parental home to forming a new family is less straightforward, with living alone and cohabitation periods in between.[4]

From both a statistical as well as a sociological perspective, 'family' is hard to nail down! However, one thing is certain – the concept of family will continue to exist and will manifest itself in varying forms over time and across countries throughout Europe. Figure 11.1 provides an overview of the many components which make up our notion of a European household.

Defining the modern family

Some experts have argued that as traditional family living arrangements have declined, people are placing even greater emphasis on the role of siblings, close friends and other relatives to provide companionship and social support.[5] In the US, some people are even joining 'intentional families', groups of strangers who meet regularly for meals and who spend holidays together. Over 500 of these communities currently operate in the US.[6]

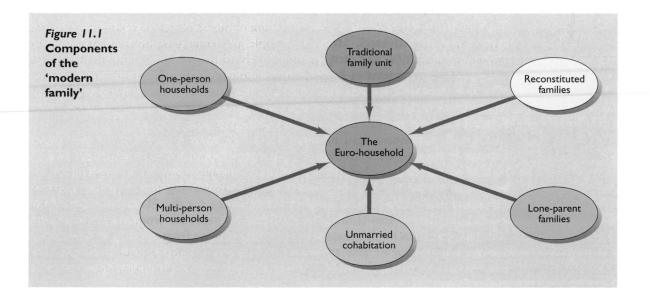

Figure 11.1 Components of the 'modern family'

Many marketers have focused on the renewed interest in family life brought about by the more flexible definitions of what constitutes a family.[7] While families were indeed out of fashion in the 1960s and 1970s, being seen by some as an infringement on personal freedom, 90 per cent of the respondents in one recent survey confirmed that family life was one of the most important things to them.[8] In a radical departure from its old, 'affluent singles' days, half of the holiday-makers who stay at Club Med resorts now bring their families along.[9]

The **extended family** was once the most common family unit. It consisted of three generations living together and often included not only the grandparents, but aunts, uncles and cousins. The **nuclear family**, a mother and a father and one or more children (perhaps with a dog thrown in for good measure), became the model family unit over time. However, many changes have occurred since the 1960s.

Just what is a household?

For statistical purposes, Eurostat has implemented the United Nation's definition of the family unit based on the 'conjugal family concept'. *The family* is defined in the narrow sense of a family nucleus as follows: 'The persons within a private or institutional household who are related as husband and wife or as parent and never-married child by blood or adoption'. Thus, a family nucleus comprises a married couple without children or a married couple with one or more never-married children of any age, or one parent with one or more never-married children of any age. The definition tries to take into account whenever possible, couples who report that they are living in consensual unions, regardless of whether they are legally married. Under the more recent European Community Household Panel, a **family household** is more broadly defined, as a 'shared residence and common housekeeping arangement'. Marketers are interested in both of these units, not only for their similarities, but as a way of understanding differences. Changes in consumers' family structures, such as cohabitation, delayed marriage and delayed child-birth, the return of mothers to the workforce and the upheaval caused by divorce, often represent opportunities for marketers as normal purchasing patterns become unfrozen and people make new choices about products and brands.[10]

Age of the family

Since 1960, the EU has seen a trend of falling numbers of marriages and an increase in the number of divorces. Moreover, people are remarrying more often than they did before the 1960s, and men are more likely to form a new family than women. Couples marry youngest in Portugal and oldest in Denmark, and the greatest age difference between husbands and wives is to be found in Greece. Figure 11.2 shows the marriage rates per thousand people for the different countries in the EU, while Figure 11.3 provides information on the divorce rates per country.[11]

Overall, consumers aged between 35 and 44 were responsible for the largest increase in the number of households, growing by almost 40 per cent since 1980.[12] Half of all family householders will fall into this age group by the year 2000. An important reason for this shift is that people are waiting longer to get married: according to Eurostat, the average age of marriage for the EU is currently 25 for women and 28 for men (compared to 24 and 26 years for women and men in the US). This trend has implications for businesses, ranging from catering to cutlery. For example, since couples tend to be married later and many already have acquired basic household items, the trend is towards giving non-traditional wedding presents such as electrical appliances for the home and PCs.[13]

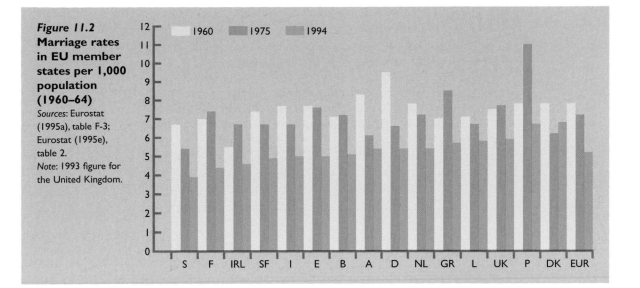

**Figure 11.2
Marriage rates
in EU member
states per 1,000
population
(1960–64)**
Sources: Eurostat
(1995a), table F-3;
Eurostat (1995e),
table 2.
Note: 1993 figure for
the United Kingdom.

Family size

Worldwide, surveys show that almost all women want smaller families than they did
a decade ago. In 1980, the average European household contained 2.8 people, but
today that number has slipped to 2.6 people. Furthermore, the current average number of children per woman is below the generational replacement threshold level,
with a fertility rate for Europe of 1.44 children per women in 1993 (compared to
almost double this in 1964). A recent UK study predicts that one in five women born
in the 1960s–1980s will remain childless – a halving of the birthrate of their
mother's generation.[14] Family size is dependent on such factors as educational level,
the availability of birth control and religion. The **fertility rate** is determined by the

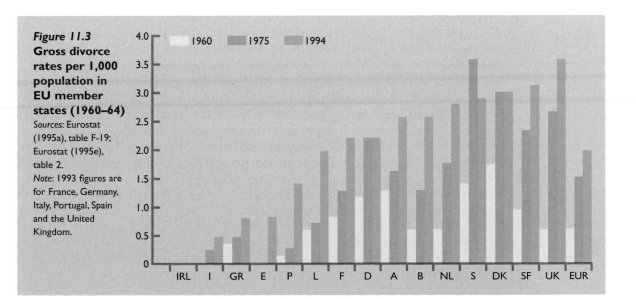

**Figure 11.3
Gross divorce
rates per 1,000
population in
EU member
states (1960–64)**
Sources: Eurostat
(1995a), table F-19;
Eurostat (1995e),
table 2.
Note: 1993 figures are
for France, Germany,
Italy, Portugal, Spain
and the United
Kingdom.

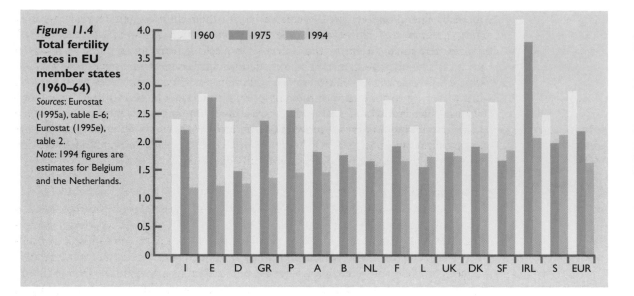

Figure 11.4 Total fertility rates in EU member states (1960–64)

Sources: Eurostat (1995a), table E-6; Eurostat (1995e), table 2.

Note: 1994 figures are estimates for Belgium and the Netherlands.

number of births per year per 1,000 women of child-bearing age. Figure 11.4 shows the trends in total fertility rates in EU member states between 1960 and 1994.[15]

Marketers keep a close eye on the population's birth rate to gauge how the pattern of births will affect demand for products in the future. Even when a married couple does live with children, families are shrinking. The number of European households comprising one or two people is increasing (from 22 per cent to 26 per cent during 1980–90) and the number of households with four or more people is falling (from 34 per cent to 25 per cent during 1980–90).[16]

The number of unmarried adults and one-person households is steadily rising (they now account for 26 per cent of European households, and are projected to be the fastest growing segment through to the year 2005). Some marketers are beginning to address the fact that this group is underrepresented in advertising.[17] Gold Blend coffee built a very popular TV ad campaign around a romance between two single neighbours, while Procter & Gamble introduced Folger's Singles 'single-serve' coffee bags for people who live alone and don't need a full pot.[18] On the other hand, many singles report that they avoid buying single-size food portions or eating alone in restaurants since both remind them of their unattached status – they prefer takeaway food.[19]

Single men and women constitute quite different markets. More than half of single men are under the age of 35, while among people over age 65, women account for 80 per cent of one-person households. Despite single males' greater incomes, single women dominate many markets because of their spending patterns. Single women are more likely than single men to own a home, and they spend more on housing-related items and furniture. Single men, in contrast, spend more overall in restaurants and on cars. However, these spending patterns are also significantly affected by age: middle-aged single women, for example, spend *more* than their male counterparts on cars.[20]

Who's living at home?

In many cases the nuclear family is being transformed to resemble the old-fashioned extended family. Many adults are being forced to care for parents as well as for children. A growing trend in the US and Europe is for middle-aged couples to be faced with the prospect of caring for both their children and their parents simultaneously.

Americans spend on average 17 years caring for their children, but 18 years assisting elderly parents.[21] Middle-aged people have been termed *'the sandwich generation'*, because they must attend to those above and below them in age. The problem of caring for ageing parents became so acute in Singapore that the government established a Tribunal for the Maintenance of Parents in 1996. A new law now requires adult offspring to take care of their parents, a practice which traditionally is a priority in Asian cultures. Two hundred cases involving neglected parents were heard by the Tribunal in its first six months of operation.[22] As the population ages and life expectancies continue to climb in developed countries, the problem of allocating resources to the support of parents will only get worse.

Non-traditional family structures

The European Community Household Panel regards any occupied housing unit as a household, regardless of the relationships among people living there. Thus, one person living alone, three roommates or two lovers all constitute households. Less traditional households will rapidly increase these if trends persist. One-parent households are increasing steadily throughout Europe (most common in the UK, Denmark and Belgium, least common in Greece). Although these households are in the majority of cases headed by women, there is also an increasing trend for fathers to take on this role.[23] In the US, 10 million children live with a step-parent or with children who are not full brothers or sisters, and 24 per cent of all children live in one-parent families.[24]

Marketing opportunity

Many people are extremely attached to pets, to the point where companion animals might be considered part of the family. Pets are seen by many as therapeutic, and often are assumed to share our emotions. Over 35 per cent of European households and over 42 per cent of American households own at least one pet.[25] Together, they spend over $30 billion a year on their pets (more than they spend on going to the cinema and home videos combined).[26] In France, there are twice as many dogs and cats as children![27]

The inclusion of pets as family members creates many marketing opportunities, ranging from bejewelled collars to professional dogwalkers. Listed below are worldwide samples of some recent attempts to cater to people's pet attachments.[28]

- Macy's department store opened a Petigree shop for dogs and cats. Says one employee, 'You can put your dog in a pink satin party dress or a 1920s flapper dress with fringe'. Other items include a wedding dress for dogs (for $100; the veil is extra), a $48 black dinner jacket or a $30 trench coat.
- A vet in Maryland offers holistic medicine for pets. He features natural foods, acupuncture and chiropractic massages. The vet also sells the 'Rodeo Drive Fragrance Collection' (named after a fashionable street in Beverly Hills), a set of spray colognes for dogs.
- A 25-minute video, 'Doggie Adventure', was produced for dogs. Shot with a camera balanced two feet off the ground, it takes viewers on a romp from a dog's perspective.
- Kennelwood Village, a day-care centre for dogs in St Louis, features a swimming pool (with a lifeguard on duty), tetherball tournaments and whirlpool therapy for arthritic canines.
- In the UK, pet insurance is a £100 million industry, with more than a million pets being covered by insurance policies.
- About 85 per cent of Swedish dogs carry health and life insurance.

Effects of family structure on consumption

A family's needs and expenditures are affected by such factors as the number of people (children and adults) in the family, their ages, and whether one, two or more adults are employed outside of the home.

Two important factors determining how a couple spend time and money are whether they have children and whether the woman works. Couples with children generally have higher expenses, and not just for the 'basics' such as for food and utilities bills. Studies in the UK estimate that the costs of keeping a teenager 'in the style to which they aspire' run close to £66,000, and the costs of getting a child to the teen years is approaching £33,000.[29] In addition, a recently married couple make very different expenditures compared to people with young children, who in turn are quite different from a couple with children in college, and so on. Families with working mothers must often make allowances for such expenses as nursery care and a working wardrobe for the woman.

Multicultural dimensions

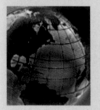

The Euro-housewife:
considerable differences between EU member states

- The percentage of women aged between 25 and 59 who describe themselves as housewives varies considerably between member states. While the EU average is 33 per cent, it ranges from a high of 60 per cent in Ireland (Spain, Greece, Italy and Luxembourg are also high), to a mere 4 per cent in Denmark.
- Barely 6 per cent of women between 25 and 39 without children stay at home, compared with 36 per cent with one child under 5 and 52 per cent with at least 2 children under 5.
- EU-wide, only 7 per cent of today's housewives stopped working because of marriage – but this number peaked at 15 per cent in Greece and 14 per cent in Spain. However, 42 per cent stop because of children.
- Family obligations, such as housework, caring for children or others are the main reason that 84 per cent of housewives are not looking for work.
- Being a housewife is strongly related to the level of education. Housewives represent 45 per cent of EU women aged from 25 to 59 with lower secondary education, 26 per cent with upper secondary education, and only 13 per cent of women with higher educational levels.[30]

The family life cycle

Recognizing that family needs and expenditures change over time, the concept of the **family life cycle (FLC)** has been widely used by marketers. The FLC combines trends in income and family composition with the changes in demands placed upon this income. As we grow older, our preferences for products and activities tend to change. In many cases, our income levels tend to rise (at least until retirement), so that we can afford more as well. In addition, many purchases that must be made at an early age do not have to be repeated very often. For example, we tend to accumulate durable goods, such as furniture, and only replace them as necessary.

A life cycle approach to the study of the family assumes that pivotal events alter role relationships and trigger new stages of life which modify our priorities. These events include the birth of a first child, the departure of the last child from the house, the death of a spouse, retirement of the principal wage earner and divorce.[31] Movement through these life stages is accompanied by significant changes in expenditures in leisure, food, durables and services, even after the figures have been adjusted to reflect changes in income.[32]

This focus on longitudinal changes in priorities is particularly valuable in predicting demand for specific product categories over time. For example, the money spent by a couple with no children on eating out and holidays will probably be diverted for quite different purchases after the birth of a child. While a number of models have been proposed to describe family life cycle stages, their usefulness has been limited because in many cases they have failed to take into account such important social trends as the changing role of women, the acceleration of alternative lifestyles, childless and delayed-child marriages and single-parent households.

Four variables are necessary to describe these changes: age, marital status, the presence or absence of children in the home, and their ages. In addition, our definition of marital status (at least for analysis purposes) must be relaxed to include any couple living together who are in a long-term relationship. Thus, while roommates might not be considered 'married', a man and woman who have established a household would be, as would two homosexual men or women who have a similar understanding.

When these changes are considered, this approach allows us to identify a set of categories that include many more types of family situations.[33] These categories, which are listed in Table 11.1, are derived by dividing consumers into groups in terms of age, whether there is more than one adult present, and whether there are children. For example, a distinction is made between the consumption needs of people in the Full Nest I category (where the youngest child is under 6), the Full Nest II category (where the youngest child is over 6), the Full Nest III category (where the youngest child is over 6 and the parents are middle-aged), and the Delayed Full Nest (where the parents are in their forties but the youngest child is under 6).

Table 11.1 The family life cycle: an updated view

| | Age of head of household | | |
	Under 35	35–64	Over 64
One adult in household	Bachelor I	Bachelor II	Bachelor III
Two adults in household	Young couple	Childless couple	Older couple
Two adults plus children in household	Full nest I Full nest II	Delayed full nest Full nest III	

Source: Adapted from Mary C. Gilly and Ben M. Enis, 'Recycling the Family Life Cycle: A Proposal for Redefinition', in Andrew A. Mitchell (ed.), *Advances in Consumer Research* 9 (Ann Arbor, MI: Association for Consumer Research, 1982): 274, Figure 1.

Life cycle effects on buying

As might be expected, consumers classified into these categories show marked differences in consumption patterns. Young bachelors and newlyweds have the most 'modern' sex-role attitudes, are the most likely to exercise regularly, to go to pubs, concerts, the cinema and restaurants, and to go dancing; and they consume more alcohol. Families with young children are more likely to consume health foods such as fruit, juice and yoghurt, while those made up of single parents and older children buy more junk foods. The monetary value of homes, cars and other durables is lowest for bachelors and single parents, but increases as people go through the full nest and childless couple stages. Perhaps reflecting the bounty of wedding gifts, newlyweds are the most likely to own appliances such as toasters, ovens and electric coffee grinders. Babysitter and day care usage is, of course, highest among single-parent and full nest households, while home maintenance services (e.g. lawnmowing) are most likely to be employed by older couples and bachelors.

The growth of these additional categories creates many opportunities for enterprising marketers. For example, divorced people undergo a process of transition to a new social role. This change is often accompanied by the disposal of possessions linked to the former role and the need to acquire a set of possessions that help to express the person's new identity as he or she experiments with new lifestyles.[34]

The intimate corporation: family decision-making

The decision process within a household unit in some ways resembles a business conference. Certain matters are put up for discussion, different members may have different priorities and agendas, and there may be power struggles to rival any tale of corporate intrigue. In just about every living situation, whether a conventional family, students sharing a house or apartment, or some other non-traditional arrangement, group members seem to take on different roles just as purchasing agents, engineers, account executives and others do within a company.

Household decisions

Two basic types of decisions are made by families.[35] In a **consensual purchase decision**, the group agrees on the desired purchase, differing only in terms of how it will be achieved. In these circumstances, the family will probably engage in problem-solving and consider alternatives until the means for satisfying the group's goal is found. For example, a household considering adding a dog to the family but concerned about who will take care of it might draw up a chart assigning individuals to specific duties.

Unfortunately, life is not always that easy. In an **accommodative purchase decision,** group members have different preferences or priorities and cannot agree on a purchase that will satisfy the minimum expectations of all involved. It is here that bargaining, coercion, compromise and the wielding of power are all likely to be used to achieve agreement on what to buy or who gets to use it. Family decisions often are characterized by an accommodative rather than a consensual decision. Conflict occurs when there is incomplete correspondence in family members' needs and preferences. While money is the most common source of conflict between marriage partners, television choices come a close second![36] Some specific factors determining the degree of family decision conflict include the following:[37]

- *Interpersonal need* (a person's level of investment in the group): a child in a family situation may care more about what his or her family buys for the house than a college student who is living in student accommodation.
- *Product involvement and utility* (the degree to which the product in question will be used or will satisfy a need): a family member who is an avid coffee drinker will obviously be more interested in the purchase of a new coffeemaker to replace a malfunctioning one than a similar expenditure for some other item.
- *Responsibility* (for procurement, maintenance, payment, and so on): people are more likely to have disagreements about a decision if it entails long-term consequences and commitments. For example, a family decision about getting a dog may involve conflict regarding who will be responsible for walking and feeding it.
- *Power* (or the degree to which one family member exerts influence over the others in making decisions): in traditional families, the husband tends to have more power than the wife, who in turn has more than the oldest child, and so on. In family decisions, conflict can arise when one person continually uses the power he or she has within the group to satisfy his or her priorities. For example, if Steen believed that his mother was not very likely to buy him both CDs, he might be willing to resort to extreme tactics to influence her, such as throwing a temper tantrum or refusing to participate in family chores.

In general, decisions will involve conflict among family members to the extent that they are important or novel and/or if individuals have strong opinions about good and bad alternatives. The degree to which these factors generate conflict determines the type of decision the family will make.[38]

Sex roles and decision-making responsibilities

Traditionally, some buying decisions, termed **autocratic decisions**, were made by one spouse. Men, for instance, often had sole responsibility for selecting a car, while most decorating choices fell to women. Other decisions, such as holiday destinations, were made jointly; these are known as **syncratic decisions**. According to a study conducted by Roper Starch Worldwide, wives tend to have the most say when buying groceries, children's toys, clothes and medicines. Syncratic decisions are common for cars, holidays, homes, appliances, furniture, home electronics, interior design and long-distance phone services. As the couple's education increases, more decisions are likely to be made together.[39]

Identifying the decision-maker

The nature of consumer decision-making within a particular product category is an important issue for marketers, so that they know whom to target and whether or not they need to reach both spouses to influence a decision. For example, when market research in the 1950s indicated that women were playing a larger role in household purchasing decisions, lawn-mower manufacturers began to emphasize the rotary mower over other power mowers. Rotary mowers, which conceal the cutting blades and engine, were often depicted being used by young women and smiling grandmothers to relieve fears of injuries.[40]

Researchers have paid special attention to which spouse plays the role of what has been called the **family financial officer (FFO)**, who keeps track of the family's bills and decides how any surplus funds will be spent. Among newlyweds, this role tends to be played jointly, and then over time one spouse or the other tends to take over these responsibilities.[41] Spouses usually exert significant influence on decision-making, even after one of them has died. An Irish study found that many widows claim to sense the continued presence of their dead husbands, and to conduct 'conversations' with them about household matters![42]

In traditional families (and especially those with low educational levels), women are primarily responsible for family financial management – the man makes it, and the woman spends it.[43] Each spouse 'specializes' in certain activities.[44] The pattern is different among families where spouses adhere to more modern sex-role norms. These couples believe that there should be more shared participation in family maintenance activities. In these cases, husbands assume more responsibility for laundering, housecleaning, day-to-day shopping, and so on, in addition to such traditionally 'male' tasks as home maintenance and waste removal.[45] Of course, cultural background is an important determinant of the dominance of the husband or wife. Husbands tend to be more dominant in decision-making among couples with a strong Mediterranean ethnic identification.[46] Even in northern Europe, the pattern of traditional 'male' and 'female' roles is still fairly strong (See Table 11.2).[47]

Four factors appear to determine the degree to which decisions will be made jointly or by one or the other spouse:[48]

1. *Sex-role stereotypes*: Couples who believe in traditional sex-role stereotypes tend to make individual decisions for sex-typed products (i.e. those considered to be 'masculine' or 'feminine').
2. *Spousal resources*: The spouse who contributes more resources to the family has the greater influence.
3. *Experience*: Individual decisions are made more frequently when the couple has gained experience as a decision-making unit.
4. *Socio-economic status*: Joint decisions are made more by middle-class families than in either higher- or lower-class families.

Table 11.2 **'New man fails to survive into the nineties'**

Divisions of household tasks, 1994	Always the woman	Usually the woman	About equal, or both together	Usually the man	Always the man	All couples
Washing and ironing	47	32	18	1	1	100
Deciding what to have for dinner	27	32	35	3	1	100
Looking after sick family members	22	26	45	–	–	100
Shopping for groceries	20	21	52	4	1	100
Small repairs around the house	2	3	18	49	25	100

Source: Nicholas Timmins, 'New Man Fails to Survive into the Nineties', *The Independent* (25 January 1996).

Multicultural dimensions

Traditional sex roles are quite prevalent in Japan, where women have less power than in any other industrialized country. The contraceptive pill is banned, and a wife is legally prohibited from using a different surname from that of her husband. Fewer than one in ten Japanese managers are women, one of the lowest ratios in the world (women are twice as likely to be managers in Mexico or Zimbabwe).

However, something of a quiet revolution is happening in Japanese homes as some obedient spouses have had enough. Recently women have started to rebel against the inevitability of getting married young and staying at home with babies. The number of unmarried people over the age of 30 has doubled in the last twenty years.

For those who do marry, things are changing as well. Traditionally, a wife would wait up all night for a drunken husband to come home so she could kneel down with her forehead touching the floor and proclaim, 'Welcome home, honourable sir'. Now, she is more likely to lock him out of the house until he sobers up. Most Japanese men are given a budget by their wives for lunch, cigarettes and girlie magazines. One housewife noted, 'Your home is managed very well if you make your men feel that they're in control when they are in front of others, while in reality you're in control'.[49]

Men's attitudes towards family life also are changing. Japanese fathers spend so much time working that more than a quarter of children surveyed said their dads never take them for a walk or play games with them. Owing to long working hours, a typical Japanese father has only 36 minutes a day to spend with his children. About 60 per cent of Japanese men typically do not eat breakfast at home, and about 30 per cent regularly miss dinner. Now, balancing work and family is becoming a heated topic, especially as recession weakens the guarantee of lifetime employment and men are re-examining their priorities.[50] This change was reflected in some recent McDonald's advertising, which showed doting fathers helping children with their bikes. This would not be noteworthy in America, but got a lot of attention in a country where fathers typically are shown as corporate warriors or even as superheroes (for example, a popular advertising character is called PepsiMan).

A hit Japanese software product called 'Princess Maker' is intended to give men more involvement in family life. The player controls the activities, hobbies and clothing of a girl character he 'raises' from childhood. He names her, picks her birthday and even chooses her blood group, which some Japanese believe determines character traits. The girl's progress is monitored in categories including sexiness, strength and intelligence. Note: This bestselling program would probably not go down too well in the West, since this 'virtual daughter' can be programmed to dress in lingerie! If the player makes unwise choices about her activities, she appears in a slinky dress and he is notified that she is destined to be a bar hostess.[51]

With many women now working outside the home, men are participating more in housekeeping activities, but women continue to do the lion's share of household chores. Ironically, this even appears to be true when the woman's income actually exceeds her husband's![52] Overall, the degree to which a couple adhere to traditional

Multicultural dimensions

Despite recent changes in decision-making responsibilities, women are still primarily responsible for the continuation of the family's **kin network system**: they perform the rituals intended to maintain ties among family members, both immediate and extended. This function includes such activities as coordinating visits among relatives, phoning and writing to family members, sending greeting cards, making social engagements, and so on.[53] This organizing role means that women often make important decisions about the family's leisure activities, and are more likely to decide with whom the family will socialize.

sex-role norms determines how much their allocation of responsibilities will fall along familiar lines and how their consumer decision-making responsibilities will be allocated.

Heuristics in joint decision-making

The *synoptic ideal* calls for the husband and wife to take a common view and act as joint decision-makers. According to this ideal, they would very thoughtfully weigh alternatives, assign to one another well-defined roles, and calmly make mutually beneficial consumer decisions. The couple would act rationally, analytically and use as much information as possible to maximize joint utility. In reality, however, spousal decision-making is often characterized by the use of influence or methods that are likely to reduce conflict. A couple 'reaches' rather than 'makes' a decision. This process has been described as 'muddling through'.[54]

One common technique for simplifying the decision-making process is the use of *heuristics* (see chapter 8). Some decision-making patterns frequently observed when a couple makes decisions in buying a new house illustrate the use of heuristics:

- The couple's areas of common preference are based upon salient, objective dimensions rather than more subtle, hard-to-define cues. For example, a couple may easily agree on the number of bedrooms they need in the new home, but will have more difficulty achieving a common view of how the home should look.
- The couple agrees on a system of *task specialization*, where each is responsible for certain duties or decision areas and does not interfere in the other's. For many couples, these assignments are likely to be influenced by their perceived sex roles. For example, the wife may seek out houses in advance that meet their requirements, while the husband determines whether the couple can obtain a mortgage.
- Concessions are based on the intensity of each spouse's preferences. One spouse will yield to the influence of the other in many cases simply because his or her level of preference for a certain attribute is not particularly intense, where in other situations he or she will be willing to exert effort to obtain a favourable decision.[55] In cases where intense preferences for different attributes exist, rather than attempt to influence each other, spouses will 'trade off' a less-intense preference for a more strongly felt one. For example, a husband who is indifferent to kitchen design may yield to his wife, but expect that in turn he will be allowed to design his own garage workshop. It is interesting to note

that many men apparently want to be very involved in making some decorating decisions and setting budgets – more than women want them to be. According to one survey, 70 per cent of male respondents felt the husband should be involved in decorating the family room, while only 51 per cent of wives wanted them to be.[56]

Children as decision-makers: consumers-in-training

Anyone who has had the 'delightful' experience of supermarket shopping with one or more children knows that children often have a say in what their parents buy, especially for products like breakfast cereal.[57] In addition, children increasingly are being recognized as a potential market for traditionally adult products. For example, Kodak is putting a lot of promotional effort into encouraging children to become photographers. Currently, only 20 per cent of children aged 5–12 own a camera, and they shoot an average of just one roll of film a year. In a new effort called 'Big Shots', ads portray photography as a cool pursuit and as a form of rebellion. Cameras are packaged with an envelope to mail the film directly back so parents can't see the photos.[58]

Parental yielding occurs when a parental decision-maker is influenced by a child's request and 'surrenders'. The likelihood of this occurring is partly dependent on the dynamics within a particular family – as we all know, parental styles range from permissive to strict, and they also vary in terms of the amount of responsibility children are given to make decisions.[59] The strategies children use to request purchases were documented in a recent study. While most children simply asked for things, other common tactics included saying they had seen it on television, saying that a sibling or friend has it, or bargaining by offering to do chores. Other actions were less innocuous; they included directly placing the object in the trolley and continuous whining – often a 'persuasive' behaviour![60]

As shown in Figure 11.5 on page 319, children begin making selections and purchases of products at an early age. By the time they reach their teens, the process of socialization and peer influence is well underway. Teenage girls and their horses are a clear example of this socialization process with respect to lifestyle choices and consumption behaviours.

Multicultural dimensions

In a controversial effort to control the size of its population, The People's Republic of China offers many incentives for parents to have only one child. One by-product of this campaign is that some claim the country is producing a pampered generation of spoiled only children, who are called 'little emperors'. Parents are trying to give these offspring a rich childhood which they themselves didn't enjoy during the dark days of the Cultural Revolution. They are spending a very large portion of family income on toys, books and computers. Baby food, which didn't exist in China a decade ago, is now a major budget item.[61]

Of course, the Chinese are not alone in viewing the child as a status symbol. In the West, as one marketing executive put it, 'Babies are the BMWs of the nineties'. Infant wear and other items for toddlers has become a $23 billion business. Dual-career couples are waiting longer to start a family and thus are able to spend more on them – the number of women aged 30 or over when the first child is born has quadrupled since 1970, and the number of first children born to women over 40 has more than doubled. As a result, children's designer clothing is booming – Versace sells a $250 black motorcycle jacket for the junior James Dean, and Nicole Miller offers a $150 cocktail dress for the petite *femme fatale*.[62] And infants are not being left out: Ralph Lauren sells a cashmere blanket for $350, L.L. Bean, the direct marketer of outdoor gear, has added toddler snow suits to its catalogues, and Nike is marketing a line of toddler athletic wear.[63]

Children often play important roles in family consumer decision-making, and they are gaining responsibility as consumers in their own right. They continue to support the toy and sweet industries, of course, but now they also buy and/or influence the purchase of many other products as well. For better or for worse, the new generation is, as the bumper sticker proclaims, 'Born to Shop'. Shopping now ranks among the top seven interests and activities of America's children.[64] Over 80 per cent of young respondents in one survey said their primary wish was to have more money to buy things.[65] In the next section, we'll consider how children learn to make these choices.

Consumer socialization

Children do not spring from the womb with consumer skills already in memory. **Consumer socialization** has been defined as the process 'by which young people acquire skills, knowledge, and attitudes relevant to their functioning in the marketplace'.[66] Where does this knowledge come from? Friends and teachers certainly participate in this process. For instance, children talk to one another about consumer products, and this tendency increases with age.[67] Especially for young children, though, the two primary socialization sources are the family and the media.

Influence of parents

Parents' influences in consumer socialization are both direct and indirect. They deliberately try to instil their own values about consumption in their children ('you're going to learn the value of the kroner/guilder/pound . . . EURO'). Parents also determine the degree to which their children will be exposed to other information sources, such as television, salespeople and peers.[68] Grownups serve as significant models for observational learning (see chapter 3). Children learn about consumption

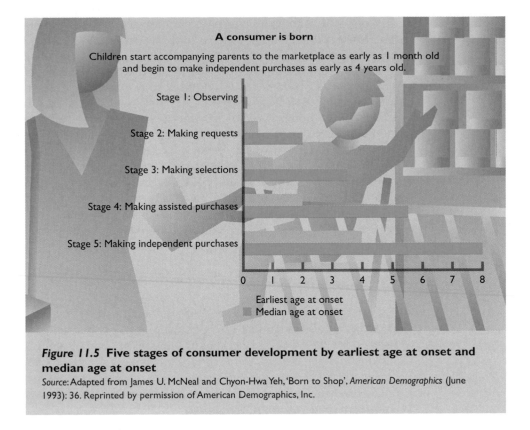

A consumer is born

Children start accompanying parents to the marketplace as early as 1 month old and begin to make independent purchases as early as 4 years old.

Stage 1: Observing

Stage 2: Making requests

Stage 3: Making selections

Stage 4: Making assisted purchases

Stage 5: Making independent purchases

0   1   2   3   4   5   6   7   8

Earliest age at onset
Median age at onset

Figure 11.5 **Five stages of consumer development by earliest age at onset and median age at onset**
Source: Adapted from James U. McNeal and Chyon-Hwa Yeh, 'Born to Shop', *American Demographics* (June 1993): 36. Reprinted by permission of American Demographics, Inc.

by watching their parents' behaviour and imitating it. This modeling is facilitated by marketers who package adult products in child versions.

The process of consumer socialization begins with infants, who accompany their parents to shops where they are initially exposed to marketing stimuli. Within the first two years of life, children begin to make requests for desired objects. As children learn to walk, they also begin to make their own selections when they are in shops. By the age of 5, most children are making purchases with the help of parents and grandparents, and by 8 most are making independent purchases and have become fully-fledged consumers.[69] The sequence of steps involved in turning children into consumers is summarized in Figure 11.5.

Marketing pitfall

Three dimensions combine to produce different 'segments' of parental styles. Parents characterized by certain styles have been found to socialize their children differently.[70] 'Authoritarian parents', who are hostile, restrictive and emotionally uninvolved, do not have warm relationships with their children, are active in filtering the types of media to which their children are exposed, and tend to have negative views about advertising. 'Neglecting parents' also do not have warm relationships, but they are more detached from their children and exercise little control over what their children do. In contrast, 'indulgent parents' communicate more with their children about consumption-related matters and are less restrictive. They believe that children should be allowed to learn about the marketplace without much interference.

Influence of television: 'the electric babysitter'

It's no secret that children watch a lot of television. As a result, they are constantly bombarded with messages about consumption, both contained in commercials and in the programmes themselves. The media teaches people about a culture's values and myths. The more a child is exposed to television, whether the programme is a local 'soap' or *Bay Watch* the more he or she will accept the images depicted there as real.[71] In Britain, *Tele-Tubbies* goes a step further – it targets viewers from 3 months to 2 years. It's unclear if this show would succeed in the US, since babies aren't seen as a lucrative market for advertising messages (yet!).[72]

In addition to the large volume of programming targeted directly at children, children also are exposed to idealized images of what it is like to be an adult. Since children over the age of 6 spend about a quarter of their television viewing during prime time, they are affected by programmes and commercials targeted at adults. For example, young girls exposed to adult lipstick commercials learn to associate lipstick with beauty.[73]

Sex-role socialization

Children pick up on the concept of gender identity at an earlier age than was previously believed – perhaps as young as age 1 or 2. By the age of 3, most children categorize driving a truck as masculine and cooking and cleaning as feminine.[74] Even cartoon characters who are portrayed as helpless are more likely to wear frilly or ruffled dresses.[75] Toy companies perpetuate these stereotypes by promoting gender-linked toys with commercials that reinforce sex-role expectations through their casting, emotional tone and copy.[76]

One function of child's play is to rehearse for adulthood. Children 'act out' different roles they might assume later in life and learn about the expectations others have of them. The toy industry provides the props children use to perform these roles.[77] Depending on which side of the debate you're on, these toys either reflect or

Champion sweatshirts, Oilily and Mexx overalls, Keds and Adidas shoes, Levi jeans. European and global brands are part of the social expression of young children, as well as their parents!

teach children about what society expects of males versus females. While preschool boys and girls do not exhibit many differences in toy preferences, after the age of 5 they part company: girls tend to stick with dolls, while boys gravitate towards 'action figures' and high-tech diversions. Industry critics charge that this is because the toy industry is dominated by males, while toy company executives counter that they are simply responding to children's natural preferences.[78]

Often 'traditional' sex roles are stressed in children's products; the same item may be designed and positioned differently for boys and girls. Huffy, for example, manufactures bicycles for both boys and girls. The boys' versions have names such as 'Sigma' and 'Vortex', and they are described as having 'maxed-out features that'll pump your pulse'. The girls' version is more demure. It is called 'Sweet Style', and comes in pink or purple. As a company executive described it in contrast to the boys' bikes, the girls' model 'is a fashion bike. It's not built for racing or jumping – just the look.'[79]

Cognitive development

The ability of children to make mature, 'adult' consumer decisions obviously increases with age (not that grownups always make mature decisions). Children can be segmented by age in terms of their **stage of cognitive development**, or ability to comprehend concepts of increasing complexity. Some recent evidence indicates that young children are able to learn consumption-related information surprisingly well, depending on the format in which the information is presented (e.g. learning is enhanced if a videotaped vignette is presented to small children repeatedly).[80]

The foremost proponent of the idea that children pass through distinct stages of cognitive development was the Swiss psychologist Jean Piaget, who believed that each stage is characterized by a certain cognitive structure the child uses to handle information.[81] In one classic demonstration of cognitive development, Piaget poured the contents of a short, squat glass of lemonade into a taller, thinner glass. Five year

Girls playing with Lego.
Photo by Søren Askegaard.

olds, who still believed that the shape of the glass determined its contents, thought this glass held more liquid than the first glass. They are in what Piaget termed a *pre-operational stage of development*. In contrast, 6 year olds tended to be unsure, but 7 year olds knew the amount of lemonade had not changed.

Many developmental specialists no longer believe that children necessarily pass through these fixed stages at the same time. An alternative approach regards children as differing in information-processing capability, or the ability to store and retrieve information from memory (see chapter 3). The following three segments have been identified by this approach:[82]

1. *Limited*: Below the age of 6, children do not employ storage and retrieval strategies.
2. *Cued*: Children between the ages of 6 and 12 employ these strategies, but only when prompted.
3. *Strategic*: Children aged 12 and older spontaneously employ storage and retrieval strategies.

This sequence of development underscores the notion that children do not think like adults, and they cannot be expected to use information in the same way. It also reminds us that they do not necessarily form the same conclusions as adults do when presented with product information. For example, children are not as likely to realize that something they see on television is not 'real,' and as a result they are more vulnerable to persuasive messages.

Marketing pitfall

Hooper's Hooch, a lemon-flavoured alcoholic beverage made by Bass PLC, is one of a dozen different brands launched in the UK that is specifically targeted to children (other popular brands include Lemonhead and Mrs Pucker's). The drink's slogan: 'One taste and you're Hooched'. These drinks, known as 'alcopops', are now being test-marketed in the US in lemonade, cola and orange flavours and contain 4–5.5 per cent alcohol in order to appeal to teenagers. In Britain, alcohol laws are less restrictive – children under 18 can't purchase alcohol, but they can drink it in their homes – than in the US. Critics argue that this marketing strategy helps those who don't have a taste for alcohol develop one, since children who grow up drinking Coke or Orangina will accept alcopops more readily than wine coolers.[83] What do you think?

Marketing research and children

Despite their buying power, relatively little real data on children's preferences or influences on spending patterns is available. Compared to adults, children are difficult subjects for market researchers. They tend to be unreliable reporters of their own behaviour, they have poor recall, and they often do not understand abstract questions.[84] This problem is compounded in Europe, where some countries restrict marketers' ability to interview children.

Still, market research can pay off, and many companies, as well as a number of specialized firms, have been successful in researching some aspects of this segment.[85] After interviewing elementary school pupils, Campbell's Soup discovered that children like soup, but don't like to admit it, because they associate it with 'nerds'. The company decided to reintroduce the Campbell kids in its advertising after a prolonged absence, but they are now slimmed down and more athletic to reflect an updated, 'un-nerdy' image.[86]

Product testing

A particularly helpful type of research with children is product testing. Young subjects can provide a valuable perspective on which products will succeed. One confectionery company has a Candy Tasters Club, composed of 1,200 kids aged 6 to 16, who evaluate its product ideas. For example, the group vetoed the idea of a Batman lollipop, claiming that the superhero was too macho to be sucked.[87] The Fisher-Price Company maintains a nursery known as the Playlab. Children are chosen from a waiting list of 4,000 to play with new toys, while staff members watch from behind a one-way mirror.[88] H.J. Heinz recently held a contest for children to create new ketchup bottle labels and received about 60,000 entries; Binney & Smith is asking children to rename its Crayola crayons after personal heroes.[89]

Other techniques include ethnographic research, where researchers spend time with children or videotape them as they shop. The most successful interviewers are those who try not to be 'adultcentric' (i.e. as an adult authority figure who assumes that children's beliefs are just unreal fantasies); they act as a friend to the children and are willing to use a variety of projective techniques and props to get children to express themselves in their own terms.[90]

Message comprehension

Since children differ in their ability to process product-related information, many serious ethical issues are raised when advertisers try to appeal directly to them.[91] Children tend to accept what they see on television as real, and they do not necessarily understand the persuasive intent of commercials – that they are paid advertisements. Preschool children may not have the ability to make any distinctions between programming and commercials.

Children's cognitive defences are not yet sufficiently developed to filter out commercial appeals, so in a sense altering their brand preferences may be likened to 'shooting fish in a barrel', as one critic put it.[92] Although some ads include a disclaimer, which is a disclosure intended to clarify a potentially misleading or deceptive statement, the evidence suggests that young children do not understand these either.[93] The Children's Advertising Review Unit (CARU) recently unveiled guidelines for child-oriented web sites after receiving complaints that children had difficulty distinguishing ads from content. These include clear identification of the sponsor and the right to cancel purchases made online.[94]

Children's level of understanding is especially hard to assess, since preschoolers are not very articulate. One way round this problem is to show pictures of children in different scenarios, and ask the subjects to point to the sketch that corresponds to what a commercial is trying to get them to do. The problem with children's processing of commercials has been exacerbated by television programming that essentially promotes toys (Transformers, for example). This format has been the target of a lot of criticism because it blurs the line between programming and commercials (much like 'infomercials' for adults, as described in chapter 8).[95] Parents' groups object to such shows because, as one mother put it, the 'whole show is one big commercial'.[96]

Chapter summary

- Many purchasing decisions are made by more than one person. Collective decision-making occurs whenever two or more people are involved in evaluating, selecting or using a product or service.

- Demographics are statistics that measure a population's characteristics. Some of the most important of these relate to family structure, e.g. the birth rate, the marriage rate and the divorce rate. In Europe, collecting reliable and comparable data regarding the family unit has not always been a straightforward process.

- A household is an occupied housing unit. The number and type of European households is changing in many ways, delays in getting married and having children, and in the composition of family households, which increasingly are headed by a single parent. New perspectives on the family life cycle, which focuses on how people's needs change as they move through different stages in their lives, are forcing marketers to consider more seriously such consumer segments as homosexuals, divorcees and childless couples when they develop targeting strategies.

- Families must be understood in terms of their decision-making dynamics. Spouses in particular have different priorities and exert varying amounts of influence in terms of effort and power. Children are also increasingly influential during a widening range of purchase decisions.

- Children undergo a process of socialization, whereby they learn how to be consumers. Some of this knowledge is instilled by parents and friends, but a lot of it comes from exposure to mass media and advertising. Since children are in some cases so easily persuaded, the ethical aspects of marketing to them are hotly debated among consumers, academics and marketing practitioners.

🔑 Key terms

Accommodative purchase decision (p. 312)
Autocratic decision (p. 313)
Cognitive development (p. 321)
Consensual purchase decision (p. 312)
Consumer socialization (p. 318)
Extended family (p. 306)
Family financial officer (FFO) (p. 313)

Family household (p. 306)
Family life cycle (FLC) (p. 310)
Fertility rate (p. 307)
Kin network system (p. 316)
Nuclear family (p. 306)
Parental yielding (p. 317)
Stage of cognitive development (p. 321)
Syncratic decisions (p. 313)

Consumer behaviour challenge

1. Review a number of popular media which are published in countries in Southern Europe as well as media targeted for Northern European countries. How do the ads' depiction of *family* seem to differ by region? In what sorts of consumption situations do they seem highly similar? Why?

2. Do you think market research should be performed on children? Give the reasons for your answer. What do you think about the practice of companies and

survey firms collecting public data (e.g. from marriage licences, birth records or even death announcements) to compile targeted mailing lists? State your opinion from both a consumer's and marketer's perspective.

3. Marketers have been criticized for donating products and services to educational institutions in exchange for free promotion. Is this a fair exchange, in your opinion, or should corporations be prohibited from attempting to influence youngsters in school?

4. For each of the following five product categories – groceries, cars, vacations, furniture and appliances – describe the ways in which you believe a married couple's choices would be affected if they had children.

5. In identifying and targeting newly divorced couples, do you think marketers are exploiting these couples' situations? Are there instances where you think marketers may actually be helpful to them? Support your answers with examples.

6. Arrange to interview two married couples, one younger and one older. Prepare a response form listing five product categories – groceries, furniture, appliances, vacations and cars – and ask each spouse to indicate, without consulting the other, whether purchases in each category are made by joint or unilateral decisions and to indicate whether the unilateral decisions are made by the husband or the wife. Compare each couples' responses for agreement between husbands and wives relative to who makes the decisions and compare both couples' overall responses for differences relative to the number of joint versus unilateral decisions. Report your findings and conclusions.

7. Collect ads for three different product categories in which the family is targeted. Find another set of ads for different brands of the same items in which the family is not featured. Prepare a report on the effectiveness of the approaches.

8. Observe the interactions between parents and children in the cereal section of a local grocery shop. Prepare a report on the number of children who expressed preferences, how they expressed their preferences and how parents responded, including the number who purchased the child's choice.

9. Watch three hours of children's programming on commercial television stations and evaluate the marketing techniques used in the commercials in terms of the ethical issues raised in the final section of this chapter. Report your findings and conclusions.

10. Select a product category, and using the life cycle stages given in the chapter, list the variables that will affect a purchase decision for the product by consumers in each stage of the cycle.

11. Consider three important changes in modern European family structure. For each, find an example of a marketer who has attempted to be conscious of this change as reflected in product communications, retailing innovations, or other aspects of the marketing mix. If possible, also try to find examples of marketers who have failed to keep up with these developments.

Finally, the big day has come! David is going home with Julia to meet her parents. David had been doing some contracting work at the publishing company where Julia works, and it was love at first sight. Even though David had attended 'The School of Hard Knocks' on the streets of Liverpool, while Julia studied Classics at Trinity College, Oxford, somehow they knew they could work things out despite their vastly different social backgrounds. Julia's been hinting that the Caldwells have money from *several* generations back, but David doesn't feel intimidated. After all, he knows plenty of guys from both Liverpool and London who have wheeled-and-dealed their way into six figures; he thinks he can handle one more big shot in a silk suit, flashing a roll of bills and showing off his expensive modern furniture with mirrors and gadgets everywhere you look.

When they arrive at the family estate 90 minutes outside of London, David looks for a Rolls-Royce parked at the end of the long, tree-lined driveway, but he sees only a Jeep Cherokee – which, he decides, must belong to one of the servants. Once inside, David is surprised by how simply the house is decorated and by how understated everything seems. The hall floor is covered with a faded Oriental rug, and all the furniture looks really old – in fact, there doesn't seem to be a new stick of furniture anywhere, just a lot of antiques.

David is even more surprised when he meets Mr Caldwell. He had half expected Julia's father to be wearing a tuxedo and holding a large glass of cognac like the people on *Lifestyles of the Rich and Famous*. In fact, David had put on his best Italian silk suit in anticipation and was wearing his large cubic zirconium ring so Mr Caldwell would know that he had money too. When Julia's father emerges from his study wearing an old rumpled cardigan and plimsolls, David realizes he's definitely not in the old neighbourhood . . .

Income and social class

As David's eye-opening experience at the Caldwells suggests, there are many ways to spend money, and a wide gulf exists between those who have it and those who don't. Perhaps an equally wide one exists between those who have had it for a long time and those who 'made it the hard way – by earning it!' This chapter begins by considering briefly how general economic conditions affect the way consumers allocate their money. Then, reflecting the adage 'The rich are different', it will explore how people who occupy different positions in society consume in very different ways. Whether a skilled worker like David or a child of privilege like Julia, a person's social class has a profound impact on what he or she does with money and on how consumption choices reflect the person's 'place' in society.

As this chapter illustrates, these choices play another purpose as well. The specific products and services we buy are often intended to make sure *other* people know what our social standing is – or what we would like it to be. Products are frequently bought and displayed as markers of social class; they are valued as status symbols. Indeed, it is quite common for a product to be positioned on the basis of its (presumed) place in the social hierarchy. The chapter concludes with an assessment of the evolving natures of such status symbols, and it considers some reasons why status-driven products are not always accurate indicators of a consumer's true social standing.

The field of behavioural economics, or economic psychology, is concerned with the 'human' side of economic decisions. Beginning with the pioneering work of the psychologist George Katona, this discipline studies how consumers' motives and their expectations about the future affect their current spending, and how these individual decisions add up to affect a society's economic well-being.[1]

Income patterns

Many Europeans would probably say that while they are comfortable, they don't earn enough money. In reality, the average European's standard of living continues to improve. Gross Domestic Product has more than doubled and in some countries quadrupled in EU countries between 1980 and 1995, although this boom is by no means shared equally among all consumer groups.[2] Individual income shifts are linked to two key factors: a shift in women's roles and increases in educational attainment.[3]

Woman's work

One reason for this increase in income is that there has also been a larger proportion of people of working age participating in the labour force. While men are more

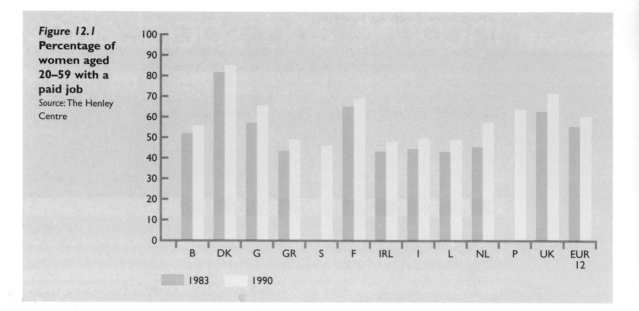

Figure 12.1 Percentage of women aged 20–59 with a paid job
Source: The Henley Centre

likely to have paid employment than women, the greatest increases in paid employment have been among women in EU countries over the past decade. This steady increase in the numbers of working women is a primary cause of the increase in household incomes. Figure 12.1 shows the steady rise in female paid workers for Europe. Yet in spite of these increases, women are more likely to be in part-time work, a situation which reflects the more traditional activities of caring for the household and children living at home – activities that are still seen as primarily their responsibility. Figure 12.2 shows the percentages of men and women part-time workers in a number of European countries. As discussed in the previous chapter, family situation, the number and age of children living at home and the educational level of women heavily influence their employment activities.

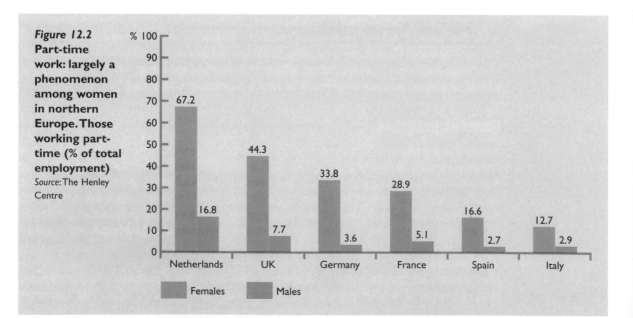

Figure 12.2 Part-time work: largely a phenomenon among women in northern Europe. Those working part-time (% of total employment)
Source: The Henley Centre

Yes, it pays to go to school!

Another factor that determines who gets a bigger slice of the pie is education. Although the expense of going to college often entails great sacrifice, it still pays in the long run. University and higher professional study graduates earn about 50 per cent more than those who have gone through secondary school only during the course of their lives. Close to half of the increase in consumer spending power during the 1990s comes from these higher education groups.

To spend or not to spend, that is the question

A basic assumption of economic psychology is that consumer demand for goods and services depends on ability to buy *and* willingness to buy. While demand for necessities tends to be stable over time, other expenditures can be postponed or eliminated if people don't feel that now is a good time to spend.[4] For example, a person may decide to 'make do' with his current car for another year rather than buy a new car now.

Discretionary spending

Discretionary income is the money available to a household over and above that required for a comfortable standard of living. European consumers are estimated to have discretionary spending power in the billions of ECUs per year, and it is consumers aged 35–55 whose incomes are at a peak which account for the greatest amounts. As might be expected, discretionary income increases as overall income goes up: while income distributions vary over different EU countries, households earning more than 100,000 ECUs account for less than 5 per cent of all families. Still, they have more than a quarter of the EU's discretionary income at their disposal.[5] While discretionary income is a powerful tool for predicting certain types of consumer behaviour, it is not always a measure for which straightforward comparisons between countries can be easily made. Factors such as different levels of sales tax (VAT) or varying levels of direct family benefits for children under 19 years living at home in various EU countries account for differences in what constitutes true discretionary income. Figure 12.3 shows the absolute amount of ECU expenditures

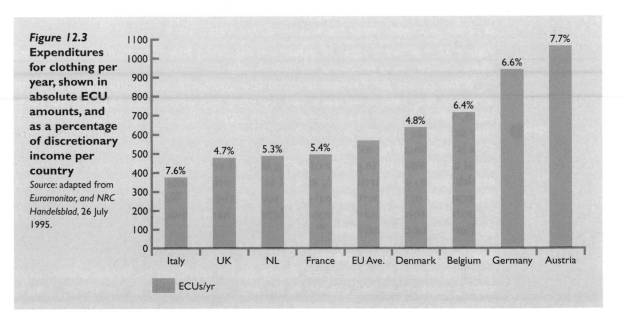

Figure 12.3 Expenditures for clothing per year, shown in absolute ECU amounts, and as a percentage of discretionary income per country
Source: adapted from Euromonitor, and NRC Handelsblad, 26 July 1995.

ECUs/yr

for clothing per year for different countries, while the figures at the top of each country graph show the percentage of discretionary income used for clothing.

Individual attitudes towards money

Many consumers are entertaining doubts about their individual and collective futures, and are anxious about holding on to what they have. A consumer's anxieties about money are not necessarily related to how much he or she actually has: acquiring and managing money is more a state of mind than of wallet. Money can have a variety of complex psychological meanings; it can be equated with success or failure, social acceptability, security, love or freedom.[6] Some clinical psychologists even specialize in treating money-related disorders, and report that people feel guilty about their success and deliberately make bad investments to ease this feeling! Other clinical conditions include atephobia (fear of being ruined), harpaxophobia (fear of becoming a victim of robbers), peniaphobia (fear of poverty) and aurophobia (fear of gold).[7] The Roper/Starch survey found that security was the attribute most closely linked to the meaning of money. Other significant associations included comfort, being able to help one's children, freedom and pleasure.[8]

Consumer confidence

A consumer's beliefs about what the future holds is an indicator of consumer confidence, which reflects the extent to which people are optimistic or pessimistic about the future health of the economy and how they will fare in the future. These beliefs influence how much money he or she will pump into the economy when making discretionary purchases.

Many businesses take forecasts about anticipated spending very seriously, and periodic surveys attempt to 'take the pulse' of the European consumer. The Henley Centre conducts a survey of consumer confidence, as does Eurostat and the EuroMonitor. The following are the types of questions posed to consumers in these surveys:[9]

- My standard of living will change for the better over the next year.
- My quality of life will improve over the next year.
- I will have a lack of money when I retire.
- I spend too much of my income, and intend to spend less next year.
- I am concerned about the amount of free time I have.

Figure 12.4 shows a sense of pessimism regarding how European consumers feel about the long-term prospects for their family.

When people are pessimistic about their prospects and about the state of the economy, they tend to cut back their spending and take on less debt. On the other hand, when they are optimistic about the future, they tend to reduce the amount they save, take on more debt and buy discretionary items. The overall savings rate thus is influenced by individual consumers' pessimism or optimism about their personal circumstances (e.g. fear of being laid off versus a sudden increase in personal wealth due to an inheritance), as well as by world events (e.g. the election of a new government or an international crisis such as the Gulf War) and cultural differences in attitudes towards saving (e.g. the Japanese have a much higher savings rate than do Europeans or Americans).[10]

Seeking value versus quality

In an era of diminished resources, Europeans are redefining traditional relationships among price, value and quality. In the past (most notably in the 1980s), people seemed to be willing to pay almost anything for products and services. Consumers

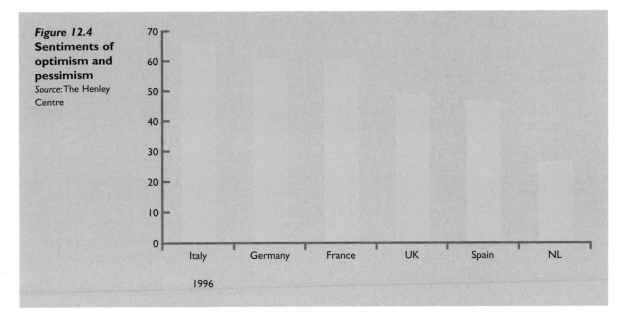

**Figure 12.4
Sentiments of
optimism and
pessimism**
Source: The Henley
Centre

1996

still claim to want quality – but at the right price. In surveys, most people report that they regret the conspicuous consumption of the 1980s and feel the need to live with less. The attitude of the 1990s is more practical and reflects a 'back to basics' orientation. People want more hard news instead of 'hype' from advertising, and they appreciate ads that feature problem-solving tips or that save money or time. European youth (age range 12–24) in particular are more sceptical of advertising messages, relative to the total population.

Reflecting this new, more sober, state of mind, consider the findings of a large-scale survey conducted by The Henley Centre of European households to determine their priorities and concerns. Some of the findings are shown in Figure 12.5.[11]

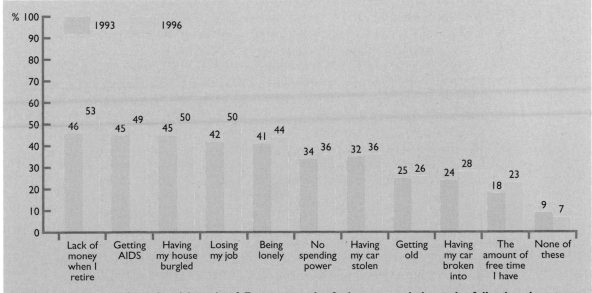

Figure 12.5 Deeper into the risk society? Europeans who feel concerned about the following threats
Source: The Henley Centre, *Frontiers: Planning for Consumer Change in Europe* (1996/97)

Social class

All societies can be roughly divided into the haves and the have-nots (though some-times 'having' is a question of degree). While social equality is a widely held value throughout Europe, the fact remains that some people seem to be more equal than others. As David's encounter with the Caldwells suggests, a consumer's standing in society, or **social class**, is determined by a complex set of variables, including income, family background and occupation.

Marketing opportunity

Winston Churchill preferred his with starched linen collars and loops on the shoulders to hold up his braces. Prince Charles has his fitted in the privacy of his palace, while fashion mogul Ralph Lauren – who, you'd imagine, could get them for free at his own shop – sometimes orders dozens at a time. And then there's the rather eccentric customer who wants his to resemble Australian prisoner uniforms – but made of cream-coloured silk.

What all these people have in common – the politicians and powerbrokers, royals and the slightly offbeat – is a desire for the simple luxury of a custom-made shirt. And not just any old made-to-measure shirt: these garments must be from the famous craftsmen of Jermyn Street, whose shops in London's SW1 district cater to connoisseurs with a passion for fine tailoring and a perfect fit. At prices from £100 to £155 per shirt, depending on the cloth, and with a minimum order of between four and six, you probably can't afford to wear anything else.

Jermyn Street tailors have been practising the art of fine service and attention to detail for over a century – it's what their customers expect from the place acknowledged as the world's capital of made-to-measure shirts. 'We have created a unique market, and have attracted the top customers, who feel quite comfortable here', notes Paul Cuss, chief patternmaker at *Turnbull and Asser*, the holder of the coveted Royal Warrant for shirtmaking, and the shop that supplies Prince Charles and former President Ronald Reagan, among others. According to Mr Cuss, 'It's very establishment, very clubby.' With its heavy wooden furniture, stuffed hunting trophies and velvet Hapsburgian smoking jackets for sale – along with ties, bathrobes and boxer shorts, and a framed picture of Winston Churchill, *Turnbull and Asser's* cosy emporium is a gentlemen's world straight out of *Country Life* magazine.

One can imagine the Jermyn Street of old, when the landed gentry and Etonian schoolboys travelled there to buy their shirts in a rite of passage for the aristocracy, and in the process, established the street's reputation. While Jermyn Street thrives on tradition, their clients come from all over the world. The French and fashion-conscious Italians come for the 'tailored English look', but the shirtmakers admit to following fashion trends: among the serious solid whites and blues are a few shocking pink, lilac and dayglow orange samples.

Precise construction of the shirt also means that it takes time to have the garment finished. After measuring, there's a wait of around two weeks for a sample to be made. Then there's a trial period of washing and wearing, to see if the fit is right. Finally, the hand-cutters and sewers get to work, and in 6–8 weeks the masterpiece is ready – and you can walk proudly down the street, knowing you've joined an exclusive club whose members say price doesn't matter when it comes to style.[12]

The place one occupies in the social structure is an important determinant not only of *how much* money is spent. It also influences *how* it is spent. David was surprised that the Caldwells, who clearly had a lot of money, did not seem to flaunt it. This understated way of living is a hallmark of so-called 'old money'. People who have had it for a long time don't need to prove they've got it. In contrast, consumers who are relative newcomers to affluence might allocate the same amount of money very differently.

A universal pecking order

In many animal species, a social organization is developed whereby the most assertive or aggressive animals exert control over the others and have the first pick of food, living space and even mating partners. Chickens, for example, develop a clearly defined dominance–submission hierarchy. Within this hierarchy, each hen has a position in which she is submissive to all of the hens above her and dominates all of the ones below her (hence, the origin of the term *pecking order*).[13]

People are no different. They also develop a pecking order where they are ranked in terms of their relative standing in society. This standing determines their access to such resources as education, housing and consumer goods. And people try to improve their ranking by moving up the social order whenever possible. This desire to improve one's lot, and often to let others know that one has done so, is at the core of many marketing strategies.

While every culture has its **social hierarchies**, variations in terms of how explicit these distinctions are can be observed. Stratification of one sort or another is universal, even in societies that officially disdain such a process. For example, in China, a supposedly classless society, many Chinese are irritated by the children of top party officials, who are called *gaoganzidi*. These offspring have a reputation for laziness, enjoying material pleasures and getting the best jobs by virtue of their family connections. They are thus a privileged class in a classless society.[14]

Multicultural dimensions

Both the top and bottom ends of American income levels are swelling. Since 1980 the wealthiest fifth of the population has increased income by 21 per cent, while wages for the bottom 60 per cent have stagnated or dipped. America's most powerful brands, from Levi's jeans to Ivory soap, were built on a mass marketing premise but now that's changing. Stores like Wal-Mart and Tiffany are reporting big earnings, while middle-class outlets like Penney have weak sales. This trend has led some companies to try to have their cake and eat it too by developing a two-tiered marketing strategy where separate marketing strategies are crafted for upmarket and downmarket consumers. For example, Walt Disney's Winnie the Pooh can be purchased as an original line-drawn figure on fine china or on pewter spoons in upmarket speciality and department stores, while a plump cartoon-like Pooh is available on plastic key chains and polyester bedsheets at Wal-Mart. The Gap is remodelling its Banana Republic stores to make them more upmarket, while simultaneously developing its Old Navy stores for the low end.[15]

Social class affects access to resources

Just as marketers try to carve society into groups for segmentation purposes, sociologists have developed ways to describe meaningful divisions of society in terms of people's relative social and economic resources. Some of these divisions involve political power, while others revolve around purely economic distinctions. Karl Marx felt that position in a society was determined by one's relationship to the *means of production*. Some people (the haves) control resources, and they use the labour of others to preserve their privileged positions. The have-nots lack control and depend on their own labour for survival, so these people have the most to gain by changing the system. Distinctions among people that entitle some to more than others are perpetuated by those who will benefit by doing so.[16]

The sociologist Max Weber showed that the rankings people develop are not one-dimensional. Some involve prestige or 'social honour' (he called these *status groups*), some rankings focus on power (or *party*) and some revolve around wealth and property (*class*).[17]

Social class affects taste and lifestyles

The term social class is now used more generally to describe the overall rank of people in a society. People who are grouped within the same social class are approximately equal in terms of their social standing in the community. They work in roughly similar occupations, and they tend to have similar lifestyles by virtue of their income levels and common tastes. These people tend to socialize with one another and share many ideas and values regarding the way life should be lived.[18]

Marketing pitfall	Stemar gazes over the expansive new verandah of his summer cottage on a tranquil island off Norway's southeastern coast, chatting on his cell phone. The 50-year-old Oslo accountant recently added a host of amenities such as hot running water to his *hytte*, as Norwegians call their rustic summer cabins. Now he plans to put in a paved road to his front door and a swimming pool in the garden. 'There's nothing wrong with a little comfort', says Stemar. Well, maybe not in other summer playgrounds such as France's Côte d'Azur, but here in austere Norway, the words 'comfort' and 'vacation' are not synonymous. Thanks to the recent oil boom, many Norwegians are spending their newfound wealth to upgrade spartan summer chalets with tennis courts, jacuzzis and even helipads. But in a country where simplicity and frugality are cherished virtues, and egalitarianism is strong, the display of wealth and money is suspect. Some politicians have suggested bulldozing the houses of the wealthy if they block access to the sea, and trade union leaders have blasted a new breed of Norwegians who favour showy yachts and life in the fast lane, and who build fences around private property.

'The rich can be quite vulgar', grumbles Stemar's neighbour Brit, who demanded that he trim a metre or so off his verandah because she and her husband Gustav could see it from their cabin lower down the hill. Both teachers, Brit and Gustav are nearing retirement, and have a more traditional Norwegian view of how to spend their summer, and how to spend their money. At stake, many say, are Norwegian ideals of equality and social democracy. They dictate that all Norwegians should have the same quality of life and equally share the national wealth. Norwegians champion austerity because they haven't always been prosperous. Before oil was discovered

Marketing pitfall *continued* about twenty years ago, only a few families were considered wealthy. This frugality is obvious even in the capital, Oslo. For all the new oil money, plus low inflation, the city isn't a brash 'Kuwait of the North'.

Summer chalets should reflect the spartan mood, diehards say, and vacation activities must be limited. Scraping down paint is popular, as is hammering down loose floorboards. So is swimming in lakes, fishing for supper and chopping wood. But not much else. As another neighbour, Aase puts it: 'We like to, uh, sit here. I'd like the rich to stay away from here. They would ruin the neighbourhood.'[19]

Social class is as much a state of being as it is of having: as David saw, class also is a question of what one *does* with one's money and how one defines his or her role in society. Although people may not like the idea that some members of society are better off or 'different' from others, most consumers do acknowledge the existence of different classes and the effect of class membership on consumption. As one wealthy woman observed when asked to define social class: 'I would suppose social class means where you went to school and how far. Your intelligence. Where you live . . . . Where you send your children to school. The hobbies you have. Skiing, for example, is higher than the snowmobile . . . . It can't be [just] money, because nobody ever knows that about you for sure'.[20]

Social stratification

In college, some students always seem to be more popular than others. They have access to many resources, such as special privileges, expensive cars, generous allowances or dates with other equally popular classmates. At work, some people are put on the fast track and are promoted to prestige jobs, given higher salaries and perhaps such perks as a parking space, a large office or the keys to the executive bathroom.

In virtually every context, some people seem to be ranked higher than others. Patterns of social arrangements evolve whereby some members get more resources than others by virtue of their relative standing, power and/or control in the group.[21] The phenomenon of social stratification refers to this creation of artificial divisions in a society: 'those processes in a social system by which scarce and valuable resources are distributed unequally to status positions that become more or less permanently ranked in terms of the share of valuable resources each receives.'[22]

Achieved versus ascribed status

If you recall groups you've belonged to, both large and small, you'll probably agree that in many instances some members seem to get more than their fair share while others are not so lucky. Some of these resources may have gone to people who earned them through hard work or diligence. This allocation is due to *achieved status*. Other rewards may have been obtained because the person was lucky enough to be born rich or beautiful. Such good fortune reflects *ascribed status*.

Whether rewards go to the 'best and the brightest' or to someone who happens to be related to the boss, allocations are rarely equal within a social group. Most groups exhibit a structure, or status hierarchy, in which some members are somehow better off than others. They may have more authority or power, or they are simply more liked or respected.

Class structure around the world

Every society has some type of hierarchical class structure, where people's access to products and services is determined by their resources and social standing. Of course, the specific 'markers' of success depend on what is valued in each culture. For the Chinese, who are just beginning to experience the bounties of capitalism, one marker of success is hiring a bodyguard to protect oneself and one's newly acquired possessions![23]

Japan is a highly status-conscious society, where upmarket, designer labels are popular, and new forms of status are always being sought. To the Japanese, owning a traditional rock garden, formerly a vehicle for leisure and tranquillity, has become a coveted item. Possession of a rock garden implies inherited wealth, since aristocrats traditionally were patrons of the arts. In addition, considerable assets are required to afford the required land in a country where property is extraordinarily expensive. The scarcity of land also helps to explain why the Japanese are fanatic golfers: since a golf course takes up so much space, membership in a golf club is extremely valuable.[24]

On the other side of the world from Japan, there is always England: England is also a class-conscious country, and at least until recently, consumption patterns were preordained in terms of one's inherited position and family background. Members of the upper class were educated at public schools such as Eton and Harrow, and had a distinctive accent. Remnants of this rigid class structure can still be found. 'Hooray Henrys' (wealthy young men) play polo at Windsor and hereditary peers still sit in the House of Lords.

The dominance of inherited wealth appears to be fading in Britain's traditionally aristocratic society. According to a recent survey, 86 of the 200 wealthiest people in England made their money the old-fashioned way: they earned it. Even the sanctity of the Royal Family, which epitomizes the aristocracy, has been diluted because of tabloid exposure and the antics of younger family members who have been transformed into celebrities more like rock stars than royalty.[25]

Social mobility

To what degree do people tend to change their social class? In some traditional societies social class is very difficult to change, but in Europe, any man or woman can become Prime Minister. **Social mobility** refers to the 'passage of individuals from one social class to another'.[26]

This passage can be upward, downward or even horizontal. *Horizontal mobility* refers to movement from one position to another roughly equivalent in social status, like becoming a nurse instead of a junior school teacher. *Downward mobility* is, of course, not very desirable, but this pattern is unfortunately quite evident in recent years as redundant workers have been forced to join the dole queue or have joined the ranks of the homeless. In the United States, a conservative estimate is that 600,000 Americans are homeless on a given day.[27]

Despite that discouraging trend, demographics decree that there must be *upward mobility* in European society. The middle and upper classes reproduce less than the lower classes (an effect known as *differential fertility*), and they tend to restrict family size below replacement level. Therefore, so the reasoning goes, positions of higher status over time must be filled by those of lower status.[28] Overall, though, the offspring of blue-collar consumers tend also to be blue-collar while the offspring of white-collar consumers also tend to be white-collar.[29] People tend to improve their positions over time, but these increases are not usually dramatic enough to catapult them from one social class to another.

Components of social class

When we think about a person's social class, there are a number of pieces of information we can consider. Two major ones are occupation and income. A third important factor is educational attainment, which is strongly related to income and occupation.

Occupational prestige

In a system where (like it or not) a consumer is defined to a great extent by what he or she does for a living, *occupational prestige* is one way to evaluate the 'worth' of people. Hierarchies of occupational prestige tend to be quite stable over time, and they also tend to be similar in different societies. Similarities in occupational prestige have been found in countries as diverse as Brazil, Ghana, Guam, Japan and Turkey.[30]

A typical ranking includes a variety of professional and business occupations at the top (e.g. director of a large corporation, doctor or college lecturer), while those jobs hovering near the bottom include shoe shiner, unskilled labourer and dustman. Because a person's occupation tends to be strongly linked to his or her use of leisure time, allocation of family resources, political orientation, and so on, this variable is often considered to be the single best indicator of social class.

Income

The distribution of wealth is of great interest to social scientists and to marketers, since it determines which groups have the greatest buying power and market potential. Wealth is by no means distributed evenly across the classes. While there is a more equitable distribution of wealth across European countries relative to Latin America, Asia and America (the top fifth of the population in the US controls about 75 per cent of all assets),[31] there is still a disportionate share of wealth controlled by a small segment of the European population. As we have seen, income *per se* is often not a very good indicator of social class, since the way money is spent is more telling. Still, people need money to allow them to obtain the goods and services that they need to express their tastes, so obviously income is still very important.

The relationship between income and social class

Although consumers tend to equate money with class, the precise relationship between other aspects of social class and income is not clear and has been the subject of debate among social scientists.[32] The two are by no means synonymous, which is why many people with a lot of money try to use it to improve their social class.

One problem is that even if a family increases household income by adding wage-earners, each additional job is likely to be of lower status. For example, a housewife who gets a part-time job is not as likely to get one that is of equal or greater status than the primary wage-earner's. In addition, the extra money earned may not be pooled for the common good of the family. Instead it is used by the individual for his or her own personal spending. More money does not then result in increased status or changes in consumption patterns, since it tends to be devoted to buying more of the same rather than upgrading to higher-status products.[33]

The following general conclusions can be made regarding the relative value of social class (i.e. place of residence, occupation, cultural interests, etc.) versus income in predicting consumer behaviour:

- Social class appears to be a better predictor of purchases that have symbolic aspects, but low-to-moderate prices (e.g. cosmetics, alcohol).
- Income is a better predictor of major expenditures that do not have status or symbolic aspects (e.g. major appliances).
- Social class and income data together are better predictors of purchases of expensive, symbolic products (e.g. cars, homes, luxury goods).[34]

Measurement of social class

Because social class is a complex concept which depends on a number of factors, not surprisingly it has proved difficult to measure. Early measures included the Index of Status Characteristics developed in the 1940s and the Index of Social Position developed by Hollingshead in the 1950s.[35] These indices used various combinations of individual characteristics (e.g. income, type of housing) to arrive at a label of class standing. The accuracy of these composites is still a subject of debate among researchers; one recent study claimed that for segmentation purposes, raw education and income measures work as well as composite status measures.[36]

Blue-collar workers with relatively high-income jobs still tend to view themselves as working-class, even though their income levels may be equivalent to many white-collar workers.[37] This fact reinforces the idea that the labels 'working-class' or 'middle-class' are very subjective. Their meanings say at least as much about self-identity as they do about economic well-being.

Problems with measures of social class

Market researchers were among the first to propose that people from different social classes can be distinguished from each other in important ways. While some of these dimensions still exist, others have changed.[38] Unfortunately, many of these measures are badly dated and are not as valid today for a variety of reasons, four of which are discussed here.[39]

Most measures of social class were designed to accommodate the traditional nuclear family, with a male wage-earner in the middle of his career and a female full-time homemaker. Such measures have trouble accounting for two-income families, young singles living alone, or households headed by women which are so prevalent in today's society (see chapter 11).

Another problem with measuring social class is attributable to the increasing anonymity of our society. Earlier studies relied on the *reputational method*, where extensive interviewing was done within a community to determine the reputations and backgrounds of individuals. This information, coupled with the tracing of interaction patterns among people, provided a very comprehensive view of social standing within a community.

This approach is virtually impossible to implement in most communities today. One compromise is to interview individuals to obtain demographic data and to combine these data with the subjective impressions of the interviewer regarding the person's possessions and standard of living. An example of this approach appears in Figure 12.6. Note that the accuracy of this questionnaire relies largely on the interviewer's judgement, especially regarding the quality of the respondent's neighbour-

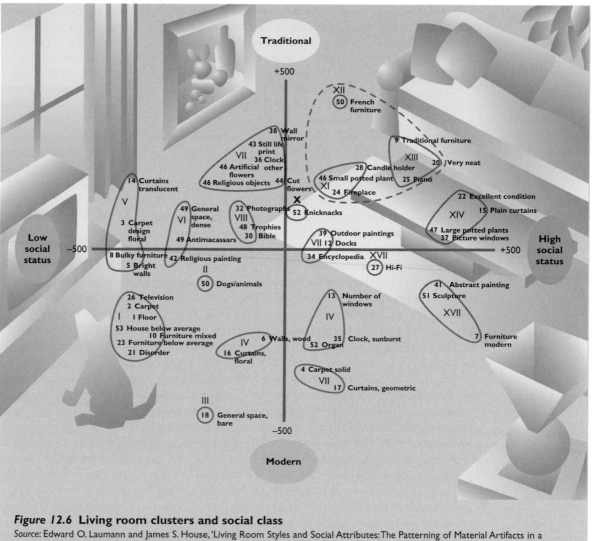

Figure 12.6 **Living room clusters and social class**
Source: Edward O. Laumann and James S. House, 'Living Room Styles and Social Attributes: The Patterning of Material Artifacts in a Modern Urban Community', *Sociology and Social Research* 54 (April 1970): 321–42.

hood. These impressions are in danger of being biased by the interviewer's own circumstances, which may affect his or her standard of comparison. This potential problem highlights the need for adequate training of interviewers, as well as for some attempt to cross-validate such data, possibly by employing multiple judges to rate the same area.

One problem with assigning people to a social class is that they may not be equal in their standing on all of the relevant dimensions. A person might come from a low-status ethnic group but have a high-status job, while another may live in a fashionable part of town but did not complete secondary school. The concept of **status crystallization** was developed to assess the impact of inconsistency on the self and social behaviour.[40] It was thought that since the rewards from each part of such an 'unbalanced' person's life would be variable and unpredictable, stress would result. People who exhibit such inconsistencies tend to be more receptive to social change than are those whose identities are more firmly rooted.

A related problem occurs when a person's social class standing creates expectations that are not met. Some people find themselves in the not unhappy position of making more money than is expected of those in their social class. This situation is known as an *overprivileged condition* and is usually defined as an income that is at least 25–30 per cent over the median for one's class.[41] In contrast, *underprivileged* consumers, who earn at least 15 per cent less than the median, must often devote their consumption priorities to sacrificing in order to maintain the appearance of living up to class expectations.

Lottery winners are examples of consumers who become overprivileged overnight. As attractive as winning is to many people, it has its problems. Consumers with a certain standard of living and level of expectations may have trouble adapting to sudden affluence and engage in flamboyant and irresponsible displays of wealth. Ironically, it is not unusual for lottery winners to report feelings of depression in the months after the win. They may have trouble adjusting to an unfamiliar world, and they frequently experience pressure from friends, relatives and business people to 'share the wealth'.

One New York winner who was featured prominently in the media is a case in point. He was employed as a mail porter until winning $5 million. After winning the lottery, he divorced his wife and married his girlfriend. She wore a $12,000 gown to the ceremony and the couple arrived in a horse-drawn carriage. Other purchases included a Cadillac with a Rolls Royce grill and a $5,000 car phone. He later denied rumours that he was heavily in debt due to his extravagant spending.[42]

The traditional assumption is that husbands define a family's social class, while wives must live it. Women borrow their social status from their husbands.[43] Indeed, the evidence indicates that physically attractive women tend to 'marry up' to a greater extent than attractive men. Women trade the resource of sexual appeal, which historically has been one of the few assets they were allowed to possess, for the economic resources of men.[44] The accuracy of this assumption in today's world must be questioned. Many women now contribute equally to the family's well-being and work in positions of comparable or even greater status than their spouses. *Cosmopolitan* magazine offered this revelation: 'Women who've become liberated enough to marry any man they please, regardless of his social position, report how much more fun and spontaneous their relationships with men have become now that they no longer view men only in terms of their power symbols.'[45]

Employed women tend to average both their own and their husband's respective positions when estimating their own subjective status.[46] Nevertheless, a prospective spouse's social class is often an important 'product attribute' when evaluating alternatives in the interpersonal marketplace (as David and Julia were to find out). *Cosmopolitan* also discussed this dilemma, implying that social class differences are still an issue in the mating game: 'You've met the (almost) perfect man. You both adore Dashiell Hammett thrillers, Mozart, and tennis. He taught you to jet ski; you taught him the virtues of tofu . . . . The problem? You're an executive earning ninety-thousand dollars a year. He's a taxi driver . . . .'[47]

Problems with social class segmentation: a summary

Social class remains an important way to categorize consumers. Many marketing strategies do target different social classes. However, marketers have failed to use social class information as effectively as they could for the following reasons:

- They have ignored status inconsistency.
- They have ignored intergenerational mobility.
- They have ignored subjective social class (i.e. the class a consumer identifies with rather than the one he or she objectively belongs to).
- They have ignored consumers' aspirations to change their class standing.
- They have ignored the social status of working wives.

How social class affects purchase decisions

Different products and stores are perceived by consumers to be appropriate for certain social classes.[48] Working-class consumers tend to evaluate products in more utilitarian terms such as sturdiness or comfort rather than style or fashionability. They are less likely to experiment with new products or styles, such as modern furniture or coloured appliances.[49] In contrast, more affluent people tend to be concerned about appearance and body image, so they are more avid consumers of diet foods and drinks compared to people in small working-class towns. These differences mean that the cola market, for example, can be segmented by social class.[50]

Class differences in worldview

A major social class difference involves the *worldview* of consumers. The world of the working class (including the lower-middle class) is more intimate and constricted. For example, working-class men are likely to name local sports figures as heroes and are less likely to take long vacation trips to out-of-the way places.[51] Immediate needs, such as a new refrigerator or TV, tend to dictate buying behaviour for these consumers, while the higher classes tend to focus on more long-term goals, such as saving for college fees or retirement.[52]

Working-class consumers depend heavily on relatives for emotional support and tend to orient themselves in terms of the community rather than the world at large. They are more likely to be conservative and family-oriented. Maintaining the appearance of one's home and property is a priority, regardless of the size of the house.

While they would like to have more in the way of material goods, working-class people do not necessarily envy those who rank above them in social standing.[53] The maintenance of a high-status lifestyle is sometimes not seen as worth the effort. As one blue-collar consumer commented: 'Life is very hectic for those people. There are more breakdowns and alcoholism. It must be very hard to sustain the status, the clothes, the parties that are expected. I don't think I'd want to take their place.'[54] Figure 12.7 shows the influences that income levels and age has on our concerns about 'the hectic life'.[55]

The blue-collar consumer quoted here may be right. While good things appear to go hand in hand with higher status and wealth, the picture is not that clear. The social scientist Emile Durkheim observed that suicide rates are much higher among the wealthy. He wrote in 1897, 'the possessors of most comfort suffer most'.[56] The quest for riches has the potential to result in depression, deviant behaviour and ruin. In fact, a recent survey of affluent American consumers (they made an average of $176,000 a year) supports this notion. Although these people are in the top 2.5 per cent income bracket in America, only 14 per cent said they are very well off.[57]

The concept of a **taste culture**, which differentiates people in terms of their aesthetic and intellectual preferences, is helpful in understanding the important yet subtle distinctions in consumption choices among the social classes. Taste cultures largely

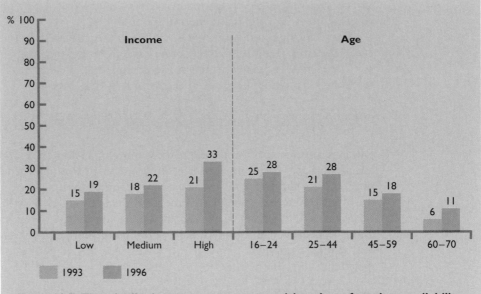

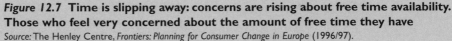

Figure 12.7 **Time is slipping away: concerns are rising about free time availability. Those who feel very concerned about the amount of free time they have**
Source: The Henley Centre, *Frontiers: Planning for Consumer Change in Europe* (1996/97).

reflect education (and also are income-related).[58] A distinction is often made between low-culture and high-culture groups (and is discussed in more detail in chapter 16).

While such perspectives have met with criticism due to the implicit value judgements involved, they are valuable because they recognize the existence of groupings based on shared tastes in literature, art, home decoration, and so on. In one of the classic studies of social differences in taste, researchers catalogued homeowners' possessions while asking more typical questions about income and occupation. Clusters of furnishings and decorative items which seemed to appear together with some regularity were identified, and different clusters were found depending on the consumer's social status. For example, religious objects, artificial flowers and still-life portraits tended to be found together in relatively lower-status living rooms, while a cluster containing abstract paintings, sculptures and modern furniture was more likely to appear in a higher-status home.[59]

Another approach to social class focuses on differences in the types of *codes* (the ways meanings are expressed and interpreted by consumers) used within different social strata. Discovery of these codes is valuable to marketers, since this knowledge allows them to communicate to markets using concepts and terms most likely to be understood and appreciated by specific consumers.

The nature of these codes varies among social classes. **Restricted codes** are dominant among the working class, while elaborated codes tend to be used by the middle and upper classes. Restricted codes focus on the content of objects, not on relationships among objects. **Elaborated codes**, in contrast, are more complex and depend upon a more sophisticated worldview. Some differences between these two general types of codes are provided in Table 12.1. As this table indicates, these code differences extend to the way consumers approach such basic concepts as time, social relationships and objects.

Table 12.1 Effects of restricted versus elaborated codes

	Restricted codes	Elaborated codes
General characteristics	Emphasize description and contents of objects	Emphasize analysis and interrelationships between objects; i.e. hierarchical organization and instrumental connections
	Have implicit meanings (context dependent)	Have explicit meanings
Language	Use few qualifiers, i.e. few adjectives or adverbs	Have language rich in personal, individual qualifiers
	Use concrete, descriptive, tangible symbolism	Use large vocabulary, complex conceptual hierarchy
Social relationships	Stress attributes of individuals over formal roles	Stress formal role structure, instrumental relationships
Time	Focus on present; have only general notion of future	Focus on instrumental relationship between present activities and future rewards
Physical space	Locate rooms, spaces in context of other rooms and places: e.g. 'front room', 'corner shop'	Identify rooms, spaces in terms of usage; formal ordering of spaces: e.g. 'dining room', 'financial district'
Implications for marketers	Stress inherent product quality, contents (or trustworthiness, goodness of 'real-type'), spokesperson	Stress differences, advantages vis-à-vis other products in terms of some autonomous evaluation criteria
	Stress implicit fit of product with total lifestyle	Stress product's instrumental ties to distant benefits
	Use simple adjectives, descriptors	Use complex adjectives, descriptors

Source: Adapted from Jeffrey F. Durgee, 'How Consumer Sub-Cultures Code Reality: A Look at Some Code Types', in Richard J. Lutz (ed.), *Advances in Consumer Research* 13 (Provo, UT: Association for Consumer Research, 1986): 332.

Marketing appeals that are constructed with these differences in mind will result in quite different messages. For example, a life insurance ad targeted at a lower-class person might depict in simple, straightforward terms a hard-working family man who feels good immediately after purchasing a policy. An upmarket appeal might depict a more affluent older couple surrounded by photos of their children and grandchildren and contain extensive copy emphasizing the satisfaction that comes from planning for the future and highlighting the benefits of a whole-life insurance policy.

Targeting the poor
While poor people obviously have less to spend than rich ones, they have the same basic needs as everyone else. Low-income families purchase such staples as milk, bread and tea at the same rates as average-income families. And minimum wage level households spend a greater than average share on out-of-pocket health care costs, rent, and food consumed at home.

The unemployed do feel alienated in a consumer society, since they are unable to obtain many of the items that our culture tells us we 'need' to be successful. However, idealized advertising portrayals don't seem to appeal to low-end consumers who have been interviewed by researchers. Apparently, one way to preserve self-esteem is by placing oneself outside the culture of consumption and emphasizing the value of a simple way of life with less emphasis on materialism. In some cases, they enjoy the advertising as entertainment without actually yearning for the products; a comment by one 32-year-old British woman is typical: 'They're not aimed at me, definitely not. It's fine to look at them, but they're not aimed at me so in the main I just pass over them.'[60]

Some marketers are developing products and services for low-income consumers. These strategies may be obvious in some cases (or even boarding on the insulting) as when S.C. Johnson & Son, manufacturers of Raid insect spray, regularly hosts 'cockroach evictions' at inner-city housing developments. Other strategies raise important ethical issues, especially when marketers of so-called 'sin products' such as alcohol and tobacco single out what many feel is a vulnerable audience. For example, manufacturers of malt liquors and fortified wines concentrate their efforts in poor areas where they know their products sell best.

Targeting the rich

We live in an age where elite department stores sell Donna Karan and Calvin Klein Barbies, and Mattel's Pink Splendor Barbie comes complete with crystal jewellery and a bouffant gown sewn with 24-carat threads.[61] To dress that 'living doll', Victoria's Secret offers its Million Dollar Miracle Bra, with over 100 carats of real diamonds.[62] *Somebody* must be buying this stuff ...

Many marketers try to target affluent markets. This practice often makes sense, since these consumers obviously have the resources to expend on costly products (often with higher profit margins). *The Robb Report*, a magazine targeted to the affluent (average reader income is $755,000) in 1996 estimated that 4.8 million American households had a net worth of at least $1 million, up 118 per cent from 1992. The magazine segments the wealthy into three markets: the marginally rich (household income $70,000 to $99,999), the comfortably rich (income of $100,000 to $249,000), and the super rich ($250,000+).[63]

However, it is a mistake to assume that everyone with a high income should be placed in the same market segment. As noted earlier, social class involves more than absolute income; it is also a way of life, and affluent consumers' interests and spending priorities are significantly affected by such factors as where they got their money, how they got it, and how long they have had it.[64] For example, the marginally rich tend to prefer sporting events to cultural activities, and are only half as likely as the super rich to frequent art galleries or the opera.[65]

The rich *are* different. But, they are different from one another as well. Income alone is not a good predictor of consumer behaviour, which reminds us that the wealthy can be further segmented in terms of attitudes, values and preferences. For example, according to industry experts drivers in the luxury car market can be segmented as follows:

● Cadillac owners want to be chauffeured. They are not very attentive to styling details or the car's colour. Their primary interests are in comfort and the impression they make on others.
● Porsche owners prefer to drive themselves. They are more interested in performance than luxury. The colour red is a favourite.

- Jaguar owners are more austere. They are interested in elegance and prefer darker colours.
- Mercedes owners like to feel they are in control. They tend to prefer muted shades of tan, grey and silver.

Multicultural dimensions 	*Avenue* is an American magazine that reports on the comings-and-goings of New York high society. Now the magazine is launching another edition – in China. *Avenue China* was launched in October 1994, and included stories about golfing in Bali, an Italian designer and profiles of top Chinese executives. The magazine cannot be found on news-stands; it is being given to the rich residents of Beijing, Shanghai, Guangzhou and Shenzhen (China's wealthiest cities). About a third of the edition's 50,000 copies will be hand-delivered to top government officials, businesspeople and celebrities. Considering that China's per-capita GDP is only $370 per year, it's obvious that *Avenue China* is targeting the cream of the crop of a new breed of Chinese success stories.[66]

Old money

When people have enough money for all intents and purposes to buy just about anything they want, ironically social distinctions no longer revolve around the amount of money one has. Instead, it appears to be important to consider *where* the money came from and *how* it is spent. The 'top out-of-sight class' (such as Julia's parents) live primarily on inherited money. People who have made vast amounts of money from their own labour do not tend to be included in this select group, though their flamboyant consumption patterns may represent an attempt to prove their wealth.[67] The mere presence of wealth is thus not sufficient to achieve social prominence. It must be accompanied by a family history of public service and philanthropy, which is often manifested in tangible markers that enable these donors to achieve a kind of immortality (e.g. Rockefeller University or the Whitney Museum).[68] 'Old money' consumers tend to make distinctions among themselves in terms of ancestry and lineage rather than wealth.[69] Old money people (like the Caldwells) are secure in their status. In a sense, they have been trained their whole lives to be rich.

The nouveaux riches

Other wealthy people do not know how to be rich. The Horatio Alger myth, where a person goes from 'rags to riches' through hard work and a bit of luck, is still a powerful force in Western society and, more recently, in Asian societies as well. Although many people do in fact become 'self-made millionaires', they often encounter a problem (although not the worst problem one could think of!) after they have become wealthy and have changed their social status: consumers who have achieved extreme wealth and have relatively recently become members of upper social classes are known as the *nouveaux riches*, a term that is sometimes used in a derogatory manner to describe newcomers to the world of wealth.

The *nouveau riche* phenomenon is also widespread in Russia and other Eastern European countries, where the transition to capitalism has paved the way for a new class of wealthy consumers who are spending lavishly on luxury items. One study of wealthy Russians identified a group of 'super-spenders', who earn about $1000 a month and spend as much on discretionary items as they do on rent. They would like to spend more money, but are frustrated by the lack of quality products and services available to them![70]

Alas, many *nouveaux riches* are plagued by *status anxiety*. They monitor the cultural environment to ensure that they are doing the 'right' thing, wearing the 'right' clothes', being seen in the 'right places', using the 'right' caterer, and so on.[72] Flamboyant consumption can thus be viewed as a form of symbolic self-completion, where the excessive display of symbols thought to denote 'class' is used to make up for an internal lack of assurance about the 'correct' way to behave.[73]

The 'get set'

While the possession of wealth is clearly an important dimension of affluence, this quality may be as much determined by attitudes towards consumption as it is by level of income. Some marketers have identified a consumer segment composed of well-off, but not rich, people who desire the best products and services, even though they may have to be more selective about those items they are able to buy. These consumers are realistic about what they can afford and prefer to sacrifice in some areas so that they can have the best in others. Various advertising and marketing research agencies have labelled this segment with such terms as *Influentials*, the *New Grown-Ups* and the *Get Set*.

While many upper-class brands tried in the past to downscale themselves to attract the mass market, there are some indications that this strategy is reversing. Because of the Get Set's emphasis on quality, one scenario is that marketers will encourage the masses to 'buy up' into products associated with the upper classes, even if they are forced to buy less. A print campaign for Waterford Crystal exemplifies this approach. The theme line, 'Steadfast in a world of wavering standards', is calculated to appeal to consumers who desire authenticity and lasting value.[74]

Status symbols

People have a deep-seated tendency to evaluate themselves, their professional accomplishments, their material well-being, and so on, relative to others. The popular phrase 'keeping up with the Joneses' (in Japan it's 'keeping up with the Satos') refers to the comparison between one's standard of living and that of one's neighbours.

Satisfaction is a relative concept, however. We hold ourselves to a standard defined by others that is constantly changing. Unfortunately, a major motivation for the purchase and display of products is not to enjoy them, but rather to let others know that we can afford them. In other words, these products function as status symbols. The desire to accumulate these 'badges of achievement' is summarized by the slogan: 'He who dies with the most toys, wins'. Status-seeking is a significant source of motivation to procure appropriate products and services that the user hopes will let others know that he or she has 'made it'.

Conspicuous consumption

The motivation to consume for the sake of consuming was first discussed by the social analyst Thorstein Veblen at the turn of the century. Veblen felt that a major role of products was for **invidious distinction** – they are used to inspire envy in others through display of wealth or power. Veblen coined the term **conspicuous consumption** to refer to people's desire to provide prominent visible evidence of their ability to afford luxury goods. Veblen's work was motivated by the excesses of his time. He wrote in the era of the robber barons, where the likes of J.P. Morgan, Henry Clay Frick, William Vanderbilt and others were building massive financial empires and flaunting their wealth by throwing lavish parties. Some of these events of excess became legendary, as described in this account:

> there were tales, repeated in the newspapers, of dinners on horseback; of banquets for pet dogs; of hundred-dollar bills folded into guests' dinner napkins; of a hostess who attracted attention by seating a chimpanzee at her table; of centerpieces in which lightly clad living maidens swam in glass tanks, or emerged from huge pies; of parties at which cigars were ceremoniously lighted with flaming banknotes of large denominations.[75]

The trophy wife

This flaunting of one's possessions even extended to wives: Veblen criticized the 'decorative' role women were often forced to play as they were bestowed with expensive clothes, pretentious homes and a life of leisure as a way to advertise the wealth of their husbands – a sort of 'walking advertisement'. Such fashions as high-heeled shoes, tight corsets, billowing trains on dresses and elaborate hairstyles all conspired to ensure that wealthy women could barely move without assistance, much less perform manual labour. Similarly, the Chinese practice of foot-binding turned women into cripples, who had to be carried from place to place.

The modern potlatch

Veblen was inspired by anthropological studies of the Kwakiutl Indians, who lived in the American Pacific Northwest. These Indians had a ceremony called a **potlatch**, a feast where the host showed off his wealth and gave extravagant presents to the guests. The more one gave away, the better one looked to the others. Sometimes, the host would use an even more radical strategy to flaunt his wealth. He would publicly destroy some of his property to demonstrate how much he had.

This ritual was also used as a social weapon: since guests were expected to reciprocate, a poorer rival could be humiliated by being invited to a lavish potlatch. The need to give away as much as the host, even though he could not afford it, would essentially force the hapless guest into bankruptcy. If this practice sounds 'primitive', think for a moment about many modern weddings. Parents commonly invest huge sums of money to throw a lavish party and compete with others for the distinction of giving their daughter the 'best' or most extravagant wedding, even if they have to save for twenty years to do so.

The leisure class

This process of conspicuous consumption was, for Veblen, most evident among what he termed the *leisure class*, people for whom productive work is taboo. In Marxist terms, this reflects a desire to link oneself to ownership or control of the means of production, rather than to the production itself. Any evidence that one actually has to work for a living is to be shunned, as suggested by the term the 'idle rich'.

Like the potlatch ritual, the desire to convince others that one has a surplus of resources creates the need for evidence of this abundance. Accordingly, priority is given to consumption activities that use up as many resources as possible in non-constructive pursuits. This *conspicuous waste* in turn shows others that one has the assets to spare. Veblen noted that 'we are told of certain Polynesian chiefs, who, under the stress of good form, preferred to starve rather than carry their food to their mouths with their own hands'.[76]

The death – and rebirth – of status symbols

While ostentatious products fell out of favour in the early part of this decade, the late 1990s are witnessing a resurgence of interest in luxury goods. European companies such as Hermes International, LVMH Hennesey Louis Vuitton and Baccarat are enjoying sales gains of between 13 and 16 per cent, as affluent consumers are once again indulging their desires for the finer things in life. One market researcher has termed this trend 'the pleasure revenge' – people are tired of buying moderately, eating low fat foods, and so on, and as a result sales are booming for self-indulgent products from fur coats to premium ice creams and caviar. As the Chairman of LVMH put it, 'The appetite for luxury is as strong as ever. The only difference is that in the 1980s, people would put a luxury trademark on anything. Today only the best sells.'[77]

Parody display

As the competition to accumulate status symbols escalates, sometimes the best tactic is to switch gears and go in reverse. One way to do this is to deliberately *avoid*

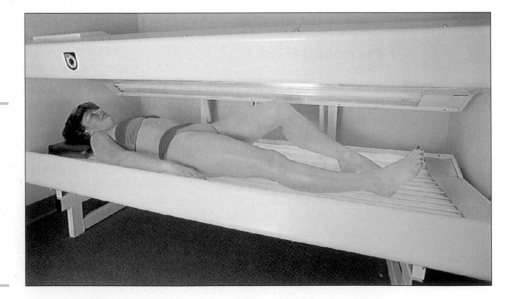

The tanning-salon industry may be said to owe its success to consumers' desire to pay for the illusion that they have idle time to soak up the sun.
© Tim Barnwell/Stock Boston.

status symbols – that is, to seek status by mocking it. This sophisticated form of conspicuous consumption has been termed parody display.[78] A good example of parody display is the home-furnishing style known as High Tech, which was in vogue a few years ago. This motif incorporated the use of industrial equipment (e.g. floors were covered with plates used on the decks of destroyers), and pipes and support beams were deliberately exposed.[79] This decorating strategy is intended to show that one is so witty and 'in the know' that status symbols aren't necessary. Hence, the popularity of old, torn blue jeans, and 'utility' vehicles such as jeeps among the upper classes. Thus, 'true' status is shown by the adoption of product symbolism that is deliberately not fashionable.

Marketing opportunity

Since the products and activities that connote high status are always changing, a significant amount of marketing effort goes into educating consumers as to what specific symbols they should be displaying and to ensuring that a product is accepted in the pantheon of status symbols.

The need to display the 'right' symbols has been a boon to the publishing industry, where a variety of 'how-to books', magazines and videos are available to school willing students of status. The concept of 'dressing for success', where detailed instructions are provided to allow people to dress as if they are members of the upper middle class (at least the authors' versions of this) was one popular example.[80] This guidance has now spread to other areas of consumption, including 'power lunching', (e.g. order steak tartare to intimidate your partner, since raw meat is a power food), office furnishings and home decoration.

Chapter summary

- The field of behavioural economics considers how consumers decide what to do with their money. In particular, *discretionary expenditures* are made only when people are able and willing to spend money on items above and beyond their basic needs. *Consumer confidence* – the state of mind consumers have about their own personal situation, as well as their feelings about their overall economic prospects – helps to determine whether they will purchase goods and services, take on debt or save their money.
- In this decade, consumers overall have been relatively pessimistic about their future prospects. A lower level of resources has caused a shift towards an emphasis on quality products that are reasonably priced. Consumers are less tolerant of exaggerated or vague product claims, and they are more sceptical about marketing activities. Consumers in their twenties are particularly sceptical about the economy and marketing targeted to their age group.
- A consumer's *social class* refers to his or her standing in society. It is determined by a number of factors, including education, occupation and income.
- Virtually all groups make distinctions among members in terms of relative superiority, power and access to valued resources. This *social stratification* creates a status hierarchy, where some goods are preferred over others and are used to categorize their owners' social class.

- While income is an important indicator of social class, the relationship is far from perfect since social class is also determined by such factors as place of residence, cultural interests and worldview.
- Purchase decisions are sometimes influenced by the desire to 'buy up' to a higher social class or to engage in the process of *conspicuous consumption*, where one's status is flaunted by the deliberate and non-constructive use of valuable resources. This spending pattern is a characteristic of the *nouveaux riches*, whose relatively recent acquisition of income, rather than ancestry or breeding, is responsible for their increased *social mobility*.
- Products are used as status symbols to communicate real or desired social class. *Parody display* occurs when consumers seek status by deliberately avoiding fashionable products.

Key terms

Behavioural economics *(p. 327)*
Conspicuous consumption *(p. 347)*
Consumer confidence *(p. 330)*
Discretionary income *(p. 329)*
Elaborated codes *(p. 342)*
Invidious distinction *(p. 347)*
Parody display *(p. 348)*
Potlatch *(p. 347)*
Restricted codes *(p. 342)*

Savings rate *(p. 330)*
Social class *(p. 332)*
Social hierarchy *(p. 333)*
Social mobility *(p. 336)*
Social stratification *(p. 335)*
Status crystallization *(p. 339)*
Status symbols *(p. 327)*
Taste culture *(p. 341)*

Consumer behaviour challenge

1. The concepts *income* and *wealth* are measured in different ways throughout Europe, in spite of the standardization of currency coming in 1999. Look through several recent issues of *Review of Income and Wealth* to get an idea of how these concepts differ across countries. For marketers, do you have any suggestions as to how to segment income groups for a European-wide strategy?

2. What are some of the obstacles to measuring social class in European society? Discuss some ways to get around these obstacles.

3. What consumption differences might you expect to observe between a family characterized as underprivileged versus one whose income is average for its social class?

4. When is social class likely to be a better predictor of consumer behaviour than mere knowledge of a person's income?

5. How do you assign people to social classes, or do you at all? What consumption cues do you use (e.g. clothing, speech, cars, etc.) to determine social standing?

6. Thorstein Veblen argued that women were often used as a vehicle to display their husbands' wealth. Is this argument still valid today?

7. Given present environmental conditions and dwindling resources, what is the future of 'conspicuous waste'? Can the desire to impress others with affluence ever be eliminated? If not, can it take on a less dangerous form?

8. Some people argue that status symbols are dead. Do you agree?

9. Compile a list of occupations, and ask a sample of students who are studying a variety of subjects (both business and non-business) to rank the prestige of these jobs. Can you detect any differences in these rankings as a function of students' subjects?

10. Compile ads that depict consumers of different social classes. What generalizations can you make about the reality of these ads and about the media in which they appear?

11. Identify a current set of fraudulent status symbols, and construct profiles of consumers who are wearing or using these products. Are these profiles consistent with the images portrayed in each product's promotional messages?

12. The chapter observes that some marketers are finding 'greener pastures' by targeting low-income people. How ethical is it to single out consumers who cannot afford to waste their precious resources on discretionary items? Under what circumstances should this segmentation strategy be encouraged or discouraged?

It's just a few months before winter weather really sets in, and Joost is lying on his bed 'channel surfing' on the TV and day dreaming about trying out his new ice-hockey skates on the frozen lakes near the flat where he and his father live in the suburbs of Amsterdam. His father tried to convince him to buy the classic 'hoge Noren' – black high-top touring skates with a long blade that have been 'classics' in Holland for decades, but Joost insisted on ice-hockey skates. His response was: 'Your skates are for middle-aged, old-fashioned skaters who are too serious about the whole thing. I want skates I can mess about in. Besides, these skates go well with my new *Fila* winter jacket.'

While Joost is switching from one channel to the next, an advertisement for a skiing holiday comes on the screen and catches his limited attention. Images of 'extreme skiing' are mixed with scenes of young people sitting around a well-stocked breakfast table. Text appears at the bottom of the screen, instructing the viewer to go to the *teletext* page for more information. The entire advertisement lasts 15 seconds. Joost uses the remote control to switch to the teletext page, and scans the ski package offerings. Great! Ten days in Austria for just 745 guilders. It includes round-trip bus transportation, twin rooms, half-pension and nine days of ski passes. Before moving on to the next channel, he notes down the travel agent's web site address. With the TV still on, he logs on to his computer and checks the web site. He can book the trip on the web. First, he needs to ask a few friends to see if they want to go during the Christmas break. Then he just needs his Dad's permission . . . and his credit card number.

Age subcultures

Age and consumer identity

The era in which a consumer is born creates for that person a cultural bond with the millions of others born during the same time period. As we grow older, our needs and preferences change, often in unision with others who are close to our own age. For this reason, a consumer's age exerts a significant influence on his or her identity. All things being equal, we are more likely than not to have things in common with others of our own age. In this chapter, we'll explore some of the important characteristics of some key age groups, and consider how marketing strategies must be modified to appeal to diverse age subcultures.

Age cohorts: 'my generation'

An age cohort consists of people of similar ages who have undergone similar experiences. They share many common memories about cultural heroes (e.g. Clint Eastwood versus Brad Pitt, or Frank Sinatra versus Kurt Cobain), important historical events (e.g. the 1969 Apollo moon landing versus the 1997 Mars mission), and

Choosing for 'hockey' style ice skates goes well beyond just product and price considerations. Review this chapter's opening consumer vignette for the more complete picture of the complex choice processes of teens.

Documenting their time together at World Cup '98, this group of young adult fans from Belgium and Holland create their own 'Paris souvenir'.

so on. Although there is no universally accepted way to divide people into age cohorts, each of us seems to have a pretty good idea of what we mean when we refer to 'my generation'.

Marketers often target products and services to one or more specific age cohorts. They recognize that the same offering will probably not appeal to people of different ages, nor will the language and images they use to reach them. In some cases separate campaigns are developed to attract consumers of different ages. For example, travel agencies throughout Europe target youth markets during the months of May and June for low-cost summer holidays to Mallorca, and then target middle-aged, more affluent consumers for the same destination during September and October. What differs in the two campaigns are the media used, the images portrayed and the prices offered.

The appeal of nostalgia

Because consumers within an age group confront crucial life changes at roughly the same time, the values and symbolism used to appeal to them can evoke powerful feelings of nostalgia (see chapter 3). Adults aged 30+ are particularly susceptible to this phenomenon.[1] However, young people as well as old are influenced by references to their past. In fact, research indicates that some people are more disposed to be nostalgic than others, regardless of age. A scale that has been used to measure the impact of nostalgia on individual consumers appears in Table 13.1.

Chapter 3 noted that product sales can be dramatically affected by linking a brand to vivid memories and experiences, especially for items that are associated with childhood or adolescence. Vespa scooters, Hornby electric trains and the coupon 'saving-points' from Douwe Egberts coffee are all examples of products which have managed to span two or more generations of loyal consumers, providing the brand a strong equity position in competitive and crowded markets.

Many advertising campaigns have played on the collective memories of consumers by using older celebrities to endorse their products, such as American Express's campaign which featured Eric Clapton and Lou Reed. In Japan, Ringo Starr (the *Beatles'* drummer) is used to help promote demand for apples. The target market is

Table 13.1 **The nostalgia scale**

Scale items

- They don't make 'em like they used to.

- Things used to be better in the good old days.

- Products are getting shoddier and shoddier.

- Technological change will ensure a brighter future (reverse coded).

- History involves a steady improvement in human welfare (reverse coded).

- We are experiencing a decline in the quality of life.

- Steady growth in GNP has brought increased human happiness (reverse coded).

- Modern business constantly builds a better tomorrow (reverse coded).

Note: Items are presented on a nine-point scale ranging from strong disagreement (1) to strong agreement (9), and responses are summed.
Source: Morris B. Holbrook and Robert M. Schindler, 'Age, Sex, and Attitude Toward the Past as Predicters of Consumers' Aesthetic Tastes for Cultural Products', *Journal of Marketing Research* 31 (August 1994): 416. Reprinted by permission of the American Marketing Association.

middle-aged consumers, and it doesn't hurt that, phonetically, 'Ringo' means *apple* in Japanese. To assess just how pervasive nostalgia is, pay attention to television commercials, and notice how often they are produced against a background of 'classic songs'. *Memories* magazine, which was founded to exploit the nostalgia boom, even offers advertisers a discount if they run old ads next to their current ones.

The teen market: it totally rules

In 1956, the label 'teenage' first entered the (American) vocabulary, as *Frankie Lymon and the Teenagers* became the first pop group to identify themselves with this new subculture. The concept of teenager is a fairly new cultural construction; throughout most of history a person simply made the transition from child to adult (often accompanied by some sort of ritual or ceremony, as we'll see in a subsequent chapter). The magazine *Seventeen*, launched in 1944, was based on the revelation that young women didn't want to look just like their mother. In the early 1960s, the teenage drama between rebellion and conformity began to unfold, pitting Elvis Presley with his greased hair and suggestive hip-swivels against more 'parentally approved' types such as Cliff Richard. Now, this rebellion is played out by being detached from the adult world, as exemplified by Beavis and Butthead or the confused, sullen teenagers appearing daily on Ricki Lake, Gerry Springer and other daytime talk shows which are broadcast on European satellite networks.[2]

Teen values and conflicts

Puberty and adolescence can be both the best of times and the worst of times. Many exciting changes happen as individuals leave the role of child and prepare to assume the role of adult. These changes create a lot of uncertainty about the self, and the need to belong and to find one's unique identity as a person becomes extremely important. At this age, choices of activities, friends and 'looks' are crucial to social acceptance. Teenagers actively search for cues from their peers and from advertising for the 'right' way to look and behave. Advertising geared to teenagers is typically action-oriented and depicts a group of 'in' teenagers using the product. Teenagers use products to express their identities, to explore the world and their newfound freedom in it, and also to rebel against the authority of their parents and other socializing agents. Joost's rejection of his father's suggestion to buy 'classic' skates, and his choice of ice-hockey skates which fashionably matched his *Fila* jacket, are mild expressions of these sorts of expressive consumption behaviours. Marketers often do their best to assist in this process. The range of consumer products targeted at teenagers (and particularly young ones) is greater than ever. Then again, so is teenagers' disposable income from part-time jobs and weekly pocket money.[3]

Teenagers in every culture grapple with fundamental developmental issues as they make the transitition from childhood to adult. According to research by Saatchi & Saatchi, there are four themes of conflict common to all teens:

1. *Autonomy versus belonging:* Teenagers need to acquire independence so they try to break away from their families. On the other hand, they need to attach themselves to a support structure, such as peers, to avoid being alone. A thriving internet subculture has developed to serve this purpose. The 'Net' (World Wide Web) is becoming the preferred method of communication for many young people, since its anonymity makes it easier to talk to people of the opposite sex, or of different ethnic and racial groups.[4]

2. *Rebellion versus conformity*: Teenagers need to rebel against social standards of appearance and behaviour, yet they still need to fit in and be accepted by others. Cult products that cultivate a rebellious image are prized for this reason. Skeleteens, a line of natural soft drinks in flavours like Brain Wash, Black Lemonade and DOA, is developing such a following thanks to its 'dangerous' mystique. This underground product was first discovered by California bikers in America, who were drawn to the images of skulls and crossbones on the labels.[5]

Teenagers in every culture grapple with personal and social issues as they make the transition from childhood to adulthood. What better way to work through issues than together, at the Snack Bar!

3. *Idealism versus pragmatism:* Teenagers tend to view adults as hypocrites, while they see themselves as being sincere. They have to struggle to reconcile their view of how the world should be with the realities they perceive around them.

4. *Narcissism versus intimacy:* Teenagers can be obsessed with their appearance and needs. On the other hand, they also feel the desire to connect with others on a meaningful level.[6]

Teenagers throughout history have had to cope with insecurity, parental authority and peer pressure. In the 1990s, however, these issues are compounded by concerns about the environment, racism, AIDS and other pressing social problems. Today's teenagers often have to cope with additional family responsibilities as well, especially if they live in non-traditional families where they must take significant responsibility for shopping, cooking and housework. It's hard work being a teenager in the 1990s. Figure 13.1 shows the results of a large European survey on some 'everyday' activities and responsibilities.

Marketing pitfall

Calvin Klein's strategy of using adolescent sexuality to sell the company's products dates back to 1980, when Brooke Shields proclaimed that 'nothing comes between her and her Calvins'. Later, ads featuring singer Marky Mark in his underwear sparked a new fashion craze. In 1995, though, Klein took this approach one very daring step further when a very controversial advertising campaign featuring young-looking models in situations dripping with sexual innuendo was unveiled. In one spot, an old man with a gravelly voice is in a basement and says to a scantily clad young boy, 'You got a real nice look. How old are you? Are you strong? You think you could rip that shirt off of you? That's a real nice body. You work out? I can tell'. The campaign ended when the Chairman of Dayton Hudson, a retail chain which co-sponsored the campaign, asked that the stores' names be removed from the ads, and *Seventeen* refused to carry them.[7] By then, of course, Klein had reaped invaluable volumes of free publicity as teenagers and adults debated the appropriateness of these images.

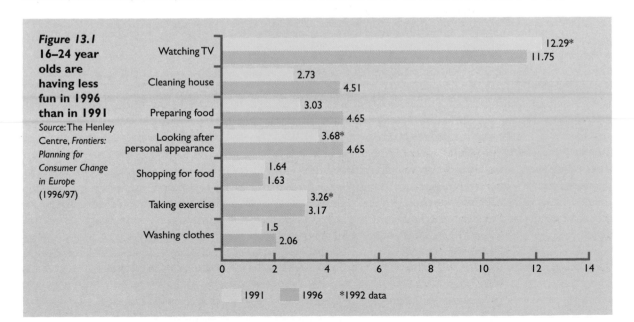

Figure 13.1 16–24 year olds are having less fun in 1996 than in 1991

Source: The Henley Centre, *Frontiers: Planning for Consumer Change in Europe* (1996/97)

Watching TV — 12.29* / 11.75
Cleaning house — 2.73 / 4.51
Preparing food — 3.03 / 4.65
Looking after personal appearance — 3.68* / 4.65
Shopping for food — 1.64 / 1.63
Taking exercise — 3.26* / 3.17
Washing clothes — 1.5 / 2.06

1991   1996   *1992 data

Appealing to the teen market

Consumers in this age subculture have a number of needs, including experimentation, belonging, independence, responsibility and approval from others. Product usage is a significant medium to express these needs. Because they are so interested in many different products and have the resources to obtain them, the teen market is avidly courted by many marketers. Much of this money goes towards 'feel-good' products: cosmetics, posters, and fast food – with the occasional nose ring thrown in as well. Table 13.2 summarizes the sorts of activities which British teenagers experiment in, and pay for with their own money.

Because today's teenagers were raised on TV and they tend to be much more canny than older generations, marketers must tread lightly when they try to reach them. As Joost illustrated with his 5 minutes of information-gathering on the TV, teletext and internet, teenagers in Europe have increasingly complex media consumption habits, and are acknowledged as being more advertising-literate. In particular, the messages must be seen as authentic and not condescending. In spite of their more critical evaluation of television advertising (see Figure 13.2), there is no doubt that TV adverts have a clear influence on youth purchases, as Figure 13.2 shows.

Marketers view teenagers as 'consumers-in-training', since brand loyalty is developed during this age. A teenager who is committed to a brand may continue to purchase it for many years to come. Such loyalty creates a barrier-to-entry for other brands that were not chosen during these pivotal years. Thus, advertisers sometimes try to 'lock in' consumers to certain brands so that they will buy these brands in the future more or less automatically. As one teen magazine ad director observed, 'We . . . always say it's easier to start a habit than stop it.'[8]

Table 13.2 Affluent lifestyles leading children into temptation
'During the last seven days, have you spent any of your own money on the following items?' (% saying yes)

	12–13 year olds		14–15 year olds	
	boys	girls	boys	girls
Crisps	38	42	43	46
Biscuits	16	10	14	8
Fast food (hot)	34	25	42	32
Arcade games (for fun)	22	7	20	7
Arcade gambling	12	3	14	4
Computer games	18	4	13	2
Leisure/sports centre	24	15	23	13
National lottery (gambling)	16	10	24	16

Source: 'Affluent Lifestyle Leading Children into Temptation', *The Independent* (23 September 1996).

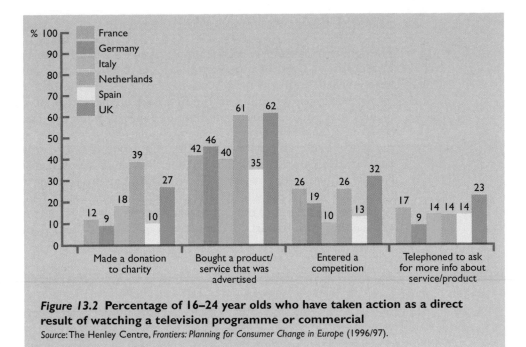

Figure 13.2 Percentage of 16–24 year olds who have taken action as a direct result of watching a television programme or commercial
Source: The Henley Centre, *Frontiers: Planning for Consumer Change in Europe* (1996/97).

Teenagers also exert a strong influence on the purchase decisions of their parents (see chapter 11).[9] In addition to providing 'helpful' advice to parents, teenagers increasingly are buying products on behalf of the family. As discussed in chapter 11, mothers are most likely to return to the workforce (most often to part-time work) once the children in the household are at school and have become more independent.[10]

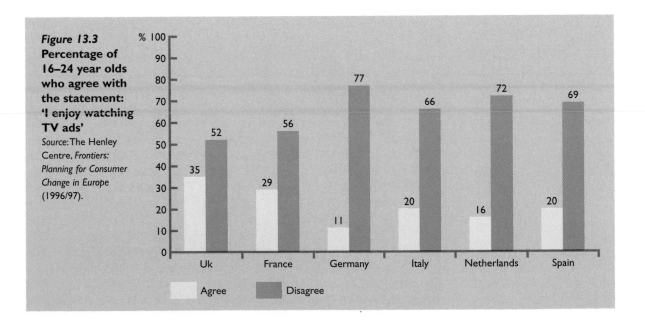

Figure 13.3 Percentage of 16–24 year olds who agree with the statement: 'I enjoy watching TV ads'
Source: The Henley Centre, *Frontiers: Planning for Consumer Change in Europe* (1996/97).

Baby busters: 'Generation X'

The cohort of consumers between the ages of 18 and 29 consists of over 30 million Europeans who will be a powerful force in years to come. This group, which has been labelled 'Generation X', 'slackers' or 'busters', has been profoundly affected by the economic downturn in the first part of the 1990s. So-called baby busters include many people, both in and out of higher education, whose tastes and priorities are beginning to be felt in fashion, popular culture, politics and marketing. Even the World Bank is sensitive to targeting this group of future policy-makers in a vernacular they can relate to. Their Public Service Advertisement for World Hunger Day which was broadcast by MTV in North America and Europe is very 'Gen-X'. Images flash by of the globe, babies, food, war, fluorescent bananas and attractive young people gazing at the camera, backed by a worldly beat with a jazz infusion and ending with words in distinctive type: 'The World Bank. Knowledge and resources for change'.[11]

Tracy in NYC. She said if she spits her gum out from up here and it hit someone below, the force would totally split them in half.

Some marketers feel the most important rule in marketing to Generation Xers is not to take yourself too seriously. This ad for Chuck Taylor All-Stars succeeded because it conveyed an irreverant attitude instead of claiming that its shoes were a 'hot' fashion statement. The company deliberately kept production values low so that readers wouldn't feel they were looking at an 'MTV clone'.

Marketing to busters or marketing bust?

Although the income of this age cohort is below expectations, they still constitute a formidable market segment – partly because so many still live at home and have more discretionary income. Busters in their twenties are estimated to have an annual spending power of $125 billion, and their purchases are essential to the fortunes of such product categories as beer, fast food and cosmetics.

Because many busters have been doing the family shopping for a long time, marketers are finding that they are much more sophisticated about evaluating advertising and products. They are turned off by advertising that either contains a lot of hype or takes itself too seriously. They see advertising as a form of entertainment but are turned off by overcommercialization.[12] As the Vice-President of Marketing for MTV put it, 'You must let them know that you know who they are, that you understand their life experiences. You want them to feel you're talking directly to them.'[13]

Nike took a soft-sell approach to woo younger buyers of its athletic shoes. Its ads show little of the product, focusing instead on encouraging readers to improve themselves through exercise. Other ads make fun of advertising: an ad created for a Maybelline eye shadow depicts supermodel Christy Turlington coolly posing in a glamorous setting. She then suddenly appears on her living room couch, where she laughs and says 'Get over it'.

One of the more successful commercials created specifically for this group was from a bank! Midland Bank's qualitative market research showed that money was one of university students' major worries. Its series of TV ads featuring Sam, 'a new student', was humorous, but avoided being patronizing. It also aimed to emphasize Midland's claim that it offers the best and cheapest deals. The message was reinforced by a no-nonsense PR campaign on student financing which received 25 editorial mentions in national publications. The success of the campaign has taken Midland to market leadership in this segment.[14]

Perhaps one reason why marketers' efforts to appeal to Xers with messages of alienation, cynicism and despair have not succeeded is that many people in their twenties aren't depressed after all! Generation Xers are quite a diverse group – they don't all wear reversed baseball caps and work in temporary, low-pay mindless jobs. Despite the birth of dozens of magazines catering to 'riot grrrls' and other angry Xers with names like *Axcess*, *Project X* and *KGB*, the most popular magazine for twenty-something women is *Cosmopolitan*. What seems to make this age cohort the angriest is constantly being labelled as angry by the media![15]

The advertising agency Saatchi & Saatchi sent teams of psychologists and cultural anthropologists into the field to study the buster subculture. These researchers identified four key segments:

1. *Cynical Disdainers* – the most pessimistic and sceptical about the world.
2. *Traditional Materialists* – the most like baby boomers in their thirties and forties, these young people are upbeat, optimistic about the future, and actively striving for what they continue to view as the desire for material prosperity.
3. *Hippies Revisited* – this group tends to espouse the non-materialistic values of the 1960s. Their priorities are expressed through music, retro fashion and a strong interest in spirituality.
4. *Fifties Machos* – these consumers tend to be young conservatives. They believe in stereotyped gender roles, are politically conservative and they are the least accepting of multi-culturalism.[16]

Multicultural dimensions

Images of Western consumption bombarding teenagers on TV screens around the world rapidly are creating a global youth culture. Some Japanese teenagers are so enamoured of West Coast American culture, they have been known to cruise down the main streets of Tokyo with surfboards on the roofs of their cars.

Spending time with friends and watching TV are ranked equally as teenagers' favourite pastimes, but eight of the ten top teen activities are media-related. Middle Easterners watch the most television (3.6 hours per day), North Americans watch 2.9 hours per day and Western Europeans log in at 2.5 hours. MTV reaches over 239 million viewers in 68 countries. Despite differences in cultures, middle-class youth worldwide can be spotted wearing their cherished Levi's and Nikes (the Japanese call this style *Amekaji*, or American casual); identification with these products helps to form tangible bonds among young people around the world. Many of these young consumers learn about America (or rather, the idealized version of it shown to us by television producers) by watching television. The soap opera *Santa Barbara* is the most popular show among 11–17-year-olds in Russia, while Brazilian teenagers are avid followers of the hospital drama *E.R.*[17] Some visitors to America are surprised to find that not all American teenagers share the lifestyle of the stars of *Beverley Hills 90210*.

Baby boomers

The **baby boomers** are the source of many fundamental cultural and economic changes. The reason: power in numbers. As the Second World War ended, they began to establish families and careers at a record pace. Imagine a large python that has swallowed a mouse; the mouse moves down the length of the python, creating a moving bulge as it goes.

The cultural impact of boomers

So it is with baby boomers. Figures 13.4 and 13.5 show the projections of the European population for both youth and boomers for a 17-year period. This increase

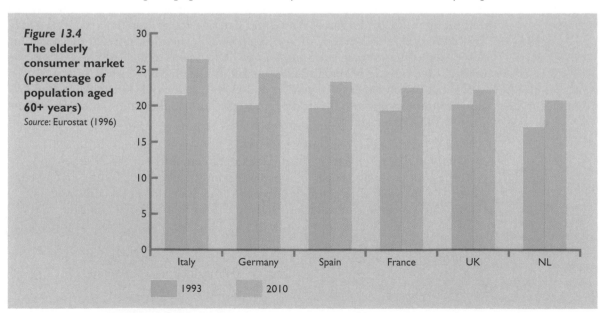

Figure 13.4 **The elderly consumer market (percentage of population aged 60+ years)**
Source: Eurostat (1996)

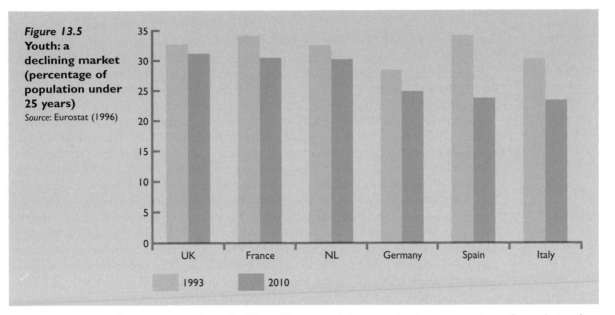

Figure 13.5
Youth: a declining market (percentage of population under 25 years)
Source: Eurostat (1996)

in the proportion of older citizens and decrease in the proportion of youth is often referred to as the 'greying and de-greening' of the European population, a structural trend which has major implications for the marketing of goods and services. Figure 13.6 shows the origins of the baby boomer age cohort.

As teenagers in the 1960s and 1970s, this generation created a revolution in style, politics and consumer attitudes. As they have aged, their collective will has been behind cultural events as diverse as the Paris student demonstrations and hippies in the 1960s, to Thatcherism and yuppies in the 1980s. Now that they are older, they continue to influence popular culture in important ways.

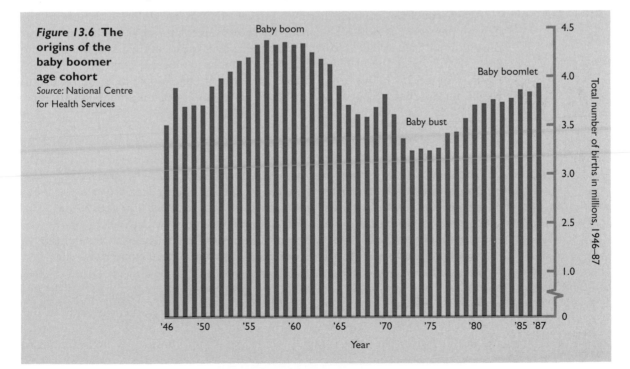

Figure 13.6 **The origins of the baby boomer age cohort**
Source: National Centre for Health Services

Economic power: he who pays the piper, calls the tune

Because of the size and buying power of the boomer group over the last twenty years, marketers focused most of their attention on the youth market. The popular slogan at the time, 'Don't trust anyone over thirty', also meant that people over thirty had trouble finding products appropriate to their age groups. Times have changed, and again it is the baby boomers who have changed them. For example, boomers tend to have different emotional and psychological needs from those who came before them. *Domain*, a high-fashion furniture chain, found that its core boomer clientele is as concerned about self-improvement as it is about home decor. The company launched a series of in-store seminars dealing with themes like women's issues and how to start a business, and found its repeat business doubled.[18]

This 'mouse in the python' has moved into its mid-thirties to fifties, and this age group is now the one that exerts the most impact on consumption patterns. Most of the growth in the market will be accounted for by people who are moving into their peak earning years. As one commercial for VH1, the music-video network that caters to those who are a bit too old for MTV, pointed out, 'The generation that dropped acid to escape reality . . . is the generation that drops antacid to cope with it'.

Consumers aged 35–44 spend the most on housing, cars and entertainment. In addition, consumers aged 45–54 spend the most of any age category on food, clothing, and personal pension plans. To appreciate the impact middle-aged consumers have and will have on the European economy, consider this: at current spending levels, a 1 per cent increase in householders aged 35–54 results in an additional $8.9 billion in consumer spending.

In addition to the direct demand for products and services created by this age group, these consumers are creating a new baby boom of their own to keep marketers busy in the future. Since fertility rates have dropped, this new boom is not as big as the one that created the baby boom generation; the new upsurge in the number of children born in comparison can best be described as a *baby boomlet*.

Many couples postponed getting married and having children because of the new emphasis on careers for women. These consumers are now beginning to hear the ticking of the biological 'clock'. They are having babies in their late twenties and early thirties, resulting in fewer (but perhaps more pampered) children per family. Couples in the 25–34 age group account for roughly one in five of all married couples in Europe, but for one in three of married couples with children living at home.

The grey market

The old widowed woman sits alone in her clean but sparsely furnished apartment, while the television blares out a soap opera. Each day, she slowly and painfully makes her way out of the apartment and goes to the corner shop to buy essentials, bread, milk and vegetables, always being careful to pick the least expensive offering. Most of the time she sits in her rocking chair, thinking sadly of her dead husband and the good times she used to have.

Is this the image you have of a typical elderly consumer? Until recently, many marketers did. As a result, they largely neglected the elderly in their feverish pursuit of the baby boomer market. But as our population ages and people are living longer and healthier lives, the game is rapidly changing. A lot of businesses are beginning to

Active Life is distributed free of charge through 1,500 main Post Offices in the United Kingdom.
Used with permission.

replace the old stereotype of the poor recluse. The newer, more accurate image is of an elderly person who is active, interested in what life has to offer, and is an enthusiastic consumer with the means and willingness to buy many goods and services.

Grey power: shattering stereotypes

By the year 2010, 20 per cent of Europeans will be 62 or older. This fastest growing age segment can be explained by the ageing of 'boomers', an increase in awareness of healty lifestyles and nutrition, coupled with improved medical diagnoses and treatment. Not only is this segment growing and living longer, older adults have large amounts of discretionary income, since they typically have paid off their mortgage, and no longer have the expense of raising and educating children.

Most elderly people lead more active, multidimensional lives than we assume. Many engage in voluntary work, continue to work and/or are involved in daily care of a grandchild. Still, outdated images of mature consumers persist. In one survey, one-third of consumers over age 55 reported that they deliberately did *not* buy a product because of the way an elderly person was stereotyped in the product's advertising.[19]

Seniors' economic clout

There is abundant evidence that the economic health of elderly consumers is good and getting better. Some of the important areas that stand to benefit from the surging grey market include holidays, cars, home improvements, cruises and tourism, cosmetic surgery and skin treatments, health, finance and legal matters, and 'how-to' books for learning to cope with retirement.

It is crucial to remember that income alone does not capture the spending power of this group. As mentioned above, elderly consumers are no longer burdened with the financial obligations that drain the income of younger consumers. Elderly consumers are much more likely to own their home, have no mortgage or have a (low-cost or subsidized) rented house or apartment. Across Europe, approximately 50 per cent of pensioners' income still comes from state pensions, yet it is clear that older consumers are time-rich, and have a significant amount of discretionary income to spend.[20]

Marketing opportunity

A few marketers are beginning to recognize the vast potential of the senior market and are designing products and services to cater to the specific needs of the elderly. A growing number of magazines are also being targeted to meet the interests of the older consumer. *Active Life*, *Saga*, *Mature Tymes* and *Plus* are all targeted at the 'over 50' market, although you wouldn't necessarily know it by the magazines, photos, advertising or articles! Most covers show vital, active 50-plussers, and the advertising focuses on quality of service, value for money and straightforward communications. With the exception of a few older faces promoting incontinence products, you're more likely to see consumers on mountain bikes than tending the garden.

Even companies that have relatively many 65-plussers as a target market don't feel the need to associate 'old' with their products for services. Advertisements for river and ocean cruises (which have a high percentage of older clientele throughout Europe) show busy discos and swimming pools, dominated by 30–40 year old clients, with a few wrinkle-free elderly in the photo. The accent to the elderly market is on product benefits, and not whether the product is best suited for a particular age group.[21]

Researchers have identified a set of key values that are relevant to older consumers. For marketing strategies to succeed, they should be related to one or more of these factors:[22]

- *Autonomy*: Mature consumers want to lead active lives and to be self-sufficient. Financial services and financial planning are increasing markets for the elderly segment, who have a strong need to remain independent. While companies are the largest purchasers of cars in the UK, the majority of private buyers are 'greys' – a further sign of their financial muscle and desire for autonomy.[23]
- *Connectedness*: Mature consumers value the bonds they have with friends and family. While the 'grey' don't relate well to their own age group (most elderly report feeling on average ten years younger than they are, and feel that 'other' elderly behave 'older' than they do), they do value information which communicates clear benefits to cohorts in their age group. Advertisements which avoid patronising stereotypes are well received.
- *Altruism*: Mature consumers want to give something back to the world. Thrifty Car Rental found in a survey that over 40 per cent of older consumers would select a rental car company if it sponsored a programme that gives discounts to senior citizens' centres. Based on this research, the company launched its highly successful 'Give a Friend a Lift' programme.

● *Personal growth*: Mature consumers are very interested in trying new experiences and developing their potential. By installing user-friendly interactive touch-screen computer stations in European stores, older consumers have become better educated about health issues, and are loyal to the GNC brand.[24]

Perceived age: you're only as old as you feel

The 'grey' market does not consist of a uniform segment of vigorous, happy, ready-to-spend consumers – nor is it a group of senile, economically marginalized, immobile people. In fact, research confirms the popular wisdom that age is more a state of mind than of body. A person's mental outlook and activity level has a lot more to do with his or her longevity and quality of life than does *chronological age*, or the actual number of years lived. In addition to these psychological dimensions of age, there are also cultural influences on what constitutes ageing, and perceptions of what is 'elderly' across different European markets.[25]

A better yardstick to categorize the elderly is **perceived age**, or how old a person feels. Perceived age can be measured on several dimensions, including 'feel-age' (i.e. how old a person feels) and 'look-age' (i.e. how old a person looks).[26] The older consumers get, the younger they feel relative to actual age. For this reason, many marketers emphasize product benefits rather than age appropriateness in marketing campaigns, since many consumers will not relate to products targeted to their chronological age.[27]

Marketing pitfall

Some marketing efforts targeted at the elderly have backfired because they reminded people of their age or presented their age group in an unflattering way. One of the more infamous blunders was committed by Heinz. A company analyst found that many elderly people were buying baby food because of the small portions and easy chewing consistency, so Heinz introduced a line of 'Senior Foods' made especially for denture wearers. Needless to say, the product failed. Consumers did not want to admit that they required strained foods (even to the supermarket cashier). They preferred to purchase baby foods, which they could pretend they were buying for a grandchild.

In Holland, a country where bicycles are an important mode of personal transportation, a specially designed 'elderly bicycle' was a resounding failure in spite of its competitive product benefits. While conventional marketing wisdom would suggest that a firm communicate its unique functional benefits to a target market, this wisdom backfired for the Dutch 'greys'. Positioning the bicycle as an easy-to-pedal 'senior bicycle' was met with a negative response, as the Dutch elderly who still ride a bicycle (a common sight in Holland!) feel too young to be riding a 'senior' bike.[28]

Segmenting seniors

The senior subculture represents an extremely large market: the number of Europeans aged 62 and over exceeds the entire population of Canada.[29] Because this group is so large, it is helpful to think of the mature market as consisting of four subsegments: an 'older' group (aged 55–64), an 'elderly' group (aged 65–74), an 'aged' group (aged 75–84) and finally a 'very old' group (85+).[30]

The elderly market is well suited for segmentation. Older consumers are easy to identify by age and stage in the family life cycle. Most receive Social Security benefits so they can be located without much effort, and many subscribe to one of the magazines targeted to the elderly, discussed earlier in this section. *Saga* in the UK has the largest circulation of any European magazine with over 750,000 monthly readers. Selling holidays and insurance to the over-50s, the parent company also makes use of a database with over 4 million over-50s.

Several segmentation approaches begin with the premise that a major determinant of elderly marketplace behaviour is the way a person deals with being old.[31] *Social ageing theories* try to understand how society assigns people to different roles across the lifespan. For example, when someone retires he/she may reflect society's expectations for someone at this life stage – this is a major transition point when people exit from many relationships.[32] Some people become depressed, withdrawn and apathetic as they age, some are angry and resist the thought of ageing, and some appear to accept the new challenges and opportunities this period of life has to offer.

Table 13.3 summarizes some selected findings from one current segmentation approach called **gerontographics** which divides the mature market into groups based on both level of physical well-being and social conditions, such as becoming a grandparent or losing a spouse.

Table 13.3 **Gerontographics**

Segment	55-plus	Profile	Marketing implications
Healthy indulgers	18%	Have experienced the fewest events related to ageing, such as retirement or widowhood, and are most likely to behave like younger consumers. Main focus is on enjoying life.	Looking for independent living and are good customers for discretionary services like home-cleaning and answering machines.
Healthy hermits	36%	React to life events like the death of a spouse by becoming withdrawn. Resent that they are expected to behave like old people.	Emphasize conformity. They want to know their appearance is socially acceptable, and tend to be comfortable with well-known brands.
Ailing outgoers	29%	Maintain positive self-esteem despite adverse life events. They accept limitations but still are determined to get the most out of life.	Have health problems that may require a special diet. Special menus and promotions will bring these people in to restaurants seen as catering to their needs.
Frail recluses	17%	Have adjusted their lifestyles to accept old age, but have chosen to cope with negative events by becoming spiritually stronger.	Like to stay put in the same house where they raised their families. Good candidates for redecorating, also for emergency response systems.

Source: Adapted from George P. Moschis, 'Life Stages of the Mature Market', *American Demographics* (September 1996): 44–50.

<table>
<tr>
<td>

Marketing pitfall

</td>
<td>

Many consumer products will encounter a more sympathetic reception from the elderly if products and the packages they come in are redesigned to be sensitive to physical limitations. While aesthetically appealing, packages are often awkward and difficult to manage, especially for those who are frail or arthritic. Also, many serving sizes are not geared to smaller families, widows or widowers and other people living alone, and coupons tend to be for family-sized products, rather than for single servings.

Older people may have difficulty with ring-pull cans and push-open milk cartons. Ziploc packages (self-sealing plastic bags) and clear plastic wrap also are difficult to handle. Packages need to be easy to read and should be made lighter and smaller. Finally, designers need to pay attention to contrasting colours. A slight yellowing of the eye's lens as one ages makes it harder to see background colours on packages. Discerning between blues, greens and violets becomes especially difficult. The closer identifying type colours are to the package's or advertisement's background colour, the less visibility and attention they will command.

</td>
</tr>
</table>

In general, the elderly have been shown to respond positively to ads that provide an abundance of information. Unlike other age groups, these consumers usually are not amused, or persuaded, by imagery-oriented advertising. A more successful strategy involves the construction of advertising that depicts the aged as well-integrated, contributing members of society, with emphasis on them expanding their horizons rather than clinging precariously to life.

Some basic guidelines have been suggested for effective advertising to the elderly. These include the following:[33]

- Keep language simple.
- Use clear, bright pictures.
- Use action to attract attention.
- Speak clearly, and keep the word count low.
- Use a single sales message, and emphasize brand extensions to tap consumers' familiarity.
- Avoid extraneous stimuli (i.e., excessive pictures and graphics can detract from the message).

Chapter summary

- Europeans have many things in common with others merely because they are about the same age or live in the same country, or same part of the country. Consumers who grew up at the same time share many cultural memories, so they may respond to marketers' *nostalgia* appeals that remind them of these experiences.
- Important age cohorts include teenagers, the 18–29 year olds, baby boomers and the elderly. *Teenagers* are making a transition from childhood to adulthood, and their self-concepts tend to be unstable. They are receptive to products that help them to be accepted and enable them to assert their independence. Because many teenagers receive allowances, and/or earn pocket

money but have few financial obligations, they are a particularly important segment for many non-essential or expressive products, ranging from chewing gum to hair gel, to clothing fashions and music. Because of changes in family structure, many teenagers are taking more responsibility for their families' day-to-day shopping and routine purchase decisions.

● *'Gen-Xers'*, consumers aged 18–29, are a difficult group to 'get a clear picture' of for marketers. They will be a powerful force in the years to come, whose tastes and priorities will be felt in fashion, popular culture, politics and marketing.

● *Baby boomers* are the most powerful age segment because of their size and economic clout. As this group ages, its interests have changed and marketing priorities have changed as well. The needs and desires of baby boomers have a strong influence on demands for housing, child care, cars, clothing and so on. Only a small proportion of boomers fit into an affluent, materialistic category.

● As the population ages, the needs of *elderly* consumers will also become increasingly influential. Many marketers traditionally ignored the elderly because of the stereotype that they are inactive and spend too little. This stereotype is no longer accurate. Most of the elderly are healthy, vigorous and interested in new products and experiences – and they have the income to purchase them. Marketing appeals to this age subculture should focus on consumers' self-concepts and perceived ages, which tend to be more youthful than their chronological ages. Marketers should emphasize the concrete benefits of products, since this group tends to be sceptical of vague, image-related promotions. Personalized service is of particular importance to this segment.

🔑 Key terms

Age cohort *(p. 353)*   **Gerontographics** *(p. 368)*
Baby boomers *(p. 362)*   **Grey market** *(p. 365)*
Generation X *(p. 360)*   **Perceived age** *(p. 367)*

Consumer behaviour challenge

1. As Europe moves further into the process of creating a single market and single currency, citizens' attitudes regarding different aspects of this complex process are monitored in all countries. See the following web site for the most recent survey findings: http://europa.eu.int/en/comm/dg10/infcom/epo/eo.html
What sorts of tentative conclusions can you make with respect to the influence that *age* has on attitudes towards single

currency, and other 'Pan-European' efforts? What are the possible implications for the marketing of goods and services using a Pan-European strategy?

2. Over the past few years, the Vatican has been involved in a variety of events, aimed at developing a closer and stronger relationship with Europe's youth. At the invitation of the Pope, Bob Dylan (who is fifty-something) gave a concert in 1997. Other Vatican-

sponsored projects, such as World Youth Day, have enlisted French fashion designers (see Amy Barrett, 'John Paul II to Share Stage with Marketers', *Wall Street Journal, Europe*, 19 August 1997, p. 4). Do a literature and web search to document the Vatican's activities which are targeted at youth. What goals do they seem to have in mind? What are the key segments? (Think in terms of age group segments, as well as geographic and cultural segmentation variables.) How successful a 'marketer' is the Vatican, in your opinion?

3. Below are a number of European retail web sites. After reviewing the sites, give an analysis of target market and age segmentation strategies used by these firms.
   www.waf.it.mall (A weekend of shopping in Florence?)
   www.one4you.be (Interested in beer from Belgium?)
   www.bexley.fr ('Trend-resistant' shoes – French classics)
   www.demon.co.uk/mace/cacmall.html (Desert plants, offered in a variety of languages)
   www.creor.com (High-value jewellery from Italy, priced in dollars)
   www.classicengland.co.uk (Anglophile heaven – historical newspapers, teapots, etc.)

4. Why have baby boomers had such an important impact on consumer culture in the second half of this century?

5. How has the baby boomlet changed attitudes towards child-rearing practices and created demand for different products and services?

6. Is it practical to assume that people age 55 and older constitute one large consumer market? What are some approaches to further segmenting this age subculture?

7. What are some important variables to keep in mind when tailoring marketing strategies to the elderly?

8. Find good and bad examples of advertising targeted to elderly consumers. To what degree does advertising stereotype the elderly? What elements of ads or other promotions appear to determine their effectiveness in reaching and persuading this group?

PART E

Culture and European lifestyles

PART OUTLINE

The final part of this book considers consumers as members of a broad cultural system. Chapter 14 starts this part by examining some of the basic building blocks of culture and consumption, and shows how consumer behaviours and culture are constantly interacting with each other. Chapter 15 focuses on the importance of understanding consumers' lifestyles throughout Europe, and illustrates the lifestyle concept and its marketing applications with a discussion of food, drink and cars. Finally, Chapter 16 looks at the production of culture, and how the 'gatekeepers' of culture help shape our sense of fashion and consumer culture. Using a variety of perspectives, including post-modernism, we try to place consumer behaviour into a European context as well as in the global marketplace. The often cited 'think global and acting local' closes the chapter, and brings our study of consumer behaviour into the new millennium.

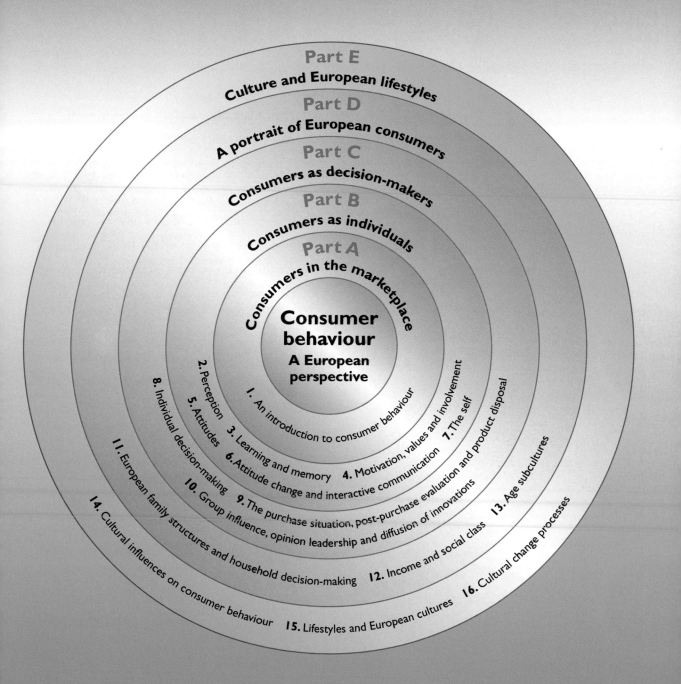

Part E
Culture and European lifestyles

Part D
A portrait of European consumers

Part C
Consumers as decision-makers

Part B
Consumers as individuals

Part A
Consumers in the marketplace

Consumer
behaviour
A European
perspective

1. An introduction to consumer behaviour

2. Perception 3. Learning and memory 4. Motivation, values and involvement 7. The self

5. Attitudes 6. Attitude change and interactive communication

8. Individual decision-making 9. The purchase situation, post-purchase evaluation and product disposal

10. Group influence, opinion leadership and diffusion of innovations

11. European family structures and household decision-making 12. Income and social class 13. Age subcultures

14. Cultural influences on consumer behaviour 15. Lifestyles and European cultures 16. Cultural change processes

CHAPTER 14

Damien McLoughlin, University College, Dublin, Ireland

It's Thursday night, 7.30. Sean puts down the phone after speaking with Colum, his study partner in his consumer behaviour class. The weekly night out for the Irish marketing students has begun! Sean has just spent the summer months travelling in Europe. He was always amazed, and delighted, to find a place claiming to be an Irish pub – regardless of how unauthentic the place was, an Irish pub always sold Guinness, a true symbol of Ireland, he reflected. Sean had begun to drink when he started university. Initially, bottled beers straight from the fridge had been his preference. However, now that he's in his third year and a more sophisticated, travelled and rounded person, he feels that those beers were just a little too – well, fashionable. He has thus recently begun to drink Guinness. His Dad, Uncle and Grandad, in fact most of the older men he knows drink Guinness. That day in consumer behaviour the lecturer had discussed the 'Guinness Time' TV commercial which had been run the previous year. It featured a young man doing a crazy dance around a settling pint of Guinness. The young man saved his most crazed expression for the point when he took his first sip. The lecturer had pointed out that the objectives of the ad were to associate Guinness with fun – an important reason why young people drink alcohol – and to encourage them to be patient with the stout, as a good pint takes a number of minutes to settle.

Sean has arranged to meet his friends in the local pub at 8.30. They will order 'three pints of the finest black stuff' and then have their own Guinness ritual. To begin they watch it being poured and then look for the rising rings of the head – the best indication of a good pint. Once settled, a small top up, and then ready for action. But they always wait and study their glasses before taking the first mouthful together – what a thing of beauty!

Cultural influences on consumer behaviour

Culture and consumption

Consumption choices cannot be understood without considering the cultural context in which they are made: culture is the 'prism' through which people view products.

Sean's beer drinking reflects his desire to associate and dissociate (with help from the media and marketers) with a certain style, attitude and trendiness. Being an Irishman, his attachment to Guinness has a very different meaning in his world than it would have in, e.g., trendy circles in continental cities, where Guinness may be associated with the very fashionability that Sean tries to avoid.

Indeed, it is quite common for cultures to modify symbols identified with other cultures and present these to a new audience. As this occurs, these cultural products undergo a process of cooptation, where their original meanings are transformed and often trivialized by outsiders. In this case, an Irish beer was to a large extent divorced from its original connection with the Irish traditional working class or rurality and is now used as a trendy way of consuming 'Irishness' abroad (but without the rural or lower-class aspect).[1]

How culture travels

Sean lives in an Irish middle-class area, but he is able to 'connect' symbolically with millions of other young consumers by relating to styles that originated far away – even though the original meanings of those styles may have little relevance to him. The spread of fashions in consumption is just one example of what happens when the meanings created by some members of a culture are interpreted and produced for mass consumption.

Take the example of rap music. Baggy jeans and outfits featuring gold vinyl skirts, huge gold chains and bejewelled baseball caps which used to be seen only on the streets of impoverished urban areas are being adapted by *haute couture* fashion designers for the catwalks of Manhattan and Paris. In addition, a high proportion of people who buy recordings of rap music are white. How did rap music and fashions, which began as forms of expression in the black urban subculture, make it to mainstream America and the rest of the world? A brief chronology is given in Table 14.1.

This chapter considers how the culture in which we live creates the meaning of everyday products and how these meanings move through a society to consumers. As Figure 14.1 shows, meaning transfer is largely accomplished by such marketing vehicles as the advertising and fashion industries, which associate functional products with symbolic qualities. These goods, in turn, impart their meanings to consumers through different forms of ritual.[2]

Table 14.1 The mainstreaming of popular music and fashion

Date	Event
1968	Hip-hop is invented in the Bronx by DJ Kool Herc.
1973–78	Urban block parties feature break dancing and graffitti.
1979	A small record company named Sugar Hill becomes the first rap label.
1980	Graffitti artists are featured in Manhattan art galleries.
1981	Blondie's song 'Rapture' hits No. 1 on the charts.
1985	Columbia Records buys the Def Jam label.
1988	MTV begins *Yo! MTV Raps*, featuring Fab 5 Freddy.
1990	Hollywood gets into the act with the hip-hop film *House Party*; Ice-T's rap album is a hit on college radio stations; amid controversy; white rapper Vanilla Ice hits the big time; NBC launches a sitcom, *Fresh Prince of Bel Air*.
1991	Mattel introduces its Hammer doll (i.e. a doll in a likeness of the rap star Hammer, formerly known as M.C. Hammer); designer Karl Lagerfeld shows shiny vinyl raincoats and chain belts in his Chanel collection; designer Charlotte Neuville sells gold vinyl suits with matching baseball caps for $800; Isaac Mizrahi features wide-brimmed caps and take-offs on African medallions (including an oversized, gold Star of David); Bloomingdale's launches Anne Klein's rap-inspired clothing line by featuring a rap performance in its Manhattan store.
1992	Rappers start to abandon this look, turning to low-fitting baggy jeans, sometimes worn backwards; white rapper Marky Mark appears in a national campaign wearing Calvin Klein underwear exposed above his hip-hugging pants; composer Quincy Jones launches a new magazine for people who are into hip-hop, and it gains a significant white readership.[1]
1993	Hip-hop fashions and slang continue to cross over into mainstream consumer culture. An outdoor ad for Coca-Cola proclaims, 'Get Yours 24–7.' The company is confident that many viewers in its target market will know that the phrase is urban slang for 'always' (i.e. 24 hours a day, 7 days a week).[2]
1994	Designers persevere in their adaptations of street fashion. Italian designer Versace, among others, pushes, oversized overalls favoured by urban kids. In one ad, he asks, 'Overalls with an oversize look, something like what rappers and homeboys wear. Why not a sophisticated version?'[3]

1. Nina Darnton, 'Where the Homegirls Are'. *Newsweek* (17 June 1991): 60; 'The Idea Chain', *Newsweek* (5 October 1992): 32.
2. Cyndee Miller, 'X Marks the Lucrative Spot, But Some Advertisers Can't Hit Target', *Marketing News* (2 August 1993): 1.
3. Ad appeared in *Elle* (September 1994).

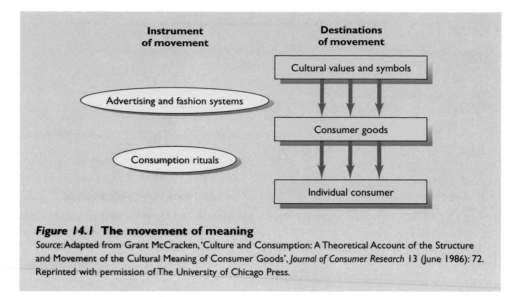

Figure 14.1 The movement of meaning
Source: Adapted from Grant McCracken, 'Culture and Consumption: A Theoretical Account of the Structure and Movement of the Cultural Meaning of Consumer Goods', *Journal of Consumer Research* 13 (June 1986): 72. Reprinted with permission of The University of Chicago Press.

The first part of the chapter reviews what is meant by culture and how cultural priorities are identified and expressed. These social guidelines often take the form of *values*, which have already been discussed in chapter 4. The second part considers the role of myths and rituals in shaping the cultural meaning of consumer products and consumption activities. The chapter concludes by exploring the concepts of the sacred and the profane and their relevance for consumer behaviour.

Understanding culture

Culture, a concept crucial to the understanding of consumer behaviour, may be thought of as the collective memory of a society. Culture is the accumulation of shared meanings, rituals, norms and traditions among the members of an organization or society. It is what defines a human community, its individuals, its social organizations, as well as its economic and political system. It includes both abstract ideas, such as values and ethics, as well as the material objects and services, such as cars, clothing, food, art and sports, that are produced or valued by a group of people. Thus, individual consumers and groups of consumers are but part of culture, and culture is the overall system within which other systems are organized.[3] Figure 14.2 provides an overview of the all encompassing influence that culture has on consumers.

Ironically, the effects of culture on consumer behaviour are so powerful and far-reaching that this importance is sometimes difficult to grasp or appreciate. We are surrounded by a lot of practices, from seemingly insignificant behaviours like pressing the start button of our walkman to larger movements like flying to an exotic honeymoon in Thailand. What is important is that these practices have meaning to us, we know how to interpret them. Culture is basically this interpretation system which we use to understand all those daily or extraordinary **signifying practices**[4] around us. Culture as a concept is like a fish immersed in water – we do not always appreciate this power until we encounter a different environment, where suddenly

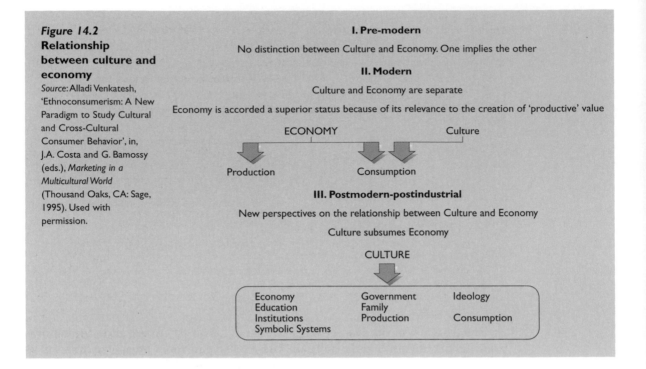

Figure 14.2 Relationship between culture and economy

Source: Alladi Venkatesh, 'Ethnoconsumerism: A New Paradigm to Study Cultural and Cross-Cultural Consumer Behavior', in, J.A. Costa and G. Bamossy (eds.), *Marketing in a Multicultural World* (Thousand Oaks, CA: Sage, 1995). Used with permission.

I. Pre-modern

No distinction between Culture and Economy. One implies the other

II. Modern

Culture and Economy are separate

Economy is accorded a superior status because of its relevance to the creation of 'productive' value

ECONOMY — Culture

Production   Consumption

III. Postmodern-postindustrial

New perspectives on the relationship between Culture and Economy

Culture subsumes Economy

CULTURE

Economy	Government	Ideology
Education	Family	
Institutions	Production	Consumption
Symbolic Systems		

many of the assumptions we had taken for granted about the clothes we wear, the food we eat, the way we address others, and so on no longer seem to apply.

The importance of these cultural expectations is only discovered when they are violated. For example, while on tour in New Zealand. The Spice Girls created a stir among New Zealand's Maoris by performing a war dance only men are supposed to do. A tribal official indignantly stated, 'It is not acceptable in our culture, and especially by girlie pop stars from another culture'.[5] Sensitivity to cultural issues, whether by rock stars or by brand managers, can only come by understanding these underlying dimensions – that is the goal of this chapter.

Consumer behaviour and culture: a two-way street

A consumer's culture determines the overall priorities he or she attaches to different activities and products. It also determines the success or failure of specific products and services. A product that provides benefits consistent with those desired by members of a culture at any point in time has a much better chance of attaining acceptance in the marketplace. It may be difficult to guess the success or failure of certain products. Some years ago, the American business magazine *Forbes* predicted the imminent bankruptcy of the Danish stereo manufacturer Bang & Olufsen, and advised everybody to sell off their stocks in the company. In addition, they mocked the company's new product as a ghettoblaster, with the difference that the price was $3000 and not $300. The product was the new 'on-the-wall' stereo with automatic sliding doors – the product was an instant success and the value of Bang & Olufsen stocks multiplied by 40![6] Here was a product that was launched when the time was right – something that *Forbes* overlooked.

The relationship between consumer behaviour and culture is a two-way street. On the one hand, products and services that resonate with the priorities of a culture at any given time have a much better chance of being accepted by consumers. On the other hand, the study of new products and innovations in product design successfully produced by a culture at any point in time provides a window on the dominant cultural ideals of that period. Consider, for example, some products that reflect underlying cultural processes at the time they were introduced.

- Convenience foods and ready-to-eat meals, hinting at changes in family structure and the decline of the full-time housewife.
- Cosmetics like those of 'The Body Shop', made of natural materials and not tested on animals, which reflected consumers' apprehensions about pollution, waste and animal rights.
- Unisex fragrances, indicating new views on sex roles and a blurring of gender boundaries, as exemplified by Calvin Klein.

Aspects of culture

Culture is not static. It is continually evolving, synthesizing old ideas with new ones. A cultural system can be said to consist of three functional areas:[7]

1. *Ecology*: the way in which a system is adapted to its habitat. This area is shaped by the technology used to obtain and distribute resources (e.g. industrialized societies versus less affluent countries).
2. *Social structure*: the way in which orderly social life is maintained. This area includes the domestic and political groups that are dominant within the culture (e.g. the nuclear family versus the extended family).
3. *Ideology*: the mental characteristics of a people and the way in which they relate to their environment and social groups. This area revolves around the belief that members of a society possess a common **worldview**. They share certain ideas about principles of order and fairness. They also share an **ethos**, or a set of moral and aesthetic principles.

One world? The theme of blurring gender boundaries is evident in several contemporary campaigns, as in this Danish shoe ad.
Artwork by Grey Århus. Courtesy of biano footwear.

How cultures vary

Although every culture is different, at lot of research has aimed at reducing the cultural variation to simpler principles. A Dutch researcher on culture, Geert Hofstede, has proposed four dimensions to account for much of this variability.[8]

1. *Power distance*: the way in which interpersonal relationships form when differences in power are perceived. Some cultures emphasize strict, vertical relationships (e.g. France), while others, such as the Scandinavian countries, stress a greater degree of equality and informality.
2. *Uncertainty avoidance*: the degree to which people feel threatened by ambiguous situations and have beliefs and institutions that help them to avoid this uncertainty (e.g. organized religion).
3. *Masculinity/Femininity*: the degree to which sex roles are clearly delineated (see chapter 7). Certain societies are more likely to possess very explicit rules about the acceptable behaviours of men and women, such as who is responsible for certain tasks within the family unit.
4. *Individualism*: the extent to which the welfare of the individual versus that of the group is valued. Cultures differ in their emphasis on individualism versus collectivism. In collectivist cultures, people subordinate their personal goals to those of a stable in-group. In contrast, consumers in individualist cultures attach more importance to personal goals, and people are more likely to change memberships when the demands of the group (e.g. workplace, church, etc.) become too costly.

However, Hofstede's approach has been much criticized. The four dimensions do not account for the differences in the meaning and the role of the concepts in each culture. That each culture has to cope with problems of power, risk and uncertainty, gender roles and the relationship between the individual and society is obvious. But that the solutions to these problems are reducible to different levels on one and the same scale is dubious, to say the least. For example, it is difficult to assume that concepts such as 'risk' or 'masculine' would mean the same in all cultures. Every culture, and hence every consumer culture, has to be understood and analyzed on the basis of its own premises, an approach known as ethnoconsumerism.[9]

Rules for behaviour

Values, as we saw in chapter 4, are very general principles for judging between good and bad goals, etc. They form the core principles of every culture. From these flow norms, or rules, dictating what is right or wrong, acceptable or unacceptable. Some norms, called *enacted norms*, are explicitly decided upon, such as the rule that a green traffic light means 'go' and a red one means 'stop'. Many norms, however, are much more subtle. These *crescive norms* are embedded in a culture and are only discovered through interaction with other members of that culture. Crescive norms include the following.[10]

● A custom is a norm handed down from the past that controls basic behaviours, such as division of labour in a household or the practice of particular ceremonies.
● Mores are customs with a strong moral overtone. Mores often involve a taboo, or forbidden behaviour, such as incest or cannibalism. Violation of mores often meets with strong censure from other members of a society.
● Conventions are norms regarding the conduct of everyday life. These rules deal with the subtleties of consumer behaviour, including the 'correct' way to furnish one's house, wear one's clothes, host a dinner party, and so on.

All three types of crescive norms may operate to define a culturally appropriate behaviour. For example, mores may tell us what kind of food is permissible to eat. Note that mores vary across cultures, so eating a dog may be taboo in Europe, while Hindus would shun beaf steak and Muslims avoid pork products. Custom dictates the appropriate hour at which the meal should be served. Conventions tell us how to eat the meal, including such details as the utensils to be used, table etiquette and even the appropriate apparel to be worn at dinnertime.

We often take these conventions for granted, assuming that they are the 'right' things to do (again, until we are exposed to a different culture!). And it is good to remember that much of what we know about these norms is learned *vicariously* (see chapter 3), as we observe the behaviours of actors and actresses in movies and TV series, but also television commercials, print ads and other popular culture media. In the long run, marketers have an awful lot to do with influencing consumers' enculturation!

Myths and rituals

Every culture develops stories and practices that help its members to make sense of the world. When we examine these activities in other cultures, they often seem strange or even unfathomable. Yet, our *own* cultural practices appear quite normal – even though a visitor may find them equally bizarre!

It works like magic!

To appreciate how so-called 'primitive' belief systems which some may consider irrational or superstitious continue to influence our supposedly 'modern', rational society, consider the avid interest of many Western consumers in magic. Marketers of health foods, anti-ageing cosmetics, exercise programmes and gambling casinos often imply that their offerings have 'magical' properties that will ward off sickness, old age, poverty or just plain bad luck. People by the millions play their 'lucky numbers' in the lottery, carry lucky charms to ward off 'the evil eye', and many have 'lucky' clothing or other products which they believe will bring them good fortune.

An interest in the occult tends to be popular, perhaps even more so when members of a society feel overwhelmed or powerless – magical remedies simplify our lives by giving us 'easy' answers. Customers at river rafting trips in America speak about the magical capacities of the river to heal psychological wounds and bring out the best in people.[11] Even a computer is regarded with awe by many consumers as a sort of 'electronic magician', with the ability to solve our problems (or in other cases to make data magically disappear!).[12] This section will discuss myths and rituals, two aspects of culture common to all societies, from the ancients to the modern world.

Myths

Every society possesses a set of myths that define that culture. A **myth** is a story containing symbolic elements that expresses the shared emotions and ideals of a culture. The story may feature some kind of conflict between two opposing forces, and its outcome serves as a moral guide. In this way, a myth reduces anxiety because it provides consumers with guidelines about their world.

An understanding of cultural myths is important to marketers, who in some cases (most likely unconsciously) pattern their strategy along a mythic structure. Consider, for example, the way that a company like McDonald's takes on 'mythical' qualities.[13] The golden arches are a universally recognized symbol, one that is virtually synonymous with American culture. Not only do they signify the possibility for the whole world symbolically to consume a bite of Americana and modernity, but they also offer sanctuary to Americans around the world, who know exactly what to expect once they enter. Basic struggles involving good versus evil are played out in the fantasy world created by McDonald's advertising, as when Ronald McDonald confounds the Hamburglar. McDonald's even has a 'seminary' (Hamburger University) where inductees go to learn appropriate behaviours.

The functions and structure of myths

Myths serve four interrelated functions in a culture.[14]

1. *Metaphysical*: they help to explain the origins of existence.
2. *Cosmological*: they emphasize that all components of the universe are part of a single picture.
3. *Sociological*: they maintain social order by authorizing a social code to be followed by members of a culture.
4. *Psychological*: they provide models for personal conduct.

Myths can be analyzed by examining their underlying structures, a technique pioneered by the anthropologist Claude Lévi-Strauss. Lévi-Strauss noted that many stories involve **binary opposition**, where two opposing ends of some dimension are represented (e.g. good versus evil, nature versus technology). Characters and products often appear in advertisements to be defined by what they *are not* rather than what they *are* (e.g. this is *not* a product for those who feel old, *not* an experience for the frightened, *not* music for the meek . . .).

Recall from the discussion of Freudian theory in chapter 4 that the ego functions as a kind of 'referee' between the opposing needs of the id and the superego. In a similar fashion, the conflict between mythical opposing forces is sometimes resolved by a *mediating figure*, who can link the opposites by sharing characteristics of each. For example, many myths contain animals that have human abilities (e.g. a talking snake) to bridge the gap between humanity and nature, just as cars (technology) are often given animal names (nature) like Jaguar or Mustang.

Myths are found everywhere in modern popular culture. While we generally equate myths with the ancient Greeks or Romans, modern myths are embodied in many aspects of popular culture, including comic books, movies, holidays, and, even commercials.

Comic book superheroes demonstrate how myths can be communicated to consumers of all ages. Indeed, some of these fictional figures represent a **monomyth**, a myth that is common to many cultures.[15] The most prevalent monomyth involves a hero who emerges from the everyday world with supernatural powers and wins a decisive victory over evil forces. He then returns with the power to bestow good things on his fellow men. This basic theme can be found in such classic heroes as Lancelot, Hercules and Ulysses. The recent success of the Disney movie *Hercules* reminds us that these stories are timeless and appeal to people through the ages.

Comic book heroes are familiar to most consumers, and they are viewed as more credible and effective than celebrity endorsers. Film spinoffs and licensing deals aside, comic books are a multi-million dollar industry. The American version of the

クリエイティブが元気です。
ッキャンエリクソン博報堂
MCCANN-ERICKSON HAKUHODO INC.

This ad used in a corporate campaign for McCann-Erickson's Tokyo office plays on the Superman myth by depicting a superhero with light beams radiating from his eyes. The headline reads: 'We're ready to rejuvenate your advertising'.
Courtesy of McCann-Erickson Hakuhodo Inc.

monomyth is best epitomized by Superman, a Christ-like figure who renounces worldly temptations and restores harmony to his community. Heroes such as Superman are sometimes used to confer a product, store or service with desirable attributes. This imagery is sometimes borrowed by marketers – currently, PepsiCo is trying to enhance its position in the Japanese market by using a figure called 'Pepsiman', a muscle-bound caricature of an American superhero in a skin-tight uniform, to promote the drink. Pepsiman even appears in a Sega game called Fighting Vipers.[16]

But there are many other, less obvious mythological figures surrounding us. For example, the role of Einstein as a mythological figure and one that is used for giving meaning to and promoting certain consumable objects such as movies or posters, or used in advertisements as a sort of indirect endorsement has been studied by consumer researchers.[17]

Many blockbuster films and hit TV programmes draw directly on mythic themes. While dramatic special effects or attractive stars certainly don't hurt, a number of these films perhaps owe their success to their presentation of characters and plot structures that follow mythic patterns. Examples of these mythic blockbusters include:[18]

- *The Big Blue*: The sea is the offspring of many myths. Its inaccessibility and depth has always inspired humans to create imagery about this other world. The film depicts the search for a lost symbiosis between man and nature, where the only person with real access to this must give up his human life to become one with the purity and the graciousness of the sea, symbolized by the dolphins.
- *E.T.: The Extraterrestrial*: E.T. represents a familiar myth involving Messianic visitation. The gentle creature from another world visits Earth and performs miracles (e.g. reviving a dying flower). His 'disciples' are local children, who help him combat the forces of modern technology and an unbelieving secular society. The metaphysical function of myth is served by teaching that the humans chosen by God are pure and unselfish.

Subcultures can even gel around fictional characters. Many fans of *Star Trek* immerse themselves in a make-believe world of Starships, phasers and Vulcan death grips. Some Trekkers have even specialized: there is an entire cult of fans devoted to Klingons, members of an aggressive warrior race that long battled the Federation. Devotees have their own language (tlhIngan, a tongue created by a linguist for one of the *Star Trek* movies), fan 'zines, food and even a summer camp. Reflecting the popularity of this subculture, a commercial for Pizza Hut in the UK ran entirely in tlhIngan. The warriors' words translate as 'Get a kid's pizza, Pepsi, and "Star Trek: The Next Generation" cup for only £2.99'.
(Erik Davis, 'tlhIngan Hol Dajatlh'a' [Do You Speak Klingon?]', *Utne Reader* [March/April] 1994: 122–9.)
Photo courtesy of Pizza Hut Inc.

- *Star Trek*: The television series and films documenting the adventures of the starship *Enterprise* are linked to myths, such as the story of the New England Puritans exploring and conquering a new continent – 'the final frontier'. Encounters with the Klingons mirror skirmishes with American Indians. In addition, the quest for Paradise was a theme employed in at least 13 of the original 79 episodes.[19]
- *Jaws*: This and films constructed around similar themes, draw on myths of the beast; the wild, dangerous and untamed nature which is culture's (human being's) enemy. Such myths are known from Christianity and other religious mythologies, such as the Norse mythology (The Midgaard Snake and the Fenris Wolf), and has played a central role in the way the Western world has regarded nature over centuries.

Commercials as myths

Commercials can be analyzed in terms of the underlying cultural themes they represent. For example, commercials for various food products ask consumers to 'remember' the mythical good old days when products were wholesome and natural. The mythical theme of the underdog prevailing over the stronger foe (i.e. David and Goliath) has been used by the car rental firm Avis in a now classic campaign where they stated 'We're only no. 2, we try harder'. Other figures of mythical narratives have been used by advertisers, such as the villain (a brand teasing its competitors), the hero (the brand in control) or the helper (the brand that helps you accomplish something).[20]

Rituals

A **ritual** is a set of multiple, symbolic behaviours that occur in a fixed sequence and that tend to be repeated periodically.[21] Although bizarre tribal ceremonies, perhaps

This Italian ad for Volkswagen plays upon the myth of the Garden of Eden, a classic struggle between virtue and temptation. The copy reads, 'Whoever said that you would have to pay dearly for giving in to temptation?'
Courtesy of Volkswagen.

involving animal or virgin sacrifice, may come to mind when people think of rituals, in reality many contemporary consumer activities are ritualistic. Four major types of rituals are possession rituals, exchange rituals, grooming rituals and divestment rituals.[22] Below, we shall take a closer look at some of these.

Rituals can occur at a variety of levels, as noted in Table 14.2. Some of the rituals described are specifically American, but the US Super Bowl may be compared to the English FA Cup Final or the traditional ski jump competition in Austria on the first day of the new year. Some rituals affirm broad cultural or religious

Table 14.2 Types of ritual experience

Primary behaviour source	Ritual type	Examples
Cosmology	Religious	Baptism, meditation, mass
Cultural values	Rites of passage	Graduation, marriage
	Cultural	Festivals, holidays (Valentine's Day), Super Bowl
Group learning	Civic	Parades, elections, trials
	Group	Business negotiations, office luncheons
	Family	Mealtimes, bedtimes, birthdays, Mother's Day, Christmas
Individual aims and emotions	Personal	Grooming, household rituals

Source: Dennis W. Rook, 'The Ritual Dimension of Consumer Behavior', *Journal of Consumer Research* 12 (December 1985): 251–64. Reprinted with permission of The University of Chicago Press.

values, like the differences in the ritual of tea drinking in Great Britain and France. Whereas tea seems a sensuous and mystical drink to the French, the drinking of coffee is regarded as having a more functional purpose. For the British, tea is a daily drink and coffee is seen more as a drink to express oneself.[23] Other kinds of ritual occur in small groups or even in isolation. Market researchers discovered that for many people the act of late-night ice cream eating has ritualistic overtones, often involving a favourite spoon and bowl![24]

Ritual artefacts

Many businesses owe their livelihoods to their ability to supply **ritual artefacts**, or items used in the performance of rituals, to consumers. Birthday candles, diplomas, specialized foods and beverages (e.g. wedding cakes, ceremonial wine, or even sausages at the stadium), trophies and plaques, band costumes, greetings cards and retirement watches are all used in consumer rituals. In addition, consumers often employ a ritual script, which identifies the artefacts, the sequence in which they are used and who uses them. But rituals are not restricted to special occasions only as described above. Daily life is full of ritualized behaviour. Wearing a tie on certain occasions can be seen as a ritual, for example. The significance attached to rituals will vary across cultures ('Mother's Day' is slowly gaining popularity in several European countries), and will often be a mixture of private and public (generally shared) symbolism.[25]

Grooming rituals

Whether brushing one's hair 100 strokes a day or talking to oneself in the mirror, virtually all consumers undergo private grooming rituals. These are sequences of behaviours that aid in the transition from the private self to the public self or back again. These rituals serve various purposes, ranging from inspiring confidence before confronting the world to cleansing the body of dirt and other profane materials.

When consumers talk about their grooming rituals, some of the dominant themes that emerge from these stories reflect the almost mystical qualities attributed to grooming products and behaviours. Many people emphasize a before-and-after phenomenon, where the person feels magically transformed after using certain products (similar to the Cinderella myth).[26]

Two sets of binary oppositions which are expressed in personal rituals are *private/public* and *work/leisure*. Many beauty rituals, for instance, reflect a transformation from a natural state to the social world (as when a woman 'puts on her face') or vice versa. In these daily rituals, women reaffirm the value placed by their culture on personal beauty and the quest for eternal youth.[27] This focus is obvious in ads for Oil of Ulay Beauty Cleanser, which proclaim: 'And so your day begins. The Ritual of Oil of Ulay'. Similarly, the bath is viewed as a sacred, cleansing time, a way to wash away the sins of the profane world.[28]

Gift-giving rituals

The promotion of appropriate gifts for every conceivable holiday and occasion provides an excellent example of the influence consumer rituals can exert on marketing phenomena. In the **gift-giving ritual**, consumers procure the perfect object (artefact), meticulously remove the price tag (symbolically changing the item from a commodity to a unique good), carefully wrap it and deliver it to the recipient.[29]

Gift-giving is primarily viewed by researchers as a form of economic exchange, where the giver transfers an item of value to a recipient, who in turn is somehow obliged to reciprocate. However, gift-giving can also involve symbolic exchange, where the giver is motivated by unselfish factors, such as love or admiration, and does not expect anything in return. Some research indicates that gift-giving evolves as a form of social expression; it is more exchange-oriented (instrumental) in the early stages of a relationship, but becomes more altruistic as the relationship develops.[30]

Every culture prescribes certain occasions and ceremonies for giving gifts, whether for personal or professional reasons. The giving of birthday presents alone is a major undertaking. Business gifts are an important component in defining professional relationships, and great care is often taken to ensure that the appropriate gifts are purchased.

Multicultural dimensions

The importance of gift-giving rituals is underscored by considering Japanese customs, where the wrapping of a gift is as important (if not more so) than the gift itself. The economic value of a gift is secondary to its symbolic meaning.[31] To the Japanese, gifts are viewed as an important aspect of one's duty to others in one's social group. Giving is a moral imperative (known as *giri*).

Highly ritualized gift-giving occurs during the giving of both household/personal gifts and company/professional gifts. Each Japanese has a well-defined set of relatives and friends with whom he or she shares reciprocal gift-giving obligations (*kosai*).[32]

Personal gifts are given on social occasions, such as at funerals, to people who are hospitalized, to mark movements from one life-stage to another (e.g. weddings, birthdays) and as greetings (e.g. when one is meeting a visitor). Company gifts are given to commemorate the anniversary of a corporation's founding or the opening of a new building, as well as being a routine part of doing business, as when rewards are given at trade meetings to announce new products.

Some of the items most desired by Japanese consumers to receive as gifts include gift coupons, beer and soap.[33] In keeping with the Japanese emphasis on saving face, presents are not opened in front of the giver, so that it will not be necessary to hide one's possible disappointment with the present.

The gift-giving ritual can be broken down into three distinct stages.[34] During *gestation*, the giver is motivated by an event to procure a gift. This event may be either *structural* (i.e. prescribed by the culture, as when people buy Christmas presents), or *emergent* (i.e. the decision is more personal and idiosyncratic). The second stage is *presentation*, or the process of gift exchange. The recipient responds to the gift (either appropriately or not), and the donor evaluates this response.

In the third stage, known as *reformulation*, the bonds between the giver and receiver are adjusted (either looser or tighter) to reflect the new relationship that emerges after the exchange is complete. Negativity can arise if the recipient feels the gift is inappropriate or of inferior quality. The donor may feel the response to the gift was inadequate or insincere or a violation of the reciprocity norm, which obliges people to return the gesture of a gift with one of equal value.[35] Both participants may feel resentful for being 'forced' to participate in the ritual.[36]

Self-gifts

People commonly find (or devise) reasons to give themselves something; they 'treat' themselves. Consumers purchase **self-gifts** as a way to regulate their behaviour. This ritual provides a socially acceptable way of rewarding themselves for good deeds, consoling themselves after negative events or motivating themselves to accomplish some goal.[37] Figure 14.3 is a projective stimulus similar to ones used in research on self-gifting. Consumers are asked to tell a story based on a picture such as this, and their responses are analyzed to discover the reasons people view as legitimate for rewarding themselves with self-gifts. For example, one recurring story that might emerge is that the woman in the picture had a particularly gruelling day at work and needs a pick-me-up in the form of a new fragrance. This theme could then be incorporated into a promotional campaign for a perfume. With the growing evidence of hedonic motives for consumption in the recent decades, self-gifts may represent a more and more important part of the overall consumption pattern.

Holiday rituals

Holidays are important rituals in both senses of the word. Going on holiday is one of the most widespread rituals and tourism one of the biggest industries of the late twentieth century. On holidays consumers step back from their everyday lives and perform ritualistic behaviours unique to those times.[38] Holiday occasions are filled with ritual artefacts and scripts and are increasingly cast as a time for giving gifts by enterprising marketers. Holidays also often mean big business to hotels, restaurants, travel agents, and so on. For example, going to Disneyland in Paris may mean a ritualized return to the memories of our own dreams of a totally free (of obligations, duties and responsibilities) fantasy-land of play.[39]

Figure 14.3 **Projective drawing to study the motivations underlying the giving of self-gifts**
Source: Based on David G. Mick, Michelle DeMoss and Ronald J. Faber, 'Latent Motivations and Meanings of Self-Gifts: Implications for Retail Management' (research report, Center for Retailing Education and Research, University of Florida, 1990).

For many businesses Christmas is the single most important season. Concerning the holidays of celebrations, most such holidays are based on a myth, and often a real (Guy Fawkes) or imaginary (Cupid on Valentine's Day) character is at the centre of the story. These holidays persist because their basic elements appeal to deep-seated patterns in the functioning of culture.[40]

The Christmas holiday is bursting with myths and rituals, from adventures at the North Pole to those that occur under the mistletoe. One of the most important holiday rituals involves Santa Claus, or an equivalent mythical figure, eagerly awaited by children the world over. Unlike Christ, this person is a champion of materialism. Perhaps it is no coincidence, then, that he appears in stores and shopping malls – secular temples of consumption. Whatever his origins, the Santa Claus myth serves the purpose of socializing children by teaching them to expect a reward when they are good and that members of society get what they deserve. Needless to say, Christmas, Santa Claus and other attached rituals and figures change when they enter into other cultural settings. Some of the transformations of Santa Claus in a Japanese context include a figure called 'Uncle Chimney', Santa Claus as a stand-in for the newborn Christ and Santa Claus crucified at the entrance of one department store with the words 'Happy Shopping' written above his head.[41] What does this tell us about the globalization process?

On *Valentine's Day*, standards regarding sex and love are relaxed or altered as people express feelings that may be hidden during the rest of the year. In addition to cards, a variety of gifts are exchanged, many of which are touted by marketers to represent aphrodisiacs or other sexually related symbols. It seems as if many people in consumer societies are always on the lookout for new rituals to fill their lives. This ritual was once virtually unknown in Scandinavia but is slowly becoming part

MET *Echte Boter* KRIJG JE ZE WEER AAN TAFEL.

The literal translation of the caption in this Dutch ad is 'With real butter, you can get them at the table'. Getting them to the table also infers in Dutch that you're getting two opponents to sit down and talk things out … this ad makes a parody of the cultural clash of the Dutch 'Sinter Klaas', which is celebrated on 5 December, and 'Santa Claus', who is becoming more and more a part of Christmas celebrations on 25 December.
Photo by Søren Askegaard.

of their consumption environment. Also, the American ritual of celebrating Hallowe'en is now becoming fashionable in Europe, where the French in particular have adopted it as an occasion for festivities, dancing and the chance to show off new fashions.[42]

Rites of passage

What does a dance for recently divorced people have in common with 'college initiation ceremonies'? Both are examples of modern **rites of passage**, or special times marked by a change in social status. Every society, both primitive and modern, sets aside times where such changes occur. Some of these changes may occur as a natural part of consumers' life cycles (puberty or death), while others are more individual in nature (divorce and re-entering the dating market).

Some marketers attempt to reach consumers on occasions in which their products can enhance a transition from one stage of life to another.[43] A series of Volkswagen ads underlined the role of the car for the freedom the women, who were leaving their husbands or boyfriends.

Stages of role transition   Much like the metamorphosis of a caterpillar into a butterfly, consumers' rites of passage consist of three phases.[44] The first stage, *separation*, occurs when the individual is detached from his or her original group or status (i.e., the first-year university student leaves home). *Liminality* is the middle stage, where the person is literally in-between statuses (i.e. the new arrival on campus tries to work out what is happening during orientation week). The last stage, *aggregation*, takes place when the person re-enters society after the rite of passage is complete (the student returns home for the Christmas vacation as a 'real university student'). Rites of passage mark many consumer activities, as exemplified by confirmation or other rites of going from the world of the child to the world of the adult. A similar transitional state can be observed when people are prepared for certain occupational roles. For example, athletes and fashion models typically undergo a 'seasoning' process. They are removed from their normal surroundings (e.g. athletes are taken to training camps, while young models often are moved to Paris or Milan), indoctrinated into a new subculture and then returned to the real world in their new roles.

The final passage: marketing death   The rites of passage associated with death support an entire industry. Survivors must make expensive purchase decisions, often at short notice and driven by emotional and superstitious concerns. Funeral ceremonies help the living to organize their relationships with the deceased, and action tends to be tightly scripted, down to the costumes (e.g. the ritual black attire, black ribbons for mourners, the body in its best suit) and specific behaviours (e.g. sending condolence cards or holding a wake). Mourners 'pay their last respects', and seating during the ceremony is usually dictated by mourners' closeness to the individual. Even the cortège is accorded special status by other motorists, who recognize its separate, sacred nature by not overtaking as it proceeds to the cemetery.[45]

Sacred and profane consumption

As we saw when considering the structure of myths, many types of consumer activity involve the demarcation, or binary opposition, of boundaries, such as good versus bad, male versus female – or even 'regular' versus 'low-fat'. One of the most important of these sets of boundaries is the distinction between the sacred and the profane. **Sacred consumption** involves objects and events that are 'set apart' from normal activities, and are treated with some degree of respect or awe. They may or may not be associated with religion, but most religious items and events tend to be regarded as sacred. **Profane consumption** involves consumer objects and events that are ordinary, everyday objects and events that do not share the 'specialness' of sacred ones. (Note that profane does not mean vulgar or obscene in this context.)

Domains of sacred consumption

Sacred consumption events permeate many aspects of consumers' experiences. We find ways to 'set apart' a variety of places, people and events. In this section, we'll consider some examples of ways that 'ordinary' consumption is sometimes not so ordinary after all.

Sacred places

Sacred places have been 'set apart' by a society because they have religious or mystical significance (e.g. Bethlehem, Mecca, Stonehenge) or because they commemorate some aspect of a country's heritage (e.g., the Kremlin, Versailles, the Colosseum in Rome). Remember that in many cases the sacredness of these places is due to the property of contamination – that is, something sacred happened on that spot, so the place itself takes on sacred qualities. Tourism is one of the most common and rapidly spreading forms of consuming the sacred.[46]

Other places are created from the profane world and imbued with sacred qualities. Graumann's Chinese Theater in Hollywood, where film stars leave their footprints in concrete for posterity, is one such place. When Ajax, the local football team of Amsterdam, moved from their old stadium, De Meern, to a larger, more modern stadium (De Arena), the turf from the old stadium was carefully lifted from the ground and sold to a local churchyard. The churchyard offers the turf to fans willing to pay a premium price to be buried under authentic Ajax turf!

Even the modern shopping mall can be regarded as a secular 'cathedral of consumption', a special place where community members come to practise shopping rituals. Theme parks are a form of mass-produced fantasy that take on aspects of sacredness. In particular, the various Disneylands are destinations for pilgrimages from consumers around the globe. Disneyland displays many characteristics of more traditional sacred places, especially for Americans, but Europeans too may consider these parks the quintessence of America. It is even regarded by some as the epitome of child(ish) happiness. A trip to the park is the most common 'last wish' for terminally ill children.[47]

In many cultures, the home is a particularly sacred place. It represents a crucial distinction between the harsh, external world and consumers' 'inner space'. In Northern and Western Europe the home is a place where you entertain guests (in Southern Europe it is more common to go out) and fortunes are spent each year on interior decorators and home furnishings; the home is thus a central part of consumers' identities.[48] Consumers all over the world go to great lengths to create a special environment that allows them to create the quality of homeliness. This effect is created by personalizing the home as much as possible, using such devices as door wreaths, mantel arrangements and a 'memory wall' for family photos.[49] Even public places, like various types of cafés and bars, strive for a home-like atmosphere which shelters customers from the harshness of the outside world.

Sacred people

People themselves can be sacred, when they are idolized and set apart from the masses. Souvenirs, memorabilia and even mundane items touched or used by sacred people take on special meanings and acquire value in their own right. Indeed, many businesses thrive on consumers' desire for products associated with famous people. There is a thriving market for celebrity autographs, and objects once owned by celebrities, whether Princess Diana's gowns or John Lennon's guitars, often are sold at auction for astronomical prices. A store called 'A Star is Worn' sells items donated by celebrities – a black bra autographed by Cher sold for $575. As one observer commented about the store's patrons, 'They want something that belonged to the stars, as if the stars have gone into sainthood and the people want their shrouds.'[50]

Marketing pitfall

The sacredness of some celebrities has spawned a secondary industry – celebrity lookalikes and sound-alikes. However, just as celebrity endorsements are risky businesses because of their dependence on the image of the celebrity, so too the lookalike industry. The death of Diana, Princess of Wales may well put 'her' lookalikes on the dole, according to one London-based booking agent. Having lookalikes perform as Diana following her death would be distasteful, it was argued.[51] Likewise, many of the charity organizations she supported may suffer in the long run after the immediate upsurge in interest in these causes has died down. On the other hand, her death is certain to bring profits to a lot of people, from biography authors and publishers, film makers and TV companies to memorabilia industries and souvenir sellers outside the palaces where she lived.

Sacred events

Many consumers' activities have taken on a special status. Public events in particular resemble sacred, religious ceremonies, as exemplified by the playing of the national anthems before a game or the reverential lighting of matches and lighters at the end of a rock concert.[52]

For many people, the world of sport is sacred and almost assumes the status of a religion. The roots of modern sports events can be found in ancient religious rites, such as fertility festivals (e.g. the original Olympics).[53] Indeed, it is not uncommon for teams to join in prayer prior to a game. The sports pages are like the Scriptures (and we describe ardent fans as reading them 'religiously'), the stadium is a house of worship, and the fans are members of the congregation. After the first Scottish victory in many years in a football match against England at Wembley Stadium, Scottish fans tore down the goals to bring pieces back home as sacred relics. Indeed, grass from stadiums of important matches, like World Cup finals, has been sold in small portions at large prices.

Devotees engage in group activities, such as tailgate parties and the 'Mexican Wave', where (resembling a revival meeting) participants on cue join the wave-like motion as it makes its way around the stadium. The athletes that fans come to see are godlike; they are reputed to have almost superhuman powers (especially football stars in Southern Europe and Latin America). Athletes are central figures in a common cultural myth, the hero tale. As exemplified by mythologies of the barefoot marathon winner (Abebe Bikila from Ethiopia, 1960), or boxing heroes (legally) fighting their way out of poverty and misery, often the person must prove him- or herself under strenuous circumstances. Victory is achieved only through sheer force of will. Of course, sports heroes are popular endorsers in commercials, but only a few of these sports personalities 'travel' very well, since sports heroes tend to be first and foremost national heroes. However, a few people are known world-wide, at least within the key target for the ads, so that they can be used in international campaigns.

If sports is one domain that is becoming increasingly sacred (cf. sacralization below), then the traditionally sacred realm of fine arts is in danger of desacralization. In a recent sale of a publishing company of classical music, various representatives voiced the fear that a takeover by one of the giants such as Sony, Polygram or EMI would mean the introduction of a market logic which would destroy its opportunities to continue to sponsor unknown artists and make long-term investments in them. It is argued that classical music is not a product which can be handled by any marketer, but requires special attention and a willingness to accept financial losses in order to secure artistic openness and creativity.[54] Such reactions (as justified as they may be) indicate that artists and managers conceive of themselves as dealing with sacred objects that cannot be subdued to what is conceived as the profane legitimacy of the market.[55]

Tourism is another example of a sacred, non-ordinary experience of extreme importance to marketers. When people travel on holiday, they occupy sacred time and space. The tourist is continually in search of 'authentic' experiences which differ from his or her normal world (think of Club Med's motto, 'The antidote to civilization').[56] This travelling experience involves binary oppositions between work and leisure and being 'at home' versus 'away'. Norms regarding appropriate behaviour are modified as tourists scramble for illicit experiences they would not dream of engaging in at home.

The desire of travellers to capture these sacred experiences in objects forms the bedrock of the souvenir industry, which may be said to be in the business of selling sacred memories. Whether a personalized matchbook from a wedding or a little piece of the Berlin Wall, souvenirs represent a tangible piece of the consumer's sacred experience.[57]

In addition to personal mementoes, such as ticket stubs saved from a favourite concert, the following are other types of sacred souvenir icons:[58]

- Local products (e.g. goose liver from Périgord or Scotch whisky)
- Pictorial images (e.g. post cards)
- 'Piece of the rock' (e.g. seashells, pine cones)
- Symbolic shorthand in the form of literal representations of the site (e.g. a miniature Little Mermaid or Eiffel Tower)
- Markers (e.g. Hard Rock Café T-shirts).

From sacred to profane, and back again

Just to make life interesting, in recent times many consumer activities have moved from one sphere to the other. Some things that were formerly regarded as sacred have moved into the realm of the profane, while other, everyday phenomena are now regarded as sacred.[59] Both these processes are relevant to our understanding of contemporary consumer behaviour.

Desacralization

Desacralization occurs when a sacred item or symbol is removed from its special place or is duplicated in mass quantities, becoming profane as a result. For example, souvenir reproductions of sacred monuments such as the leaning Tower of Pisa or the Eiffel Tower, 'pop' artworks of the Mona Lisa or adaptations of important symbols such as the Union Jack by clothing designers, tend to eliminate their special aspects by turning them into unauthentic commodities, produced mechanically and representing relatively little value.[60]

Religion itself has to some extent been desacralized. Religious symbols, such as stylized crosses or New Age crystals, have moved into the mainstream of fashion jewellery.[61] Religious holidays, particularly Christmas, are regarded by many (and criticized by some) as having been transformed into secular, materialistic occasions devoid of their original sacred significance. Benetton, the Italian clothing manufacturer, has been at the forefront in creating vivid (and often controversial) messages exposing us to our cultural categories and prejudices, but also at times have touched upon the issue of desacralization.[62]

Even the clergy are increasingly adopting secular marketing techniques. Especially in the United States, televangelists rely upon the power of television, a secular medium, to convey their messages. The Catholic Church generated a major controversy after it hired a prominent public relations firm to promote its anti-abortion campaign.[63] None the less, many religious groups have taken the secular route, and are now using marketing techniques to increase the number of believers. The question is whether the use of marketing changes the 'product' or 'service' of the churches: true belief and salvation?[64]

Desacralization? This controversial Benetton ad was rejected by some magazines because of what some perceived to be offensive religious symbolism.
Photographer: O. Toscani for Benetton.

Multicultural dimensions

The American 'market for religious belief' with its televangelists and its heavy promotion of various churches and sects is a very exotic experience for many Europeans. The ad depicted below for a Minneapolis church to help recruit worshippers is typical of the American trend towards secular practices being observed by many organized religions. It even uses a pun (on the curing of a headache?) to pass the message of salvation.

Sacralization

Sacralization occurs when objects, events and even people take on sacred meaning to a culture or to specific groups within a culture. For example, events like the Cannes Film Festival or Wimbledon and people like Elvis Presley or Princess Diana have become sacralized to some consumers.

Objectification occurs when sacred qualities are attributed to mundane items. One way that this process can occur is through *contamination*, where objects associated with sacred events or people become sacred in their own right. This reason explains the desire by many fans for items belonging to, or even touched by, famous people. One standard procedure through which objects become sacralized occurs when they become included in the collection of a museum.

In addition to museum exhibits displaying rare objects, even mundane, inexpensive things may be set apart in private *collections*, where they are transformed from profane items to sacred ones. Name an item, and the odds are that a group of collectors are lusting after it. The contents of collections range from various popular culture memorabilia, rare books and autographs, to Barbie dolls, tea bags, lawn

The ad for The Episcopal Church discussed in the Multicultural dimensions block above.
Courtesy of Church Ad Project, 1021 Diffley, Eagan, MN 55123.

mowers and even junk mail.[65] The 1200 members of the American McDonald's collectors' club collect 'prizes' like sandwich wrappers and Happy Meal trinkets – rare ones like the 1987 Potato Head Kids Toys sell for $25.[66] Consumers often are ferociously attached to their collections; this passion is exemplified by the comment made in one study by a woman who collects teddy bears: 'If my house ever burns down, I won't cry over my furniture, I'll cry over the bears.'[67]

An item is sacralized as soon as it enters a collection, and it takes on special significance to the collector that, in some cases, may be hard to comprehend by the outsider. **Collecting** refers to the systematic acquisition of a particular object or set of objects, and this widespread activity can be distinguished from hoarding, which is merely unsystematic collecting.[68] Collecting typically involves both rational and emotional components, since collectors are fixed by their objects, but they also carefully organize and exhibit them.[69]

Some consumer researchers feel that collectors are motivated to acquire their 'prizes' in order to gratify a high level of materialism in a socially acceptable manner. By systematically amassing a collection, the collector is allowed to 'worship' material objects without feeling guilty or petty. Another perspective is that collecting is an aesthetic experience; for many collectors the pleasure emanates from being involved in creating the collection, rather than from passively admiring the items one has scavenged or bought. Whatever the motivation, hard-core collectors often devote a great deal of time and energy to maintaining and expanding their collections, so for many this activity becomes a central component of their extended selves (see chapter 7).[70]

Marketing opportunity

Marketers continue to find new ways to indulge consumers' passions for collecting. Some of the hottest new collectibles are phone cards; sales of these pre-paid cards are projected to reach around $3 billion by the year 2000. Telephone companies sell advertising space on the cards and go into licensing agreements with film and cartoon producers in order to issue cards with images from these productions. The attractiveness of these cards to the phone companies is magnified because many of them will never actually be redeemed as they are far more valuable to collectors if they are 'virgins'.[71]

Chapter summary

- A society's *culture* includes its values, ethics and the material objects produced by its people. It is the accumulation of *shared meanings* and traditions among members of a society. A culture can be described in terms of ecology (the way people adapt to their habitat), its social structure and its ideology (including people's moral and aesthetic principles). This chapter describes some aspects of culture and focuses on how cultural meanings are created and transmitted across members of a society.

- Members of a culture share a system of *beliefs* and *practices*, including *values*. The process of learning the values of one's culture is called enculturation. Each culture can be described by a set of core values. Values can be identified by several methods, though it is often difficult to apply these results directly to marketing campaigns due to their generality.

- *Myths* are stories containing symbolic elements that express the shared ideals of a culture. Many myths involve some binary opposition, where values are defined in terms of what they are and what they are not (e.g. nature versus technology). Modern myths are transmitted through advertising, films and other media.
- A *ritual* is a set of multiple, symbolic behaviours which occur in a fixed sequence and tend to be repeated periodically. Rituals are related to many consumption activities which occur in popular culture. These include holiday observances, gift-giving and grooming.
- A *rite of passage* is a special kind of ritual which involves the transition from one role to another. These passages typically entail the need to acquire products and services, called ritual artefacts, to facilitate the transition. Modern rites of passage include graduations, initiation ceremonies, weddings and funerals.
- Consumer activities can be divided into *sacred* and *profane* domains. Sacred phenomena are 'set apart' from everyday activities or products. People, events or objects can become sacralized. *Objectification* occurs when sacred qualities are ascribed to products or items owned by sacred people. *Sacralization* occurs when formerly sacred objects or activities become part of the everyday, as when 'one-of-a-kind' works of art are reproduced in large quantities. *Descralization* occurs when objects that previously were considered sacred become commercialized and integrated into popular culture.
- *Collecting* is one of the most common ways of experiencing sacred consumption in daily life. It is simultaneously one of the domains where consumption and passions are most heavily intertwined.

🔑 Key terms

Binary opposition *(p. 382)*	**Monomyth** *(p. 382)*
Collecting *(p. 396)*	**Mores** *(p. 380)*
Collectivist cultures *(p. 380)*	**Myth** *(p. 381)*
Conventions *(p. 380)*	**Profane consumption** *(p. 391)*
Cooptation *(p. 375)*	**Rites of passage** *(p. 390)*
Culture *(p. 377)*	**Ritual** *(p. 384)*
Custom *(p. 380)*	**Ritual artefacts** *(p. 386)*
Desacralization *(p. 394)*	**Sacralization** *(p. 395)*
Ethnoconsumerism *(p. 380)*	**Sacred consumption** *(p. 391)*
Ethos *(p. 379)*	**Self-gifts** *(p. 387)*
Gift-giving ritual *(p. 386)*	**Signifying practices** *(p. 377)*
Individualist cultures *(p. 380)*	**Worldview** *(p. 379)*

Consumer behaviour challenge

1. Culture can be thought of as a society's personality. If your culture were a person, could you describe its personality traits?

2. What is the difference between an enacted norm and a crescive norm? Identify the set of crescive norms operating when a man and woman in

your culture go out for dinner on a first date. What products and services are affected by these norms?

3. How do the consumer decisions involved in gift-giving differ from other purchase decisions?

4. The chapter argues that not all gift-giving is positive. In what ways can this ritual be unpleasant or negative?

5. Construct a ritual script for a wedding in your culture. How many artefacts can you list that are contained in this script?

6. What are some of the major motivations for the purchase of self-gifts? Discuss some marketing implications of these.

7. Describe the three stages of the rite of passage associated with graduating from the university.

8. Identify the ritualized aspects of various kinds of sports that are employed in advertising.

9. Some people have raised objections to the commercial exploitation of cultural figures. For example, in the US many consumers deplored the profits that filmmakers and businesspeople have made from films such as *Malcolm X* (e.g. by selling a 'Malcolm X' air freshener). Others argued that this commercialization merely helps to educate consumers about what such people stood for, and is inevitable in our society. What do you think?

10. Interview two or three of your fellow students about collecting, talking about either their own collections or a collection of somebody they know of. Use concepts about the sacred to analyze the responses.

Tina and Caroline are both executives in an advertising agency. After a particularly gruelling week, they are looking forward to a well-deserved weekend off. Tina is enthusiastically telling Caroline about her plans. Since she won't have to get up early in the morning, she's going to sleep late in her new apartment. Then she's planning to go window shopping and maybe meet some friends for lunch in one of the cafés where she knows that some of them will be. Then she'll go back and rest in the afternoon until it's time to join her friend Anna to go to the new techno and rave place, which she heard about the other day. There, they'll dance their hearts out all night.

Caroline just chuckles to herself: while Tina's wasting her time in bed in the city, *she's* going to get up early to join a tour to a nearby bird sanctuary organized by the environmental group of which she's a member. She has heard that it will also be possible to see some rare orchids. By four o'clock, she plans to be comfortably planted in front of the computer in order to write an open letter to the municipal authorities concerning the current debate on whether to stop using pesticides in public parks and along the roadsides. Then she'll just sit back and relax, perhaps watch a rented video of one of the good films she missed due to lack of time . . .

Caroline is sometimes amazed at how different she is from Tina, though both think of themselves as sophisticated and in touch with the times. They also earn the same salary and do almost the same things at work all week long. How can their tastes be so different at the weekend? Oh well, Caroline sighs to herself, that's why they make chocolate and vanilla.

Lifestyles and European cultures

Caroline and Tina strongly resemble one another demographically. They were both raised in middle-class households, have similar educational backgrounds, are about the same age and they share the same occupation and income. However, as their leisure choices show, it would be a mistake to assume that their consumption choices are similar as well. Caroline and Tina each choose products, services and activities that help them define a unique *lifestyle*. This chapter first explores how marketers approach the issue of lifestyle and then how they use information about these consumption choices to tailor products and communications to individual lifestyle segments. It then considers how lifestyle choices are affected by where people live, and it considers some issues that occur when firms attempt to market their products in unfamiliar cultures.

Lifestyle: who we are, what we do

In traditional societies, which place a high value on a collective mentality, consumption options are largely dictated by class, caste, village or family. In a modern consumer society, however, people are freer to select the products, services and activities that define themselves and, in turn, create a social identity that is communicated to others. One's choice of goods and services makes a statement about who one is and about the types of people with which one wishes to identify – as well as those with whom we wish to maintain some distance!

Lifestyle refers to a pattern of consumption reflecting a person's choices of how he or she spends time and money, but in many cases also to the attitudes and values attached to these behavioural patterns. Many of the factors discussed in this book, such as a person's self-concept, reference group and social class, are used as 'raw ingredients' to fashion a unique lifestyle. In an economic sense, one's lifestyle represents the way one has elected to allocate income, both in terms of relative allocations to different products and services and to specific alternatives within these categories.[1] Other distinctions have been made to describe consumers in terms of their broad patterns of consumption, such as those differentiating consumers in terms of how proportions of their income are allocated to various sectors of consumption. Often, these allocations create a new kind of status system based less on income than on accessibility to information about goods and how these goods function as social markers.[2]

Lifestyles may be considered as group identities. Marketers use demographic and economic approaches in tracking changes in broad societal priorities, but these approaches do not begin to embrace the symbolic nuances that separate lifestyle groups. Lifestyle is more than the allocation of discretionary income. It is a statement about who one is in society and who one is not. Group identities, whether of hobbyists, athletes, or drug users, take their form based on acts of expressive symbolism. The self-definitions of group members are derived from the common symbol system to which the group is dedicated. Such self-definitions have been described by a number of terms, including *lifestyle, taste public, consumer group, symbolic community* and *status culture*.[3]

Each lifestyle is (somewhat) unique. Patterns of consumption based on lifestyles are often composed of many ingredients that are shared by others in similar social and economic circumstances. Still, each person provides a unique 'twist' to this pattern which allows him or her to inject some individuality into a chosen lifestyle. For example, a 'typical' student (if there is such a thing) may dress much like his or her friends, go to the same places and like the same foods, yet still indulge a passion for running marathons, stamp collecting or community service, activities which make him or her unique.

Lifestyles don't last forever, and are not set in stone – unlike deep-seated values, people's tastes and preferences evolve over time, so that consumption patterns that were viewed favourably at one point in time may be laughed or sneered at a few years later. If you don't believe that, simply think back to what you, your friends and your family were wearing, doing and eating five or ten years ago: where *did* you find those clothes? Because people's attitudes regarding physical fitness, social activism, sex roles for men and women, the importance of home life and family, and many other things, do change, it is vital for marketers to monitor the social landscape continually to try to anticipate where these changes will lead.

Consumption as a goal

Members of 'cargo cults' in the South Pacific literally worshipped cargo that was salvaged from crashed aircraft or washed ashore from ships. These people believed that the ships and planes passing near their islands were piloted by their ancestors, and they tried to attract them to their villages. During the Second World War, they went so far as to construct fake planes from straw in the hope of luring real ones.[4]

While not everyone literally worships material goods in this way, things do play a central role in many people's lives. Materialism refers to the importance people attach to worldly possessions. Westerners in general (and Americans in particular) are often stereotyped as being members of a highly materialistic society where people often gauge their worth and that of others in terms of how much they own.

In Europe, we often take the existence of an abundance of products and services for granted, until we remember how recent many of these developments are. The commonness of ownership of cars, freezers, telephones and televisions are all post-1950s phenomena. In fact, one way to think about marketing is as a system that provides a certain standard of living to consumers. To some extent, then, our lifestyles are influenced by the standard of living we have come to expect and desire.

The living standard of consumers in many countries, particularly in Asia, has also increased considerably in recent years. And new products are steadily becoming 'necessities'. A Gallup study of 22,500 adults in 17 European countries found that ownership of such items as microwave ovens, VCRs and cellular phones has 'exploded' in recent years.[5] Advertising encourages this emphasis on consumption and increasingly portrays consumption as an end in itself, rather than as a means to attain well-being.[6]

Of course, not everyone stresses the value of materialism to the same degree. Individual differences have been found among consumers in terms of this emphasis. One approach partitions the value of materialism into three categories: success, centrality and happiness.[7] The scale items used to measure these categories are shown in Table 15.1.

Cross-cultural differences have also been analyzed. One study including twelve countries resulted in the following ranking in degree of materialism from highest to lowest: Romania, USA, New Zealand, Ukraine, Germany, Turkey, Israel, Thailand, India, UK, France and Sweden.[8] From these results, several conclusions can be drawn. First of all, materialism is not directly linked to affluence, as has often been proposed. On the contrary, some of the most materialistic cultures are the ones where most consumers (feel that they) lack a lot of things. But this obviously is not

Table 15.1 A scale to measure categories of materialism

Category	Scale items
Success	I admire people who own expensive homes, cars and clothes.
	Some of the most important achievements in life include acquiring material possessions.
	I don't put much emphasis on the amount of material objects people own as a sign of success.*
	The things I own say a lot about how well I'm doing in life.
	I like to own things that impress people.
	I don't pay much attention to the material objects other people own.*
	I usually buy only the things I need.*
Centrality	I try to keep my life simple, as far as possessions are concerned.*
	The things I own aren't all that important to me.*
	I enjoy spending money on things that aren't practical.
	Buying things gives me a lot of pleasure.
	I like a lot of luxury in my life.
	I put less emphasis on material things than most people I know.*
	I have all the things I really need to enjoy life.*
Happiness	My life would be better if I owned certain things I don't have.
	I wouldn't be any happier if I owned nicer things.*
	I'd be happier if I could afford to buy more things.
	It sometimes bothers me quite a bit that I can't afford to buy all the things I'd like.

Source: Adapted from Marsha L. Richins and Scott Dawson, 'A Consumer Values Orientation for Materialism and Its Measurement: Scale Development and Validation', *Journal of Consumer Research* 20 (December 1992), Table 3. Reprinted with permission of The University of Chicago Press.
Note: Respondents indicate whether they agree or disagree with each item on a five-point scale.
*Items with an asterisk are reverse scored.

the only explanation, since the US, New Zealand and Germany score relatively high as well, and India scores low. Since neither wealth, 'westernness' nor any other single variable can explain these differences, it must be concluded that materialism is a consequence of several factors, including such things as social stability, access to information, reference models, as well as historical developments and cultural values.

Lifestyle marketing

The lifestyle concept is one of the most widely used in modern marketing activities. It provides a way to understand consumers' everyday needs and wants, and a mechanism to allow a product or service to be positioned in terms of how it will allow a person to pursue a desired lifestyle. A **lifestyle marketing perspective** recognizes that people are increasingly conscious about the fact that we all sort ourselves and each other into groups on the basis of the things we/they like to do, how we/they like to spend their leisure time and how we/they choose to spend disposable income.[9] These choices in turn create opportunities for market segmentation strategies that recognize the potency of a consumer's chosen lifestyle in determining both the types of products purchased and the specific brands more likely to appeal to a designated lifestyle segment.

Products are the building blocks of lifestyles

To study lifestyles is to appreciate the profoundness of the superficial, as one lifestyle analyst has put it.[10] Consumers often choose products, services and activities over others because they are associated with a certain lifestyle. For this reason, lifestyle marketing strategies attempt to position a product by fitting it into an existing pattern of consumption. According to a German survey of 291 of the biggest marketing research and advertising agencies, 68 per cent of those used lifestyle research of some kind, mostly for the sectors of food, cosmetics, cars, drinks and fashion and clothing.[11]

Because a goal of lifestyle marketing is to provide consumers with opportunities to pursue their chosen ways to enjoy their lives and express their social identities, a key aspect of this strategy is to focus on product usage in desirable social settings (see chapter 10). The goal of associating a product with a social situation is a long-standing one for advertisers, whether the product is included in a round of golf, a family barbecue or a night at a glamorous disco surrounded by 'jetsetters'.[12] Thus people, products and settings are combined to express a certain consumption style, as shown in Figure 15.1.

Product complementarity

The adoption of a lifestyle marketing perspective implies that we must look at *patterns* of behaviour to understand consumers. We can get a clearer picture of how people use products to define lifestyles by examining how they make choices in a variety of product categories. Indeed, many products and services do seem to 'go together', usually because they tend to be selected by the same types of people. In many cases, products do not seem to 'make sense' if unaccompanied by companion products (e.g. fast food and paper plates, or a suit and tie) or are incongruous in the presence of others (e.g. a big upholstered chair in a high-tech office or Chivas Regal Whisky at the local café, as illustrated in the French ad seen here). Therefore, an

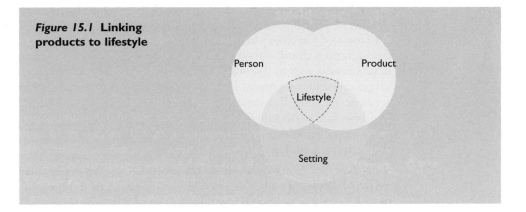

Figure 15.1 Linking products to lifestyle

Person

Product

Lifestyle

Setting

important part of lifestyle marketing is to identify the *set* of products and services that seems to be linked in consumers' minds to a specific lifestyle. As one study noted, 'all goods carry meaning, but none by itself . . . . The meaning is in the relations between all the goods, just as music is in the relations marked out by the sounds and not in any one note.'[13]

Product complementarity occurs when the symbolic meanings of different products are related to each other.[14] These sets of products, termed **consumption constellations**, are used by consumers to define, communicate and perform social roles.[15] For example, the (American) 'yuppie' of the 1980s was defined by such products as a Rolex watch, BMW car, Gucci briefcase, a squash racket, fresh pesto, white wine and brie. The yuppie culture eventually spread to Europe and somewhat similar constellations could be found for what were called 'Sloane Rangers' in the United Kingdom and 'Bon Chic Bon Gens' in France. While people today take pains to avoid being classified as yuppies, this social role had a major influence on defining cultural values and consumption priorities in the 1980s.[16] What consumption constellations might characterize you and your friends today?

ON TROUVE CHIVAS REGAL AU CAFÉ DE LA JATTE*

MAIS PAS CHEZ ROBERT*

This ad illustrates how the product is complementary with a certain environment and not with another, exemplified by two actually existing Parisian restaurants.
Courtesy of Chivas Regal.

Psychographics

As Tina and Caroline's lifestyle choices demonstrated, consumers can share the same demographic characteristics and still be very different people. For this reason, marketers need a way to 'breathe life' into demographic data to identify, understand and target consumer segments that will share a set of preferences for their products and services. Chapter 7 discussed some of the important differences in consumers' self-concepts and personalities that play a big role in determining product choices. When personality variables are combined with knowledge of lifestyle preferences, marketers have a tool with which to view consumer segments. This tool is known as **psychographics**, which involves the description of consumers based mainly on such psychological and social psychological factors as values, beliefs and attitudes, and used to explain why these consumers have a propensity to consume certain products or brands, use certain services, devote time to certain activities and use certain media.[17]

Psychographic research was first developed in the 1960s and 1970s to address the shortcomings of two other types of consumer research: motivational research and quantitative survey research. *Motivational research*, which involves intensive personal interviews and projective tests, yields a lot of information about individual consumers. The information gathered, however, was often idiosyncratic and deemed not very useful or reliable.[18] At the other extreme, *quantitative survey research*, or large-scale demographic surveys, yields only a little information about a lot of people. As some researchers observed, 'The marketing manager who wanted to know why people ate the competitor's corn flakes was told "32 per cent of the respondents said *taste*, 21 per cent said *flavour*, 15 per cent said *texture*, 10 per cent said *price*, and 22 per cent said *don't know* or *no answer*".'[19]

In many applications, the term psychographics is used interchangeably with lifestyle to denote the separation of consumers into categories based on differences in choices of consumption activities and product usage. While there are many psychographic variables that can be used to segment consumers, they all share the underlying principle of going beyond surface characteristics to understand consumers' motivations for purchasing and using products.

Conducting a psychographic analysis

Some early attempts at lifestyle segmentation 'borrowed' standard psychological scales (often used to measure pathology or personality disturbances) and tried to relate scores on these tests to product usage. As might be expected, such efforts were largely disappointing (see chapter 7). These tests were never intended to be related to everyday consumption activities and yielded little in the way of explanation for purchase behaviours. The technique is more effective when the variables included are more closely related to actual consumer behaviours. If you want to understand purchases of household cleaning products, you are better off asking people about their attitudes towards household cleanliness than testing for personality disorders.

Most contemporary psychographic research attempts to group consumers according to some combination of three categories of variables – Activities, Interests and Opinions – which are known as **AIOs**. Using data from large samples, marketers create profiles of customers who resemble each other in terms of their activities and patterns of product usage.[20] The dimensions used to assess lifestyle are listed in Table 15.2.

***Table 15.2* Lifestyle dimensions**

Activities	Interests	Opinions	Demographics
Work	Family	Themselves	Age
Hobbies	Home	Social issues	Education
Social events	Job	Politics	Income
Holiday	Community	Business	Occupation
Entertainment	Recreation	Economics	Family size
Club membership	Fashion	Education	Dwelling
Community	Food	Products	Geography
Shopping	Media	Future	City size
Sports	Achievements	Culture	Stage in life cycle

Source: William D. Wells and Douglas J. Tigert, 'Activities, Interests and Opinions', *Journal of Advertising Research* 11 (August 1971): 27–35. © 1971 by The Advertising Research Foundation.

To group consumers into common AIO categories, respondents are given a long list of statements and are asked to indicate how much they agree with each one. Lifestyle is thus teased out by discovering how people spend their time, what they find interesting and important and how they view themselves and the world around them, as well as demographic information.

Typically, the first step in conducting a psychographic analysis is to determine which lifestyle segments are producing the bulk of customers for a particular product. Researchers attempt to determine who uses the brand and try to isolate heavy, moderate and light users. They also look for patterns of usage and attitudes towards the product. In some cases, just a few lifestyle segments account for the majority of brand users.[21]

After the heavy users are identified and understood, the brand's relationship to them is considered. Heavy users may have quite different reasons for using the product; they can be further subdivided in terms of the *benefits* they derive from using the product or service. For instance, marketers at the beginning of the walking shoe craze assumed that purchasers were basically burned-out joggers. Subsequent psychographic research showed that there were actually several different groups of 'walkers', ranging from those who walk to get to work to those who walk for fun. This realization resulted in shoes aimed at different segments.

Psychographic segmentation can be used in a variety of ways.

- *To define the target market*: This information allows the marketer to go beyond simple demographic or product usage descriptions (e.g. middle-aged men or frequent users).
- *To create a new view of the market*: Sometimes marketers create their strategies with a 'typical' customer in mind. This stereotype may not be correct because the actual customer may not match these assumptions. For example, marketers of a facial cream for women were surprised to find their key market

was composed of older, widowed women rather than the younger, more sociable women to whom they were pitching their appeals.

- *To position the product*: Psychographic information can allow the marketer to emphasize features of the product that fit in with a person's lifestyle. Products targeted to people whose lifestyle profiles show a high need to be around other people might focus on the product's ability to help meet this social need.
- *To communicate product attributes better*: Psychographic information can offer very useful input to advertising creatives who must communicate something about the product. The artist or writer obtains a much richer mental image of the target consumer than that obtained through dry statistics, and this insight improves his or her ability to 'talk' to that consumer. For example, an American study conducted for one beer brand found that heavy beer drinkers tended to feel that life's pleasures were few and far between. Commercials were developed using the theme that told these drinkers: 'You only go around once, so reach for all the gusto you can'.[22]
- *To develop overall strategy*: Understanding how a product fits, or does not fit, into consumers' lifestyles allows the marketer to identify new product opportunities, chart media strategies and create environments most consistent and harmonious with these consumption patterns.
- *To market social and political issues*: Psychographic segmentation can be an important tool in political campaigns and can also be employed to find similarities among types of consumers who engage in destructive behaviours, such as drug use or excessive gambling.

Lifestyle segmentation typologies

Marketers are constantly on the lookout for new insights that will allow them to identify and reach groups of consumers that are united by a common lifestyle. To meet this need, many research companies and advertising agencies have developed their own *segmentation typologies* which divide people into segments. Respondents answer a battery of questions that allow the researchers to cluster them into a set of distinct lifestyle groups. The questions usually include a mixture of AIOs, plus other items relating to their perceptions of specific brands, favourite celebrities, media preferences, and so on. These systems are usually sold to companies wanting to learn more about their customers and potential customers.

At least at a superficial level, many of these typologies are fairly similar to one another, in that a typical typology breaks up the population into roughly 5–10 segments. Each cluster is given a descriptive name and a profile of the 'typical' member is provided to the client. For example, McCann-Erickson London, a British advertising agency, segments male and female consumers separately. Lifestyle categories in this system include such segments as 'avant guardians' (interested in change), 'pontificators' (traditionalists, very British), 'chameleons' (follow the crowd) and 'sleepwalkers' (contented under-achievers). Unfortunately, it is often difficult to compare or evaluate different typologies, since the methods and data used to devise these systems frequently are *proprietary* – this means that the information is developed and owned by the company, and the company feels that it would not be desirable to release this information to outsiders.

Lifestyle analyses are widely used in Europe. For example, one British company recently unveiled ConsumerBank, a database with 240 pieces of information each on 40 million consumers.[23] Increasingly sophisticated efforts are being made to develop lifestyle typologies that transcend national borders. Many of these systems have been developed to understand European buying habits, and in particular to determine if it is possible to identify 'Euroconsumers', who share the same lifestyle orientations despite living in, say, France versus Italy. These studies have had mixed success, with most researchers reporting that people in each nation still have a lot of idiosyncrasies that make it difficult to group them together.[24] Below we will provide some examples of such international lifestyle segmentation efforts.

RISC

Since 1978, the *Research Institute on Social Change* (**RISC**) has conducted international measurements of socio-cultural change in more than forty countries, including most European countries. The basis for RISC are representative surveys in the various countries including questions on values and attitudes, behaviour, socio-demographics, media usage and proprietary questions for subscribing clients. The information, which is comparable across countries and over time, provides a broad understanding of the social context in which consumers make decisions and of the character and the direction of the currents of change which modify that social context. It can support marketing efforts within a particular country, but is most powerful in transnational marketing contexts. This information also provides a platform for segmenting populations in terms of their attitudes, beliefs and concerns.

The long-term measurement of the social climate across many countries makes it possible to give more qualified guesses and anticipations of future change. It makes it possible to see signs of change in one country before it eventually spreads to other countries. For example, concern for the environment appeared in Sweden in the early 1970s, then in Germany in the late 1970s, in France in the beginning of the 1980s and in Spain in the early 1990s.[25]

The values and attitudes questions are the foundation of the measurement of 'trends', defined as the degree of agreement or disagreement with a set of attitudes that have been selected to define this trend. Based on statistical analysis of the respondents' score on each trend, each individual is located in a virtual space described by three axes, representing the three most discriminating dimensions in the data material. The vertical axis (Exploration/Stability) separates people motivated by change, creativity, volatility and openness from people motivated by stability, familiarity, tradition and structure. The horizontal axis (Social/Individual) distinguishes people oriented towards collective needs from people oriented more towards satisfaction of individual needs. The third axis (Global/Local) indicates a distance between people who are comfortable with broad and unfamiliar environments, multiple loose connections, large-scale networking from people preferring close-knit relationships and a desire for the elements of life to be connected in a predictable manner. The population is then divided into ten segments referring to their position in this virtual space. Figure 15.2 illustrates the ten segments (G for global, L for Local (behind)) and their main life aspirations.

The percentage of the population in each segment varies over time and among countries. In Figure 15.3, one can see the percentage of the British population who were located in each cell in 1989 and 1996. In these seven years, according to RISC, the British have moved in the direction of stability (down), ethics and community (left) and towards a more globally oriented view of the world (front). This shift may be seen in recent events such as the election of a government without a Thatcherist legacy and more sympathetic to the idea of the European Union.

Each of the forty trends can also be located in the space according to the gravity point of the people who scored highest on the particular trend. Trends that are

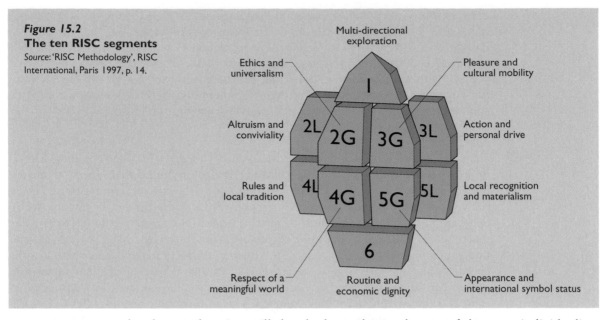

Figure 15.2
The ten RISC segments
Source: 'RISC Methodology', RISC International, Paris 1997, p. 14.

related to exploration will thus be located near the top of the map, individualism trends to the right, locality trends are smaller because they are at the back, and so on. While the position of the trends tend not to vary greatly, the percentage of various populations (countries, age groups, heavy users of a brand) supporting each trend will differ greatly. In the example in Figure 15.4, the indices are for the United Kingdom as compared to the European total. Darker colours indicate the trends which are more important in Britain as compared to the European average: cultural mobility, expanded vitality, narrow bounds, law and order, social recognition, well-being and epicurism (a quality-of-life orientation towards 'the finer things' in life).

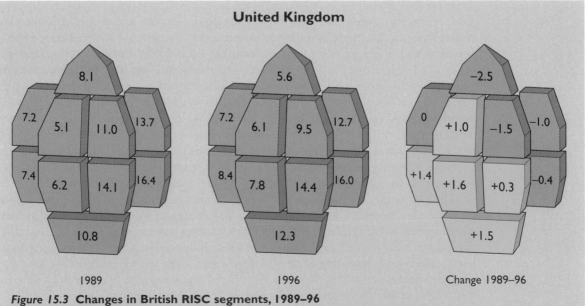

Figure 15.3 **Changes in British RISC segments, 1989–96**
Source: RISC International, Paris 1997.

Figure 15.4 **Trend map of the UK**
Source: RISC International, Paris 1997.

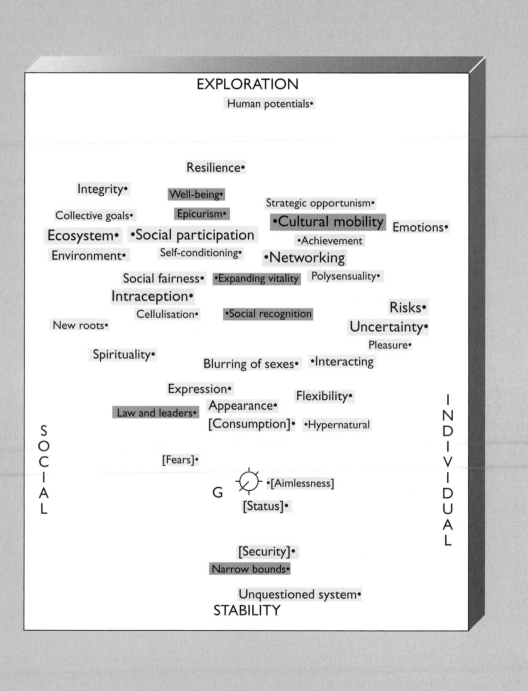

The use of RISC typically involves identifying users of a brand and understanding those users better, and also to monitor changes in the profiles of users over time. Furthermore, potential target groups, the product benefits and the kind of communication that would attract and reach them can be indicated by systems such as RISC. In the example in Figure 15.5 we see the lifestyle profiling of German car brand B (approximately 21 per cent of the population) and car brand M (approximately 19 per cent) as their first, second or third choice if they were going to buy a new car. Car brand B has a strong profile, individual and experimental, with both global and local orientations. Car brand M, in contrast, has a more uniform profile, with evidence of popularity across all segments of the population. However, there is a very strong presence in cell one; the group which is most interested in new designs, technologies and functions.

As an example of a longitudinal analysis, consider Figure 15.6. Between 1995 and 1996, the profile for car brand B has sharpened and become more distinct. In 1995, it was chosen as the potential 'next car purchase' almost equally by all segments. Only cell 4L (under-representation) and cell 3G (over-representation) showed any real difference. In 1996, the right-hand top of the lifestyle map is strongly over-represented, and the preference among locally oriented consumers has also increased. This kind of shift might suggest a strong and successful advertising campaign or some other widely recognized and approved event (successful new model, good PR, etc.).

The discussion of RISC is not an attempt to promote this system at the expense of other, often rather similar systems such as EuroStyles of the CCA, the 4Cs (Cross Cultural Consumer Characteristics) of Young and Rubicam, and GlobalScan of the Bates group. It is meant as an illustration of what such syndicated large-scale international lifestyle approaches have to offer clients. Needless to say, this is only a glimpse of the data material accessible to clients.

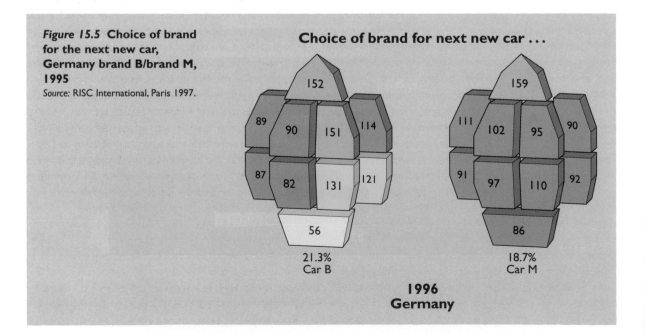

Figure 15.5 **Choice of brand for the next new car, Germany brand B/brand M, 1995**
Source: RISC International, Paris 1997.

Choice of brand for next new car ...

21.3%
Car B

18.7%
Car M

**1996
Germany**

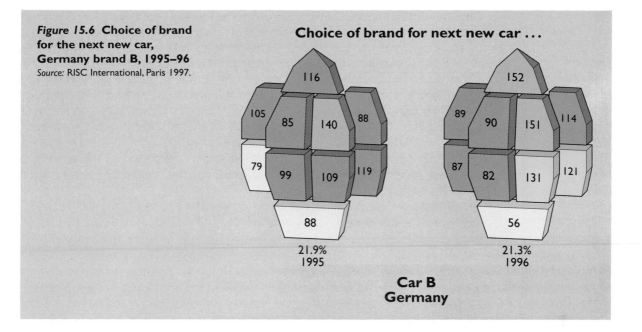

Figure 15.6 Choice of brand for the next new car, Germany brand B, 1995–96
Source: RISC International, Paris 1997.

Choice of brand for next new car ...

	116					152	
105	85	140	88		89	90	151	114
79	99	109	119		87	82	131	121
	88					56	

21.9%
1995

21.3%
1996

**Car B
Germany**

A class-based lifestyle approach: SocioConsult

One leading French sociologist, Pierre Bourdieu, has proposed a lifestyle concept which is closely linked to social class. In a major empirical study, he tried to demonstrate how people's tastes and lifestyles in French society are dependent on what he named **habitus** (systems of classification of phenomena adopted from our socialization processes) and our economic and cultural capital.[26] Although Bourdieu has been much quoted in academia, no lifestyle analysis system has been constructed directly from his research. However, a project to develop a typology of consumers based on such combinations of social class and lifestyles has been developed by the French company SocioConsult. Based in Paris, this company attempts to identify segments of consumers in different countries who share common values and outlooks on life. Respondents answer a battery of questions designed to assess their outlook on life (including work, leisure, family, consumption and aesthetics). Based on the responses received, consumers are grouped into what the company calls 'social milieux'. The nine social milieux obtained for Great Britain are derived by using two types of information: (1) social level (i.e. income and social class) and (2) value orientation, which is related to attitudes towards change and outlook on life. They are depicted in Figure 15.7. Each of these nine clusters exhibits different attitudes and behaviours. This information is provided to the company's clients, who select segments to target and who design product and promotional strategies calculated to appeal to members of that 'social milieu'.

Lifestyles outside Western Europe

VALS

The most well-known and widely used segmentation system in America is **VALS** (*Values and Lifestyles*), developed at what is now SRI International in California. Originally, VALS combined two perspectives to create lifestyle clusters. One was

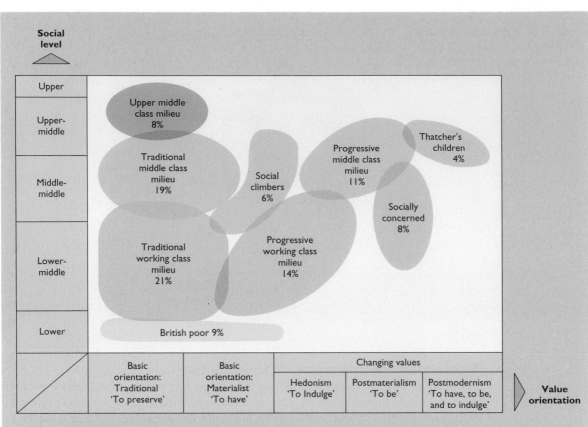

SocioConsult, based in Paris, attempts to identify segments of consumers in different countries who share common values and outlooks on life. Respondents answer a battery of questions that are designed to assess their outlook on life (including work, leisure, family, consumption, and aesthetics). Based upon the responses received, consumers are grouped into what the company calls 'social milieux'. The nine social milieux obtained for Great Britain are shown here. These clusters are derived by using two types of information: (1) social level (i.e., income and social class) and (2) value orientation, which is related to attitudes toward change and outlook on life. Each of the nine clusters exhibits different attitudes and behaviours; this information is then provided to the company's clients, who select segments to target and who design product and promotional strategies calculated to appeal to members of that 'social milieu'.

Figure 15.7 **Social milieux: an example of international lifestyle segmentation**
Source: SocioConsult, Paris 1994.

based on the Maslow hierarchy of needs (discussed in chapter 4). Maslow's hierarchy stipulates that people's needs must be satisfied sequentially – that is, companionship is not a priority until physical needs are met, and so on. The second perspective was based on the distinction made by the sociologist David Riesman between *inner-directed* people, who value personal expression and individual taste, and *outer-directed* people, who tend to be swayed by the behaviour and reactions of others.

Responding to criticisms of the VALS model, as well as to economic and demographic changes, the developers decided to update the system. The changes include the evolution of a global economy and the increasing diversity of products and media that result in greater fragmentation of lifestyles.

The so-called VALS 2 divides people into eight groups determined both by psychological characteristics and 'resources', which include such factors as income, education, energy levels and eagerness to buy. VALS 2 appears to be easier to use, but it has abandoned some of the conceptual foundation on which the original VALS was based. In the VALS 2 structure, groups are arrayed vertically by resources and horizontally by self-orientation, as shown in Figure 15.8. The new top group are termed *actualizers*; these are successful consumers with many resources. The group are concerned with social issues and are open to change. The next three groups also have sufficient resources but differ in their outlooks on life:[27]

- *Fulfilleds* are satisfied, reflective and comfortable. They tend to be practical and value functionality.
- *Achievers* are career-oriented and prefer predictability over risk or self-discovery.
- *Experiencers* are impulsive, young and enjoy offbeat or risky experiences.

The next three groups have fewer resources:

- *Believers* have strong principles and favour proven brands.
- *Strivers* are like achievers, but with fewer resources. They are very concerned about the approval of others.
- *Makers* are action-oriented and tend to focus their energies on self-sufficiency. They will often be found working on their cars, canning their own vegetables, or building their own houses.
- *Strugglers* are at the bottom of the ladder. They are most concerned with meeting the needs of the moment, and thus strongly resemble the survivor and sustainer groups they replaced.

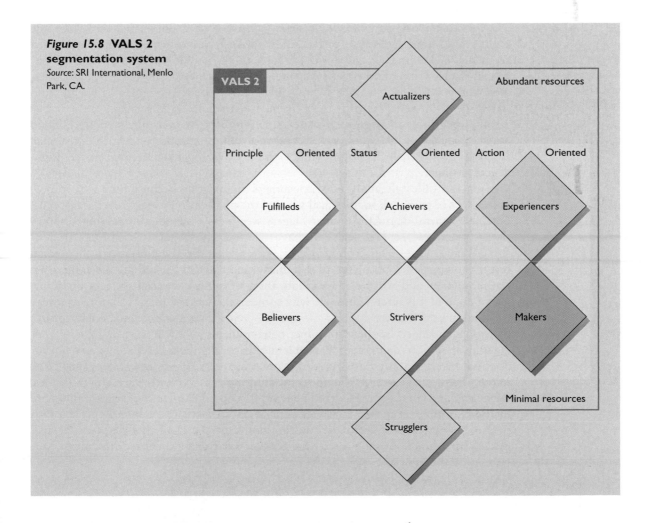

Figure 15.8 **VALS 2 segmentation system**
Source: SRI International, Menlo Park, CA.

Other international lifestyle segmentations

Japanese culture values conformity; one way to refer to the desire to fit in is *hiton-ami consciousness*, which translates as 'aligning oneself with other people'. Despite this overall emphasis, there is a growing segment of Japanese consumers who are swimming against the tide. These people have been called 'life designers' to reflect their interest in crafting their own lifestyle patterns. One Japanese segmentation scheme divides consumers into 'tribes' and includes among others the 'crystal tribe' (which prefers well-known brands), 'my home tribe' (family-oriented) and 'impulse buyer tribe'.[28]

As countries in *Eastern Europe* convert to free market economies, many marketers are exploring ways to segment these increasingly consumption-oriented societies. Some Western products such as Marlboro cigarettes and McDonald's are already firmly entrenched in Russia. The D'Arcy Masius Benton & Bowles Advertising Agency, which has offices in Moscow and St Petersburg, conducted a psychographic study of Russian consumers, and has proclaimed that the country's 150 million consumers can be divided into five segments, including 'Cossacks' (status-seeking nationalists who drive BMWs, smoke Dunhill cigarettes and drink Rémy Martin cognac), *Kuptsi* (merchants who value practical products and tend to drive Volkswagens, smoke Chesterfields and drink Stolichnaya vodka) and 'Russian Souls' (passive consumers who drive Lada cars, smoke Marlboros and drink Smirnoff).[29]

A *cross-country psychographic segmentation* project conducted jointly by the Ogilvy and Mather advertising agency and an Australian research firm identified ten segments, including such categories as 'basic needs' (traditional and passive), 'look-at-me' (seek exciting and prosperous life), 'visible achievement' (traditional values, seek 'the good life'), 'socially aware' (involved in environmental movements) and 'fairer deal' (dissatisfied with their lives). Relatively few Australians were in the 'visible achievement' segment, while high numbers of consumers in the United States, Canada and Japan were. A disproportionate number of British consumers fell into the 'fairer deal' group, while Germans were over-represented in the 'look-at-me' segment.[30]

Generally, lifestyle analyses of consumers are exciting because they seek to provide a sort of complete sociological view of the market and its segments and trends, but their general character is their biggest weakness, since the underlying assumption – that these general segments have relatively homogeneous patterns of consumer behaviour – is far from proven.[31] Add to this the generally weak theoretical foundation and the problems of reliability and validity linked to the large-scale questionnaires and to the operationalization of complex social process in simple variables, and it is understandable why some marketers see lifestyles more as a way of 'thinking the market' and as an input to creative strategies than as descriptions of segments defined by their consumer behaviour.[32]

One attempt to overcome the problem of generally defined segments is the introduction of sectorial lifestyles, an idea proposed by the French research agency CCA in the 1980s. The principle behind sectorial lifestyles is that only variables (attitudes, behaviour, etc.) that are considered relevant to a specific domain of consumption are included in the survey. The lifestyles defined on the basis of such an approach thus pertain to this specific sector of consumption only. Later in this chapter, we shall discuss an example of such a sectorial lifestyle system: food-related lifestyles.

Geographic influences on lifestyles

The consumption patterns of different countries' regions have been shaped by unique climates, cultural influences and resources. These national and regional differences can exert a major impact on consumers' lifestyles, since many of our preferences in foods, entertainment, and so on are dictated by local customs and the availability of some diversions rather than others. The lifestyles of people in each country and each region differ in a variety of ways, some quite subtle and some quite noticeable, some easy to explain and some not so obvious.

Regional consumption differences: the macro-level

In some cases, it may make sense to distinguish between larger regions comprising several countries. For example, many companies operating in Europe consider Scandinavia (Denmark, Norway and Sweden) or The Benelux (Belgium, The Netherlands and Luxembourg) to be more or less one market due to the perceived similarities among the countries. That there are relative similarities among these countries is a matter of fact, but marketers should beware of over-estimating the homogeneity of such macro-regions. Portraits of macro-regions can be drawn with rough strokes only with a very big brush. In the following section we will look at a couple of examples of such macro-regions in Europe.

One syndicated survey indicated that when having a dinner with friends, going out for dinner was more popular in southern Europe, whereas entertaining at home is more popular in northern Europe.[33] Combining such data with other related data, such as average time spent for meal preparation and emotional aspects involved in food preparation and consumption, three general types of 'food styles' were suggested for European countries: 'express train', 'party' and 'candlelit'. The first group of countries (Spain, Portugal, Italy, Germany, Belgium, Austria, Hungary, Greece and the UK) are characterized by little time being spent on cooking, a preference to go out and predominance of classic family values. The 'party' countries (France, Ireland, Norway, Sweden, Poland, and the former Czechoslovakia) emphasize the pleasure of the meal, they like to entertain family and friends at home and will spend some but not too much time preparing it. Lastly, the 'candlelit' countries (Switzerland, The Netherlands, Denmark and Finland) show a preference for the intimate dinner with a few friends at home, and a focus on high product quality and the importance of the setting (silverware, the candlelit room, etc.). What should one think of such a grouping?

Since food consumption is traditionally linked to geographical conditions such as climate, or distance from the sea or mountains, another study hypothesized the importance of local or regional patterns of consumption across national borders compared to national consumption patterns.[34] The results of an analysis of 138 food-related variables from 15 countries, however, showed that national or linguistic borders seem more significant in defining patterns of food consumption. Figure 15.9 illustrates the twelve general food cultures in Europe suggested by this study. To list a few of the defining characteristics of some of the food cultures, the French/French-Swiss, Wallonian and Italian clusters are characterized by, among other things, the importance of the sensory pleasure and high consumption of red wine; the Germanic cluster of countries of a high degree of health consciousness; the Portuguese and

Greek food cultures by relatively traditional eating patterns with a fascination for new 'global' food; the Norwegian and Danish food cultures by their openness to convenience products (and, for the Danes, also for the love of beer); and the British and Irish for their extraordinary desire for sweets and tea.

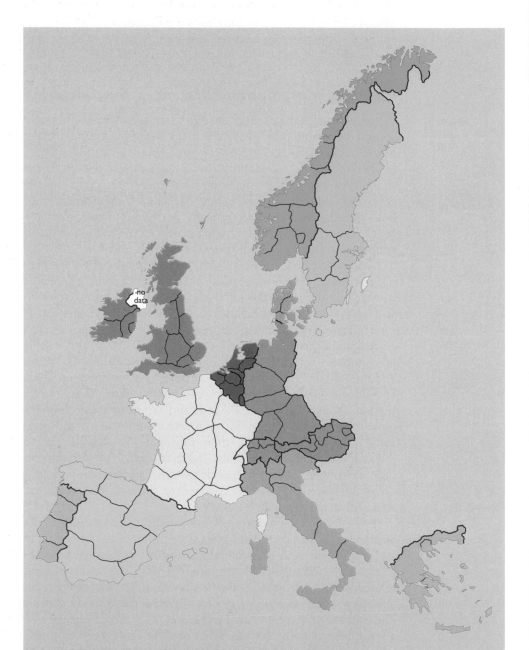

Figure 15.9 **Twelve possible European food cultures?**
Source: Søren Askegaard and Tage Koed Madsen, 'The Local and the Global: Exploring Traits of Homogeneity and Heterogeneity in European Food Cultures', *International Business Review*, vol. 7 (6), 1998.

Interestingly, it is predominantly in the centre of Europe that food cultures exhibit overlapping national borders (France–Switzerland; Germany–Switzerland–Austria; The Netherlands–Flanders), the only exception being the British–Irish food culture. The more geographically peripheral countries (Scandinavia, Iberia, Italy and Greece) show 'national food cultures'. Is this due to more exchange and inter-relationship historically among the people in the 'crossroads of Europe'? Or is it language that decides basic cultural patterns? If so, this would confirm the famous Whorf–Sapir hypothesis that language is not only a means for expressing culture but actually creates it by instituting certain schemes of classification of events, things and people. The fact that the food cultures defined in this study exactly follow linguistic lines of division (with the exception of there being two French-speaking clusters) could point in that direction. Or it could reflect the simple fact that the language of the questionnaire is very decisive for the response pattern. If the latter is the case, then it would be a strong criticism of the way in which marketers use surveys as a cross-national research instrument.[35] The truth probably lies somewhere in between the two.

We have seen that the fact that grand traits of differences can be located between certain regions in Europe, for instance a distinction between Teutonic, Gallic and Anglo-Saxon styles of communicating,[36] stressing the logical strictness of the argument, its rhetorical qualities and its empirical validity respectively. Such grand traits of similarities do not necessarily permit us to conclude that there are broad similarities in the food consumption or other consumption areas as well. Obviously it is a matter of scope. Certain parts of Europe tend to have consumption patterns similar to each other compared to China, for example. But whether these similarities are detailed enough to be useful to marketers other than in a very broad sense is another question.

National consumption differences

A series of articles recently discussed 'the changing consumer' in various European countries. The focus in these articles was predominantly macro-oriented changes in demography and economy, aggregate family expenditures or size of distribution outlets and similar information.[37] However relevant such information is, it does not provide a very vivid 'flesh-and-blood' portrait of European consumers in various countries. Needless to say, such portraits are extremely difficult to draw unless one wants to fall back on the most simple use of stereotypes: the French with baguette, cheese and Renault; the Spanish with paella, tapas and Seat, the British with tea, biscuits and Rover; the German with sauerkraut, sausage and Volkswagen.

We will try to refrain from such portraits here, and instead provide a set of examples that should illustrate some similarities and differences among European countries. We will do that by referring to research results pertaining to consumer behaviour from four different market sectors.

Food

Food is one of the most important fields of consumption when it comes to the impact on the structure of people's daily lives. The wealth of symbolic meanings attached to various kinds of food and hence food's capacity as a 'marker' of certain roles, status, situations, rituals, etc. is well documented.[38] How is the meal prepared and eaten? How often do we eat and at what times during the day? What do we drink with the meals? What is the social function of eating? These are questions for which the answers vary from country to country and from segment to segment.

Western European households spend typically between 14 and 17 per cent of their income on food, although the UK (10.1 per cent) and The Netherlands (11.0 per cent) are exceptions to this rule.[39] How this sum is spent varies greatly from country to country, depending on local production and local culinary patterns. The per capita consumption of different food products in European countries varies several hundred per cent in all categories. For example, the consumption of fresh fish in Spain and Portugal is about ten times that of Austria or the UK, and the consumption of pork in Denmark about ten times that of France. The consumption of potatoes is high in Ireland, but it is actually higher in Greece, and by far the lowest in Italy, which consumes approximately four times more pasta per inhabitant than the number two in the European market (Switzerland)![40]

A group of researchers developed a food-related lifestyle instrument based on means–end theory (cf. chapter 4).[41] The instrument includes attitude statements concerning five different domains: quality aspects, ways of shopping, cooking methods, consumption situations and purchasing motives. Tests of its cross-cultural validity showed reasonable results, at least within north-western Europe.[42] An application of the food-related lifestyle model in four European countries between 1993 and 1995 suggested that certain segments are found in all countries, some are found in three countries and some only in one country. The size of the segments, however, varies significantly, as seen in Table 15.3. These differences may shed some light on the differences between the national food cultures in question.

The 'uninvolved' segment (predominately in Germany and France) have little interest in food, do not attach importance to quality, they tend to nibble and graze rather than eat 'real meals' and use convenience products and fast food more than the average. Single males with low education level are over-represented in this segment. The 'careless' segment (predominately in the UK and Denmark) are spontaneous food shoppers, tempted by new products. They are attracted by convenience foods, are younger, single and have relatively high incomes. The 'rational consumers' segment

Table 15.3 Food-related lifestyle segments in four countries

	France	Germany	UK	Denmark
Uninvolved	18%	21%	9%	11%
Careless		11%	27%	23%
Rational	35%	26%	33%	11%
Moderate	16%			
Ecological moderate				20%
Conservative	13%	18%	19%	11%
Adventurous		24%	12%	25%
Hedonistic	18%			

Source: Adapted from Karen Brunsø, Klaus G. Grunert and Lone Bredahl, 'An Analysis of National and Cross-National Consumer Segments Using the Food-Related Lifestyle Instrument in Denmark, France, Germany and Great Britain', MAPP Working paper no. 35 (The Aarhus School of Business, January 1996).

(predominantly in France and the UK) are very interested in food and are careful planners of both dinner and shopping. They try to maximize the quality/price ratio of their purchases, and get self-fulfilment from cooking. They tend to be female, with families, working part-time. The 'conservative' segment (predominantly the UK and Germany) consider cooking a woman's task. They plan their meals and shopping, eat at fixed hours and seek security in their eating behaviour by sticking to traditions. They are older, rural and with lower income and education. The 'adventurous' segment (predominantly Denmark and Germany) like to try new (exotic) recipes and products, they go for quality products and often shop in specialized stores. The whole family takes part in the cooking, and the social aspects of eating are considered very important. They are generally well-educated families with double income and children.

Apart from the relative distributions of the segments, two of the segments found may tell us something specific about the national consumption environments. In Denmark the 'ecologically moderate' (moderately involved in food, highly involved in environmentally friendly produce) indicate the strength of the market share of ecological produce (35 per cent increase in sales volume in 1996). The hedonists in France are a little less adventurous than their 'sister segments' of that name in other countries, but they are more focused on the sensory pleasure of eating, indicating a gastronomic sophistication. For example, it has been suggested that French consumers have more sophisticated purchasing behaviour for beef than consumers in Germany, UK and Spain.[43]

Research such as this food-related lifestyle study may be taken as evidence that it is easier to define segments across countries and cultures based on psychological rather than behavioural variables. This would seem to be the case, since similar motivations may result in very different kinds of behaviour, which are influenced by Europe's varying cultural norms and habits.

Mexican cuisine is popular in Scandinavia. This ad appeared in a Swedish magazine.
Courtesy of Nordfalks AB.

An anthropological study of developments in the British food culture revealed four different types of consumption practices which are currently shaping the way local and foreign products and practices enter into the British way of creating a self-identity through food.[44] The **global food** culture, represented mainly by American fast food, indicates a willingness either to buy into the particular context of Americana, or quite the opposite, to join a wave of globally uniform consumption patterns that are found everywhere and therefore belong nowhere in particular. **Expatriate food** refers to the search for authentic meals and products from other cultures – a 'real Tuscan evening for you and your partner'. Thus it also depends on global knowledge of food cultures, but focuses on the differences among local food cultures. Thirdly, **nostalgia food** represents a search for local authenticity – Stilton cheese, toffee puddings – from the cultural heritage, which is threatened by the internationalization of British cooking patterns. The study quotes *The Sunday Times*: 'Having shamefully neglected our own traditional dishes for 40 years, we now have a flashy, meretricious cuisine based, for the most part, on ersatz imitations of Mediterranean food'.[45] Finally, **creolization** of food involves blending various traditions into new ones, such as Chinese dishes omitting ingredients considered unappetizing in Western culture, Mexican food with less chilli, or Indianized versions of sandwiches. This creolization, or 'localizing' of foods, is found in many European countries. In The Netherlands, Indonesian food has been adapted to fit the tastes of the mainstream culture, just as Turkish sandwiches have been modified in Germany.[46]

These trends probably exist in all European countries but vary in importance and in their influence and outcomes in terms of eating behaviour. It is interesting to note that all four are related to globalization trends, but only global food leads to a tendency to standardize consumption patterns.

Drink

Drinking, like eating, is an activity full of symbolic dimensions linked to gender, class, lifestyle, situations and rituals.[47] The drinking cultures in Europe differ highly in terms of what is drunk, how and when. One of the most obvious differences in the European drinking pattern is the distinction between beer cultures and wine cultures. Countries such as Germany, Belgium, Austria, Denmark and Ireland have the highest per capita consumption of beer, whereas Italy, France, Portugal and Luxembourg lead the way in wine consumption.[48] To explain such huge differences, it has been argued that in some of these countries, such as Germany, France and Italy, consumption of beer and wine is so interwoven in daily lifestyles and the cultural fabric that it is hard to imagine those cultures without them. Economic and public policy factors are also important, and reflect attitudes towards alcohol in governmental institutions. In countries such as Finland, Norway and Sweden, alcoholic beverages stronger than 'light beer' (around 2 per cent alcohol) are sold only in state monopolies and are heavily taxed. Hence, the figures in Table 15.4, may be understated by up to 30 per cent due to legal and illegal duty-free imports and home production.[49]

It has been suggested that we should distinguish between two kinds of drinking traditions in Europe: multidimensional drinking patterns characterize drinking which occurs in connection with other social activities. Examples would be wine with meals in southern Europe, beer and wine festivals in Germany, or drinking while socializing in pubs in the UK and Ireland. Drinking in these countries is traditionally not related to excess or to special occasions only. On the other hand,

Table 15.4 **Beer and wine consumption per capita in nineteen countries**

Ranked in order of per capita consumption in 1991 (wine in litres)			Ranked in order of per capita consumption in 1991 (beer in litres)		
Rank	*Country*	*1991*	*Rank*	*Country*	*1991*
1.	France	66.8	1.	Germany	142.7
2.	Portugal	62.0	2.	Denmark	125.9
3.	Luxembourg	60.3	3.	Austria	123.7
4.	Italy	56.8	4.	Ireland	123.0
5.	Switzerland	48.7	5.	Luxembourg	116.1
6.	Spain	34.3	6.	Belgium	111.3
7.	Austria	33.7	7.	United Kingdom	106.2
8.	Greece	32.4	8.	Netherlands	88.5
9.	Germany	24.9	9.	USA	87.4
10.	Belgium	23.9	10.	Finland	85.3
11.	Denmark	22.0	11.	Spain	70.9
12.	Netherlands	15.3	12.	Switzerland	70.1
13.	Sweden	12.3	13.	Portugal	67.4
14.	United Kingdom	11.5	14.	Sweden	59.3
15.	Finland	7.4	15.	Norway	52.8
16.	USA	7.2	16.	France	40.5
17.	Norway	6.9	17.	Greece	40.0
18.	Ireland	4.6	18.	Iceland	24.2
19.	Iceland	4.4	19.	Italy	22.5

Source: Adapted from David Smith and J. Robert Skalnik, 'Changing Patterns in the Consumption of Alcoholic Beverages in Europe and the United States', in Flemming Hansen (ed.), *European Advances in Consumer Research* (Provo, UT: Association for Consumer Research, 1995): 343–55. Used with permission.

unidimensional drinking patterns occur in countries where moderate continuous drinking linked to daily social activities is replaced by occasional drinking (weekends or holidays only) but is characterized by people drinking excessively.[50]

Other major variations in drink consumption patterns are revealed by statistics. Carbonated drinks are most popular in Great Britain, Ireland and Denmark, whereas mineral water consumption is especially high in France, Belgium and Italy. The Germans, Dutch, Finns and Greeks consume most spirits among the Western Europeans compared to the Italians, who have the lowest consumption level of such drinks.[51] Obviously, statistics of this kind do not reveal much about the types of product consumed, nor the consumption situations. For example, schnapps may account for the spirits consumption in Germany, ouzo in Greece, genever in The Netherlands and vodka in Finland. Furthermore, the commonness of various consumption situations for such drinks vary across countries and among lifestyles. Wine may be used at religious ceremonies or at dinner each evening, beer on the beach or in a bar after working hours, carbonated drinks after sports or for children's birthday parties, and so on. What kinds of various rituals involving drinking can you think of in your country?

Trends in European drinking patterns seems to indicate that increasing health consciousness leads to a trend in drinking lower alcohol content beverages. This may also be due to increasingly blurred borders between multidimensional and unidimensional drinking patterns. In general drinking patterns are becoming more similar across Europe. Traditional wine-drinking countries show the largest increase in beer consumption over time, while an increase in wine drinking is occuring in traditional beer countries.[52]

Cars

The car is the third, highly symbolic good with a great deal of cultural significance attached to it. Again, consumption differs among European countries for various reasons, such as local infrastructure, local production facilities, taxation or traditions. For instance, the percentage of families owning two cars is highest in Italy (41 per cent), France (30 per cent), the UK (29 per cent) and (West) Germany (26 per cent). The numbers reflect, among many other factors, the power and importance of local car industries to shape conditions so that car ownership is feasible. But industry efforts to facilitate car ownership only help explain a general 'car culture' in these countries. The reasons for a low number of families with two cars may vary from relative poverty (Greece, Portugal, Spain) to small distances (The Netherlands) and high taxation (Denmark).[53]

In the car market, as in many other markets, the discussion continues as to whether it makes sense to segment consumers across countries. One argument for segmentation which cuts across countries is that the benefits of private car ownership are strongly felt, regardless of the differing driving habits and transportation circumstances in different countries. Thus, in principle, all car consumers should be found in one of the basic proposed categories: pleasure seekers, image seekers and functionality seekers.

The German car manufacturer BMW has argued that although their customers' demographic and economic profiles are quite similar, they do not operate with a standard European consumer market and standardized marketing activities.[54] This is due to two reasons: first, they argue that the differences in size of the various segments are so great that it makes no sense to target the same segment in various countries; but more importantly, they also argue that they have discovered variations between the *benefits ultimately sought* by car drivers in different countries.

As a consequence of a study conducted in Italy, France, The Netherlands, Switzerland, and Austria, BMW can break purchase criteria down into three levels: criteria which are important in *all* countries, criteria which are important to all motorists in *one* country, and criteria important to *some consumers in all* countries. On the pan-European level the following criteria were detected: reliability, safety, quality and advanced technology. These are thus necessary minimum requirements to be considered as a potential supplier. On the national level, the following set of differences were detected. In The Netherlands, much importance is attached to the car's overall integrity rather than to qualities such as interior design. Furthermore, the reputation of the brand turned out to be very important for the Dutch. In France, special importance was attached to the self-confidence provided by the car and to its road-holding abilities. Both Austrian and Swiss customers were very demanding, but, unlike the Austrians, the Swiss wanted a car to be discreet while Austrians placed importance on a car as a prestigious status symbol. Finally, the Italians looked for a car in accordance with their personal style and with dynamic driving capacities. In general, the study's conclusions were that BMW drivers are more demanding in terms of styling, exclusiveness, driving dynamics and advanced technology than average European drivers, but that, within this segment, special importance was attached to different dimensions across different countries. In the five countries studied, BMW discovered a total of seven common segments whose names speak more or less for themselves: The unpretentious car fan (18 per cent); the prestige-oriented sporty driver (25 per cent); the hedonist (9 per cent); the utilitarian thinker (13 per cent); the traditionalist (17 per cent); the prestige-oriented achiever (10 per cent); and the understatement buyer (9 per cent). However, as shown in Figure 15.10, the size of each of the segments varies considerably in each country. The country-specific results indicate that different models appeal to different segments in different countries. For example, it could be types 6 and 2 in Austria whereas it could be types 1 and 4 in Switzerland. The case of BMW is a good combination of pan-European and country-specific approaches to analyzing consumer behaviour.

European advertising preferences and regulations

Consumers in different countries are accustomed to different forms of advertising. In many cases, advertising content is regulated by the government. For example, tobacco advertising in Denmark is not allowed to depict young people, and Swedish tobacco advertising targeted at end-users must not show any people at all. At present, the European Commission in Brussels are discussing initiatives to make even stricter controls on advertising, introducing among other things a total ban on tobacco advertising in Europe.

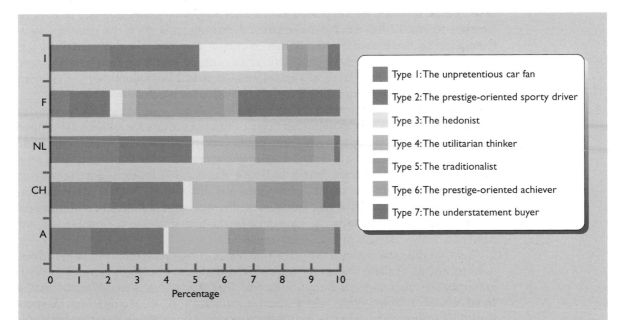

Figure 15.10 Distribution of car segments in five European countries
Source: Horst Kern, Hans-Christian Wagner and Roswitha Harris, 'European Aspects of a Global Brand: The BMW Case', *Marketing and Research Today* (February 1990): 47–57. Used with permission.

In Germany, pricing is controlled, and special sales can be held only for a particular reason, such as going out of business or the end of the season. Advertising also focuses more on the provision of factual information rather than on the aggressive hard sell. Indeed, it is illegal to mention the names of competitors.[55] Unlike the Anglo-Saxon advertising culture, comparative advertising is banned in most Latin and Germanic countries in Europe.

But the differences among European countries are not restricted to the legal area. There are also differences concerning which type of television advertising spots and print-ads will work best in various European countries. A comparative study of French and German TV spots revealed a distinct profile of the ads in these two countries. French TV ads tended to have less product information, to have a less direct way of communicating about socially sensitive topics, to rely more on non-verbal and implicit communication types and to present women in a more seductive and sexually alluring manner.[56] The same differences concerning the general image of French communication as seductive and imaginative versus a more factual and sober German style were confirmed when looking at other types of communication such as television news programmes and news magazines.

One possible explanation for this difference may be due to the distinction between **low-context** and **high-context cultures**.[57] In a high-context culture, messages tend to be more implicit, and built into the communication context, whereas communication in low-context cultures tends to be more explicit, specific and direct. France, according to this perspective of classifying culture, is relatively high-context compared to Germany, which belongs among the most low-context cultures in the world.

In comparison, the British have a more favourable attitude to advertising than both French and Germans. They tend to think of advertising as a humorous and entertaining part of daily life, and have less concerns about its manipulative capacities.[58] These findings are supported by another source, concluding that, relative to Americans, the British tended to regard advertising as a form of entertainment. Compared to the United States, British television commercials also contained less information.[59] One advertising executive stated outright that from watching a sample reel of German and British car ads respectively, it would be evident that the German ones would be much more rational and the British ones much more emotional.[60]

Not only do attitudes about ads vary across Europe, the same can be said for preferences of media. For example, in France outdoor posters are a highly developed and popular medium for creative campaigns. Cinema advertising is also enjoyable to the French. In the UK, adverts in daily newspapers are more important compared to other European countries, and in Germany the radio medium is more important than elsewhere.[61] But the use of various media is difficult to compare among countries due to variations in the regulation of media use. For example, interrupting programmes with advertising is not permitted in the Scandinavian countries, and not practised in the German public TV channels.

Cultural differences may influence actual reader comprehension of a certain advertisement. Most of these studies have concluded that ads, like other pictures or communications, are understood culturally, and that readership is so different that a standardized execution of the ad becomes problematic.[62] When two different TV spots (called 'Hitchhiker' and 'Quackers') for the chocolate bar *KitKat* were tested in six different countries, the consumers (all younger people) showed significant differences in what they retained as the main idea of the ad and the main product characteristic (see Table 15.5).[63]

Table 15.5 **Differences in message decoding of two ads in six European countries**

	Main idea	
	Hitchhiker	*Quackers*
Belgium	Product for young people	You can share it
England	A break with KitKat	
Holland	Product for young people	A break with KitKat
Italy	Product quality	
Germany	To relax	A break with KitKat
France	'Magic effect'	To relax

© Copyright GfK
Source: ESOMAR, Madrid 1992

	Main product characteristics	
	Hitchhiker	*Quackers*
Belgium	Good product	Crispy bar
England	Chocolate bar with wafer	A snack
Holland	Little	
Italy	Good product	
Germany	Relax with KitKat	Chocolate bar
France	Crispy bar	Good product

© Copyright GfK
Source: ESOMAR, Madrid 1992.
Source: J. Andrew Davison and Erik Grab, 'The Contributions of Advertising Testing to the Development of Effective International Advertising: The KitKat Case Study', *Marketing and Research Today* (February 1993): 15–24. Used with permission.

The variations could be explained by different factors such as relative familiarity with the product concept (in Italy), the small size of the product in relation to local competitors (The Netherlands), popularity of English-style humour (Germany) and the prevailing advertising style in the country (France). Another study comparing Danish and American readings of international ads has detected similar variations in readership due to cultural backgrounds. For example, an ad for a lemon-flavoured soft drink featuring young people enjoying themselves on a beach was interpreted by the Danes as showing the strength of the community and by Americans as showing individual freedom.[64] It is probably safe to conclude that, although there are often certain similarities in the way ads are understood across cultures, the readership tends to focus on different themes in different countries.[65]

Regional consumption differences: the micro-level

Geodemography

The term **geodemography** refers to analytical techniques that combine data on consumer expenditures and other socioeconomic factors with geographic information about the areas in which people live in order to identify consumers who share common consumption patterns.

Geodemography is based on the assumption that 'birds of a feather flock together' – that people who have similar needs and tastes tend to live near one another. Given this, it should be possible to locate 'pockets' of like-minded people who can then be reached more economically by direct mail and other methods. Important dimensions in differentiating between neighbourhoods or townships are factors such as income level, ethnic background and demographics (most notably age). Geographic information increasingly is being combined with other data to paint an even more complete picture of the consumer. Several marketing research ventures now employ **single-source data** where information about a person's actual purchasing history is combined with geodemographic data, thus allowing marketers to learn even more about the types of marketing strategies that motivate some people to respond.

Ethnic and religious subcultures

Sevgi, waking up early on Saturday morning, braces herself for a long day of errands and chores. As usual, her mother expects her to do the shopping while she is at work, and then help prepare the food for the big family get-together tonight. Of course, her older brother would never be asked to do the shopping or help out in the kitchen – these are woman's jobs.

Family gatherings make a lot of work, and Sevgi wishes that her mother would use prepared foods once in a while, especially on a Saturday when Sevgi has an errand or two of her own to do. But no, her mother insists on preparing most of her food from scratch; she rarely uses any convenience products to ensure that the meals she serves are of the highest quality .

Resigned, Sevgi watches TRTint on the family's cable-TV while she's getting dressed, and then she heads down to the local newsshop in 'De Pijp' to buy a magazine – there are dozens of Turkish magazines and newspapers for sale, and she likes to pick up new ones occasionally. Then Sevgi buys the grocery items her mother wants; the Islamic Halal butcher is a long-time family friend and already has the cuts of lamb prepared for her. The vendors at the open air stalls on the Albert Cuyp Market where she and her mother shop all the time know her, and provide her with choice quality olives and vegetables. One quick stop at the local sweet shop to pick up the family's favourite *drop* (licorice) and she's almost done. With any luck, she'll have a few minutes to stop at the music store and pick up 'Bridges to Babylon', the latest CD from The Rolling Stones. She'll listen to it in the kitchen while she chops, peels and stirs. Sevgi smiles to herself: despite a busy day preparing the house and meal for the family party, she feels that Amsterdam is a great place to live.

Subcultures and consumer identity

Yes, Sevgi lives in Amsterdam, not Ankara. However, this consumer vignette could have just as easily taken place in London, Berlin, Stockholm, Marseilles or thousands of other cities throughout Europe. There are well over 25 million Europeans who belong to an ethnic sub-group, and in several European countries such as France, Belgium and Germany, they collectively account for around 10 per cent of the total population. In the UK, the ethnic communities represented are forecast to double in population to over 6 million within the next 30 years.[66]

Turkish consumers have much in common with members of other racial and ethnic groups who live in Europe. These groups of consumers observe the same national holidays, their expenditures are affected by the country's economic health and they may join together in rooting for their host country's national team in the Olympics. None the less, while European residency (and in most cases European citizenship) provides the raw material for some consumption decisions, others profoundly affect (see Figure 15.11) and are profoundly affected by the enormous variations in the social fabric of the country where they live.

Consumers' lifestyles are affected by group memberships *within* the society at large. These groups are known as **subcultures**, whose members share beliefs and common experiences that set them apart from others. While subcultural group memberships often have a significant impact on consumer behaviour, some subcultural identifications are more powerful than others. Major subcultural consumer groups based on age have already been discussed in chapter 13.

Ethnic and racial subcultures

Ethnic and religious identity is a significant component of a consumer's self-concept. An **ethnic or racial subculture** consists of a self-perpetuating group of consumers who are held together by common cultural and/or genetic ties, and is identified both by its members and by others as being a distinguishable category.[67]

In some countries, such as Japan, ethnicity is almost synonymous with the dominant culture, since most citizens claims the same homogeneous cultural ties (although Japan has sizeable minority populations, most notably people of Korean ancestry). In heterogeneous societies like those found in Europe, many different cultures are represented, and consumers may expend great effort to keep their subcultural identification from being submerged into the mainstream of the dominant society.

Ethnicity and marketing strategies

Although some companies may feel uncomfortable at the notion that people's racial and ethnic differences should be explicitly taken into account when formulating marketing strategies, the reality is that these subcultural memberships frequently are paramount in shaping people's needs and wants. Membership in these groups is often predictive of such consumer variables as level and type of media exposure, food preferences, the wearing of distinctive apparel, political behaviour, leisure activities and even willingness to try new products.

Furthermore, research evidence indicates that members of minority groups are more likely to find an advertising spokesperson from their own group to be more trustworthy, and this enhanced credibility in turn translates into more positive brand attitudes.[68] In addition, the way marketing messages should be structured depends on subcultural differences in how meanings are communicated. As discussed earlier in

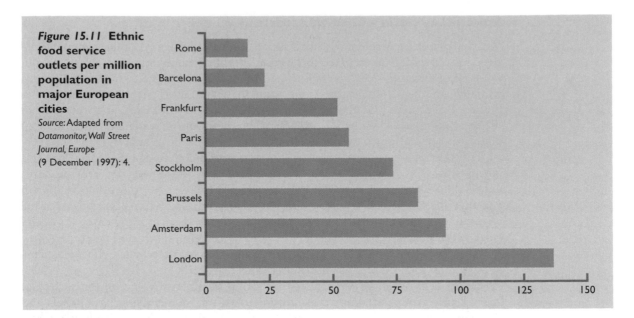

***Figure 15.11* Ethnic food service outlets per million population in major European cities**
Source: Adapted from *Datamonitor, Wall Street Journal, Europe* (9 December 1997): 4.

Multicultural dimensions

Just as marketers have discovered that it is a mistake to group together all members of racial minorities, the same wisdom can be applied to Caucasian consumers: white is made up of many shades of grey, and there are big differences among ethnic whites. Consider, for example, differences in income levels among subcultures of various European extractions. These differences often reflect the length of time members of a subculture have been settled in the United States, since groups who have been there longer have had more time to develop business networks and amass wealth. French-Americans are the most likely to be affluent – almost 42 per cent have a household income greater than $75,000, while Polish-Americans have the lowest income among these segments.

Some organizations are beginning to develop campaigns to target various Caucasian ethnic groups. For example, casino gambling is most popular among those of German, Italian or Portuguese extraction, so some gaming operations are reaching out to them. AT&T discovered that using singer Whitney Houston in its successful 'your true voice' campaign did not appeal to Russian-Americans, so the company instead used a Russian comedian in commercials it aired on Russian-language television. Even the US Postal Service is trying to target ethnic whites after its research found that European-Americans are more likely than others to use money-transfer programmes and parcel post. The Postal Service is advertising in foreign language papers and directories to compete with UPS for these customers.[70]

this chapter, sociologists make a distinction between *high-context cultures* and *low-context cultures*. In a high-context culture, group members tend to be tightly-knit, and they are likely to infer meanings that go beyond the spoken word. Symbols and gestures, rather than words, carry much of the weight of the message. Many minority cultures are high-context and have strong oral traditions, so perceivers will be more sensitive to nuances in advertisements that go beyond the message copy.[69]

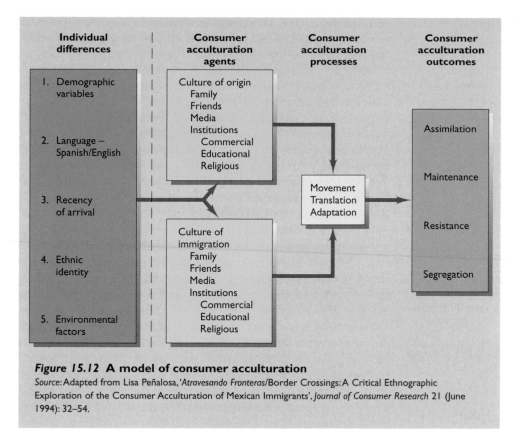

Figure 15.12 A model of consumer acculturation

Source: Adapted from Lisa Peñalosa, '*Atravesando Fronteras*/Border Crossings: A Critical Ethnographic Exploration of the Consumer Acculturation of Mexican Immigrants', *Journal of Consumer Research* 21 (June 1994): 32–54.

'To be or not to be: that is the answer'

One important way to distinguish among members of a subculture is to consider the extent to which they retain a sense of identification with their country of origin versus their host country. **Acculturation** refers to the process of movement and adaptation to one country's cultural environment by a person from another country.[71] The nature of this transition process is affected by many factors. Individual differences, such as whether the person speaks the host country language, influence how difficult the adjustment will be.

The person's contact with **acculturation agents** – people and institutions that teach the ways of a culture – also are crucial. Some of these agents are aligned with the *culture of origin* (in Sevgi's case, Turkey). These include family, friends, the mosque, local businesses and Turkish-language media that keep the consumer in touch with his or her country of origin. Other agents are associated with the *culture of immigration* (in this case, The Netherlands), and help the consumer to learn how to navigate in the new environment. These include state schools and Dutch-language media.

As immigrants adapt to their new surroundings, several processes come into play. *Movement* refers to the factors motivating people to uproot themselves physically from one location and go to another. Although many ethnic members throughout Europe are second-generation (born in the country where they live), their parents are more likely to have been the first to arrive in the new country. On arrival, immigrants encounter a need for *translation*. This means attempting to master a set of rules for operating in the new environment, whether learning how to decipher a different currency or understanding the social meanings of unfamiliar clothing styles. This cultural learning leads to a process of *adaptation*, where new consumption patterns are formed.

As consumers undergo acculturation, several things happen. Many immigrants undergo (at least some extent) *assimilation*, where they adopt products that are identified with the mainstream culture. At the same time, there is an attempt at *maintenance* of practices associated with the culture of origin. Immigrants stay in touch with people in their country, and many continue to eat ethnic foods and read ethnic newspapers. Their continued identification with their home culture may cause *resistance*, as they resent the pressure to submerge their identities and take on new roles. Figure 15.12 provides an overview of the processes involved in consumer acculturation.

These processes illustrate that ethnicity is a fluid concept, and the boundaries of a subculture constantly are being recreated. An *ethnic pluralism* perspective argues that ethnic groups differ from the mainstream in varying degrees, and that adaptation to the larger society occurs selectively. Research evidence argues against the notion that assimilation necessarily involves losing identification with the person's original ethnic group. For example, Sevgi feels comfortable in expressing her 'Turkishness' in a variety of consumption-related ways: the magazines she buys, the TV programmes on the Turkish network she chooses to watch, her choice of ethnically appropriate gifts for events such as weddings and holidays. Alternatively, she has no problems at all in expressing consumption behaviours of the mainstream culture – she loves eating *drop* (Dutch licorice), buys 'Western' music and has her favourite outfits for going out to the cinema and clubs. The best indicator of ethnic assimilation, these researchers argue, is the extent to which members of an ethnic group have social interactions with members of other groups in comparison to their own.[72]

The impact of religion on consumption

Religion *per se* has not been studied extensively in marketing, possibly because it is seen as a taboo subject. The very low-key or nonexistent approach by large multinational or pan-European companies reflects the same sort of caution that these companies have in targeting ethnic groups – companies are having to decide whether religiously- or ethnic-tailored programmes foster greater brand loyalty or whether any advantage is outweighed by the risks of misreading the target market and causing offence. Without question, the most successful companies targeting and serving both ethnic and religious segments are small businesses, whose managers and owners often are members of the group.[73] However, the little evidence that has been accumulated indicates that religious affiliation has the *potential* to be a valuable predictor of consumer behaviour.[74] Religious subcultures have been shown to exert an impact on such consumer variables as personality, attitudes towards sexuality, birth rates and household formation, income and political attitudes.

Putting together descriptive demographic profiles of Europe's major religious groups is not an exact science. For example, French law prohibits any question on religion in national censuses, although with an estimated 4–5 million Muslim inhabitants France undoubtedly has the biggest Islamic community in Western Europe. As a faith, Islam is now second only to Roman Catholicism in France.[75] Similar problems with taking a census are found in the UK. Britain's one million-strong Muslim population is small, but has the fastest growth rate of all religions in the country. The thousand or so existing mosques are likely to be converted warehouses, churches or community halls. The hundreds of new mosques being built feature traditional Islamic domes and minarets – a trend which signals the growing economic vitality of British Muslims, as well as local authorities' growing acceptance of mosques.[76] While Islam is the fastest-growing religion in Europe, it is difficult to generalize about Muslims beyond belief in the teachings of the Koran, identifying holidays and periods of fasting such as Ramadan, and certain dietary restrictions. Coming from more than 120 countries and a variety of ethnic groups (Blacks, Asians, Arabs, Europeans) they are like many groups of consumers in Europe – diverse in their celebrations of consumption habits!

Christianity has dominated the history and cultural development of Europe, and has played an important role in the shaping of the European continent. While the many denominations of Christians make it the largest religious grouping in Europe, active membership is on the decline, with fewer and fewer adults attending services on any given Sunday.[77] In response to this trend, the Vatican has been involved in a variety of events aimed at developing closer and more active relationships with Europe's youth. Enlisting French fashion designers for World Youth Day, having Bob Dylan perform at a Vatican-sponsored rock concert, and having Easter Mass and information about the Vatican on a World Wide Web Site are recent attempts to get youth involved with the church.[78] Divided roughly along the more Protestant North, and predominantly Catholic South, Christianity still makes up the majority religion in Europe in terms of claimed membership. Its major holidays of Easter and Christmas and celebrations such as 'Carnival' (*Faschung* in Germany) are celebrated or observed to such an extent that large industries such as travel and retailing rely on these seasons as the time of year when they earn the most revenues.

| Marketing pitfall | There are mixed feelings in the Catholic community about the spread of religious imagery in popular culture. On the one hand, The Vatican museum recently opened its first boutique outside Vatican walls, and is now selling silk ties and scarves designed for the Vatican by Salvatore Ferragamo.[79] On the other hand, an ad in a Danish campaign for the French car manufacturer Renault had to be withdrawn after protests from the Catholic community. The ad described a dialogue during confession between a Catholic priest and a repenting man. The man's sins can be atoned by reciting Ave Marias until he confesses to having scratched the paint of the priest's new Renault – at which point the priest shouts 'heathen' and orders the man to pay a substantial penalty to the church.[80] |

Euro-consumers: do they exist?

A number of trends seem to be valid for all Western European markets.[81] These include:

- a tendency to more unevenly distributed income
- an increasing number of older people
- a decrease in household size

- a growing proportion of immigrants
- increase in environmental concern and consumption of 'green' products
- relatively increasing consumption of services compared to durable goods

In spite of these common trends, there are, as we have seen, big differences in the local contexts in which these trends are found as well as differences in the degree to which the trend is significant in each individual country.

Many European managers expect an increase in the importance of Euro-brands and Euro-consumers.[82] However, *why* and *when* companies should or could adopt pan-European strategies or not remains a complex matter. One study suggested 21 influencing factors on pan-European marketing standardization, including management characteristics, firm characteristics, industry characteristics and government characteristics, but not market characteristics![83]

We believe that consumer behaviour analysis must play an important role in the decision to standardize or adapt marketing strategies. All consumers to some extent will differ in what they buy, why they buy, who makes the purchase decision, how they buy, when they buy and where they buy.[84] Some of these differences may be explained at the lifestyle level and less so on the national level, and some are very obviously related to national or regional differences. It is also obvious that some differences are disappearing, due to the increasingly international supply of goods and the increasing internationalization of the retailing system in Europe.[85] However, not even the fact that similar goods are bought in similar stores across European countries permits us to confirm the existence of the Euro-consumer. Product usage and knowledge, and to a certain extent imagery, may be relatively shared among Europeans, but as soon as one takes the contexts of acquisition, consumption and disposal contexts into account, the actual role and meaning of the product in daily life becomes coloured by the local culture. No lifestyle survey has yet demonstrated a truly European profile in any of the lifestyles; European segments continue to be defined in rather abstract common denominators.

It is often asserted that segments such as international businesspeople, or younger people mainly influenced by trends from MTV and other 'global youth culture' phenomena, are especially prone to standardized marketing. European managers are people who tend to be prime consumers of pan-European media, like business magazines or CNN (in the hotel rooms).[86] So there may be a tendency to a higher degree of internationalization among younger, wealthier and more educated people. The question is how deep the similarity really is. A study of consumption of luxury goods in five major European markets concluded that the pan-European consumer of luxury brands is between 35 and 49 years old, lives in a major city, has a high income and a university education, and occupies a managerial job. On the other hand, there were big differences among the various countries in the level of brand awareness and purchase level, and the degree of significance of socio-economic factors for purchase of luxury brands. For example, Spain and Italy are strongly segmented due to socio-economic differences, while France, the UK and Germany are less useful in explaining luxury consumption. The level of purchase and awareness was found to be high in France, the UK and Italy, and low in Germany and Spain. The most 'mature' market for luxury brands was France, the UK and a narrow Italian segment, whereas the rest of the Italians lacked the money, the Germans lacked the motivation and the Spanish lacked both.[87]

In general, the absence of the Euro-consumer does not mean that Svensson of Sweden, Smith of the UK, Smit of Holland, Simón of Spain and Schultz of Germany cannot have more in common in certain aspects than they have with their compatriots. But it means that these similarities can be analyzed and understood only with methods that are also able to take the differences into consideration.

Chapter summary

- A consumer's *lifestyle* refers to the ways he or she chooses to spend time and money and how his or her values, attitudes and tastes are reflected by consumption choices. Lifestyle research is useful to track societal consumption preferences and also to position specific products and services to different segments.
- Marketers segment by lifestyle differences, often by grouping consumers in terms of their *AIOs* (activities, interests, and opinions).
- *Psychographic techniques* attempt to classify consumers in terms of psychological, subjective variables in addition to observable characteristics (demographics). A variety of systems, such as RISC, have been developed to identify consumer 'types' and to differentiate them in terms of their brand or product preferences, media usage, leisure time activities, and attitudes towards such broad issues as politics and religion.
- Interrelated sets of products and activities are associated with social roles to form *consumption constellations*. People often purchase a product or service because it is associated with a constellation which, in turn, is linked to a lifestyle they find desirable.
- Where one comes from is often a significant determinant of lifestyle. Many marketers recognize national or regional differences in product preferences, and develop different versions of their products for different markets.
- Because a consumer's culture exerts such a big influence on his or her lifestyle choices, marketers must learn as much as possible about differences in cultural norms and preferences when marketing in more than one country. One important issue is the extent to which marketing strategies must be tailored to each culture, versus standardized across cultures.
- Consumers identify with many groups that share common characteristics and identities. These large groups that exist within a society are *subcultures*, and membership in them often gives marketers a valuable clue about individuals' consumption decisions. A large component of a person's identity is determined by his or her ethnic origins, racial identity and religious background. The growing numbers of people who claim multi-ethnic backgrounds are beginning to blur the traditional distinctions drawn among these subcultures.
- Recently, several minority groups have caught the attention of marketers as their economic power has grown. Segmenting consumers by their *ethnicity* can be effective, but care must be taken not to rely on inaccurate (and sometimes offensive) ethnic stereotypes.
- Because a consumer's culture exerts such a major influence on his or her lifestyle choices, marketers must learn as much as possible about differences in cultural norms and preferences when marketing in more than one country.
- Given that we, as consumers, must take part in many activities that reflect our local cultures, Euro-consumers as an overall segment do not exist. The existence of a Euro-consumer is at best limited to certain segments of the population, the young and the (international) managerial class, and to certain situations.

1

🔑 Key terms

Acculturation *(p. 431)*
Acculturation agents *(p. 431)*
AIOs *(p. 407)*
Consumption constellations
  (p. 405)
Creolization *(p. 422)*
Ethnic subculture *(p. 429)*
Expatriate food *(p. 422)*
Geodemography *(p. 428)*
Global food *(p. 422)*
Habitus *(p. 413)*
High context culture *(p. 426)*
Lifestyle *(p. 401)*

Lifestyle marketing perspective
  (p. 404)
Low context culture *(p. 426)*
Materialism *(p. 402)*
Nostalgia food *(p. 422)*
Product complementarity *(p. 405)*
Psychographics *(p. 406)*
Racial subculture *(p. 429)*
RISC *(p. 409)*
Single-source data *(p. 428)*
Subcultures *(p. 429)*
VALS *(p. 413)*

Consumer behaviour challenge

1. Compare and contrast the concepts of lifestyle and social class.
2. In what situations is demographic information likely to be more useful than psychographic data, and vice versa?
3. Discuss some concrete situations in which international similarities in lifestyles may be more relevant than national cultural differences for market segmentation and for the understanding of consumer behaviour.
4. Describe the underlying principles used to construct the RISC system. What are some positive and negative aspects of this approach to lifestyle segmentation?
5. Compile a set of recent ads that attempt to link consumption of a product with a specific lifestyle. How is this goal usually accomplished?
6. The chapter mentions that psychographic analyses can be used to market politicians. Conduct research on the marketing strategies used in a recent, major election. How were voters segmented in terms of values? Can you find evidence that communications strategies were guided by this information?
7. Using media targeted to the group, construct a consumption constellation for the social role of university students.

What set of products, activities and interests tend to appear in advertisements depicting 'typical' university students? How realistic is this constellation?
8. Administer the Materialism Scale in Table 15.1 to a sample of business students and another group of, say, humanities students. What predictions might you make regarding group differences on this value? For each statement, ask respondents to circle a number on a scale:

Strongly disagree   Strongly agree

1   2   3   4   5

Note: When scoring, remember that items marked with an asterisk are reverse scored. That is, a response of '5' should be scored as a '1,' a '4' as a '2', and so on. Sum each person's score for each scale item, and calculate the average response for each sample. Do the two groups differ in terms of their mean responses?
9. If you were segmenting European consumers in terms of their relative level of materialism, how might your advertising and promotional strategy take this difference into account? Construct two versions of an ad for a

suntan lotion, one to appeal to a high materialism country and one to appeal to a low materialism country (under the untenable assumption of all other things being equal).

10. There are, of course, people of all RISC types in all European countries, but their numbers vary. Try to determine which lifestyles are the most common in some European countries that you know.

11. If you have access to foreign TV channels, try to compare the advertising in the ones from your own country with the foreign ones. Are the styles different? Are the predominant products different? Is the use of a certain style of advertisement for a certain type of product similar or dissimilar?

12. Locate one or more consumers (perhaps family members) who have immigrated from another country. Interview them about how they adapted to their host culture. In particular, what changes did they make in their consumption practices over time?

CHAPTER 16

Güliz Ger, Bilkent University, Ankara, Turkey

Six weeks before St Valentine's Day, called the Lovers' Day in Turkey, Ayşe starts planning for that special romantic evening. She remembers that last year she and her husband could not find a table in any restaurant in Ankara, all hotels and restaurants had been fully booked and florists had run out of red roses. So she acts early and makes a reservation for two at a good restaurant. She starts window shopping for a gift that she would like to receive. She sees a St Valentine's Day Swatch that she really likes. Two weeks before Lovers' Day she starts asking her husband what he is thinking of getting her. She takes him to the shopping mall and shows him the St Valentine's Day Swatch and tells him that she'd like that very much. On Lovers' Day Ayşe's husband remembers that he has not yet bought anything, goes to get the St Valentine's Day Swatch – only to discover that the shop has run out of them. Instead he buys a much more expensive Swatch. When he comes home, he finds his wife, dressed up ready to go out for dinner. Excited, she closes her eyes and puts her arm forward, confident that he will put a watch around her wrist. And he does. But when she opens her eyes and sees that it is not the St Valentine's Day Swatch, she is upset – and furious. She bursts into tears; they have an argument; and Ayşe goes to the bedroom and takes off her nice clothes. They spend the evening at home, in separate rooms, not talking to each other. Some Lovers' Day she thinks.

Later, Ayşe tells the story to her friends, some of whom think it's very funny . . .

Cultural change processes

The Rolling Stones. Miniskirts. Kipper ties. Fast food. High-tech furniture. Postmodern architecture. James Bond. We inhabit a world brimming with different styles and possibilities. The food we eat, the cars we drive, the clothes we wear, the places we live and work, the music we listen to – all are influenced by the ebb and flow of popular culture and fashion. Consumers may at times feel overwhelmed by the sheer choice in the marketplace. A person trying to decide on something as routine as a tie has many hundreds of alternatives from which to choose. Despite this seeming abundance, however, the options available to consumers at any point in time actually represent only a *small fraction* of the total set of possibilities.

The opening vignette illustrates some of the processes related to cultural change that are discussed in this chapter: fashions, new consumption opportunities and globalization. Lovers' Day started to be celebrated in Turkey about a decade ago, first by exchanging cards among school friends. It has become more widespread in the last few years, mostly among the urban middle class who now exchange gifts and make a special evening of it. St Valentine's Day, appropriated as Lovers' Day, is taking root among married and unmarried couples in this Muslim country where traditional norms of respectability did not allow dating – dating is not what 'nice' girls were supposed to do, and many from conservative or lower-middle-class families still frown on it.

Cultural selection

The selection of certain alternatives over others – whether cars, dresses, computers, recording artists, political candidates, religions or even scientific methodologies – is the culmination of a complex filtration process resembling a funnel, as depicted in Figure 16.1. Many possibilities initially compete for adoption, and these are steadily narrowed down as they make their way down the path from conception to consumption in a process of **cultural selection**.

Our tastes and product preferences are not formed in a vacuum. Choices are driven by the images presented to us in mass media, our observations of those around us, and even by our desires to live in the fantasy worlds created by marketers. These options are constantly evolving and changing. A clothing style or type of cuisine that is 'hot' one year may be 'out' the next.

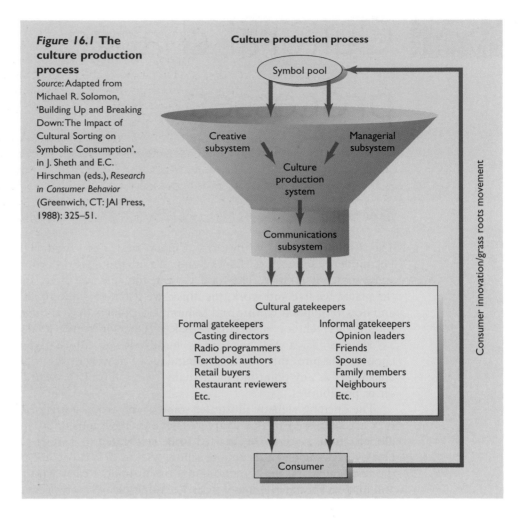

Figure 16.1 The culture production process
Source: Adapted from Michael R. Solomon, 'Building Up and Breaking Down: The Impact of Cultural Sorting on Symbolic Consumption', in J. Sheth and E.C. Hirschman (eds.), *Research in Consumer Behavior* (Greenwich, CT: JAI Press, 1988): 325–51.

Culture production systems

No single designer, company or advertising agency is solely responsible for creating popular culture. Every product, whether a hit record, a car or a new fashion, requires the input of many different participants. The set of individuals and organizations responsible for creating and marketing a cultural product is a **cultural production system (CPS)**.[1]

The nature of these systems helps to determine the types of product that eventually emerge from them. Factors such as the number and diversity of competing systems and the amount of innovation versus conformity that is encouraged are important. For example, an analysis of the Country & Western music industry has shown that the hit records it produces tend to be similar to one another during periods when it is dominated by a few large companies, whereas there is more diversity when a greater number of producers are competing within the same market.[2]

The different members of a culture production system may not necessarily be aware of or appreciate the roles played by other members, yet many diverse agents work together to create popular culture.[3] Each member does his or her best to anticipate which particular images will be most attractive to a consumer market. Of course, those who are able to forecast consumers' tastes consistently will be successful over time.

Components of a CPS

A culture production system has three major subsystems: (1) a *creative subsystem* responsible for generating new symbols and/or products; (2) a *managerial subsystem* responsible for selecting, making tangible, mass producing and managing the distribution of new symbols and/or products; and (3) a *communications subsystem* responsible for giving meaning to the new product and providing it with a symbolic set of attributes that are communicated to consumers.

An example of the three components of a culture production system for a record would be (1) a singer (e.g. Madonna, a creative subsystem); (2) a company (e.g. Sire Records, which manufactures and distributes Madonna's records, a managerial subsystem); and (3) the advertising and publicity agencies hired to promote the albums (a communications subsystem). Table 16.1 illustrates some of the many *cultural specialists*, who operate in different subsystems, who are required to create a hit CD.

Table 16.1 **Cultural specialists in the music industry**

Specialist	Functions
Songwriter(s)	Compose music and lyrics; must reconcile artistic preferences with estimates of what will succeed in the marketplace
Performer(s)	Interpret music and lyrics; may be formed spontaneously, or may be packaged by an agent to appeal to a predetermined market (e.g. New Kids on the Block and the Spice Girls)
Teachers and coaches	Develop and refine performers' talents
Agent	Represent performers to record companies
A&R (artist & repertoire) executive	Acquire artists for the record label
Publicists, image consultants, designers, stylists	Create an image for the group that is transmitted to the buying public
Recording technicians, producers	Create a recording to be sold
Marketing executives	Make strategic decisions regarding performer's appearances, ticket pricing, promotional strategies, and so on
Video director	Interpret the song visually to create a music video that will help to promote the record
Music reviewers	Evaluate the merits of a recording for listeners
Disc jockeys, radio programme directors	Decide which records will be given airplay and/or placed in the radio stations' regular rotations
Record shop owner	Decide which of the many records produced will be stocked and/or promoted heavily in the retail environment

Cultural gatekeepers

Many judges or 'tastemakers' influence the products that are eventually offered to consumers. These judges, or **cultural gatekeepers**, are responsible for filtering the overflow of information and materials intended for consumers. Gatekeepers include film, restaurant and car reviewers, interior designers, disc jockeys, retail buyers and magazine editors. Collectively, this set of agents is known as the *through-put sector*.[4]

Speaking the language of beauty

A recent study of cultural gatekeepers in the fashion and beauty industry illustrates how some cultural 'products' (in this case, fashion models) are selected and championed over other stylistic possibilities.[5] Editors at such women's magazines as *Cosmopolitan*, *Marie Claire*, *Depêche Mode* and *Elle* play an important role in selecting the specific variations of beauty that will appear in the pages of these 'bibles of fashion'. These images, in turn, will be relied on by millions of readers to decide what 'look' they would like to adopt – and, of course, which particular products and services (such as hairstyles, cosmetics, clothing styles, exercise programmes) they will need to attain these images.

In this study, decision-makers at a group of influential magazines identified a small set of 'looks' that characterize many of the diverse fashion models they evaluate on a daily basis – what is more, though each editor was studied independently, overall respondents exhibited a very high level of agreement among themselves regarding what the 'looks' are, what they are called, which are more or less desirable *and* which they expect to be paired with specific product advertisements. This research suggests that cultural gatekeepers tend to rely on the same underlying cultural ideals and priorities when making the selections that in turn get passed down the channel of distribution for consideration by consumers.

High culture and popular culture

Do Beethoven and Björk have anything in common? While both the famous composer and the Icelandic singer are associated with music, many would argue that the similarity stops here. Culture production systems create many diverse kinds of products, but some basic distinctions can be offered regarding their characteristics.

Arts and crafts

One distinction can be made between arts and crafts.[6] An **art product** is viewed primarily as an object of aesthetic contemplation without any functional value. A **craft product**, in contrast, is admired because of the beauty with which it performs some function (e.g. a ceramic ashtray or hand-carved fishing lures). A piece of art is original, subtle and valuable, and is associated with the elite of society. A craft tends to follow a formula that permits rapid production. According to this framework, elite culture is produced in a purely aesthetic context and is judged by reference to recognized classics. It is high culture – 'serious art'.[7]

High art versus low art

The distinction between high and low culture is not as clear as it may first appear. In addition to the possible class bias that drives such a distinction (i.e. we assume that the rich have culture while the poor do not), high and low culture are blending together in interesting ways. Popular culture reflects the world around us; these phenomena touch rich and poor. In many places in Europe, advertising is widely appreciated as an artform and the TV/cinema commercials have their own Cannes festival. In France and Great Britain certain advertising executives are public figures in their respective countries. For over ten years, Europeans in different countries have paid relatively high entrance fees to watch an all-night programme in a cinema consisting of nothing but television commercials.[8]

The arts are big business. All cultural products that are transmitted by mass media become a part of popular culture.[9] Classical recordings are marketed in much the same way as Top forty albums, and museums use mass-marketing techniques to sell their wares. The Parisian museums even run a satellite gift shop at the Charles de Gaulle airport.

Marketers often incorporate high art imagery to promote products. They may sponsor artistic events to build public goodwill or feature works of art on shopping bags.[10] When observers from Toyota watched customers in luxury car showrooms, the company found that these consumers tended to view a car as an art object. This theme was then used in an ad for the Lexus with the caption: 'Until now, the only fine arts we supported were sculpture, painting and music'.[11]

Cultural formulae

Mass culture, in contrast, churns out products specifically for a mass market. These products aim to please the average taste of an undifferentiated audience and are predictable because they follow certain patterns. As illustrated in Table 16.2 many popular art forms, such as detective stories or science fiction, generally follow a **cultural formula**, where certain roles and props often occur consistently.[12] Computer programs even allow users to 'write' their own romances by systematically varying certain set elements of the story. Romance novels are an extreme case of a cultural formula. The romance novel and other formula reflect the consumer society by the way consumption events and different brands play a role in the story and in the construction of the different atmospheres described.[13]

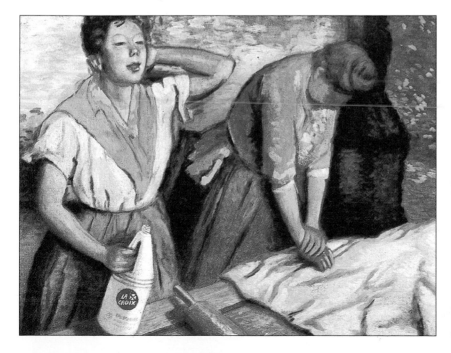

This French advertisement demonstrates the adaptation of famous paintings ('high art') to sell products ('low art'). In this version of Edgar Degas' 'The Ironers', a brand of bleach replaces a bottle of wine.
Courtesy of Colgate-Palmolive.

These Absolut ads featuring popular artists help to blur the boundaries between marketing activities and popular culture. Courtesy of V&S Vin & Spirit AB.

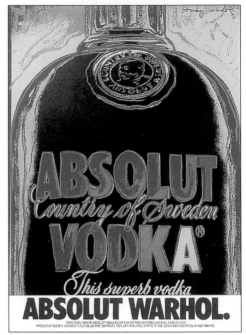

Table 16.2 **Cultural formulae in public artforms**

Artform/ genre	Classic western	Science fiction	Hard-boiled detective	Family sitcom
Time	1800s	Future	Present	Anytime
Location	Edge of civilization	Space	City	Suburbs
Protagonist	Cowboy (lone individual)	Astronaut	Detective	Father (figure)
Heroine	Schoolmistress	Spacegirl	Damsel in distress	Mother (figure)
Villain	Outlaws, killers	Aliens	Killer	Boss, neighbour
Secondary characters	Townsfolk, Indians	Technicians in spacecraft	Police, underworld	Children, dogs
Plot	Restore law and order	Repel aliens	Find killer	Solve problem
Theme	Justice	Triumph of humanity	Pursuit and discovery	Chaos and confusion
Costume	Cowboy hat, boots, etc.	High-tech uniforms	Raincoat	Normal clothes
Locomotion	Horse	Spaceship	Beat-up car	Family estate car
Weaponry	Sixgun, rifle	Rayguns	Pistol, fists	Insults

Source: Arthur A. Berger, *Signs in Contemporary Culture: An Introduction to Semiotics* (New York: Longman, 1984): 86. Copyright © 1984. Reissued 1989 by Sheffield Publishing Company, Salem, WI. Reprinted with permission of the publisher.

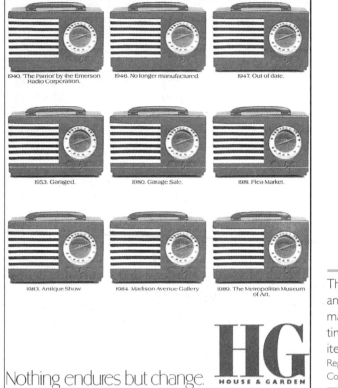

1940. 'The Patriot' by the Emerson Radio Corporation.

1946. No longer manufactured.

1947. Out of date.

1953. Garaged.

1980. Garage Sale.

1981. Flea Market.

1983. Antique Show.

1984. Madison Avenue Gallery.

1989. The Metropolitan Museum of Art.

Nothing endures but change.

HG HOUSE & GARDEN

This *House & Garden* ad illustrates the life cycle of an Emerson radio to show how ideas about a mass-produced cultural product can change over time and create a classic and valuable collector's item.

Reprinted by permission of HG Magazine, Copyright © 1989 Condé Nast Publications Inc.

Artists and companies in the popular music or film industry may be more guided by ideas of what could make a 'hit' than by any wish for artistic expression. And creators of aesthetic products are increasingly adapting conventional marketing methods to fine tune their mass market offerings. In the United States, market research is used, for example, to test audience reactions to film concepts. Although testing cannot account for such intangibles as acting quality or cinematography, it can determine if the basic themes of the movie strike a responsive chord in the target audience. This type of research is most appropriate for blockbuster movies, which usually follow one of the formulae described earlier.

Even the content of films is sometimes influenced by this consumer research. Typically, free invitations to pre-screenings are handed out in malls and cinemas. Attendees are asked a few questions about the film, then some are selected to participate in focus groups. Although groups' reactions usually result in only minor editing changes, occasionally more drastic effects result. When initial reaction to the ending of the film *Fatal Attraction* was negative, Paramount Pictures spent an additional $1.3 million to shoot a new one.[14]

The fashion system

The **fashion system** consists of all those people and organizations involved in creating symbolic meanings and transferring these meanings to cultural goods. Although people tend to equate fashion with clothing, it is important to keep in mind that fashion processes affect *all* types of cultural phenomena, including music, art, architecture and even science (i.e. certain research topics and scientists are 'hot' at any point in time). Even business practices are subject to the fashion process; they evolve and change depending on which management techniques are in vogue, such as total quality management or Business Process Re-engineering.

Fashion can be thought of as a *code*, or language, that helps us to decipher these meanings.[15] However, fashion seems to be *context-dependent* to a larger extent than language. That is, the same item can be interpreted differently by different consumers and in different situations.[16] The meaning of many products is *undercoded* – that is, there is no one precise meaning, but rather plenty of room for interpretation among perceivers.

At the outset, it may be helpful to distinguish among some confusing terms. **Fashion** is the process of social diffusion by which a new style is adopted by some group(s) of consumers. In contrast, *a fashion* (or style) refers to a particular combination of attributes. And, to be *in fashion* means that this combination is currently positively evaluated by some reference group. Thus, the term *Danish Modern* refers to particular characteristics of furniture design (i.e. a fashion in interior design); it does not necessarily imply that Danish Modern is a fashion that is currently desired by consumers.[17]

Cultural categories

The meaning that does get imparted to products reflects underlying **cultural categories**, which correspond to the basic ways we characterize the world.[18] Our culture makes distinctions between different times, between leisure and work, between genders, and so on. The fashion system provides us with products that signify these categories. For example, the clothing industry gives us clothing to denote certain times (e.g. evening wear, resort wear), it differentiates between leisure clothes and work clothes, and it promotes masculine, feminine or unisex styles.

Interdependence among product meanings

These cultural categories affect many different products and styles. As a result, it is common to find that dominant aspects of a culture at any point in time tend to be reflected in the design and marketing of very different products. This concept is hard to grasp, since on the surface a clothing style, say, has little in common with a piece of furniture or with a car. However, an overriding concern with a value such as achievement or environmentalism can determine the types of product likely to be accepted by consumers at any point in time. These underlying or latent themes then surface in various aspects of design. A few examples of this interdependence will help to demonstrate how a dominant fashion motif reverberates across industries.

- Costumes worn by political figures or film and rock stars can affect the fortunes of the apparel and accessory industries. The appearance of the actor Clark Gable in a film not wearing a vest (unusual at that time) dealt a severe setback to the men's apparel industry, while Jackie Kennedy's famous 'pillbox' hat prompted a rush for hats by women in the 1960s. Other cross-category effects include the craze for ripped sweatshirts instigated by the movie *Flashdance*, the influence on fashion from such figures as Diana, Princess of Wales or the singer Madonna's legitimization of lingerie as an acceptable outerwear clothing style.

- Some years ago, the Louvre in Paris was remodelled to include a controversial glass pyramid at the entrance designed by the architect I.M. Pei. Shortly thereafter, several designers unveiled pyramid-shaped clothing at Paris fashion shows.[19]
- In the 1950s and 1960s, much of the Western world was preoccupied with science and technology. This concern with 'space-age' mastery was fuelled by the Russians' launching of the Sputnik satellite, which prompted fears that the West (and here, most importantly the US) was falling behind in the technology race. The theme of technical mastery of nature and of futuristic design became a motif that cropped up in many aspects of popular culture – from car designs with prominent tailfins to high-tech kitchen styles.

Collective selection

Fashions tend to sweep through countries; it seems that all of a sudden 'everyone' is doing the same thing or wearing the same styles. Some sociologists view fashion as a form of *collective behaviour*, or a wave of social conformity. How do so many people get tuned in to the same phenomenon at once, as happened with hip-hop styles?

Remember that creative subsystems within a culture production system attempt to anticipate the tastes of the buying public. Despite their unique talents, members of this subsystem are also members of mass culture. Like the fashion magazine editors discussed earlier, cultural gatekeepers are drawing from a common set of ideas and symbols, and are influenced by the same cultural phenomena as the eventual consumers of their products.

 The process by which certain symbolic alternatives are chosen over others has been termed **collective selection**.[20] As with the creative subsystem, members of the managerial and communications subsystems also seem to develop a common

A cultural emphasis on science in the late 1950s affected product designs, as seen in the design of cars with large tail fins (to resemble rockets).
R. Gates/Frederic Lewis.

frame of mind. Although products within each category must compete for acceptance in the marketplace, they can usually be characterized by their adherence to a dominant theme or motif – be it the Grunge look, sixties nostalgia, Danish Modern or nouvelle cuisine.

Behavioural science perspectives on fashion

Fashion is a very complex process which operates on many levels. At one extreme, it is a macro, societal phenomenon affecting many people simultaneously. At the other, it exerts a very personal effect on individual behaviour. A consumer's purchase decisions are often motivated by his or her desire to be in fashion. Fashion products are aesthetic objects, and their origins are rooted in art and history. For this reason, there are many perspectives on the origin and diffusion of fashion. Although these cannot be described in detail here, some major approaches can be briefly summarized.[21]

Psychological models of fashion

Many psychological factors help to explain why people are motivated to be in fashion. These include conformity, variety-seeking, personal creativity and sexual attraction. For example, many consumers seem to have a 'need for uniqueness': they want to be different, but not too different.[22] For this reason, people often conform to the basic outlines of a fashion, but try to improvize and make a personal statement within these guidelines.

One of the earliest theories of fashion proposed that 'shifting **erogenous zones**' (sexually arousing areas of the body) accounted for fashion changes. Different parts of the female body are the focus of sexual interest, and clothing styles change to highlight or hide these parts. For example, people in the Victorian era found shoulders exciting, a 'well-turned ankle' was important in the beginning of this century, while the back was the centre of attention in the 1930s. Some contemporary fashions suggest that the midriff is now an erogenous zone. (Note: until very recently, the study of fashion focused almost exclusively on its impact on women. Hopefully, this concentration will broaden as scholars and practitioners begin to appreciate that men are affected by many of the same fashion influences.)

While these shifts may be due to boredom, some have speculated that there are deeper reasons for changes in focus; body areas symbolically reflect social values. In medieval times, for example, a rounded belly was desirable. This preference was most likely a reflection of the fact that multiple pregnancies were necessary to maintain population growth in an age when infant mortality was high. Interest in the female leg in the 1920s and 1930s coincided with women's new mobility and independence, while the exposure of breasts in the 1970s signalled a renewed interest in breast feeding.[23]

Economic models of fashion

Economists approach fashion in terms of the model of supply and demand. Items that are in limited supply have high value, while those readily available are less desirable. Rare items command respect and prestige.

Veblen's notion of **conspicuous consumption** proposed that the wealthy consume to display their prosperity, for example by wearing expensive (and at times impractical) clothing. The functioning of conspicuous consumption seems more complex in today's society, since wealthy consumers often engage in *parody display*,

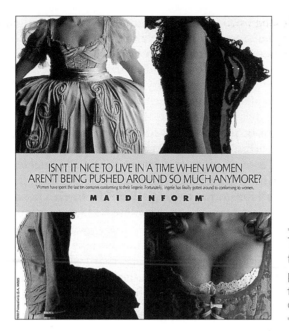

ISN'T IT NICE TO LIVE IN A TIME WHEN WOMEN
AREN'T BEING PUSHED AROUND SO MUCH ANYMORE?
Women have spent the last ten centuries conforming to their lingerie. Fortunately, lingerie has finally gotten around to conforming to women.

M A I D E N F O R M

This ad for Maidenform illustrates that fashions have accentuated different parts of the female anatomy throughout history.
Copyright © 1990 by Maidenform, Inc.

where they deliberately adopt formerly low status or inexpensive products, such as jeeps or jeans. On the other hand, new hierarchies develop between generic jeans signalling a traditional, work-oriented, class-less or lower-class environment and designer jeans expressing an urban, upmarket, class-distinctive and more contemporary lifestyle.[24] Other factors also influence the demand curve for fashion-related products. These include a *prestige-exclusivity effect*, where high prices still create high demand, and a *snob effect*, where lower prices actually reduce demand ('only a cheapskate would pay so little for that!').[25]

Sociological models of fashion

The collective selection model discussed previously is an example of a sociological approach to fashion. In addition, much attention has been focused on the relationship between product adoption and class structure.

The **trickle-down theory**, first proposed in 1904 by Georg Simmel, has been one of the most influential approaches to understanding fashion. It states that there are two conflicting forces that drive fashion change. First, subordinate groups try to adopt the status symbols of the groups above them as they attempt to climb up the ladder of social mobility. Dominant styles thus originate with the upper classes and *trickle down* to those below. However, this is where the second force comes into play: those people in the superordinate groups are constantly looking below them on the ladder to ensure that they are not imitated. They respond to the attempts of lower classes to 'impersonate' them by adopting even *newer* fashions. These two processes create a self-perpetuating cycle of change – the engine that drives fashion.[26]

The trickle-down theory was quite useful for understanding the process of fashion changes when applied to a society with a stable class structure which permitted the easy identification of lower- versus upper-class consumers. This task is not so easy in modern times. In contemporary Western society, then, this approach must be modified to account for new developments in mass culture.[27]

- A perspective based on class structure cannot account for the wide range of styles that are simultaneously made available in our society. Modern consumers have a much greater degree of individualized choice than in the past because of advances in technology and distribution. Just as an adolescent is almost instantly aware of the latest style trends by watching MTV, *elite fashion* has been largely replaced by *mass fashion*, since media exposure permits many groups to become aware of a style at the same time.
- Consumers tend to be more influenced by opinion leaders who are similar to them. As a result each social group has its own fashion innovators who determine fashion trends. It is often more accurate to speak of a *trickle-across effect*, where fashions diffuse horizontally among members of the same social group.[28]
- Finally, current fashions often originate with the lower classes and *trickle up*. Grassroots innovators typically are people who lack prestige in the dominant culture (like urban youth). Since they are less concerned with maintaining the status quo, they are more free to innovate and take risks.[29] Whatever the direction of the trickling, one thing is sure: that fashion is always a complex process of variation, of imitation and differentiation, of adoptions and rejections in relation to one's social surroundings.[30]

This blurring of origins of fashion has been attributed to the condition of post-modernity when there is no fashion, only fashions and no rules, only choices,[31] and where the norms and rules can no longer be dictated solely from the *haute couture* or other cultural gatekeepers but where the individual allows him- or herself more freedom in creating a personal look by mixing elements from different styles.[32] We shall discuss the issue of postmodernity and consumption later in this chapter.

Cycles of fashion adoption

In 1997, a little digital animal swept across the planet. After enjoying considerable success in Japan in 1996 with about 3 million units sold, it spread throughout the world during 1997 where the population by the summer had increased to a total of 7 million with approximately twice that number in back orders. The Tamagochi, as it is known, is an electronic pet that must be nurtured, played with and taken care of just as a living being. Failure to do so means it will weaken and show signs of maltreatment until it eventually dies. That is, in the Japanese version it dies. This unhappy ending did not appeal to Americans who therefore created their own version where it flies off to another planet if not treated well. Needless to say, the Japanese 'authentic' versions quickly became collector's items (cf. the discussion of collections in chapter 14).

The story of the Tamagochi shows how quickly a consumer craze can catch on globally. Although the longevity of a particular style can range from a month to a century, fashions tend to flow in a predictable sequence. The **fashion life cycle** is quite similar to the more familiar product life cycle. An item or idea progresses through basic stages from birth to death, as shown in Figure 16.2.

Variations in fashion life cycles

Chapter 10 described the *diffusion of innovations*, where products are adopted by groups of consumers over time. This diffusion process is intimately related to the popularity of fashion-related items. To illustrate how this process works, consider how the **fashion acceptance cycle** works in the popular music business. In the *introduction stage*, a song is listened to by a small number of music innovators. It

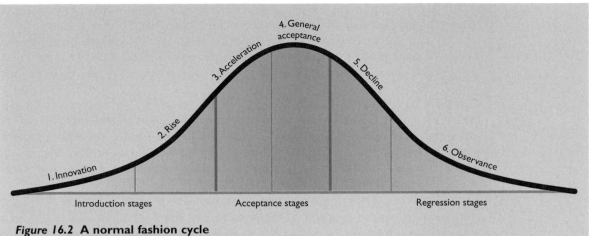
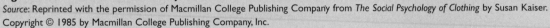

Figure 16.2 A normal fashion cycle
Source: Reprinted with the permission of Macmillan College Publishing Company from *The Social Psychology of Clothing* by Susan Kaiser.
Copyright © 1985 by Macmillan College Publishing Company, Inc.

may be played in clubs or on 'cutting-edge' radio stations, which is exactly how 'grunge rock' groups such as Nirvana got their start. During the *acceptance stage*, the song enjoys increased social visibility and acceptance by large segments of the population. A record may get wide airplay on 'Top 40' stations, steadily rising up the charts 'like a bullet'. This process may of course be supported or even generated by marketing efforts from the record company.

This Jim Beam ad illustrates the cyclical nature of fashion.
Courtesy of Jim Beam Brand, Inc.

In the *regression stage*, the item reaches a state of social saturation as it becomes overused, and eventually it sinks into decline and obsolescence as new songs rise to take its place. A hit record may be played once an hour on a Top 40 station for several weeks. At some point, though, people tend to get sick of it and focus their attention on newer releases. The former hit record eventually winds up in the discount rack at the local record store.

Figure 16.3 illustrates that fashions are characterized by slow acceptance at the beginning, which (if the fashion is to 'make it') rapidly accelerates and then tapers off. Different classes of fashion can be identified by considering the relative length of the fashion acceptance cycle. While many fashions exhibit a moderate cycle, taking several years to work their way through the stages of acceptance and decline, others are extremely long-lived or short-lived.

A **classic** is a fashion with an extremely long acceptance cycle. It is in a sense 'anti-fashion', since it guarantees stability and low risk to the purchaser for a long period of time. Keds sneakers, classical so-called 'tennis shoes' introduced in the US in 1917, have been successful because they appeal to those who are turned off by the high-fashion, trendy appeal of L.A. Gear, Reebok and others. When consumers in focus groups were asked to project what kind of building Keds would be, a common response was a country house with a white picket fence. In other words, the shoes are seen as a stable, classic product. In contrast, Nikes were often described as steel-and-glass skyscrapers, reflecting their more modernistic image.[33]

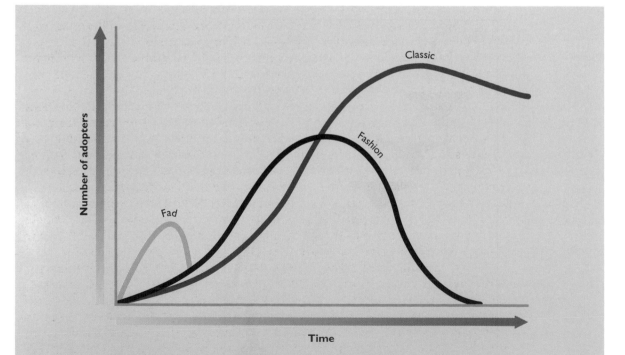

Figure 16.3 **Comparison of the acceptance cycle of fads, fashions and classics**
Source: Reprinted with the permission of Macmillan College Publishing Company from *The Social Psychology of Clothing* by Susan Kaiser. Copyright © 1985 by Macmillan College Publishing Company, Inc.

A **fad** is a very short-lived fashion. Fads are usually adopted by relatively few people. Adopters may all belong to a common subculture, and the fad 'trickles across' members but rarely breaks out of that specific group. Some successful fad products include 'this summer's toy' kinds of things like hula hoops, yo yo's and the like. Streaking was a fad that hit university campuses in America in the mid-1970s. This term referred to students running naked through classrooms, cafeterias and dorms. Although streaking quickly spread across many campuses, it was primarily restricted to college settings there. (In England it is associated with major sports events, especially cricket.) Streaking highlights several important characteristics of fads.[34]

- The fad is non-utilitarian – that is, it does not perform any explicit purpose function.
- The fad is often adopted on impulse; people do not undergo stages of rational decision-making before joining in.
- The fad diffuses rapidly, gains quick acceptance, and is short-lived.

Reality engineering

Many of the environments in which we find ourselves, whether shopping centres, sports stadiums or theme parks, are composed at least partly of images and characters drawn from products, marketing campaigns or the mass media. **Reality engineering** occurs as elements of popular culture are appropriated by marketers and converted to vehicles for promotional strategies.[35] These elements include sensory and spatial aspects of everyday existence, whether in the form of products appearing in films, odours pumped into offices and shops, advertising hoardings, theme parks, video monitors attached to shopping trolleys, and so on.

The people of Disney Corporation are probably the best world-wide known reality engineers, through their theme parks in California and Florida, and their newer parks in Japan and Europe. Disneyland-Paris was off to a problematic start when it opened in 1991. Fewer visitors and especially too few clients for the hotel and congress facilities created economic problems. But the conceptualization of the park was changed, made less American and more European, and now the park is drawing huge crowds. Also other consumption facilities and housing areas have been created around it, including a giant shopping centre where one of the streets will be a recreation of a 'typical street' of one of the local villages.[36] But other themed environments like the Asterix park, future parks or artificially created tropical environments are becoming increasingly popular for shorter vacations throughout Europe. The British-owned chain Center Parks now has 13 villages in Europe – five in The Netherlands, three in the UK, two in Belgium and France, and one in Germany – all of them built on the concept of constructing a happy and safe environment for the confirmation of family values – a life 'in brackets' away from the risks and hassles of the 'real society'.[37]

The Lost City, a new resort in South Africa, blurs the boundaries even further; it has created a 'fake' Africa for affluent guests. The complex is drought-proof and disease-proof, and it features a three-storey water slide, an 'ocean' with a panic button that will stop the wave motion on command, and a nightly volcanic eruption complete with 'non-allergenic' smoke.[38] The melding of marketing activity with popular culture is evident in other contexts as well. A British coffee ad recently borrowed the words from the Beatles' song 'A Day in the Life' and went so far as to include a shot of John Lennon's signature round-framed glasses sitting on a table. The British Boy Scouts announced that they would begin accepting corporate sponsorships for merit badges.

Multicultural dimensions

One of the most controversial intersections between marketing and society occurs when companies provide 'educational materials' to schools. In the United States, many firms, including such companies as Nike and Nintendo, provide free book covers covered with ads. Almost 40 per cent of secondary schools in the US start the day with a 'video feed' from Channel One, which exposes students to commercials in the classroom in exchange for educational programming. The Seattle School Board voted to accept corporate advertising in middle and high schools, and students in Colorado Springs travel in buses adorned with company logos. In some schools 9-year-olds practise maths by counting Tootsie Rolls (a brand of sweets), and use reading software that sports logos from KMart, Coke, Pepsi and Cap'n Crunch cereal.

Corporate involvement with schools is hardly new – in the 1920s Ivory Soap sponsored soap-carving competitions for students. But, the level of intrusion is sharply increasing as companies scramble to compensate for the decrease in children's viewership of television on Saturday mornings and weekday afternoons and find themselves competing with videos and computer games for their attention. Many educators argue that these materials are a godsend for resource-poor schools that otherwise would have hardly any other way to communicate with students. What do you think?[39]

Marketing sometimes seems to exert a self-fulfilling prophecy on popular culture. As commercial influences on popular culture increase, marketer-created symbols make their way into our daily lives to a greater degree. Historical analyses of plays, best-selling novels and the lyrics of hit songs, for example, clearly show large increases in the use of brand names over time.[40]

Reality engineering is accelerating due to the current popularity of product placements by marketers. It is quite common to see real brands prominently displayed or to hear them discussed in films and on television. In many cases, these 'plugs' are no accident. **Product placement** refers to the insertion of specific products and/or the use of brand names in film and TV scripts. Perhaps the greatest product placement success story was Reese's Pieces; sales jumped by 65 per cent in the American market after it appeared in the film *E.T.*[41]

Since that time, products are popping up everywhere, for example an Apple PowerBook can clearly be seen in *Mission: Impossible* (in return, Apple underwrote a television advertising campaign for the film, and also created an online web site for the release free of charge). Sometimes, these placements even result in changes to the programme itself. The film *Flipper* shows a Coke can in one scene. When producers signed a marketing deal with Pizza Hut, which is owned by PepsiCo, they had to spend about $40,000 to change the drink label digitally to Pepsi.[42]

Some critics argue that the practice of product placement has got out of hand: shows are created with the purpose of marketing products rather than for their entertainment value. Some children's shows have been berated for essentially being extended commercials for a toy. One major film company sent a letter to large consumer products companies to solicit product placements for forthcoming film production and even provided a fee scale: US$ 20,000 for the product to be seen in the film; US$ 40,000 for an actor to mention the product by name; and US$ 60,000 for the actor to use the product.[43] The director of strategic planning at Saatchi &

Saatchi New York predicts, 'any space you can take in visually, anything you hear in the future will be branded, I believe. It's not going to be the Washington Monument. It's going to be the *Washington Post* Monument'.[44] From various countries (and the film *Fierce Creatures*!) it is known how companies sponsor zoo animals; often animals are attached to the company through the company logo or name. The live penguin in the Copenhagen zoo thus becomes a representation of the penguin logo of a Danish bank! The 'original' symbolizes the 'copy'!

Media images significantly influence consumers' perceptions of reality, affecting viewers' notions about such issues as dating behaviour, racial stereotypes and occupational status.[45] Studies of the **cultivation hypothesis**, which relates to media's ability to shape consumers' perceptions of reality, have shown that heavy television viewers tend to overestimate the degree of affluence in the country, and these effects also extend to such areas as perceptions of the amount of violence in one's culture.[46] Also, the depiction of consumer environments in programmes and advertisements may lead to further marginalization of e.g. unemployed people, who cannot afford to buy into the depicted lifestyle,[47] or to outright addicted consumers, who cannot refrain from constantly buying various goods, although they may not use these at all.

Consumer addiction is a physiological and/or psychological dependency on products or services. While most people equate addiction with drugs, virtually any product or service can be seen as relieving some problem or satisfying some need to the point where reliance on it becomes extreme. In some cases, it is fairly safe to say that the consumer, not unlike a drug addict, has little or no control over consumption. The products, whether alcohol, cigarettes, chocolate or diet colas, control the consumer. Even the act of shopping itself is an addictive experience for some consumers.[48]

As much advertising and TV programming and many films travel very far, predominantly from the United States to the rest of the world, but also among many other countries, all of these issues are related to the processes of globalization.

Global marketing and culture

Learning about the practices of other cultures is more than just interesting – it is an essential task for any company in the 1990s that wishes to expand its horizons and become part of the international or global marketplace. In this section, we'll consider some of the issues confronting marketers who seek to use a global marketing approach. We'll also consider the consequences of the 'Americanization' or 'Westernization' of global culture, as marketers continue to export Western popular culture to a globe of increasingly affluent consumers, many of whom are eagerly waiting to replace their traditional products and practices with the offerings of Benetton, Levi's, McDonald's, Nestlé and Unilever.

Think globally, act locally

As corporations increasingly find themselves competing in many markets around the world, the debate has intensified regarding the necessity of developing separate marketing plans for each culture. A lively debate has ensued regarding the need to 'fit in' to the local culture. Let's briefly consider each viewpoint.

This Brazilian ad for Electrolux points to the global strength of this company and its products.
Courtesy of Electrolux.

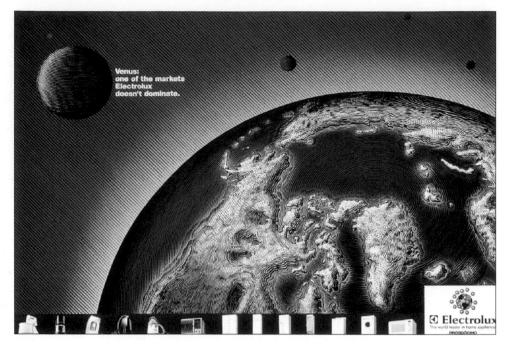

Venus:
one of the markets
Electrolux
doesn't dominate.

Electrolux
The world leader in home appliance

Adopting a standardized strategy

Proponents of a standardized marketing strategy argue that many cultures, especially those of relatively industrialized countries, have become so homogenized that the same approach will work throughout the world. By developing one approach for multiple markets, a company can benefit from economies of scale, since it does not have to incur the substantial time and expense of developing a separate strategy for each culture.[49] This viewpoint represents an **etic perspective**, which focuses on commonalities across cultures. An etic approach to a culture is objective and analytical; it reflects impressions of a culture as viewed by outsiders, which assumes that there are common, general categories and measurements which are valid for all cultures under consideration.

Adopting a localized strategy

On the other hand, many marketers choose to study and analyze a culture using an **emic perspective**, which focuses on variations within a culture. This approach assumes that each culture is unique, with its own value system, conventions and

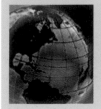

Multicultural dimensions

The *etic* approach has been chosen by many companies who have adopted a standardized strategy for marketing products in Europe. Although the unification of the European Community (in to the European Union) has not happened as smoothly as some predicted, the prospect of many separate economies eventually being massed into one market of 325 million consumers has led many companies to begin to standardize their prices, brand names and advertising.[50]

Many companies are responding to this dramatic change by consolidating the different brands sold in individual countries into common *Eurobrands*. In the United

Multicultural dimensions *continued*

Kingdom and France, for example, the Marathon chocolate bar sold by Mars, Inc., is now called Snickers (a somewhat risky move, considering that the British refer to women's underwear as 'knickers').[51]

Major pan-European or global campaigns in 1996 and 1997 have been launched by such companies, brands and organizations as American Express, Ciba-Geigy, Dockers, Eurotunnel, Hewlett-Packard, Lee Jeans, Mazda, Pepsi, TDK, Visa International, Volvo and WorldWide Fund for Nature.[52]

regulations. This perspective argues that each country has a **national character**, a distinctive set of behaviour and personality characteristics.[53] An effective strategy must be tailored to the sensibilities and needs of each specific culture. An emic approach to a culture is subjective and experiential; it attempts to explain a culture as it is experienced by insiders.

Given the sizeable variations in tastes within a relatively homogeneous country such as the US market, it is hardly surprising that people around the world have developed their own preference. Unlike Americans, for example, Europeans favour plain chocolate over milk chocolate, which they regard as suitable only for children. Whisky is considered a 'classy' drink in France and Italy, but not in England. Crocodile bags are popular in Asia and Europe, but not in the US. Americans' favourite tie colours are red and blue, while the Japanese prefer olive, brown and bronze. Even global brands are perceived differently across markets. In The Netherlands and UK, Heineken beer is positioned (and perceived) as a middle-priced, mainstream beer, while in the US and the rest of Europe, it is perceived (and priced) as a premium beer. Alternatively, Budweiser Beer (the American brand, not the original Czech brand) has a very middle-price and mainstream position in the US, yet is a premium priced beer in Europe and South America.[54]

Superstitions and cultural sensitivities

Marketers must be aware of a culture's norms regarding such sensitive topics as taboos and sexuality. For example, the Japanese are superstitious about the number four. *Shi*, the Japanese word for four, also means death. For this reason, in Japan Tiffany sells glassware and china in sets of five.

The consequences of ignoring these issues became evident during the 1994 soccer World Cup, when both McDonald's and Coca-Cola made the mistake of reprinting the Saudi Arabian flag, which includes sacred words from the Koran, on disposable packaging used in promotions. Despite their delight at having a Saudi team in contention for the Cup, and the satisfaction with Coca-Cola sponsoring the team, Muslims around the world protested at this borrowing of sacred imagery, and both companies had to scramble to rectify the situation.[55]

Cultures vary sharply in the degree to which references to sex and bodily functions is permitted. Many American consumers would blush at much European advertising, where sexuality is much more explicit. This dimension is particularly interesting in Japan, which is a culture of contradictions. On the one hand, the Japanese are publicly shy and polite. On the other hand, sexuality plays a significant role in this society. *Manga*, the extremely popular Japanese comic books which comprise a billion dollar industry, stress themes of sex and violence. Nudity is quite commonplace in Japanese advertising and general media.[56]

In contrast, a recent controversy in India illustrates problems that can arise in a more conservative culture. The government-run television network rejected a spot for KamaSutra condoms which showed a couple sitting on a bed playing chess. As the woman sweeps the pieces off the board, she mouths the word 'Check' while he mouths the word 'Mate'. The tagline reads, 'For the pleasure of making love'.[57]

Multicultural dimensions

Strongly held values can make life very difficult for marketers, especially when they are selling sensitive products. This is the case with tampons; while 70 per cent of American women use them, only 100 million out of a potential market of 1.7 billion eligible women around the world use this product. Resistance to the product posed a major problem for *Tambrands*, which does not make other products and must expand its customer base to remain viable.

The company has found it difficult to sell its feminine hygiene products in some cultures such as Brazil, where many young women fear they will lose their virginity if they use a tampon. A commercial developed for this market included an actress who says in a reassuring voice, 'Of course, you're not going to lose your virginity', while a second woman adds, 'That will happen in a much more romantic way'.

To counteract this problem prior to launching a new global advertising campaign for Tampax in 26 countries, the firm's advertising agency conducted research and divided the world into three clusters based on residents' resistance to using tampons (resistance was so intense in Muslim countries that the agency didn't even attempt to reach women in these markets).

In Cluster One (including the US, the UK and Australia), women felt comfortable with the idea and offered little resistance. A teaser ad was developed to encourage more frequency of use: 'Should I sleep with it, or not?'

In Cluster Two (including France, Israel and South Africa), about 50 per cent of women use the product, but some concerns about virginity remain. To counteract these objections, the marketing strategy focused on obtaining the endorsements of gynaecologists within each country.

In Cluster Three (including Brazil, China and Russia), the greatest resistance was encountered. To try to make inroads in these countries, the researchers found that the first priority is simply to explain how to use the product without making women feel squeamish – a challenge they still are trying to puzzle out.[58]

Does global marketing work?

So, after briefly considering some of the many differences one encounters across cultures globally, the often voiced question still remains – 'does global marketing work'? Given the growth of global brands and global marketing strategies over the past few decades, the practical answer has to be 'yes'. But this doesn't add much in terms of insights for managers. Perhaps the more appropriate question is, '*when* and *why* does it work?'

Although the argument for a homogeneous world culture is appealing in principle, in practice it has met with mixed results. We have discussed how one reason for the difficulties of using a global marketing approach is that consumers in differ-ent countries have different conventions and customs, which may mean that they simply do not use products the same way. Kellogg, for example, discovered that in Brazil big breakfasts are not traditional – cereal is more commonly eaten as a dry snack.

Some large corporations, such as Coca-Cola, have been successful in crafting a single, international image. Still, even Coca-Cola must make minor modifications to the way it presents itself in each culture. Although Coke commercials are largely standardized, local agencies are permitted to edit them to highlight close-ups of local faces.[59]

As the world's borders seem to shrink due to advances in communications, many companies continue to develop global advertising campaigns. In some cases they are encountering obstacles to acceptance, especially in less-developed countries or in those areas, such as Central and Eastern Europe, that are only beginning to embrace Western-style materialism as a way of life.[60]

To maximize the chances of success for these multicultural efforts, marketers must locate consumers in different countries who none the less share a common worldview. This is more likely to be the case among people whose frame of refer-ence is relatively more international or cosmopolitan, and/or who receive much of their information about the world from sources that incorporate a world-wide perspective.

Who is likely to fall into this category? The same two segments which were candidates for pan-European marketing: (1) affluent people who are 'global citizens' and who are exposed to ideas from around the world through their travels, business contacts, and media experiences, and as a result share common tastes, and (2) young people whose tastes in music and fashion are strongly influenced by inter-national pop culture broadcasting many of the same images and sounds to multiple countries.[61]

Marketing pitfall

The language barrier is one problem confronting marketers who wish to break into foreign markets. One technique that is used to avoid this problem is where a translated ad is retranslated into the original language by a different interpreter to catch errors. Some specific translation obstacles that have been encountered around the world include the following.[62]

- Wrigley's Spearmint Gum reads as 'Shark's sperm' in some East European countries.
- When Vauxhall launched its 'Nova' model in Spain, it realized that the name meant 'doesn't go' in Spanish.
- Also in Spain, Mitsubishi discovered that its four-wheel drive model Pajero would be known as 'Wanker'.
- When Rolls Royce introduced its 'Silver Mist' model in Germany, it found that the word 'mist' is translated as excrement. Similarly, Sunbeam's hair curling iron, called the 'Mist-Stick', translated as manure wand. To add insult to injury, Vicks is German slang for sexual intercourse, so that company's name had to be changed to Wicks in this market.

The Coca-Cola invasion: exporting Western lifestyles

The allure of Western consumer culture has spread throughout the world, as people in other societies slowly but surely fall under the spell of far-reaching advertising campaigns, contact with tourists and the desire to form attachments with other parts of the world. This attraction sometimes results in bizarre permutations of products and services, as they are modified to be compatible with local customs. Consider these events:[63]

- In Peru, Indian boys can be found carrying rocks painted to look like transistor radios.
- In Papua New Guinea, some tribesmen put Chivas Regal wrappers on their drums and wear Pentel pens through their nose, instead of traditional nose bones.
- Bana tribesmen in the remote highlands of Kako, Ethiopia, pay to watch 'Pluto the Circus Dog' on a Viewmaster.
- When a Swazi princess marries a Zulu king, she wears red touraco wing feathers around her forehead and a cape of windowbird feathers and oxtails. He is wrapped in a leopard skin. All is recorded on a Kodak movie camera while the band plays 'The Sound of Music'.
- In addition to traditional gifts of cloth, food and cosmetics, Nigerian Hausa brides receive cheap quartz watches although they cannot tell the time.

'I'd like to buy the world a Coke'

As indicated by these examples, many formerly isolated cultures now incorporate Western objects into their traditional practices. In the process, the meanings of these objects are transformed and adapted to local tastes (at times in seemingly bizarre ways). Sometimes the process enriches local cultures, sometimes it produces painful stresses and strains the local fabric.

The West (and especially the US) is a *net exporter* of popular culture. Western symbols in the form of images, words and products have diffused throughout the world. This influence is eagerly sought by many consumers, who have learned to equate Western lifestyles in general and the English language in particular with modernization and sophistication. As a result, people around the world are being exposed to a blizzard of Western products that are attempting to become part of local lifestyles.

For example, American-inspired TV game shows are popular around the world: *Geh Aufs Ganze* (Let's Make a Deal) is one of Germany's top shows. Although *The Dating Game* went off the air in the US in 1989, it is now seen in ten foreign countries and is top in its time slot in Poland, Finland and England, where it's called *Blind Date*. In Singapore a cult has formed around locally produced broadcasts of *The $25,000 Pyramid*, while in France *Le Juste Prix* (The Price is Right) attracts almost half the country's viewers. Not everyone in these countries is happy with the Western influence – producers of *The Dating Game* in Turkey received death threats from Muslim fundamentalists.[64]

The American appeal is so strong that some non-US companies go out of their way to create an American image. A British ad for Blistex lip cream, for example, includes a fictional woman named 'Miss Idaho Lovely Lips' who claims Blistex is 'America's best-selling lip cream'.[65] Recent attempts by American marketers to 'invade' other countries include:

As this Swedish ad for Wrangler jeans shows, products associated with the 'authentic' American West are in demand around the world.
Courtesy of Wrangler Europe.

- Kellogg is trying to carve out a market for breakfast cereal in India, even though currently only about 3 per cent of Indian households eat such products. Most middle-class Indians eat a traditional hot breakfast which includes such dishes as chapatis (unleavened bread) and *dosas* (a fried pancake), but the company is confident that it can entice them to make the switch to Corn Flakes, Froot Loops and other American delicacies.[66]
- The National Basketball Association is fast becoming the first truly global sports league. Nearly $500 million of licensed merchandise was sold *outside* the US in 1996. A survey of 28,000 teenagers in 45 countries conducted by the DMB&B advertising agency found that Michael Jordan is by far the world's favourite athlete. In China, his Chicago Bulls team (translated as 'The Red Oxen') is virtually everyone's favourite.[67]
- The British are avid tea drinkers, but how will they react to American-style iced tea? US companies like Snapple are hoping they can convince the British that iced tea is more than hot tea that's gone cold. These firms may have some way to go, based on the reactions of one British construction worker who tried a canned iced tea for the first time: 'It was bloody awful'.[68]
- Pizza Hut is invading, of all places, Italy. The country that invented pizza will be exposed to the American mass-produced version, quite a different dish from the local pizza, which is often served on porcelain dishes and eaten with a knife and fork. On the other hand, one of Pizza Hut's top performing restaurants is now located in Paris, a centre of fine cuisine, so only time will tell if Italians will embrace pizza 'American-style'.[69]

The West invades Asia

Although a third of the world's countries have a per capita GNP of less than $500, people around the world now have access to Western media, where they can watch reruns of shows like *Lifestyles of the Rich and Famous* and *Dallas*, idealized tributes to the opulence of Western lifestyles. To illustrate the impact of this imagery around the world, it is interesting to compare its impact in two very different Asian countries.

Consider how the material expectations of consumers in the People's Republic of China have escalated. Twenty years ago, the Chinese strove to attain what they called the 'three bigs': bikes, sewing machines and wristwatches. This wish list was later modified to become the 'new big six', adding refrigerators, washing machines and televisions. At the last count, the ideal is now the 'eight new things'. The list now includes *colour* televisions, cameras and video recorders.[70] Chinese women are starting to demand Western cosmetics costing up to a quarter of their salaries, ignoring domestically produced competitors. As one Chinese executive noted, 'Some women even buy a cosmetic just because it has foreign words on the package'.[71]

In contrast to China, the Japanese have already become accustomed to a bounty of consumer goods. Still, the Japanese are particularly enthusiastic borrowers of Western culture. American music and films are especially popular, perhaps because they are the best way to experience US lifestyles and popular culture. They have even recreated an entire Dutch village (complete with real Dutch people who 'perform' daily), which is one of Japan's top honeymoon destinations.

The Japanese often use Western words as a shorthand for anything new and exciting, even if they do not understand their meaning. The resulting phenomenon is known as 'Japlish', where new Western-sounding words are merged with Japanese. Cars are given names like Fairlady, Gloria and Bongo Wagon. Consumers buy *deodoranto* (deodorant) and *appuru pai* (apple pie). Ads urge shoppers to *stoppu rukku* (stop and look), and products are claimed to be *yuniku* (unique).[72] Coca-Cola cans say 'I feel Coke & sound special', and a company called Cream Soda sells products with the slogan 'Too old to die, too young to be happy'.[73] Other Japanese products with English names include Mouth Pet (breath freshener), Pocari Sweat ('refreshment water'), Armpit (electric razor), Brown Gross Foam (hair-colouring mousse), Virgin Pink Special (skin cream), Cow Brand (beauty soap) and Mymorning Water (canned water).[74]

Mainland China is one of the newest markets opening up to Western business and culture. When McDonald's opened in Beijing in the early 1990s, this new restaurant became their largest outlet in the world with more than 700 seats and 1,000 employees. Many competed for these highly valued positions that are perceived to offer prestige and upward mobility.

Photo courtesy of © Kees/Sygma.

This poster promotes the Tom Cruise film *Far and Away* to the Japanese, who are huge fans of American popular culture.
© Jeffrey Aaronson/Aspen Network.

Emerging consumer cultures in transitional economies

In the early 1980s the American TV show *Dallas* was broadcast by the Romanian Communist government to show the decadence of Western capitalism. The strategy backfired, and instead the devious (but rich!) J.R. became a revered icon in parts of Eastern Europe and the Middle East – to the extent that a tourist attraction outside Bucharest includes a big white log gate that announces (in English) the name: 'South Fork Ranch'.[75] Western 'decadence' appears to be infectious.[76]

After the collapse of communism, Eastern Europeans emerged from a long winter of deprivation into a springtime of abundance. The picture is not all rosy, however, since attaining consumer goods is not easy for many in **transitional economies**, where the economic system is still 'neither fish nor fowl', and governments ranging from China to Portugal struggle with the difficult adaptation from a controlled, centralized economy to a free market system. These problems stem from such factors as the unequal distribution of income among citizens, as well as striking rural–urban differences in expectations and values. The key aspect of a transitional economy is the rapid change required on social, political and economic dimensions as the populace is suddenly exposed to global communications and external market pressures.[77]

Some of the consequences of the transition to capitalism include a loss of confidence and pride in the local culture, as well as alienation, frustration and an increase in stress as leisure time is sacrificed to work ever harder to buy consumer goods. The yearning for the trappings of Western material culture is perhaps most evident in parts of Eastern Europe, where citizens who threw off the shackles of communism now have direct access to coveted consumer goods from the US and Western Europe – if they can afford them. One analyst observed, 'as former subjects of the Soviet empire dream it, the American dream has very little to do with liberty and justice for all and a great deal to do with soap operas and the Sears Catalogue'.[78]

In 1990 more than sixty countries had a GNP of *less* than $10 billion. In contrast, more than 135 transnational companies had revenues greater than that figure. The dominance of these marketing powerhouses has helped to create a *globalized consumption ethic*. As people the world over increasingly are surrounded by goods and tempting images of them, a material lifestyle becomes more important to attain. Shopping evolves from being a weary, task-oriented struggle to locate even basic necessities to one of a leisure activity, where possessing consumer goods becomes a mechanism to display one's status – often at great personal sacrifice. In Turkey one researcher met a rural consumer, a mother who deprived her child of nutritious milk from the family's cow and instead sold it in order to be able to buy sweets for her child because 'what is good for city kids is also good for my child'.[79] As the global consumption ethic spreads, the products wished for in different cultures become homogenized – Christmas now is celebrated among some urbanites in Muslim Turkey, even though gift-giving (even on birthdays) is not customary in many parts of that country.

In some cases, the meanings of these desired products are adapted to local customs and needs. In Turkey some urban women use ovens to dry clothes and dishwashers to wash muddy spinach. The process of **creolization** occurs when foreign influences are absorbed and integrated with local meanings – just as modern Christianity incorporated the pagan Christmas tree into its own rituals. Thus, a traditional clothing style such as a *bilum* worn in Papua New Guinea may be combined with Western items like Mickey Mouse shirts or baseball caps.[80] These processes make it unlikely that global homogenization will overwhelm local cultures, but rather that there will be multiple consumer cultures, each blending global icons such as Nike's pervasive 'swoosh', with indigenous products and meanings.

Consumption of global products and symbols: Japanese motorcyclists with 'chopped' bikes, jackets, jeans and that 'rebel' look.
Harley Davidson Inc. Used with permission.

Consumer resistance: back to the roots?

Despite the proliferation of Western culture around the world, there are signs that this invasion is slowing. Japanese consumers are beginning to show signs of waning interest in foreign products as the health of their country's economy declines. Some of the latest 'hot' products in Japan now include green tea and *yukata*, traditional printed cotton robes donned after the evening bath.[81] Several locally made products are catching on in parts of Eastern Europe due to their lower prices, improved quality, combined with the perceptions that sometimes the imported products are inferior versions. Some Muslims are rejecting Western symbols as they adhere to a green Islamic philosophy which includes using natural, traditional products.[82]

Some critics in other countries deplore the creeping Americanization of their cultures. Debates continue in many countries on the imposition of quotas that limit American television programming.[83] The conflict created by exporting American culture was brought to a head in recent trade negotiations on WTO (the global trade agreement), which deadlocked over the export of American films to Europe (the US share of the European cinema market is about 75 per cent). As one French official put it, 'French films are the cinema of creation. American films are products of marketing.'[84]

In Europe the French have been the most outspoken opponents of creeping Americanization. They have even tried to ban the use of such 'Franglish' terms as *le drugstore*, *le fast food* and even *le marketing*, though this effort was recently ruled unconstitutional.[85] The French debate over cultural contamination was brought to a head by the 1991 opening of Euro Disney in a Paris suburb. In addition to the usual attractions, hotels with names like The Hotel New York, The Newport Bay Club and The Hotel Cheyenne attempt to recreate regions of America. The park seems to have rebounded after a shaky start, including renaming it Disneyland Paris since Euro Disney somehow seemed incompatible. But some Europeans have been less than enthusiastic about the cultural messages being sent by the Disney organization. One French critic described the theme park as 'a horror made of cardboard, plastic and appalling colours – a construction of hardened chewing gum and idiotic folklore taken straight out of a comic book written for obese Americans'.[86]

Marketing pitfall

Cigarettes are among the most successful of Western exports. Asian consumers alone spend $90 billion a year on cigarettes, and Western tobacco manufacturers continue to push relentlessly into these markets. Cigarette advertising, often depicting glamorous Western models and settings, is found just about everywhere, on hoardings, buses, shopfronts and clothing, and many major sports and cultural events are sponsored by tobacco companies. Some companies even hand out cigarettes and gifts in amusement areas, often to pre-teens.

A few countries have taken steps to counteract this form of Westernization. Singapore bans all promotions that mention a product's name. Hong Kong has prohibited cigarette ads from appearing on radio and TV. Japan and South Korea do not allow ads to appear in women's magazines. Industry executives argue that they are simply competing in markets that do little to discourage smoking (e.g. Japan issues health warnings like 'Please don't smoke too much'), often against heavily subsidized local brands with names like Long Life (Taiwan). The warnings and restrictions are likely to increase, however; smoking-related deaths have now overtaken communicable diseases for the 'honour' of being Asia's No. 1 killer.[87]

Postmodernism?

Many of the themes mentioned earlier in this chapter, such as the globalization process, reality engineering or the blurring of the fashion picture have been linked to larger social processes dominating the last part of the twentieth century. One proposed summary term for these processes is **postmodernism** – one of the most widely discussed and disputed terms in consumer research in the past five years.[88]

Postmodernists argue that we live in a modern era where we share beliefs in certain central values of modernism and industrialism. Examples of these values include the benefits of economic growth and industrial production, and the infallibility of science. In opposition, postmodernism questions the search for universal truths and values, and the existence of objective knowledge.[89] Thus a keyword is **pluralism**, indicating the coexistence of various truths, styles and fashions. Consumers (and producers) are relatively free to combine elements from different styles and domains to create their own personal expression.

There have been several attempts to sum up features of postmodernism and their implications for marketing and consumer behaviour.[90] Together with pluralism, one European researcher has suggested that postmodernism can be described by six key features:[91]

- **Fragmentation.** The splitting up of what used to be simpler and more mass-oriented, exemplified by the ever-growing product ranges and brand extensions in more and more specialized variations. Even within the retailing environment we experience the proliferation of outlets within the concentration of bigger outlets (shopping malls). Such specialized and stylized outlets often carry an in-depth assortment of a very narrow product range, such as teas or ties. The advertising media has also become fragmented, with more and more specialized TV channels, magazines, radio stations and web sites for placing one's advertising.
- **De-differentiation.** Postmodernists are interested in the blurring of distinctions between hierarchies such as 'high and low culture', or 'politics and show business'. Examples would be the use of artistic works in advertising and the celebration of advertising as artistic works. Companies such as Coca-Cola, Nike and Guinness have their own museums. Another clear example is the blurring of advertisements and TV programmes, wherein more and more TV programmes feature advertising for themselves (in order to increase viewer ratings) and TV commercials look like 'real' programming, as in the ongoing soap opera with a couple spun around the coffee brand 'Gold Blend'. The blurring of gender categories also refer to this aspect of postmodernism.
- **Hyperreality.** The spreading of simulations and the loss of sense of the 'real' and 'authentic' as in the cases of re-engineered environments discussed earlier in this chapter. Shopping centres simulating ancient Rome (The *Forum* in Las Vegas), a Parisian street (West Edmonton Mall, Canada). Finally, products can be hyperreal to the extent that they simulate something else. For instance, sugarless sugar, fat-free fat (olestra) or the butter replacement brand 'I can't believe it's not butter!'. In fact, it has been argued that marketing may be the most important contributor to the creation of hyperreality, since the essence of marketing and particularly advertising is to create a simulated reality by resignifying words, situations and brands.[92]

The seventeenth-century Danish landmark of the 'round tower' of Copenhagen has been recreated (in a slightly smaller version) in the simulated Danish environment of Solvang, California, founded as a 'little Denmark' by Danish immigrants in the nineteenth century, but gradually becoming more of a hyperreal theme park under the influence of marketing in the post-war period. The tower in Solvang houses a local pizza restaurant: Tower Pizza, of course!
Photo: Søren Askegaard.

Marketing pitfall

Sometimes companies may fall victim to their own hyperreality. It is the dream of many producers to create a strong brand with a thorough position in the cultural life. But as they do so, their brand images are incorporated into the general cultural sign system, and the company loses control over the signs attached to the brand name. For example, the name 'Barbie' today is much more than a brand name – it has almost become a name for a personality type. When a Danish pop group, Aqua, enjoyed a huge success with the song 'Barbie' containing lyrics alluding to the sex life of this hyperreal personality (e.g. 'you can dress my hair, undress me everywhere') the Mattel Inc. Company was not amused. They sued the pop group for abuse of the Barbie name and for destroying the pure and positive image of Barbie's world created through a long range of expensive campaigns. This is yet another example of the blurring of marketing and popular culture, and the question is: Can you patent culture?[93]

● **Chronology.** This refers to the consumers' search for the authentic and a preoccupation with the past – like real or authentic Chinese or Italian foods or the search for one's nostalgic roots in foods (or other consumer goods) as we 'used to know it'.[94] Likewise, the increase in the 'no-nonsense' formats of various advertising campaigns may be seen as a return to a simpler, less contrived period of the past. What appeals to consumers here is that in a period of accelerating change, the stability of the good old days remains comforting.

- **Pastiche.** The playful and ironic mixing of existing categories and styles is typical of pastiche. An example would be one advertisement doing a parody of another or making references to slogans or other elements borrowed from other campaigns. Pastiche also involves self-referentiality (i.e. the advertisement recognizes itself as being an ad, by showing (mock) scenes from its own creative process). Table 16.3 provides a set of examples of such parodies and self-referentialities from British advertising. Self-referentiality may create hyperreality, as when a British ad for the yellow pages featured an author searching for a retail store where he could find a copy of his own old book about fly fishing actually led to the writing of such a book. Needless to say, when the book was launched, the advertisement was re-run![95]

  Other pastiches flourish, as when we see deliberate blurring of styles such as advertisements borrowing from films, or films and TV programmes borrowing from the advertisement style, all of it done 'tongue-in-cheek'. A British ad for cream depicted a Mona Lisa looking first to one side, then to the other, then she would draw out an eclair (cake with cream) and munch it followed by the pay-off line: 'Naughty but nice'.[96] Indeed, one discussion of postmodernism and its impact on marketing was in itself a pastiche using a lot of cinematic metaphors and changed film titles to structure its chapters.[97]

- **Anti-foundationalism.** This last feature of postmodern marketing efforts refers not to parody but to an outright 'anti-campaign campaign' – for example campaigns encouraging the receiver of the message *not* to take notice of the message since somebody is trying to seduce and take advantage of him/her. Other examples include anti-product products like 'death brand

Table 16.3 **A few examples of pastiche in British advertising**

Category	Content	Examples
Parody		
Direct	One advertisement parodies another	Carling Black Label (lager) spoof of Levi's (jeans) celebrated 'laundrette' sequence
Indirect	Advert 'appropriates' byline/icon etc. of another	Do It All (DIY superstores) advertised 'the united colors of Do It All' (Benetton)
Self-referentiality		
Direct	Adverts about advertising (set in advertising agency; adverts for forthcoming ads, etc.)	Next 'instalment' of advertising soap operas (Renault 21 family; Gold Blend couple, etc.) advertised beforehand
Indirect	Retransmission of old adverts that have acquired new meanings in the interim, or stylistic evocation of old ads	Repeat showings of 'I'm going well, I'm going Shell' series featuring Bing Crosby etc. Once innovative, now quaint

cigarettes', Jolt Cola ('with all the caffeine and twice the sugar'[98]) or the Icelandic Aquavit brand's appropriation of its own nickname 'black death', complete with new labels including skulls. Finally, there's 'anti-fashion' – consumers' claim that they search for certain types of ugliness when buying shoes and clothing in order to construct a very personal and ostentatious style (sound like anyone you know?).[99] The green movement and the political consumer discussed above, as well as groups involved in movements of voluntary simplicity (particularly active in the United States) or the like, can be seen as anti-foundational in their rejection of standard products in favour of alternative choices which they perceive as less harmful to the natural and human environments.

Postmodernism has also been attached to such themes as the ability of readers to look through the hype of advertising.[100] This may suggest that we are becoming more skilled consumers and readers/interpreters of advertising, recognising ads as hyperreal persuasion or seduction attempts which do not intend to reflect our own daily experiences. This skilled readership may have sparked various of the tendencies to anti-ads or pastiches discussed above. Another process attached to postmodernism is the greater appreciation of the aesthetics of everyday life,[101] referring to the tendency to focus more and more on the design and appearance of goods or buildings.

Certain postmodernists stress the liberatory aspects of postmodernism – that consumers are free to play with symbols and create their own constellations of products and lifestyles from available elements while being less concerned with norms and standards. Since there is an inherent scepticism in postmodernism, a postmodernist attitude is also a critical attitude.[102] Others point to the fact that the refusal to accept, indeed to *care* about values, may lead to passivity and political degener-

Self-parody is one approach to communication in our postmodern era.
Used with permission.

ation of societies[103] and to the inherent contradictions within the positions taken by postmodernists.[104] Whether one sees the 'postmodern consumer' as a critical and creative person, or as a passive, entertainment-seeking 'couch potato', the changes in marketing and consumption referred to in the postmodern framework are fundamental for understanding changes in our European markets as we race towards the end of the twentieth century.

Chapter summary

- The styles prevalent in a culture at any point in time often reflect underlying political and social conditions. The set of agents responsible for creating stylistic alternatives is termed a culture production system. Factors such as the types of people involved in this system and the amount of competition by alternative product forms influence the choices that eventually make their way to the marketplace for consideration by end consumers.

- Culture is often described in terms of high (or elite) forms and low (or popular) forms. Products of popular culture tend to follow a cultural formula and contain predictable components. On the other hand, these distinctions are blurring in modern society as imagery from 'high art' is increasingly being incorporated into marketing efforts and marketed products (or even marketing products like advertisements) are treated and evaluated as high art.

- The fashion system includes everyone involved in the creation and transference of symbolic meanings. Meanings that express common cultural categories (e.g. gender distinctions) are conveyed by many different products. New styles tend to be adopted by many people simultaneously in a process known as collective selection. Perspectives on motivations for adopting new styles include psychological, economic and sociological models of fashion.

- Fashions tend to follow cycles that resemble the product life cycle. The two extremes of fashion adoption, classics and fads, can be distinguished in terms of the length of this cycle.

- Followers of an *etic perspective* believe that the same universal messages will be appreciated by people in many cultures. Believers in an *emic perspective* argue that individual cultures are too unique to permit such standardization; marketers instead must adapt their approaches to be consistent with local values and practices. Attempts at global marketing have met with mixed success; in many cases this approach is more likely to work if the messages appeal to basic values and/or if the target markets consist of consumers who are more internationally rather than locally oriented.

- The Western world is a net exporter of popular culture. Consumers around the world have eagerly adopted Western products, especially entertainment vehicles and items that are linked symbolically to a uniquely Western lifestyle (e.g., Marlboro, Levi's, BMW, Nestlé). Despite or because of the continuing 'Americanization' or 'Westernization' of cultures in the world, some consumers are alarmed by this influence, and are instead emphasizing a return to local products and customs.

- Postmodernism involves processes of social change in an era, where the 'grand truths' of modernism, such as scientific knowledge or the progressiveness of economic growth are no longer taken for granted. Postmodernism includes social processes such as fragmentation, de-differentiation, hyperreality, chronology, pastiche and anti-foundationalism.

---🔑 **Key terms**

Anti-foundationalism *(p. 468)*
Art product *(p. 442)*
Chronology *(p. 467)*
Classic *(p. 452)*
Collective selection *(p. 447)*
Conspicuous consumption *(p. 448)*
Consumer addiction *(p. 455)*
Craft product *(p. 442)*
Creolization *(p. 464)*
Cultivation hypothesis *(p. 455)*
Cultural categories *(p. 446)*
Cultural formula *(p. 443)*
Cultural gatekeepers *(p. 442)*
Cultural production system (CPS) *(p. 440)*
Cultural selection *(p. 439)*
De-differentiation *(p. 466)*
Emic perspective *(p. 456)*

Erogenous zones *(p. 448)*
Etic perspective *(p. 456)*
Fad *(p. 453)*
Fashion *(p. 446)*
Fashion acceptance cycle *(p. 450)*
Fashion life cycle *(p. 450)*
Fashion system *(p. 445)*
Fragmentation *(p. 466)*
Hyperreality *(p. 466)*
National character *(p. 457)*
Pastiche *(p. 468)*
Pluralism *(p. 466)*
Postmodernism *(p. 466)*
Product placement *(p. 454)*
Reality engineering *(p. 453)*
Transitional economies *(p. 463)*
Trickle-down theory *(p. 449)*

Consumer behaviour challenge

1. Construct a 'biography' of a product, tracing its progress from the time it was introduced. How long did it take to diffuse to the mass market? Do the same consumers use the product now as did those who first adopted it? What are its future prospects – is it destined for obsolescence? Would you characterize the product as either a classic or a fad?

2. Some consumers complain that they are 'at the mercy' of designers: they are forced to buy whatever styles are in fashion, because nothing else is available. Do you agree that there is such a thing as a 'designer conspiracy'?

3. What is the basic difference between a fad, a fashion and a classic? Provide examples of each.

4. What is the difference between an art and a craft? Where would you characterize advertising within this framework?

5. The chapter mentions some instances where market research findings influenced artistic decisions, as when a film ending was reshot to accommodate consumers' preferences. Many people would oppose this use of consumer research, claiming that books, films, records or other artistic endeavours should not be designed merely to conform to what people want to read, see or hear. What do you think?

6. What role does the globalization process play in your personal consumption profile? After reflecting on that, take a walk in your nearest shopping area and look for signs of the global and the local. What is from 'somewhere else'? What is distinctively local? Are there mixtures, or are these two domains separate?

7. Try to collect advertisements that reflect the postmodern features of fragmentation, de-differentiation, hyperreality, chronology, pastiche and anti-foundationalism.

8. Reflect on your and your friends' consumption patterns in the same light. What do you see?

Case study problems

CASE STUDY I

Tatlises Lahmacun

Toygun Ozdem, Bilkent University, Ankara

The Turkish public first became aware of Ibrahim Tatlises from listening to his folk songs, performed in an impressive voice and with a distinctive style of interpretation. He performed in a style of music known as 'Arabesk', of Arabic origin and depicting the lives, loves and fortunes of poor and deprived people. This style of music captured the attention of Turkish people and his cassettes were sold in large numbers. This came as something of a surprise to him, as he became famous while still employed as a plasterer in the construction industry, thus adding to his 'folk' appeal.

While maintaining his singing career, he began making appearances in films and working as a film producer. Then he established his own public transportation company, known as Tatlises Bus Tourism Company, followed by a Tatlises Radio Channel. But the most important of his enterprises, in terms of profitability and growth potential, was the establishment of a fast-food restaurant chain known as Tatlises Lahmacun.

Following the success of the first Tatlises Lahmacun fast-food restaurant, a franchise system was implemented. The franchisees would pay $100,000 as brand equity (the equivalent charged by McDonalds is $35,000). Under this system, a percentage of the revenue is returned to the parent company. The first restaurant was established in 1993. The number of restaurants now stands at 21 nationwide, 14 of which are in Istanbul. *Tatlises* is now a familiar household name despite the absence of an advertising campaign for the Lahmacun restaurants. The management is planning to increase the number of restaurants to 63, and to expand into the wider European market in 1998.

One of the secrets underlying the success of Tatlises Lahmacun is the perception of lahmacun in the minds of the Turkish people as being a traditional,[1] tasty[2] and popular[3] Turkish meal. Lahmacun is prepared by laying a mixture of minced meat, onion, tomato and various spices (a mixture of 12 ingredients) on a thin, round-shaped dough. It is baked in a wood burning oven. Although it is still traditional fare in rural areas, it has been almost forgotten by urbanites. Establishing the restaurants has repopularised lahmacun as a familiar and typically Turkish snack.

The increasing interest in local and regional foods and music is significant in this achievement. The recent increase in publications and sales of new cookery books on regional and local foods, and new songs drawing on traditional musical elements, are evidence of the need by Turkish people to acknowledge their heritage. Lahmacun is a traditional food from the south-east of Turkey, the homeland of Tatlises.

As with the rest of the world, the issue of ethnic origin has become a growing concern in the Turkish national psyche. Turkish people have been publicly examining their cultural backgrounds. The aim is not to deny the Turk identity, rather to acknowledge individual local heritages as well. In this way, cultural variations are being rediscovered and practised. Thus Lahmacun represents not just a traditional dish, but also the cultural values of its region.

Another factor in the success of Tatlises Lahmacun could be Ibrahim Tatlises himself. He is well known by everybody and, on the whole, is well-liked. There is some unease with regard to the cultural values that Arabesk music embraces. If a cultural map of Turkey is drawn, a clear gap emerges between west and east. People in western Turkey are more like Europeans and are receptive to European lifestyles, possibly as a result of their exposure to European technology, wealth and culture. They perceive Western culture as modern and adopt Western behaviours. One of these is listening to foreign pop music, so Arabesk music is seen as regressive. A second reason is related to Tatlises' tough, macho behaviour, his distinctive accent and his 'humble peasant' persona. This causes some resentment. However, generally the public's feelings towards him are neutral and some very positive. As a result, his restaurants command a brand loyalty over imitators, many of whom copy Tatlises Lahmacun's characteristic green and yellow colours.

At a typical Tatlises Lahmacun restaurant, one can have lahmacun with lemon slices and parsley leaves, künefe,[4] ayran[5] or cola. However, there are variations in the menus depending on local demand and the local competitive environment. While some of the restaurants may even serve döner,[6] soup and offer a salad bar, others only serve lahmacun. Although the management of Tatlises Lahmacun fast-food restaurants has been trying to vary the menu by adding some extra options such as döner, salad bar and soup to the menu, they realise that this kind of diversification may degrade the image of Tatlises Lahmacun restaurants, such that they are perceived as ordinary kebap[7] restaurants. Besides, the management has been trying to develop new types of lahmacun made with chicken meat or diet lahmacun (including soybean, etc. without meat) or frozen lahmacun to be sold in department stores.

All Tatlises Lahmacun restaurants adopt modern fast-food restaurant decor. The dominant colour of the furniture and walls is yellow and green, the colour of Tatlises' hometown football team. Some of the restaurants provide customers with a convivial atmosphere enhanced by flowers and small trees, a playing area for children and popular Turkish and foreign music. Continual cleaning is maintained by uniformed employees. Survey results showed that this activity is highly valued by customers.

The kitchen is on full view to the public, who can see lahmacun being hand-made and baked in an oven. The self-service nature of the restaurant means that food is provided quickly. Some respondents noted that two portions of lahmacun are as satisfying as one BigMac, at nearly half the price.

The company has an all-embracing target market of mixed-age and income customers, who have a liking for lahmacun and are familiar with the notion of fast-food. Customers state that they feel at home and in a comfortable atmosphere in the restaurants. The management believes that by offering top quality and service, premium prices can be justified.

Interested parties in countries such as Germany, UK, Israel and Japan have sought permission to franchise new lahmacun restaurants. However, senior management are reluctant to commit to rapid expansion. On the other hand, Turkey's tourists are willing to sample the country's cuisine. This, coupled with outside interest, will result in management exploring the possibility of expansion into the European market in 1998.

Expanding the concept into the European market highlights some questions:

Questions

1. Discuss various options Tatlises lahmacun has in order to develop a positive image among Europe's fast food consumers?

2. On which cultural foundations could such an image be constructed?

3. How is consumer culture, notably myths and rituals, relevant for Tatlises lahmacun?

4. According to which of the following criteria should countries be selected for the expansion: geographic proximity? buying power of segments? pre-established fast-food culture? food culture in general?

5. Should the menu be adapted to local conditions or kept 'Turkish'?

6. Should the interior design be kept global or 'Turkeyfied' in order to convey the message of exoticism?

Notes

1. It is traditional and popular, has been eaten for years and is still the preferred food at some occasions. At wedding ceremonies in eastern Turkish villages, it has always been included on the menu.

2. In the survey, nearly all of the respondents stated that if it is properly prepared, it can be really delicious.

3. It is well known and people tend to have it if available. Most of the respondents said that they would eat it if there were quality lahmacun restaurants to hand. However, the perception of availability varied between respondents.

4. Künefe is a baked dessert that has a soft cheese filling inside layers of dough filaments and is eaten hot. Originating from south-east Anatolia, it is not commonly available in other parts of Turkey and is hence a speciality item.

5. Ayran is a very traditional drink which is a mixture of yoghurt and water.

6. Döner is meat roasted on a revolving vertical spit and after being cut in thin slices, is served with pilaff rice or inside bread.

7. At an ordinary kebap restaurant, it takes time to prepare the main meal, so appetizers are served with special breads. Salads are offered with the main meal. Turkish people go to these restaurants with their friends and have long chats while waiting for the meal. After the meal tea or Turkish coffee is served.

CASE STUDY 2

Attention to and perception of cinema commercials

Christian Alsted, Alsted Marketing Research, Copenhagen

In a recent survey carried out among Danish cinema-goers it was demonstrated that 93 per cent of them were seated before the first commercial was shown. Also, ongoing research has demonstrated much higher recall and understanding of basic intended messages in cinema advertising than in TV commercials. In short, Danish cinema-goers love to watch the commercials before a movie, which is not the case for TV commercials. Therefore it is likely that commercials aired in cinemas have much more potential for influencing viewers than TV commercials have. Up until now, no explanations of this phenomenon had been provided.

In an attempt to clarify this issue, six measures were made of certain commercials which were aired for the first time simultaneously in cinemas and on TV. In addition to a simple ad recollection test, the quality of respondents' memory were measured. Did respondents understand the messages of the commercials? Results from these measurements indicate that cinema commercials have three times the communication value of their TV-aired counterparts (see Figure 1).

Figure 1
Communication value, 13–29 year olds: comparison between 6 commercials shown on television and in the cinema

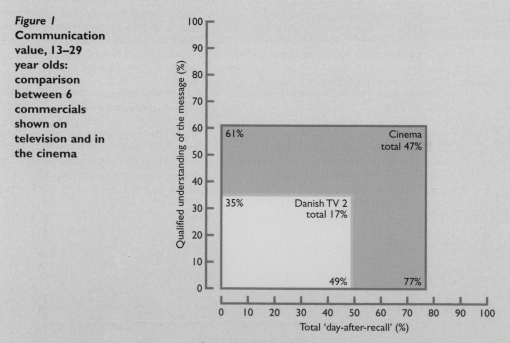

Cinema has 2.8 times better communication value than television

The survey thus demonstrated that audiences in cinemas are mentally more ready to process new stimuli. It was also shown that this cinema-context has a positive effect on the commercials in the cinemas. Viewing commercials in cinemas is a part of the overall 'cinema experience' and a conscious or subconscious transfer occurs from viewers' positive expectations towards the movie they are about to see, to the commercial.

When it was subsequently qualitatively examined which specific qualities viewers associate with cinema commercials six different values were detected: high quality, opening, entertainment, actions, novelty, luxury. The positive associations with cinema commercials are transferred to the advertised products. In other words the products advertised are met with a positive attitude and can rely on a positive initial reception by viewers.

When the lights go out and the commercials start, an instant and drastic increase in attention among the audience can be observed (see Figure 2). This heightened attention reaches its first peak in the beginning of the set of commercials and then flattens out. This contrasts with the attention-pattern found with TV commercials where attention is more fragmented. With TV it is more a case of floating peaks and troughs in the attention of the audience (see Figure 3).

Going to the cinema is seen as an 'event', and viewing the advertisements is considered as part of this event. This is important because 'events' are associated with positive expectations. The event itself can be split into three parts (Figure 2). First there is the warm-up with commercials. Then trailers ensue which are also important. They are seen less as 'commercials' for coming films and more as 'appetisers' of coming cultural events. Finally, there is the film. In this tripartite construct all parts are important. Young people in particular see commercials and trailers as a good warm-up to the film. Many young

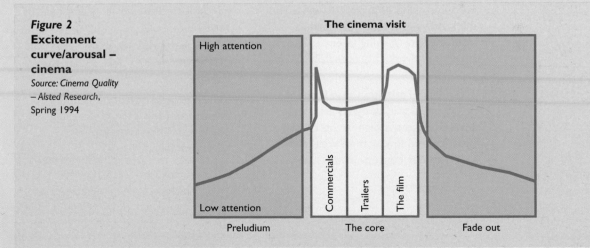

Figure 2
Excitement curve/arousal – cinema
Source: Cinema Quality – Alsted Research, Spring 1994

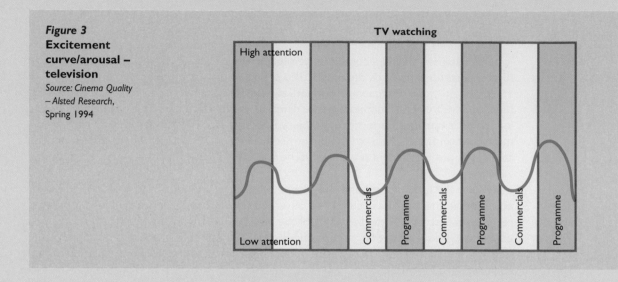

Figure 3
Excitement curve/arousal – television
Source: Cinema Quality – Alsted Research, Spring 1994

people perceive cinema commercials as good entertainment and link the fact of advertising in the cinema to a luxurious, high quality, entertaining and/or exciting image of the advertised product.

Questions

1. For which kind of products would you think that the transfer of meaning from the 'film-viewing' event to the advertised product is especially successful?

2. The focus of attention was found to be crucial in this study. Focus on the advertisements is high in the cinema situation and low in the TV situation. Which other concept from psychological theory is reminiscent of this?

3. Which factors of attraction and distraction may be decisive for the experience of the cinema-going event?

4. Which general conclusions could be drawn from this case, concerning consumers' 'consumption' of advertisements?

CASE STUDY 3

Alessi: Italian design and the re-enchantment of every day objects

Benoît Heilbrunn, Assistant Professor of Marketing, E.M. Lyon

One of the main characteristics of consumer society is the serialization of objects and their subsequent loss of uniqueness, distinctness and authenticity due to their ever increasing reproduction and diffusion. The fact that objects are repeatedly produced leads to a fade-out of meaning of most of these everyday objects, which in turn become mere commodities and thus lose their substance. This loss of meaning of most consumer objects is partly due to a societal shift from craftsmanship to industrialization which leads to the serialization of objects, and partly due to a marketing approach based on the design of objects which respond most closely to consumer needs and therefore exclude a surprise effect. This phenomenon inevitably leads to an impoverishment of sensory experience and a loss of a relationship with objects. Consider the fact that at the beginning of the nineteenth century, a four-person, average-income family was surrounded by only 150 to 200 objects at the most (including crockery and clothes), and that nowadays, a similar family owns between 2,500 and 3,000 objects, including electrical appliances and decorative objects. Today, a person is said to come into daily contact with approximately 20,000 products. Consumers thus often seem to be immersed in an uncontrolled number of signs and confronted with a well known phenomenon of semiotic pollution.

Therefore, designers have to invent products and design signs which can survive in a consumption and societal environment saturated with a tremendous and ever-increasing number of products and signs. Design thus has an essential role in giving meaning to objects, through the shapes, colours and materials. Also, the penetration of science and technology into our daily environment has eliminated most technical barriers to the production of objects. New forms and functions can now be used, thus enlarging the field of possibilities and the creative abilities of designers.

One of the most remarkable examples of this will to poetize life through object design is the Italian company Alessi which was founded in 1921 by Giovanni Alessi. The first articles produced were coffee pots and trays that were soon followed by a large series of accessories for table service. The company, now in its fourth generation, is headed by Alberto Alessi who has recruited renowned industrial designers and architects to create signature products for the company. This venture has been extremely successful with many objects becoming cult objects such as Aldo Rossi's conical kettle, Philippe Starck's juicer and Michael Graves' bird kettle. At present the production is grouped under the trademarks Alessi (mass production, mainly of steel and plastic), Officina Alessi (small or middle series production in different metals: silver, nickel-silver, titanium, brass, stainless steel, iron, tin-plate), Tendentse (porcelain) and Twergi (wood).

Officina Alessi is extremely representative of a design tradition which focuses more on existential values than on the mere utilitarian approach to objects. This new Alessi trade-mark was introduced in 1983 to identify an aspect of the company's activity which in the past had remained in books of blue prints or at the prototype stage. Their objective is to research and experiment with innovative forms, styles functions and methods of manufacture, free from the limits usually imposed by industrial mass production. The company wants to offer a wide range of products which combine both sophisticated industrial technology and traditional handicraft processes to a keen and culturally curious public. In particular the use of 'historical' metals such a nickel silver, brass, copper, silver and tin are chosen not only for their intrinsic value, but also to match the characteristics of each design (Presentation catalogue of Officina Alessi, 1994). According to the circumstances, the results take the form of standard production, or a limited series or even unique pieces. For instance, Officina Alessi launched a series of Tea and Coffee Piazzas which were commissioned from eleven internationally recognized architects. The eleven sets were each produced in limited editions of 99, priced individually at about £12,000, and in 1983, galleries in Milan and New York simultaneously hosted their launch thus reinforcing the cultural status and economic exclusivity of the objects.

What this example of design innovation illustrates is that, even though the shape of an object more or less follows its function, the shape of an object may by far overlap its function. There is always a degree of freedom which gives the designer the opportunity to disconnect (sometimes quite radically) from form function. If the shape of the object always more or less indicates its use, it also adds an inescapable aesthetic dimension which may contribute to a real redefinition of the object. Therefore design really means 'to illuminate, to clarify, to modify, to dignify, to dramatize, to persuade, and perhaps even to amuse' (Rand, 1993: 3). This definition, given by an American designer, points out two approaches to design which refer to two distinct traditions in Europe. The first approach considers design as a way to clarify and to persuade. This approach may be said to be characteristic of German and Nordic design of which companies like Braun and Bang & Olufsen may be considered as very representative. In these countries, design appears to be more functional in the sense it aims at expressing the mere function of the object. The approach to the object is essentially seen as utilitarian because the object design has to persuade the user that it serves particular functions. The role of design is to convey an impression of effectiveness, solidity, through appropriate features, colours and materials.

The second approach, which is usually more representative of Southern European countries (Italy, Spain, partly France) tends to develop objects with stronger existential connotations, such as emotional values (the object design has to arouse feelings and affective states), ludic values (the object is considered as a potential game) and epistemic values (the ability of the product to arouse curiosity and to provide novelty). This approach to design refers to the necessity of consumers to live new experiences through the use of products which provide innovative combinations of shape, materials, colours, etc. The importance of these existential values in the choice of products and brands, and therefore in the way consumers perceive the design of products, is also related to hedonistic consumption which is a very important paradigm of consumption in these countries.

The design philosophy promoted by Alberto Alessi is highly representative of this second approach in the sense that it aims at overcoming both technological and marketing constraints which dominate the actual production of consumer goods and result in a world of anonymous and impassive objects. The company's mission is hence seen as a way to literally poetize everyday objects. At the same time, the company is also preoccupied with the functional dimension of objects as illustrated by this quote from Alessandro Mendini (who designed the Falstaff pots for Alessi):

> with their simple elegance the Falstaff pots seek to present a group of utensils, that harmonise with the kitchen surroundings and at the same time enhance the practise of that supreme domestic culinary art of gastronomy . . . They are model pots of the latest generation, a design intended as a multiple art form, a kitchen landscape with pots . . . At work and at rest, they form a bouquet of reflectively polished, convex objects, discreetly present; sometimes slightly invisible; sometimes brilliantly present perhaps poetic kitchen sculptures. Actors perhaps, that tell us mysterious tales while they cook . . . Stressing the idea of play, of magic, invention and ritual, present today in the pleasure of performing numerous ancient actions that are no longer a chore but actually fun – for example, the act of cooking itself. (Presentation catalogue of the Falstaff collection)

The implicit objective is to transform everyday consumer objects into objects of aesthetic contemplation through the application of colour, pattern and additional elements. It also means there is no single meaning assigned to an object, but on the contrary, a plurality of meanings. An object is different from a tool in the sense that it does not necessarily boil down to a mere utilitarian function. The objective of a brand like Alessi is to break the conventional codes of representation of the object to transform an apparently boring practise (cooking) into a joy and a pleasing activity.

This leads to a real exploration of the communicative boundaries of design illustrated by the juicer designed by Philippe Starck, which looks like a rocket, or the Conical kettle designed by Michael Graves. These objects propose totally new approaches to familiar

Alessi's rocket-style juicer, designed by Philippe Starck, 1990–91

objects. By breaking the usual codes of representation, the designer opens the object to a multitude of meanings, which contribute to re-semantizing the objects beyond their functional purpose. Thus the design of any object implies two dimensions: (1) an *endophoric* dimension which guarantees that the object belongs to a certain class and organizes the invariable elements, and (2) an *exophoric* dimension which allows for radical formal innovation in the object category. On the one hand, the endophoric axis limits, crystallizes and adjusts; it is more or less related to utilitarian values. On the other hand, the exophoric axis invents, diffuses and disorientates. The first axis makes the object recognizable and has a reassurance function, whereas the second axis destructures the object, which responds to new expectations. Consider, for instance, the kettle designed by Michael Graves for Alessi: this object is very strongly exophoric because of its very cone shape which destabilizes the idea of a kettle, but also because of the little bird sitting on the spout which conveys the idea of lightness and defies the geometric rigidity of the object. Looking at the kettle for the first time, one is disorientated by the object whose identity as a kettle is seriously questioned and searches for a new identity outside the functional aspect. Playing with the exophoric dimension, the designer does nothing less than break the endophoric codes in order to open the object to new interpretations. One could even say that such objects may be considered as postmodern objects, in the way Robert Venturi defines them:

> elements which are hybrid rather than 'pure', compromising rather than 'clear', distorted rather than 'straightforward', ambiguous rather than 'articulated', perverse as well as 'impersonal', conventional rather than 'designed', accommodating rather than 'excluding', redundant rather than simple, vestigal as well as innovating, inconsistent rather than direct and clear. (Venturi, 1966, quoted in Woodham, 1997: 191)

Alessi's bird kettle and related items, designed by Michael Graves, 1985–88

The other interesting phenomenon is that despite the fact Alessi's objects seem at first glance to be very much culturally bound, they met a wide success in most European countries. Furthermore, the growing success of such objects lead to the notion of a 'New International Style' which initially emerged in the 1980s due to the influence of such designers as Ettore Sottsass and Andrea Branzi from Italy, Hans Hollein from Austria, Michael Graves from the United States, Xavier Mariscal from Spain, Philippe Starck from France. During the 1980s, shows of the group work were held in the major museums in the capital cities around the world and its products marketed under the banner of the 'New International Style'. This notion indicated the commodification of particular concepts within a global concept (Woodham, 1997: 161). This notion of 'design as art' was generally collected for its visual identity and implicit cultural values rather than any premium on function or practicality. Specializing on what has been termed the 'tabletop industry' or 'micro-architecture', companies like Alessi focused on the commissioning of small-scale pieces of decorative arts by well known architects and designers. Most products were exposed in museums all around the world which also means a collapse of the boundaries between art and everyday life. This phenomenon has been said to be very representative of the postmodern condition, as Mike Featherstone emphasizes it as 'the effacement of the boundary between art and everyday life . . . a general stylistic promiscuity, and playful mixing codes' (Featherstone, 1991: 65).

Questions

1. How would you explain the fact that despite their focus on intangible and aesthetic product features, Alessi's objects are successful in nearly all European countries? Can you identify key target markets based on gender, age, income or lifestyle?

2. To what extent would you agree with the idea that objects represent communication devices?

3. Do you think that consumers from each European country would be willing to pay a price premium to get a product from one of Alessi's collections? Why or why not?

4. Alessi's objects are said to be very postmodern. To what extent would you agree with this assertion?

Sources

Alessi, various promotional material

Cova, Bernard and Sventfelt, Christian, 'Societal Innovations and the Postmodern Aesteticization of Everyday life', *International Journal of Research in Marketing* 10 (1993): 297–310.

Featherstone, Mike, *Consumer Culture and Postmodernism* (London, Sage, 1991).

Heilbrunn, Benoît, 'In Search of the Lost Aura: The Object in the Age of Marketing Re-Illumination', in Stephen Brown *et al.* (eds), *Romancing the Market* (London, Routledge, 1998).

Polinoro, Laura, *L'officina Alessi* (F.A.O. spa, Crusinello, 1989).
Rand, Paul, *Design, Form & Chaos* (Yale University Press, New Haven & London, 1993).
Venturi, Robert, *Complexity and Contradiction in Architecture* (Museum of Modern Art, New York, 1996).
Woodham, Jonathan M., *Twentieth-Century Design* (Oxford, Oxford University Press, 1997).

CASE STUDY 4

From *Mille lire to Mille et Une Nuits*: inventing 'disposable' books

Benoît Heilbrunn, Assistant Professor of Marketing, E.M. Lyon

'A book for the price of an *espresso*' is Marcello Baraghini's idea. In the 1970s, he created a small publishing company called Stampa Alternativa, close to the left wing anti-establishment movements. After beginning with political pamphlets in the 1980s, Baraghini changed his stand and went into publishing luxury hardbacks ranging from art and poetry to music and fairy tales. In 1990, he came up with the idea of launching a series of books with very low production costs (200 lire) which would allow them to be sold at a very low price. The idea of *Mille lire* books was born: paperbacks with no more than 100 pages of text, printed on recycled paper, with no pictures. Fifty thousand copies of each title were printed. The authors published included Freud, Shakespeare, Garcia Lorca, Stendhal and Poe. The books were sold for the price of an espresso: 1,000 lire, cheaper than a pack of cigarettes!

What an amazing phenomenon and a very innovative move in a country where the average selling price of a book ranges from 10,000 lire for a paperback to 34,000 lire for a hardback. The success of the *Mille lire* books was inevitable. For example, the *Lettera sulla felicita* translated from Epicurus sold 500,000 copies and was among the Italian best sellers of the year. In 1992, over 2 million *Mille lire* books were sold in Italy. This new concept of books was successful because it created a new category of readers by overcoming the psychological hindrance of high prices. But this phenomenon also influenced the behaviour of regular book buyers, simply because the risk of buying an uninteresting book is considerably reduced with such low prices. This contributed to shift the buying decision criterion from price (which is predominant in the book sector together with the author's reputation or the front cover impact) to situation. People would thus buy a *Mille lire* as they buy an espresso or a pack of cigarettes depending on their consumption situation. The publisher was required to adapt his choice of retail outlets according to these situation factors. It was therefore decided to sell the *Mille lire* in the traditional newsagents on every main street. People waiting for a date, an appointment or a train would be tempted to buy on impulse such books just as they would buy any 'disposable' product such as newspapers, cigarettes or chewing gum. You use them once and throw them away.

This new concept of books, which responds to a sudden and rapid decision process, corresponds to the evolution in the status of books in western cultures. In European history, the first printed books were sacred (the first book printed by Gutenberg was a Bible), scarce (there were only 7 copies printed of Gutenberg's Bible), and very expensive. With the evolution of printing techniques and the increase in paper production, the average production price of books began to slowly decrease which made it possible for books to be more widely available. The democratization of books also meant that the natural place of books gradually shifted from libraries to family homes. The book which had been for a long time collectively read started to become an individual object. Also the evolution of the size of books – and mainly the appearance of paperbacks in the 1960s –

Sample covers of *Mille lire* titles

allowed books to be carried about in a pocket. The rise of such cheap books illustrate three important features of European societies. The first is the individualization of consumption activities which means that the purchase decision for most consumer goods is made individually. This individual choice is also very much influenced by situation variables such as the time and place of consumption, the consumer's mood, the consumer's occupation at the time of purchase, etc. The individualization of societies goes with new lifestyles such as nomadism, consumers tend to have fewer social links and to build autonomous consumption activities. The concept of *Mille lire* books is very representative of this change in society. Depending on his/her situation, mood, available time, the consumer would buy a *Mille lire*, read it and get rid of it. It means that *Mille lire* books may be considered more or less disposable as such items as pens, razors, lighters or even cameras. The main criticism targeted at the *Mille lire* operation was that this would depreciate the concept of the book, making it just another disposable product among so many others. Many people in Italy were shocked at the idea that a book could become consumable merchandise which could be used and then thrown away like any plain object. However, it was argued that this new book concept was aimed at new segments of customers, people that wouldn't buy 'normal' books because of their prohibitive price.

The effect of these books was quite paradoxical because on the one hand they depreciated the idea of culture, being cheap and easily consumed cultural products, and on the other hand, they helped to rediscover Ancient authors who were not read any more and also encouraged new people towards reading.

Due to an enormous success in Italy, the idea rapidly spread and crossed the French border. In July 1993, a new collection of similar books was launched by *Mille et Une Nuits* in France, a small and newly born publisher. The concept was slightly adapted and the books were sold for 10 francs.

Sample covers of
*Mille et Une
Nuits* titles

In France, the situation of the market was quiet. The 'livres de poche' ('pocket books', paperbacks) were celebrating their 30th birthday. The concept of 'pocket book' first appeared there in 1963, with two major characteristics: the books were sold at a very low price and their size enabled them to be carried in a pocket hence the name given to them. This market grew rapidly in France with a great number of collections being created. However, the extension of the concept also saw the price range rapidly widen. Nowadays there are approximately 100 collections of 'livres de poche' with prices ranging from 12 francs to 120 francs. This simply means that the 'livre de poche' no longer represents or federates a unique concept.

The dilution of the original concept allowed a market niche to emerge with very low-priced books such as *Mille et Une Nuits*, which appeared to be the first brand to explicitly pre-empt this market segment. The books launched by *Mille et Une Nuits* contain up to 96 pages (in fact 32, 64 or 96 pages) printed on ecological, recycled paper with an illustrated cover, some black and white plates in the text, a presentation of the text, a bibliography and a short presentation of the author's life. The first title to be printed was *Lettre sur le bonheur* (The Letter on Happiness) by Epicurus which had been a tremendous success in Italy. In order to promote and to build the awareness of this new concept, the first title was given as a free supplement (425,000 copies) with an issue of a weekly magazine called *Le Nouvel Observateur* (no. 1496, 14 July 1993). The launch of a whole collection was announced: 12 titles coming out in September 1993. These first titles were new editions of forgotten or out-of-print books by very famous authors such as Maupassant, Baudelaire, Sade, Perrault, Kleist, Cervantes and London.

The positioning of the concept was expressed in the motto written on the last page of each book: 'Mille et Une Nuits propose des chefs-d'oeuvre pour le temps d'une attente, d'un voyage, d'une insomnie.' (Mille et Une Nuits offers you a masterpiece for a wait, a trip, a night). The retail outlets used were the bookstores and some superstores, but not the newsagents as in Italy. This simply means that the *Mille et Une Nuits* products were real books and not newspapers. But very soon the publisher had to face problems due to the choice of such a distribution strategy. First, the margin the booksellers were left with was unusually thin because it amounted to one-third of the retail price (average ratio in this sector) which meant only 3 francs. This was more than three times less than an average paperback, while the storage space and effort to sell required were almost the same. Second, these books were fragile, easily damaged, and the soft cover made it almost impossible to stand them upright. They had to be laid flat on a table, the whole collection taking up a lot of space. Thus, many booksellers were reluctant to promote these books even if the publisher offered to provide them with a counter display, which enabled them to present the entire collection in a very convenient and elegant way.

Despite this reluctance, the launch was a success. The original print run was 25,000 but this was rapidly increased to 35,000. The collection was distributed in 12,000 bookstores and superstores.

However, the small publisher will soon have to face several threats faced by his new product. First, how to avoid being a mere fad product? Second, how to survive competition? Many large publishers were willing to counterattack by launching similar books targeted at different publics. Retailers were also thinking of launching their own brand of cheap books.

Discussion questions

1. What are the main factors of success for this particular product?

2. What would be the life-cycle of such a product? Do you think this product is going to last or is it doomed to have a very short life span similar to a fad product.

3. Do you think it is possible to build brand loyalty for the publisher? Or loyalty for the product category of cheap books? Why or why not?

4. Is this product transferable to any country in Europe? What factors would be critical success factors in your country? Why? How do you think those factors might differ for other European countries?

CASE STUDY 5

'The medium is the message . . . or are you what you drink?'

The impact of self-monitoring on image congruence and product/brand evaluation

Margaret K. Hogg and Alastair J. Cox, Manchester School of Management

Context[1]

The drinks market for young adults in the UK is characterized by innovation as well as by sharp swings in tastes and trends, with the rapid diffusion of new or fashionable products. This is clearly illustrated by the rapid growth in retail sales of alcoholic soft drinks since their launch in the UK in June 1995 (Mintel 1996). Within this market it is possible to segment drinks brands by their flavour, alcoholic strength and packaging. The early entrants and market leaders were alcoholic lemonades although there has recently been a shift towards alcoholic sodas. Most of the brands sold in this category in the UK are comparable to premium bottled largers with between 4 and 5% ABV (alcohol by volume). Although some brands are available in 330 ml bottles and cans, most drinks brands in this category are sold in glass bottles. Most alcoholic drinks have both a heavy usage and penetration rate in age groups that are under 34; and are particularly strong in age groups below 24. These drinks, regarded as a refreshing alternative to beer, are associated with fashion and young people (Mintel 1996). A recent introduction into this market was a range of products which contained extracts from plants (such as caffeine, guarana and damiana). The naturally based stimulants in these alcopops were intended to give drinkers added vitality and energy as they spent the night clubbing and dancing.

Scenario

Vicky, Katherine, Chloe, Daniel and Robert were sitting around chatting, as they often did, after supper on a Sunday evening. Usually they talked about the last football match which the lads had been to; or the latest film they had all seen. However, on this occasion the discussion had started to get rather heated, and they were now close to having a real argument. Last time this had happened, they had ended up with a row about vegetarianism and animal testing. This time, it had begun with an off-the-cuff remark from Rob about the recent craze for alcoholic lemonades, which he had dismissed as 'nasty, fizzy drinks'.

The previous evening, while out clubbing, Chloe had tried one of the new 'alcopop' products which contained natural stimulants and which were meant to keep clubbers going all night. Rob hadn't meant to start an argument, with his remark to Chloe:

Rob: How can anyone bear to be seen drinking that stuff – it's got a dreadful image, and it's an awful drink, not to put too fine a point upon it ...

Chloe: Excuse me, it's not awful. If you must know – I rather liked it. Anyway when did you try it?

Rob: No way, I wouldn't be seen dead drinking that stuff.

Chloe: So how would you know what it's like then? How can you say it's awful when you haven't even tried it?

Rob: Everyone knows those alcopops are horribly sweet and sickly; and anyway, they're all women's drinks.

Chloe: I don't see how you can say that when you admit you have not even tasted them.

[Katherine tried to calm things down a little, by moving the discussion away from the strictly personal, onto a more general level.]

Katherine: Alright, alright, alright – no need to get quite so cross. Surely, Chloe though, it's pretty obvious that what you drink reflects the type of person you are: financially, socially and probably sexually, even if it is only subconsciously.

[However, Katherine only succeeded in making Chloe even more mad; and Vicky quite scathing.]

Chloe: Well that just doesn't make any sense.

Vicky: It doesn't make any sense to me either. I think it's pretty obvious that some people are just more susceptible to media manipulation and fashion trends than others – but they're just sad people really.

Katherine: No, I think you've both got it wrong. It's obvious, surely – we all behave differently according to the situation we are in. I mean I change the way I behave to fit in, especially when I am out with some of my more flamboyant friends.

Vicky: Now why on earth do you do that, Katherine, what's the point? You are who you are, surely?

Katherine: Well I think the way I behave does depend on who I am with – an awful lot depends on the type of people you're with for instance, and the place you're in – whether it's a bar or a club. It's also important where the place is, its location and whether it has a dress code. I mean these are all mixed up together and you behave accordingly.

Daniel: Vicky look, I know when I'm out with my mates I would look really stupid if I ordered whisky when everyone else was drinking lager – I'd just look and feel like a right idiot.

Katherine: That's it, Dan, that's precisely the point I'm trying to make. Like, for instance, when I'm in a wine bar or restaurant I would almost always choose wine or cocktails to drink, but when I'm in a pub I usually drink beer ... I mean you want to make sure you're not out of place by the way you are behaving or by what you're drinking. It's rather like what you wear, it's everything ... honestly, Vicky.

Daniel: Oh, come on, Vicky, you've got to admit Katherine's right you know. People choose drinks which fit into the kind of places they are in and the people they're with.

Vicky: Look, I think that might have been true in the eighties, when it was all image, mobile phones and bottles of *Budweiser*. But I think it's a lot different now, there's much more sense of a free spirit and of free choice.

Daniel: I don't know that you can really say that, Vicky – not really, I mean look at Chloe. Chloe, you wouldn't drink beer from a pint glass in a trendy bar now would you? You'd look like an old man with a pint glass in your hand. You wouldn't want people to associate you with that type of image would you?

Chloe: Of course I wouldn't drink a pint in a trendy bar, but that's because it would probably get spilt everywhere. Anyway I have never really liked the taste of those beers and lagers. I really can't say that I'm interested in what other people think about what I drink, and I find it hard to believe that other people are really seriously interested in what I drink.

Robert: Chloe, I really think you're quite wrong, you know. You're really completely missing the point here. You can definitely read meanings into people's product or brand choices, certainly some of their choices, anyway. Look at alcopops for instance. They are definitely a woman's drink. They've got such a female image, though you certainly won't see many older women drinking alcopops and you definitely don't see many blokes drinking them either. That's why it would look rather odd for me to stand at a bar drinking alcopops.

Chloe: Don't be so ridiculous, Rob – how can you read so much into one bottle of alcopops? You'll be saying next that the clothes I wear and the music I listen to send messages about me – that's really nonsense. What about these jeans, for instance – what meaning can you see in this pair of blue jeans?

Rob: Well for a start, they're Levi 501s which are about as trendy as you can get in branded jeans – apart from the designer labels like Calvin Klein and Armani.

Chloe: Well, you see you're wrong. I chose this pair of branded jeans simply for the cut and the quality. I am not worried about what people think the label says about me, and I am not really bothered about what you all think of me wearing this brand of jeans . . . as long as you think they suit me and fit well.

Katherine: But Chloe, I really can't imagine you in an ordinary pair of jeans, I mean would you buy ordinary jeans – say from the market or from a department store? I bet you never have.

Chloe: But that's my point, surely. I wouldn't buy jeans which didn't have the cut and quality I wanted, and these just happen to be the brand I like.

Katherine: Well, Chloe maybe you're the exception to the rule, but I definitely think people's choices of things like jeans and drinks (not to mention cars) are influenced by the people around them, even if it is only subconsciously. Everything changes depending on the people you associate with and the situation you're in.

Vicky: Oh come on Katherine, now that really is a ridiculous idea – it's an incredible notion to suggest everyone changes all the time – I mean, you might change your behaviour slightly to fit in, but you're still the same person underneath after all. I know I am, and I am sure you are.

[At this point, Daniel decided to try another tack.]

Daniel: OK Vicky and Chloe, why don't we try looking at it another way, and then you might be able to see what Katherine, Rob and I are trying to get at. Let's assume you're at that popular bar in the centre of town – it's busy as it always is on a Saturday night. You're planning to spend a couple of hours there before meeting up with some friends and going on to a club. Imagine you are just about to go up and buy a drink. There are lots of people around who will be able to see what brand you choose to drink – what influences your choice of drink in those circumstances?

Vicky: Well it depends . . .

Daniel: Yes, but what on . . .

Vicky: Well I don't know – how I feel I suppose, what I feel like drinking, how much I've already had to drink, what's available, what I can afford – oh, I don't know, lots of things. . .

Daniel: What about you Chloe, like last night for instance, what made you choose the new alcopops drink?

Chloe: Someone else bought it for me, actually, and I did not like to refuse it. It was not necessarily something that I would have chosen myself. I am not very keen on fizzy drinks if I am going dancing. But it was OK – a bit sweet maybe, but not bad; and besides it didn't cost me anything. I switched back to one of those bottled beers afterwards, I must admit – it certainly tasted a lot better, though it is a bit expensive for what you get. It was the same as the stuff you are drinking now Rob. By the way Rob, what made you choose that brand?

By the end of this case study, you should be able to:
- Define and illustrate symbolic consumption.
- Define and evaluate the role of self-monitoring in consumer behaviour.
- Recognize and explain the situational factors which influence product and brand choices.
- Identify the meanings and interpretations which consumers often associate with their choice of products and brands.
- Access the impact of symbolic consumption on consumer behaviour.

Class preparation: It is recommended that you should have at least read the chapters in Part B. In particular, chapter 7 ('The self') will provide some useful concepts and theory for analysis and discussion.

Case study questions

1. What are the factors which influence product/brand evaluation and choice in this case study?

2. Assess the importance of self-image and product image in product/brand evaluation and choice.

3. To what extent can the 'self-image congruence models' discussed in Chapter 7 help us understand the interaction between consumers and product/brands in this case study?

4. Discuss the different levels of self-monitoring displayed by Katherine, Vicky, Chloe, Daniel and Robert (review *symbolic interactionism* and *self-consciousness* in Chapter 7).

5. How far can the products and brands in this case study be seen as social stimuli and/or as responses?

6. Why is symbolic consumption so central to our understanding of consumer behaviour?

Case study exercises

1. **Preliminary task:** As preparation for the class, prepare short market research reports on the market for alcopops in Europe, using industry reports and concentrating particularly on the consumer behaviour aspects when reporting your findings.

2. **Follow-up task:** After the class discussion of the case material, work in small groups to undertake some market research of your own, by interviewing ten users and ten non-users of alcopops, around the themes identified in the class discussion.

Notes

The authors acknowledge the support of *GSM Marketing* Leeds and *Hard Times* Leeds for the research project on which this case study material is based. © Hogg and Cox, January 1998

1. This background information is based on company documents (personal correspondence) and a Mintel report (1996) on the alcoholic soft drinks industry.

Glossary

Absolute threshold the minimum amount of stimulation that can be detected on a sensory channel *(p. 49)*

Accommodative purchase decision the process to achieve agreement among a group whose members have different preferences or priorities *(p. 312)*

Acculturation the process of learning the beliefs and behaviours endorsed by another culture *(pp. 106, 431)*

Acculturation agents friends, family, local businesses and other reference groups which facilitate the learning of cultural norms *(p. 431)*

Activation models of memory approaches to memory stressing different levels of processing that occur and activate some aspects of memory rather than others, depending on the nature of the processing task *(p. 78)*

Actual self a person's realistic appraisal of his or her qualities *(p. 177)*

Adaptation the process that occurs when a sensation becomes so familiar that it is no longer the focus of attention *(p. 52)*

Affect the way a consumer feels about an attitude object *(p. 123)*

Age cohort a group of consumers of the same approximate age who have undergone similar experiences *(p. 353)*

Agentic goals goals that stress self-assertion and mastery and are associated with males *(p. 184)*

AIOs (Activities, Interests and Opinions) the psychographic variables used by researchers in grouping consumers *(p. 407)*

Androgyny the possession of both masculine and feminine traits *(p. 186)*

Anti-foundationalism an anti-campaign campaign encouraging the consumer not to take notice of a message *(p. 468)*

Art product a creation viewed primarily as an object of aesthetic contemplation without any functional value *(p. 442)*

Atmospherics the use of space and physical features in store design to evoke certain effects in buyers *(p. 252)*

Attention the assignment of cognitive capacity to selected stimuli *(p. 52)*

Attitude a lasting, general evaluation of people (including oneself), objects or issues *(p. 121)*

Attitude object (A_o) anything towards which one has an attitude *(p. 121)*

Attitude towards the act of buying (A_{act}) the perceived consequences of a purchase *(p. 138)*

Attitude towards the advertisement (A_{ad}) a predisposition to respond favourably to a particular advertising stimulus during an exposure situation *(p. 126)*

Autocratic decisions purchase decisions that are made exclusively by one spouse *(p. 313)*

Baby boomers a large cohort of people born between 1946 and 1964 who are the source of many important cultural and economic changes *(p. 362)*

Balance theory considers relations among elements a person might perceive as belonging together and people's tendency to change relations among elements in order to make them consistent or balanced *(p. 131)*

Behaviour a consumer's actions with regard to an attitude object *(p. 123)*

Behavioural economics the study of the behavioural determinants of economic decisions *(p. 327)*

Behavioural influence perspective the view that consumer decisions are learned responses to environmental cues *(p. 209)*

Behavioural learning theories the perspectives on learning that assume that learning takes place as the result of responses to external events *(p. 65)*

Binary opposition a defining structural characteristic where two opposing ends of a dimension are presented (p. 382)

Body cathexis a person's feelings about aspects of his or her body (p. 192)

Body image a consumer's subjective evaluation of his or her physical appearance (p. 192)

Brand equity a brand that has strong positive associations and consequently commands a lot of loyalty (p. 71)

Brand loyalty a pattern of repeat product purchases accompanied by an underlying positive attitude towards the brand (p. 231)

Bubble drawings a projective research technique in which respondents provide a caption to explain a picture (p. 27)

Causal research research performed to obtain evidence of cause-and-effect relationships (p. 30)

Chronology the consumer's search for the authentic and a preoccupation with the past (p. 467)

Classic a fashion with an extremely long acceptance cycle (p. 452)

Classical conditioning the learning that occurs when a stimulus eliciting a response is paired with another stimulus which initially does not elicit a reponse on its own but will cause a similar response over time because of its association with the first stimulus (p. 66)

Cognition the beliefs a consumer has about an attitude object (p. 123)

Cognitive development the ability to comprehend concepts of increasing complexity as a person ages (p. 321)

Cognitive learning the learning that occurs as a result of internal mental processes (p. 69)

Cognitive structure the factual knowledge or set of beliefs about a product and the way these are organized (p. 222)

Collecting the accumulation of rare or mundane and inexpensive objects, which transforms profane items into sacred ones (p. 396)

Collective selection the process whereby certain symbolic alternatives tend to be chosen jointly in preference to others by members of a group (p. 447)

Collectivist culture a cultural orientation which encourages people to subordinate their personal goals to those of a stable in-group (p. 380)

Communal goals goals that stress affiliation and the fostering of harmonious relations and are associated with females (p. 184)

Communications model a framework specifying that a number of elements are necessary for communication to be achieved including a source, message, medium, receivers and feedback (p. 147)

Comparative influence the process whereby a reference group influences decisions about specific brands or activities (p. 271)

Compatibility a prerequisite for a product's adoption; the product should fit the consumers' lifestyle (p. 295)

Compensatory decision rules allow information about attributes of competing products to be averaged; poor standing on one attribute may be offset by good standing on another (p. 233)

Complexity ease of understanding and use of a product; greater ease lowers the effort and perceived risk in adoption (p. 296)

Conformity a change in beliefs or actions as a reaction to real or perceived group pressure (p. 276)

Consensual purchase decision a decision in which the group agrees on the desired purchase and differs only in terms of how it will be achieved (p. 312)

Conspicuous consumption the purchase and prominent display of luxury goods as evidence of the consumer's ability to afford them (pp. 347, 448)

Consumer addiction a physiological and/or psychological dependency on products or services (p. 455)

Consumer behaviour the processes involved when individuals or groups select, purchase use or dispose of products, services ideas or experiences to satisfy needs or desires (p. 8)

Consumer confidence the state of mind of consumers relative to their optimism or pessimism about economic decisions; people tend to make more discretionary purchases when their confidence in the economy is high (p. 330)

Consumer satisfaction/dissatisfaction (CS/D) the overall attitude a person has about a product after it has been purchased (p. 256)

Consumer socialization the process by which people acquire skills that enable them to function in the marketplace (p. 318)

Consumption constellations a set of products and activities used by consumers to define, communicate and perform social roles (p. 405)

Continuous innovation a product change or new product that requires relatively little adaptation in the consumer's behaviour (p. 295)

Convention norms regarding the conduct of everyday life *(p. 380)*

Cooptation a cultural process where the original meaning of a product or other symbol associated with a subculture are modified by members of mainstream culture *(p. 375)*

Craft product a creation valued because of the beauty with which it performs some function; this type of product tends to follow a formula that permits rapid production; it is easier to understand than an art product *(p. 442)*

Creolization the blending of various eating traditions with new ones to make national food tastes fit the tastes of mainstream culture *(pp. 442, 464)*

Cultivation hypothesis a perspective emphasizing media's ability to distort consumers' perceptions of reality *(p. 455)*

Cultural categories the grouping of ideas and values that reflect the basic ways members of society characterize the world *(p. 446)*

Cultural formula where certain roles and props often occur consistently in many popular art forms, such as detective stories or science fiction *(p. 443)*

Cultural gatekeepers individuals who are responsible for determining the types of message and symbolism to which members of mass culture are exposed *(p. 442)*

Cultural production system (CPS) the set of individuals or organizations responsible for creating and marketing a cultural product *(p. 440)*

Cultural selection the process where some alternatives are selected in preference to those selected by cultural gatekeepers *(p. 439)*

Culture the values, ethics, rituals, traditions, material objects and services produced or valued by members of society *(p. 377)*

Custom a norm that is derived from a traditional way of doing something *(p. 380)*

Database marketing involves tracking consumers' buying habits and crafting products and information tailored to people's wants and needs *(p. 15)*

De-differentiation the blurring of distinctions between hierarchies such as high and low cultures or politics and show business *(p. 466)*

Deindividuation the process whereby individual identities are submerged within a group, reducing inhibitions against socially inappropriate behaviour *(p. 279)*

Demographics the observable measurements of a population's characteristics, such as birth rates, age distribution income *(p. 11)*

Dependent variables in causal research the variables that are affected when independent variables are manipulated *(p. 31)*

Desacralization the process that occurs when a sacred item or symbol is removed or is duplicated in mass quantities and as a result becomes profane *(p. 394)*

Descriptive research research done to describe something without necessarily explaining the reason for the phenomenon *(p. 30)*

Desire to wish or long for consumer goods which contribute to the formation of consumers' self-image; also refers to the sociogenic nature of needs *(p. 94)*

Differential threshold the ability of a sensory system to detect changes or differences among stimuli *(p. 50)*

Discontinuous innovation a product change or new product that requires a significant amount of adaptation of behaviour by the adopter *(p. 295)*

Discretionary income the money available to an individual or household over and above that required for maintaining a standard of living *(p. 329)*

Drive theory focuses on the desire to satisfy a biological need in order to reduce physiological arousal *(p. 92)*

Dynamically continuous innovation a product change or new product that requires a moderate amount of adaptation of behaviour by the adopter *(p. 295)*

Early adopters people receptive to new styles because they are involved in the product category and place high value on being fashionable *(p. 293)*

Ego involvement the importance of a product to a consumer's self-concept *(p. 101)*

Ego that system that mediates between the id and the superego *(p. 112)*

Elaborated codes the ways of expressing and interpreting meanings that are complex and depend on a sophisticated worldview; they tend to be used by the middle and upper classes *(p. 342)*

Elaboration likelihood model (ELM) the approach that one of two routes to persuasion (central versus peripheral) will be followed, depending on the personal relevance of a message; the route taken determines the relative importance of message contents versus other characteristics, such as source attractiveness *(p. 169)*

Emic perspective an approach to studying cultures that stresses the unique aspects of each culture (p. 456)

Encoding the process in which information from short-term memory is entered into long-term memory in recognizable form (p. 75)

Enculturation the process of learning the beliefs and behaviours endorsed by one (p. 106)

Erogenous zones areas of the body considered by members of a culture to be focuses of sexual attractiveness (p. 448)

Ethnic subculture a self-perpetuating group of consumers held together by common cultural ties (p. 429)

Ethnoconsumerism the understanding and analysis of each culture, including consumer culture, on the basis of its own premises (p. 380)

Ethnography an in-depth study of a group's behaviours, social rules and beliefs performed when in a natural environment (p. 29)

Ethos a set of moral, aesthetic and evaluative principles (p. 379)

Etic perspective an approach to studying culture that stresses the commonalities across cultures (p. 456)

Evaluative criteria the dimensions used by consumers to compare competing product alternatives (p. 224)

Evoked set those products already in memory plus those prominent in the retail environment that are actively considered during a consumer's choice process (pp. 78, 221)

Exchange the process whereby two or more organizations or people give and receive something of value (p. 9)

Exchange theory the perspective that every interaction involves an exchange of value (p. 255)

Expatriate food the search for authentic food (and products) from other cultures (p. 422)

Expectancy disconfirmation model the perspective that consumers form beliefs about product performance based on prior experience with the product and/or communications about the product that imply a certain level of quality; their actual satisfaction depends on the degree to which performance is consistent with these expectations (p. 257)

Expectancy theory the perspective that behaviour is largely 'pulled' by expectations of achieving desirable 'outcomes' or positive incentives, rather than 'pushed' from within (p. 93)

Experiential perspective an approach stressing the gestalt or totality of the product or service experience, focusing on consumers' affective responses in the market place (p. 209)

Experimentation problem-solving research design either in the laboratory or field (p. 31)

Exploratory research a type of consumer research performed to learn more about a consumer issue; usually the researcher does not have a prediction in advance but is collecting data in order to help design future research (p. 26)

Exposure an initial stage of perception where some sensations come within range of consumers' sensory receptors (p. 51)

Extended family traditional family structure where several generations and/or relatives such as aunts, uncles and cousins live together (p. 306)

Extended problem-solving an elaborate decision-making process often initiated by a motive that's fairly central to the self-concept and accompanied by perceived risk; the consumer tries to collect as much information as possible and carefully weighs product alternatives (p. 209)

Extended self the definition of self created by the external objects with which one surrounds oneself (p. 182)

Extinction the process whereby learned connections between a stimulus and response are eroded so that the response is no longer reinforced (p. 66)

Fad a short-lived fashion (p. 453)

Family financial officer (FFO) the family member who is in charge of making financial decisions (p. 313)

Family household a housing unit containing at least two people who are related by blood or marriage (p. 306)

Family life cycle (FLC) a classification scheme that segments consumers in terms of changes in income and family composition and the changes in demands placed on this income (p. 310)

Fantasy a self-induced shift in consciousness, often focusing on an unattainable or improbable goal; sometimes fantasy is a way of compensating for a lack of external stimulation or for dissatisfaction with the actual self (p. 177)

Fashion the process of social diffusion by which a new style is adopted by a group or groups of consumers (p. 446)

Fashion acceptance cycle the diffusion process of a style through three stages: introduction, acceptance and regression *(p. 450)*

Fashion life cycle the 'career' or stages in the life of a fashion as it progresses from launch to obsolescence *(p. 450)*

Fashion system those people or organizations involved in creating symbolic meanings and transferring these meanings to cultural goods *(p. 445)*

Fear appeal an attempt to change attitudes or behaviour through the use of threats or by the highlighting of negative consequences of non-compliance with the request *(p. 166)*

Fertility rate a rate determined by the number of births per year per 1,000 women of child-bearing age *(p. 307)*

Figure-ground principle the gestalt principle whereby one part of a stimulus configuration dominates a situation while other aspects recede into the background *(p. 56)*

Focus groups a qualitative research technique that gathers information from group interaction focused on a series of topics introduced by a discussion leader or moderator *(p. 26)*

Foot-in-the-door technique based on the observation that a consumer is more likely to comply with a request if she or he has first agreed to comply with a smaller request *(p. 131)*

Fragmentation the splitting up of what used to be simple and mass-oriented, exemplified by ever-growing product ranges and brand extensions *(p. 466)*

Frequency marketing a marketing technique that reinforces regular purchases by giving them prizes with values that increase along the amount purchased *(p. 74)*

Functional theory of attitudes a pragmatic approach that focuses on how attitudes facilitate social behaviour; attitudes exist because they serve some function for the person *(p. 122)*

Generation X (Gen-Xers or baby busters) the cohort of consumers aged 18–29, who were profoundly affected by the economic recession of the early 1990s *(p. 360)*

Geodemography techniques that combine consumer demographic information with geographic consumption patterns to permit precise targeting of consumers with specific characteristics *(p. 428)*

Gerontographics a research tool which divides the mature market into groups based on level of physical well-being and social conditions *(p. 368)*

Gestalt psychology a school of thought that maintains people derive meaning from the totality of a set of stimuli rather than from an individual stimulus *(p. 55)*

Gift-giving ritual the events involved in the selection, presentation, acceptance and interpretation of a gift *(p. 386)*

Global food culture, represented largely by American fast food, indicates a willingness to join a globally uniform consumption pattern *(p. 422)*

Goal a consumer's desired end-state *(p. 92)*

Green movement a movement expressing a general concern for the environment as it is affected by all aspects of production and consumption processes *(p. 261)*

Grey market term used to describe the phenomenon of a fast-growing segment of consumers aged 62 or older *(p. 365)*

Habitual decision-making the consumption choices that are made out of habit, without additional information search or deliberation among products *(p. 209)*

Habitus systems of classification of phenomena adopted from our socialization processes *(p. 413)*

Hedonic consumption the multisensory, fantasy and emotional aspects of consumers' interactions with products *(p. 43)*

Hermeneutics an interpretative research method which stresses that perceivers evaluate messages by drawing on many preconceived notions and which focuses on how people's notions about themselves, the world and the source of the message may be changed after being exposed to a message *(p. 29)*

Heuristics the mental rules of thumb that lead to a speedy decision *(p. 226)*

Hierarchy of effects a fixed sequence of steps that occurs during attitude formation; this sequence varies depending on such factors as the consumer's level of involvement with the attitude object *(p. 123)*

High context culture group members tend to be tightly knit and messages and meanings are implicit and built into the communication context *(p. 426)*

Homeostasis the state of being where the body is in physiological balance; goal-oriented behaviour attempts to reduce or eliminate an unpleasant motivational state and returns to a balanced one *(p. 92)*

Hyperreality a phenomenon associated with modern advertising in which what is initially stimulation or hype becomes real *(pp. 60, 466)*

Icon a sign that resembles the product in some culturally meaningful way *(p. 57)*

Id the system oriented to immediate gratification *(p. 112)*

Ideal of beauty a model, or exemplar, of appearance valued by a culture *(p. 193)*

Ideal self a person's conception of how he or she would like to be *(p. 177)*

Impulse buying a process that occurs when the consumer experiences a sudden urge to purchase an item that he or she cannot resist *(p. 252)*

Independent variables the factors manipulated in causal research that are hypothesized to affect the dependent variables *(p. 31)*

In-depth interview an important tool of qualitative research *(p. 26)*

Individualist culture a cultural orientation that encourages people to attach more importance to personal goals than to group goals; values such as personal enjoyment and freedom are stressed *(p. 380)*

Inertia the process whereby purchase decisions are made out of habit because the consumer lacks the motivation to consider alternatives *(pp. 100, 230)*

Information power power given simply because one knows something others would like to know *(p. 275)*

Information search the process whereby a consumer searches for appropriate information to make a reasonable decision *(p. 212)*

Informational social influence the conformity that occurs because the group's behaviour is taken as evidence about reality *(p. 277)*

Innovative communicators opinion leaders who are also early purchasers *(p. 288)*

Instrumental values those goals that are endorsed because they are needed to achieve desired end-states or terminal values *(p. 107)*

Interactionist a perspective on human communication which relies on three basic premises about communication, i.e. the meaning of things, ideas and actions *(p. 149)*

Interference a process whereby additional learned information displaces earlier information resulting in memory loss for the item learned previously *(p. 82)*

Interpretivism a research perspective that produces a 'thick' description of a consumers' subjective experiences and stresses the importance of the individuals' social construction of reality *(p. 24)*

Interpretant the meaning derived from a symbol *(p. 57)*

Interpretation the process whereby meanings are assigned to stimuli *(p. 54)*

Invidious distinction the display of wealth or power to inspire envy in others *(p. 347)*

Involvement the motivation to process product-related information *(p. 99)*

ISO standards a set of quality criteria developed in 1987 to regulate product quality by the International Standards Organization *(p. 256)*

JND (Just Noticeable Difference) the minimum change in a stimulus that can be detected by a perceiver *(p. 50)*

Kin network system the rituals intended to maintain ties among family members, both immediate and extended *(p. 316)*

Knowledge structures organized systems of concepts relating to brands, stores and other concepts *(p. 78)*

Laddering a technique for uncovering consumers' associations between specific attributes and general consequences *(p. 109)*

Lateral cycling a process where already purchased objects are sold to others or exchanged for other items *(p. 261)*

Latitudes of acceptance and rejection formed around an attitude standard; ideas that fall with a latitude will be favourably received, while those falling outside this zone will not *(p. 131)*

Learning a relatively permanent change in a behaviour as a result of experience *(p. 65)*

Lifestyle a set of shared values or tastes exhibited by a group of consumers especially as these are reflected in consumption patterns *(p. 401)*

Lifestyle marketing perspective a perspective that recognizes that people are increasingly conscious that we sort ourselves and each other into groups on the basis of the things we/they like to do and how we/they spend our/their disposable income *(p. 404)*

Limited problem-solving a problem-solving process in which consumers are not motivated to search for information or evaluate rigorously each alternative; instead they use simple decision rules to arrive at a purchase decision *(p. 209)*

Long-term memory the system that allows us to retain information for a long period *(p. 78)*

Looking-glass self the process of imagining the reaction of others towards oneself *(p. 179)*

LOV (list of values) a scale developed to isolate values with more direct marketing applications *(p. 107)*

Low context culture messages tend to be more explicit, specific and direct *(p. 426)*

Market beliefs the specific beliefs of decision rules pertaining to marketplace phenomena *(p. 226)*

Market maven a person who often serves as a source of information about marketplace activities *(p. 288)*

Match-up hypothesis in a celebrity ad campaign, the celebrity's image and that of the product he or she endorses should be similar for the campaign to be effective *(p. 155)*

Materialism the importance consumers attach to worldly possessions *(p. 402)*

Means–end chain a research approach that assumes that very specific product attributes are linked at levels of increasing abstraction to terminal values *(p. 109)*

MECCAs (Means–end Conceptualization of the Components of Advertising Strategy) a research approach in which researchers generate a map depicting relationships between functional product or service attributes and terminal values and then use this information to develop advertising strategy *(p. 110)*

Memory a process of acquiring information and storing it over time *(p. 75)*

Metaphor the use of an explicit comparison between a product and some other person, place or thing *(p. 168)*

Monomyth a myth with basic characteristics that are found in many cultures *(p. 382)*

Mores norms with strong moral overtones *(p. 380)*

Motivation an internal state that activates goal-oriented behaviour *(p. 91)*

Motivational research a qualitative research approach based on psychoanalytical (Freudian) interpretations with a heavy emphasis on unconscious motives for consumption *(p. 113)*

Multiattribute attitude models those models that assume that a consumer's attitude (evaluation) of an attitude object depends on the beliefs he or she has about several or many attributes of the object; the use of a multiattribute model implies that an attitude towards a product or brand can be predicted by identifying these specific beliefs and combining them to derive a measure of the consumer's overall attitude *(p. 134)*

Myth a story containing symbolic elements which expresses the shared emotion and ideals of a culture *(p. 381)*

National character a distinctive set of behaviour and personality characteristics that describe a country's people or culture *(pp. 381, 457)*

Naturalistic inquiry the attempt to generate a 'thick' description of the real-life experiences of people *(p. 29)*

Negative reinforcement the process whereby a negative reward weakens responses to stimuli so that inappropriate behaviour is avoided in the future *(p. 67)*

Non-compensatory decision rules a set of simple rules used to evaluate competing alternatives; a brand with a low standing on one relevant attribute is eliminated from the consumer's choice set *(p. 232)*

Normative influence the process in which a reference group helps to set and enforce basic standards of conduct *(p. 271)*

Normative social influence the conformity that occurs when a person alters his or her behaviour to meet the expectations of a person or group *(p. 277)*

Norms the informal rules that govern what is right and wrong *(p. 276)*

Nostalgia a bittersweet emotion when the past is viewed with sadness and longing; many 'classic' products appeal to consumers' memories of their younger days *(p. 83)*

Nostalgia food search for local authenticity from the cultural heritage, which is threatened by internationalization *(p. 422)*

Nuclear family a contemporary living arrangement composed of a married couple and their children *(p. 306)*

Object a semiotic term, the product that is the focus of the message *(p. 57)*

Observability the visibility of a product *(p. 297)*

Observational learning the process in which people learn by watching the actions of others and noting the reinforcements they receive for their behaviours *(p. 70)*

Operant conditioning the process by which the individual learns to perform behaviours that produce positive outcomes and to avoid those that yield negative outcomes *(p. 70)*

Opinion leaders those people who are knowledgeable about products and who are frequently able to influence others' attitudes or behaviours with regard to a product category *(p. 286)*

Opinion seekers usually opinion leaders who are also involved in a product category and actively search for information *(p. 288)*

Paradigm a widely accepted view or model of phenomena being studied. The perspective that regards people as *rational information processors* is currently the dominant paradigm, though this approach is now being challenged by a new wave of research that emphasizes the frequently subjective nature of consumer decision-making *(p. 24)*

Parental yielding the process that occurs when a parental decision-maker is influenced by a child's product request *(p. 317)*

Parody display the deliberate avoidance of widely used status symbols, whereby the person seeks status by mocking it *(p. 348)*

Pastiche the playful and ironic mixing of existing categories and styles *(p. 468)*

Perceived age how old a person feels rather than his or her chronological age *(p. 367)*

Perceived risk the belief that use of a product has potentially negative consequence, either physical or social *(p. 218)*

Perception the process by which stimuli are selected, organized or interpreted *(p. 40)*

Perceptual map a research tool used to understand how a brand is positioned in consumers' minds relative to competitors *(p. 42)*

Perceptual selectivity the process in which people attend to only a small portion of the stimuli to which they are exposed *(p. 51)*

Persuasion an active attempt to change attitudes *(p. 146)*

Pluralism the coexistence of various styles, truths and fashions *(p. 466)*

Point-of-purchase stimuli (POP) the promotional materials that are deployed in shops or other outlets to influence consumers; decisions at the time products are purchased *(p. 253)*

Political consumer the political consumer uses his or her buying pattern as a weapon against or support for companies which share the person's own values *(p. 263)*

Popular culture the music, films, sports, books, celebrities and other forms of entertainment consumed by the mass market *(p. 16)*

Positive reinforcement the process whereby rewards provided by the environment strengthen response to stimuli *(p. 67)*

Positivism a research perspective that relies on the principles of the 'scientific method' and assumes that a single reality exists; events in the world can be objectively measured; and the causes of behaviour can be identified, manipulated and predicted *(p. 24)*

Postmodernism a theory that questions the search for universal truths and values and the existence of objective knowledge *(p. 466)*

Potlatch a Kwakiutl Indian feast at which the host displays his wealth and gives extravagant gifts *(p. 347)*

Primary data any information that is collected specifically for the purposes of the present study *(p. 31)*

Priming the process in which certain properties of a stimulus are more likely to evoke a schema than others *(p. 54)*

Principle of closure implies that consumers tend to perceive an incomplete picture as complete *(p. 55)*

Principle of cognitive consistency the belief that consumers value harmony among their thoughts, feelings and behaviours and that they are motivated to maintain uniformity among these elements *(p. 128)*

Principle of similarity the gestalt principle that describes how consumers tend to group objects that share similar physical characteristics *(p. 56)*

Problem recognition the process that occurs whenever the consumer sees a significant difference between his or her current state and some desired or ideal state; this recognition initiates to the decision-making process *(p. 211)*

Problem-solving research research designed to test specific hypotheses; the information needed is clearly defined and the sample consumer population is intended to be representative of some larger group; findings in this type of research are often used as input to decision-making *(p. 26)*

Product complementarity the view that products in different functional categories have symbolic meanings that are related to one another *(p. 405)*

Product placement the process of obtaining exposure for a product by arranging for it to be inserted into a film, television programme or some other medium *(p. 454)*

Profane consumption the process of consuming objects and events that are ordinary or of the everyday world (p. 391)

Projective techniques the presentation of an ambiguous, unstructured object, activity or person to which the consumer responds in some way (explainingthe object, telling a story, drawing a picture, etc.); projectives are used when it is believed that a consumer will not or cannot respond meaningfully to direct questions (p. 26)

Psychodrawing a projective technique that allows the respondent to express his or her perceptions of products or usage situations in pictorial format (p. 27)

Psychographics the use of psychological, sociological and anthropological factors to construct market segments (pp. 12, 406)

Psychophysics the science that focuses on how the physical environment is integrated into the consumer's subjective experience (p. 49)

Punishment the process or outcome that occurs when a response is followed by unpleasant events (p. 68)

Qualitative research research performed to acquire in-depth knowledge about consumer behaviour, to generate ideas for future studies or to test the researcher's original hypothesis (p. 26)

Quantitative research a research process involving the gathering of data and its subsequent (statistical) analyses so that a researcher can make a definite statement about quantities, or the relationship among variables (p. 30)

Racial subculture a self-perpetuating group held together by ties of common culture and/or genetics, identified by its members and others as a distinguishable category (p. 429)

Rational perspective a view of the consumer as a careful, analytical decision-maker who tries to maximize utility in purchase decisions (p. 207)

Reactance a boomerang effect that may occur when consumers are threatened with a loss of freedom of choice; they respond by doing the opposite of the behaviour advocated in a persuasive message (p. 280)

Reality engineering the process whereby elements of popular culture are appropriated by marketers and become integrated into marketing strategies (e.g. product placement) (p. 453)

Recycling the re-use of resources in order to protect the environment (p. 258)

Reference group an actual or imaginary individual or group which has a significant effect on an individual's evaluations, aspirations or behaviour (p. 269)

Referent power the power of prominent people to affect others' consumption behaviours by virtue of product endorsements, distinctive fashion statements or championing causes (p. 274)

Relationship marketing the strategic perspective that stresses the long-term, human side of buyer/seller interactions (p. 255)

Relative advantage the belief that a product's use will provide a benefit other products cannot offer (p. 297)

Resonance a literary device, frequently used in advertising, which uses a play on words to communicate a product benefit (p. 168)

Response bias a form of contamination in survey research where some factor, such as the desire to make a good impression on the experimenter, leads respondents to modify their true answers (p. 86)

Restricted codes the ways of expressing and interpreting meanings that focus on the content of objects and tend to be used by the working class (p. 342)

Retrieval the process whereby desired information is accessed from long-term memory (p. 76)

RISC (Research Institute on Social Change) an organization that conducts international measurements of socio-cultural change in more than forty countries (p. 409)

Risky shift group members show a greater willingness to consider riskier alternatives following group discussions than they would if each member made his or her own decision without prior discussion (p. 279)

Rites of passage sacred times marked by a change in social status (p. 390)

Ritual a set of multiple, symbolic behaviours that occur in fixed sequence and that tend to be repeated periodically (p. 384)

Ritual artefacts items or consumer goods used in the performance of rituals (p. 386)

Role theory the perspective that much of consumer behaviour resembles action in a play (p. 8)

Rumour a word-of-mouth campaign to promote one product and criticize its competitors (p. 283)

Sacralization a process that occurs when ordinary objects, events or people take on sacred meaning to a culture or to specific groups within a culture (p. 395)

Sacred consumption the process of consuming objects and events that are set apart from normal life and treated with some degree of respect or awe (p. 391)

Savings rate the amount of money saved for later use influenced by consumers' pessimism or optimism about their personal circumstances and perceptions of the economy (p. 330)

Schema an organized collection of beliefs and feelings represented in a cognitive category *(pp. 40, 79)*

Secondary data pre-existing information in some form; it was originally collected for another purpose but may be useful to the present research *(p. 31)*

Self-concept the attitude a person holds to him- or herself *(p. 176)*

Self-gifts the products or services bought by consumers for their own use as a reward or consolation *(p. 387)*

Self-image congruence models the approaches based on the prediction that products will be chosen when their attributes match some aspect of the self *(p. 182)*

Self-perception theory an alternative explanation of dissonance effects; it assumes that people use observations of their own behaviour to infer their attitudes towards an object *(p. 129)*

Semiotics a field of study that examines the correspondence between a sign and the meaning(s) it conveys *(p. 57)*

Sensation the immediate response of sensory receptors to such basic stimuli as light, colour and sound *(p. 40)*

Sensory memory the temporary storage of information received from the senses *(p. 77)*

Sex-typed traits characteristics that are stereotypically associated with one sex or another *(p. 185)*

Shopping orientation a consumer's general attitudes and motivations regarding the act of shopping *(p. 248)*

Short-term memory the system that allows us to retain information for a short period *(p. 77)*

Sign the sensory imagery that represents the intended meanings of the object *(p. 57)*

Signifying practices practices that have meaning to individuals, who know how to interpret them, thanks to the understanding of culture as the interpreting system *(p. 377)*

Single-source data a compilation of information that includes different aspects of consumption and demographic data for a common consumer segment *(p. 428)*

Sleeper effect the process whereby differences in attitude change between positive and negative sources seem to diminish over time *(p. 157)*

Social class the overall rank of people in society; people who are grouped within the same social class are approximately equal in terms of their social standing, occupations and lifestyles *(p. 332)*

Social comparison theory the perspective that people compare their outcomes with others' as a way to increase the stability of their own self-evaluation, especially when physical evidence is unavailable *(p. 278)*

Social hierarchy a ranking of social desirability in terms of consumers' access to such resources as money, education and luxury goods *(p. 333)*

Social judgement theory the perspective that people assimilate new information about attitude objects in the light of what they already know or feel; the initial attitude as a frame of reference and new information are categorized in terms of this standard *(p. 131)*

Social marketing the promotion of causes and ideas (social products), such as energy conservation, charities and population control *(p. 121)*

Social mobility the movement of individuals from one social class to another *(p. 336)*

Social stratification the process in a social system by which scarce and valuable resources are distributed unequally to status positions which become more or less permanently ranked in terms of the share of valuable resources each receives *(p. 335)*

Sociometric methods the techniques for measuring group dynamics that involve tracing of communication patterns in and among groups *(p. 291)*

Source attractiveness the dimensions of a communicator which increase his or her persuasiveness; these include expertise and attractiveness *(p. 153)*

Source credibility a communication source's perceived expertise, objectivity or trustworthiness *(p. 153)*

Stage of cognitive development segmentation of children by age or their ability to comprehend concepts of increasing complexity *(p. 321)*

Status crystallization the extent to which different indicators of a person's status are consistent with one another *(p. 339)*

Status symbols products that are purchased and displayed to signal membership in a desirable social class *(p. 327)*

Stereotype technique a projective technique where respondents are given a description of a typical family or person and asked to supply related information *(p. 28)*

Stimulus ambiguity a condition occurring when the meanings conveyed by an ad are unclear; ambiguous stimuli will usually be interpreted in a way that's consistent with the consumer's own set of needs and motives *(p. 54)*

Stimulus discrimination the process that occurs when behaviour caused by two stimuli is different as when consumers learn to differentiate a brand from its competitors *(p. 67)*

Stimulus generalization the process that occurs when the behaviour caused by a reaction to one stimulus occurs in the presence of other, similar stimuli *(p. 67)*

Storage the process that occurs when knowledge entered in long-term memory is integrated with what is already in memory and 'warehoused' until needed *(p. 75)*

Store gestalt consumers' global evaluation of a store *(p. 251)*

Store image the 'personality' of a shop composed of attributes such as location, merchandise suitability and the knowledge and congeniality of the sales staff *(p. 251)*

Subculture a group whose members share beliefs and common experiences that set them apart from the members of the main culture *(p. 429)*

Superego the system that internalizes society's rules which works to prevent the id from seeking selfish gratification *(p. 112)*

Surrogate consumer a professional who is retained to evaluate and/or make purchases on behalf of a consumer *(p. 288)*

Surveys a form of primary data collection in which a respondent is presented with a questionnaire usually in the form of a set of statements and is asked to respond to them *(p. 31)*

Symbolic interactionism a sociological approach stressing that relationships with people play a large part in forming the self; people live in a symbolic environment and the meaning attached to any situation or object is determined by a person's interpretation of those symbols *(p. 179)*

Symbolic self-completion theory the perspective that people who have an incomplete self-definition in some context will compensate by acquiring symbols associated with a desired social identity *(p. 181)*

Syncratic decisions purchase decisions that are made jointly by spouses *(p. 313)*

Taste culture a group of consumers who share aesthetic and intellectual preferences *(p. 341)*

Terminal values end-states desired by members of a culture *(p. 107)*

Theory of cognitive dissonance a theory based on the premise that people have a need for order and consistency in their lives and that a state of tension is created when beliefs or behaviours conflict with one another *(p. 96)*

Theory of reasoned action a version of the Fishbein multi-attitude theory that considers such factors as

social pressure and the attitude towards the act of buying a product rather than attitudes towards just the product itself *(p. 138)*

Time style determined by an individual's priorities, it incorporates such dimensions as economic time, past or future orientation, time submissiveness and time anxiety *(p. 242)*

Transitional economies countries that are in the process of transforming their economic system from a controlled, centralized system to a free market one *(p. 463)*

Trialability the likelihood of experimenting with an innovation prior to making a commitment *(p. 296)*

Trickle-down theory the perspective that fashions spread as a result of status symbols associated with the upper classes trickling down to the other social classes as these consumers try to emulate those with higher status *(p. 449)*

Two-factor theory the perspective that two separate psychological processes are operating when a person is repeatedly exposed to an ad; repetition increases familiarity and thus reduces uncertainty about the product, but over time boredom increases with each exposure and at some point the level of boredom begins to exceed the amount of uncertainty reduced, resulting in wear-out *(p. 161)*

Unobtrusive measures methods of data collection that do not require direct human responses. These techniques are sometimes called *trace analysis* because they rely on the physical traces, or evidence, of past behaviour *(p. 33)*

Uses and gratifications theory argues that consumers are an active, goal-directed audience who draw on mass media as a resource to satisfy needs *(p. 148)*

Value a belief that some condition is preferable to its opposite *(p. 104)*

Value system a culture's ranking of the relative importance of values *(p. 105)*

Values and Lifestyles (VALS) a psychographic segmentation system used to categorize consumers into clusters *(p. 413)*

Want the particular form of consumption chosen to satisfy a need *(p. 92)*

Weber's Law the ideas shared by members of a culture about principles of order and fairness *(p. 50)*

Word-of-mouth communication (WOM) the information transmitted by individual consumers on an informal basis *(p. 281)*

Worldview the ideas shared by members of a culture about principles of order and fairness *(p. 379)*

Notes

Chapter 1

1. Christian Alsted, 'De unge, smukke og rige – oldies', *Markedsføring* 11(1992): 30.
2. Mike Featherstone (ed.) *Global Culture. Nationalism, Globalization, and Modernity* (London: Sage, 1990).
3. Daniel Miller: 'Consumption as the Vanguard of History', in D. Miller (ed.), *Acknowledging Consumption* (London: Routledge, 1995): 1–57.
4. Erving Goffman, *The Presentation of Self in Everyday Life* (Garden City, N.Y.: Doubleday, 1959); George H. Mead, *Mind, Self, and Society* (Chicago: University of Chicago Press, 1934); Michael R. Solomon, 'The Role of Products as Social Stimuli: A Symbolic Interactionism Perspective', *Journal of Consumer Research* 10 (December 1983): 319–29.
5. William F. Schoell and Joseph P. Guiltinan, *Marketing: Contemporary Concepts and Practices*, 4th edn (Boston: Allyn & Bacon, 1990).
6. Jeffrey F. Durgee, 'On Cézanne, Hot Buttons, and Interpreting Consumer Storytelling', *Journal of Consumer Marketing* 5 (Fall 1988): 47–51.
7. Joshua Levine, 'Desperately Seeking Jeepness', *Forbes* (15 May 1989): 134; Anthony Ramirez, 'New Cigarettes Raising Issue of Target Market', *New York Times* (18 February 1990): 28; Howard Schlossberg, 'Segmenting Becomes Constitutional Issue', *Marketing News* (16 April 1990): 1.
8. Annetta Miller, 'You Are What You Buy', *Newsweek* (4 June 1990) 2: 59.
9. Natalie Perkins, 'Zeroing in on Consumer Values', *Ad Age* (22 March 1993): 23.
10. Quoted in March Magiera, 'Levi's Broadens Appeal', *Ad Age* (17 July 1989): 1(2).
11. Jennifer Lawrence, 'Gender-specific Works for Diapers – Almost Too Well', *Ad Age* (8 February 1993): S-10 (2).
12. 'Wrangler Ad Ropes in Men', *Marketing* (27 March 1997).
13. Richard P. Coleman, 'The Continuing Significance of Social Class to Marketing', *Journal of Consumer Research*, 10 (December 1983): 265–80.
14. BBS Radio, 4 January 1997.
15. Jean-Claude Usunier, *Marketing across Cultures* (Hemel Hempstead: Prentice Hall, 1996).
16. Euromonitor, *European Marketing Data and Statistics*, 32nd edition (1997).
17. Rena Bartos, 'International Demographic Data? Incomparable!', *Marketing and Research Today* (November 1989): 205–12.
18. Søren Askegaard and Tage Koed Madsen, 'European Food Cultures: An Exploratory Analysis of Food Related Preferences and Behaviour in European Regions', *MAPP Working Paper no. 26* (Aarhus: The Aarhus Business School, 1995).
19. *Information*, 4 February 1997.
20. *Weekendavisen*, 21–25 March 1997.
21. Richard Vezina, Alain d'Astous and Sophie Deschamps, 'The Physically Disabled Consumer: Some Preliminary Findings and an Agenda for Future Research', in F. Hansen (ed.), *European Advances in Consumer Research*, vol. 2 (Provo, UT: Association for Consumer Research, 1995): 277–81.
22. 'Suited, Surfing and Shopping', *The Economist*, (25 January 1997): 69; *Markedsføring*, Internetsektionen, no. 6 (1996).
23. *Samvirke*, no. 3 (March 1997).
24. 'Play Your Cards Right', *Marketing* (17 April 1997): 32–3.
25. Jonathan Berry, 'Database Marketing', *Business Week* (5 September 1994): 56 (7).
26. Barry Leventhal, 'An Approach to Fusing Market Research with Database Marketing', *Journal of the Market Research Society*, 39(4) (1997): 545–58.
27. Susan Fournier, 'A Consumer–Brand Relationship Framework for Strategic Brand Management',

Doctoral Dissertation (Dept of Marketing, University of Florida, 1994).

28. Douglas B. Holt, 'How Consumers Consume: A Typology of Consumption Practices', *Journal of Consumer Research*, 22(1) (June 1995): 1–16.

29. For a recent discussion of this trend, see Russell W. Belk, 'Hyperreality and Globalization: Culture in the Age of Ronald McDonald', *Journal of International Consumer Marketing*, 8 (3/4) (1995): 23–37.

30. Bernard Dubois and Gilles Laurent, 'Is there a Euro Consumer for Luxury Goods?', in W.F. van Raaij and G. Bamossy (eds.), *European Advances in Consumer Research*, vol. 1 (Provo, UT: Association for Consumer Research, 1993): 58–69.

31. *Politiken* (14 November 1997): 13.

32. Pasi Falk, 'The Advertising Genealogy', in P. Sulkunen, J. Holmwood, H. Radner and G. Schulze (eds.), *Constructing the New Consumer Society* (London: Macmillan, 1997): 81–107.

33. *Morgenavisen Jyllands-Posten* (22 November 1996): 1, 6, 7.

34. Larry Edwards, 'The Decision Was Easy', Advertising Age, 2 (26 August 1987): 106.

35. For scientific consumer research and discussions related to public policy issues, there is a special European journal, the *Journal of Consumer Policy*.

36. Andrew Pollack, 'Japan Debates Broader Power for Consumers', *New York Times* (8 March 1993): A1 (2).

37. Morris B. Holbrook, 'The Consumer Researcher Visits Radio City: Dancing in the Dark', in E.C. Hirschman and M.B. Holbrook (eds.), *Advances in Consumer Research*, 12 (Provo, UT: Association for Consumer Research, 1985): 28–31.

38. Cf. Philip Kotler and Alan R. Andreasen, *Strategic Marketing for Nonprofit Organizations*, 4th edn (Englewood Cliffs, NJ: Prentice Hall, 1991); Jeff B. Murray and Julie L. Ozanne, 'The Critical Imagination: Emancipatory Interests in Consumer Research', *Journal of Consumer Research* 18 (September 1991): 192–44; William D. Wells, 'Discovery-Oriented Consumer Research', *Journal of Consumer Research* 19 (March 1993): 489–504.

39. Jean-Claude Usunier, 'Integrating the Cultural Dimension into International Marketing', Proceedings of the Second Conference on the Cultural Dimension of International Marketing (Odense: Odense University, 1995): 1–23.

40. Flemming Hansen (ed.), *European Advances in Consumer Research*, vol. 2 (Provo, UT: Association for Consumer Research, 1995).

41. Some of the material in this section is adapted from Naresh K. Malhotra, *Marketing Research:*

An Applied Orientation (Englewood Cliffs, N.J.: Prentice Hall, 1993). The reader is encouraged to consult this or the other excellent textbooks currently available for further information on the field of marketing research.

42. Wendy Gordon and Roy Langmaid, *Qualitative Market Research* (Aldershot: Gower, 1988).

43. Grant McCracken, *The Long Interview* (Thousand Oaks: Sage, 1988).

44. Deborah D. Heisley and Sidney J. Levy, 'Autodriving: a Photoelicitation Technique', *Journal of Consumer Research* 18 (December 1989): 257–72.

45. Suzanne C. Grunert-Beckmann and Søren Askegaard, 'Consumers' Experience of Financial Management Services: A Qualitative Study', *Proceedings of XXII International Association for Research in Economic Psychology Conference*, ed. R. Luna (Valencia: Universidad de Valencia, 1997): 93–106.

46. Mason Haire, 'Projective Techniques in Marketing Research', *Journal of Marketing* 14 (April 1950): 649–50.

47. Stephen J. Arnold and Eileen Fischer, 'Hermeneutics and Consumer Research', *Journal of Consumer Research* (June 1994): 55–70; Craig J. Thompson, Howard R. Pollio and William B. Locander, 'The Spoken and the Unspoken: A Hermeneutic Approach to Understanding the Cultural Viewpoints That Underlie Consumers' Expressed Meanings', *Journal of Consumer Research* 21 (December 1994): 432–52.

48. For a detailed discussion of ethnography and its potential for strategic applications, see Eric J. Arnould and Melanie Wallendorf, 'Market-Oriented Ethnography: Interpretation Building and Marketing Strategy Formulation', *Journal of Marketing Research* (November 1994): 484–504.

49. Russell W. Belk (ed.), *Highways and Buyways: Naturalistic Research from the Consumer Behavior Odyssey* (Provo, UT: Association for Consumer Research, 1991).

50. Cf. Ronald Groves and Russell W. Belk, 'Special Session Summary. The Odyssey Downunder: A Qualitative Study of Aboriginal Consumers', F.R. Kardes and M. Sujan (eds.), *Advances in Consumer Research* XXII (Provo, UT: Association for Consumer Research 1995): 303–5.

51. Elizabeth Roberts, 'This Ad's For You', *Newsweek* (24 February 1992): 40.

52. John Thøgersen, 'A Model of Recycling Behaviour, with Evidence from Danish Source Separation Programmes', *International Journal of Research in Marketing*, 11 (1994): 145–63.

Chapter 2

1. Kim Foltz, 'Campaign on Harmony Backfires for Benetton', *New York Times* (20 November 1989): D8.
2. Jerome S. Bruner, 'On Perceptual Readiness', *Psychological Review* 64 (March 1957): 123–52.
3. Joseph Pereira and Barbara Carton, 'Toys 'R' Us to Banish some "Realistic Toy" Guns', *Wall Street Journal* (October 1994): B1 (2 pp.).
4. Elizabeth C. Hirschman and Morris B. Holbrook, 'Hedonic Consumption: Emerging Concepts, Methods, and Propositions', *Journal of Marketing* 46 (Summer 1982): 92–101.
5. Stephen Brown, *Postmodern Marketing* (London: Routledge, 1995).
6. Maryon Tysoe, 'What's Wrong with Blue Potatoes?', *Psychology Today* (December 1985) 2: 6.
7. *Markedsføring* 1 (1995): 18.
8. 'Crystal Clear Persuasion', *Tufts University Diet & Nutrition Letter* (January 1993): 1.
9. Dianne Solis, 'Cost No Object for Mexico's Makeup Junkies', *The Wall Street Journal* (7 June 1994): B1.
10. Tysoe, 'What's Wrong with Blue Potatoes?'.
11. Meg Rosen and Frank Alpert, 'Protecting Your Business Image: The Supreme Court Rules on Trade Dress', *Journal of Consumer Marketing* 11(1) (1994): 50–5.
12. 'Ny emballage og nyt navn fordoblede salget', *Markedsføring* 12 (1992): 24.
13. Quoted in Cynthia Morris, 'The Mystery of Fragrance', *Essence* 71 (May 1988) 3: 71.
14. Suein L. Hwang, 'Seeking Scents that No One Has Smelled', *The Wall Street Journal* (10 August 1994): B1 2.
15. 'En duft af træ', *Markedsføring* 13 (1996): 6.
16. Gail Tom, 'Marketing with Music', *Journal of Consumer Marketing* 7 (Spring 1990): 49–53; J. Vail, 'Music as a Marketing Tool', *Advertising Age* (4 November 1985): 24.
17. Joan E. Rigdon, 'Hallmark Cards Can Send a Message That's a Real Earful for a Loved One', *The Wall Street Journal* (5 November 1993): A5I.
18. *Marketing* (3 April 1997).
19. For research in time compression, see James MacLachlan and Michael H. Siegel, 'Reducing the Costs of Television Commercials by Use of Time Compression', *Journal of Marketing Research* 17 (February 1980): 52–7; James MacLachlan, 'Listener Perception of Time Compressed Spokespersons', *Journal of Advertising Research* 2 (April/May 1982): 47–51; Danny L. Moore,

Douglas Hausknecht and Kanchana Thamodaran, 'Time Compression, Response Opportunity, and Persuasion', *Journal of Consumer Research* 13 (June 1986): 85–99.
20. Jean-Claude Usunier, *Marketing Across Cultures* (Hemel Hempstead: Prentice Hall, 1996).
21. Anne C. Bech, Erling Engelund, Hans Jørn Juhl, Kai Kristensen and Carsten Stig Poulsen, 'QFood. Optimal Design of Food Products', *MAPP Working Paper* no. 19 (Aarhus: The Aarhus School of Business, 1994); Hans Jørn Juhl, 'A Sensory Analysis of Butter Cookies – An Application of Generalized Procrustes Analysis', *MAPP Working Paper* no. 20 (Aarhus: The Aarhus School of Business, 1994).
22. Andreas Scharf, 'Positionierung neuer bzw. modifizierter Nahrungs- und Genußmittel durch integrierte Markt- und Sensorik-forschung', *Marketing ZFP*, 1 (1st quarter 1995): 5–17.
23. See Tim Davis, 'Taste Tests: Are the Blind Leading the Blind?', *Beverage World* (April 1987) 3: 43.
24. Quoted in Davis, 'Taste Tests', 44.
25. '$10 Sure Thing', *Time* (4 August 1980): 51.
26. David Kilburn, 'Japanese VCR Edits Out the Ads', *Advertising Age* (20 August 1990): 16.
27. Craig Reiss, 'Fast-Forward Ads Deliver', *Advertising Age* (27 October 1986) 2: 3; Steve Sternberg, 'VCR's: Impact and Implications', *Marketing and Media Decisions* 22 (December 1987) 5: 100.
28. 'It's All in the Mind', *Marketing* (27 March 1997): 31–4.
29. Quoted in Stuart Elliott, 'When Up Is Down, Does It Sell?', *New York Times* (21 February 1992) 2: D1.
30. 'Reklamer i det skjulte', *Markedsføring* 7 (1996): 28.
31. 'Toilet Ads', *Marketing* (5 December 1996): 11.
32. 'Rare Media Well Done', *Marketing* (16 January 1997): 31.
33. 'Contact Lenses', *Marketing* (29 August 1996): 7.
34. Kim Foltz, *New York Times* (23 October 1989): D11.
35. *El Mundo Deportivo* (5 March 1997).
36. Michael Lev, 'Music Industry Broadens Its Campaigns', *New York Times* (17 January 1992): D15.
37. 'Realkredit for mennesker', *Markedsføring* 4 (1996): 10.
38. Brown, *Postmodern Marketing*.
39. See David Mick, 'Consumer Research and Semiotics: Exploring the Morphology of Signs, Symbols, and Significance', *Journal of Consumer Research* 13 (September 1986): 196–213.

40. Teresa J. Domzal and Jerome B. Kernan, 'Reading Advertising: The What and How of Product Meaning', *Journal of Consumer Marketing* 9 (Summer 1992): 48–64, p. 49.

41. Winfried Nöth, *Handbook of Semiotics* (London: Sage, 1994); Mick, 'Consumer Research and Semiotics'; Charles Sanders Peirce, in Charles Hartshorne, Paul Weiss and Arthur W. Burks (eds.), *Collected Papers* (Cambridge, MA: Harvard University Press, 1931–58).

42. Jacques Durand, 'Rhetorical Figures in the Advertising Image', in Jean Umiker-Sebeok (ed.), *Marketing and Semiotics. New Directions in the Study of Signs for Sale* (Berlin: Mouton de Gruyter, 1987): 295–318.

43. Christian Alsted and Hanne Hartvig Larsen, 'Toward a Semiotic Typology of Advertising Forms', *Marketing and Semiotics. Selected Papers from the Copenhagen Symposium*, ed. Hanne Hartvig Larsen, David Glen Mick and Christian Alsted (Copenhagen: Handelshøjskolens forlag, 1991): 75–103.

44. Winfried Nöth, 'The Language of Commodities. Groundwork for a Semiotics of Consumer Goods', *International Journal of Research in Marketing* 4 (1988): 173–86.

45. Cf. the early introduction of the field: Elisabeth C. Hirschman and Morris B. Holbrook (eds.), *Symbolic Consumer Behavior* (Ann Arbor, MI: Association for Consumer Research, 1981).

46. Odile Solomon, 'Semiotics and Marketing. New Directions in Industrial Design Applications', *International Journal of Research in Marketing* 4 (1988): 201–15.

47. Jean-Marie Floch, 'The Contribution of Structural Semiotics to the Design of a Hypermarket', *International Journal of Research in Marketing* 4 (1988): 233–52.

48. James Ogilvy, 'This Postmodern Business', *Marketing and Research Today* (February 1990): 4–22.

49. Chantal Cinquin, 'Homo Coca-Colens: From Marketing to Semiotics and Politics', in Jean Umiker-Sebeok (ed.), *Marketing and Semiotics. New Directions in the Study of Signs for Sale* (Berlin: Mouton de Gruyter, 1987): 485–95.

50. A. Fuat Fırat and Alladi Venkatesh, 'Postmodernity: The Age of Marketing', *International Journal of Research in Marketing*, 10(3) (1993): 227–49.

51. Jean Baudrillard, *Simulations* (New York: Semiotext(e), 1983).

Chapter 3

1. Robert A. Baron, *Psychology: The Essential Science* (Boston: Allyn & Bacon, 1989).

2. Richard A. Feinberg, 'Credit Cards as Spending Facilitating Stimuli: A Conditioning Interpretation', *Journal of Consumer Research* 13 (December 1986): 348–56.

3. R. A. Rescorla, 'Pavlovian Conditioning: It's Not What You Think It Is', *American Psychologist* 43 (1988): 151–60; Elnora W. Stuart, Terence A. Shimp and Randall W. Engle, 'Classical Conditioning of Consumer Attitudes: Four Experiments in an Advertising Context', *Journal of Consumer Research* 14 (December 1987): 334–9; Terence A. Shimp, Elnora W. Stuart and Randall W. Engle, 'A Program of Classical Conditioning Experiments Testing Variations in the Conditioned Stimulus and Context', *Journal of Consumer Research* 18(1) (June 1991): 1–12.

4. 'Anemic Crocodile', *Forbes* (15 August 1994): 116.

5. Baron, *Psychology*.

6. For a comprehensive approach to consumer behaviour based on operant conditioning principles, see Gordon R. Foxall, 'Behavior Analysis and Consumer Psychology', *Journal of Economic Psychology* 15 (March 1994): 5–91. Foxall also sets out some consumer behaviour based on a neo-behaviourist perspective. By identifying environmental determinants, he develops four classes of consumer behaviour: *accomplishment*, *pleasure*, *accumulation* and *maintenance*. For an extensive discussion on this approach, see the entire special issue of: Gordon R. Foxall, 'Science and Interpretation in Consumer Behavior: A Radical Behaviourist Perspective', *European Journal of Marketing*, 29(9) (1995): 3–99.

7. Ellen J. Langer, *The Psychology of Control* (Beverly Hills, CA: Sage, 1983); Klaus G. Grunert, 'Automatic and Strategic Processes in Advertising Effects', *Journal of Marketing* 60 (1996): 88–91.

8. Robert B. Cialdini, *Influence: Science and Practice*, 2nd edn (New York: William Morrow, 1984).

9. Chris T. Allen and Thomas J. Madden, 'A Closer Look at Classical Conditioning', *Journal of Consumer Research* 12 (December 1985): 301–15.

10. Albert Bandura, *Social Foundations of Thought and Action: A Social Cognitive View* (Englewood Cliffs, NJ: Prentice Hall, 1986); Baron, *Psychology*.

11. Allen and Madden, 'A Closer Look at Classical Conditioning'; Chester A. Insko and William F. Oakes, 'Awareness and the Conditioning of Attitudes', *Journal of Personality and Social Psychology* 4 (November 1966): 487–96; Carolyn K. Staats and Arthur W. Staats, 'Meaning Established by Classical Conditioning', *Journal of Experimental Psychology* 54 (July 1957): 74–80.

12. Kevin Lane Keller, 'Conceptualizing, Measuring, and Managing Customer-Based Brand Equity', *Journal of Marketing* 57 (January 1993): 1–22; Patrick Bawise 'Brand Equity: Snark or Boojum?', *International Journal of Research in Marketing*, 10 (1993) 93–104; W. Fred van Raaij and Wim Schoonderbeer, 'Meaning Structure of Brand Names and Extensions', in W. Fred van Raaij and Gary J. Bamossy (eds.), *European Advances in Consumer Research* (Provo, UT, Association for Consumer Research, 1993): 479–84; Gil McWilliam, 'The Effect of Brand Typology on Brand Extension Fit: Commercial and Academic Research Findings', in *European Advances in Association for Consumer Research* (1993): 485–91; Elyette Roux and Frederic Lorange, 'Brand Extension Research: A Review', in W. Fred van Raaij and Gary J. Bamossy (eds.), *European Advances in Consumer Research* (Provo, UT: Association for Consumer Research, 1993): 492–500; 'The Art of Perception', *Marketing* (28 November 1996): 25–9.

13. Herbert Krugman, 'Low Recall and High Recognition of Advertising', *Journal of Advertising Research* (February/March 1986): 79–86.

14. Gerald J. Gorn, 'The Effects of Music in Advertising on Choice Behavior: A Classical Conditioning Approach', *Journal of Marketing* 46 (Winter 1982): 94–101.

15. Calvin Bierley, Frances K. McSweeney and Renee Vannieuwkerk, 'Classical Conditioning of Preferences for Stimuli', *Journal of Consumer Research* 12 (December 1985): 316–23; James J. Kellaris and Anthony D. Cox, 'The Effects of Background Music in Advertising: A Reassessment', *Journal of Consumer Research* 16 (June 1989): 113–18.

16. Frances K. McSweeney and Calvin Bierley, 'Recent Developments in Classical Conditioning', *Journal of Consumer Research* 11 (September 1984): 619–31.

17. Basil G. Englis, 'The Reinforcement Properties of Music Videos: "I Want My . . . I Want My . . . I Want My . . . MTV"' (paper presented at the meetings of the Association for Consumer Research, New Orleans, 1989).

18. 'Giving Bad Puns the Business', *Newsweek* (11 December 1989): 71.

19. Bernice Kanner, 'Growing Pains – and Gains: Brand Names Branch Out', *New York* (13 March 1989): 22.

20. Peter H. Farquhar, 'Brand Equity', *Marketing Insights* (Summer 1989): 59.

21. John Marchese, 'Forever Harley', *New York Times* (17 October 1993): 10; 'Spamming the Globe', *Newsweek* (29 August 1994): 8.

22. Quoted in 'Look-Alikes Mimic Familiar Packages', *New York Times* (9 August 1986): D1; 'Action Fails to Match Spirit of Lookalike Law', *Marketing* (27 March 1997): 19.

23. Laurie Hays, 'Too Many Computer Names Confuse Too Many Buyers', *Wall Street Journal* (29 June 1994): B1 (2 pp.).

24. Blaise J. Bergiel and Christine Trosclair, 'Instrumental Learning: Its Application to Customer Satisfaction', *Journal of Consumer Marketing* 2 (Fall 1985): 23–8.

25. Terence A. Shimp, 'Neo-Pavlovian Conditioning and Its Implications for Consumer Theory and Research', in Thomas S. Robertson and Harold H. Kassarjian (eds.), *Handbook of Consumer Behavior* (Englewood Cliffs, NJ: Prentice Hall, 1991).

26. R. C. Atkinson and R. M. Shiffrin, 'Human Memory: A Proposed System and Its Control Processes', in K. W. Spence and J. T. Spence (eds.), *The Psychology of Learning and Motivation: Advances in Research and Theory* (New York: Academic Press, 1968): 89–195.

27. James R. Bettman, 'Memory Factors in Consumer Choice: A Review', *Journal of Marketing* (Spring 1979): 37–53. For a study that explored the relative impact of internal versus external memory on brand choice, cf. Joseph W. Alba, Howard Marmorstein and Amitava Chattopadhyay, 'Transitions in Preference Over Time: The Effects of Memory on Message Persuasiveness', *Journal of Marketing Research* 29 (November 1992): 406–17. For other research on memory and advertising, see H. Shanker Krishnan and Dipankar Chakravarti, 'Varieties of Brand Memory Induced by Advertising: Determinants, Measures, and Relationships', in David A. Aaker and Alexander L. Biel (eds.), *Brand Equity & Advertising: Advertising's Role in Building Strong Brands* (Hillsdale, NJ: Lawrence Erlbaum Associates, 1993): 213–31; Bernd H. Schmitt, Nader T. Tavassoli and Robert T. Millard, 'Memory for Print Ads: Understanding Relations Among Brand Name,

Copy, and Picture', *Journal of Consumer Psychology* 2(1) (1993): 55–81; Marian Friestad and Esther Thorson, 'Remembering Ads: The Effects of Encoding Strategies, Retrieval Cues, and Emotional Response', *Journal of Consumer Psychology* 2 (1) (1993): 1–23; Surendra N. Singh, Sanjay Mishra, Neeli Bendapudi and Denise Linville, 'Enhancing Memory of Television Commercials Through Message Spacing', *Journal of Marketing Research* 31 (August 1994): 384–92.

28. Kim Robertson, 'Recall and Recognition Effects of Brand Name Imagery', *Psychology & Marketing* 4 (Spring 1987): 3–15.

29. Endel Tulving, 'Remembering and Knowing the Past', *American Scientist* 77 (July/August 1989): 361.

30. Baron, *Psychology*.

31. George A. Miller, 'The Magical Number Seven, Plus or Minus Two: Some Limits on Our Capacity for Processing Information', *Psychological Review* 63 (1956): 81–97.

32. James N. MacGregor, 'Short-Term Memory Capacity: Limitation or Optimization?', *Psychological Review* 94 (1987): 107–8.

33. See Catherine A. Cole and Michael J. Houston, 'Encoding and Media Effects on Consumer Learning Deficiencies in the Elderly', *Journal of Marketing Research* 24 (February 1987): 55–64; A. M. Collins and E. F. Loftus, 'A Spreading Activation Theory of Semantic Processing', *Psychological Review* 82 (1975): 407–28; Fergus I. M. Craik and Robert S. Lockhart, 'Levels of Processing: A Framework for Memory Research', *Journal of Verbal Learning and Verbal Behavior* 11 (1972): 671–84.

34. Walter A. Henry, 'The Effect of Information-Processing Ability on Processing Accuracy', *Journal of Consumer Research* 7 (June 1980): 42–8.

35. Anthony G. Greenwald and Clark Leavitt, 'Audience Involvement in Advertising: Four Levels', *Journal of Consumer Research* 11 (June 1984): 581–92.

36. Kevin Lane Keller, 'Memory Factors in Advertising: The Effect of Advertising Retrieval Cues on Brand Evaluations', *Journal of Consumer Research* 14 (December 1987): 316–33. For a discussion of processing operations that occur during brand choice, see Gabriel Biehal and Dipankar Chakravarti, 'Consumers' Use of Memory and External Information in Choice: Macro and Micro Perspectives', *Journal of Consumer Research* 12 (March 1986): 382–405.

37. Susan T. Fiske and Shelley E. Taylor, *Social Cognition* (Reading, MA: Addison-Wesley, 1984).

38. Deborah Roedder John and John C. Whitney, Jr, 'The Development of Consumer Knowledge in Children: A Cognitive Structure Approach', *Journal of Consumer Research* 12 (March 1986): 406–17.

39. Michael R. Solomon, Carol Surprenant, John A. Czepiel and Evelyn G. Gutman, 'A Role Theory Perspective on Dyadic Interactions: The Service Encounter', *Journal of Marketing* 49 (winter 1985): 99–111.

40. Roger W. Morrell, Denise C. Park and Leonard W. Poon, 'Quality of Instructions on Prescription Drug Labels: Effects on Memory and Comprehension in Young and Old Adults', *The Gerontologist* 29 (1989): 345–54.

41. Frank R. Kardes, Gurumurthy Kalyanaram, Murali Chandrashekaran and Ronald J. Dornoff, 'Brand Retrieval, Consideration Set Composition, Consumer Choice, and the Pioneering Advantage' (unpublished manuscript, the University of Cincinnati, OH, 1992).

42. Nijar Dawar and Philip Parket 'Marketing Universals: Consumers' Use of Brand Name, Price, Physical Appearance, and Retailer Reputation as Signals of Product Quality', *Journal of Marketing* 58 (1994) 81–95; Judith Lynne Zaichkowsky and Padma Vipat, 'Inferences from Brand Names' in W. Fred van Raaij and Gary J. Bamossy (eds.), *European Advances in Consumer Research* (Provo, UT: Association for Consumer Research, 1993): 534–40.

43. Krugman, 'Low Recall and High Recognition of Advertising'.

44. Eric J. Johnson and J. Edward Russo, 'Product Familiarity and Learning New Information', *Journal of Consumer Research* 11 (June 1984): 542–50.

45. Eric J. Johnson and J. Edward Russo, 'Product Familiarity and Learning New Information', in Kent Monoe (ed.), *Advances in Consumer Research* 8 (Ann Arbor, MI: Association for Consumer Research, 1981): 151–5; John G. Lynch and Thomas K. Srull, 'Memory and Attentional Factors in Consumer Choice: Concepts and Research Methods', *Journal of Consumer Research* 9 (June 1982): 18–37.

46. Julie A. Edell and Kevin Lane Keller, 'The Information Processing of Coordinated Media Campaigns', *Journal of Marketing Research* 26 (May 1989): 149–64.

47. Lynch and Srull, 'Memory and Attentional Factors in Consumer Choice'.

48. Joseph W. Alba and Amitava Chattopadhyay, 'Salience Effects in Brand Recall', *Journal of Marketing Research* 23 (November 1986): 363–70; Elizabeth C. Hirschman and Michael R. Solomon, 'Utilitarian, Aesthetic, and Familiarity Responses to Verbal Versus Visual Advertisements', in *Advances in Consumer Research* 11, ed. Thomas C. Kinnear (Provo, UT: Association for Consumer Research, 1984): 426–31.

49. Susan E. Heckler and Terry L. Childers, 'The Role of Expectancy and Relevancy in Memory for Verbal and Visual Information: What is Incongruency?', *Journal of Consumer Research* 18 (March 1992): 475–92.

50. Russell H. Fazio, Paul M. Herr and Martha C. Powell, 'On the Development and Strength of Category-Brand Associations in Memory: The Case of Mystery Ads', *Journal of Consumer Psychology* 1(1) (1992): 1–13.

51. Hirschman and Solomon, 'Utilitarian, Aesthetic, and Familiarity Responses to Verbal Versus Visual Advertisements'.

52. Terry Childers and Michael Houston, 'Conditions for a Picture-Superiority Effect on Consumer Memory', *Journal of Consumer Research* 11 (September 1984): 643–54; Terry Childers, Susan Heckler and Michael Houston, 'Memory for the Visual and Verbal Components of Print Advertisements', *Psychology & Marketing* 3 (Fall 1986): 147–50.

53. Werner Krober-Riel, 'Effects of Emotional Pictorial Elements in Ads Analyzed by Means of Eye Movement Monitoring', in Thomas C. Kinnear (ed.), *Advances in Consumer Research* 11 (Provo, UT: Association for Consumer Research, 1984): 591–6.

54. Hans-Bernd Brosius, 'Influence of Presentation Features and News Context on Learning from Television News', *Journal of Broadcasting & Electronic Media* 33 (Winter 1989): 1–14.

55. Raymond R. Burke and Thomas K. Srull, 'Competitive Interference and Consumer Memory for Advertising', *Journal of Consumer Research* 15 (June 1988): 55–68.

56. Burke and Srull, 'Competitive Interference and Consumer Memory for Advertising'.

57. Johnson and Russo, 'Product Familiarity and Learning New Information'.

58. Joan Meyers-Levy, 'The Influence of Brand Names Association Set Size and Word Frequency on Brand Memory', *Journal of Consumer Research* 16 (September 1989): 197–208.

59. Michael H. Baumgardner, Michael R. Leippe, David L. Ronis and Anthony G. Greenwald, 'In Search of Reliable Persuasion Effects: II. Associative Interference and Persistence of Persuasion in a Message-Dense Environment', *Journal of Personality and Social Psychology* 45 (September 1983): 524–37.

60. Alba and Chattopadhyay, 'Salience Effects in Brand Recall'.

61. Margaret Henderson Blair, Allan R. Kuse, David H. Furse and David W. Stewart, 'Advertising in a New and Competitive Environment: Persuading Consumers to Buy', *Business Horizons* 30 (November/December 1987): 20.

62. Lynch and Srull, 'Memory and Attentional Factors in Consumer Choice'.

63. Russell W. Belk, 'Possessions and the Extended Self', *Journal of Consumer Research* 15 (September 1988): 139–68.

64. Russell W. Belk, 'The Role of Possessions in Constructing and Maintaining a Sense of Past', in Marvin E. Goldberg, Gerald Gorn and Richard W. Pollay (eds.), *Advances in Consumer Research* 16 (Provo, UT: Association for Consumer Research, 1989): 669–78.

65. Hans Baumgartner, Mita Sujan and James R. Bettman, 'Autobiographical Memories, Affect and Consumer Information Processing', *Journal of Consumer Psychology* 1 (January 1992): 53–82; Mita Sujan, James R. Bettman and Hans Baumgartner, 'Influencing Consumer Judgments Using Autobiographical Memories: A Self-Referencing Perspective', *Journal of Marketing Research* 30 (November 1993): 422–36.

66. Kevin Goldman, 'New Campaigns Tip the Hat to Nostalgia', *Wall Street Journal* (9 August 1994): B4.

67. Gabriella Stern, 'VW Hopes Nostalgia will Spur Sales of Retooled Beetle, Fuel US Comback', *The Wall Street Journal, Europe* (7 May 1997): 4; 'Ostalgie for the Day When They'd Never Had it so Good', *The Independent* (10 February 1997); Almar Latour, 'Shelf Wars', *Central European Economic Review* (4) (Dow Jones, May 1997); G. Morello, 'The Hidden Dimensions of Marketing' (Amsterdam: Vrije Universiteit, 1993): 13.

68. Morris B. Holbrook and Robert M. Schindler, 'Some Exploratory Findings on the Development of Musical Tastes', *Journal of Consumer Research* 16 (June 1989): 119–24.

69. Randall Rothenberg, 'The Past is Now the Latest Craze', *New York Times* (29 November 1989): D1.

70. Cf. Morris B. Holbrook, 'Nostalgia and Consumption Preferences: Some Emerging Patterns of Consumer Tastes', *Journal of Consumer Research* 20 (September 1993): 245–56; Robert M. Schindler and Morris B.

Holbrook, 'Critical Periods in the Development of Men's and Women's Tastes in Personal Appearance', *Psychology & Marketing* 10(6) (November/December 1993): 549–64; Morris B. Holbrook and Robert M. Schindler, 'Age, Sex, and Attitude Toward the Past as Predictors of Consumers' Aesthetic Tastes for Cultural Products', *Journal of Marketing Research* 31 (August 1994): 412–22.

71. 'Only 38% of T.V. Audience Links Brands with Ads', *Marketing News* (6 January 1984): 10.

72. 'Terminal Television', *American Demographics* (January 1987): 15.

73. Richard P. Bagozzi and Alvin J. Silk, 'Recall, Recognition, and the Measurement of Memory for Print Advertisements', *Marketing Science* (1983): 95–134.

74. Adam Finn, 'Print Ad Recognition Readership Scores: An Information Processing Perspective', *Journal of Marketing Research* 25 (May 1988): 168–77.

75. Bettman, 'Memory Factors in Consumer Choice'.

76. Mark A. deTurck and Gerald M. Goldhaber, 'Effectiveness of Product Warning Labels: Effects of Consumers' Information Processing Objectives', *Journal of Consumer Affairs* 23(1) (1989): 111–25.

77. Finn, 'Print Ad Recognition Readership Scores'.

78. Surendra N. Singh and Gilbert A. Churchill, Jr, 'Response-Bias-Free Recognition Tests to Measure Advertising Effects', *Journal of Advertising Research* (June/July 1987): 23–36.

79. William A. Cook, 'Telescoping and Memory's Other Tricks', *Journal of Advertising Research* 27 (February/March 1987): 5–8.

80. 'On a Diet? Don't Trust Your Memory', *Psychology Today* (October 1989): 12.

81. Hubert A. Zielske and Walter A. Henry, 'Remembering and Forgetting Television Ads', *Journal of Advertising Research* 20 (April 1980): 7–13.

Chapter 4

1. Ronald Paul Hill and Harold Robinson, 'Fanatic Consumer Behavior: Athletics as a Consumption Experience', *Psychology & Marketing* 8 (Summer 1991): 79–100.

2. Robert A. Baron, *Psychology: The Essential Science* (Needham, MA: Allyn & Bacon, 1989).

3. Jean Baudrillard, 'La genèse idéologique des besoins', *Cahiers internationaux de sociologie* (47, 1969): 45–68.

4. Søren Askegaard and A. Fuat Fırat, 'Towards a Critique of Material Culture, Consumption, and Markets', S. Pearce (ed.), *Experiencing Material Culture in the Western World* (London: Leicester University Press): 114–39.

5. Robert Bocock, *Consumption* (London: Routledge 1993).

6. Russell W. Belk, Güliz Ger and Søren Askegaard, 'Consumer Desire in Three Cultures', in D. MacInnis and M. Brucks (eds.), *Advances in Consumer Research*, XXIV (Provo, UT: Association for Consumer Research, 1997): 24–8.

7. Leon Festinger, *A Theory of Cognitive Dissonance* (Stanford, CA: Stanford University Press, 1957).

8. Mary Kay Ericksen and M. Joseph Sirgy, 'Achievement Motivation and Clothing Preferences of White-Collar Working Women', in Michael R. Solomon (ed.), *The Psychology of Fashion* (Lexington, MA: Lexington Books, 1985), 357–69.

9. Abraham H. Maslow, *Motivation and Personality*, 2nd edn (New York: Harper & Row, 1970).

10. Richard Maddock, 'A Theoretical and Empirical Substructure of Consumer Motivation and Behaviour', in Flemming Hansen (ed.), *European Advances in Consumer Research* II (Provo, UT: Association for Consumer Research, 1995): 29–37.

11. John H. Antil, 'Conceptualization and Operationalization of Involvement', in Thomas C. Kinnear (ed.), *Advances in Consumer Research* 11 (Provo, UT: Association for Consumer Research, 1984), 203–9. The literature offers numerous approaches to the construct of involvement. See also Peter H. Bloch, 'Involvement beyond the Purchase Process: Conceptual Issues and Empirical Investigation', in Kent Monroe (ed.), *Advances in Consumer Research* 8 (Provo, UT: Association for Consumer Research, 1981), 61–5; George S. Day, *Buyer Attitudes and Brand Choice Behavior* (Chicago: Free Press, 1970); Michael J. Houston and Michael L. Rothschild, 'Conceptual and Methodological Perspectives on Involvement', in S.C. Jain (ed.), *Research Frontiers in Marketing: Dialogues and Directions* (Chicago: American Marketing Association, 1978), 184–7; John L. Lastovicka and David Gardner, 'Components of Involvement', in John C. Maloney and Bernard Silverman (eds.), *Attitude Research Plays for High Stakes* (Chicago: American Marketing Association, 1979), 53–73.

12. Andrew Mitchell, 'Involvement: A Potentially Important Mediator of Consumer Behavior', in William L. Wilkie (ed.), *Advances in Consumer Research* 6 (Provo, UT: Association for Consumer Research, 1979), 191–6.

13. Richard L. Celsi and Jerry C. Olson, 'The Role of Involvement in Attention and Comprehension Processes', *Journal of Consumer Research* 15 (September 1988): 210–24.

14. Ton Otker: 'The Highly Involved Consumer: A Marketing Myth?', *Marketing and Research Today* (February 1990): 30–6.

15. Anthony G. Greenwald and Clark Leavitt, 'Audience Involvement in Advertising: Four Levels', *Journal of Consumer Research* 11 (June 1984): 581–92.

16. For a discussion of interrelationships between situational and enduring involvement, see Marsha L. Richins, Peter H. Bloch and Edward F. McQuarrie, 'How Enduring and Situational Involvement Combine to Create Involvement Responses', *Journal of Consumer Psychology* 1 (1992)2: 143–53.

17. Rajeev Batra and Michael L. Ray, 'Operationalizing Involvement as Depth and Quality of Cognitive Responses', in Alice Tybout and Richard Bagozzi (eds.), *Advances in Consumer Research* 10 (Ann Arbor, MI: Association for Consumer Research, 1983), 309–13.

18. Herbert E. Krugman, 'The Impact of Television Advertising: Learning without Involvement', *Public Opinion Quarterly* 29 (Fall 1965): 349–56.

19. Bruce Crumley, 'Multipoints Add Up for Quick Burger', *Advertising Age* (November 29, 1993): 14.

20. Marsha L. Richins and Peter H. Bloch, 'After the New Wears off: The Temporal Context of Product Involvement', *Journal of Consumer Research* 13 (September 1986): 280–5.

21. Kevin J. Clancy, 'CPMs Must Bow to "Involvement" Measurement', *Advertising Age* (20 January 1992): 26.

22. For a newer, modified version of this scale, see Edward F. McQuarrie and J. Michael Munson, 'A Revised Product Involvement Inventory: Improved Usability and Validity', in John F. Sherry, Jr and Brian Sternthal (eds.), *Advances in Consumer Research* 19 (Provo, UT: Association for Consumer Research, 1992): 108–15.

23. Gilles Laurent and Jean-Noel Kapferer, 'Measuring Consumer Involvement Profiles', *Journal of Marketing Research* 22 (February 1985): 41–53; this scale was later validated on an American sample as well, cf. William C. Rodgers and Kenneth C. Schneider, 'An Empirical Evaluation of the Kapferer–Laurent Consumer Involvement Profile Scale', *Psychology & Marketing* 10 (July/August 1993) 4: 333–45.

24. Data adapted from Judith Lynne Zaichkowsky and James H. Sood, 'A Global Look at Consumers' Involvement and Use of Products', *International Marketing Review* 6 (1989)1: 20–34.

25. Culture clash experienced by one of the authors.

26. Morris B. Holbrook and Elizabeth C. Hirschman, 'The Experiential Aspects of Consumption: Consumer Fantasies, Feelings, and Fun', *Journal of Consumer Research* 9 (September 1982): 132–40.

27. Deborah J. MacInnis, Christine Moorman and Bernard J. Jaworski, 'Enhancing and Measuring Consumers' Motivation, Opportunity, and Ability to Process Brand Information from Ads', *Journal of Marketing* 55 (October 1991): 332–53.

28. Shalom H. Schwartz and Warren Bilsky, 'Toward a Universal Psychological Structure of Human Values', *Journal of Personality and Social Psychology*, 53 (1987): 550–62.

29. Bernard Cova and Robert Salle, 'Buying Behaviour in European and American Industry: Contrasts'; *European Management Journal* 9(4) (1991): 433–6.

30. Christian Dussart, 'Capitalism against Capitalism: Political and Economic Implications of Marketing Practice in Europe', in M.J. Baker (ed.), *Perspectives on Marketing Management*, vol. 4 (London: John Wiley & Sons, 1994): 119–34.

31. Richard W. Pollay, 'Measuring the Cultural Values Manifest in Advertising', *Current Issues and Research in Advertising* (1983): 71–92.

32. Milton Rokeach, *The Nature of Human Values* (New York: Free Press, 1973).

33. Suzanne C. Grunert and Gerhard Scherhorn, 'Consumer Values in West Germany: Underlying Dimensions and Cross Cultural Comparison with North America', *Journal of Business Research*, 20 (1990): 97–107.

34. Donald E. Vinson, Jerome E. Scott and Lawrence R. Lamont, 'The Role of Personal Values in Marketing and Consumer Behavior', *Journal of Marketing* 41 (April 1977): 44–50.

35. Milton Rokeach, *Understanding Human Values* (New York: The Free Press, 1979); see also J. Michael Munson and Edward McQuarrie, 'Shortening the Rokeach Value Survey for Use in Consumer Research', in Michael J. Houston (ed.), *Advances in Consumer Research* 15 (Provo, UT: Association for Consumer Research, 1988): 381–6.

36. Jacques-Marie Aurifeille, 'Value Changes and Their Marketing Implications: A Russian Survey', in W.F. van Raaij and G. Bamossy (eds.), *European Advances in Consumer Research* I (Provo, UT: Association for Consumer Research, 1993): 249–61.

37. B.W. Becker and P.E. Conner, 'Personal Values of the Heavy User of Mass Media', *Journal of Advertising Research* 21 (1981): 37–43; Vinson, Scott and Lamont, 'The Role of Personal Values in Marketing and Consumer Behavior'.

38. Sharon E. Beatty, Lynn R. Kahle, Pamela Homer and Shekhar Misra, 'Alternative Measurement Approaches to Consumer Values: The List of Values and the Rokeach Value Survey', *Psychology & Marketing* 2 (1985): 181–200.

39. Pierre Valette-Florence, Suzanne C. Grunert, Klaus G. Grunert and Sharon Beatty, 'Une comparaison franco-allemande de l'adhésion aux valeurs personnelles', *Recherce et Applications en Marketing* 6 (3) (1991): 5–20.

40. Klaus G. Grunert, Suzanne C. Grunert and Sharon Beatty, 'Cross-cultural Research on Consumer Values', *Marketing and Research Today* (17, 1989): 30–9.

41. Suzanne C. Grunert, Klaus G. Grunert and Kai Kristensen, 'Une méthode d'estimation de la validité interculturelle des instruments de mesure: Le cas de la mésure des valeurs des consommateurs par la liste des valeurs LOV', *Recherce et Applications en Marketing* 8 (4) (1993): 5–28.

42. Shalom L. Schwartz and Warren Bilsky, 'Toward a Theory of Universal Content and Structure of Values: Extensions and Cross Cultural Replications', *Journal of Personality and Social Psychology* 58 (1990): 878–91.

43. Suzanne C. Grunert and Hans Jørn Juhl, 'Values, Environmental Attitudes, and Buying of Organic Foods', *Journal of Economic Psychology* 16 (1995): 39–62.

44. Quoted in 'New Japanese Fads Blazing Trails in Cleanliness', *Montgomery Advertiser* (28 September 1996): 10A; cf. also Andrew Pollack, 'Can the Pen Really be Mightier than the Germ?', *The New York Times* (27 July 1995): A4.

45. Thomas J. Reynolds and Jonathan Gutman, 'Laddering Theory, Method, Analysis, and Interpretation', *Journal of Advertising Research* 28 (February/March 1988): 11–34; Beth Walker, Richard Celsi and Jerry Olson, 'Exploring the Structural Characteristics of Consumers' Knowledge', in Melanie Wallendorf and Paul Anderson (eds.), *Advances in Consumer Research* 14 (Provo, UT: Association for Consumer Research, 1986): 17–21.

46. Andreas Hermann, 'Wertorientierte Produkt- und Werbegestaltung', *Marketing ZFP* (3, 3rd quarter 1996): 153–63.

47. Klaus G. Grunert and Suzanne C. Grunert, 'Measuring Subjective Meaning Structures by the Laddering Method: Theoretical Considerations and Methodological Problems', *International Journal of Research in Marketing* 12 (3) (1995): 209–25. This volume of *IJRM* is a special issue on means-end chains and the laddering technique.

48. Roger Mason, 'Measuring the Demand for Status Goods: An Evaluation of Means–End Chains and Laddering', in Flemming Hansen (ed.), *European Advances in Consumer Research* II (Provo, UT: Association for Consumer Research, 1995): 78–82.

49. Thomas J. Reynolds and Alyce Byrd Craddock, 'The Application of the MECCAs Model to the Development and Assessment of Advertising Strategy: A Case Study', *Journal of Advertising Research* (April/May 1988): 43–54.

50. Elin Sørensen, Klaus G. Grunert and Niels Asger Nielsen, 'The Impact of Product Experience, Product Involvement and Verbal Processing Style on Consumers' Cognitive Structures with Regard to Fresh Fish', *MAPP Working Paper* no. 42 (Aarhus: The Aarhus School of Business, October 1996).

51. Reported on the 3rd MAPP research centre conference (October 1996).

52. Ernest Dichter, *A Strategy of Desire* (Garden City, NY: Doubleday, 1960); Ernest Dichter, *The Handbook of Consumer Motivations* (New York: McGraw-Hill, 1964); Jeffrey J. Durgee, 'Interpreting Dichter's Interpretations: An Analysis of Consumption Symbolism in The Handbook of Consumer Motivations', *Marketing and Semiotics. Selected Papers from the Copenhagen Symposium*, ed. Hanne Hartvig Larsen, David G. Mick and Christian Alsted (Copenhagen: Handelshøjskolens forlag 1991): 52–74; Pierre Martineau, *Motivation in Advertising* (New York: McGraw-Hill, 1957).

53. Vance Packard, *The Hidden Persuaders* (New York: D. McKay, 1957).

54. Harold Kassarjian, 'Personality and Consumer Behavior: A Review', *Journal of Marketing Research* 8 (November 1971): 409–18.

55. Bill Schlackman, 'An Historical Perspective', in Sue Robson and Angela Foster, *Qualitative Research in Action* (London: Edward Arnold, 1988): 15–23.

56. Cf. also Russell W. Belk, Güliz Ger and Søren Askegaard, 'Metaphors of Consumer Desire', Kim P. Corfman and John Lynch, Jr (eds.), *Advances in Consumer Research* XXIII (Provo, UT:

Association for Consumer Research, 1996): 368–73.

57. Roger Crisp, 'Persuasive Advertising, Autonomy, and the Creation of Desire', *Journal of Business Ethics* 6 (1987): 413–18.

58. Søren Askegaard and A. Fuat Fırat, 'Towards a Critique of Material Culture, Consumption and Markets'.

59. William Leiss, Stephen Kline and Sut Jhally, *Social Communication in Advertising: Persons, Products, & Images of Well-Being* (Toronto: Methuen, 1986); Jerry Mander, *Four Arguments for the Elimination of Television* (New York: William Morrow, 1977).

60. Matthew L. Wald, 'Looking for Savings as Gas Prices Rise', *New York Times* (27 May 1989): 48.

61. Raymond Williams, 'Advertising: The Magic System', in *Problems in Materialism and Culture* (London: New Left Books, 1962).

62. Steven Engelberg, 'Advertising Pervades Poland, Turning Propoganda to Glitz', *New York Times* (26 May 1992) 2: A1.

Chapter 5

1. Robert A. Baron and Donn Byrne, *Social Psychology: Understanding Human Interaction*, 5th edn (Boston: Allyn & Bacon, 1987).

2. Seymour H. Fine, *Social Marketing: Promoting the Causes of Public and Nonprofit Agencies* (Boston: Allyn & Bacon, 1990); Katryna Malafarina and Barbara Loken, 'Progress and Limitations of Social Marketing: A Review of Empirical Literature on the Consumption of Social Ideas', in Leigh McAllister and Michael Rothschild (eds.), *Advances in Consumer Research* 20 (Provo, UT: Association for Consumer Research, 1993): 397–404.

3. Each country in the EU runs campaigns which involve information dissemination with an underlying attitude change strategy. A wide range of issues (alcohol, drug use and abuse, safe sex, healthy eating, exercise, etc.) are typically covered in these campaigns. Contact regional and national health authorities and ministries for more details on campaigns in your own country.

4. Dennis T. Lowry and David E. Towles, 'Prime Time TV Portrayals of Sex, Contraception and Venereal Diseases', *Journalism Quarterly* 86 (Summer 1989): 347–52.

5. Quoted in Molly O'Neill, 'Words to Survive Life With: None of This, None of That', *New York Times* (27 May 1990): 1.

6. Bill Carter, 'A Message on Drinking is Seen and Heard', *New York Times* (11 September 1989): D11.

7. Daniel Katz, 'The Functional Approach to the Study of Attitudes', *Public Opinion Quarterly* 24 (Summer 1960): 163–204; Richard J. Lutz, 'Changing Brand Attitudes through Modification of Cognitive Structure', *Journal of Consumer Research* 1 (March 1975): 49–59.

8. Russell H. Fazio, T. M. Lenn and E. A. Effrein, 'Spontaneous Attitude Formation', *Social Cognition* 2 (1984): 214–34.

9. Mason Haire, 'Projective Techniques in Marketing Research', *Journal of Marketing* 14 (April 1950): 649–56.

10. Sharon Shavitt, 'The Role of Attitude Objects in Attitude Functions', *Journal of Experimental Social Psychology* 26 (1990): 124–48; see also J. S. Johar and M. Joseph Sirgy, 'Value-Expressive versus Utilitarian Advertising Appeals: When and Why to Use Which Appeal', *Journal of Advertising* 20 (September 1991): 23–34.

11. Michael Ray, 'Marketing Communications and the Hierarchy-of-Effects', in P. Clarke (ed.), *New Models for Mass Communications* (Beverly Hills, CA: Sage, 1973): 147–76.

12. Herbert Krugman, 'The Impact of Television Advertising: Learning Without Involvement', *Public Opinion Quarterly* 29 (Fall 1965): 349–56; Robert Lavidge and Gary Steiner, 'A Model for Predictive Measurements of Advertising Effectiveness', *Journal of Marketing* 25 (October 1961): 59–62.

13. Punam Anand, Morris B. Holbrook and Debra Stephens, 'The Formation of Affective Judgments: The Cognitive–Affective Model Versus the Independence Hypothesis', *Journal of Consumer Research* 15 (December 1988): 386–91; Richard S. Lazarus, 'Thoughts on the Relations Between Emotion and Cognition', *American Psychologist* 37(9) (1982): 1019–24.

14. Robert B. Zajonc, 'Feeling and Thinking: Preferences Need No Inferences', *American Psychologist* 35(2) (1980): 151–75.

15. Banwari Mittal, 'The Role of Affective Choice Mode in the Consumer Purchase of Expressive Products', *Journal of Economic Psychology* 4(9) (1988): 499–524.

16. Scot Burton and Donald R. Lichtenstein, 'The Effect of Ad Claims and Ad Context on Attitude Toward the Advertisement', *Journal of Advertising* 17(1) (1988): 3–11; Karen A. Machleit and R. Dale Wilson, 'Emotional Feelings and Attitude Toward the Advertisement: The Roles of Brand Familiarity and Repetition', *Journal of Advertising* 17(3) (1988): 27–35; Scott B. Mackenzie and Richard J. Lutz, 'An Empirical Examination of the Structural Antecedents of

Attitude toward the Ad in an Advertising Pretesting Context', *Journal of Marketing* 53 (April 1989): 48–65; Scott B. Mackenzie, Richard J. Lutz and George E. Belch, 'The Role of Attitude Toward the Ad as a Mediator of Advertising Effectiveness: A Test of Competing Explanations', *Journal of Marketing Research* 23 (May 1986): 130–43; Darrel D. Muehling and Russell N. Laczniak, 'Advertising's Immediate and Delayed Influence on Brand Attitudes: Considerations Across Message-Involvement Levels', *Journal of Advertising* 17(4) (1988): 23–34; Mark A. Pavelchak, Meryl P. Gardner and V. Carter Broach, 'Effect of Ad Pacing and Optimal Level of Arousal on Attitude Toward the Ad', in Rebecca H. Holman and Michael R. Solomon (eds.), *Advances in Consumer Research* 18 (Provo, UT: Association for Consumer Research, 1991): 94–9. Some research evidence indicates that a separate attitude is also formed regarding the brand name itself; see George M. Zinkhan and Claude R. Martin, Jr, 'New Brand Names and Inferential Beliefs: Some Insights on Naming New Products', *Journal of Business Research* 15 (1987): 157–72.

17. John P. Murry, Jr, John L. Lastovicka and Surendra N. Singh, 'Feeling and Liking Responses to Television Programs: An Examination of Two Explanations for Media-Context Effects', *Journal of Consumer Research* 18 (March 1992): 441–51.

18. Barbara Stern and Judith Lynne Zaichkowsky, 'The Impact of Entertaining Advertising on Consumer Responses', *Australian Marketing Researcher* 14 (August 1991): 68–80.

19. For a recent study that examined the impact of scepticism on advertising issues, see David M. Boush, Marian Friestad and Gregory M. Rose, 'Adolescent Skepticism Toward TV Advertising and Knowledge of Advertiser Tactics', *Journal of Consumer Research* 21 (June 1994): 165–75; see also Lawrence Feick and Heribert Gierl, 'Skepticism about Advertising: A Comparison of East and West German Consumers', *International Journal of Research in Marketing* 13 (1996): 227–35; Rik Pieters and Hans Baumgartner 'The Attitude Toward Advertising of Advertising Practitioners, Homemakers and Students in The Netherlands and Belgium', in W. Fred van Raaij and Gary J. Bamossy (eds.), *European Advances in Consumer Research* (Provo, UT: Association for Consumer Research, 1993): 39–45.

20. Basil G. Englis, 'Consumer Emotional Reactions to Television Advertising and Their Effects on Message Recall', in S. Agres, J. A. Edell and T. M. Dubitsky (eds.), *Emotion in Advertising:*

Theoretical and Practical Explorations (Westport, CT: Quorum Books, 1990): 231–54.

21. Morris B. Holbrook and Rajeev Batra, 'Assessing the Role of Emotions as Mediators of Consumer Responses to Advertising', *Journal of Consumer Research* 14 (December 1987): 404–20.

22. Marian Burke and Julie Edell, 'Ad Reactions over Time: Capturing Changes in the Real World', *Journal of Consumer Research* 13 (June 1986): 114–18.

23. Herbert Kelman, 'Compliance, Identification, and Internalization: Three Processes of Attitude Change', *Journal of Conflict Resolution* 2 (1958): 51–60.

24. See Sharon E. Beatty and Lynn R. Kahle, 'Alternative Hierarchies of the Attitude–Behaviour Relationship: The Impact of Brand Commitment and Habit', *Journal of the Academy of Marketing Science* 16 (Summer 1988): 1–10.

25. Leon Festinger, *A Theory of Cognitive Dissonance* (Stanford, CA: Stanford University Press, 1957).

26. Chester A. Insko and John Schopler, *Experimental Social Psychology* (New York: Academic Press, 1972).

27. Robert E. Knox and James A. Inkster, 'Postdecision Dissonance at Post Time', *Journal of Personality and Social Psychology* 8(4) (1968): 319–23.

28. Daryl J. Bem, 'Self-Perception Theory', in Leonard Berkowitz (ed.), *Advances in Experimental Social Psychology* (New York: Academic Press, 1972): 1–62.

29. Jonathan L. Freedman and Scott C. Fraser, 'Compliance without Pressure: The Foot-in-the-Door Technique', *Journal of Personality and Social Psychology* 4 (August 1966): 195–202; for further consideration of possible explanations for this effect, see William DeJong, 'An Examination of Self-Perception Mediation of the Foot-in-the-Door Effect', *Journal of Personality and Social Psychology* 37 (December 1979): 221–31; Alice M. Tybout, Brian Sternthal and Bobby J. Calder, 'Information Availability as a Determinant of Multiple-Request Effectiveness', *Journal of Marketing Research* 20 (August 1988): 280–90.

30. David H. Furse, David W. Stewart and David L. Rados, 'Effects of Foot-in-the-Door, Cash Incentives and Follow-ups on Survey Response', *Journal of Marketing Research* 18 (November 1981): 473–8; Carol A. Scott, 'The Effects of Trial and Incentives on Repeat Purchase Behavior', *Journal of Marketing Research* 13 (August 1976): 263–9.

31. Muzafer Sherif and Carl I. Hovland, *Social Judgment: Assimilation and Contrast Effects in Communication and Attitude Change* (New Haven, CT: Yale University Press, 1961).

32. For a recent treatment, see Joan Meyers-Levy and Brian Sternthal, 'A Two-Factor Explanation of Assimilation and Contrast Effects', *Journal of Marketing Research* 30 (August 1993): 359–68.

33. Mark B. Traylor, 'Product Involvement and Brand Commitment', *Journal of Advertising Research* (December 1981): 51–6.

34. Fritz Heider, *The Psychology of Interpersonal Relations* (New York: Wiley, 1958).

35. William L. Wilkie, *Consumer Behavior* (New York: Wiley, 1986).

36. A number of criteria beyond the scope of this book are important in evaluating methods of attitude measurement, including such issues as reliability, validity and sensitivity. For an excellent treatment of attitude-scaling techniques, see David S. Aaker and George S. Day, *Marketing Research*, 4th edn (New York: Wiley, 1990).

37. Martin Fishbein, 'An Investigation of the Relationships Between Beliefs About an Object and the Attitude Toward that Object', *Human Relations* 16 (1983): 233–40.

38. Allan Wicker, 'Attitudes Versus Actions: The Relationship of Verbal and Overt Behavioral Responses to Attitude Objects', *Journal of Social Issues* 25 (Autumn 1969): 65.

39. Laura Bird, 'Loved the Ad. May (or May Not) Buy the Product', *Wall Street Journal* (7 April 1994): B1 (2 pp.); 'Which Half?', *The Economist* (8 June 1996): 80.

40. Icek Ajzen and Martin Fishbein, 'Attitude–Behavior Relations: A Theoretical Analysis and Review of Empirical Research', *Psychological Bulletin* 84 (September 1977): 888–918.

41. Morris B. Holbrook and William J. Havlena, 'Assessing the Real-to-Artificial Generalizability of Multi-Attribute Attitude Models in Tests of New Product Designs', *Journal of Marketing Research* 25 (February 1988): 25–35; Terence A. Shimp and Alican Kavas, 'The Theory of Reasoned Action Applied to Coupon Usage', *Journal of Consumer Research* 11 (December 1984): 795–809.

42. Richard P. Bagozzi, Hans Baumgartner and Youjae Yi, 'Coupon Usage and the Theory of Reasoned Action', in Rebecca H. Holman and Michael R. Solomon (eds.), *Advances in Consumer Research* 18, (Provo, UT: Association for Consumer Research, 1991): 24–7; Edward F. McQuarrie, 'An Alternative to Purchase

Intentions: The Role of Prior Behavior in Consumer Expenditure on Computers', *Journal of the Market Research Society* 30 (October 1988): 407–37; Arch G. Woodside and William O. Bearden, 'Longitudinal Analysis of Consumer Attitude, Intention, and Behavior Toward Beer Brand Choice', in William D. Perrault, Jr (ed.), *Advances in Consumer Research* 4 (Ann Arbor, MI: Association for Consumer Research, 1977): 349–56.

43. Michael J. Ryan and Edward H. Bonfield, 'The Fishbein Extended Model and Consumer Behavior', *Journal of Consumer Research* 2 (1975): 118–36.

44. Blair H. Sheppard, Jon Hartwick and Paul R. Warshaw, 'The Theory of Reasoned Action: A Meta-Analysis of Past Research with Recommendations for Modifications and Future Research', *Journal of Consumer Research* 15 (December 1988): 325–43.

45. Joseph A. Cote, James McCullough and Michael Reilly, 'Effects of Unexpected Situations on Behavior–Intention Differences: A Garbology Analysis', *Journal of Consumer Research* 12 (September 1985): 188–94.

46. Russell H. Fazio, Martha C. Powell and Carol J. Williams, 'The Role of Attitude Accessibility in the Attitude-to-Behavior Process', *Journal of Consumer Research* 16 (December 1989): 280–8; Robert E. Smith and William R. Swinyard, 'Attitude–Behavior Consistency: The Impact of Product Trial Versus Advertising', *Journal of Marketing Research* 20 (August 1983): 257–67.

47. Joseph A. Cote and Patriya S. Tansuhaj, 'Culture Bound Assumptions in Behavior Intention Models', in Thom Srull (ed.), *Advances in Consumer Research* 16 (Provo, UT: Association for Consumer Research, 1989): 105–9.

48. Matthew Greenwald and John P. Katosh, 'How to Track Changes in Attitudes', *American Demographics* (August 1987): 46.

Chapter 6

1. Tim Triplett, 'Women and Cigars: Puffery or Promise?', *Marketing News* (4 December 1995): 1 (3).

2. Gert Assmus, 'An Empirical Investigation into the Perception of Vehicle Source Effects', *Journal of Advertising* 7 (Winter 1978): 4–10; for a more thorough discussion of the pros and cons of different media, see Stephen Baker, *Systematic Approach to Advertising Creativity* (New York: McGraw Hill, 1979).

3. Alladi Venkatesh, Ruby Roy Dholakia and Nikhilesh Dholakia, 'New Visions of Information Technology and Postmodernism: Implications for Advertising and Marketing Communications', in Walter Brenner and Lutz Kolbe (eds.), *The Information Superhighway and Private Households: Case Studies of Business Impacts* (Heidelberg: Physical-Verlag, 1996): 319–37; Donna L. Hoffman and Thomas P. Novak, 'Marketing in Hypermedia Computer-Mediated Environments: Conceptual Foundations', *Journal of Marketing* 60(3) (July 1996): 50–68; for an early theoretical discussion of interactivity in communications paradigms, cf. R. Aubrey Fisher, *Perspectives on Human Communication* (New York: Macmillan, 1978).

4. First proposed by Elihu Katz, 'Mass Communication Research and the Study of Popular Culture: An Editorial Note on a Possible Future for this Journal', *Studies in Public Communication* 2 (1959): 1–6. For a recent discussion of this approach cf. Stephanie O'Donohoe, 'Advertising Uses and Gratifications', *European Journal of Marketing* 28 (8/9) (1994): 52–75.

5. Quoted in Stephanie O'Donohoe, 'Advertising Uses and Gratifications', *European Journal of Marketing* 28, 8/9 (1994): 52–75, p. 66.

6. Herbert Blumer, *Symbolic Interactionism: Perspective and Method* (Berkeley: University of California Press, 1969): 2.

7. B. Aubrey Fischer, *Perspectives on Human Communication* (New York: Macmillan, 1978): 174–8.

8. Michael Wilke, 'A Radio Entrepreneur Reaches for the Interactive Age', *The New York Times* (4 September 1994): F7.

9. Joshua Quittner, 'Hot 'Zines on the Web', *Time* (4 September 1995): 64.

10. This section is adapted from a discussion in Michael R. Solomon and Elnora W. Stuart, *Marketing: Real People, Real Choices* (Upper Saddle River, NJ: Prentice Hall, 1997).

11. Thomas L. Harris, 'PR Gets Personal', *Direct Marketing* (April 1994): 29–32.

12. Carl I. Hovland and W. Weiss, 'The Influence of Source Credibility on Communication Effectiveness', *Public Opinion Quarterly* 15 (1952): 635–50.

13. Herbert Kelman, 'Processes of Opinion Change', *Public Opinion Quarterly* 25 (Spring 1961): 57–78; Susan M. Petroshuis and Kenneth E. Crocker, 'An Empirical Analysis of Spokesperson Characteristics on Advertisement and Product Evaluations', *Journal of the Academy of Marketing Science* 17 (Summer 1989): 217–26.

14. Kenneth G. DeBono and Richard J. Harnish, 'Source Expertise, Source Attractiveness, and the Processing of Persuasive Information: A Functional Approach', *Journal of Personality and Social Psychology* 55(4) (1988): 541–6.

15. Hershey H. Friedman and Linda Friedman, 'Endorser Effectiveness by Product Type', *Journal of Advertising Research* 19 (5) (1979): 63–71.

16. S. Ratneshwar and Shelly Chaiken, 'Comprehension's Role in Persuasion: The Case of its Moderating Effect on the Persuasive Impact of Source Cues', *Journal of Consumer Research* 18 (June 1991): 52–62.

17. 'Reach for the Stars', *Marketing Today* (September 1996): 104–5.

18. 'Robber Makes it Biggs in Ad', *Advertising Age* (29 May 1989): 26.

19. Alice H. Eagly, Andy Wood and Shelly Chaiken, 'Causal Inferences About Communicators and Their Effect in Opinion Change', *Journal of Personality and Social Psychology* 36(4) (1978): 424–35.

20. Judith Graham, 'Sponsors Line Up for Rockin' Role', *Advertising Age* (11 December 1989): 50.

21. Nicole Dickenson, 'Can Celebrities Ruin a Launch?', *Campaign* (3 May 1996): 34.

22. Michael A. Kamins, 'Celebrity and Noncelebrity Advertising in a Two Sided Context', *Journal of Advertising Research* 29 (June–July 1989): 34; Joseph M. Kamen, A.C. Azhari and J.R. Kragh, 'What a Spokesman Does for a Sponsor', *Journal of Advertising Research* 15(2) (1975): 17–24; Lynn Langmeyer and Mary Walker, 'A First Step to Identify the Meaning in Celebrity Endorsers', in Rebecca H. Holman and Michael R. Solomon (eds.), *Advances in Consumer Research* 18 (Provo, UT: Association for Consumer Research, 1991): 364–71.

23. Jeffrey Burroughs and Richard A. Feinberg, 'Using Response Latency to Assess Spokesperson Effectiveness', *Journal of Consumer Research* 14 (September 1987): 295–9.

24. Grant McCracken, 'Who is the Celebrity Endorser? Cultural Foundations of the Endorsement Process', *Journal of Consumer Research* 16(3) (December 1989): 310–21.

25. Thomas R. King, 'Credibility Gap: More Consumers Find Celebrity Ads Unpersuasive', *Wall Street Journal* (5 July 1989): B5; Bruce Haring, 'Company Totes up Popularity Quotients', *Billboard Magazine* 101 (1989): 12.

26. Marie Okabe, 'Fading Yen for Foreign Stars in Ads', *Singapore Straits-Times* (1986).

27. Michael A. Kamins, 'An Investigation into the "Match-Up" Hypothesis in Celebrity Advertising:

When Beauty May be Only Skin Deep', *Journal of Advertising* 19, 1 (1990): 4–13; Lynn R. Kahle and Pamela M. Homer, 'Physical Attractiveness of the Celebrity Endorser: A Social Adaptation Perspective', *Journal of Consumer Research* 11 (March 1985): 954–61.

28. Bruce Haring, 'Company Totes Up Popularity Quotients', *Billboard* (1989): 12.
29. Larry Armstrong, 'Still Starstruck', *Business Week* (4 July 1994): 38; Jeff Giles, 'The Risks of Wishing Upon a Star', *Newsweek* (6 September 1993): 38.
30. Pamela G. Hollie, 'A Rush for Singers to Promote Goods', *New York Times* (14 May 1984): D1.
31. Dominique Midgely, 'Variety Performers Avoid Over-exposure', *Marketing* (February 1996): 9.
32. Ashmore, Richard D., Michael R. Solomon and Laura Longo, 'Thinking about Female Fashion Models' Looks: A Multidimensional Approach to the Structure of Perceived Physical Attractiveness', *Personality and Psychology Bulletin*, 22(11) (November 1996) 1083–104; Basil G. Englis, Michael R. Solomon and Richard D. Ashmore, 'Beauty Before the Eyes of Beholders: The Cultural Encoding of Beauty Types in Magazine Advertising and Music Television', *Journal of Advertising*, 23 (June 1994), 49–64; Michael R. Solomon, Richard Ashmore and Laura Longo 'The Beauty Match-up Hypothesis: Congruence between Types of Beauty and Product Images in Advertising', *Journal of Advertising* 21 (December 1992): 23–34.
33. Ernest Beck, 'Shaving Industry Targets European Women', *Wall Street Journal Europe* (6 May 1977): 4.
34. Karen K. Dion, 'What is Beautiful is Good', *Journal of Personality and Social Psychology* 24 (December 1972): 285–90. See also: Christian Derbaix and Lennart Sjöberg, 'Movie Stars in Space: A Comparison of Preference and Similarity Judgments', *International Journal of Research in Marketing* 11 (1994): 261–74.
35. Michael J. Baker and Gilbert A. Churchill, Jr, 'The Impact of Physically Attractive Models on Advertising Evaluations', *Journal of Marketing Research* 14 (November 1977): 538–55; Marjorie J. Caballero and William M. Pride, 'Selected Effects of Sales-person Sex and Attractiveness in Direct Mail Advertisements', *Journal of Marketing* 48 (January 1984): 94–100; W. Benoy Joseph, 'The Credibility of Physically Attractive Communicators: A Review', *Journal of Advertising* 11(3) (1982): 15–24; Lynn R. Kahle and Pamela M. Homer, 'Physical Attractiveness of the Celebrity Endorser: A Social Adaptation Perspective', *Journal of Consumer Research* 11(4)

(1985): 954–61; Judson Mills and Eliot Aronson, 'Opinion Change as a Function of Communicator's Attractiveness and Desire to Influence', *Journal of Personality and Social Psychology* 1 (1965): 173–7.
36. Leonard N. Reid and Lawrence C. Soley, 'Decorative Models and the Readership of Magazine Ads', *Journal of Advertising Research* 23(2) (1983): 27–32.
37. Marjorie J. Caballero, James R. Lumpkin and Charles S. Madden, 'Using Physical Attractiveness as an Advertising Tool: An Empirical Test of the Attraction Phenomenon', *Journal of Advertising Research* (August/September 1989): 16–22.
38. Baker and Churchill, Jr, 'The Impact of Physically Attractive Models on Advertising Evaluations'; George E. Belch, Michael A. Belch and Angelina Villareal, 'Effects of Advertising Communications: Review of Research', in *Research in Marketing* (Greenwich, CT: JAI Press, 1987): 9, 59–117; A.E. Courtney and T.W. Whipple, *Sex Stereotyping in Advertising* (Lexington, MA: Lexington Books, 1983).
39. Kahle and Homer, 'Physical Attractiveness of the Celebrity Endorser'.
40. Anthony R. Pratkanis, Anthony G. Greenwald, Michael R. Leippe and Michael H. Baumgardner, 'In Search of Reliable Persuasion Effects: III. The Sleeper Effect is Dead, Long Live the Sleeper Effect', *Journal of Personality and Social Psychology* 54 (1988): 203–18.
41. Herbert C. Kelman and Carl I. Hovland, 'Reinstatement of the Communication in Delayed Measurement of Opinion Change', *Journal of Abnormal Psychology* 4(48) (1953) 3: 327–35.
42. Darlene Hannah and Brian Sternthal, 'Detecting and Explaining the Sleeper Effect', *Journal of Consumer Research* (September 1984) 11: 632–42.
43. David Mazursky and Yaacov Schul, 'The Effects of Advertisment Encoding on the Failure to Discount Information: Implications for the Sleeper Effect', *Journal of Consumer Research* 15 (June 1988): 24–36.
44. For an excellent review of the country of origin literature, see: Nicholas Papadopoulos and Louise Heslop, *Product and Country Images: Research and Strategy* (New York, The Haworth Press, 1993). See also Israel D. Nebenzahl, Eugene D. Jaffe and Shlomo I. Lampert, 'Towards a Theory of Country Image Effect on Product Evaluation', *Management International Review* 37 (1997): 27–49; Johny K. Johansson, 'Why Country of Origin Effects are Stronger than Ever', Basil Englis and Anna Olofsson (eds.), *Association for*

Consumer Research, European Conference, Stockholm (June 1997); Allan Jaeger, 'Crafting the Image of the Netherlands Abroad', *The Netherlander* (31 May 1997): 13.

45. David W. Stewart and David H. Furse, 'The Effects of Television Advertising Execution on Recall, Comprehension, and Persuasion', *Psychology & Marketing* 2 (Fall 1985): 135–60.

46. R.C. Grass and W.H. Wallace, 'Advertising Communication: Print vs. TV', *Journal of Advertising Research* 14 (1974): 19–23.

47. Elizabeth C. Hirschman and Michael R. Solomon, 'Utilitarian, Aesthetic, and Familiarity Responses to Verbal versus Visual Advertisements', in Thomas C. Kinnear (ed.), *Advances in Consumer Research* 11 (Provo, UT: Association for Consumer Research, 1984): 426–31.

48. Andrew A. Mitchell and Jerry C. Olson, 'Are Product Attribute Beliefs the Only Mediator of Advertising Effects on Brand Attitude?', *Journal of Marketing Research* 18 (1981) 3: 318–32.

49. Terry L. Childers and Michael J. Houston, 'Conditions for a Picture-Superiority Effect on Consumer Memory', *Journal of Consumer Research* 11 (September 1984): 643–54.

50. Andrew A. Mitchell, 'The Effect of Verbal and Visual Components of Advertisements on Brand Attitudes and Attitude Toward the Advertisement', *Journal of Consumer Research* 13 (June 1986): 12–24.

51. John R. Rossiter and Larry Percy, 'Attitude Change through Visual Imagery in Advertising', *Journal of Advertising Research* 9 (1980) 2: 10–16.

52. Jolita Kiselius and Brian Sternthal, 'Examining the Vividness Controversy: An Availability-Valence Interpretation', *Journal of Consumer Research* 12 (March 1986): 418–31.

53. Scott B. Mackenzie, 'The Role of Attention in Mediating the Effect of Advertising on Attribute Importance', *Journal of Consumer Research* 13 (September 1986): 174–95.

54. Robert B. Zajonc, 'Attitudinal Effects of Mere Exposure', Monograph, *Journal of Personality and Social Psychology* 8 (1968): 1–29.

55. George E. Belch, 'The Effects of Television Commercial Repetition on Cognitive Response and Message Acceptance', *Journal of Consumer Research* 9 (June 1982): 56–65; Marian Burke and Julie Edell, 'Ad Reactions Over Time: Capturing Changes in the Real World', *Journal of Consumer Research* 13 (June 1986): 114–18; Herbert Krugman, 'Why Three Exposures May Be Enough', *Journal of Advertising Research* 12 (December 1972): 11–14.

56. Robert F. Bornstein, 'Exposure and Affect: Overview and Meta-Analysis of Research, 1968–1987', *Psychological Bulletin* 106 (1989) 2: 265–89; Arno Rethans, John Swasy and Lawrence Marks, 'Effects of Television Commercial Repetition, Receiver Knowledge, and Commercial Length: A Test of the Two-Factor Model', *Journal of Marketing Research* 23 (February 1986): 50–61.

57. Linda L. Golden and Mark I. Alpert, 'Comparative Analysis of the Relative Effectiveness of One- and Two-Sided Communication for Contrasting Products', *Journal of Advertising* 16 (1987); Kamins, 'Celebrity and Noncelebrity Advertising in a Two-Sided Context'; Robert B. Settle and Linda L. Golden, 'Attribution Theory and Advertiser Credibility', *Journal of Marketing Research* 11 (May 1974): 181–5.

58. See Alan G. Sawyer, 'The Effects of Repetition of Refutational and Supportive Advertising Appeals', *Journal of Marketing Research* 10 (February 1973): 23–33; George J. Szybillo and Richard Heslin, 'Resistance to Persuasion: Inoculation Theory in a Marketing Context', *Journal of Marketing Research* 10 (November 1973): 396–403.

59. Lawrence M. Fisher, 'Winery's Answer to Critics: Print Good and Bad Reviews', *New York Times* (9 January 1991): D5.

60. Golden and Alpert, 'Comparative Analysis of the Relative Effectiveness of One- and Two-Sided Communication for Contrasting Products'.

61. Belch *et al.*, 'Effects of Advertising Communications'.

62. Frank R. Kardes, 'Spontaneous Inference Processes in Advertising: The Effects of Conclusion Omission and Involvement on Persuasion', *Journal of Consumer Research* 15 (September 1988): 225–33.

63. Michael Lev, 'For Car Buyers, Technology or Zen', *New York Times* (22 May 1989): D1.

64. 'Connecting Consumer and Product', *New York Times* (18 January 1990): D19.

65. Edward F. Cone, 'Image and Reality', *Forbes* (14 December 1987): 226.

66. H. Zielske, 'Does Day-After Recall Penalize "Feeling" Ads?', *Journal of Advertising Research* 22 (1982): 19–22.

67. Roger Thurow, 'In Global Push, Nike Finds its Brash Ways Don't Always Pay Off', *Wall Street Journal Europe* (6 May 1997): A1.

68. Cone, 'Image and Reality'.

69. Belch *et al.*, 'Effects of Advertising Communications'; Courtney and Whipple, 'Sex

Stereotyping in Advertising'; Michael S. LaTour, 'Female Nudity in Print Advertising: An Analysis of Gender Differences in Arousal and Ad Response', *Psychology & Marketing* 7 (1990) 1: 65–81; B.G. Yovovich, 'Sex in Advertising – The Power and the Perils', *Advertising Age* (2 May 1983): M4–M5.

70. Marc G. Weinberger and Harlan E. Spotts, 'Humor in U.S. versus U.K. TV Commercials: A Comparison', *Journal of Advertising* 18 (1989) 2: 39–44.

71. Thomas J. Madden, 'Humor in Advertising: An Experimental Analysis', working paper no. 83–27 (University of Massachusetts, 1984); Thomas J. Madden and Marc G. Weinberger, 'The Effects of Humor on Attention in Magazine Advertising', *Journal of Advertising* 11 (1982) 3: 8–14; Weinberger and Spotts, 'Humor in U.S. versus U.K. TV Commercials'.

72. David Gardner, 'The Distraction Hypothesis in Marketing', *Journal of Advertising Research* 10 (1970): 25–30.

73. 'Funny Ads Provide Welcome Relief During These Gloom and Doom Days', *Marketing News* (17 April 1981): 3.

74. Lynette S. Unger and James M. Stearns, 'The Use of Fear and Guilt Messages in Television Advertising: Issues and Evidence', in *1983 AMA Educators' Proceedings*, ed. Patrick E. Murphy *et al.* (Chicago: American Marketing Association, 1983): 16–20.

75. Michael L. Ray and William L. Wilkie, 'Fear: The Potential of an Appeal Neglected by Marketing', *Journal of Marketing* 34 (1970) 1: 54–62.

76. Ronald Paul Hill, 'An Exploration of the Relationship Between AIDS Related Anxiety and the Evaluation of Condom Advertisements', *Journal of Advertising* 17 (1988) 4: 35–42.

77. Randall Rothenberg, 'Talking Too Tough on Life's Risks?' *New York Times* (16 February 1990): D1.

78. Judith Waldrop, 'They're Coming to Take You Away (Fear as a Form of Persuasion)', *American Demographics* (15 June 1988): 2; John F. Tanner, Jr, James B. Hunt and David R. Eppright, 'The Protection Motivation Model: A Normative Model of Fear Appeals', *Journal of Marketing* 55 (July 1991): 36–45.

79. Brian Sternthal and C. Samuel Craig, 'Fear Appeals: Revisited and Revised', *Journal of Consumer Research* 1 (December 1974): 22–34.

80. Anonymous, 'A Drive to Woo Women – And Invigorate Sales', *New York Times* (2 April 1989).

81. Carrie Goerne, 'Gun Companies Target Women: Foes Call it "Marketing to Fear"; *Marketing News* (31 August 1992) 2: 1.

82. Stern, 'Medieval Allegory'.

83. Edward F. McQuarrie and David Glen Mick, 'On Resonance: A Critical Pluralistic Inquiry into Advertising Rhetoric', *Journal of Consumer Research* 19 (September 1992): 180–97.

84. See Linda M. Scott, 'The Troupe: Celebrities as Dramatis Personae in Advertisements', in Rebecca H. Holman and Michael R. Solomon (eds.), *Advances in Consumer Research* 18 (Provo, UT: Association for Consumer Research, 1991), 355–63; Barbara Stern, 'Literary Criticism and Consumer Research: Overview and Illustrative Analysis', *Journal of Consumer Research* 16 (1989): 322–34; Judith Williamson, *Decoding Advertisements* (Boston: Marion Boyars, 1978).

85. John Deighton, Daniel Romer and Josh McQueen, 'Using Drama to Persuade', *Journal of Consumer Research* 16 (December 1989): 335–43.

86. Richard E. Petty, John T. Cacioppo and David Schumann, 'Central and Peripheral Routes to Advertising Effectiveness: The Moderating Role of Involvement', *Journal of Consumer Research* 10 (1983) 2: 135–46.

87. Jerry C. Olson, Daniel R. Toy and Philip A. Dover, 'Do Cognitive Responses Mediate the Effects of Advertising Content on Cognitive Structure?', *Journal of Consumer Research* 9 (1982) 3: 245–62.

88. Julie A. Edell and Andrew A. Mitchell, 'An Information Processing Approach to Cognitive Responses', in S.C. Jain (ed.), *Research Frontiers in Marketing: Dialogues and Directions* (Chicago: American Marketing Association, 1978).

89. See Mary Jo Bitner and Carl Obermiller, 'The Elaboration Likelihood Model: Limitations and Extensions in Marketing', in Elizabeth C. Hirschman and Morris B. Holbrook (eds.), *Advances in Consumer Research* 12 (Provo, UT: Association for Consumer Research, 1985), 420–5; Meryl P. Gardner, 'Does Attitude Toward the Ad Affect Brand Attitude under a Brand Evaluation Set?', *Journal of Marketing Research* 22 (1985): 192–8; C.W. Park and S.M. Young, 'Consumer Response to Television Commercials: The Impact of Involvement and Background Music on Brand Attitude Formation', *Journal of Marketing Research* 23 (1986): 11–24; Petty, Cacioppo and Schumann, 'Central and Peripheral Routes to Advertising Effectiveness'; for a discussion of how different kinds of involvement

interact with the ELM, see Robin A. Higie, Lawrence F. Feick and Linda L. Price, 'The Importance of Peripheral Cues in Attitude Formation for Enduring and Task-Involved Individuals', in Rebecca H. Holman and Michael R. Solomon (eds.), *Advances in Consumer Research* 18 (Provo, UT: Association for Consumer Research, 1991), 187–93.

90. J. Craig Andrews and Terence A. Shimp, 'Effects of Involvement, Argument Strength, and Source Characteristics on Central and Peripheral Processing in Advertising', *Psychology & Marketing* 7 (Fall 1990): 195–214.

91. Richard E. Petty, John T. Cacioppo, Constantine Sedikides and Alan J. Strathman, 'Affect and Persuasion: A Contemporary Perspective', *American Behavioral Scientist* 31 (1988) 3: 355–71.

Chapter 7

1. Daniel Goleman, 'When Ugliness is Only in Patient's Eye, Body Image Can Reflect Mental Disorder', *New York Times* (2 October 1991): C13.

2. Harry C. Triandis, 'The Self and Social Behavior in Differing Cultural Contexts', *Psychological Review* 96 (1989) 3: 506–20; H. Markus and S. Kitayamak, 'Culture and the Self: Implications for Cognition, Emotion, and Motivation', *Psychological Review* 98 (1991): 224–53.

3. Hazel R. Markus and S. Kitayama, 'Culture and the Self: Implications for Cognition, Emotion, and Motivation', *Psychological Review* 98 (1991): 224–53.

4. Nancy Wong and Aaron Ahuvia, 'A Cross-Cultural Approach to Materialism and the Self', in Dominique Bouchet (ed.), *Cultural Dimensions of International Marketing* (Odense University, Denmark, 1995): 68–89.

5. Anthony G. Greenwald and Mahzarin R. Banaji, 'The Self as a Memory System: Powerful, but Ordinary', *Journal of Personality and Social Psychology* 57 (1989)1: 41–54; Hazel Markus, 'Self Schemata and Processing Information About the Self', *Journal of Personality and Social Psychology* 35 (1977): 63–78.

6. Morris Rosenberg, *Conceiving the Self* (New York: Basic Books, 1979); M. Joseph Sirgy, 'Self-Concept in Consumer Behavior: A Critical Review', *Journal of Consumer Research* 9 (December 1982): 287–300.

7. Emily Yoffe, 'You Are What You Buy', *Newsweek* (4 June 1990): 59.

8. Roy F. Baumeister, Dianne M. Tice and Debra G. Hutton, 'Self-Presentational Motivations and Personality Differences in Self-Esteem', *Journal of Personality* 57 (September 1989): 547–75; Ronald J. Faber, 'Are Self-Esteem Appeals Appealing?' in *Proceedings of the 1992 Conference of The American Academy of Advertising*, ed. Leonard N. Reid (1992): 230–5.

9. B. Bradford Brown and Mary Jane Lohr, 'Peer-Group Affiliation and Adolescent Self-Esteem: An Integration of Ego Identity and Symbolic-Interaction Theories', *Journal of Personality and Social Psychology* 52 (1987) 1: 47–55.

10. Marsha L. Richins, 'Social Comparison and the Idealized Images of Advertising', *Journal of Consumer Research* 18 (June 1991): 71–83; Mary C. Martin and Patricia F. Kennedy, 'Advertising and Social Comparison: Consequences for Female Preadolescents and Adolescents', *Psychology & Marketing* 10 (November/December 1993) 6: 513–30.

11. Philip N. Myers, Jr and Frank A. Biocca, 'The Elastic Body Image: The Effect of Television Advertising and Programming on Body Image Distortions in Young Women', *Journal of Communication* 42 (Summer 1992): 108–33.

12. Jeffrey F. Durgee, 'Self-Esteem Advertising', *Journal of Advertising* 14 (1986) 4: 21.

13. Ernest Dichter, *Handbook of Consumer Motivations* (New York: McGraw-Hill, 1964).

14. Sigmund Freud, *New Introductory Lectures in Psychoanalysis* (New York: Norton, 1965).

15. Harrison G. Gough, Mario Fioravanti and Renato Lazzari, 'Some Implications of Self versus Ideal-Self Congruence on the Revised Adjective Check List', *Journal of Personality and Social Psychology* 44 (1983) 6: 1214–20.

16. Steven Jay Lynn and Judith W. Rhue, 'Daydream Believers', *Psychology Today* (September 1985): 14.

17. Erving Goffman, *The Presentation of Self in Everyday Life* (Garden City, N.Y.: Doubleday, 1959); Michael R. Solomon, 'The Role of Products as Social Stimuli: A Symbolic Interactionism Perspective', *Journal of Consumer Research* 10 (December 1983), 319–29.

18. Julie Skur Hill, 'Purchasing Habits Shift for Execs', *Advertising Age* (27 April 1992): 1–16.

19. George H. Mead, *Mind, Self and Society* (Chicago: University of Chicago Press, 1934).

20. Charles H. Cooley, *Human Nature and the Social Order* (New York: Scribner's, 1902).

21. J.G. Hull and A.S. Levy, 'The Organizational Functions of the Self: An Alternative to the Duval and Wicklund Model of Self-Awareness', *Journal of Personality and Social Psychology* 37 (1979):

756–68; Jay G. Hull, Ronald R. Van Treuren, Susan J. Ashford, Pamela Propsom and Bruce W. Andrus, 'Self-Consciousness and the Processing of Self-Relevant Information', *Journal of Personality and Social Psychology* 54 (1988) 3: 452–65.

22. Arnold W. Buss, *Self-Consciousness and Social Anxiety* (San Francisco: W.H. Freeman, 1980); Lynn Carol Miller and Cathryn Leigh Cox, 'Public Self-Consciousness and Makeup Use', *Personality and Social Psychology Bulletin* 8 (1982) 4: 748–51; Michael R. Solomon and John Schopler, 'Self-Consciousness and Clothing', *Personality and Social Psychology Bulletin* 8 (1982) 3: 508–14.

23. Morris B. Holbrook, Michael R. Solomon and Stephen Bell, 'A Re-Examination of Self-Monitoring and Judgments of Furniture Designs', *Home Economics Research Journal* 19 (September 1990): 6–16; Snyder, 'Self-Monitoring Processes'.

24. Mark Snyder and Steve Gangestad, 'On the Nature of Self-Monitoring: Matters of Assessment, Matters of Validity', *Journal of Personality and Social Psychology* 51 (1986): 125–39.

25. Timothy R. Graeff, 'Image Congruence Effects on Product Evaluations: The Role of Self-Monitoring and Public/Private Consumption', *Psychology & Marketing* 13(5) (August 1996): 481–99.

26. Richard G. Netemeyer, Scot Burton and Donald R. Lichtenstein, 'Trait Aspects of Vanity: Measurement and Relevance to Consumer Behavior', *Journal of Consumer Research* 21 (March 1995): 612–26.

27. Michael R. Solomon and Henry Assael, 'The Forest or the Trees?: A Gestalt Approach to Symbolic Consumption', in Jean Umiker-Sebeok (ed.), *Marketing and Semiotics: New Directions in the Study of Signs for Sale* (Berlin: Mouton de Gruyter, 1987): 189–218.

28. Jack L. Nasar, 'Symbolic Meanings of House Styles', *Environment and Behavior* 21 (May 1989): 235–57; E.K. Sadalla, B. Verschure and J. Burroughs, 'Identity Symbolism in Housing', *Environment and Behavior* 19 (1987): 599–87.

29. Michael R. Solomon, 'The Role of Products as Social Stimuli: A Symbolic Interactionism Perspective', *Journal of Consumer Research* 10 (December 1983): 319–28; Robert E. Kleine, III, Susan Schultz-Kleine and Jerome B. Kernan, 'Mundane Consumption and the Self: A Social-Identity Perspective', *Journal of Consumer Psychology* 2 (1993) 3: 209–35; Newell D. Wright, C.B. Claiborne and M. Joseph Sirgy, 'The Effects of Product Symbolism on Consumer Self-

Concept', in John F. Sherry, Jr and Brian Sternthal (eds.), *Advances in Consumer Research* 19 (Provo, UT: Association for Consumer Research, 1992), 311–18; Susan Fournier, 'A Person-Based Relationship Framework for Strategic Brand Management', PhD Dissertation (University of Florida, 1994).

30. A. Dwayne Ball and Lori H. Tasaki, 'The Role and Measurement of Attachment in Consumer Behavior', *Journal of Consumer Psychology* 1 (1992) 2: 155–72.

31. William B. Hansen and Irwin Altman, 'Decorating Personal Places: A Descriptive Analysis', *Environment and Behavior* 8 (December 1976): 491–504.

32. R.A. Wicklund and P.M. Gollwitzer, *Symbolic Self-Completion* (Hillsdale, N.J.: Lawrence Erlbaum, 1982).

33. Erving Goffman, *Asylums* (New York: Doubleday, 1961).

34. Quoted in Floyd Rudmin, 'Property Crime Victimization Impact on Self, on Attachment, and on Territorial Dominance', *CPA Highlights, Victims of Crime Supplement* 9 (1987) 2: 4–7.

35. Barbara B. Brown, 'House and Block as Territory', paper presented at the Conference of the Association for Consumer Research (San Francisco, 1982).

36. Quoted in Shay Sayre and David Horne, 'I Shop, Therefore I Am: The Role of Possessions for Self Definition', in Shay Sayre and David Horne (eds.), *Earth, Wind, and Fire and Water: Perspectives on Natural Disaster* (Pasadena CA: Open Door Publishers, 1996): 353–70.

37. Deborah A. Prentice, 'Psychological Correspondence of Possessions, Attitudes, and Values', *Journal of Personality and Social Psychology* 53 (1987) 6: 993–1002.

38. Sak Onkvisit and John Shaw, 'Self-Concept and Image Congruence: Some Research and Managerial Implications', *The Journal of Consumer Marketing* 4 (Winter 1987): 13–24. For a related treatment of congruence between advertising appeals and self-concept, see George M. Zinkhan and Jae W. Hong, 'Self-Concept and Advertising Effectiveness: A Conceptual Model of Congruency, Conspicuousness, and Response Mode', in Rebecca H. Holman and Michael R. Solomon (eds.) *Advances in Consumer Research* 18 (Provo, UT: Association for Consumer Research, 1991), 348–54.

39. C.B. Claiborne and M. Joseph Sirgy, 'Self-Image Congruence as a Model of Consumer Attitude Formation and Behavior: A Conceptual Review and Guide for Further Research', paper presented

at the Academy of Marketing Science Conference (New Orleans, 1990).

40. Liz Hunt, 'Rise in Infertility Linked to Craze for Body Building', *The Independent* (12 July 1995): 12.

41. Al E. Birdwell, 'A Study of Influence of Image Congruence on Consumer Choice', *Journal of Business* 41 (January 1964): 76–88; Edward L. Grubb and Gregg Hupp, 'Perception of Self, Generalized Stereotypes, and Brand Selection', *Journal of Marketing Research* 5 (February 1986): 58–63.

42. Ira J. Dolich, 'Congruence Relationship Between Self-Image and Product Brands', *Journal of Marketing Research* 6 (February 1969): 80–4; Danny N. Bellenger, Earle Steinberg and Wilbur W. Stanton, 'The Congruence of Store Image and Self Image as it Relates to Store Loyalty', *Journal of Retailing* 52 (1976) 1: 17–32; Ronald J. Dornoff and Ronald L. Tatham, 'Congruence between Personal Image and Store Image', *Journal of the Market Research Society* 14 (1972) 1: 45–52.

43. Naresh K. Malhotra, 'A Scale to Measure Self-Concepts, Person Concepts, and Product Concepts', *Journal of Marketing Research* 18 (November 1981): 456–64.

44. Ernest Beaglehole, *Property: A Study in Social Psychology* (New York: Macmillan, 1932).

45. M. Csikszentmihalyi and Eugene Rochberg Halton, *The Meaning of Things: Domestic Symbols and the Self* (Cambridge, MA: Cambridge University Press, 1981).

46. Russell W. Belk, 'Possessions and the Extended Self', *Journal of Consumer Research* 15 (September 1988): 139–68.

47. Janeen Arnold Costa 'Introduction', in J.A. Costa (ed.), *Gender Issues and Consumer Behavior* (Thousand Oaks: Sage Publications, 1994).

48. Joan Meyers Levy, 'The Influence of Sex Roles on Judgment', *Journal of Consumer Research* 14 (March 1988): 522–30.

49. Kimberly J. Dodson and Russell W. Belk, 'Gender in Children's Birthday Stories', in Janeen Costa (ed.), *Gender, Marketing, and Consumer Behavior* (Salt Lake City, UT: Association for Consumer Research, 1996): 96–108.

50. Elizabeth C. Hirschman, 'A Feminist Critique of Marketing Theory: Toward Agentic-Communal Balance', working paper (School of Business, Rutgers University, New Brunswick, NJ, l990).

51. Eileen Fischer and Stephen J. Arnold, 'Sex, Gender Identity, Gender Role Attitudes, and Consumer Behavior', *Psychology & Marketing* 11 (March/April 1994) 2: 163–82.

52. Kathleen Debevec and Easwar Iyer, 'Sex Roles and Consumer Perceptions of Promotions, Products, and Self: What Do We Know and Where Should We Be Headed', in Richard J. Lutz (ed.), *Advances in Consumer Research* 13 (Provo, UT: Association for Consumer Research, 1986), 210–14; Joseph A. Bellizzi and Laura Milner, 'Gender Positioning of a Traditionally Male-Dominant Product', *Journal of Advertising Research* (June/July 1991): 72–9.

53. Janeen Arnold Costa and Teresa M. Pavia, 'Alpha-Numeric Brand Names and Gender Stereotypes', *Research in Consumer Behavior* 6 (1993): 85–112.

54. Helga Dittmar, Jane Beattie and Susanne Friese, 'Gender Identity and Material Symbols: Objects and Decision Considerations in Impulse Purchases', *Journal of Economic Psychology* 16 (1995): 491–511; Jason Cox and Helga Dittmar, 'The Functions of Clothes and Clothing (Dis)Satisfaction: A Gender Analysis Among British Students', *Journal of Consumer Policy* 18 (1995): 237–65.

55. Sandra L. Bem, 'The Measurement of Psychological Androgyny', *Journal of Consulting and Clinical Psychology* 42 (1974): 155–62; Deborah E.S. Frable, 'Sex Typing and Gender Ideology: Two Facets of the Individual's Gender Psychology That Go Together', *Journal of Personality and Social Psychology* 56 (1989) 1: 95–108.

56. See D. Bruce Carter and Gary D. Levy, 'Cognitive Aspects of Early Sex-Role Development: The Influence of Gender Schemas on Preschoolers' Memories and Preferences for Sex-Typed Toys and Activities', *Child Development* 59 (1988): 782–92; Bernd H. Schmitt, France Le Clerc and Laurette Dube-Rioux, 'Sex Typing and Consumer Behavior: A Test of Gender Schema Theory', *Journal of Consumer Research* 15 (June 1988): 122–7.

57. Carol Gilligan, *In a Different Voice: Psychological Theory and Women's Development* (Cambridge, MA: Harvard University Press, 1982); Joan Meyers-Levy and Durairaj Maheswaran, 'Exploring Differences in Males' and Females' Processing Strategies', *Journal of Consumer Research* 18 (June 1991): 63–70.

58. Lynn J. Jaffe and Paul D. Berger, 'Impact on Purchase Intent of Sex-Role Identity and Product Positioning', *Psychology & Marketing* (Fall 1988): 259–71; Lynn J. Jaffe, 'The Unique Predictive Ability of Sex-Role Identity in Explaining Women's Response to Advertising', *Psychology & Marketing* 11 (September/October 1994) 5: 467–82.

59. Leila T. Worth, Jeanne Smith and Diane M. Mackie, 'Gender Schematicity and Preference for Gender-Typed Products', *Psychology & Marketing* 9 (January 1992): 17–30.

60. Laurel Anderson and Marsha Wadkins, 'The New Breed in Japan: Consumer Culture', unpublished manuscript (Arizona State University, Tempe, 1990); Doris L. Walsh, 'A Familiar Story', *American Demographics* (June 1987): 64.

61. Julie Candler, 'Woman Car Buyer – Don't Call Her a Niche Anymore', *Advertising Age* (21 January 1991): S-8; see also Robin Widgery and Jack McGaugh, 'Vehicle Message Appeals and the New Generation Woman', *Journal of Advertising Research* (September/October 1993): 36–42; Blayne Cutler, 'Condom Mania', *American Demographics* (June 1989): 17.

62. B. Abrams, 'American Express is Gearing New Ad Campaign to Women', *Wall Street Journal* (4 August 1983): 23.

63. 'Ads' Portrayal of Women Today is Hardly Innovative', *Marketing News* (6 November 1989): 12; Jill Hicks Ferguson, Peggy J. Kreshel and Spencer F. Tinkham, 'In the Pages of Ms.: Sex Role Portrayals of Women in Advertising', *Journal of Advertising* 19 (1990) 1: 40–51.

64. Richard Elliott, Abigail Jones, Andrew Benfield and Matt Barlow 'Overt Sexuality in Advertising: A Discourse Analysis of Gender Responses', *Journal of Consumer Policy*, 18 (1995): 187–217. Sonia Livingstone and Gloria Greene, 'Television Advertisements and the Portrayal of Gender', *British Journal of Social Psychology* 25 (1986): 149–54; for one of the original articles on this topic, see L.Z. McArthur and B.G. Resko, 'The Portrayal of Men and Women in American Television Commercials', *Journal of Social Psychology* 97 (1975): 209–20.

65. Richard Edel, 'American Dream Vendors', *Advertising Age* (9 November 1988): 153.

66. Stuart Elliott, 'Avon Products is Abandoning Its Old-Fashioned Image in an Appeal to Contemporary Women', *The New York Times* (27 April 1993): D21.

67. Daniel J. Brett and Joanne Cantor, 'The Portrayal of Men and Women in U.S. Television Commercials: A Recent Content Analysis and Trends Over 15 Years', *Sex Roles* 18 (1988): 595–609.

68. Kyle Pope, 'High-Tech Marketers Try to Attract Women Without Causing Offense', *The Wall Street Journal* (17 March 1994): B1 (2).

69. Gordon Sumner, 'Tribal Rites of the American Male', *Marketing Insights* (Summer 1989): 13.

70. Margaret G. Maples, 'Beefcake Marketing: The Sexy Sell', *Marketing Communications* (April 1983): 21–5.

71. Cyndee Miller, 'Cosmetics Makers to Men: Paint Those Nails', *Marketing News* (12 May 1997): 14, 18.

72. Alan Farnham, 'You're so Vain', *Fortune* (9 September 1996): 66 (10).

73. Amy M. Spindler, 'It's a Face-Lifted, Tummy-Tucked Jungle Out There', *The New York Times* (9 June 1996): Sec. 3, 1 (3).

74. 'Changing Conceptions of Fatherhood', *USA Today* (May 1988): 10.

75. Quoted in Kim Foltz, 'In Ads, Men's Image Becomes Softer', *New York Times* (26 March 1990): D12.

76. Quoted in Jennifer Foote, 'The Ad World's New Bimbos', *Newsweek* (25 January 1988): 44.

77. Maples, 'Beefcake Marketing'.

78. Quoted in Lynn G. Coleman, 'What Do People Really Lust After in Ads?', *Marketing News* (6 November 1989): 12.

79. Riccardo A. Davis, 'Marketers Game for Gay Events', *Advertising Age* (30 May 1994): S-1 (2); Cyndee Miller, 'Top Marketers Take Bolder Approach in Targeting Gays', *Marketing News* (4 July 1994): 1 (2); see also Douglas L. Fugate, 'Evaluating the US Male Homosexual and Lesbian Population as a Viable Target Market Segment', *Journal of Consumer Marketing* 10 (1993) 4: 46–57; Laura M. Milner, 'Marketing to Gays and Lesbians: A Review', unpublished manuscript (The University of Alaska, 1990).

80. Kate Fitzgerald, 'IKEA Dares to Reveal Gays Buy Tables, Too', *Advertising Age* (28 March 1994): 3 (2); Cyndee Miller, 'Top Marketers Take Bolder Approach in Targeting Gays', *Marketing News* (4 July 1994): 1(2); Paula Span, 'ISO the Gay Consumer', *The Washington Post* (19 May 1994): D1 (2).

81. Elliott, 'A Sharper View of Gay Consumers'; Kate Fitzgerald, 'AT&T Addresses Gay Market', *Advertising Age* (16 May 1994): 8.

82. James S. Hirsch, 'New Credit Cards Base Appeals on Sexual Orientation and Race', *The Wall Street Journal* (6 November 1995): B1 (2).

83. Projections of the incidence of homosexuality in the general population often are influenced by assumptions of the researchers, as well as the methodology they employ (e.g. self-report, behavioural measures, fantasy measures). For a discussion of these factors, see Edward O. Laumann, John H. Gagnon, Robert T. Michael and Stuart Michaels, *The Social Organization of Homosexuality* (Chicago: University of Chicago Press, 1994).

84. Lisa Peñaloza, 'We're Here, We're Queer, and We're Going Shopping! A Critical Perspective on the Accommodation of Gays and Lesbians in the U.S. Marketplace', *Journal of Homosexuality* 31, 1/2 (1966): 9–41.

85. D.L. Fugate, 'Evaluating the U.S. Male Homosexual and Lesbian Population as a Viable Target Market Segment: A Review with Implications' *Journal of Consumer Marketing* 10 (4) (1993): 46–57. Projections of the incidence of homosexuality in the general population often are influenced by assumptions of the researchers, as well as the methodology they employ (e.g. self-report, behavioural measures, fantasy measures). For a discussion of these factors, see Edward O. Laumann, John H. Gagnon, Robert T. Michael and Stuart Michaels, *The Social Organization of Homosexuality* (Chicago: University of Chicago Press, 1994).

86. Peñaloza, 'We're Here, We're Queer, and We're Going Shopping! A Critical Perspective on the Accommodation of Gays and Lesbians in the U.S. Marketplace'.

87. Michael Wilke, 'Subaru Adds Lesbians to Niche Marketing Drive', *Advertising Age* (4 March 1996): 8.

88. Dennis W. Rook, 'Body Cathexis and Market Segmentation', in Michael R. Solomon (ed.), *The Psychology of Fashion* (Lexington, MA: Lexington Books, 1985): 233–41.

89. 'Nederlandse vrouw krijt lachend rimpels', *De Telegraaf* (26 April 1997): TA5.

90. Jane E. Brody, 'Notions of Beauty Transcend Culture, New Study Suggests', *The New York Times* (21 March 1994): A14.

91. Geoffrey Cowley, 'The Biology of Beauty', *Newsweek* (3 June 1996): 61–6.

92. Michael Fay and Christopher Price, 'Female Body-Shape in Print Advertisements and the Increase in Anorexia Nervosa', *European Journal of Marketing* 28 (1994): 12.

93. Lois W. Banner, *American Beauty* (Chicago: The University of Chicago Press, 1980); for a philosophical perspective, see Barry Vacker and Wayne R. Key, 'Beauty *and* the Beholder: The Pursuit of Beauty Through Commodities', *Psychology & Marketing* (10 November/December 1993) 6: 471–94.

94. David M. Garner, Paul E. Garfinkel, Donald Schwartz and Michael Thompson, 'Cultural Expectations of Thinness in Women', *Psychological Reports* 47 (1980): 483–91.

95. Kathleen Boyes, 'The New Grip of Girdles is Lightened by Lycra', *USA Today* (25 April 1991): 6D.

96. Stuart Elliott, 'Ultrathin Models in Coca-Cola and Calvin Klein Campaigns Draw Fire and a Boycott Call', *The New York Times* (26 April 1994): D18; Cyndee Miller, 'Give Them a Cheeseburger', *Marketing News* (6 June 1994): 1 (2).

97. Jill Neimark, 'The Beefcaking of America', *Psychology Today* (November/December 1994): 32 (11).

98. Richard H. Kolbe and Paul J. Albanese, 'Man to Man: A Content Analysis of Sole-Male Images in Male-Audience Magazines', *Journal of Advertising* 25, 4 (Winter 1996): 1–20.

99. 'Girls at 7 Think Thin, Study Finds', *New York Times* (11 February 1988): B9.

100. Sarah McBride, 'Turn On! Tune In! Eat Up!: Antidiet Trend Gets Militant', *The Wall Street Journal* Interactive Edition (2 May 1997).

101. Elaine L. Pedersen and Nancy L. Markee, 'Fashion Dolls: Communicators of Ideals of Beauty and Fashion', paper presented at the International Conference on Marketing Meaning (Indianapolis, IN, 1989); Dalma Heyn, 'Body Hate', *Ms.* (August 1989): 34; Mary C. Martin and James W. Gentry, 'Assessing the Internalization of Physical Attractiveness Norms', *Proceedings of the American Marketing Association Summer Educators' Conference* (Summer 1994): 59–65.

102. Debra A. Zellner, Debra F. Harner and Robbie I. Adler, 'Effects of Eating Abnormalities and Gender on Perceptions of Desirable Body Shape', *Journal of Abnormal Psychology* 98 (February 1989): 93–6.

103. Robin T. Peterson, 'Bulimia and Anorexia in an Advertising Context', *Journal of Business Ethics* 6 (1987): 495–504.

104. Christian S. Crandall, 'Social Contagion of Binge Eating', *Journal of Personality and Social Psychology* 55 (1988): 588–98.

105. Judy Folkenberg, 'Bulimia: Not For Women Only', *Psychology Today* (March 1984): 10.

106. Eleanor Grant, 'The Exercise Fix: What Happens When Fitness Fanatics Just Can't Say No?', *Psychology Today* 22 (February 1988): 24.

107. John W. Schouten, 'Selves in Transition: Symbolic Consumption in Personal Rites of Passage and Identity Reconstruction', *Journal of Consumer Research* 17 (March 1991): 412–25.

108. Monica Gonzalez, 'Want a Lift?', *American Demographics* (February 1988): 20.

109. Annette C. Hamburger and Holly Hall, 'Beauty Quest', *Psychology Today* (May 1988): 28.

110. Emily Yoffe, 'Valley of the Silicon Dolls', *Newsweek* (26 November 1990): 72.

111. Norihiko Shirouzu, 'Reconstruction Boom in Tokyo: Perfecting Imperfect Bellybuttons', *The Wall Street Journal* (4 October 1995): B1.

112. Keith Greenberg, 'What's Hot: Cosmetic Surgery', *Public Relations Journal* (June 1988): 23.

113. Ruth P. Rubinstein, 'Color, Circumcision, Tattoos, and Scars', in Michael R. Solomon (ed.), *The Psychology of Fashion* (Lexington, MA: Lexington Books, 1985): 243–54; Peter H. Bloch and Marsha L. Richins, 'You Look "Mahvelous": The Pursuit of Beauty and Marketing Concept', *Psychology & Marketing* 9 (January 1992): 3–16.

114. Kathy H. Merrell, 'Saving Faces', *Allure* (January 1994): 66 (2).

115. 'White Weight', *Psychology Today* (September/ October 1994): 9.

116. Sondra Farganis, 'Lip Service: The Evolution of Pouting, Pursing, and Painting Lips Red', *Health* (November 1988): 48–51.

117. Michael Gross, 'Those Lips, Those Eyebrows; New Face of 1989 (New Look of Fashion Models)', *New York Times Magazine* (13 February 1989): 24.

118. Quoted in 'High Heels: Ecstasy's Worth the Agony', *New York Post* (31 December 1981).

119. Quoted in Wendy Bounds, 'Body-Piercing Gets Under America's Skin', *The Wall Street Journal* (4 April 1994): B1 (2), p. B4.

Chapter 8

1. John C. Mowen, 'Beyond Consumer Decision Making', *Journal of Consumer Marketing* 5 (1988) 1: 15–25.

2. Richard W. Olshavsky and Donald H. Granbois, 'Consumer Decision Making – Fact or Fiction', *Journal of Consumer Research* 6 (September 1989): 93–100.

3. James R. Bettman, 'The Decision Maker Who Came In from the Cold', Presidential Address, in Leigh McAllister and Michael Rothschild (eds.), *Advances in Consumer Research* 20 (Provo, UT: Association for Consumer Research, in press); John W. Payne, James R. Bettman and Eric J. Johnson, 'Behavioral Decision Research: A Constructive Processing Perspective', *Annual Review of Psychology* 4 (1992): 87–131; for an overview of recent developments in individual choice models, see Robert J. Meyer and Barbara E. Kahn, 'Probabilistic Models of Consumer Choice Behavior', in Thomas S. Robertson and Harold H. Kassarjian (eds.), *Handbook of Consumer Behavior* (Englewood Cliffs, NJ: Prentice-Hall, 1991): 85–123.

4. Mowen, 'Beyond Consumer Decision Making'; Kordelia Spies, Friedrich Hesse and Kerstin Loesch, 'Store Atmosphere, Mood and Purchasing Behavior', *International Journal of Research in Marketing*, 14 (1997): 1–17; José M.M. Bloemer and Hans D.P. Kasper, 'The Complex Relationship between Consumer Satisfaction and Brand Loyalty', *Journal of Economic Psychology*, 16 (1995): 311–29.

5. Joseph W. Alba and J. Wesley Hutchinson, 'Dimensions of Consumer Expertise', *Journal of Consumer Research* 13 (March 1988): 411–54; Jouni T. Kujala and Michael D. Johnson, 'Price Knowledge and Search Behavior for Habitual, Low Involvement Food Purchases', *Journal of Economic Psychology*, 14 (1993): 249–65.

6. Gordon C. Bruner III and Richard J. Pomazal, 'Problem Recognition: The Crucial First Stage of the Consumer Decision Process', *Journal of Consumer Marketing* 5 (1988) 1: 53–63.

7. Ross K. Baker, 'Textually Transmitted Diseases', *American Demographics* (December 1987): 64.

8. Julia Marlowe, Gary Selnow and Lois Blosser, 'A Content Analysis of Problem-Resolution Appeals in Television Commercials', *The Journal of Consumer Affairs* 23 (1989) 1: 175–94.

9. Peter H. Bloch, Daniel L. Sherrell and Nancy M. Ridgway, 'Consumer Search: An Extended Framework', *Journal of Consumer Research* 13 (June 1986): 119–26.

10. Girish Punj, 'Presearch Decision Making in Consumer Durable Purchases', *Journal of Consumer Marketing* 4 (Winter 1987): 71–82.

11. H. Beales, M.B. Jagis, S.C. Salop and R. Staelin, 'Consumer Search and Public Policy', *Journal of Consumer Research* 8 (June 1981): 11–22.

12. Thomas E. Miller, 'New Markets for Information', *American Demographics* (April 1995): 46–50.

13. Amy Cortese, 'A Way Out of the Web Maze', *Business Week* (24 February 1997): 93 (8); Rebecca H. Patterson, 'No Lines at Britain's First On-Line Grocery', *Wall Street Journal*, Europe (25–26 July 1997): 4.

14. Thomas E. Weber, 'Advertising: New Software Lets Marketers Target Their Ads on Internet', *The Wall Street Journal Interactive Edition* (21 April 1997).

15. Itamar Simonson, Joel Huber and John Payne, 'The Relationship Between Prior Brand Knowledge and Information Acquisition Order', *Journal of Consumer Research* 14 (March 1988): 566–78.

16. John R. Hauser, Glen L. Urban and Bruce D. Weinberg, 'How Consumers Allocate Their Time

When Searching for Information', *Journal of Marketing Research* 30 (November 1993): 452–66; George J. Stigler, 'The Economics of Information', *Journal of Political Economy* 69 (June 1961): 213–25.

17. Cathy J. Cobb and Wayne D. Hoyer, 'Direct Observation of Search Behaviour', *Psychology & Marketing* 2 (Fall 1985): 161–79.

18. Sharon E. Beatty and Scott M. Smith, 'External Search Effort: An Investigation across Several Product Categories', *Journal of Consumer Research* 14 (June 1987): 83–95; William L. Moore and Donald R. Lehmann, 'Individual Differences in Search Behavior for a Nondurable', *Journal of Consumer Research* 7 (December 1980): 296–307.

19. Geoffrey C. Kiel and Roger A. Layton, 'Dimensions of Consumer Information Seeking Behavior', *Journal of Marketing Research* 28 (May 1981): 233–9; see also Narasimhan Srinivasan and Brian T. Ratchford, 'An Empirical Test of a Model of External Search for Automobiles', *Journal of Consumer Research* 18 (September 1991): 233–42; Mari Niva, Eva Heiskanen and Päivi Timonen, 'Environmental Information in Consumer Decision Making', *National Consumer Research Centre* (Helsinki, July 1996).

20. David F. Midgley, 'Patterns of Interpersonal Information Seeking for the Purchase of a Symbolic Product', *Journal of Marketing Research* 20 (February 1983): 74–83.

21. Cyndee Miller, 'Scotland to U.S.: "This Tennent's for You"', *Marketing News* (29 August 1994): 26.

22. Satya Menon and Barbara E. Kahn, 'The Impact of Context on Variety Seeking in Product Choices', *Journal of Consumer Research* 22 (December 1995): 285–95; Barbara E. Kahn and Alice M. Isen, 'The Influence of Positive Affect on Variety Seeking Among Safe, Enjoyable Products', *Journal of Consumer Research* 20 (September 1993): 257–70; Hans Baumgartner and Jan-Benedict E.M. Steenkamp, 'Exploratory Consumer Buying Behavior: Conceptualization and Measurement', *International Journal of Research in Marketing*, 13 (1996): 121–37; Gordon Foxall and Seema Bhate, 'Cognitive Style and Personal Involvement as Explicators of Innovative Purchasing of "Healthy" Food Brands', *European Journal of Marketing* 27(2) (1993).

23. Michael Laroche, Chankon Kim and Lianxi Zhou, 'Brand Familiarity and Confidence as Determinants of Purchase Intention: An Empirical Test in a Multiple Brand Context', *Journal of Business Research* 37 (1996): 115–120.

24. Barbara E. Kahn, 'Understanding Variety-Seeking Behavior From a Marketing Perspective', unpublished manuscript (University of Pennsylvania, University Park, 1991); Leigh McAlister and Edgar A. Pessemier, 'Variety-Seeking Behavior: An Interdisciplinary Review', *Journal of Consumer Research* 9 (December 1982): 311–22; Fred M. Feinberg, Barbara E. Kahn and Leigh McAlister, 'Market Share Response When Consumers Seek Variety', *Journal of Marketing Research* 29 (May 1992): 228–37; Barbara E. Kahn and Alice M. Isen, 'The Influence of Positive Affect on Variety Seeking Among Safe, Enjoyable Products', *Journal of Consumer Research* 20 (September 1993) 2: 257–70.

25. Gary Belsky, 'Why Smart People Make Major Money Mistakes', *Money* (July 1995): 76 (10); Richard Thaler and Eric J. Johnson, 'Gambling with the House Money or Trying to Break Even: The Effects of Prior Outcomes on Risky Choice', *Management Science* 36 (June 1990): 643–60; Richard Thaler, 'Mental Accounting and Consumer Choice', *Marketing Science* 4 (Summer 1985): 199–214.

26. Daniel Kahneman and Amos Tversky, 'Prospect Theory: An Analysis of Decision under Risk', *Econometrica* 47 (March 1979): 263–91; Timothy B. Heath, Subimal Chatterjee and Karen Russo France, 'Mental Accounting and Changes in Price: The Frame Dependence of Reference Dependence', *Journal of Consumer Research* 22 (1) (June 1995): 90–7.

27. Quoted in Richard Thaler, 'Mental Accounting and Consumer Choice', *Marketing Science* 4 (Summer 1985): 199–214, p. 206.

28. Girish N. Punj and Richard Staelin, 'A Model of Consumer Search Behavior for New Automobiles', *Journal of Consumer Research* 9 (March 1983): 366–80.

29. Cobb and Hoyer, 'Direct Observation of Search Behavior'; Moore and Lehmann, 'Individual Differences in Search Behavior for a Nondurable'; Punj and Staelin, 'A Model of Consumer Search Behavior for New Automobiles'.

30. James R. Bettman and C. Whan Park, 'Effects of Prior Knowledge and Experience and Phase of the Choice Process on Consumer Decision Processes: A Protocol Analysis', *Journal of Consumer Research* 7 (December 1980): 234–48.

31. Alba and Hutchinson, 'Dimensions of Consumer Expertise'; Bettman and Park, 'Effects of Prior Knowledge and Experience and Phase of the Choice Process on Consumer Decision Processes'; Merrie Brucks, 'The Effects of Product Class

Knowledge on Information Search Behavior',
Journal of Consumer Research 12 (June l985):
1–16; Joel E. Urbany, Peter R. Dickson and
William L. Wilkie, 'Buyer Uncertainty and
Information Search', *Journal of Consumer
Research* 16 (September 1989): 208–15.

32. Cyndee Miller, 'HIV Kits Target Untested Market',
Marketing News (20 January 1997): 1, 11.

33. Mary Frances Luce, James R. Bettman and John
W. Payne, 'Choice Processing in Emotionally
Difficult Decisions', *Journal of Experimental
Psychology* 23(2) (1997): 384–405.

34. John R. Hauser and Birger Wernerfelt, 'An
Evaluation Cost Model of Consideration Sets',
Journal of Consumer Research 16 (March 1990):
393–408.

35. Robert J. Sutton, 'Using Empirical Data to
Investigate the Likelihood of Brands Being
Admitted or Readmitted Into an Established
Evoked Set', *Journal of the Academy of
Marketing Science* 15 (Fall 1987): 82.

36. Alba and Hutchison, 'Dimensions of Consumer
Expertise'; Joel B. Cohen and Kunal Basu
'Alternative Models of Categorization: Toward a
Contingent Processing Framework', *Journal of
Consumer Research* 13 (March 1987): 455–72.

37. Robert M. McMath, 'The Perils of Typecasting',
American Demographics (February 1997): 60.

38. Eleanor Rosch, 'Principles of Categorization', in
E. Rosch and B.B. Lloyd (eds.), *Recognition and
Categorization* (Hillsdale, NJ: Lawrence Erlbaum,
1978).

39. Michael R. Solomon, 'Mapping Product
Constellations: A Social Categorization Approach
to Symbolic Consumption', *Psychology &
Marketing* 5 (1988) 3: 233–58.

40. Robert M. McMath, 'The Perils of Typecasting',
American Demographics (February 1997): 60.

41. Elizabeth C. Hirschman and Michael R. Solomon,
'Competition and Cooperation Among Culture
Production Systems', in Ronald F. Bush and
Shelby D. Hunt (eds.), *Marketing Theory:
Philosophy of Science Perspectives* (Chicago:
American Marketing Association, 1982): 269–72.

42. Michael D. Johnson, 'The Differential Processing
of Product Category and Noncomparable Choice
Alternatives', *Journal of Consumer Research* 16
(December 1989): 300–9.

43. Mita Sujan, 'Consumer Knowledge: Effects on
Evaluation Strategies Mediating Consumer
Judgments', *Journal of Consumer Research* 12
(June 1985): 31–46.

44. Rosch, 'Principles of Categorization'.

45. Joan Meyers-Levy and Alice M. Tybout, 'Schema
Congruity as a Basis for Product Evaluation',

Journal of Consumer Research 16 (June 1989):
39–55.

46. Mita Sujan and James R. Bettman, 'The Effects of
Brand Positioning Strategies on Consumers'
Brand and Category Perceptions: Some Insights
from Schema Research', *Journal of Marketing
Research* 26 (November 1989): 454–67.

47. Cf. William P. Putsis, Jr and Narasimhan
Srinivasan, 'Buying or Just Browsing? The
Duration of Purchase Deliberation', *Journal of
Marketing Research* 31 (August 1994): 393–402.

48. Robert E. Smith, 'Integrating Information from
Advertising and Trial: Processes and Effects on
Consumer Response to Product Information',
Journal of Marketing Research 30 (May 1993):
204–19.

49. Jack Trout, 'Marketing in Tough Times',
Boardroom Reports (October 1992) 2: 8.

50. Amna Kirmani and Peter Wright, 'Procedural
Learning, Consumer Decision Making and
Marketing Communication', *Marketing Letters*
(1992).

51. Robert A. Baron, *Psychology: The Essential
Science* (Boston: Allyn & Bacon, 1989); Valerie S.
Folkes, 'The Availability Heuristic and Perceived
Risk', *Journal of Consumer Research* 15 (June
1989): 13–23; Daniel Kahneman and Amos
Tversky, 'Prospect Theory: An Analysis of
Decision Under Risk', *Econometrica* 47 (1979):
263–91.

52. Wayne D. Hoyer, 'An Examination of Consumer
Decision Making for a Common Repeat Purchase
Product', *Journal of Consumer Research* 11
(December 1984): 822–29; Calvin P. Duncan,
'Consumer Market Beliefs: A Review of the
Literature and an Agenda for Future Research', in
Advances in Consumer Research 17, ed. Marvin
E. Goldberg, Gerald Gorn and Richard W. Pollay
(Provo, UT: Association for Consumer Research,
1990): 729–35; Frank Alpert, 'Consumer Market
Beliefs and Their Managerial Implications: An
Empirical Examination', *Journal of Consumer
Marketing* 10 (1993) 2: 56–70.

53. Michael R. Solomon, Sarah Drenan and Chester
A. Insko, 'Popular Induction: When is Consensus
Information Informative?', *Journal of Personality*
49 (1981) 2: 212–24.

54. Folkes, 'The Availability Heuristic and Perceived
Risk'.

55. Beales *et al.*, 'Consumer Search and Public
Policy'.

56. Gary T. Ford and Ruth Ann Smith, 'Inferential
Beliefs in Consumer Evaluations: An Assessment
of Alternative Processing Strategies', *Journal of
Consumer Research* 14 (December 1987):

363–71; Deborah Roedder John, Carol A. Scott and James R. Bettman, 'Sampling Data for Covariation Assessment: The Effects of Prior Beliefs on Search Patterns', *Journal of Consumer Research* 13 (June 1986): 38–47; Gary L. Sullivan and Kenneth J. Berger, 'An Investigation of the Determinants of Cue Utilization', *Psychology & Marketing* 4 (Spring 1987): 63–74.

57. John *et al.*, 'Sampling Data for Covariation Assessment'.

58. Duncan, 'Consumer Market Beliefs'.

59. Chr. Hjorth Andersen, 'Price as a Risk Indicator', *Journal of Consumer Policy* 10 (1987): 267–81.

60. David M. Gardner, 'Is There a Generalized Price–Quality Relationship?', *Journal of Marketing Research* 8 (May 1971): 241–3; Kent B. Monroe, 'Buyers' Subjective Perceptions of Price', *Journal of Marketing Research* 10 (1973): 70–80.

61. Durairaj Maheswaran, 'Country of Origin as a Stereotype: Effects of Consumer Expertise and Attribute Strength on Product Evaluations', *Journal of Consumer Research* 21 (September 1994): 354–65; Ingrid M. Martin and Sevgin Eroglu, 'Measuring a Multi-Dimensional Construct: Country Image', *Journal of Business Research* 28 (1993): 191–210; Richard Ettenson, Janet Wagner and Gary Gaeth, 'Evaluating the Effect of Country of Origin and the "Made in the U.S.A." Campaign: A Conjoint Approach', *Journal of Retailing* 64 (Spring 1988): 85–100; C. Min Han and Vern Terpstra, 'Country-of-Origin Effects for Uni-National & Bi-National Products', *Journal of International Business* 19 (Summer 1988): 235–55; Michelle A. Morganosky and Michelle M. Lazarde, 'Foreign-Made Apparel: Influences on Consumers' Perceptions of Brand and Store Quality', *International Journal of Advertising* 6 (Fall 1987): 339–48.

62. See Richard Jackson Harris, Bettina Garner-Earl, Sara J. Sprick and Collette Carroll, 'Effects of Foreign Product Names and Country-of-Origin Attributions on Advertisement Evaluations', *Psychology & Marketing* 11 (March/April 1994) 2: 129–45; Terence A. Shimp, Saeed Samiee and Thomas J. Madden, 'Countries and Their Products: A Cognitive Structure Perspective', *Journal of the Academy of Marketing Science* 21 (Fall 1993) 4: 323–30. For an excellent review of the country of origin literature, see Nicholas Papadopoulos and Louise Heslop, *Product and Country Images: Research and Strategy* (New York, The Haworth Press, 1993). See also Israel D. Nebenzahl, Eugene D. Jaffe and Shlomo I.

Lampert, 'Towards a Theory of Country Image Effect on Product Evaluation', *Management International Review*, 37(1997): 27–49; Johny K. Johansson, 'Why Country of Origin Effects are Stronger than Ever', *Association for Consumer Research*, European Conference, Stockholm (June 1997), Basil Englis and Anna Olofsson (eds.) in press; Allan Jaeger, 'Crafting the Image of the Netherlands Abroad', *The Netherlander* (31 May 1997): 13.

63. 'American Pie', *Business Week* (27 June 1994): 6.

64. Durairaj Maheswaran, 'Country of Origin as a Stereotype: Effects of Consumer Expertise and Attribute Strength on Product Evaluations', *Journal of Consumer Research* 21 (September 1994): 354–65.

65. Joshua Levine, 'The Dance Drink', *Forbes* (12 September 1994): 232.

66. Sung-Tai Hong and Robert S. Wyer, Jr, 'Effects of Country-of-Origin and Product–Attribute Information on Product Evaluation: An Information Processing Perspective', *Journal of Consumer Research* 16 (September 1989): 175–87; Marjorie Wall, John Liefeld and Louise A. Heslop, 'Impact of Country-of-Origin Cues on Consumer Judgments in Multi-Cue Situations: A Covariance Analysis', *Journal of the Academy of Marketing Science* 19 (1991) 2: 105–13.

67. Wai-Kwan Li and Robert S. Wyer, Jr, 'The Role of Country of Origin in Product Evaluations: Informational and Standard-of-Comparison Effects', *Journal of Consumer Psychology* 3(2) (1994): 187–212.

68. Durairaj Maheswaran, 'Country of Origin as a Stereotype: Effects of Consumer Expertise and Attribute Strength on Product Evaluations', *Journal of Consumer Research* 21 (September 1994): 354–65.

69. *Images of Europe: A Survey of Japanese Attitudes Toward European Products*, Report prepared by Dentsu Inc. for the Commission of the European Communities (Brussels, 1994).

70. Richard W. Stevenson, 'The Brands With Billion-Dollar Names', *New York Times* (28 October 1988): A1.

71. Ronald Alsop, 'Enduring Brands Hold Their Allure by Sticking Close to Their Roots', *Wall Street Journal*, centennial edn (1989): B4.

72. 'Assessing Brands: Broad, Deep, Long and Heavy', *The Economist* (16 November 1996): 84–5.

73. 'What's in a Name?', *The Economist* (27 August 1988): 62.

74. Stuart Elliott, 'What's in a Name? Perhaps Billions', *New York Times* (12 August 1992): D6.

75. Jacob Jacoby and Robert Chestnut, *Brand Loyalty: Measurement and Management* (New York: Wiley, 1978).

76. Anne B. Fisher, 'Coke's Brand Loyalty Lesson', *Fortune* (5 August 1985): 44.

77. Jacoby and Chestnut, *Brand Loyalty*.

78. Ronald Alsop, 'Brand Loyalty is Rarely Blind Loyalty', *Wall Street Journal* (19 October 1989): B1.

79. Betsy Morris, 'The Brand's the Thing', *Fortune* (4 March 1996): 72 (8).

80. C. Whan Park, 'The Effect of Individual and Situation Related Factors on Consumer Selection of Judgmental Models', *Journal of Marketing Research* 13 (May 1976): 144–51.

81. Joseph W. Alba and Howard Marmorstein, 'The Effects of Frequency Knowledge on Consumer Decision Making', *Journal of Consumer Research* 14 (June 1987): 14–25.

Chapter 9

1. 'Consumers Hit at Poor Service', *Marketing* (5 December 1996): 4.

2. Pradeep Kakkar and Richard J. Lutz, 'Situational Influence on Consumer Behavior: A Review', in Harold H. Kassarjian and Thomas S. Robertson (eds.), *Perspectives in Consumer Behavior*, 3rd edn (Glenview, IL.: Scott, Foresman and Company, 1981): 204–14.

3. Carolyn Turner Schenk and Rebecca H. Holman, 'A Sociological Approach to Brand Choice: The Concept of Situational Self-Image', in Jerry C. Olson (ed.), *Advances in Consumer Research* 7 (Ann Arbor, MI: Association for Consumer Research, 1980), 610–14.

4. Russell W. Belk, 'An Exploratory Assessment of Situational Effects in Buyer Behavior', *Journal of Marketing Research* 11 (May 1974): 156–63; U.N. Umesh and Joseph A. Cote, 'Influence of Situational Variables on Brand-Choice Models', *Journal of Business Research* 16 (1988) 2: 91–9; see also J. Wesley Hutchinson and Joseph W. Alba, 'Ignoring Irrelevant Information: Situational Determinants of Consumer Learning', *Journal of Consumer Research* 18 (December 1991): 325–45.

5. Gordon Foxall, 'Science and Interpretation in Consumer Research: A Radical Behaviorist Perspective', *European Journal of Marketing* 29 (9) (1995): 1–90; Gordon Foxall, 'The Consumer Situation as Interpretive Device', in Flemming Hansen (ed.), *European Advances in Consumer Research* II (Provo, UT: Association for Consumer Research, 1995): 104–8.

6. Laura Bird, 'Grey Poupon Tones Down Tory Image', *The Wall Street Journal* (22 July 1994): B2.

7. Peter R. Dickson, 'Person-Situation: Segmentation's Missing Link', *Journal of Marketing* 46 (Fall 1982): 56–64.

8. Daniel Stokols, 'On the Distinction Between Density and Crowding: Some Implications for Future Research', *Psychological Review* 79 (1972): 275–7.

9. Keith Bradsher, 'There's More to Coin Laundries Than Just Getting the Wash Done', *New York Times* (7 January 1990): 38.

10. Carol F. Kaufman, Paul M. Lane and Jay D. Linquist, 'Exploring More Than 24 Hours a Day: A Preliminary Investigation of Polychronic Time Use', *Journal of Consumer Research* 18 (December 1991): 392–401.

11. Michelle M. Bergadaa, 'The Role of Time in the Action of the Consumer', *Journal of Consumer Research* 17 (December 1990): 289–302; see also Laurence P. Feldman and Jacob Hornik, 'The Use of Time: An Integrated Conceptual Model', *Journal of Consumer Research* 7 (March 1981): 407–19.

12. Jean-Claude Usunier and Pierre Valette-Florence, 'Individual Time Orientation: A Psychometric Scale', *Time and Society* 3 (2) (1994): 219–41.

13. Robert J. Samuelson, 'Rediscovering the Rat Race', *Newsweek* (15 May 1989): 57.

14. Quoted in Judann Dagnoli, 'Time – The Currency of the 90's', *Advertising Age* (13 November 1989): S-2.

15. Leonard L. Berry, 'Market to the Perception', *American Demographics* (February 1990): 32.

16. Quoted in Isabel Wilkerson, 'New Funeral Options for Those in a Rush', *New York Times* (25 February 1989): A16.

17. Lane, Kaufman and Lindquist, 'Exploring More Than 24 Hours a Day'.

18. Quoted in Kleiman, 'Fast Food? It Just Isn't Fast Enough Anymore', *New York Times* (6 December 1989): A1.

19. Allison James, 'Cooking the Books. Global or Local Identities in Contemporary British Food Cultures', in David Howes (ed.), *Cross-Cultural Consumption. Global Markets, Local Realities* (London: Routledge 1996): 77–92.

20. Agnès Durande-Moreau and Jean-Claude Usunier, 'Individual Time-Styles and Customer Satisfaction: The Case of the Waiting Experience', *Marketing for an Expanding Europe*, Proceedings of the 25th EMAC Conference, ed. J. Berács, A. Bauer and J. Simon (Budapest: Budapest University of Economic Sciences): 371–90; cf. also

Shirley Taylor, 'Waiting for Service: The Relationship Between Delays and Evaluations of Service', *Journal of Marketing* 58 (April 1994): 56–69.

21. Quoted in Gabriele Morello, 'Sicilian Time', *Time and Society*, 6 (1) (1997): 55–69. However, Morello concludes that in spite of such indications of traditional time perceptions, modernization is showing up in changed paces and attitudes towards time also in Sicily.

22. David H. Maister, 'The Psychology of Waiting Lines', in John A. Czepiel, Michael R. Solomon and Carol F. Surprenant (eds.), *The Service Encounter: Managing Employee/Customer Interaction in Service Businesses* (Lexington, MA: Lexington Books, 1985): 113–24.

23. A.Th.H. Pruyn and A. Smids, 'Customers' Evaluations of Queues: Three Exploratory Studies', in W.F. van Raaij and G. Bamossy (eds.), *European Advances in Consumer Research* I (Provo, UT: Association for Consumer Research, 1993): 371–82.

24. Robert J. Graham, 'The Role of Perception of Time in Consumer Research', *Journal of Consumer Research* 7 (March 1981): 335–42.

25. Alan Zarembo, 'What if There Weren't Any Clocks to Watch?', *Newsweek* (30 June 1997): 14; based on research reported in Robert Levine, *A Geography of Time: The Temporal Misadventures of a Social Psychologist, or How Every Culture Keeps Time Just a Little Bit Differently* (New York: Basic Books, 1997).

26. Cf. Gabriele Morello, 'Sicilian Time'.

27. Sigmund Grønmo, 'Concepts of Time: Some Implications for Consumer Research', in Thomas K. Srull (ed.), *Advances in Consumer Research* XVI (Provo, UT: Association for Consumer Research 1989): 339–45.

28. 'Lukkeloven flytter handel for milliarder', *Børsen* (26 September 1996): 8.

29. Gabriele Morello and P. van der Reis, 'Attitudes Towards Time in Different Cultures: African Time and European Time', *Proceedings of the Third Symposium on Cross-Cultural Consumer and Business Studies* (Honolulu: University of Hawaii, 1990); Gabriele Morello, 'Our Attitudes Towards Time', *Forum 96/2* (European Forum for Management Development 1996): 48–51.

30. Gary Davies, 'What Should Time Be?', *European Journal of Marketing* 28 (8/9) (1994): 100–13.

31. Esther S. Page-Wood, Carol J. Kaufman and Paul M. Lane, 'The Art of Time', in *Proceedings of the Academy of Marketing Science* (1990).

32. Eric N. Berg, 'Fight on Quick Pizza Delivery Grows', *New York Times* (29 August, 1989): D6.

33. Søren Askegaard and Tage Koed Madsen, 'European Food Cultures: An Exploratory Analysis of Food Related Preferences and Behaviour in European Regions', *MAPP Working Paper* no. 26 (Aarhus: The Aarhus School of Business, September 1995); for a thorough discussion of food culture, see Claude Fischler: *L'homnivore* (Paris: Odile Jacob, 1990).

34. Laurette Dube and Bernd H. Schmitt, 'The Processing of Emotional and Cognitive Aspects of Product Usage in Satisfaction Judgments', in Rebecca H. Holman and Michael R. Solomon (eds.), *Advances in Consumer Research* 18 (Provo, UT: Association for Consumer Research, 1991): 52–6; Lalita A. Manrai and Meryl P. Gardner, 'The Influence of Affect on Attributions for Product Failure', in Rebecca H. Holman and Michael R. Solomon (eds.), *Advances in Consumer Research* 18 (Provo, UT: Association for Consumer Research, 1991): 249–54.

35. Peter J. Burke and Stephen L. Franzoi, 'Studying Situations and Identities Using Experimental Sampling Methodology', *American Sociological Review* 53 (August 1988): 559–68.

36. Kevin G. Celuch and Linda S. Showers, 'It's Time To Stress *Stress*: The Stress-Purchase/ Consumption Relationship', in Rebecca H. Holman and Michael R. Solomon (eds.), *Advances in Consumer Research* 18 (Provo, UT: Association for Consumer Research, 1991): 284–9; Lawrence R. Lepisto, J. Kathleen Stuenkel and Linda K. Anglin, 'Stress: An Ignored Situational Influence', in Rebecca H. Holman and Michael R. Solomon (eds.), *Advances in Consumer Research* 18 (Provo, UT: Association for Consumer Research, 1991): 296–302.

37. See Eben Shapiro, 'Need a Little Fantasy? A Bevy of New Companies Can Help', *New York Times* (10 March 1991): F4.

38. John D. Mayer and Yvonne N. Gaschke, 'The Experience and Meta-Experience of Mood', *Journal of Personality and Social Psychology* 55 (July 1988): 102–11.

39. Meryl Paula Gardner, 'Mood States and Consumer Behavior: A Critical Review', *Journal of Consumer Research* 12 (December 1985): 281–300; Scott Dawson, Peter H. Bloch and Nancy M. Ridgway, 'Shopping Motives, Emotional States, and Retail Outcomes', *Journal of Retailing* 66 (Winter 1990): 408–27; Patricia A. Knowles, Stephen J. Grove and W. Jeffrey Burroughs, 'An Experimental Examination of Mood States on Retrieval and Evaluation of Advertisement and Brand Information', *Journal of the Academy of Marketing Science* 21 (April

1993); Paul W. Miniard, Sunil Bhatla and Deepak Sirdeskmuhk, 'Mood as a Determinant of Postconsumption Product Evaluations: Mood Effects and Their Dependency on the Affective Intensity of the Consumption Experience', *Journal of Consumer Psychology* 1 (1992) 2: 173–95; Mary T. Curren and Katrin R. Harich, 'Consumers' Mood States: The Mitigating Influence of Personal Relevance on Product Evaluations', *Psychology & Marketing* 11 (March/April 1994) 2: 91–107; Gerald J. Gorn, Marvin E. Rosenberg and Kunal Basu, 'Mood, Awareness, and Product Evaluation', *Journal of Consumer Psychology* 2 (1993) 3: 237–56.

40. Gordon C. Bruner, 'Music, Mood, and Marketing', *Journal of Marketing* 54 (October 1990): 94–104; Basil G. Englis, 'Music Television and its Influences on Consumers, Consumer Culture, and the Transmission of Consumption Messages', in Rebecca H. Holman and Michael R. Solomon (eds.), *Advances in Consumer Research* 18 (Provo, UT: Association for Consumer Research, 1991).

41. Marvin E. Goldberg and Gerald J. Gorn, 'Happy and Sad TV Programs: How They Affect Reactions to Commercials', *Journal of Consumer Research* 14 (December 1987): 387–403; Gerald J. Gorn, Marvin E. Goldberg and Kunal Basu, 'Mood, Awareness, and Product Evaluation', *Journal of Consumer Psychology* 2 (1993) 3: 237–56; Mary T. Curren and Katrin R. Harich, 'Consumers' Mood States: The Mitigating Influence of Personal Relevance on Product Evaluations', *Psychology & Marketing* 11(March/April 1994) 2: 91–107.

42. For a scale that was devised to assess these dimensions of the shopping experience, see Barry J. Babin, William R. Darden and Mitch Griffin, 'Work and/or Fun: Measuring Hedonic and Utilitarian Shopping Value', Journal of Consumer Research 20 (March 1994): 644–56.

43. Barry J. Babin, William R. Darden, and Mitch Griffin, 'Work and/or Fun: Measuring Hedonic and Utilitarian Shopping Value', *Journal of Consumer Research* 20 (March 1994): 644–56.

44. Edward M. Tauber, 'Why Do People Shop?', *Journal of Marketing* 36 (October 1972): 47–8.

45. Quoted in Robert C. Prus, *Making Sales: Influence as Interpersonal Accomplishment* (Newbury Park, CA: Sage Library of Social Research, Sage Publications, Inc., 1989): 225.

46. Gregory P. Stone, 'City Shoppers and Urban Identification: Observations on the Social Psychology of City Life', *American Journal of Sociology* 60 (1954): 36–45; Danny Bellenger and Pradeep K. Korgaonkar, 'Profiling the Recreational Shopper', *Journal of Retailing* 56 (1980)3: 77–92.

47. Nina Gruen, 'The Retail Battleground: Solutions for Today's Shifting Marketplace', *Journal of Property Management* (July–August 1989): 14.

48. 'Petrol Selling: Pump Action', *The Economist* (27 January 1996): 62.

49. 'Tankpasserne er forvandlet til købmænd', *Børsen* (28 September 1996): 9.

50. Hanne Hartvig Larsen and Sanni Grych, 'Fødevaredetailhandelen i Storbritannien. Analyse og beskrivelse af udvalgte detailhandelsorganisationer', *MAPP Project Paper* (Aarhus: The Aarhus School of Business, March 1997).

51. Personal communication with a Finnish reviewer.

52. 'Slaget om Europa', *Jyllands Posten* (12 February 1997).

53. Jane Gould, 'Driven to Shop? The Role of Transportation in Future Home Shopping', *Centre for Marketing Working Paper*, 96–801 (London Business School, September 1996).

54. Kelly Shermach, 'Study Identifies Types of Interactive Shoppers', *Marketing News* (25 September 1995): 22.

55. Arieh Goldman, 'The Shopping Style Explanation for Store Loyalty', *Journal of Retailing* 53 (Winter 1977–78): 33–46, 94; Robert B. Settle and Pamela L. Alreck, 'Hyperchoice Shapes the Marketplace', *Marketing Communications* (May 1988): 15.

56. 'Kundekort som konkurrencevåben', *Export* 36 (6 September 1996): 4–6.

57. An excellent collection of articles on this topic is found in Pasi Falk and Colin Campbell (eds.), *The Shopping Experience* (London: Sage, 1997).

58. C. Gardner and J. Sheppard, *Consuming Passion: The Rise of Retail Culture* (London: Unwin Hyman, 1989).

59. Stephen Brown, 'Sex 'n' Shopping', Working Paper 9501 (University of Stirling: Institute for Retail Studies, 1995); see also Stephen Brown, 'Consumption Behaviour in the Sex 'n' Shopping Novels of Judith Krantz: A Post-structuralist Perspective', in Kim P. Corfman and John G. Lynch, Jr (eds.), *Advances in Consumer Research* XXIII (Provo, UT: Association for Consumer Research, 1996): 43–8.

60. Véronique Aubert-Gamet, 'Twisting Servicescapes: Diversion of the Physical Environment in a Re-Appropriation Process', *International Journal of Service Industry Management* 8 (1) (1997): 26–41.

61. Stephen Brown, *Postmodern Marketing* (London: Routledge, 1995), discussion on pp. 50ff; Lars Thøger Christensen and Søren Askegaard, 'Flexibility in the Marketing Organization: The Ultimate Consumer Orientation or Ford Revisited?', *Marketing Today and for the 21st Century*, Proceedings of the XIV EMAC Conference, ed. Michelle Bergadaà (Cergy-Pontoise: ESSEC, 1995): 1507–14.

62. For a recent study of consumer shopping patterns in a mall that views the mall as an ecological habitat, see Peter N. Bloch, Nancy M. Ridgway and Scott A. Dawson, 'The Shopping Mall as Consumer Habitat', *Journal of Retailing* 70 (1994) 1: 23–42.

63. Turo-Kimmo Lehtonen and Pasi Mäenpää, 'Shopping in the East Centre Mall', in Pasi Falk and Colin Campbell (eds.), *The Shopping Experience* (London: Sage, 1997): 136–65.

64. See for instance Fabian Csaba, *Designing the Retail-Entertainment Complex: A Marketing Ethnography of the Mall Of America*, Doctoral Dissertation (Odense University: School of Business and Economics, 1998).

65. Quoted in Jacquelyn Bivins, 'Fun and Mall Games', *Stores* (August 1989): 35.

66. Sallie Hook, 'All the Retail World's a Stage: Consumers Conditioned to Entertainment in Shopping Environment', *Marketing News* 21 (31 July 1987): 16.

67. Stephen Brown, 'Marketing as Multiplex: Screening Postmodernism', *European Journal of Marketing* 28 (8/9) (1994): 27–51.

68. David Chaney, 'The Department Store as a Cultural Form', *Theory, Culture and Society* 1 (3) (1983): 22–31.

69. Cecilia Fredriksson, 'The Making of a Swedish Department Store Culture', in Pasi Falk and Colin Campbell (eds.), *The Shopping Experience*, (London: Sage, 1997): 111–35.

70. Michael Lev, 'Store of the Future: It Also Sells Shoes', *New York Times* (17 June 1991) 2: D1.

71. 'Enticing Europe's Shoppers: U.S. Way of Dressing and of Retailing Spreading Fast', *The New York Times* (24 April 1996): D1(2).

72. Patrick Hetzel and Veronique Aubert, 'Sales Area Design and Fashion Phenomena: A Semiotic Approach', W.F. van Raaij and G. Bamossy (eds.), *European Advances in Consumer Research* I (Provo, UT: Association for Consumer Research, 1993): 522–33.

73. Søren Askegaard and Güliz Ger, 'Product-Country Images as Stereotypes: A Comparative Analysis of the Image of Danish Food Products in Germany and Turkey', *MAPP Working paper* no. 45 (Aarhus: The Aarhus School of Business, 1997).

74. Susan Spiggle and Murphy A. Sewall, 'A Choice Sets Model of Retail Selection', *Journal of Marketing* 51 (April 1987): 97–111; William R. Darden and Barry J. Babin, 'The Role of Emotions in Expanding the Concept of Retail Personality', *Stores* 76 (April 1994) 4: RR7–RR8.

75. Most measures of store image are quite similar to other attitude measures, as discussed in chapter 5. For an excellent bibliography of store image studies, see Mary R. Zimmer and Linda L. Golden, 'Impressions of Retail Stores: A Content Analysis of Consumer Images', *Journal of Retailing* 64 (Fall 1988): 265–93.

76. Zimmer and Golden, 'Impressions of Retail Stores'.

77. Philip Kotler, 'Atmospherics as a Marketing Tool', *Journal of Retailing* (Winter 1973–74): 10–43, 48–64, 50; for a review of some recent research, see Peter McGoldrick and Christos Pieros, 'The Atmospherics-Customer Behaviour Relationship: Role of Response Moderators', in J. Berács, A. Bauer and J. Simon (eds.), *Marketing for an Expanding Europe*, Proceedings of the 25th EMAC Conference (Budapest: Budapest University of Economic Sciences, 1996): 735–53.

78. Joseph A. Bellizzi and Robert E. Hite, 'Environmental Color, Consumer Feelings, and Purchase Likelihood', *Psychology & Marketing* 9 (September/October 1992) 5: 347–63.

79. Deborah Blumenthal, 'Scenic Design for In-Store Try-Ons', *New York Times* (9 April 1988).

80. Judy I. Alpert and Mark I. Alpert, 'Music Influences on Mood and Purchase Intentions', *Psychology & Marketing* 7 (Summer 1990): 109–34.

81. Brad Edmondson, 'Pass the Meat Loaf', *American Demographics* (January 1989): 19.

82. 'Butikken er en slagmark', *Berlingske Tidende* (15 July 1996): 3.

83. Marianne Meyer, 'Attention Shoppers!' *Marketing and Media Decisions* 23 (May 1988): 67.

84. Easwar S. Iyer, 'Unplanned Purchasing: Knowledge of Shopping Environment and Time Pressure', *Journal of Retailing* 65 (Spring 1989): 40–57; C. Whan Park, Easwar S. Iyer and Daniel C. Smith, 'The Effects of Situational Factors on In-Store Grocery Shopping', *Journal of Consumer Research* 15 (March 1989): 422–33.

85. Francis Piron, 'Defining Impulse Purchasing', in Rebecca H. Holman and Michael R. Solomon (eds.), *Advances in Consumer Research* 18 (Provo, UT: Association for Consumer Research, 1991): 509–14; Dennis W. Rook, 'The Buying Impulse', *Journal of Consumer Research* 14 (September 1987): 189–99.

86. Michael Wahl, 'Eye POPping Persuasion', *Marketing Insights* (June 1989): 130.

87. 'Zipping Down the Aisles', *The New York Times Magazine* (6 April 1997).

88. Cathy J. Cobb and Wayne D. Hoyer, 'Planned Versus Impulse Purchase Behavior', *Journal of Retailing* 62 (Winter 1986): 384–409; Easwar S. Iyer and Sucheta S. Ahlawat, 'Deviations from a Shopping Plan: When and Why Do Consumers Not Buy as Planned', in Melanie Wallendorf and Paul Anderson (eds.), *Advances in Consumer Research* 14 (Provo, UT: Association for Consumer Research, 1987), 246–49.

89. 'Effective Demands', *Marketing* (5 December 1996): 34–8.

90. 'A Never-Ending Toy Story', *Marketing*, (5 December 1996): 33.

91. Bernice Kanner, 'Trolling in the Aisles', *New York* (16 January 1989): 12; Michael Janofsky, 'Using Crowing Roosters and Ringing Business Cards to Tap a Boom in Point-of-Purchase Displays', *The New York Times* (21 March 1994): D9.

92. John P. Cortez, 'Media Pioneers Try to Corral On-the-Go Consumers', *Advertising Age* (17 August 1992): 25.

93. Cyndee Miller, 'MTV "Video Capsule" Features Sports for Music Retailers, Corporate Sponsors', *Marketing News* (3 February 1992): 5.

94. William Keenan, Jr 'Point-of-Purchase: From Clutter to Technoclutter', *Sales and Marketing Management* 141 (April 1989): 96.

95. Meyer, 'Attention Shoppers!'.

96. Cyndee Miller, 'Videocart Spruces Up for New Tests', *Marketing News* (19 February 1990): 19; William E. Sheeline, 'User-Friendly Shopping Carts', *Fortune* (5 December 1988): 9.

97. Paco Underhill, 'In-Store Video Ads Can Reinforce Media Campaigns', *Marketing News* (May 1989): 5.

98. James Sterngold, 'Why Japanese Adore Vending Machines', *New York Times* (5 January 1992) 2: A1.

99. See Robert B. Cialdini, *Influence: Science and Practice*, 2nd edn (Glenview, IL: Scott, Foresman and Company, 1988).

100. Richard P. Bagozzi, 'Marketing as Exchange', *Journal of Marketing* 39 (October 1975): 32–9; Peter M. Blau, *Exchange and Power in Social Life* (New York: Wiley, 1964); Marjorie Caballero and Alan J. Resnik, 'The Attraction Paradigm in Dyadic Exchange', *Psychology & Marketing* 3 (1986) 1: 17–34; George C. Homans, 'Social Behavior as Exchange', *American Journal of Sociology* 63 (1958): 597–606; Paul H. Schurr and Julie L. Ozanne, 'Influences on Exchange Processes: Buyers' Preconceptions of a Seller's Trustworthiness and Bargaining Toughness', *Journal of Consumer Research* 11 (March 1985): 939–53; Arch G. Woodside and J.W. Davenport, 'The Effect of Salesman Similarity and Expertise on Consumer Purchasing Behavior', *Journal of Marketing Research* 8 (1974): 433–6.

101. Paul Busch and David T. Wilson, 'An Experimental Analysis of a Salesman's Expert and Referent Bases of Social Power in the Buyer–Seller Dyad', *Journal of Marketing Research* 13 (February 1976): 3–11; John E. Swan, Fred Trawick, Jr, David R. Rink and Jenny J. Roberts, 'Measuring Dimensions of Purchaser Trust of Industrial Salespeople', *Journal of Personal Selling and Sales Management* 8 (May 1988): 1.

102. For a recent study in this area, see Peter H. Reingen and Jerome B. Kernan, 'Social Perception and Interpersonal Influence: Some Consequences of the Physical Attractiveness Stereotype in a Personal Selling Setting', *Journal of Consumer Psychology* 2 (1993) 1: 25–38.

103. Mary Jo Bitner, Bernard H. Booms and Mary Stansfield Tetreault, 'The Service Encounter: Diagnosing Favorable and Unfavorable Incidents', *Journal of Marketing* 54 (January 1990): 7–84; Robert C. Prus, *Making Sales* (Newbury Park, CA: Sage Publications, 1989); Arch G. Woodside and James L. Taylor, 'Identity Negotiations in Buyer–Seller Interactions', in Elizabeth C. Hirschman and Morris B. Holbrook (eds.), *Advances in Consumer Research* 12 (Provo, UT: Association for Consumer Research, 1985): 443–9.

104. Gilbert A. Churchill, Jr, Neil M. Ford, Steven W. Hartley and Orville C. Walker, Jr, 'The Determinants of Salesperson Performance: A Meta-Analysis', *Journal of Marketing Research* 22 (May 1985): 103–18.

105. Siew Meng Leong, Paul S. Busch and Deborah Roedder John, 'Knowledge Bases and Salesperson Effectiveness: A Script-Theoretic Analysis', *Journal of Marketing Research* 26 (May 1989): 164; Harish Sujan, Mita Sujan and James R. Bettman, 'Knowledge Structure Differences Between More Effective and Less Effective Salespeople', *Journal of Marketing Research* 25 (February 1988): 81–6; Robert Saxe and Barton Weitz, 'The SOCCO Scale: A Measure of the Customer Orientation of Salespeople', *Journal of Marketing Research* 19 (August 1982): 343–51; David M. Szymanski,

'Determinants of Selling Effectiveness: The Importance of Declarative Knowledge to the Personal Selling Concept', *Journal of Marketing* 52 (January 1988): 64–77; Barton A. Weitz, 'Effectiveness in Sales Interactions: A Contingency Framework', *Journal of Marketing* 45 (Winter 1981): 85–103.

106. Jagdish M. Sheth, 'Buyer–Seller Interaction: A Conceptual Framework', in *Advances in Consumer Research* (Cincinatti, OH: Association for Consumer Research, 1976): 382–6; Kaylene C. Williams and Rosann L. Spiro, 'Communication Style in the Salesperson–Customer Dyad', *Journal of Marketing Research* 22 (November 1985): 434–42.

107. Marsha L. Richins, 'An Analysis of Consumer Interaction Styles in the Marketplace', *Journal of Consumer Research* 10 (June 1983): 73–82.

108. Evert Gummesson, 'The New Marketing – Developing Long-Term Interactive Relationships', *Long Range Planning*, 20 (4) (1987): 10–20; see also Robert M. Morgan and Shelby D. Hunt, 'The Commitment–Trust Theory of Relationship Marketing', *Journal of Marketing* 58 (July 1994): 20–38.

109. Brown, *Postmodern Marketing*: discussion on pp. 57–8.

110. Robert F. Dwyer, Paul H. Schurr and Sejo Oh, 'Developing Buyer–Seller Relationships', *Journal of Marketing* 51 (April 1987): 11–27.

111. Rama Jayanti and Anita Jackson, 'Service Satisfaction: Investigation of Three Models', in Rebecca H. Holman and Michael R. Solomon (eds.), *Advances in Consumer Research* 18 (Provo, UT: Association for Consumer Research, 1991), 603–10; David K. Tse, Franco M. Nicosia and Peter C. Wilton, 'Consumer Satisfaction as a Process', *Psychology & Marketing* 7 (Fall 1990): 177–93.

112. Eugene W. Anderson, Claes Fornell and Donald R. Lehmann, 'Customer Satisfaction, Market Share, and Profitability: Findings from Sweden', *Journal of Marketing* 58 (July 1994) 3: 53–66.

113. Robert Jacobson and David A. Aaker, 'The Strategic Role of Product Quality', *Journal of Marketing* 51 (October 1987): 31–44; for a recent review of issues regarding the measurement of service quality, see J. Joseph Cronin, Jr and Steven A. Taylor, 'Measuring Service Quality: A Reexamination and Extension', *Journal of Marketing* 56 (July 1992): 55–68.

114. Anna Kirmani and Peter Wright, 'Money Talks: Perceived Advertising Expense and Expected Product Quality', *Journal of Consumer Research* 16 (December 1989): 344–53; Donald R. Lichtenstein and Scot Burton, 'The Relationship Between Perceived and Objective Price-Quality', *Journal of Marketing Research* 26 (November 1989): 429–43; Akshay R. Rao and Kent B. Monroe, 'The Effect of Price, Brand Name, and Store Name on Buyers' Perceptions of Product Quality: An Integrative Review', *Journal of Marketing Research* 26 (August 1989): 351–57.

115. Shelby Hunt, 'Post-Transactional Communication and Dissonance Reduction', *Journal of Marketing* 34 (January 1970): 46–51; Daniel E. Innis and H. Rao Unnava, 'The Usefulness of Product Warranties for Reputable and New Brands', in Rebecca H. Holman and Michael R. Solomon (eds.), *Advances in Consumer Research* 18 (Provo, UT: Association for Consumer Research, 1991): 317–22; Terence A. Shimp and William O. Bearden, 'Warranty and Other Extrinsic Cue Effects on Consumers' Risk Perceptions', *Journal of Consumer Research* 9 (June 1982): 38–46.

116. Holbrook and Corfman, 'Quality and Value in the Consumption Experience'; Robert M. Pirsig, *Zen and the Art of Motorcycle Maintenance: An Inquiry into Values* (New York: Bantam Books, 1974).

117. W.F. van Raaij, 'The Formation and Use of Expectations in Consumer Decision Making', in T.S. Robertson and H.H. Kassarjian (eds.), *Handbook of Consumer Behavior* (Englewood Cliffs, NJ: Prentice-Hall, 1991): 401–18.

118. John W. Gamble, 'The Expectations Paradox: The More You Offer Customer, Closer You are to Failure', *Marketing News* (14 March 1988): 38.

119. Franz Bailom, Hans H. Hinterhuber, Kurt Matzler and Elmar Sauerwein, 'Das Kano-Modell der Kundenzufriedenheit', *Marketing ZFP* 2 (2nd quarter 1996): 117–26.

120. Marit G. Engeset, Kjell Grønhaug and Morten Heide, 'The Impact of Experience on Customer Satisfaction as Measured in Direct Surveys', *Marketing for an Expanding Europe*, Proceedings of the 25th EMAC Conference, ed. J. Berács, A. Bauer and J. Simon (Budapest: Budapest University of Economic Sciences): 403–17.

121. Kjell Grønhaug and Alladi Venkatesh, 'Products and Services in the Perspectives of Consumer Socialisation'; *European Journal of Marketing* 21 (10); Folke Ölander, 'Consumer Satisfaction – A Sceptic's View', in H.K. Hunt (ed.), *Conceptualization and Measurement of*

Consumer Satisfaction and Dissatisfaction (Cambridge, MA: Marketing Science Institute, 1977): 453–88.

122. Mary C. Gilly and Betsy D. Gelb, 'Post-Purchase Consumer Processes and the Complaining Consumer', *Journal of Consumer Research* 9 (December 1982): 323–8; Diane Halstead and Cornelia Dröge, 'Consumer Attitudes Toward Complaining and the Prediction of Multiple Complaint Responses', in Rebecca H. Holman and Michael R. Solomon (eds.), *Advances in Consumer Research* 18 (Provo, UT: Association for Consumer Research, 1991): 210–16; Jagdip Singh, 'Consumer Complaint Intentions and Behavior: Definitional and Taxonomical Issues', *Journal of Marketing* 52 (January 1988): 93–107.

123. Alan Andreasen and Arthur Best, 'Consumers Complain – Does Business Respond?', *Harvard Business Review* 55 (July–August 1977): 93–101.

124. Ingrid Martin, 'Expert–Novice Differences in Complaint Scripts', in Rebecca H. Holman and Michael R. Solomon (eds.), *Advances in Consumer Research* 18 (Provo, UT: Association for Consumer Research, 1991): 225–31; Marsha L. Richins, 'A Multivariate Analysis of Responses to Dissatisfaction', *Journal of the Academy of Marketing Science* 15 (Fall 1987): 24–31.

125. John A. Schibrowsky and Richard S. Lapidus, 'Gaining a Competitive Advantage by Analyzing Aggregate Complaints', *Journal of Consumer Marketing* 11 (1994) 1: 15–26.

126. Russell W. Belk, 'The Role of Possessions in Constructing and Maintaining a Sense of Past', in Marvin E. Goldberg, Gerald Gorn and Richard W. Pollay (eds.), *Advances in Consumer Research* 17 (Provo, UT: Association for Consumer Research, 1989): 669–76.

127. David E. Sanger, 'For a Job Well Done, Japanese Enshrine the Chip', *New York Times* (11 December 1990): A4.

128. Jacob Jacoby, Carol K. Berning and Thomas F. Dietvorst, 'What About Disposition?', *Journal of Marketing* 41 (April 1977): 22–8.

129. Mike Tharp, 'Tchaikovsky and Toilet Paper', *U.S. News and World Report* (December 1987): 62; B. Van Voorst, 'The Recycling Bottleneck', *Time* (14 September 1992): 52–4; Richard P. Bagozzi and Pratibha A. Dabholkar, 'Consumer Recycling Goals and Their Effect on Decisions to Recycle: A Means–End Chain Analysis', *Psychology & Marketing* 11 (July/August1994) 4: 313–40.

130. 'Finally, Something at McDonald's You Can Actually Eat', *Utne Reader* (May–June 1997): 12.

131. Debra J. Dahab, James W. Gentry and Wanru Su, 'New Ways to Reach Non-Recyclers: An Extension of the Model of Reasoned Action to Recycling Behaviors', in Frank Kardes and Mita Sujan (eds.), *Advances in Consumer Research* XXII (Provo, UT: Association for Consumer Research, 1994): 251–6

132. Rik G.M. Pieters, 'Changing Garbage Disposal Patterns of Consumers: Motivation, Ability, and Performance', *Journal of Public Policy and Marketing* 10 (2) (1991): 59–76.

133. Richard P. Bagozzi and Pratibha A. Dabholkar, 'Consumer Recycling Goals and Their Effect on Decisions to Recycle: A Means–End Chain Analysis', *Psychology & Marketing* 11 (July/August 1994): 5; see also L.J. Shrum, Tina M. Lowrey and John A. McCarty, 'Recycling as a Marketing Problem: A Framework for Strategy Development', *Psychology & Marketing* 11 (July/August 1994) 4: 393–416.

134. John Thøgersen, 'Wasteful Food Consumption: Trends in Food and Packaging Waste', in W.F. van Raaij and G. Bamossy (eds.), *European Advances in Consumer Research* I (Provo, UT: Association for Consumer Research, 1993): 434–9.

135. Suzanne C. Grunert, 'Antecedents of Source Separation Behaviour: A Comparison of Two Danish Municipalities', *Marketing for an Expanding Europe*, Proceedings of the 25th EMAC Conference, ed. J. Berács, A. Bauer and J. Simon (Budapest: Budapest University of Economic Sciences): 525–37.

136. 'Global markedsføring af danske miljøløsninger', *Markedsføring* 8 (1995): 12.

137. Manfred Kirchgeorg, 'Kreislaufwirtschaft – Neue Herausforderungen für das Marketing', *Marketing ZFP*, 4 (4th quarter 1995): 232–48.

138. 'Incentive Schemes. Jam Today', *The Economist* (12 April 1997): 67.

139. Timothy Aeppel, 'From License Plates to Fashion Plates', *The Wall Street Journal* (21 September 1994): B1 (2).

140. John F. Sherry, Jr, 'A Sociocultural Analysis of a Midwestern American Flea Market', *Journal of Consumer Research* 17 (June 1990): 13–30.

141. Diane Crispell, 'Collecting Memories', *American Demographics* (November 1988): 38–42.

142. Allan J. Magrath, 'If Used Product Sellers Ever Get Organized, Watch Out', *Marketing News* (25 June 1990): 9; Kevin McCrohan and James D. Smith, 'Consumer Participation in the Informal Economy', *Journal of the Academy of Marketing Science* 15 (Winter 1990): 62.

143. *Advertising Age* (2 May 1992).

144. Giampaolo Fabris, 'Consumer Studies: New Perspectives', *Marketing and Research Today* (June 1990): 67–73.

145. Walter Hopfenbeck, *The Green Management Revolution: Lessons in Environmental Excellence* (Englewood Cliffs, NJ: Prentice-Hall, 1993).

146. Armin Herker, 'Eine Erklärung des Umweltbewußten Konsumentenverhaltens', *Marketing ZFP*, 3 (3rd Quarter, 1995): 149–61.

147. Suzanne C. Grunert, 'Everybody Seems Concerned About the Environment: But is This Concern Reflected in (Danish) Consumers Food Choice?', in W. Fred van Raaij and Gary Bamossy (eds.), *European Advances in Consumer Research* I (Provo, UT: Association for Consumer Research): 428–33.

148. Carolyn Strong, 'A Preliminary Investigation: A Step Towards an Understanding of Children as Environmentally Conscious Consumers', *Marketing for an Expanding Europe*, Proceedings of the 25th EMAC Conference, ed. J. Berács, A. Bauer and J. Simon (Budapest: Budapest University of Economics, 1996): 2139–49.

149. Paul M.W. Hackett, 'Consumers' Environmental Concern Values: Understanding the Structure of Contemporary Green Worldviews', in W. Fred van Raaij and Gary Bamossy (eds.), *European Advances in Consumer Research* I (Provo, UT: Association for Consumer Research): 416–27.

150. Jean-Luc Gianneloni, 'The Combined Effect of Age, Level of Education and Personal Values on the Attitude Towards the Protection of the Environment', *Marketing Today and for the 21st Century*, Proceedings of the 24th EMAC Conference, ed. Michelle Bergadaà (Cergy-Pontoise: ESSEC, 1995): 373–389.

151. Suzanne C. Grunert and Kai Kristensen, 'The Green Consumer: Some Danish Evidence', *Marketing for Europe – Marketing for the Future*, Proceedings of the 21st EMAC Conference, ed. K.G. Grunert and D. Fuglede (Aarhus: The Aarhus School of Business, 1992): 525–39.

152. J. Robert Skalnik, Patricia Skalnik and David Smith, 'Growth Hormones in Milk-Producing Cows: For the Consumer, Much Ado About Nothing ... Perhaps', in Flemming Hansen (ed.), *European Advances in Consumer Research* II (Provo, UT: Association for Consumer Research): 201–3.

153. *Information* (9 January 1997): 3.

154. 'Vand for livet – et unikt kampagnesamarbejde', *Markedsføring* 5 (1996): 2.

155. 'BT Pushes Community Role', *Marketing* (12 December 1996): 9.

156. 'Crossing the Moral Minefield', *Marketing* (22 June 1995): 11.

Chapter 10

1. Joel B. Cohen and Ellen Golden, 'Informational Social Influence and Product Evaluation', *Journal of Applied Psychology* 56 (February 1972): 54–9; Robert E. Burnkrant and Alain Cousineau, 'Informational and Normative Social Influence in Buyer Behavior', *Journal of Consumer Research* 2 (December 1975): 206–15; Peter H. Reingen, 'Test of a List Procedure for Inducing Compliance with a Request to Donate Money', *Journal of Applied Psychology* 67 (1982): 110–18. C. Whan Park and V. Parker Lessig, 'Students and Housewives: Differences in Susceptibility to Reference Group Influence', *Journal of Consumer Research* 4 (September 1977): 102–10.

2. Kenneth J. Gergen and Mary Gergen, *Social Psychology* (New York: Harcourt Brace Jovanovich, 1981).

3. Harold H. Kelley, 'Two Functions of Reference Groups', in *Basic Studies in Social Psychology*, ed. Harold Proshansky and Bernard Siedenberg (New York: Holt, Rinehart and Winston, 1965): 210–14.

4. David Murrow, 'Dewar's Profiles Travel Well', *Advertising Age* (14 August 1989): 28.

5. 'Flere vil spise mere fisk', *Markedsføring*, 18 (1996): 18.

6. L. Festinger, S. Schachter and K. Back, *Social Pressures in Informal Groups: A Study of Human Factors in Housing* (New York: Harper, 1950).

7. R.B. Zajonc, H.M. Markus and W. Wilson, 'Exposure Effects and Associative Learning', *Journal of Experimental Social Psychology* 10 (1974): 248–63.

8. D.J. Stang, 'Methodological Factors in Mere Exposure Research', *Psychological Bulletin* 81 (1974): 1014–25; R.B. Zajonc, P. Shaver, C. Tavris and D. Van Kreveid, 'Exposure, Satiation and Stimulus Discriminability', *Journal of Personality and Social Psychology* 21 (1972): 270–80.

9. J.E. Grush, K.L. McKeogh and R.F. Ahlering, 'Extrapolating Laboratory Exposure Research to Actual Political Elections', *Journal of Personality and Social Psychology* 36 (1978): 257–70.

10. A. Benton Cocanougher and Grady D. Bruce, 'Socially Distant Reference Groups and Consumer Aspirations', *Journal of Marketing Research* 8 (August 1971): 79–81; James E. Stafford, 'Effects of Group Influences on Consumer Brand Preferences', *Journal of Marketing Research* 3 (February 1966): 68–75.

11. Cocanaugher and Bruce, 'Socially Distant Reference Groups and Consumer Aspirations'.

12. Anne F. Jensen and Søren Askegaard, 'In Pursuit of Ugliness: On the Complexity of the Fashion Concept', Paper presented at the ITAA Colloquium 'Confluences Fashioning Intercultural Perspectives' (Lyons: Université de la Mode, 10–12 July 1997).

13. Jeffrey D. Ford and Elwood A. Ellis, 'A Re-examination of Group Influence on Member Brand Preference', *Journal of Marketing Research* 17 (February 1980): 125–32; Thomas S. Robertson, *Innovative Behavior and Communication* (New York: Holt, Rinehart and Winston, Inc., 1980): chapter 8.

14. William O. Bearden and Michael J. Etzel, 'Reference Group Influence on Product and Brand Purchase Decisions', *Journal of Consumer Research* 9 (1982) 2: 183–94.

15. Robert D. Hof, 'Special Report: Internet Communities', *Business Week* 63 (8) (5 May 1997).

16. Gergen and Gergen, *Social Psychology*, 312.

17. J.R.P. French, Jr and B. Raven, 'The Bases of Social Power', in *Studies in Social Power*, ed. D. Cartwright (Ann Arbor, MI: Institute for Social Research, 1959): 150–67.

18. 'Getting a Charge Out of Rock'n'Roll', *Forbes* (19 December 1994): 302.

19. B. Macchiette and A. Roy, 'Affinity Marketing: What Is It and How Does It Work?', *Journal of Product and Brand Management* 2 (1) (1993): 55–66.

20. Michael R. Solomon, 'Packaging the Service Provider', *The Service Industries Journal* 5 (March 1985): 64–72.

21. Lars Thøger Christensen and Søren Askegaard, 'Identities and Images of Products and Organizations: A Semiotic Exercise', paper presented at the European Group of Organizational Studies 14th colloquium (Maastricht, 9–11 July 1998).

22. See Robert B. Cialdini, *Influence: Science and Practice*, 2nd edn (New York: Scott, Foresman, 1988), for an excellent and entertaining treatment of this process.

23. For the seminal work on conformity and social influence, see Solomon E. Asch, 'Effects of Group Pressure Upon the Modification and Distortion of Judgments', in D. Cartwright and A. Zander (eds.), *Group Dynamics* (New York: Harper and Row, 1953); Richard S. Crutchfield, 'Conformity and Character', *American Psychologist* 10 (1955): 191–8; Muzafer Sherif, 'A Study of Some Social Factors in Perception', *Archives of Psychology* 27 (1935): 187.

24. Burnkrant and Cousineau, 'Informational and Normative Social Influence in Buyer Behavior'.

25. For a recent attempt to measure individual differences in proclivity to conformity, see William O. Bearden, Richard G. Netemeyer and Jesse E. Teel, 'Measurement of Consumer Susceptibility to Interpersonal Influence', *Journal of Consumer Research* 15 (March 1989): 473–81.

26. Douglas B. Holt, Søren Askegaard and Torsten Ringberg, '7ups and Downs', Unpublished manuscript, Penn State University.

27. John W. Thibaut and Harold H. Kelley, *The Social Psychology of Groups* (New York: John Wiley, 1959); W.W. Waller and R. Hill, *The Family, a Dynamic Interpretation* (New York: Dryden, 1951).

28. William O. Bearden, Richard G. Netemeyer and Jesse E. Teel, 'Measurement of Consumer Susceptibility to Interpersonal Influence', *Journal of Consumer Research* 9 (3) (1989): 183–94; Lynn R. Kahle, 'Observations: Role-Relaxed Consumers: A Trend of the Nineties', *Journal of Advertising Research* (March/April 1995): 66–71; Lynn R. Kahle and Aviv Shoham, 'Observations: Role-Relaxed Consumers: Empirical Evidence', *Journal of Advertising Research* 35 (3) (May/June 1995): 59–62.

29. Leon Festinger, 'A Theory of Social Comparison Processes', *Human Relations* 7 (May 1954): 117–40.

30. Chester A. Insko, Sarah Drenan, Michael R. Solomon, Richard Smith and Terry J. Wade, 'Conformity as a Function of the Consistency of Positive Self-Evaluation with Being Liked and Being Right', *Journal of Experimental Social Psychology* 19 (1983): 341–58.

31. Abraham Tesser, Murray Millar and Janet Moore, 'Some Affective Consequences of Social Comparison and Reflection Processes: The Pain and Pleasure of Being Close', *Journal of Personality and Social Psychology* 54 (1988) 1: 49–61.

32. L. Wheeler, K.G. Shaver, R.A. Jones, G.R. Goethals, J. Cooper, J.E. Robinson, C.L. Gruder and K.W. Butzine, 'Factors Determining the Choice of a Comparison Other', *Journal of Experimental Social Psychology* 5 (1969): 219–32.

33. George P. Moschis, 'Social Comparison and Informal Group Influence', *Journal of Marketing Research* 13 (August 1976): 237–44.

34. Burnkrant and Cousineau, 'Informational and Normative Social Influence in Buyer Behavior'; M. Venkatesan, 'Experimental Study of Consumer Behavior Conformity and

Independence', *Journal of Marketing Research* 3 (November 1966): 384–7.

35. Harvey London, *Psychology of the Persuader* (Morristown, NJ: Silver Burdett/General Learning Press, 1973); William J. McGuire, 'The Nature of Attitudes and Attitude Change', in G. Lindzey and E. Aronson (eds.), *The Handbook of Social Psychology* (Reading, MA: Addison-Wesley, 1968): 3; N. Miller, G. Naruyama, R.J. Baebert and K. Valone, 'Speed of Speech and Persuasion', *Journal of Personality and Social Psychology* 34 (1976): 615–24.

36. J.L. Freedman and S. Fraser, 'Compliance Without Pressure: the Foot-in-the-Door Technique', *Journal of Personality and Social Psychology* 4 (1966): 195–202.

37. R.B. Cialdini, J.E. Vincent, S.K. Lewis, J. Catalan, D. Wheeler and B.L. Darby, 'Reciprocal Concessions Procedure for Inducing Compliance: The Door-in-the-Face Effect', *Journal of Personality and Social Psychology* 31 (1975): 200–15.

38. Nathan Kogan and Michael A. Wallach, 'Risky Shift Phenomenon in Small Decision-Making Groups: A Test of the Information Exchange Hypothesis', *Journal of Experimental Social Psychology* 3 (January 1967): 75–84; Nathan Kogan and Michael A. Wallach, *Risk Taking* (New York: Holt, Rinehart and Winston, 1964); Arch G. Woodside and M. Wayne DeLozier, 'Effects of Word-of-Mouth Advertising on Consumer Risk Taking', *Journal of Advertising* (Fall 1976): 12–19.

39. Kogan and Wallach, *Risk Taking*.

40. Roger Brown, *Social Psychology* (New York: The Free Press, 1965).

41. David L. Johnson and I.R. Andrews, 'Risky Shift Phenomenon Tested with Consumer Product Stimuli', *Journal of Personality and Social Psychology* 20 (1971): 382–5; see also Vithala R. Rao and Joel H. Steckel, 'A Polarization Model for Describing Group Preferences', *Journal of Consumer Research* 18 (June 1991): 108–18.

42. Donald H. Granbois, 'Improving the Study of Customer In-Store Behavior', *Journal of Marketing* 32 (October 1968): 28–32.

43. Len Strazewski, 'Tupperware Locks in New Strategy', *Advertising Age* (8 February 1988): 30.

44. Gergen and Gergen, *Social Psychology*.

45. L.J. Strickland, S. Messick and D.N. Jackson, 'Conformity, Anticonformity and Independence: Their Dimensionality and Generality', *Journal of Personality and Social Psychology* 16 (1970): 494–507.

46. Jack W. Brehm, *A Theory of Psychological Reactance* (New York: Academic Press, 1966).

47. R.D. Ashmore, V. Ramchandra and R. Jones, 'Censorship as an Attitude Change Induction', paper presented at meetings of Eastern Psychological Association, New York, 1971; R.A. Wicklund and J. Brehm, *Perspectives on Cognitive Dissonance* (Hillsdale, NJ: Lawrence Erlbaum, 1976).

48. C.R. Snyder and H.L. Fromkin, *Uniqueness: The Human Pursuit of Difference* (New York: Plenum Press, 1980).

49. Quoted in Raymond Serafin, 'Non-conformity Sparks Saab', *Advertising Age* (3 April 1995): 27.

50. 'The Mild Ones', *Forbes* (19 December 1994): 300–1.

51. Johan Arndt, 'Role of Product-Related Conversations in the Diffusion of a New Product', *Journal of Marketing Research* 4 (August 1967): 291–5.

52. 'Word-of-Mouth' to Become True Measure of Ads', *Marketing* (9 February 1995): 7.

53. Quoted in Barbara B. Stern and Stephen J. Gould, 'The Consumer as Financial Opinion Leader', *Journal of Retail Banking* 10 (Summer 1988): 43–52.

54. Elihu Katz and Paul F. Lazarsfeld, *Personal Influence* (Glencoe, IL: Free Press, 1955).

55. John A. Martilla, 'Word-of-Mouth Communication in the Industrial Adoption Process', *Journal of Marketing Research* 8 (March 1971): 173–8; see also Marsha L. Richins, 'Negative Word-of-Mouth by Dissatisfied Consumers: A Pilot Study', *Journal of Marketing* 47 (Winter 1983): 68–78.

56. Arndt, 'Role of Product-Related Conversations in the Diffusion of a New Product'.

57. James H. Myers and Thomas S. Robertson, 'Dimensions of Opinion Leadership', *Journal of Marketing Research* 9 (February 1972): 41–6.

58. 'Black Sheep of the Theakston Family', *Marketing* (3 December 1992): 24.

59. James F. Engel, Robert J. Kegerreis and Roger D. Blackwell, 'Word of Mouth Communication by the Innovator', *Journal of Marketing* 33 (July 1969): 15–19.

60. Bill Barol, 'Batmania', *Newsweek* (26 June 1989): 70.

61. Dorothy Leonard-Barton, 'Experts as Negative Opinion Leaders in the Diffusion of a Technological Innovation', *Journal of Consumer Research* 11 (March 1985): 914–26.

62. Chip Walker, 'Word of Mouth', *American Demographics* (July 1995): 38–44.

63. Richard J. Lutz, 'Changing Brand Attitudes through Modification of Cognitive Structure', *Journal of Consumer Research* 1 (March 1975): 49–59; for some suggested remedies to bad publicity, see Mitch Griffin, Barry J. Babin and Jill S. Attaway, 'An Empirical Investigation of the Impact of Negative Public Publicity on Consumer Attitudes and Intentions', in Rebecca H. Holman and Michael R. Solomon (eds.), *Advances in Consumer Research* 18 (Provo, UT: Association for Consumer Research, 1991): 334–41; Alice M. Tybout, Bobby J. Calder and Brian Sternthal, 'Using Information Processing Theory to Design Marketing Strategies', *Journal of Marketing Research* 18 (1981): 73–9.

64. Robert E. Smith and Christine A. Vogt, 'The Effects of Integrating Advertising and Negative Word-of-Mouth Communications on Message Processing and Response', *Journal of Consumer Psychology* 4 (2) (1995): 133–51; Paula Fitzgerald Bone, 'Word-of-Mouth Effects on Short-Term and Long-Term Product Judgments', *Journal of Business Research* 32 (1995): 213–23.

65. Charles W. King and John O. Summers, 'Overlap of Opinion Leadership Across Consumer Product Categories', *Journal of Marketing Research* 7 (February 1970): 43–50.

66. Jan Møller Jensen, 'A Strategic Framework for Analysing Negative Rumors in the Market Place: The Case of Wash & Go in Denmark', J. Sirgy, K.D. Bahn and T. Erem (eds.), *World Marketing Congress*, vol. VI (Istanbul: Proceedings of the Sixth Bi-Annual Conference of the Academy of Marketing Science 1993): 559–63.

67. John F. Sherry Jr, 'Some Implications of Consumer oral Tradition for Reactive Marketing', in Thomas Kinnear (ed.), *Advances in Consumer Research*, vol. 11 (Ann Arbor, MI: Association for Consumer Research, 1984): 741–7.

68. Jan Møller Jensen, 'A Strategic Framework ...'

69. This rumour is wonderfully and profoundly analysed in Edgar Morin: *La Rumeur d'Orléans* (Paris: Seuil, 1969).

70. John Leo, 'Psst! Wait 'Till You Hear This: A Scholar Says Rumors Reveal Our Fears and Desires', *Time* (16 March 1987): 76.

71. Sid Astbury, 'Pork Rumors Vex Indonesia', *Advertising Age* (16 February 1989): 36.

72. Craig S. Smith, 'A Beer Tampering Scare in China Shows a Peril of Global Marketing', *The Wall Street Journal* (3 November 1995): B1.

73. 'Oil and Troubled Waters', *Marketing* (29 June 1995): 13.

74. 'Bordeaux vil generobre den tabte hyldeplads', *Markedsføring* 12 (1996): 6.

75. Marcus Mabry, 'Do Boycotts Work?', *Newsweek* (6 July 1992) 3: 35.

76. 'Beware Yanks Bearing Drinks', *Marketing* (5 March 1992): 23–4.

77. 'Nike Ambushes Sports Limelight', *Marketing* (25 July 1996): 2.

78. Everett M. Rogers, *Diffusion of Innovations*, 3rd edn (New York: Free Press, 1983).

79. Leonard-Barton, 'Experts as Negative Opinion Leaders in the Diffusion of a Technological Innovation'; Rogers, *Diffusion of Innovations*.

80. Herbert Menzel, 'Interpersonal and Unplanned Communications: Indispensable or Obsolete?', in *Biomedical Innovation* (Cambridge, MA: MIT Press, 1981): 155–63.

81. Meera P. Venkatraman, 'Opinion Leaders, Adopters, and Communicative Adopters: A Role Analysis', *Psychology & Marketing* 6 (Spring 1989): 51–68.

82. Niraj Dawar, Philip M. Parker and Lydia J. Price, 'A Cross-Cultural Study of Interpersonal Information Exchange', *Journal of International Business Studies* (3rd quarter 1996): 497–516.

83. Robert Merton, *Social Theory and Social Structure* (Glencoe, IL: Free Press, 1957).

84. King and Summers, 'Overlap of Opinion Leadership Across Consumer Product Categories'; see also Ronald E. Goldsmith, Jeanne R. Heitmeyer and Jon B. Freiden, 'Social Values and Fashion Leadership', *Clothing and Textiles Research Journal* 10 (Fall 1991): 37–45; J.O. Summers, 'Identity of Women's Clothing Fashion Opinion Leaders', *Journal of Marketing Research* 7 (1970): 178–85.

85. Gerrit Antonides and Gulden Asugman, 'The Communication Structure of Consumer Opinions', in Flemming Hansen (ed.), *European Advances in Consumer Research* II (Provo, UT: Association for Consumer Research, 1995): 132–7.

86. Steven A. Baumgarten, 'The Innovative Communicator in the Diffusion Process', *Journal of Marketing Research* 12 (February 1975): 12–18.

87. Russell W. Belk, 'Occurrence of Word-of-Mouth Buyer Behavior as a Function of Situation and Advertising Stimuli', in Fred C. Allvine (ed.), *Combined Proceedings of the American Marketing Association*, Series No. 33 (Chicago: American Marketing Association, 1971): 419–22.

88. Lawrence F. Feick, Linda L. Price and Robin A. Higie, 'People Who Use People: The Other Side of Opinion Leadership', in Richard J. Lutz (ed.), *Advances in Consumer Research* 13 (Provo, UT: Association for Consumer Research, 1986): 301–5.

89. For discussion of the market maven construct, see Lawrence F. Feick and Linda L. Price, 'The Market Maven', *Managing* (July 1985): 10; scale items adapted from Lawrence Feick and Linda Price, 'The Market Maven: A Diffuser of Marketplace Information', *Journal of Marketing* 51 (January 1987), 83–7.

90. Michael R. Solomon, 'The Missing Link: Surrogate Consumers in the Marketing Chain', *Journal of Marketing* 50 (October 1986): 208–18.

91. Andra Adelson, 'A French Skin-Care Line Seeks to Take America by First Winning Over Pharmacists', *New York Times* (14 February 1994): D7.

92. Stern and Gould, 'The Consumer as Financial Opinion Leader'.

93. William R. Darden and Fred D. Reynolds, 'Predicting Opinion Leadership for Men's Apparel Fashions', *Journal of Marketing Research* 1 (August 1972): 324–8. A modified version of the opinion leadership scale with improved reliability and validity can be found in Terry L. Childers, 'Assessment of the Psychometric Properties of an Opinion Leadership Scale', *Journal of Marketing Research* 23 (May 1986), 184–8.

94. 'Connect', *Newsweek* (5 May 1997): 11.

95. Peter H. Reingen and Jerome B. Kernan, 'Analysis of Referral Networks in Marketing: Methods and Illustration', *Journal of Marketing Research* 23 (November 1986): 370–8.

96. Susan B. Kaiser, *The Social Psychology of Clothing* (New York: Macmillan, 1985); Thomas S. Robertson, *Innovative Behavior and Communication* (New York: Holt, Rhinehart and Winston, 1971).

97. Eric J. Arnould, 'Toward a Broadened Theory of Preference Formation and the Diffusion of Innovations: Cases from Zinder Province, Niger Republic', *Journal of Consumer Research* 16 (September 1989): 239–67.

98. Susan L. Holak, Donald R. Lehmann and Farena Sultan, 'The Role of Expectations in the Adoption of Innovative Consumer Durables: Some Preliminary Evidence', *Journal of Retailing* 63 (Fall 1987): 243–59.

99. Hubert Gatignon and Thomas S. Robertson, 'A Propositional Inventory for New Diffusion Research', *Journal of Consumer Research* 11 (March 1985): 849–67.

100. Frank Huber, 'Ein Konzept zur Ermittlung und Bearbeitung des Frühkäufersegments im Bekleidungsmarkt', *Marketing ZFP* 2 (2nd Quarter 1995): 110–121.

101. Gordon R. Foxall and Seema Bhate, 'Cognitive Style and Personal Involvement as Explicators of Innovative Purchasing of Health Food Brands', *European Journal of Marketing* 27 (2) (1993): 5–16.

102. Elisabeth C: Hirschman, 'Symbolism and Technology as Sources of the Generation of Innovations', in Andrew Mitchell (ed.), *Advances in Consumer Research* 9 (Provo, UT: Association for Consumer Research, 1981): 537–41.

103. Søren Askegaard and A. Fuat Fırat, 'Towards a Critique of Material Culture, Consumption and Markets', in Susan M. Pearce (ed.), *Experiencing Material Culture in the Western World* (London: Leicester University Press, 1997): 114–39.

104. Stephen Brown, *Postmodern Marketing* (London: Routledge, 1995).

105. Everett M. Rogers, *Diffusion of Innovations*, 3rd edn (New York: Free Press, 1983).

106. Robert J. Fisher and Linda L. Price, 'An Investigation into the Social Context of Early Adoption Behavior', *Journal of Consumer Research* 19 (December 1992): 477–86.

107. Güliz Ger and Russell W. Belk, 'I'd Like to Buy the World a Coke: Consumptionscapes of the "Less Affluent World"', *Journal of Consumer Policy* 19 (1996): 271–304.

108. W. Chan Kim and Renée Mauborgne, 'Value Innovation: The Strategic Logic of High Growth', *Harvard Business Review* (January–February 1997): 103–12.

109. 'Dare to Be Different', *Marketing* (13 February 1997): 22–3.

Chapter 11

1. Nancy Marx Better, 'Green Teens', *The New York Times Magazine* (8 March 1992) 3: 44; Howard Schlossberg, 'Kids Teach Parents How to Change Their Buying Habits', *Marketing News* (1992): 8.

2. T. Eggerickx, and F. Bégeot, 'Les recensements en Europe dans les années 1990. De la diversité des pratiques nationales à la comparabilité internationales des résulats', *Population* 41(2) (1993): 327–48.

3. F. Simoes-Casimiro and M.G. Calado-Lopes, 'Concepts and Typologies of Household and Family in the 1981 and 1991 Population Censuses in the Twelve Community Countries'. Unpublished report for Eurostat (Lisbon:

Instituto Superior de Estatistica e Gescao de Informação, 1995); 'Gezinsleven binner de EU onder druk', *Nederlandse Dagblad* (7 July 1995); 'Statistics in Focus: Population and Social Conditions', *Eurostat* (Luxembourg: Office for Official Publications of the European Communities, 1996).

4. 'Statistics in Focus: Population and social conditions' *Eurostat* (Luxembourg: Office for Official Publications of the European Communities, 1996).

5. Robert Boutilier, 'Diversity in Family Structures', *American Demographics Marketing Tools* (1993): 4–6; W. Bradford Fay, 'Families in the 1990s: Universal Values, Uncommon Experiences', *Marketing Research: A Magazine of Management & Applications* 5(Winter 1993) 1: 47.

6. Ellen Graham, 'Craving Closer Ties, Strangers Come Together as Family', *The Wall Street Journal* (4 March 1996): B1 (2).

7. David Cheal, 'The Ritualization of Family Ties', *American Behavioral Scientist* 31 (July/August 1988): 632.

8. 'Women and Men in the European Union: A Statistical Portrait' (Luxembourg: Office for Official Publications of the European Communities, 1996); 'Families Come First', *Psychology Today* (September 1988): 11.

9. Christy Fisher, 'Kidding Around Making Sense', *Advertising Age* (27 June 1994): 34.

10. Alan R. Andreasen, 'Life Status Changes and Changes in Consumer Preferences and Satisfaction', *Journal of Consumer Research* 11 (December 1984): 784–94; James H. McAlexander, John W. Schouten and Scott D. Roberts, 'Consumer Behavior and Divorce', *Research in Consumer Behavior* 6 (1993): 153–84.

11. 'Men and Women in the European Union: A Statistical Portrait', *EUROSTAT*; 'The Population of the EU on 1 January, 1995', *Statistics in Focus. Population and Social Conditions*, no. 8 (Luxembourg: Office for Official Publications of the European Communities, 1995).

12. 'Men and Women in the European Union: A Statistical Portrait' (Luxembourg: Office for Official Publications of the European Communities, 1995); 'The Big Picture', *American Demographics* (March 1989): 22–7; Thomas G. Exter, 'Middle-Aging Households', *American Demographics* (July 1992): 63.

13. Cyndee Miller, ''Til Death Do They Part', *Marketing News* (27 March 1995): 1–2.

14. 'The Population of the EU on 1 January, 1995', *Statistics in Focus. Population and Social Conditions*, no. 8 (Luxembourg: Office for Official Publications of the European Communities, 1995); Nicholas Timmins, 'One in Five Women to Remain Childless', *The Independent* (4 October 1995).

15. 'The Population of the EU on 1 January, 1995', *Statistics in Focus. Population and Social Conditions*, no. 8 (Luxembourg: Office for Official Publications of the European Communities, 1995).

16. 'Men and Women in the European Union: A Statistical Portrait' (Luxembourg: Office for Official Publications of the European Communities, 1995): 72.

17. Peg Masterson, 'Agency Notes Rise of Singles Market', *Advertising Age* (9 August 1993): 17.

18. Christy Fisher, 'Census Data May Make Ads More Single Minded', *Advertising Age* (20 July 1992): 2.

19. Calmetta Y. Coleman, 'The Unseemly Secrets of Eating Alone', *The Wall Street Journal* (6 July 1995): B1 (2).

20. Stephanie Shipp, 'How Singles Spend', *American Demographics* (April 1988): 22–7; Patricia Braus, 'Sex and the Single Spender', *American Demographics* (November 1993): 28–34.

21. 'Mothers Bearing a Second Burden', *New York Times* (14 May 1989): 26.

22. Seth Mydans, 'A Tribunal to Get Neglected Parents Smiling Again', *The New York Times* (27 December 1996): A4.

23. 'Men and Women in the European Union: A Statistical Portrait' (Luxembourg: Office for Official Publications of the European Communities, 1995): 76.

24. 'Census Paints a New Picture of Family Life', *The New York Times* (30 August 1994): 22.

25. Diane Crispell, 'Pet Projections', *American Demographics* (September 1994): 59.

26. Howard G. Chua-Eoan, 'Reigning Cats and Dogs', *Time* (16 August 1993): 50 (2); Patricia Braus, 'Cat Beats Dog, Wins Spot in House', *American Demographics* (September 1993): 24 (2).

27. Quoted in Youssef M. Ibrahim, 'French Love for Animals: Too Fervent?', *New York Times* (2 February 1990): A5.

28. Woody Hochswender, 'The Cat's Meow', *New York Times* (16 May 1989): B7; Judann Dagnoli, 'Toothcare for Terriers', *Advertising Age* (20 November 1989): 8; 'For Fido, Broccoli and Yogurt', *New York Times* (16 April 1989); Howard G. Chua-Eoan, 'Reigning Cats and Dogs', *Time* (16 August 1993): 50 (2); William E. Schmidt, 'Right, Then: Your Policy Covers Fido for Therapy', *The New York Times* (15 May 1994): 4.

29. A. Waldrop, 'Lesson in Home Economics'; Gary Younge, 'Parents face a £66,000 Bill', *The Guardian* (27 May 1996); Liz Hunt, 'The Cost of Growing: Schoolchildren Need Huge Sums', *The Independent* (19 August 1996).

30. 'Key Figures: Bulletin of Economic Trends in Europe and Summaries, 7/97' (Luxembourg: Office for Official Publications of the European Communities, 1997).

31. Mary C. Gilly and Ben M. Enis, 'Recycling the Family Life Cycle: A Proposal for Redefinition', in Andrew A. Mitchell (ed.), *Advances in Consumer Research* 9 (Ann Arbor, MI: ACR, 1982): 271–6.

32. Charles M. Schaninger and William D. Danko, 'A Conceptual and Empirical Comparison of Alternative Household Life Cycle Models', *Journal of Consumer Research* 19 (March 1993): 580–94; Robert E. Wilkes, 'Household Life-Cycle Stages, Transitions, and Product Expenditures', *Journal of Consumer Research* 22 (1) (June 1995): 27–42.

33. These categories are an adapted version of an FLC model proposed by Gilly and Enis (1982). Based on a recent empirical comparison of several competing models, Schaninger and Danko found that this framework outperformed others, especially in terms of its treatment of non-conventional households, though they recommend several improvements to this model as well. See Mary C. Gilly and Ben M. Enis, 'Recycling the Family Life Cycle: A Proposal for Redefinition', in *Advances in Consumer Research* 9, ed. Andrew A. Mitchell (Ann Arbor, MI: Association for Consumer Research, 1982), 271–6; Charles M. Schaninger and William P. Drake, 'A Conceptual and Empirical Comparison of Alternate Household Life Cycle Markets', *Journal of Consumer Research* 19 (March 1993): 580–94; Scott D. Roberts, Patricia K. Voli and KerenAmi Johnson, 'Beyond the Family Life Cycle: An Inventory of Variables for Defining the Family as a Consumption Unit', in Victoria L. Crittenden (ed.), *Developments in Marketing Science* 15 (Coral Gables, FL: Academy of Marketing Science, 1992): 71–5.

34. James H. McAlexander, John W. Schouten and Scott D. Roberts, 'Consumer Behavior and Divorce', in *Research in Consumer Behavior* (Greenwich, CT: JAI Press, 1992); Michael R. Solomon, 'The Role of Products as Social Stimuli: A Symbolic Interactionism Perspective', *Journal of Consumer Research* 10 (December 1983): 319–29; Melissa Martin Young, 'Disposition of Possession During Role Transitions', in Rebecca H. Holman and Michael R. Solomon (eds.), *Advances in Consumer Research* 18 (Provo, UT: Association for Consumer Research, 1991), 33–9.

35. Harry L. Davis, 'Decision Making Within the Household', *Journal of Consumer Research* 2 (March 1972): 241–60; Michael B. Menasco and David J. Curry, 'Utility and Choice: An Empirical Study of Wife/Husband Decision Making', *Journal of Consumer Research* 16 (June 1989): 87–97; for a recent review, see Conway Lackman and John M. Lanasa, 'Family Decision-Making Theory: An Overview and Assessment', *Psychology & Marketing* 10 (March/April 1993) 2: 81–94.

36. Shannon Dortch, 'Money and Marital Discord', *American Demographics* (October 1994): 11 (3).

37. Daniel Seymour and Greg Lessne, 'Spousal Conflict Arousal: Scale Development', *Journal of Consumer Research* 11 (December 1984): 810–21.

38. For recent research on factors influencing how much influence adolescents exert in family decision-making, see Ellen Foxman, Patriya Tansuhaj and Karin M. Ekstrom, 'Family Members' Perceptions of Adolescents' Influence in Family Decision Making', *Journal of Consumer Research* 15 (March 1989) 4: 482–91; Sharon E. Beatty and Salil Talpade, 'Adolescent Influence in Family Decision Making: A Replication with Extension', *Journal of Consumer Research* 21 (September 1994) 2: 332–41.

39. Diane Crispell, 'Dual-Earner Diversity', *American Demographics* (July 1995): 32–7.

40. Thomas Hine, *Populuxe* (New York: Alfred A. Knopf, 1986).

41. Robert Boutilier, *Targeting Families: Marketing To and Through the New Family* (American Demographics, 1993).

42. Darach Turley, 'Dialogue with the Departed', *European Advances in Consumer Research* 2 (1995): 10–13.

43. Dennis L. Rosen and Donald H. Granbois, 'Determinants of Role Structure in Family Financial Management', *Journal of Consumer Research* 10 (September 1983): 253–58.

44. Robert F. Bales, *Interaction Process Analysis: A Method for the Study of Small Groups* (Reading, MA: Addison-Wesley, 1950); for a cross-gender comparison of food shopping strategies, see Rosemary Polegato and Judith L. Zaichkowsky, 'Family Food Shopping: Strategies Used by Husbands and Wives', *The Journal of Consumer Affairs* 28 (1994): 2.

45. Alma S. Baron, 'Working Parents: Shifting Traditional Roles', *Business* 37 (January/March 1987): 36; William J. Qualls, 'Household

Decision Behavior: The Impact of Husbands' and Wives' Sex Role Orientation', *Journal of Consumer Research* 14 (September 1987): 264–79; Charles M. Schaninger and W. Christian Buss, 'The Relationship of Sex Role Norms to Household Task Allocation', *Psychology & Marketing* 2 (Summer 1985): 93–104.

46. Cynthia Webster, 'Effects of Hispanic Ethnic Identification on Marital Roles in the Purchase Decision Process', *Journal of Consumer Research* 21 (September 1994) 2: 319–31; for a recent study that examined the effects of family depictions in advertising among Hispanic consumers, cf. Gary D. Gregory and James M. Munch, 'Cultural Values in International Advertising: An Examination of Familial Norms and Roles in Mexico', *Psychology & Marketing* 14(2) (March 1997): 99–120.

47. John B. Ford, Michael S. LaTour and Tony L. Henthorne, 'Perception of Marital Roles in Purchase Decision Processes: A Cross-Cultural Study', *Journal of the Academy of Marketing Science* 23(2) (Spring 1995): 120–31; for a recent study of husband–wife dyad decision-making for home purchase decisions, cf. Chankon Kim and Hanjoon Lee, 'A Taxonomy of Couples Based on Influence Strategies: The Case of Home Purchase', *Journal of Business Research* 36(2) (June 1996): 157–68.

48. Gary L. Sullivan and P.J. O'Connor, 'The Family Purchase Decision Process: A Cross-Cultural Review and Framework for Research', *Southwest Journal of Business & Economics* (Fall 1988): 43; Marilyn Lavin, 'Husband-Dominant, Wife-Dominant, Joint', *Journal of Consumer Marketing* 10 (1993) 3: 33–42; Nicholas Timmins, 'New Man Fails to Survive into the Nineties', *The* Independent (25 January 1996). See also Roger J. Baran, 'Patterns of Decision Making Influence for Selected Products and Services Among Husbands and Wives Living in the Czech Republic', in F. Hansen (ed.), *European Advances in Consumer Research* 2; Jan Pahl 'His Money, Her Money: Recent Research on Financial Organization in Marriage', *Journal of Economic Psychology* 16 (1995): 361–76; Carole B. Burgoyne, 'Financial Organization and Decision-making within Western "households"', *Journal of Economic Psychology* 16 (1995): 421–30; Erich Kirchler, 'Spouses' joint purchase decisions: Determinants of influence tactics for muddling through the process', *Journal of Economic Psychology* 14 (1993): 405–38.

49. Quoted in Nicholas D. Kristof, 'Japan is a Woman's World Once the Front Door is Shut', *The New York Times* (19 June 1996): A1 (2), p. A8.

50. Yumiko Ono, 'McDonald's Doting Dads Strike a Chord in Japan', *The WSJ Interactive Edition* (8 May 1997).

51. The Associated Press, 'Hit Japanese Software lets Players Raise "Daughter"', *Montgomery Advertiser* (7 April 1996): 14A.

52. Tony Bizjak, 'Chore Wars Rage On – Even When Wife Earns the Most', *The Sacramento Bee* (1 April, 1993): A1 (3).

53. Micaela DiLeonardo, 'The Female World of Cards and Holidays: Women, Families, and the Work of Kinship', *Signs* 12 (Spring 1942): 440–53.

54. C. Whan Park, 'Joint Decisions in Home Purchasing: A Muddling Through Process', *Journal of Consumer Research* 9 (September 1982): 151–62; see also William J. Qualls and Françoise Jaffe, 'Measuring Conflict in Household Decision Behavior: Read My Lips and Read My Mind', in *Advances in Consumer Research* 19, ed. John F. Sherry Jr and Brian Sternthal (Provo, UT: Association for Consumer Research, 1992).

55. Kim P. Corfman and Donald R. Lehmann, 'Models of Cooperative Group Decision-Making and Relative Influence: An Experimental Investigation of Family Purchase Decisions', *Journal of Consumer Research* 14 (June 1987):

56. Alison M. Torrillo, 'Dens are Men's Territory', *American Demographics* (January 1995): 11 (2).

57. Charles Atkin, 'Observation of Parent–Child Interaction in Supermarket Decision-Making', *Journal of Marketing* 42 (October 1978).

58. Emily Nelson, 'Kodak Aims to Put Kids Behind its Cameras', *The WSJ Interactive Edition* (6 May 1997).

59. Les Carlson, Ann Walsh, Russell N. Laczniak and Sanford Grossbart, 'Family Communication Patterns and Marketplace Motivations, Attitudes, and Behaviors of Children and Mothers', *The Journal of Consumer Affairs* 28(1) (Summer 1994): 25–53; cf. also Roy L. Moore and George P. Moschis, 'The Role of Family Communication in Consumer Learning', *Journal of Communication* 31 (Autumn 1981): 42–51.

60. Leslie Isler, Edward T. Popper and Scott Ward, 'Children's Purchase Requests and Parental Responses: Results From a Diary Study', *Journal of Advertising Research* 27 (October/November 1987).

61. Patrick E. Tyler, 'As a Pampered Generation Grows Up, Chinese Worry', *The New York Times* (25 June 1996): A1, A6.

62. Robert Berner, 'Toddlers Dress to the Nine and Designers Rake it In', *The WSJ Interactive Edition* (27 May 1997).

63. Quoted in Lisa Gubernick and Marla Matzer, 'Babies as Dolls', *Forbes* (27 February 1995): 78–82, p.79.

64. Horst H. Stipp, 'Children as Consumers', *American Demographics* (February 1988): 27.

65. Melissa Turner, 'Kids' Marketing Clout Man-Sized', *Atlanta Journal* (18 February 1988): E10.

66. Scott Ward, 'Consumer Socialization', in *Perspectives in Consumer Behavior*, ed. Harold H. Kassarjian and Thomas S. Robertson (Glenville, IL: Scott, Foresman, 1980): 380.

67. Thomas Lipscomb, 'Indicators of Materialism in Children's Free Speech: Age and Gender Comparisons', *Journal of Consumer Marketing* (Fall 1988): 41–6.

68. George P. Moschis, 'The Role of Family Communication in Consumer Socialization of Children and Adolescents', *Journal of Consumer Research* 11 (March 1985): 898–913.

69. James U. McNeal and Chyon-Hwa Yeh, 'Born to Shop', *American Demographics* (June 1993): 34–9.

70. See Les Carlson, Sanford Grossbart and J. Kathleen Stuenkel, 'The Role of Parental Socialization Types on Differential Family Communication Patterns Regarding Consumption', *Journal of Consumer Psychology* 1 (1992) 1: 31–52.

71. See Patricia M. Greenfield, Emily Yut, Mabel Chung, Deborah Land, Holly Kreider, Maurice Pantoja and Kris Horsley, 'The Program-Length Commercial: A Study of the Effects of Television/Toy Tie-Ins on Imaginative Play', *Psychology & Marketing* 7 (Winter 1990): 237–56 for a study on the effects of commercial programming on creative play.

72. Jill Goldsmith, 'Ga, Ga, Goo, Goo, Where's the Remote? TV Show Targets Tots', *Dow Jones Business News* (5 February 1997), accessed via *The Wall Street Journal Interactive Edition* (6 February 1997).

73. Gerald J. Gorn and Renee Florsheim, 'The Effects of Commercials for Adult Products on Children', *Journal of Consumer Research* 11 (March 1985): 9, 62–7; for a recent study that assessed the impact of violent commercials on children, see V. Kanti Prasad and Lois J. Smith, 'Television Commercials in Violent Programming: An Experimental Evaluation of Their Effects on Children', *Journal of the Academy of Marketing Science* 22 (1994) 4: 340–51.

74. Glenn Collins, 'New Studies on "Girl Toys" and "Boy Toys"', *New York Times* (13 February 1984): D1.

75. Susan B. Kaiser, 'Clothing and the Social Organization of Gender Perception: A Developmental Approach', *Clothing and Textiles Research Journal* 7 (Winter 1989): 46–56.

76. D.W. Rajecki, Jill Ann Dame, Kelly Jo Creek, P.J. Barrickman, Catherine A. Reid and Drew C. Appleby, 'Gender Casting in Television Toy Advertisements: Distributions, Message Content Analysis, and Evaluations', *Journal of Consumer Psychology* 2 (1993) 3: 307–27.

77. Lori Schwartz and William Markham, 'Sex Stereotyping in Children's Toy Advertisements', *Sex Roles* 12 (January 1985): 157–70.

78. Joseph Pereira, 'Oh Boy! In Toyland, You Get More if You're Male', *The Wall Street Journal* (23 September 1994): B1 (2); Joseph Pereira, 'Girls' Favorite Playthings: Dolls, Dolls, and Dolls', *The Wall Street Journal* (23 September 1994): B1 (2).

79. Brad Edmondson, 'Snakes, Snails, and Puppy Dogs' Tails', *American Demographics* (October 1987): 18.

80. Laura A. Peracchio, 'How Do Young Children Learn to be Consumers? A Script-Processing Approach', *Journal of Consumer Research* 18 (March 1992): 4, 25–40; Laura A. Peracchio, 'Young Children's Processing of a Televised Narrative: Is a Picture Really Worth a Thousand Words?', *Journal of Consumer Research* 20 (September 1993) 2: 281–93; see also M. Carole Macklin, 'The Effects of an Advertising Retrieval Cue on Young Children's Memory and Brand Evaluations', *Psychology & Marketing* 11 (May/June 1994) 3: 291–311.

81. Jean Piaget, 'The Child and Modern Physics', *Scientific American* 196 (1957) 3: 46–51; see also Kenneth D. Bahn, 'How and When Do Brand Perceptions and Preferences First Form? A Cognitive Developmental Investigation', *Journal of Consumer Research* 13 (December 1986): 382–93.

82. Deborah L. Roedder, 'Age Differences in Children's Responses to Television Advertising: An Information Processing Approach', *Journal of Consumer Research* 8 (September 1981): 1, 44–53; see also Deborah Roedder John and Ramnath Lakshmi-Ratan, 'Age Differences in Children's Choice Behavior: The Impact of Available Alternatives', *Journal of Marketing Research* (29 May 1992): 216–26; Jennifer Gregan-Paxton and Deborah Roedder John, 'Are Young Children Adaptive Decision Makers? A Study of Age Differences in Information Search Behavior', *Journal of Consumer Research* (1995).

83. Tara Parker-Pope, 'Spiked Sodas, an Illicit Hit with Kids In U.K., Head for U.S.', *The Wall Street Journal* (12 February 1996): B1.

84. Janet Simons, 'Youth Marketing: Children's Clothes Follow the Latest Fashion', *Advertising Age* (14 February 1985): 16.

85. Stipp, 'Children as Consumers'; See Laura A. Peracchio, 'Designing Research to Reveal the Young Child's Emerging Competence', *Psychology & Marketing* 7 (Winter 1990): 257–76, for details regarding the design of research on children.

86. 'Kid Power', *Forbes* (30 March 1987): 9–10.

87. Dena Kleiman, 'Candy to Frighten Your Parents With', *New York Times* (23 August 1989): C1.

88. Laura Shapiro, 'Where Little Boys Can Play with Nail Polish', *Newsweek* (28 May 1990): 62.

89. Matt Murray, 'Marketers Want Kids' Help and Their Parents' Loyalty', *The WSJ Interactive Edition* (6 May 1997).

90. Cindy Clark, 'Putting Aside Adultcentrism: Child-Centered Ethnographic Research', unpublished manuscript (C.D. Clark Limited, 1991); Cindy Clark, 'Some Practical In's and Out's of Studying Children as Consumers', paper presented at the AMA Research Roundtable (March 1986).

91. Gary Armstrong and Merrie Brucks, 'Dealing with Children's Advertising: Public Policy Issues and Alternatives', *Journal of Public Policy and Marketing* 7 (1988): 98–113.

92. Bonnie Reece, 'Children and Shopping: Some Public Policy Questions', *Journal of Public Policy and Marketing* (1986): 185–94.

93. Mary Ann Stutts and Garland G. Hunnicutt, 'Can Young Children Understand Disclaimers in Television Commercials', *Journal of Advertising* 16 (Winter 1987): 41–6.

94. Ira Teinowitz, 'CARU to Unveil Guidelines for Kid-Focused Web Sites', *Ad Age* (21 April 1997): 8.

95. Steve Weinstein, 'Fight Heats Up Against Kids' TV "Commershows"', *Marketing News* (9 October 1989): 2.

96. Alan Bunce, 'Are TV Ads Turning Kids Into Consumers?', *Christian Science Monitor* (11 August 1988): 1.

Chapter 12

1. Fred van Raaij, 'Economic Psychology', *Journal of Economic Psychology* 1 (1981): 1–24.

2. Peter S.H. Leeflang and W. Fred van Raaij, 'The Changing Consumer in the European Union: A Meta-analysis', *International Journal of Research in Marketing* 12 (1995): 373–87.

3. Data in this section are adapted from Fabian Linden, *Consumer Affluence: The Next Wave* (New York: The Conference Board, Inc., 1994); 'Women and Men in the European Union: A Statistical Portrait' *Eurostat*, (Luxembourg: Office for Official Publications of the European Communities, 1995).

4. Christopher D. Carroll, 'How Does Future Income Affect Current Consumption?', *Quarterly Journal of Economics* 109 (February 1994) 1: 111–47.

5. 'Demographic Statistics, 1997: Population and Social Conditions Series', *Eurostat* (Luxembourg: Office for Official Publications of the European Communities, 1997). See also the Europa Server at: *http://europa.eu.int*

6. Jose J.F. Medina, Joel Saegert and Alicia Gresham, 'Comparison of Mexican-American and Anglo-American Attitudes Toward Money', *The Journal of Consumer Affairs* 30 (1) (1996): 124–45.

7. Kirk Johnson, 'Sit Down. Breathe Deeply. This is *Really* Scary Stuff', *The New York Times* (16 April 1995): F5.

8. Robert Sullivan, 'Americans and Their Money', *Worth* (June 1994): 60 (12).

9. 'Frontiers: Planning or Consumer Change in Europe 96/97', vol. 2 (London: The Henley Centre, 1996).

10. George Katona, 'Consumer Saving Patterns', *Journal of Consumer Research* 1 (June 1974): 1–12.

11. 'Frontiers: Planning or Consumer Change in Europe 96/97', vol. 2 (London: The Henley Centre, London, 1996): 4.

12. Ernest Beck, 'Why Custom-Made Shirts Are a Cut Above', *The Wall Street Journal Europe* (4–5 April 1997): 8.

13. Floyd L. Ruch and Davidip G. Zimbardo, *Psychology and Life*, 8th edn (Glenview, IL: Scott Foresman, 1971).

14. Louise Do Rosario, 'Privilege in China's Classless Society', *World Press Review* 33 (December 1986): 58.

15. David Leonhardt, 'Two-Tier Marketing', *Business Week* 82 (7) (17 March 1997).

16. Jonathan H. Turner, *Sociology: Studying the Human System*, 2nd edn (Santa Monica, CA: Goodyear, 1981).

17. Turner, *Sociology*.

18. Richard P. Coleman, 'The Continuing Significance of Social Class to Marketing', *Journal of Consumer Research* 10 (December 1983): 265–80; Turner, *Sociology*.

19. Ernest Beck, 'Cabin Fever Swirls Around Posh Cottages on Norwegian Coast', *The Wall Street Journal Europe* (6 August 1997): 1.

20. Quoted by Richard P. Coleman and Lee Rainwater, *Standing in America: New Dimensions of Class* (New York: Basic Books, 1978): 89.

21. Coleman and Rainwater, *Standing in America*.
22. Turner, *Sociology*.
23. Nicholas D. Kristof, 'Women as Bodyguards: In China, It's All the Rage', *The New York Times* (1 July 1993): A4.
24. James Sterngold, 'How Do You Define Status? A New BMW in the Drive. An Old Rock in the Garden', *New York Times* (28 December 1989): C1.
25. Robin Knight, 'Just You Move Over, 'Enry 'Iggins; A New Regard for Profits and Talent Cracks Britain's Old Class System', *U.S. News & World Report* 106 (24 April 1989): 40.
26. Turner, *Sociology*, 260.
27. See Ronald Paul Hill and Mark Stamey, 'The Homeless in America: An Examination of Possessions and Consumption Behaviors', *Journal of Consumer Research* 17 (December 1990): 303–21.
28. Joseph Kahl, *The American Class Structure* (New York: Holt, Rinehart and Winston, 1961).
29. Beeghley, *Social Stratification in America*.
30. Coleman and Rainwater, *Standing in America*, 220.
31. Turner, *Sociology*.
32. See Coleman 'The Continuing Significance of Social Class to Marketing'; Charles M. Schaninger, 'Social Class Versus Income Revisited: An Empirical Investigation', *Journal of Marketing Research* 18 (May 1981): 192–208.
33. Coleman, 'The Continuing Significance of Social Class to Marketing'.
34. Bernard Dubois and Gilles Laurent, 'Is There a Euroconsumer for Luxury Goods?', in W. Fred van Raaij and Gary J. Bamossy (eds.), *European Advances in Consumer Research*, 1 (Provo, UT: Association for Consumer Research, 1993): 59–69; Bernard Dubois and Gilles Laurent, 'Luxury Possessions and Practices: An Empirical Scale', in F. Hansen (ed.), *European Advances in Consumer Research* 2 (Provo, UT: Association for Consumer Research, 1995): 69–77; Bernard Dubois and Patrick Dusquesne 'The Market for Luxury Goods: Income versus Culture', *European Journal of Marketing* 27(1) (1993): 35–44.
35. August B. Hollingshead and Fredrick C. Redlich, *Social Class and Mental Illness: A Community Study* (New York: John Wiley, 1958).
36. John Mager and Lynn R. Kahle, 'Is the Whole More than the Sum of the Parts? Re-evaluating Social Status in Marketing', *Journal of Business Psychology*, in press.
37. R. Vanneman and F.C. Pampel, 'The American Perception of Class and Status', *American Sociological Review* 42 (June 1977): 422–37.
38. Donald W. Hendon, Emelda L. Williams, and Douglas E. Huffman, 'Social Class System Revisited', *Journal of Business Research* 17 (November 1988): 259.
39. Coleman, 'The Continuing Significance of Social Class to Marketing'.
40. Gerhard E. Lenski, 'Status Crystallization: A Non-Vertical Dimension of Social Status', *American Sociological Review* 19 (August 1954): 405–12.
41. Richard P. Coleman, 'The Significance of Social Stratification in Selling', in *Marketing: A Maturing Discipline, Proceedings of the American Marketing Association 43rd National Conference*, ed. Martin L. Bell (Chicago: American Marketing Association, 1960), 171–84.
42. Melinda Beck and Richard Sandza, 'The Lottery Craze: Multimillion Dollar Prizes Raise New Concerns That the Games Prey on the Poor', *Newsweek* (2 September 1985): 16; Rhoda E. McKinney, 'Has Money Spoiled the Lottery Millionaires', *Ebony* (December 1988): 150.
43. E. Barth and W. Watson, 'Questionable Assumptions in the Theory of Social Stratification', *Pacific Sociological Review* 7 (Spring 1964): 10–16.
44. Zick Rubin, 'Do American Women Marry Up?', *American Sociological Review* 33 (1968): 750–60.
45. Sue Browder, 'Don't be Afraid to Marry Down', *Cosmopolitan* (June 1987): 236.
46. K.U. Ritter and L.L. Hargens, 'Occupational Positions and Class Identifications of Married Working Women: A Test of the Asymmetry Hypothesis', *American Journal of Sociology* 80 (January 1975): 934–48.
47. Browder, 'Don't Be Afraid to Marry Down': 236.
48. J. Michael Munson and W. Austin Spivey, 'Product and Brand-User Stereotypes Among Social Classes: Implications for Advertising Strategy', *Journal of Advertising Research* 21 (August 1981): 37–45.
49. Stuart U. Rich and Subhash C. Jain, 'Social Class and Life Cycle as Predictors of Shopping Behavior', *Journal of Marketing Research* 5 (February 1968): 41–49.
50. Thomas W. Osborn, 'Analytic Techniques for Opportunity Marketing', *Marketing Communications* (September 1987): 49–63.
51. Coleman, 'The Continuing Significance of Social Class to Marketing'.
52. Jeffrey F. Durgee, 'How Consumer Sub-Cultures Code Reality: A Look at Some Code Types', in Richard J. Lutz (ed.), *Advances in Consumer Research* 13 (Provo, UT: Association for Consumer Research, 1986): 332–7.

53. David Halle, *America's Working Man: Work, Home, and Politics Among Blue-Collar Owners* (Chicago: The University of Chicago Press, 1984); David Montgomery, 'America's Working Man', *Monthly Review* (1985): 1.

54. Quoted in Coleman and Rainwater, *Standing in America*, 139.

55. 'Frontiers: Planning for Consumer Change in Europe 96/97' (London: The Henley Centre, 1996): 14.

56. Durkheim (1958), quoted in Roger Brown, *Social Psychology* (New York: The Free Press, 1965).

57. Lenore Skenazy, 'Affluent, Like Masses, Are Flush with Worries', *Advertising Age* (10 July 1989): 55.

58. Herbert J. Gans, 'Popular Culture in America: Social Problem in a Mass Society or Social Asset in a Pluralist Society?', in *Social Problems: A Modern Approach*, ed. Howard S. Becker (New York: Wiley, 1966); Helga Dittmar, 'Material Possessions as Stereotypes: Material Images of Different Socio-economic Groups', *Journal of Economic Psychology* 15 (1994): 561–85; Helga Dittmar and Lucy Pepper 'To Have Is to Be: Materialism and Person Perception in Working Class and Middle Class British Adolescents', *Journal of Economic Psychology* 15 (1994): 233–5.

59. Edward O. Laumann and James S. House, 'Living Room Styles and Social Attributes: The Patterning of Material Artifacts in a Modern Urban Community', *Sociology and Social Research* 54 (April 1970): 321–42; see also Stephen S. Bell, Morris B. Holbrook and Michael R. Solomon, 'Combining Esthetic and Social Value to Explain Preferences for Product Styles with the Incorporation of Personality and Ensemble Effects', *Journal of Social Behavior and Personality* (1991) 6: 243–74.

60. Quoted in Richard Elliott, 'How do the Unemployed Maintain Their Identity in a Culture of Consumption?', *European Advances in Consumer Research* 2 (1995): 1–4, p. 3.

61. Cyndee Miller, 'New Line of Barbie Dolls Targets Big, Rich Kids', *Marketing News* (17 June 1996): 6.

62. Cyndee Miller, 'Baubles are Back', *Marketing News* (14 April 1997): 1 (2).

63. Anita Sharpe, 'Magazines for the Rich Rake in Readers', *The Wall Street Journal* (16 February 1996): B1 (2).

64. 'Reading the Buyer's Mind', *U.S. News & World Report* (16 March 1987): 59.

65. Rebecca Piirto Heath, 'Life on Easy Street', *American Demographics* (April 1997): 33–8.

66. Sally D. Goll, 'Ignoring the Masses, Avenue Magazine Launches an Edition for China's Elite', *The Wall Street Journal* (28 September 1994): B1.

67. Paul Fussell, *Class: A Guide Through the American Status System* (New York: Summit Books, 1983): 29.

68. Elizabeth C. Hirschman, 'Secular Immortality and the American Ideology of Affluence', *Journal of Consumer Research* 17 (June 1990): 31–42.

69. Coleman and Rainwater, *Standing in America*, 150.

70. M.H. Moore, 'Homing in on Russian "Super Spenders"', *Adweek* (28 February 1994): 14–16.

71. Jerry Adler, 'For Sale: The Rich Look', *Newsweek* (22 June 1987): 80.

72. Jason DeParle, 'Spy Anxiety; The Smart Magazine That Makes Smart People Nervous About Their Standing', *Washingtonian Monthly* (February 1989): 10.

73. For a recent examination of retailing issues related to the need for status, see Jacqueline Kilsheimer Eastman, Leisa Reinecke Flynn and Ronald E. Goldsmith, 'Shopping for Status: The Retail Managerial Implications', *Association of Marketing Theory and Practice* (Spring 1994): 125–30.

74. Dennis Rodkin, 'Wealthy Attitude Wins Over Healthy Wallet: Consumers Prove Affluence is a State of Mind', *Advertising Age* (9 July, 1990): S-4.

75. John Brooks, *Showing off in America* (Boston: Little, Brown, 1981): 13.

76. Thorstein Veblen, *The Theory of the Leisure Class* (1899; reprint, New York: New American Library, 1953): 45.

77. Quoted in Cyndee Miller, 'Baubles are Back', *Marketing News* (14 April 1997): 1 (2). Elaine Underwood, 'Luxury's Tide Turns', *Brandweek* (7 March 1994): 18–22.

78. Brooks, *Showing off in America*.

79. Brooks, *Showing off in America*, 31–32.

80. For examples, see John T. Molloy, *Dress for Success* (New York: Warner Books, 1975); Vicki Keltner and Mike Holsey, *The Success Image* (Houston, TX: Gulf Publishing, 1982); and William Thourlby, *You Are What You Wear* (New York: New American Library, 1978).

Chapter 13

1. Bickley Townsend, 'Où sont les neiges d'antan? (Where are the snows of yesteryear?)', *American Demographics* (October 1988): 2.

2. Stephen Holden, 'After the War the Time of the Teen-Ager', *The New York Times* (7 May 1995): E4.

3. 'Same Kids, More Money', *Marketing* (29 June 1995): 37; also see the following web sites for some overviews of allowances: *http://www.kiplinger.com/drt.drthome.html* and *http://pages.prodigy.com/kidsmoney/*

4. 'Same Kids, More Money'. Scott McCartney, 'Society's Subcultures Meet by Modem', *The Wall Street Journal* (8 December 1994): B1 (2).

5 . Sara Olkon, 'Black Soda with Skulls on Label Isn't Aimed at the Pepsi Generation', *The Wall Street Journal* (24 May 1995): B1.

6. Junu Bryan Kim, 'For Savvy Teens: Real Life, Real Solutions', *Advertising Age* (23 August 1993): S-1 (3pp.).

7. Margaret Carlson, 'Where Calvin Crossed the Line', *Time* (11 September 1995): 64.

8. Ellen Goodman, 'The Selling of Teenage Anxiety', *Washington Post* (24 November 1979).

9. Ellen R. Foxman, Patriya S. Tansuhaj and Karim M. Ekstrom, 'Family Members' Perceptions of Adolescents' Influence in Family Decision Making', *Journal of Consumer Research* 15 (March 1989): 482–91.

10. 'Men and Women in the European Union: A Statistical Portrait' (Luxembourg: Office for Official Publications of the European Communities, 1995).

11. Deborah Klosky, 'World Bank Ads Target Youths', *Wall Street Journal, Europe* (7 October 1997): 4; Karen Ritchie, *Marketing to Generation X* (New York: Lexington Books, 1995); Rob Nelson, *Revolution X: Survival Guide for Our Generation* (New York: Penguin Books, 1994); for a 'Gen-X' website, see http://www.acent.net/in-mtl/v04n03/generax.htm; Laura Zinn, 'Move Over, Boomers', *Business Week* (14 December 1992): 7.

12. 'Generation Next', *Marketing* (16 January 1997): 25.

13. Quoted in T.L. Stanley, 'Age of Innocence ... Not', *PROMO* (February 1997): 28–33, p. 30.

14. 'Generation Next', 26.

15. Scott Donaton, 'The Media Wakes Up to Generation X', *Advertising Age* (1 February 1993): 16 (2); Laura E. Keeton, 'New Magazines Aim to Reach (and Rechristen) Generation X', *Wall Street Journal* (17 October 1994): B1.

16. Faye Rice, 'Making Generational Marketing Come of Age', *Fortune* (26 June 1995): 110–14.

17. Chip Walker, 'Can TV Save the Planet?', *American Demographics* (May 1996): 42–50. See also Shawn Tully, 'Teens: The Most Global Segment of All', *Fortune* (16 May 1994): 90–6.

18. Faye Rice, 'Making Generational Marketing Come of Age', *Fortune* (26 June 1995): 110–14.

19. 'Shades of Grey', *Marketing* (24 April 1997); 'Baby boom generatie moet oud-zijn modieus maken' ('Baby boom generation has to make "old" in fashion'), *NRC Handelsblad* (2 May 1996): 7; Melinda Beck, 'Going for the Gold', *Newsweek* (23 April 1990): 74.

20. 'Shades of Grey', *Marketing* (24 April 1997).

21. 'Shades of Grey'; 'Baby boom generatie moet oud-zijn modieus maken'.

22. David B. Wolfe, 'Targeting the Mature Mind', *American Demographics* (March 1994): 32–6.

23. 'Shades of Grey'.

24. Allyson Steward-Allen 'Marketing in Europe to the Consumer Over Age Fifty', *Marketing News* 31(16) (4 August 1997): 18.

25. Gabriele Morello, 'Old is Gold, But What is Old?', ESOMAR Seminar on 'The Untapped Gold Mine: The Growing Importance of the Over-50s', ESOMAR, Amsterdam, 1989; Gabriele Morello, 'Sicilian Time', in *Time and Society* (London: Sage Publications, 1997), 6(1): 55–69.

26. Benny Barak and Leon G. Schiffman, 'Cognitive Age: A Nonchronological Age Variable', in *Advances in Consumer Research* 8, ed. Kent B. Monroe (Provo, UT: Association for Consumer Research, 1981) 8: 602–6.

27. David B. Wolfe, 'An Ageless Market', *American Demographics* (July 1987): 27–55.

28. 'Baby boom generatie moet oud-zijn modieus maken'.

29. 'Demographic Statistics 1997' (Luxembourg: Office for Official Publications of the European Communities, 1997); see also http://europa.eu.int; Lenore Skenazy, 'These Days, It's Hip to be Old', *Advertising Age* (15 February 1988).

30. This segmentation approach is based on the US population and follows Lazer and Shaw, 'How Older Americans Spend Their Money'. See also 'Shades of Grey' for a two-segment approach of the UK elderly market.

31. Ellen Day, Brian Davis, Rhonda Dove and Warren A. French, 'Reaching the Senior Citizen Market(s)', *Journal of Advertising Research* (December/January 1987/88): 23–30; Warren A. French and Richard Fox, 'Segmenting the Senior Citizen Market', *Journal of Consumer Marketing* 2 (1985): 61–74; Jeffrey G. Towle and Claude R. Martin, Jr, 'The Elderly Consumer: One Segment or Many?', in Beverlee B. Anderson (ed.), *Advances in Consumer Research* 3 (Provo, UT: Association for Consumer Research, 1976): 463.

32. Catherine A. Cole and Nadine N. Castellano, 'Consumer Behavior', *Encyclopedia of Gerontology*, vol. 1 (1996): 329–39.

33. Ward, 'Marketers Slow to Catch Age Wave'.

Chapter 14

1. See, e.g. A. Fuat Fırat, 'Consumer Culture or Culture Consumed', Janeen A. Costa and G. Bamossy (eds.), *Marketing in a Multicultural World: Ethnicity, Nationalism, and Cultural Identity* (Thousand Oaks, CA: Sage, 1995): 105–25.

2. Grant McCracken, 'Culture and Consumption: A Theoretical Account of the Structure and Movement of the Cultural Meaning of Consumer Goods', *Journal of Consumer Research* 13 (June 1986): 71–84; see also Grant McCracken, *Culture and Consumption* (Bloomington: Indiana University Press, 1988).

3. For another excellent discussion on culture and consumption, see Alladi Venkatesh, 'Ethnoconsumerism: A New Paradigm to Study Cultural and Cross-Cultural Consumer Behavior', in Janeen A. Costa and Gary J. Bamossy (eds.), *Marketing in a Multicultural World* (Thousand Oaks, Sage, 1995): 26–67.

4. Paul du Gay, Stuart Hall, Linda Janes, Hugh MacKay and Keith Negus, *Doing Cultural Studies. The Story of the Sony Walkman* (London: Sage, 1997).

5. 'Spice Girls Dance into Culture Clash', *Montgomery Advertiser* (29 April 1997): 2A.

6. Personal communication with Jens Bernsen, 29 October 1997.

7. Clifford Geertz, *The Interpretation of Cultures* (New York: Basic Books, 1973); Marvin Harris, *Culture, People and Nature* (New York: Crowell, 1971); John F. Sherry, Jr, 'The Cultural Perspective in Consumer Research', in Richard J. Lutz (ed.), *Advances in Consumer Research* 13 (Provo, UT: Association for Consumer Research, 1985): 573–75.

8. Geert Hofstede, *Culture's Consequences* (Beverly Hills, CA: Sage, 1980); see also Laura M. Milner, Dale Fodness and Mark W. Speece, 'Hofstede's Research on Cross-Cultural Work-Related Values: Implications for Consumer Behavior', in W.F. van Raaij and G. Bamossy (eds.), *European Advances in Consumer Research* I (Provo, UT: Association for Consumer Research, 1993): 70–6.

9. Alladi Venkatesh, 'Ethnoconsumerism: A Proposal for a New Paradigm to Study Cross Cultural Consumer Behavior', J.A. Costa and G. Bamossy (eds.), *Marketing in a Multicultural World* (Thousand Oaks: Sage, 1995): 26–67.

10. George J. McCall and J.L. Simmons, *Social Psychology: A Sociological Approach* (New York: The Free Press, 1982).

11. Eric Arnould and Linda Price, 'River Magic: Extraordinary Experience and the Extended Service Encounter', *Journal of Consumer Research*, 20 (June 1993): 24–45.

12. Molly O'Neill, 'As Life Gets More Complex, Magic Casts a Wider Spell', *The New York Times* (13 June, 1994): A1 (2).

13. Conrad Phillip Kottak, 'Anthropological Analysis of Mass Enculturation', in Conrad P. Kottak (ed.), *Researching American Culture* (Ann Arbor, MI: University of Michigan Press, 1982): 40–74.

14. Joseph Campbell, *Myths, Dreams, and Religion* (New York: E.P. Dutton, 1970).

15. Jeffrey S. Lang and Patrick Trimble, 'Whatever Happened to the Man of Tomorrow? An Examination of the American Monomyth and the Comic Book Superhero', *Journal of Popular Culture* 22 (Winter 1988): 157.

16. Yumiko Ono, 'PepsiCo's "American" Superhero in Japanese Ads is Alien to U.S.', *The WSJ Interactive Edition* (23 May 1997).

17. James Fitchett, Douglas Brownlie and Michael Saren, 'On the Cultural Location of Consumption: The Case of Einstein as a Commodity', *Marketing for an Expanding Europe*, ed. J. Berács, A. Bauer & J. Simon, Proceedings of the 25th EMAC Conference (Budapest: Budapest University of Economic Sciences, 1996): 435–53.

18. Elizabeth C. Hirschman, 'Movies as Myths: An Interpretation of Motion Picture Mythology', in Jean Umiker-Sebeok (ed.), *Marketing and Semiotics: New Directions in the Study of Signs for Sale* (Berlin: Mouton de Guyter, 1987): 335–74.

19. See William Blake Tyrrell, 'Star Trek as Myth and Television as Mythmaker', in Jack Nachbar, Deborah Weiser and John L. Wright (eds.), *The Popular Culture Reader* (Bowling Green, OH: Bowling Green University Press, 1978): 79–88.

20. Benoît Heilbrunn, 'My Brand the Hero? A Semiotic Analysis of the Consumer-Brand Relationship', *Marketing for the 21st Century*, Proceedings of the 24th EMAC Conference, ed. M. Bergadaà (Cergy-Pontoise: ESSEC): 451–70; see also Bernie Whalen, 'Semiotics: An Art or Powerful Marketing Research Tool?', *Marketing News* (13 May 1983): 8.

21. See Dennis W. Rook, 'The Ritual Dimension of Consumer Behavior', *Journal of Consumer Research* 12 (December 1985): 251–64; Mary A. Stansfield Tetreault and Robert E. Kleine III, 'Ritual, Ritualized Behavior, and Habit: Refinements and Extensions of the Consumption Ritual Construct', in Marvin Goldberg, Gerald Gorn and Richard W. Pollay (eds.), *Advances in Consumer Research* 17 (Provo, UT: Association for Consumer Research, 1990): 31–8.

22. Grant McCracken, *Consumption and Culture* (Bloomington, IN: Indiana University Press).

23. 'The Skill of the Chase', *Marketing Week*, (30 April 1993): 38–40.

24. Kim Foltz, 'New Species for Study: Consumers in Action', *New York Times* (18 December 1989): A1.

25. Robert Grafton Small, 'Consumption and Significance: Everyday Life in a Brand-new Second-hand Bow Tie'; *European Journal of Marketing* 27 (8) (1993): 38–45.

26. Dennis W. Rook and Sidney J. Levy, 'Psychosocial Themes in Consumer Grooming Rituals', in Richard P. Bagozzi and Alice M. Tybout (eds.), *Advances in Consumer Research* 10 (Provo, UT: Association for Consumer Research, 1983): 329–33.

27. Diane Barthel, *Putting on Appearances: Gender and Attractiveness* (Philadelphia: Temple University Press, 1988).

28. Quoted in Barthel, *Putting on Appearances: Gender and Advertising*.

29. Russell W. Belk, Melanie Wallendorf and John Sherry, Jr, 'The Sacred and the Profane in Consumer Behavior: Theodicy on the Odyssey', *Journal of Consumer Research* 16 (June 1989): 1–38.

30. Russell W. Belk and Gregory S. Coon, 'Gift Giving as Agapic Love: An Alternative to the Exchange Paradigm Based on Dating Experiences', *Journal of Consumer Research* 20 (December 1993) 3: 393–417.

31. Colin Camerer, 'Gifts as Economic Signals and Social Symbols', *American Journal of Sociology* 94 (Supplement 1988): 5180–214.

32. Robert T. Green and Dana L. Alden, 'Functional Equivalence in Cross-Cultural Consumer Behavior: Gift Giving in Japan and the United States', *Psychology & Marketing* 5 (Summer 1988): 155–68.

33. Hiroshi Tanaka and Miki Iwamura, 'Gift Selection Strategy of Japanese Seasonal Gift Purchasers: An Explorative Study', paper presented at the Association for Consumer Research, Boston (October 1994).

34. John F. Sherry, Jr, 'Gift Giving in Anthropological Perspective', *Journal of Consumer Research* 10 (September 1983): 157–68.

35. Daniel Goleman, 'What's Under the Tree? Clues to a Relationship', *New York Times* (19 December 1989): C1.

36. John F. Sherry, Jr, Mary Ann McGrath and Sidney J. Levy, 'The Dark Side of the Gift', *Journal of Business Research* (1993).

37. David Glen Mick and Michelle DeMoss, 'Self-Gifts: Phenomenological Insights from Four Contexts', *Journal of Consumer Research* 17 (December 1990): 327; John F. Sherry, Jr, Mary Ann McGrath and Sidney J. Levy, 'Egocentric Consumption: Anatomy of Gifts Given to the Self', in *Contemporary Marketing and Consumer Behavior: An Anthropological Sourcebook* (Thousand Oaks, CA: Sage, 1995).

38. See, for example, Russell W. Belk, 'Halloween: An Evolving American Consumption Ritual', in Richard Pollay, Jerry Gorn and Marvin Goldberg (eds.), *Advances in Consumer Research* 17 (Provo, UT: Association for Consumer Research, 1990), 508–17; Melanie Wallendorf and Eric J. Arnould, 'We Gather Together: The Consumption Rituals of Thanksgiving Day', *Journal of Consumer Research* 18 (June 1991): 13–31.

39. Marc Augé, 'Un ethnologue à Euro Disneyland', *Le Monde Diplomatique* (September 1994).

40. Bruno Bettelheim, *The Uses of Enchantment: The Meaning and Importance of Fairy Tales* (New York: Alfred A. Knopf, 1976).

41. Brian Moeran and Lise Skov, 'Cinderella Christmas: Kitsch, Consumerism and Youth in Japan', in D. Miller (ed.), *Unwrapping Christmas* (Oxford: Oxford University Press, 1993): 105–33.

42. Anne Swardson, 'Trick or Treat? In Paris, It's Dress, Dance, Eat', *International Herald Tribune* (31 October 1996): 2.

43. Michael R. Solomon and Punam Anand, 'Ritual Costumes and Status Transition: The Female Business Suit as Totemic Emblem', in Elizabeth C. Hirschman and Morris Holbrook (eds.), *Advances in Consumer Research* 12 (Washington, D.C.: Association for Consumer Research, 1985): 315–18.

44. Arnold Van Gennep, *The Rites of Passage*, trans. Maika B. Vizedom and Gabrielle L. Caffee (London: Routledge and Kegan Paul, 1960; orig. published 1908); Solomon and Anand, 'Ritual Costumes and Status Transition'.

45. Walter W. Whitaker III, 'The Contemporary American Funeral Ritual', in Ray B. Browne (ed.), *Rites and Ceremonies in Popular Culture* (Bowling Green, OH: Bowling Green University Popular Press, 1980): 316–25; for a recent examination of funeral rituals, see Larry D. Compeau and Carolyn Nicholson, 'Funerals: Emotional Rituals or Ritualistic Emotions', paper presented at the Association of Consumer Research (Boston, October 1994).

46. On tourism, see, e.g., John Urry, *The Tourist Gaze* (London: Sage, 1988).

47. Conrad Phillip Kottak, 'Anthropological Analysis of Mass Enculturation', in Conrad P. Kottak (ed.), *Researching American Culture* (Ann Arbor, MI: University of Michigan Press, 1982): 40–74.

48. Gerry Pratt, 'The House as an Expression of Social Worlds', in James S. Duncan (ed.), *Housing and Identity: Cross-Cultural Perspectives* (London: Croom Helm, 1981): 135–79; Michael R. Solomon, 'The Role of the Surrogate Consumer in Service Delivery', *The Service Industries Journal* 7 (July 1987): 292–307.

49. Grant McCracken, "Homeyness": A Cultural Account of One Constellation of Goods and Meanings', in Elizabeth C. Hirschman (ed.), *Interpretive Consumer Research* (Provo, UT: Association for Consumer Research, 1989): 168–84.

50. James Hirsch, 'Taking Celebrity Worship to New Depths', *New York Times* (9 November 1988): C1.

51. 'One Certain Legacy of Diana is Industry Exploiting Her Life', *The Wall Street Journal Europe* (2 September 1997): 1–2.

52. Emile Durkheim, *The Elementary Forms of the Religious Life* (New York: Free Press, 1915).

53. Susan Birrell, 'Sports as Ritual: Interpretations from Durkheim to Goffman', *Social Forces* 60 (1981) 2: 354–76; Daniel Q. Voigt, 'American Sporting Rituals', in *Rites and Ceremonies in Popular Culture*: 125–40.

54. 'Sales of UK Publisher of Classical Music Strikes a Sour Note', *The Wall Street Journal Europe* (9 September 1997): 1, 4.

55. Søren Askegaard, *Marketing, The Performing Arts, and Social Change: Beyond the Legitimacy Crisis*, Working papers in Marketing, no. 13 (Odense University: School of Business and Economics, 1997).

56. John Urry, *The Tourist Gaze: Leisure and Travel in Contemporary Societies* (London: Sage, 1990).

57. Belk *et al.*, 'The Sacred and the Profane in Consumer Behavior'.

58. Beverly Gordon, 'The Souvenir: Messenger of the Extraordinary', *Journal of Popular Culture* 20 (1986) 3: 135–46.

59. Belk *et al.*, 'The Sacred and the Profane in Consumer Behavior'.

60. Belk *et al.*, 'The Sacred and the Profane in Consumer Behavior'.

61. Deborah Hofmann, 'In Jewelry, Choices Sacred and Profane, Ancient and New', *New York Times* (7 May 1989).

62. Roberto Grandi, 'Benetton's Advertising: A Case History of Postmodern Communication', Unpublished manuscript, Center for Modern Culture & Media (University of Bologna, 1994); Shawn Tully, 'Teens: The Most Global Market of All', *Fortune* (16 May 1994): 90–7.

63. Quoted in 'Public Relations Firm to Present Anti-Abortion Effort to Bishops', *New York Times* (14 August 1990): A12.

64. Per Østergaard, 'The Broadened Concept of Marketing as a Manifestation of the Postmodern Condition', in *Marketing Theory and Applications*, Proceedings of the AMA Winter Educators Conference, IV, ed. R. Varandarajan and B. Jaworski (Chicago: American Marketing Association): 234–9.

65. For an extensive bibliography on collecting, see Russell W. Belk, *Collecting in a Consumer Culture* (London: Routledge, 1995) or Russell W. Belk, Melanie Wallendorf, John F. Sherry, Jr and Morris B. Holbrook, 'Collecting in a Consumer Culture', in Russell W. Belk (ed.), *Highways and Buyways* (Provo, UT: Association for Consumer Research, 1991): 178–215. See also Janine Romina Lovatt, 'The People's Show Festival 1994: A Survey', S. Pearce (ed.), *Experiencing Material Culture in the Western World* (London: Leicester University Press, 1997): 196–254; Werner Muensterberg, *Collecting: An Unruly Passion* (Princeton, NJ: Princeton University Press, 1994); Melanie Wallendorf and Eric J. Arnould, '"My Favorite Things": A Cross-Cultural Inquiry into Object Attachment, Possessiveness, and Social Linkage', *Journal of Consumer Research* 14 (March 1988): 531–47.

66. Calmetta Y. Coleman, 'Just Any Old Thing from McDonald's Can be a Collectible', *The Wall Street Journal* (29 March 1995): B1 (2).

67. Quoted in Ruth Ann Smith, 'Collecting as Consumption: A Grounded Theory of Collecting Behavior,' unpublished manuscript (Virginia Polytechnic Institute and State University, 1994): 14.

68. Dan L. Sherrell, Alvin C. Burns and Melodie R. Phillips, 'Fixed Consumption Behavior: The Case of Enduring Acquisition in a Product Category', in Robert L. King (ed.), *Developments in Marketing Science* XIV (1991): 36–40.

69. Russell W. Belk, 'Acquiring, Possessing, and Collecting: Fundamental Processes in Consumer Behavior', in Ronald F. Bushard and Shelby D. Hunt (eds.), *Marketing Theory: Philosophy of Science Perspectives* (Chicago: AMA, 1982): 185–90.

70. Cf. Belk, *Collecting in a Consumer Culture*.

71. Glenn J. Kalinoski, 'Collecting Sales', *PROMO: The Magazine of Promotion Marketing* (May 1996): 41–7.

Chapter 15

1. Pierre Valette-Florence, *Les styles de vie* (Paris: Nathan, 1994). Benjamin Zablocki and Rosabeth Moss Kantter, 'The Differentiation of Life-Styles', *Annual Review of Sociology* (1976): 269–97.

2. Mary T. Douglas and Baron C. Isherwood, *The World of Goods* (New York: Basic Books, 1979).

3. Richard A. Peterson, 'Revitalizing the Culture Concept', *Annual Review of Sociology* 5 (1979): 137–66.

4. Russell W. Belk, 'Possessions and the Extended Self', *Journal of Consumer Research* 15 (September 1988): 139–68; Melanie Wallendorf and Eric J. Arnould, "My Favourite Things": A Cross-Cultural Inquiry into Object Attachment, Possessiveness, and Social Linkage', *Journal of Consumer Research* 14 (March 1988): 531–47.

5. 'Europeans More Active as Consumers', *Marketing News* (10 June 1994): 17.

6. Russell W. Belk and Richard W. Pollay, 'Images of Ourselves: The Good Life in Twentieth Century Advertising', *Journal of Consumer Research* 11 (March 1985): 887–97.

7. Marsha L. Richins and Scott Dawson, 'A Consumer Values Orientation for Materialism and Its Measurement: Scale Development and Validation', *Journal of Consumer Research* 20 (December 1992).

8. Güliz Ger and Russell Belk, 'Cross-Cultural Differences in Materialism', *Journal of Economic Psychology* 17 (1996): 55–77.

9. Søren Askegaard, 'Livsstilsundersøgelser: Henimod et teoretisk fundament', Doctoral Dissertation (Odense University: School of Business and Economics, 1993).

10. Henrik Dahl, *Hvis din nabo var en bil* (Copenhagen: Akademisk Forlag, 1997).

11. Thomas Drieseberg, 'Lebensstile in der Marktforschung – eine empirische Bestandsaufnahme', *Soziologie – planung und analyse* 5 (1992): 18–26.

12. William Leiss, Stephen Kline and Sut Jhally, *Social Communication in Advertising* (Toronto: Methuen, 1986).

13. Douglas and Isherwood, *The World of Goods*: 72–3.

14. Michael R. Solomon, 'The Role of Products as Social Stimuli: A Symbolic Interactionism Perspective', *Journal of Consumer Research* 10 (December 1983): 319–29.

15. Michael R. Solomon and Henry Assael, 'The Forest or the Trees?: A Gestalt Approach to Symbolic Consumption', in Jean Umiker-Sebeok (ed.), *Marketing and Semiotics: New Directions in the Study of Signs for Sale* (Berlin: Mouton de Gruyter, 1988): 189–218; Michael R. Solomon, 'Mapping Product Constellations: A Social Categorization Approach to Symbolic Consumption', *Psychology & Marketing* 5 (1988) 3: 233–58; see also Stephen C. Cosmas, 'Life

Styles and Consumption Patterns', *Journal of Consumer Research* 8 (March 1982) 4: 453–5.

16. Russell W. Belk, 'Yuppies as Arbiters of the Emerging Consumption Style', in Richard J. Lutz (ed.), *Advances in Consumer Research* 13 (Provo, UT: Association for Consumer Research, 1986): 514–19.

17. Askegaard, 'Livsstilsundersøgelser: Henimod et teoretisk fundament': 103–5.

18. Bill Schlackman, 'An Historical Perspective', in S. Robson and A. Foster (eds.), *Qualitative Research in Action* (London: Edward Arnold, 1989): 15–23.

19. William D. Wells and Douglas J. Tigert, 'Activities, Interests, and Opinions', *Journal of Advertising Research* 11 (August 1971): 27.

20. Alfred S. Boote, 'Psychographics: Mind Over Matter', *American Demographics* (April 1980): 26–9; William D. Wells, 'Psychographics: A Critical Review', *Journal of Marketing Research* 12 (May 1975): 196–213.

21. Joseph T. Plummer, 'The Concept and Application of Life Style Segmentation', *Journal of Marketing* 38 (January 1974): 33–7.

22. Berkeley Rice, 'The Selling of Lifestyles', *Psychology Today* (March 1988): 46.

23. 'CMT "Lifestyle" Launch', *Marketing* (3 February 1994): 4.

24. Valerie Latham, 'Do Euroconsumers Exist?', *Marketing* (24 June 1993): 3.

25. Document, RISC.

26. Pierre Bourdieu, *La distinction. Critique social du jugement* (Paris: Editions de Minuit, 1979).

27. Martha Farnsworth Riche, 'VALS 2', *American Demographics* (July 1989): 25.

28. Leiss *et al.*, 'Social Communication in Advertising'.

29. Stuart Elliott, 'Sampling Tastes of a Changing Russia', *New York Times* (1 April 1992) 2: D1.

30. 'Value Segments Help Define International Market', *Marketing News* (21 November 1988): 17.

31. Pierre Valette-Florence, *Les styles de vie*.

32. Askegaard, 'Livsstilsundersøgelser: Henimod et teoretisk fundament'.

33. 'One Flew Over a Continent to See What Was Cooking', *IP Network International Newsletter* 5 (Spring 1993): 5–8.

34. Søren Askegaard and Tage Koed Madsen, 'The Local and the Global: Patterns of Homogeneity and Heterogeneity in European Food Cultures', *International Business Review* (in press).

35. Cf. discussions in the following: Alladi Venkatesh, 'Ethnoconsumerism'; Jean-Claude Usunier, *Marketing Across Cultures* (Hemel Hempstead:

Prentice Hall, 1995): 140–74; Askegaard and Madsen, 'The Local and the Global: Patterns of Homogeneity and Heterogeneity in European Food Cultures'; Klaus Grunert, Suzanne Grunert and Sharon Beatty: 'Cross-Cultural Research on Consumer Values', *Marketing and Research Today* 17 (1989): 30–9.

36. Jean-Claude Usunier, *Marketing Across Cultures*.
37. Peter S.H. Leeflang and W. Fred van Raaij, 'The Changing Consumer in the European Union: A "Meta-Analysis"', *International Journal of Research in Marketing* 12 (5) (1996): 373–87.
38. Cf. among many sources M. Douglas, 'Food as a System of Classification', *In the Active Voice* (London: Routledge & Kegan Paul, 1982): 82–124; P. Farb and G. Armelagos, *Consuming Passions: The Anthropology of Eating* (Boston: Houghton Mifflin, 1980); P. Fieldhouse, *Food and Nutrition: Customs and Culture* (London: Croom Helm, 1986); C. Fischler, *L'Homnivore* (Paris: Ed. Odile Jacob, 1990); A. Warde, *Consumption, Food, and Taste* (London: Sage, 1997).
39. Euromonitor, *European Marketing Data and Statistics* (1997): 6, 254.
40. Euromonitor, *European Marketing Data and Statistics* (1997): 328–31.
41. Klaus G: Grunert, Karen Brunsø and Søren Bisp, 'Food-Related Lifestyle: Development of a Cross-Culturally Valid Instrument for Market Surveillance', in L. Kahle and L. Chiagouris (eds.), *Values, Lifestyles and Psychographics* (Mahwah, NJ: Lawrence Erlbaum Associates, 1997): 337–54.
42. See, however, Søren Askegaard, Karen Brunsø, Kaye Crippen and Reinti Liang, 'Food-Related Lifestyle in Singapore: Testing a Western European Research Instrument in Southeast Asia' (in press).
43. Klaus G. Grunert, 'What's in a Steak? A Cross-Cultural Study on the Quality Perception of Beef', *MAPP Working Paper* 39 (Aarhus: The Aarhus School of Business, 1996).
44. Allison James, 'Cooking the Books. Global or Local Identities in Contemporary British Food Cultures?', David Howes (ed.), *Cross-Cultural Consumption* (London: Routledge, 1996): 77–92.
45. James, 'Cooking the Books', p. 89.
46. Ayse S. Caglar, 'McDöner Kebap and the Social Positioning Struggle of German Turks', in J.A. Arnold and G.J. Bamossy (eds.), *Marketing in a Multicultural World: Ethnicity, Nationalism, and Cultural Identity* (London: Sage, 1995): 209–30.
47. Mary Douglas (ed.), *Constructive Drinking. Perspectives on Drink from Anthropology* (Cambridge: Cambridge University Press, 1987).

48. David Smith and J. Robert Skalnik, 'Changing Patterns in the Consumption of Alcoholic Beverages in Europe and the United States', in Flemming Hansen (ed.), *European Advances in Consumer Research* II (Provo, UT: Association for Consumer Research, 1995): 343–55.
49. David Smith and J. Robert Skalnik, 'Changing Patterns in the Consumption of Alcoholic Beverages in Europe and the United States'.
50. Pekka Sulkunen, 'Drinking Patterns and the Level of Alcohol consumption: An International Overview', in R.J. Gibbins *et al.* (eds.), *Research Advances in Alcohol and Drug Problems*, vol. 3 (New York: John Wiley).
51. Euromonitor, *European Marketing Data and Statistics* (1997): 334.
52. David Smith and J. Robert Skalnik, 'Changing Patterns in the Consumption of Alcoholic Beverages in Europe and the United States'.
53. Yves Marbeau, 'Eurodemographics? Nearly There!', *Marketing and Research Today* (March 1992): 47–57.
54. Horst Kern, Hans-Christian Wagner and Roswitha Harris, 'European Aspects of a Global Brand: The BMW Case', *Marketing and Research Today* (February 1990): 47–57.
55. Matthias D. Kindler, Ellen Day and Mary R. Zimmer, 'A Cross-Cultural Comparison of Magazine Advertising in West Germany and the U.S.', unpublished manuscript (The University of Georgia, Athens, 1990).
56. Michael Schroeder, 'Germany–France: Different Advertising Styles – Different Communication Concepts', in W.F. van Raaij and G. Bamossy (eds.), *European Advances in Consumer Research* 1 (Provo, UT: Association for Consumer Research, 1993): 77–83.
57. Edward T. Hall, *Beyond Culture* (New York: Doubleday, 1976).
58. Hans Heyder, Karl Georg Musiol and Klaus Peters, 'Advertising in Europe – Attitudes Towards Advertising in Certain Key East and West European Countries', *Marketing and Research Today* (March 1992): 58–68.
59. Marc G. Weinberger and Harlan E. Spotts, 'A Situational View of Information Content in TV Advertising in the U.S. and U.K.', *Journal of Marketing* 53 (January 1989): 89–94; see also Abhilasha Mehta, 'Global Markets and Standardized Advertising: Is It Happening? An Analysis of Common Brands in USA and UK', in *Proceedings of the 1992 Conference of the American Academy of Advertising* (1992): 170.
60. 'Abroadminded', *Marketing* (24 April 1997): 20–1.

61. Hans Heyder, Karl Georg Musiol and Klaus Peters, 'Advertising in Europe – Attitudes Towards Advertising in Certain Key East and West European Countries'.

62. Wendelin G. Müller, 'Die Standardisierbarkeit internationaler Werbung: Kulturen verlangen Adaptionen', *Marketing ZFP*, 3 (3rd Quarter 1996): 179–90.

63. J. Andrew Davison and Erik Grab, 'The Contributions of Advertising testing to the Development of Effective International Advertising: The KitKat Case Study', *Marketing and Research Today* (February 1993): 15–24.

64. Douglas B. Holt, Søren Askegaard and Torsten Ringberg, '7Ups and Downs: Cross Cultural Differences in the Reading Profile of Advertising' (in press).

65. Eduardo Camargo, 'The Measurement of Meaning: Sherlock Holmes in Pursuit of the Marlboro Man', Jean Umiker Sebeok (ed.), *Marketing and Semiotics. New Directions in the Study of Signs for Sale* (Berlin: Mouton de Gruyter, 1987): 463–83.

66. Demographic Statistics 1997: Population and social conditions Series, Luxembourg: Office for Official Publications of the European Communities, 1997; 'Colour Blind', *Marketing Week* (21 June 1996): 38–40.

67. See Frederik Barth, *Ethnic Groups and Boundaries: The Social Organization of Culture Difference* (London: Allen and Unwin, 1969); D. Bell, 'Ethnicity and Social Change', in N. Glazer and D.P. Moynihan (eds.), *Ethnicity: Theory and Experience* (Cambridge, MA: Harvard University Press, 1975): 141–74; D.L. Horowitz, 'Ethnic Identity', in N. Glazer and D.P. Moynihan (eds.), *Ethnicity: Theory and Experience* (Cambridge, MA: Harvard University Press, 1975): 109–40; J. Kotkin, *Tribes* (New York: Random House, 1993); Alladi Venkatesh, 'Ethnoconsumerism: A New Paradigm to Study Cultural and Cross-Cultural Consumer Behavior', in J.A. Costa and G.J. Bamossy (eds.), *Marketing in a Multicultural World: Ethnicity, Nationalism, and Cultural Identity* (London: Sage, 1995): 26–67; Michel Laroche, Annamma Joy, Michael Hui and Chankon Kim, 'An Examination of Ethnicity Measures: Convergent Validity and Cross-Cultural Equivalence', in Rebecca H. Holman and Michael R. Solomon (eds.), *Advances in Consumer Research* 18 (Provo, UT: Association for Consumer Research, 1991): 150–7; Melanie Wallendorf and Michael Reilly, 'Ethnic Migration, Assimilation, and Consumption', *Journal of Consumer Research* 10 (December 1983): 292–302; Milton J. Yinger, 'Ethnicity', *Annual Review of Sociology* 11 (1985): 151–80.

68. Rohit Desphandé and Douglas M. Stayman, 'A Tale of Two Cities: Distinctiveness Theory and Advertising Effectiveness', *Journal of Marketing Research* 31 (February 1994): 57–64; Stephen Riggins, 'The Media Imperative: Ethnic Minority Survival in the Age of Mass Communication', in S.H. Riggins (ed.), *Ethnic Minority Media: An International Perspective* (London: Sage, 1992): 1–22.

69. Steve Rabin, 'How to Sell Across Cultures', *American Demographics* (March 1994): 56–7.

70. Shelly Reese, 'When Whites *Aren't* a Mass Market', *American Demographics* (March 1997): 51–4.

71. Cf. Lisa Peñaloza, '*Atravesando Fronteras*/Border Crossings: A Critical Ethnographic Exploration of the Consumer Acculturation of Mexican Immigrants', *Journal of Consumer Research* 21 (June 1994) 1: 32–54.

72. A. Fuat Fırat, 'Consumer Culture or Culture Consumed?', in J.A. Costa and G.J. Bamossy (eds.), *Marketing in a Multicultural World: Ethnicity, Nationalism, and Cultural Identity* (London: Sage, 1995): 105–25; Michael Laroche, Chankon Kim, Michael K. Hui and Annamma Joy, 'An Empirical Study of Multidimensional Ethnic Change: The Case of the French Canadians in Quebec', *Journal of Cross-Cultural Psychology* 27 (1) (January 1996): 114–31.

73. Elizabeth C. Hirschman, 'Religious Affiliation and Consumption Processes: An Initial Paradigm', *Research in Marketing* (Greenwich, CT: JAI Press, 1983): 131–70.

74. See, for example, Nejet Delener, 'The Effects of Religious Factors on Perceived Risk in Durable Goods Purchase Decisions', *Journal of Consumer Marketing* 7 (Summer 1990): 27–38.

75. 'The Muslims in France: Rejecting their Ancestors the Gauls', *The Economist* (16 November 1996): 113–14.

76. Clare Garner, 'Builders Answer Islam's Growing Call to Prayer', *The Independent* (4 February 1997): 7.

77. Madeline Bunting, 'Churchgoing Bottoms Out', *The Guardian* (10 August 1996): 2; 'Catholic Church Loses Mass Appeal', *The Guardian* (30 January 1996): 4; 'België is niet langer katholiek' ('Belgium is no longer Catholic') *Trouw* (19 September 1996); Madeline Bunting, 'Revolving Door Throws Doubt on Evangelical Churches' Revival', *The Guardian* (28 August 1996).

78. Amy Barrett, 'John Paul II to Share Stage with Marketers', *Wall Street Journal, Europe* (19 August 1997): 4; see also *www.mix.it/rai/papa*

79. 'Vatican Opens Boutique Outside Walls', *Montgomery Advertiser* (10 June 1996): 4A.

80. *Markedsføring* 10 (1996): 22.

81. Peter S.H. Leeflang and W. Fred van Raaij, 'The Changing Consumer in the European Union: A "Meta-Analysis"', *International Journal of Research in Marketing* 12 (5) (1995): 373–87.

82. Massoud Saghafi and Donald Sciglimpaglia, 'Marketing in an Integrated Europe', in M. Bergadaà (ed.), *Marketing Today and for the 21st Century*, vol. 1 (ESSEC: Proceedings of the 24th EMAC Conference, 1995): 1069–76.

83. Fred van Eenennaam, 'Standardization of International Marketing Processes in a pan-European Context: Some Research Hypotheses', in M. Bergadaà (ed.), *Marketing Today and for the 21st Century*, vol. 2 (ESSEC: Proceedings of the 24th EMAC Conference, 1995): 1221–41.

84. Vern Terpstra and Kenneth David, *The Cultural Environment of International Business*, 2nd edn, (Cincinnati: Southwestern, 1985).

85. André Tordjman, 'European Retailing: Convergences, Differences, and Perspectives', in P.J. McGoldrick and G. Davies (eds.), *International Retailing. Trends and Strategies* (London: Pitman, 1995): 17–50.

86. 'Abroadminded', *Marketing* (24 April 1997): 20–1.

87 Bernard Dubois and Gilles Laurent, 'Is There a Euroconsumer for Luxury Goods?', in W.F. van Raaij and G. Bamossy (eds.), *European Advances in Consumer Research*, vol. 1 (Provo, UT: Association for Consumer Research, 1993): 58–69.

Chapter 16

1. Richard A. Peterson, 'The Production of Culture: A Prolegomenon', in Richard A. Peterson (ed.), *The Production of Culture*, Sage Contemporary Social Science Issues (Beverly Hills, CA: Sage, 1976) 33: 7–22.

2. Richard A. Peterson and D.G. Berger, 'Entrepreneurship in Organizations: Evidence from the Popular Music Industry', *Administrative Science Quarterly* 16 (1971): 97–107.

3. Elizabeth C. Hirschman, 'Resource Exchange in the Production and Distribution of a Motion Picture', *Empirical Studies of the Arts* 8 (1990) 1: 31–51; Michael R. Solomon, 'Building Up and Breaking Down: The Impact of Cultural Sorting on Symbolic Consumption', in J. Sheth and E.C. Hirschman (eds.), *Research in Consumer Behavior* (Greenwich, CT: JAI Press, 1988): 325–51.

4. See Paul M. Hirsch, 'Processing Fads and Fashions: An Organizational Set Analysis of Cultural Industry Systems', *American Journal of Sociology* 77 (1972) 4: 639–59; Russell Lynes, *The Tastemakers* (New York: Harper and Brothers, 1954); Michael R. Solomon, 'The Missing Link: Surrogate Consumers in the Marketing Chain', *Journal of Marketing* 50 (October 1986): 208–19.

5. Michael R. Solomon, Richard Ashmore and Laura Longo (1992), 'The Beauty Match-Up Hypothesis: Congruence Between Types of Beauty and Product Images in Advertising', *Journal of Advertising* 21 (December): 23–34.

6. Howard S. Becker, 'Arts and Crafts', *American Journal of Sociology* 83 (January 1987): 862–89.

7. Herbert J. Gans, 'Popular Culture in America: Social Problem in a Mass Society or Social Asset in a Pluralist Society?' in Howard S. Becker (ed.), *Social Problems: A Modern Approach* (New York: Wiley, 1966).

8. Peter S. Green, 'Moviegoers Devour Ads', *Advertising Age* (26 June 1989): 36.

9. Michael R. Real, *Mass-Mediated Culture* (Englewood Cliffs, NJ: Prentice-Hall, 1977).

10. Annetta Miller, 'Shopping Bags Imitate Art: Seen the Sacks? Now Visit the Museum Exhibit', *Newsweek* (23 January 1989): 44.

11. Kim Foltz, 'New Species for Study: Consumers in Action', *New York Times* (18 December 1989): A1.

12. Arthur A. Berger, *Signs in Contemporary Culture: An Introduction to Semiotics* (New York: Longman, 1984).

13. Stephen Brown, 'Psycho Shopper: A Comparative Literary Analysis of "the Dark Side"', in Flemming Hansen (ed.), *European Advances in Consumer Research* 2 (Provo, UT: Association for Consumer Research, 1995): 96–103; Stephen Brown, 'Consumption Behaviour in the Sex'n'Shopping Novels of Judith Krantz: A Post-structuralist perspective', in J. Lynch and K. Corfman (eds.), *Advances in Consumer Research* 23 (Provo, UT: Association for Consumer Research, 1996): 96–103.

14. Helene Diamond, 'Lights, Camera . . . Research!', *Marketing News* (11 September 1989): 10.

15. Umberto Eco, *A Theory of Semiotics* (Bloomington, IN: Indiana University Press, 1979).

16. Fred Davis, 'Clothing and Fashion as Communication', in Michael R. Solomon (ed.), *The Psychology of Fashion* (Lexington, MA: Lexington Books, 1985): 15–28.

17. Melanie Wallendorf, 'The Formation of Aesthetic Criteria Through Social Structures and Social Institutions', in Jerry C. Olson (ed.), *Advances in Consumer Research* 7 (Ann Arbor, MI: Association for Consumer Research, 1980): 3–6.

18. Grant McCracken, 'Culture and Consumption: A Theoretical Account of the Structure and Movement of the Cultural Meaning of Consumer Goods', *Journal of Consumer Research* 13 (June 1986): 71–84.

19. 'The Eternal Triangle', *Art in America* (February 1989): 23.

20. Herbert Blumer, *Symbolic Interactionism: Perspective and Method* (Englewood Cliffs, NJ: Prentice-Hall, 1969); Howard S. Becker, 'Art as Collective Action', *American Sociological Review* 39 (December 1973); Richard A. Peterson, 'Revitalizing the Culture Concept', *Annual Review of Sociology* 5 (1979): 137–66.

21. For more details, see Susan Kaiser, *The Social Psychology of Clothing*; George B. Sproles, 'Behavioral Science Theories of Fashion', in Michael R. Solomon (ed.), *The Psychology of Fashion* (Lexington, MA: Lexington Books, 1985): 55–70.

22. C.R. Snyder and Howard L. Fromkin, *Uniqueness: The Human Pursuit of Difference* (New York: Plenum Press, 1980).

23. Alison Lurie, *The Language of Clothes* (New York: Random House, 1981).

24. John Fiske, *Understanding Popular Culture* (Boston: Unwin Hyman, 1989): especially 1–21.

25. Harvey Leibenstein, *Beyond Economic Man: A New Foundation for Microeconomics* (Cambridge, MA: Harvard University Press, 1976).

26. Georg Simmel, 'Fashion', *International Quarterly* 10 (1904): 130–55.

27. Grant D. McCracken, 'The Trickle-Down Theory Rehabilitated', in Michael R. Solomon (ed.), *The Psychology of Fashion* (Lexington, MA: Lexington Books, 1985): 39–54.

28. Charles W. King, 'Fashion Adoption: A Rebuttal to the "Trickle-Down" Theory', in Stephen A. Greyser (ed.), *Toward Scientific Marketing* (Chicago: American Marketing Association, 1963): 108–25.

29. Alf H. Walle, 'Grassroots Innovation', *Marketing Insights* (Summer 1990): 44–51.

30. Patrick Hetzel, 'The Role of Fashion and Design in a Postmodern Society: What Challenges for Firms?', in M.J. Baker (ed.), *Perspectives on Marketing Management*, vol. 4 (London: John Wiley & Sons Ltd, 1994): 97–118.

31. Stuart and Elizabeth Ewen, cited in Mike Featherstone, *Consumer Culture and Postmodernism* (London: Sage, 1993): 83.

32. Patrick Hetzel, 'The Role of Fashion and Design in a Postmodern Society: What Challenges for Firms?'.

33. Anthony Ramirez, 'The Pedestrian Sneaker Makes a Comeback', *New York Times* (14 October 1990): F17.

34. B.E. Aguirre, E.L. Quarantelli and Jorge L. Mendoza, 'The Collective Behavior of Fads: The Characteristics, Effects, and Career of Streaking', *American Sociological Review* (August 1989): 569.

35. Michael R. Solomon and Basil G. Englis, 'Reality Engineering: Blurring the Boundaries Between Marketing and Popular Culture', *Journal of Current Issues and Research in Advertising* 16 (Fall 1994) 2: 1–17.

36. 'Hollywood-sur-Brie', *Le nouvel observateur* (14 November 1996): 18–19.

37. 'Les "mondes artificiels" attirent toujours plus de vacanciers', *Le Monde* (22–23 December 1996); cf. also John Urry, 'Cultural Change and Contemporary Holiday Making', *Theory, Culture, and Society* 5 (1) (1988).

38. Bill Keller, 'For Rich Tourists (and Not Too African)', *New York Times* (3 December 1992) 2: A1.

39. Suzanne Alexander Ryan, 'Companies Teach All Sorts of Lessons with Educational Tools They Give Away', *The Wall Street Journal* (19 April 1994): B1 (2); Cyndee Miller, 'Marketers Find a Seat in the Classroom', *Marketing News* (20 June 1994): 2.

40. T. Bettina Cornwell and Bruce Keillor, 'Contemporary Literature and the Embedded Consumer Culture: The Case of Updike's Rabbit', in Roger J. Kruez and Mary Sue MacNealy (eds.), *Empirical Approaches to Literature and Aesthetics: Advances in Discourse Processes* 52 (Norwood, NJ: Ablex Publishing Corporation, 1996): 559–72; Monroe Friedman, 'The Changing Language of a Consumer Society: Brand Name Usage in Popular American Novels in the Postwar Era', *Journal of Consumer Research* 11 (March 1985): 927–37; Monroe Friedman, 'Commercial Influences in the Lyrics of Popular American Music of the Postwar Era', *Journal of Consumer Affairs* 20 (Winter 1986): 193.

41. Benjamin M. Cole, 'Products That Want to Be In Pictures', *Los Angeles Herald Examiner* (5 March

1985): 36; see also Stacy M. Vollmers and Richard W. Mizerski, 'A Review and Investigation into the Effectivenss of Product Placements in Films', in Karen Whitehill King (ed.), *Proceedings of the 1994 Conference of the American Academy of Advertising*: 97–102; Michael R. Solomon and Basil G. Englis, 'Reality Engineering: Blurring the Boundaries Between Marketing and Popular Culture', *Journal of Current Issues and Research in Advertising* 16 (Fall 1994) 2: 1–17.

42. David Leonhardt, 'Cue the Soda Can', *Business Week* (24 June 1996): 64 (2).

43. Randall Rothenberg, 'Is it a Film? Is it an Ad? Harder to Tell?', *New York Times* (13 March 1990): D23.

44. Quoted in Mary Kuntz and Joseph Weber, 'The New Hucksterism', *Business Week* (1 July 1996): 75 (7), 78.

45. George Gerbner, Larry Gross, Nancy Signorielli and Michael Morgan, 'Aging with Television: Images on Television Drama and Conceptions of Social Reality', *Journal of Communication* 30 (1980): 37–47.

46. Stephen Fox and William Philber, 'Television Viewing and the Perception of Affluence', *Sociological Quarterly* 19 (1978): 103–12; W. James Potter, 'Three Strategies for Elaborating the Cultivation Hypothesis', *Journalism Quarterly* 65 (Winter 1988): 930–9; Gabriel Weimann, 'Images of Life in America: The Impact of American T.V. in Israel', *International Journal of Intercultural Relations* 8 (1984): 185–97.

47. Stephanie O'Donohue, 'On the Outside Looking In: Advertising Experiences Among Young Unemployed Adults', in Flemming Hansen (ed.), *European Advances in Consumer Research* II (Provo, UT: Association for Consumer Research): 264–72; Richard Elliott, 'How Do the Unemployed Maintain Their Identity in a Culture of Consumption?', in Flemming Hansen (ed.), *European Advances in Consumer Research* II (Provo, UT: Association for Consumer Research): 273–6.

48. Richard Elliott, 'Addictive Consumption: Function and Fragmentation in Postmodernity', *Journal of Consumer Policy*, 17 (1994), 159–79; Thomas C. O'Guinn and Ronald J. Faber, 'Compulsive Buying: A Phenomenological Exploration', *Journal of Consumer Research*, 16 (1989): 147–57.

49. Theodore Levitt, *The Marketing Imagination* (New York: The Free Press, 1983).

50. Kevin Cote, 'The New Shape of Europe', *Advertising Age* (9 November 1988): 98.

51. Steven Prokesch, 'Selling in Europe: Borders Fade', *New York Times* (31 May 1990): D1.

52. 'Abroadminded', *Marketing* (24 April 1997): 20–1.

53. Terry Clark, 'International Marketing and National Character: A Review and Proposal for an Integrative Theory', *Journal of Marketing* 54 (October 1990): 66–79.

54. Julie Skur Hill and Joseph M. Winski, 'Goodby Global Ads: Global Village is Fantasy Land for Marketers', *Advertising Age* (16 November 1987): 22; Margaret K. Hogg, and Maria H. Savolainen, 'Symbolic Consumption and the Situational Self', in Basil Englis and Anna Olofsson (ed.), *European Advances in Consumer Research* (Provo, UT: Association for Consumer Research, 1998).

55. 'Packaging Draws Protest', *Marketing News* (4 July 1994): 1.

56. Laurel Anderson Hudson and Marsha Wadkins, 'Japanese Popular Art as Text: Advertising's Clues to Understanding the Consumer', *International Journal of Research in Marketing* 4 (1988): 259–72.

57. David Alexander, 'Condom Controversy: Suggestive KamaSutra Ads Arouse India', *Advertising Age International* (27 April 1992): I-12.

58. Yumiko Ono, 'Tambrands Ads Try to Scale Cultural, Religious Obstacles', *The Wall Street Journal Interactive Edition* (17 March 1997), http://interactive4.wsj.com/archive

59. Hill and Winski, 'Goodbye Global Ads'.

60. See, for example, Russell W. Belk and Güliz Ger, 'Problems of Marketization in Romania and Turkey', *Research in Consumer Behavior* 7 (Greenwich, CT: JAI Press, 1994): 123–55.

61. See e.g. Ulf Hannerz, 'Cosmopolitans and Locals in World Culture', Mike Featherstone (ed.), *Global Culture* (London: Sage, 1990): 237–52.

62. 'Abroadminded', *Marketing* (24 April 1997): 20–1.

63. Eric J. Arnould and Richard R. Wilk, 'Why Do the Natives Wear Adidas?: Anthropological Approaches to Consumer Research', in Elisabeth C. Hirschman and Morris B Holbrook (eds.), *Advances in Consumer Research* 12 (Provo, UT: Association for Consumer Research, 1985): 748–52.

64. Robert LaFranco, 'Long-Lived Kitsch', *Forbes* (26 February 1996): 68.

65. Dana Milbank, 'Made in America Becomes a Boast in Europe', *The Wall Street Journal* (19 January 1994): B1 (2)

66. Suman Dubey, 'Kellogg Invites India's Middle Class to Breakfast of Ready-to-Eat Cereal', *The Wall Street Journal* (29 August 1994): B3B.

67. 'They All Want to be Like Mike', *Fortune* (21 July 1997): 51–3.

68. Tara Parker-Pope, 'Will the British Warm up to Iced Tea? Some Big Marketers are Counting on It', *The Wall Street Journal* (22 August 1994): B1 (2).

69. John Tagliabue, 'Proud Palaces of Italian Cusine Await Pizza Hut', *The New York Times* (1 September 1994): A4.

70. David K. Tse, Russell W. Belk and Nan Zhou, 'Becoming a Consumer Society: A Longitudinal and Cross-Cultural Content Analysis of Print Ads from Hong Kong, the People's Republic of China, and Taiwan', *Journal of Consumer Research* 15 (March 1989): 457–72; see also Annamma Joy, 'Marketing in Modern China: an Evolutionary Perspective', CJAS (June 1990): 55–67, for a review of changes in Chinese marketing practices since the economic reforms of 1978.

71. Quoted in Sheryl WuDunn, 'Cosmetics from the West Help to Change the Face of China', *New York Times* (6 May 1990): 16.

72. John F. Sherry, Jr and Eduardo G. Camargo, '"May Your Life be Marvelous": English Language Labeling and the Semiotics of Japanese Promotion', *Journal of Consumer Research* 14 (September 1987): 174–88.

73. Bill Bryson, 'A Taste for Scrambled English', *New York Times* (22 July 1990): 10; Rose A. Horowitz, 'California Beach Culture Rides Wave of Popularity in Japan', *Journal of Commerce* (3 August 1989): 17; Elaine Lafferty, 'American Casual Seizes Japan: Teenagers Go for N.F.L. Hats, Batman and the California Look', *Time* (13 November 1989): 106.

74. Lucy Howard and Gregory Cerio, 'Goofy Goods,' *Newsweek* (15 August 1994): 8.

75. Prof. Russell Belk, University of Utah, personal communication, 25 July 1997.

76. Material in this section adapted from Ger and Belk, 'I'd Like to Buy the World a Coke: Consumptionscapes of the "Less Affluent World"'; Russell W. Belk, 'Romanian Consumer Desires and Feelings of Deservingness', in Lavinia Stan (ed.), *Romania in Transition* (Hanover, NH: Dartmouth Press, 1997): 191–208; cf. Also Güliz Ger, 1997, 'Human Development and Humane Consumption: Well Being Beyond the Good Life', *Journal of Public Policy and Marketing*, Vol. 16, No. 1, 110–25.

77. Prof. Güliz Ger, Bilkent University, Turkey, personal communication, 25 July 1997.

78. Erazim Kohák, 'Ashes, Ashes … Central Europe After Forty Years', *Daedalus* 121 (Spring 1992): 197–215, p. 219, quoted in Belk, 'Romanian Consumer Desires and Feelings of Deservingness'.

79. Güliz Ger, 'The Positive and Negative Effects of Marketing on Socioeconomic Development: The Turkish Case', *Journal of Consumer Policy* 15 (1992): 229–54.

80. This example courtesy of Prof. Russell Belk, University of Utah, personal communication, 25 July 1997.

81. Jennifer Cody, 'Now Marketers in Japan Stress the Local Angle', *The Wall Street Journal* (23 February 1994): B1 (2).

82. Güliz Ger and Russell W. Belk, 'I'd Like to Buy the World a Coke: Consumptionscapes of the "Less Affluent World"', *Journal of Consumer Policy* 19 (3) (1996): 271–304.

83. Steven Greenhouse, 'The Television Europeans Love, and Love to Hate', *New York Times* (13 August 1989): 24.

84. Charles Goldsmith and Charles Fleming, 'Film Industry in Europe Seeks Wider Audience', *The Wall Street Journal* (6 December 1993): B1 (2).

85. Sherry and Camargo, '"May Your Life Be Marvelous"; French Council Eases Language Ban', *The New York Times* (31 July 1994): 12.

86. Quoted in Alan Riding, 'Only the French Elite Scorn Mickey's Debut', *New York Times* (1992) 2: A1.

87. Mike Levin, 'U.S. Tobacco Firms Push Eagerly into Asian Market', *Marketing News* (21 January 1991) 2: 2.

88. Two special issues of *International Journal of Research in Marketing* 10 (3) (1993) and 11 (4) (1994), both edited by A. Fuat Fırat, John F. Sherry, Jr and Alladi Venkatesh have been decisive for the introduction of themes of postmodernism in marketing and consumer research

89. Craig J. Thompson, 'Modern Truth and Postmodern Incredulity: A Hermeneutic Deconstruction of the Metanarrative of "Scientific Truth" in Marketing Research', *International Journal of Research in Marketing* 10 (3) (1993): 325–38.

90. See, for example, A. Fuat Fırat and Alladi Venkatesh, 'Postmodernity: The Age of Marketing', *International Journal of Research in Marketing* 10 (3) (1993): 227–49; James Ogilvy, 'This Postmodern Business, *Marketing and Research Today* (February 1990): 4–22; W. Fred van Raaij, 'Postmodern Consumption', *Journal of Economic Psychology* 14 (1993), 541–63.

91. Stephen Brown, *Postmodern Marketing* (London: Routledge, 1995): 106ff.

92. Fuat Fırat and Venkatesh, 'Postmodernity: The Age of Marketing'.

93. Eric Arnould and Søren Askegaard, 'HyperCulture: The Next Stage in the

Globalization of Consumption', Paper presented at the 1997 Annual Association for Consumer Research conference in Denver, Colorado, 16–19 October.

94. Cf. Allison James, 'Cooking the Books: Global or Local Identities in Contemporary British Food Cultures', in David Howes (ed.), *Cross-Cultural Consumption* (London: Routledge, 1996): 77–92.

95. Brown, *Postmodern Marketing*.

96. Judith Williamson, *Consuming Passions. The Dynamics of Popular Culture* (London: Marion Boyars, 1988).

97. Stephen Brown, 'Marketing as Multiplex: Screening Postmodernism', *European Journal of Marketing* 28 (8/9) (1994): 27–51.

98. Brown, *Postmodern Marketing*.

99. Anne F. Jensen and Søren Askegaard, *In Pursuit of Ugliness: On the Complexity of the Fashion Concept After the Era of Good Taste*, Working Paper in Marketing, no. 14 (Odense University: School of Business and Economics, 1997).

100. Richard Elliott, Susan Eccles and Michelle Hodgson, 'Re-coding Gender Representations: Women, Cleaning Products, and Advertising's "New Man"', *International Journal of Research in Marketing* 10 (3) (1993): 311–24.

101. Mike Featherstone, *Consumer Culture and Postmodernisn* (London: Sage, 1991).

102. Fuat Fırat and Venkatesh, 'Liberatory Postmodernism'.

103. Dominique Bouchet, 'Rails Without Ties: The Social Imaginary and Postmodern Culture. Can Postmodern Consumption replace Modern Questioning?', *International Journal of Research in Marketing* 11 (4) (1993): 405–22.

104. Brown, 'Marketing as Multiplex: Screening Postmodernism'.

Indexes

Author index

Product/company/name index

Subject index

and disposal and environmentalism 263–4
dolls 15, 16, 196, 199, 250, 254, 263–4, 395
and family structure and household decision-making 320–1, 323
and group influence 284
guns 42
and individual decision-making 228
and purchase situation 250, 251, 254
see also play
traditional family *see* nuclear and traditional family
transformational advertising 169
transitional economies 463, *504*
translation of immigrants 431
transport *see* vehicles
travel agents *see* leisure and holidays
triads of attitudes 131–3
trialability 296, *504*
trickle-down theory 449, *504*
trickle-up and trickle-across 450, 453
trophy wife 347
Turkey 94–5, 337
and cultural change processes 438, 439, 460, 464
immigrants in Netherlands 428–9, 432
and lifestyles 403, 422
restaurant case study 473–5
two-factor theory 160, *504*
two-sided argument 161–2
two-tiered marketing 333
two-way street and understanding cultural influences 377–9

UCS (unconditioned stimulus) 66, 67, 70, 72
Ukraine 403
unanimity, group 277
unbalanced triad 132–3
uncertainty avoidance 380
unconditioned stimulus 66, 67, 70, 72
undercoding 446
underpriviledged condition 339
understanding 25, 232, 377–81
unemployment 344
uniqueness, need for 280–1
unit relations of attitudes 132
United Nations 306
United States 5, 7
and age subcultures 355, 362
and attitudes 121–2, 123, 140, 142
and interactive communications 150, 153, 156–8, 159, 163, 164, 167
and cultural change processes 445–7
and cultural influences 375–6, 378, 381–5, 390, 391, 394–6
and design 485
and diffusion of innovations 293, 297
and disposal and environmentalism 260, 261, 262, 264
and family structure and household decision-making 305, 308–9, 318, 322–3
and group influence 277, 281, 285
and income 337, 339, 341, 344–5, 346
and individual decision-making 214, 216, 221, 225, 228, 230
and involvement 103
and lifestyles 402–7, 423, 426, 427, 430
segmentation 413–14, 416
and magazines for women 5, 7–8
and memory 84
and motivation 94–5, 114, 115
and opinion leadership 286–7, 289
and perception 38, 42, 51, 57–8, 60, 229
and purchase environment 249–52

and purchase situation 241, 243
and research 10, 24
and self, gender and body 177, 182, 187–8, 190, 192, 197, 198–9
and social class 333, 336, 346, 347
and values 105, 108
universality of ideals of beauty 193–4
unobtrusive measures 33
unplanned purchase 252
see also impulse
unusual advertising 54, 60, 81
unusual products 224
UPC (Universal Product Code) 33
upward mobility 336–7
user 9
uses and gratifications theory 148–9, *504*
utility/utilitarian 115
attitude function 122–3
exceeding costs 215
influence 269–70
need 91, 92, 94
product 159, 313
shopping 247

valence 95
see also negative; positive
Valentine's Day 389
VALS (Values and Lifestyles) 413–15, *504*
value (monetary) and quality 330–1
value(s) 6, 91, **104–11**, 153, *504*
bibliographical references 513–14
and consumer behaviour 106–10
core 105–6
and cultural change processes 466
and cultural influences 377
-expressive attitude 122–3
-expressive influence 269–70
hypothesis 279
instrumental 107, 108, 259, *499*
and lifestyles 409–16, *504*
List of Values scale 107–8, *499*
means–end chain model 109–10
MECCAs 110–11, *499*
profile 262
Rokeach Value Survey 107, 108
Schwarz Value Survey 108–9
system 105, *504*
teenagers 355–7
terminal 107, 108, *503*
see also beliefs; consistency
vanity 180
variable-interval reinforcement 69
variable-ratio reinforcement 69
variables
dependent 31, *496*
independent 31, *498*
variations, cultural 380
variety seeking 216
Vatican 433
vehicles and transport 462
bicycles 367
motor bikes and scooters 271, 281, 354
see also airlines; cars
vending machines 254, 262
verbal
advertising 159
cues and recall 82
projection in research 28
responses 30, 258
vicarious reinforcement 74–5, 381
video *see* television and videos
vigilance, perceptual 52
virtual communities 274;
see also internet
virtual reality 43

visibility 297
vision 44–5, 369
colour 44–5, 53, 175, 252, 369, 475
visual advertising 159
see also television advertising
vividness of message 160
voice response and dissatisfaction 258
voluntary, activities not 140
von Restorff effect 81

waiting time 242–3
wants 92, *504*
marketers' manipulation of 114–18
and needs 92, 93–5, 117
waste
conspicuous 348
see also disposal
watches and jewellery
and attitudes 152, 160
and cultural change processes 438, 462
and disposal and environmentalism 260
and group influence 274
and lifestyles 405
and purchase environment 254
and self 190
Webcasting 215
see also internet
Weber's Law 50, *504*
weighted additive rule 233
welfare, consumer 20–1
westernization *see* marketing *under* global
Whorf-Sapir hypothesis 419
widows 314
WOM *see* word-of-mouth
women 187–8
in advertisements 188
and beauty 193–7
and body 448
and cars 13, 308, 390
and computers 188
and eating disorders 197
and food preferences 184
and guns 167
and housework and child care 310, 314–17, 327, 329
and kin network system 316, *499*
and sanitary products 20, 117, 458
and search 217
and self, gender and body 176–7, 185
and shaving/hair removal 117, 156–7
single 308
and smoking 144–5, 146–7, 153, 177, 188
and social class 339
and touch 48
working 187, 310, 327–8, 337, 339
see also magazines; perfume; roles *under* sex
word-of-mouth communication 281–5, 291, *504*
dominance of 281
efficiency of 282
factors encouraging 282
negative 258, 282–5
World Bank 360
World Hunger Day 360
world view 340–3, 379, *504*
see also global
World Wide Web *see* internet
World Wildlife Fund 15
World Youth Day 433
WorldWide Fund for Nature 457

young people *see* children; teenagers
Yugoslavia, former 103

Zimbabwe 315